Luigi Lablache portrait oil painting by Friedrich Lieder, 1823
Dr. Stephen Stanley-Little

The Great Lablache

Nineteenth Century Operatic Superstar
His Life and His Times

Clarissa Lablache Cheer

Copyright © 2009 by Clarissa Lablache Cheer.

COVER: Luigi Lablache in Costa's *Don Carlos*, oil painting by Franz Xaver Winterhalter (*Simonette Lablache de la Fuente*)

Library of Congress Control Number:		2009900234
ISBN:	Hardcover	978-1-4415-0215-5
	Softcover	978-1-4415-0214-8

All rights reserved. No part of this book may be reproduced or transmitted in any form or by any means, electronic or mechanical, including photocopying, recording, or by any information storage and retrieval system, without permission in writing from the copyright owner.

This book was printed in the United States of America.

To order additional copies of this book, contact:
Xlibris Corporation
1-888-795-4274
www.Xlibris.com
Orders@Xlibris.com
48096

CONTENTS

Epigraph ix
Foreword xi
Preface xiii
Acknowledgments xvii

BOOK ONE

Chapter One	Beginnings 1
Chapter Two	Early Years 6
Chapter Three	The Family 12
Chapter Four	The Young Lablache 17
Chapter Five	Early Successes 23
Chapter Six	San Carlo to La Scala 36
Chapter Seven	Rome, Rossini and Vienna 44
Chapter Eight	Naples, Vienna and Beethoven 50
Chapter Nine	Fame at the San Carlo 63
Chapter Ten	Parma 71

BOOK TWO

Chapter Eleven	London Debut 111
Chapter Twelve	Paris and High Society 117
Chapter Thirteen	Paganini and Lablache 125
Chapter Fourteen	Return to Naples 137
Chapter Fifteen	Concerts in Naples 147
Chapter Sixteen	I Puritani 162

BOOK THREE

Chapter Seventeen	The Princess Victoria and Lablache 207
Chapter Eighteen	Victoria's Lessons 217
Chapter Nineteen	Frédéric and Fanny 232
Chapter Twenty	Coronation Year 240

Chapter Twenty-One	William Tell in London	254
Chapter Twenty-Two	Thalberg and Napoleon's Funeral	268
Chapter Twenty-Three	Dublin	280
Chapter Twenty-Four	Stabat Mater	291
Chapter Twenty Five	Don Pasquale	298
Chapter Twenty-Six	Concerts and Concerns	311
Chapter Twenty-Seven	Difficulty at Her Majesty's	325
Chapter Twenty-Eight	Jenny Lind and Lablache	335
Chapter Twenty-Nine	More Concerts and Chopin's Death	346
Chapter Thirty	La Tempesta	361

BOOK FOUR

Chapter Thirty-One	Russia	423
Chapter Thirty-Two	London Debut at Covent Garden	440
Chapter Thirty-Three	The End of the Career	455

BOOK FIVE

Chapter Thirty-Four	Final Days	479
Chapter Thirty-Five	Remembrance	494
Chapter Thirty-Six	The Thalbergs	502
Chapter Thirty-Seven	The Estate	510
Chapter Thirty-Eight	The Descendants	519

Appendix A: Compositions by Luigi Lablache	569
Appendix B: Lablache Family Musical Compositions	570
Appendix C: Luigi Lablache Images in Objets d'art	572
Appendix D: Lablache on English Music	576
Appendix E: Queen Victoria's Gift to the Lablache Family	581
Appendix F: Family Tree	582
Chronology A: Lablache Operatic Appearances with Casts	583
Chronology B: Lablache Performances By Composer	618
Chronology C: Lablache Family Concerts	625
Notes	651
Bibliography	677
Index	689

To my parents
Thomas Colyer Lablache Stanley-Little
Cerita Ida Claire Stanley-Little

*Naples! thou Heart of men which ever pantest
Naked, beneath the lidless eye of Heaven!
Elysian City, which to calm enchantest
The mutinous air and sea: they round thee, even
As Sleep round Love, are driven.*

—Shelley, Ode to Naples

*Many singers of my time were great artists . . .
But there were only three true geniuses:
Lablache, Rubini, and that child so spoiled by nature,
Maria Felicita Malibran.*

—Gioacchino Rossini

Foreword

The following is an article from London's The Musical World, 1850, written almost forty years after Luigi Lablache's operatic debut in Italy. The author is unknown, but he clearly conveys the admiration and affection for Lablache in England at the time.

Lablache is the oldest and the best-established favorite at Her Majesty's theatre. He made his first appearance in this country some twenty years ago, and from that time, with an exception, we believe, of one year's secession, he has returned hither every spring, with increased popularity. Twenty years is a long test applied to public performers; and he that could pass such an ordeal of time must possess merits of the very highest order, which could conquer the appetite for novelty, and overcome the fickleness of popular applause. All this Lablache has effected. The public, so far from being wearied at the long-continued cry of "Lablache the Great," as were the Athenians of hearing Aristides everlastly called "The Just," elevates him, if possible, into greater popularity yearly. His place is not to be supplied; no other *artiste,* not even Formes, could compensate for his loss. Independently of his powers as an actor and a singer, so great a lover is he of his art, that he will undertake with delight the most trifling character in order to ensure the success of a piece. From this it follows that no great singer has, within our recollection, undertaken such a variety of characters. We find him in every possible grade of representation. From the loftiest tragedy to the most burlesque comedy he is equally great and efficient. From Brabantio to Don Pasquale—from Marino Faliero to Dandolo. Through all the gradations of passion and humour he exhibits a superior insight into humanity, and with the finest dramatic artifice and discrimination he siezes on the insalient points, and strikes them out in bold relief, giving life and verisimilitude to his abstractions. In a comic part he fills up the stage with his acting, no less than with his voice and size. Every character around him seems merely subsidiary. "He is the sun of humour," about which the rest, as planets, perform their revolutions, deriving heat and light from him. He is the centre of gravity that attracts all the laughing humours from his auditory. Yes, we say gravity, nor therein are we guilty of a bull. In his most whimsical efforts his countenance is as serious as that of a mid-day owl. While all around are covulsed with cachinnations, his face is composed as a Chinese mandarin's, or a Spanish hidalgo's sitting for a genealogical portrait. His comedy is not sparkling and effervescent like champagne, it partakes more of the body and flavour of tokay; you may sip it—the smallest taste is palatable. He possesses somewhat of the stolidity of Liston, with occasionally the rich raciness of Dowden. His humour is as rotund as his person, and his person is a hogshead of wit and mirth. Lablache's voice is an organ of the most extraordinary power. It is impossible by description to give any notion of its volume of sound. He is an ophicleide among singers. One may have some idea of this power of tone, when it may be truly asserted that, with the entire opera, band and chorus playing and singing forte, his voice may be as distinctly and separately heard above them all as a trumpet among violins. He is the very Stentor of vocalists. When he sings he rouses the audience as the bugle doth the warhorse, or as the songs of Tyrtaeus reanimated the Spartans. With this prodigious vehicle of sound, his singing is distinquished by superior softness and expression. Lablache is a thorough musician, and no other *artiste* on the stage excels him in the knowledge and appliances of his art.

Preface

This book is a celebration of the life of the legendary nineteenth century operatic superstar—basso Luigi Lablache—my direct ancestor. Remembered as King of Basses, this is the first biography of Lablache in English. Here I not only attempt to explore the past and bring new details of his brilliant operatic life into focus, but also recall the long forgotten lives of his talented theatrical family through five generations. To me, one of the most facinating periods of musical and operatic history was realized during the time when Lablache was singing. It was a New Age; the French Revolution was over; Napoleon was gone and Rossini's operas set the whole of Italy ablaze. Opera was the major entertainment of the time, and everyone was celebrating the glorious world of Italian opera.

Knowing nothing of those early times, it was later, during World War II, as my cousin and I wandered around our grandparents' huge house in England, the faded glory of our ancestry was pervasive. Our grandmother often recounted fascinating tales of past family glories and remembrances of when she was a young Edwardian beauty. Gazing up at the huge family paintings on the walls, we had the notion that our generation had missed out on the intriguing life of the family's theatrical history. We were fascinated by the portrait of a handsome figure in Spanish costume—Luigi Lablache—by Franz Winterhalter that hung neglected in an empty bedroom. Our child's minds imagined he was watching us, like the *Laughing Cavalier*. But as children we did not realize all that he really was.

Upon the deaths of my parents later, certain family mementoes passed down to me stirred my interest in the family history. I decided to research my ancestors, and the path to that heritage ran straight through the world of opera. This was a daunting task. Stories were forgotten after two world wars, records were scattered, fabulous antiques had long ago been reliquished, and fine homes—even the one that had been in the family for over a hundred years—were gone. Our family has always loved music, and my search for Lablache and my heritage soon led me to discover Italian opera. Never did I realize at the start that I would become an aficionado of bel canto opera.

My search of over twenty-eight years led me through all the major opera centers of Europe and America, combing records in libraries and historic sites and meeting all the remarkable and generous people who have helped me in this effort.

Lablache was unparalleled in the entire history of Italian opera; his extraordinary talent and genius dominated the opera world all through the first half of the nineteenth century. Stage-struck, Lablache had dedicated his life to be a singer, and he immediately showed a natural genius for the gems of opera buffa so popular in the traditional repertoire of the Neapolitan theatres. Opera had an irresistible attraction to him as a precocious young student long before 1812, when he formally entered the operatic scene. Everything about Lablache was dynamic: his thundering voice, his enormous size (over six feet and a barrel of a man), his dark handsome looks, strength and intelligence. Admired as a superb actor in serious operatic roles, it was his unique racy humor and wit that earned him the title of first comedian in Europe. From early in his career, Lablache's powerful but purely natural voice dazzled his audiences and brought new excitement to the stage, along with international recognition for the principal Italian bel canto composers of the time, Rossini, Pacini, Donizetti and Bellini. The last three wrote operas specifically for his talent. These operas swept him into the limelight during the greatest musical period the world has ever known. Proving himself as a consummate vocalist, his experiences were drawn from his galley years performing the old masters like Pavesi, Mosca, Cimarosa, Paisello in Palermo, Messina and the little dialect theatres of Naples. However, it was his youth and special rendering of Rossini's buffo roles, like Figaro, that first put him on the road to international success as a famed Rossini bass. Rossini's early reputation was established in *commedia*, and Verdi wrote that the "finest opera buffa in existence is *Il Barbiere di Siviglia*."

Italian vocalists ruled supreme over the operatic theatre during most of the nineteenth century. Successful singers were especially all-powerful and controlled the outcome of the operas they sang. While demanding the highest fees, these singers aroused strong public passion and could fill an empty theater or close it; composers and impresarios alike were all at their disposal.

Life for musicians must have been difficult, especially when on tour. Enduring long hours of singing under appalling conditions, in smoke-filled, dirty, candlelit concert rooms and theaters with little heat during the winter seasons. Traveling between cities by horse-drawn carriages presented increased danger when crossing known robber terrains. They survived without the modern-day luxury of microphones, radio, TV, or recordings, or even antibiotics if they fell ill.

Of all the lyric Italian artists of that time, Lablache was beyond comparison. His reputation as the greatest actor and comedian spread across Europe and could not be denied. Figaro was his signature role when young; reviews of the time established that he sang the part better than anyone. Later his Bartolo was considered the best. Perhaps in no branch of vocal art did Lablache so triumphantly declare his genius as in recitativo, whether accompanied or parlante. Other bass roles he made his own were Geronimo, Mustifa, Dulcamara, Leporello, Don Pasquale, Don Magnifico. Early in his career he brought a new importance to bass roles by his voice and expressive acting abilities, enchanting audiences by his unique approach. Few could decide in which roles he excelled most. Called Magnificent, he was formidable realizing melodramatic characters such as Donizetti's Henry VIII and Rossini's Assur and he was admired in heroic, tragic, or father-figure lead roles such as William Tell, Saul, Noah, Samson, Georgio, Faliero, Elmiro, Maomento, Moses and Gritzenzo (his last role). His singing career spanned forty-five years, and he was still receiving impressive reviews even while singing into his sixties. By his death, he had scored fifty world premieres and his repertoire shone with over 170 known different roles.

The fame and reputation of Lablache was so immense that he was chosen by Queen Victoria of England to teach her singing for over twenty years. As a young woman, she looked up to him as her beloved master. She often wrote about how eagerly she awaited his visits and looked forward to her lessons. It was known that he also taught Queen Adelaide singing, and consort Prince Albert. Lablache earned a position as trusted confidant to royalty, colleagues and impresarios. Anecdotes vouch for his honesty, generosity, playfulness and good humor. What emerges is that "Papa Lablache" was a larger-than-life figure both on and off the stage.

Unfortunately for those who are interested in singer biographies, overall, few illuminating books in English about Italian nineteenth century bassos have emerged. Many factors hinder writers from recounting the lives of those early singers. Distance, language and time complicate the research, especially when following the trail of these singers, who, like Lablache, were always crossing oceans and international borders. Few writers can sustain the years of exhaustive inquiry and scrutiny, piecing together hard-to-find reviews, letters and family information.

Some biographies that exist are fairly inadequate and lack proper documentation such as clear performance chronologies, good illustrations or press reports. Early biographers of Italian opera composers—though always few and far between—tend to disregard the importance of the singers when writing about bel canto operas. Biographers today scorn or dismiss early singers almost entirely, feeling more comfortable writing about more recent artists that have made voice recordings. It is only in the last two decades that a few books have emerged about nineteenth-century Italian vocalists in English. Still those are mainly about sopranos, one exception being the two-volume amazing biography on the tenor Giovanni Battista Rubini (written in Italian). All these artists deserve more recognition, including the instrumentalists of the times.

Since I am not a trained musician, my focus in this book has not been on technical vocal analysis. Rather, I have attempted to provide a glimpse of opera in its golden age through the saga of one of its greatest interpreters. All information fades away with time; therefore I chose to preserve his life through this book.

This is not the definitive book on this huge family of singers; there are many stories and mysteries untold. Regretably, vast amounts of information cannot be included, like many letters, playbills, etc.; this material is beyond the scope of one book. In illuminating the many details of his life and those close to him, this year-by-year account reflects the atmosphere of his times. I hope to have shed some light briefly on this vibrant singer and his genius. One thing is certain—Lablache's place in history is secure; he lived every minute of his life to the fullest—a superstar of his age.

Clarissa Lablache Cheer
Sanford, Florida
September, 2008

Acknowledgments

This biography would not have been realized without the help of many individuals over the preceding years. I wish to thank and express my deep gratitude and appreciation for all the generous help given to me since I began writing this book.

Naples has always fascinated me—the birthplace of my ancestor Luigi Lablache. I was captivated by its interesting Roman past and early operatic history, the mysteries and legends at the end of the eighteenth century, and the following decades when Naples was part of the Kingdom of the Two Sicilies. The Bourbon royal family and our family ancestors struggled against a background of revolution and the changes brought on by the French and that event. So I feel it is natural that I should start by thanking all those who helped with this book from Naples and Italy who are direct and indirect descendants and friends. First and foremost is Princess di Strongoli Donna Francesca Ferrara Pignatelli and her husband Prince Fernando Ferrara Pignatelli di Strongoli. The Princess Pignatelli's hospitality while showing her private collection of Sigismund Thalberg's photos and piano was delightful, and I very much appreciate her help with our family tree. Prince Francesco d'Alba was kind enough to supply me with photos of the bust of Lablache, which stands in the lobby of the Naples Conservatorio San Pietro a Majella. Famed pianist Francesco Nicolosi and his family for their hospitality, which included a visit to the huge mausoleum of Sigismund Thalberg and wife Francesca (daughter of Lablache) buried in the famed Poggioreale above Naples and a tour of Posillipo and the original Lablache-Thalberg villa still standing today.

I am deeply indebted to Daniel L. Hitchcock of Wichita, Kansas, a Thalberg expert, because without his help none of the Naples experience would have been possible. Also in Naples, I have to thank both Sergio Ragni and Luigi Cuono for putting their superb private Neapolitan opera collection at my disposal. In Pesaro, Italy, I was helped in research by the distinguished Prof. Bruno Cagli, artistic director of the Rossini Foundation, former director of the Accademia Santa Cecilia Rome; Prof. Philip Gossett at La Casa di Rossini and Patricia B. Brauner, his assistant. At the opera archives and museum of La Scala, Milan, I must thank archivist G. Tintori Gambini for his help with Lablache's letters. In Turin, help came from Giorgio Gualerzi and wonderful assistance from Dr. Giorgio Appolonia of Castellanza. Generous assistance from Battista De Paoli, Presidente della Cassa Rurale ed Artigiani di Calcio e di Covo. Dott. Museum assistance came from Daniella Moschini, Dott. Raffaella Nardella, Biblioteca Palatina Parma; Prof. Nicola Spinosa, Dott. Pierluigi Petrobelli, Angela Barducci of Montefalco. My deep gratitude and special thanks go to my cousin Simonette Lablache de la Fuente of Rome and Massa Martana, Umbria, formally of FAO United Nations, and her husband Ottoreino Caramazza for all their work and encouragement while translating Lablache's letters.

In London, I wish to acknowledge the gracious permission of Her Majesty Queen Elizabeth II to quote from the journals of Queen Victoria in the Royal Archives at Windsor Castle, and the Royal Picture collections for giving permission to feature the Franz Winterhalter painting of Lablache in the book. Next, I wish to thank Mirella Stephens for the long translations from Florimo, The Donizetti Society of London and its member-chairman and editor Prof. Alex Weatherson and members John Watts, Pip Clayton, Angela Penfold, Ken Hebben, John Carter, Colin Craig, Keith Lawson. Producer and artistic director of Opera Rara, Patric Schmid, and the general administrator Don White. The kindness and overwhelming support of ambassador Dudley Cheke and the encouragement and help from his son, Dr. Robert A. Cheke. Katharine Hogg, archivist of the Royal Academy London, and Oliver Davies, archivist. Dr. Simon Maguire of Sotheby's and Vivian Liff of the Isle of Man. Thanks to Melanie Trifona Christoudia of the London's Theatre Museum. Barry Norman and Joanna Wallace of the Victoria and Albert Museum, London. Dr. Richard Copeman, London and Dr. John Rossilli, Cambridge.

My great appreciation and thanks go to my brother, Dr. Stephen Stanley-Little of Suffolk, England, for his early editing, translating, and constant help and encouragement. James Stanley-Little, my grandfather, and T.C. Stanley-Little, my father, whose writings and research also made this book possible. My thanks to my daughter, Georgia P. Cheer in Hampshire for her assistance. My cousin Dominique de Friston, Devon, for his help with the family archives and family history. Adrian de Friston from the Royal College of Arms and Jean-Paul de la Fuente. April Fitzlyon and opera collectors Richard Bebb and Jo Waters of London. Brook Davies of Brighton, Rosslyn Glassman, Prof. Denis William Stevens and his daughter Daphne Stevens-Pascucci, all of London. My cousin Virginia French and her husband Paul French of Bournemouth for their help. Derek Walsh in Ireland.

In Paris, my thanks to the present owner of the Lablache house in Maisons-Laffitte, Monique Denavit Saubié, for her extended tour of the house and property and undying efforts in listing the house as a landmark location in French history. Descendant of Lablache, Mme. Marie Balsan of Neuilly-Seine and her family. The Dantan collection's Jean-Marie Bruson, conservateur du Patrimoine Carnvalet Museum de la ville de Paris. And I have to thank Brian Meringo for his tireless, incredible research and translations in Paris. Bruce Brewer and Christopher Sale of Normandy, for their hospitality and help. Descendant and cousin Baron Christian de Caters of Lisbon. Descendant and cousin Henri Goüin. Daniele Maillard of Paris for her help. Thanks to Alfred de Cock of Bruxelles for his endless research on Marie Battu Lablache. Fulvio Stefano Lo Presti of Bruxelles for his help. Giovanni Christian of Zurich for his help in locating rare books.

In the United States, Los Angeles, I'm deeply indebted to my son, Mark Cheer, of Fox TV, and Bob Kluge for their valuable assistance with an expert computer transfer; without them, this book would not be possible. Also in Los Angeles, thanks to my daughter Venise Woodward for her assistance: and Jay Galbrieth and Ralph Ellis for sharing their knowledge of obscure operas through their delightful soirés. Tom and Beatice Byrne-McKiernan for letter translations. Also, the baritone Robert Heydecker of Manhattan Beach for his soirés and instructions on singing. I gratefully recall support of famed film star Stewart Granger of Hollywood, my second cousin. Ray Myles, Mike Richter, Evan Baker of Los Angeles. The patient editing of Rosemary Kingsfather and Marcene Anderson was outstanding. Carol Russell Law of the Malibran Society of Los Angeles, and Prof. Janet Johnson of USC-LA. The help of Jack Belson and George Dansker, both of New Orleans. Also with the help of my daughter, Tina Griffith, of Sanford, Florida. Singers Peter Strummer and Linda Roark-Strummer, of Oklahoma, for their interest and encouragement. Dr. James Jenkin, of Huntington Beach, California, for years of encouragement. Stan Golden and Lim Lai of San Francisco, for use of their fabulous opera collections. For his encouragement, I thank Andrew S. Pope of Menden, Louisiana, and Basil Walsh of Delray Beach, Florida, for help and research. To Eugene Galvin of Washington DC and his wife Mary Lou for arranging, singing and playing in the delightful two hundredth birthday Lablache celebration concert and their generous hospitality. Alain Letort of Washington DC. Conductor Micaele Sparacino. Maria Roffo of Lakewood, California. John Mazzarélla and Herbert Cahoon of New York City. Stephen Herx of Paramus, New Jersey. Jon R. Skinner of Portland, Oregon. Prof. William Ashbrook for all his interest and help.

Reggie Mosser's incredible, dedicated help provided the final push toward publication. I am also extremely grateful to Pierre Bellemare of Ottawa, Canada. Dr. Alison Geyser of Australia. The times I spent as president of the Chris Merritt Fan Club brought a closer friendship with Chris over the years, and his singing inspired my love of bel canto opera.

Without the encouragement and constant help of my dear friend Jack Rokahr and use of his incredibly fine collection of scores and books in his archives in Los Angeles for over twenty years, this book would not be possible.

My sincere thanks go to my dear friend, chronology expert, and musicologist Tom Kaufman for his valuable help and encouragement and for sharing his incredible chronologies. Tom inspired me from the start to what seemed an impossible task—to trace the hundreds of performances of Luigi Lablache and his huge theatrical and operatic family across Europe, the Americas, Australia, and Russia for nearly two hundred years.

Last but not least, I am indebted to my husband, Sam, without whose patience, help, and encouragement this book would have been equally impossible.

Clarissa Lablache Cheer,
Sanford, Florida.

Book One

Chapter One

Beginnings

1793-1795

Luigi Nicola Giuseppe Lablache remains unparalleled in the entire history of opera.[1] Born in Naples, Italy, on 6 December 1795,[2] the second son of Nicola and Catherine Maria Francesca Lablache,[3] he became the foremost opera bass, both comic and tragic, of his era. Throughout his life, he was referred to simply by family and friends alike as the Great Lablache.

    At the time of his birth, Lablache's parents lived in a humble house on the Riviera di Chiaia in Naples, just at the corner of the Arco Merelli.[4] This imposing street has remained almost unchanged since the eighteenth century. The houses face onto the park beside the bay. Catherine Maria Francesca Bietagh, the mother of Lablache, was also born in Naples. Reliable records in the little church of St. Maria della Nevia Chiaia nearby show her to have been baptized on the 28 September 1770[5] and that her parents' names were Tobia and Giuserra Reale Bietagh,[6] descendants of an Irish family who had immigrated to France after its male representatives had fought for King James II at the Battle of the Boyne in 1689.[7] There is evidence, principally from family history, that they had pursued their Jacobite traditions. In 1746, one of these family members joined the French forces that were defeated in the famous battle of Culloden Muir in Scotland while fighting for "Bonnie Prince Charlie."[8]

    Nicola Lablache, the father of Luigi Lablache, was a merchant who traded with the East Indies; but, unfortunately, most facts about him remain rather unclear. Nicola's life remains a mystery mainly because of his French background and his undoubtedly Jacobite persuasion. Two things are certain: he was French, and he became established in Naples in the early 1790s.[9] According to a short biography of Lablache written up in *La scuola musicale di Napoli* by Francesco Florimo in 1892, then related to him by the eldest daughter of Luigi, Francesca Lablache,

> After the French Revolution at the end of the last century, the two brothers Lablache, who had already lost their father to the guillotine, left Marseilles in 1794, and came to settle in Naples. They belonged to a noble family who could claim the title of Count. Having arrived in Naples, they entered a commercial company trading with the Indian continent; so therefore it was believed by some that Lablache was the son of a merchant . . . it is well known that at the French Revolution all titles of nobility had been abolished in France. Nicola had not the time to resume his title, and Luigi Lablache never did so perhaps because he was proud of having obtained a great name by his genius and could better adorn his family by his own fame.

However, there is conflicting evidence here: for sure, the date in Florimo's statement is incorrect. Nicola was known to have lived in Naples long before the 1790s; however, lack of specific records of Nicola's foreign transactions as a merchant have made him a rather difficult individual to trace. At that time in history, when the French Revolution was in full swing, anyone with a title and living on French soil was doomed, not only in Paris but in every French city. Certainly one can presume he was wisely maintaining a low profile.

Nicola Lablache was a stormy character from all accounts with plenty of personality and a vigorous mind. His portrait yet survives and supports this description. From Marseilles, he had been trading with the East Indies and America since the age of twenty-three. The British were at war with the French, and in 1793, their ships blockaded the southern French ports making it impossible for Nicola to trade with anyone.[10]

Toulon was then recaptured by the forces of the revolutionary government on 19 December 1793, after the Allies—Englishmen, Sardinians, Neapolitans, and French Royalists—attempted unsuccessfully to subdue France. Lyon and Marseilles had resisted the central revolutionary authority, suffered terrible reprisals, and thousands had gone to the guillotine.[11]

Reliable records of Nicola's birth have not been found, but military documents bearing seals and handwritten notes found in the family's belongings date to the de la Blache family in France during the eighteenth century. It is not certain that family tradition is correct in declaring him to be the son of a Count Simon de la Blache and one of the last positively known descendants of the de la Blache family who came originally from the region of the south of France, known today as Isere.[12] Here, there is confusion. Records in Marseilles point in another direction: a Simon Lablache (not de la Blache) born there in 1709 was the secretary of the Compagnie Royale d'Afrique in 1744. In 1748, he was the head accountant and in 1750, we find him chief director of the Compagnie Royale d'Afrique. In 1755, records show he retired[13] and in 1769, records from Marseilles state as follows:

> Simon Lablache appeared on this date in Marseilles in front of a Notary to give power of attorney to a legal representative to collect in his name the interests on a loan subscribed by him for the city of Marseilles.

This led the archivist in the Marseilles Hall of Records to assume that Simon Lablache did not reside permanently in Marseilles. The fact that his name does not appear on the records of properties seized for the crime of emigration or any other reason leads to the possibility that he left France or Marseilles before the revolution. That has never been confirmed either. However, it is most likely that part of the family were living abroad, possibly Madrid.

The records of the Archives Communales Ville de Marseilles cease there. Should we then presume that Simon was guillotined in 1793? This information could not be verified. According to records from Marseilles, Simon Lablache, possibly the father of Nicola vanished, he would have been then in his eighties. Futher research might turn up some trace of him. About this time the last Count Falcoz Alexander de la Blache was arrested in Paris, imprisoned, then released. He escaped the guillotine after the execution of Robespierre (1794). He was dead by the end of the century. Did he have a son or brother named Simon?

Confirmed by descendants of the family in 1902 to be one of the de la Blache family residences (there were four), an old chateau is known to exist near Anjou, a small village east of Vienne near the river Rhone now in the present county of Isere in the center of southern France. In 1902, nothing was left but a crumbling ruin, standing sadly in a cow pasture. Now it has been restored, but only a tower remains of the original massive structure. The other chateaus dating from the twelfth siecle is the Le Chateau Jarcieu nearby. Not far away stands the Chateau de la Blache in Beaulieu, Isere. All these, plus the Chateau de Plaisance Nogent-sur-Marne in Paris, belonged at one time to the Falcoz de la Blache family. Originally of the Dauphine, the family had an extremely picturesque history going back to the thirteenth century. Unfortunately, most of this long history of the de la Blache family is lost in time. The family has vanished from the area, leaving no trace of an ancient noble family who were created counts. The first, Alexandre de Falcoz de la Blache, Baron D'Anjou, was raised to Comte d'Anjou in 1679.[14]

Nicola Lablache was back in Naples by 1791. Perhaps he could already see that France was a very dangerous place to be at that time, for surely he could see that what might have happened to his father could also be his fate. Or did he care as he was plainly a Jacobin himself and a republican. Certainly later on it appeared that way.

On the 26 July 1793, archiepiscopal records confirm that Nicola signed a sworn deposition; and upon that date, he obtained a license to marry a woman of Irish Italian descent, Catherina Maria Francesca Bietagh.[15] Married in the parish church of San Giuseppe a Chiaia on the Riviera, the deposition reads as follows:

> Nicola Lablache, son of Simon Lablache and Catherine Deborde (certificate of birth wanting, born in Madrid). At the age of 10 years (on 16 May 1776) he entered the seminary of Pozzuoli, near Naples. Therefore he was born in 1766, and left the seminary in 1778. At the time of his marriage, he belonged to the parish church of St. Francesco e Matteo ai Quarieri di Toledo, a church in old Naples near the centre of the city.[16]

The following year on 12 February 1794, a son was born to the couple; he was named Simone Raimondo Tobia Andrea Giuseppe Lablache. This boy died five and a half months later, and his death was recorded in the register of the church of San Giuseppe a Chiaia.[17]

The city of Naples lies under the shadow of the huge volcano Vesuvius. Dating from ancient times, when Naples was a Greek colony, the mountain has had a long and deadly history of eruptions. The most famous of these was in the year AD 79, when the cities of Pompeii and Herculaneum were not only destroyed, but almost totally buried. Even the location of these cities was lost.

That year on 15 June, 1794 Vesuvius chose to make one of its great paroxysmal eruptions. It was a violent one from all accounts and one of the most violent ever recorded.[18] First, there was the usual earthquake; then three days later great sprays of fire shot up, and lava came pouring out, rushing down the mountainside into the sea. There were deep rumbling noises and flashes of lightning. The clouds of black smoke and ash that ensued plunged all of Naples into darkness for days.[19] When the smoke cleared and the ashes settled, it was noticed that the top of Vesuvius was blown away, leaving a huge jagged crater. The town of Torre del Greco was nearly buried in volcanic ash. During those dreadful months, Simon, the Lablaches' first child, died.

The parish church of Giuseppe a Chiaia, one of the oldest churches in Naples, still stands today with a slight Spanish flavor to its weather-beaten architecture. Outwardly, the facades of the houses on the Riviera di Chiaia are shabby and show little of their bygone glory when the street was a fashionable address and high society would ride past resplendent in their carriages on their journey to the San Carlo opera house. The Bourbon King Ferdinand of Naples and his queen Maria-Carolina accompanied Lord Horatio Nelson and Lady Hamilton there to view the British fleet anchored beside the Santa Lucia.

The long street is bordered by a pleasant park between the rocky promenade and the famous curve of the bay. While handsome old statues of the Roman emperors still decorate the park, now sadly, graffiti of all different colours spoil the figures. Near the end of the long facade of houses and shops, not far from the church, stands the Lablache house: curious and narrow, it leans slightly over the corner with typical sun-baked, faded green shutters.

In this humble house, within the curve of the Bay of Naples and within sight of the Santa Lucia, on 6 December 1795,[20] another son was born to Nicola and Francesca Lablache. The child was christened Luigi Nicola Giuseppe Lablache. Naples was the city of his birth and where he rose to international fame in the world of opera. And it was to the city of Naples he returned to die sixty-three years later.[21]

Chapter Two

Early Years

1795-1799

Naples in the late eighteenth century was a beautiful city, unlike the vast sprawling metropolis it is today. From tempera paintings of the time, by such artists as P. Fabris and J. Hackert, we can visualize the scenario:

> Naples lies beside crystal blue waters, nestled against green hills. There sheep graze peacefully in the care of idle shepherds. Olive plantations tucked away behind the hills are abundant with fruit, next to arbors loaded with grapes. A lonely peasant flicks his whip at a donkey laden with baskets of fruit, as he rides along a dusty road, past prickly pears growing up against the crumbling walls of ancient Roman ruins.

From paintings of the time, we see tier upon tier of pastel-colored houses with rust-red tile roofs overlooking the sea.

Lazy *lazzaroni*, wearing red stocking caps, fish in the sunlit bay while men of war lurk in the distance protecting the sleepy populace. The mighty Vesuvius towers over the city, belching great bellows of smoke, always on the brink of eruption. How like the city below, peaceful and pretty as a picture postcard on the surface, but a delusion. Naples was on the brink of disaster. Cecil Headlam describes another aspect of the Siren City in his *Story of Naples*:

> Naples as a mediaeval city lasted well into the nineteenth century. Before the *Risorgimento* it was mediaeval in government, or misgovernment; mediaeval in sanitation, or the lack of it; mediaeval in the individuality of the costumes and characteristics of its population; mediaeval in picturesqueness and the squalor

of its narrow, crowded streets; mediaeval in its social and political inequality; mediaeval in its crime and its passions, in its superstitions, and its light hearted abandonment.[22]

During the closing of the century the courts of Europe were nervous and unsettled by the dreadful news coming from France. The French Revolution had erupted and was now in full swing; the French were calling for revolution everywhere. The royalty of Naples was distinctly uncomfortable and fearful, afraid that their decadent and luxurious lifestyle might be interrupted or worse.

In the great forests surrounding the city, the Bourbon king Ferdinand and his court happily hunted deer, wild boar, and pheasant. As king of the Kingdom of the Two Sicilies,[23] he ruled not only a city, but a state, one of the largest, extending all the way from south of Rome to include the island of Sicily (at that time northern Italy was under Austrian rule).[24]

The Bourbon dynasty was at the height of its power and, though corrupt, was rather popular with the masses. There were always those who would grumble about their sovereigns, but these were the poor people and most of them were fanatically loyal. Life in Naples was carefree and gay for the aristocracy with their carnivals, operas, and masked balls. International high society came to Naples, often as part of the grand tour, and to escape colder northern climates. Poets and painters flocked there, inspired by the crumbling ruins of Pompei and Herculaneum under majestic Vesuvius. Goethe said of the city: "Naples is a paradise, in which everyone lives in a sort of intoxicated self-forgetfulness." In 1805, the writer Augustus von Kotzebue explains the most important concerns of the populace:

> There were food and lemonade stalls in every street. Macaroni was the staple diet, with plenty of fruit and vegetables. Calves, pigs and chickens foraged everywhere, milk was supplied from the cow on the doorstep. The bread was tolerable and the wine, the famous *Lachrima Cristi*, sweet. When a Neapolitan sits down to dinner, twelve dishes were considered a plain meal. At fetes and balls, there was an unending flow of little cakes, sweets and ices, claret cup, Madeira and champagne. The higher classes in Naples are indeed the "savages" of Europe. They eat, drink, sleep and game.[25]

King Ferdinand of Naples was the second son of King Philip V of Spain while his wife Maria Carolina was the daughter of the Empress Maria

Theresa of Austria and the sister of the unlucky Queen Marie Antoinette of France. They were an odd couple to say the least. Ferdinand, an unkingly comic person, had interests that were simple and democratic. He left it to his wife to take care of the affairs of state while he did pretty much as he pleased. Like all the Bourbons, his passion was hunting and shooting in the forests, slaughtering animals and birds by the hundreds. On other occasions, he was just as happy fishing in the Bay of Naples or smoking his pipe in the company of his cronies, mostly old fishermen. Often, he would go out fishing with them all day. Upon returning, he would set up a little stall on the jetty and sell his fish, enjoying haggling for hours over his catch to the delight of the locals. The Queen was not amused by all this, but as she had become the real power behind the throne, she was too busy with ruling the country, giving birth to seventeen children, and overseeing to the great feasts and endless court balls.

Living in Naples, for the rich and idle, was a carnival of pleasure. Now, however, the shadow of the French Revolution hung over these festivities. French émigrés, bearing tales of unbelievable horror, were fleeing to Naples in larger and larger numbers. Soon the Queen heard of the terrible fate of her sister, Queen Marie Antoinette. The news sent a wave of fear through the courts of Europe.[26]

That year, 1793, was remembered as a year of terrible violence perpetrated against the royal family of France. It was the year, infamous in history, in which Louis XVI, King of France, went to the guillotine, followed by his wife and sister. Then the French quite openly declared that other nations should follow suit and take up arms. Soon England and France were at war again. There had never been much love between them, considering they had been at war from 1688 through 1715. Later, there were many unsuccessful Jacobite attempts to take over the throne of England. The most famous of these was the failed Rebellion of Forty-Five when the Highlanders of Scotland rose up to support Prince Charles, hoping to place a Stuart king on the throne of England and Scotland.

The British first went to war against the French in the Mediterranean in 1793. Under Admiral Hood, they hoped to strike a blow for the Royalist cause by seizing Toulon. The expedition was a disaster, and they were driven out by the republicans. There, thousands of Royalists, including hundreds of Neapolitans were brutally slaughtered.[27] The British were forced to flee by the French under the command of a ferocious republican, the twenty-four-year-old young captain Napoleon Bonaparte. At once, he was rewarded with the title Brigadier General Bonaparte.[28] Later, the wars took a different turn when Horatio Nelson entered the scene.

It is hard to say when Nicola Lablache surfaced in Naples or to answer the question whether he was a Royalist émigré or not. The Reign of Terror had still a year or two to run. But here we find out that Nicola was a man of the times and later belonged to a French party that was radical and antimonarchist. Most likely he wanted to play down his aristocratic French background for in Naples he was starting a new family and a new life.[29] Living under the shadow of an erupting Vesuvius—beside the Toulon disaster—was pressure enough to dampen the spirits of the pleasure-loving Neapolitans that year. To crown that came the news of the fate of the French royal family. Times were not normal, and now there was an atmosphere of great discontent, fear, and impending doom. French biographer of the times, Henri Beyle, known as Stendhal remarked:

> At the earliest rumour of the first Napoleonic victories, the Kingdom of the Two Sicilies was stricken with terror—the government implored, and indeed obtained, conditions of peace. A republican Ambassador set foot in Naples; and in the timid breast of the Sovereign, humiliation poured oil upon the flames of hatred. One Friday night, the King of Naples chanced to pay a visit to the *teatro dei Fiorentini,* in order to see Pinotti,[30] the celebrated comic actor. From his seat in the Royal Box, which was set hard against the stage, he could observe *citoyen* Trouvé who sat exactly facing him, at the opposite extreme of the proscenium arch. His Citizen Excellency, the republican Ambassador, was dressed in the uniform of the Court whose interests he represented: namely, in his own hair, unpowdered, and tight trousers. His Majesty, terror-stricken at the sight of *unpowdered hair,* promptly quitted the theatre, but not before he'd had time to observe, among the spectators who thronged the pit, some fifteen or twenty heads of ominous darkness. Summoning the Officer of the Guard, His Majesty whispered a word in his ear; whereupon the Officer of the Guard, in his turn, proceeded to summon the notorious Cancelieri, the *factotum* of the military police. Quietly, the *teatro dei Fiorentini* was surrounded. As soon as the performance was ended and the spectators began to emerge, each in turn was brought face to face with Cancelieri, who asked but one question: Are you *a Neapolitan?* As a result of this inquisition, seven young men, one and all scions of the noblest families in the Kingdom, one and all with hair unpowdered, were conducted to the Fortress of St Elmo. On the following

morning, each was forced to put on a common military greatcoat; a horse-hair pigtail eighteen inches long was attached to the collar of his jacket; and all seven were promptly dispatched aboard an outward-bound troopship to serve as private soldiers in a regiment stationed in Sicily.[31]

Napoleon Bonaparte rose to power and soon after set out to conquer all of Europe. Victorious everywhere, his armies swept into northern Italy in 1797, taking first Milan and then Venice, driving the Austrians out. Hailed as liberators by the Milanese, Buonaparte had come into Italy as the representative of the forces of nationalism and political freedom. He was received with enthusiasm by all who wished for a united Italy and hoped for an end to the corruptly autocratic rulers of the petty states into which the nation was then divided, most of whom depended upon Austria for their hold on power.[32]

At first, Rome had been indifferent to the French Revolution and the French invasion of Rome. But when the pope was removed and died in exile, the Romans woke up to find a city not only looted of everything of value, but that the French had done nothing for them other than to make the Roman Republic bankrupt.[33]

The King and Queen of Naples were now feeling more and more insecure. The city was filled with pro-French supporters, who were prepared to rebel against the monarchy should the opportunity occur. They were mostly members of the middle class, not to be confused with the *lazzaroni* who were very loyal to the royal family. In November 1798, King Ferdinand, seeing his power on the brink of crumbling and the French grip on Italy weakening with Napoleon's departure for more important battles, was determined to strike a blow for the old order by invading central Italy and marching on Rome. There King Ferdinand expected to be successful. He intended to drive the French out and deliver Rome back to the Romans. The events that followed had the atmosphere of an opera buffa! Ferdinand's army marched north and entered Rome from the south side of the city where they met with little resistance—the French were caught unprepared. The proud liberator, King Ferdinand, strutted around and took as much plunder as he could lay his hands on. However, when he marched north into the stronghold of the enemy, he was easily defeated, his army dissolving at the first impact. The officers were the first to flee, and then all the motley crew of his undisciplined soldiery fled back to Naples.[34]

Fortunately for him, the famous British admiral Nelson was in Naples after having won the battle of Aboukir Bay (Battle of the Nile). Here followed the famous liaison between Nelson and Lady Emma Hamilton. King Ferdinand, finding his subjects on the verge of rebellion, hoped the presence of Nelson would stabilize the situation; his presence was a godsend to the old king and his queen. The hated French were getting closer and closer, and when it became a foregone conclusion that they would take Naples, the royal family fell into a state of panic.[35] It seemed that the inevitable would take place and that they would have to flee. There were mob uprisings in the streets; Royalists and pro-French elements were at each other's throats. Roving bands of cutthroats lurked in every dark alley looking for trouble. The royal family was so terrified they became hysterical, fearing for their lives. Soon, Nelson came to their rescue and arranged for a secret departure to Sicily, where they would be safe as long as the kindly English held command of the seas. Just before Christmas, 21 December 1798, Nelson's war-battered ship, the *Vanguard,* with her decks crammed with so-called personal effects, swept them off to Palermo.[36] There were barrels containing the royal treasury, gold and silver coins, and objets d'art from the palace. They had all escaped in a terrible storm, late at night through a secret passageway from the palace to the beach, led and arranged by none other than the charming soon-to-be mistress of Horatio Nelson—Lady Hamilton.[37] Nelson noted, "It blew harder than I have ever experienced since I have been at sea."[38] Next morning, the Neapolitans discovered to their anger and disgust that they were not only without their monarchs but abandoned to the mercy of the fast encroaching French troops.

Chapter Three

The Family

1799-1800

Naples was given up to insurgency until the French army arrived. At the head of the anti-Royalists, who were prepared to welcome them into the city, was Nicola Lablache and his wife Francesca. In the ensuing street fighting, the French succeeded in gaining control. At once, they set up the Parthenopian Republic (the Latin phrase comes from the epitaph on Virgil's tomb "of fair Parthenope"), essentially a military dictatorship. Order was restored, and at last there was peace.[39] Florimo writes:

> Francesca Lablache shared the same liberal pro French ideas as her husband, and during the proclamation of the Republic of Naples she embroidered a large flag, in the middle of which was the tree of freedom, crowned by the Phebian cap of liberty. This flag was flying outside the Royal Palace after the revolution. Then the composor Domenico Cimarosa was comissioned by the heads of the Neapolitan Republic to compose a patriotic hymn to words by Luigi Rossi.[40]

The people of Naples gathered together in the central square, now called Piazza del Plebiscito, for the ceremonial burning of the royal flag. On this solemn occasion, the hymn was sung and the republican flag raised in front of the royal palace (19 May). Later, Francesca Lablache, Cimarosa, and others were to pay dearly for their assocation with the French.[41]

However, the republic was doomed from the start and did not have an easy time of it. The cowardly king, and his hysterical queen, could not give their beloved city up to the French without a tremendous fight. They may have fled, but they were already plotting their return and the downfall of the hated French. The royal monarchs were understandably livid at reports that Naples was settling down without its rulers. How could the French be driven out was the question. Soon they realized it could be done with the right leadership, and a certain Cardinal Ruffo offered his services to the king.

The powerful cardinal Ruffo was a prince of the church and the owner of vast estates in Calabria. During the spring of that year, he organized a great army. Many soldiers were his own tenants; many were bandits, murderers, and robbers, all willing to fight to liberate the capital and restore the monarchy to power. Ruffo's bandits had high hopes, and the teeming conglomeration of adventurers soon controlled the whole countryside.[42]

In late spring 1799, the French general Championnet was compelled to withdraw all but a token force from the capital because of renewed war between Austria and the French. This was the chance the Royalists had been waiting for; and on 13 June 1799, Ruffo's undisciplined mass of brigands, some seventeen thousand strongmen, stormed the city.[43]

The Parthenopeans held strong. The royal insurgents poured in, their numbers swollen by many *lazzaroni* thirsting for revenge and plunder. The army was indistinguishable in its elements from the extreme Jacobins whom it opposed. The *lazzaroni,* the beggars, and the prisoners who had been let out of their dungeons at St. Elmo and elsewhere added to the indescribable scene. Radicals and Royalists, moderates and extremists, were all at each other's throats. They fought fiercely in the alleys, on rooftops, and in the streets, but the main resistance was in front of the royal palace.[44]

Finally, the French were defeated, and Naples was liberated.[45] Florimo writes that it was sometime after 13 June 1799:

> Nicola Lablache, who had taken on an active part in the fight that sad day, was wounded, or believed to be wounded. To escape the fury and persecution of Cardinal Ruffo he was hidden with his wife by a close friend, together with the dancer Duport and composer Cimarosa, under the wooden floor of the Royal Theatre del Fondo. Many days passed, and not knowing the situation in Naples generally, Duport foolishly climbed up on to a high window above the stage overlooking the road beneath, fell, and was killed instantly. His companions, terrified and upset, decided to hide the body under the stage as a temporary measure. However after five days the smell of the decaying body became intolerable, and, as they had finished the food a friend had brought them at great risk and obviously could not expect further supplies, they decided that the only thing to do was to surrender to the authorities. They were

aware of their liberal principles and also of what they had done during the revolt to help the French. Cimarosa was imprisoned in the Castel Nuova, and Lablache, being French, was condemned to exile. He did not go however because shortly afterwards, on Christmas day, while dining with his family, he died of an aneurysm, a young man of thirty-three.[46]

Another more lurid account of his death is that upon the entry of Ruffo and his cutthroats into Naples, Nicola was taken prisoner after fighting fiercely for many hours:

He was confined in the Castle of St. Elmo. Later he was taken out with others and shot, and buried in the prison enclosure, no stone marking his grave. When his son, years later wished to remove his body to a more befitting resting place and raise a monument over it, the place of his interment could not be discovered.[47]

This account is also unsupported. It is possible that he had been part of a French group of Jacobins that Queen Carolina had arrested after the news of Marie Antoinette's execution. Vowing vengeance on all the Jacobins in Naples, she arranged for them to be thrown into the dungeons of the St. Elmo Castle and forced to dig their own graves. "This done, each was chained to a stake in his separate hole, and left to rot. Those who survived did so due to the secret kindnesses of their friends, who included many jailers and officers of the fort."[48]

A more valid account from other researches suggests that Nicola survived the year of the fatal revolution and was alive until 8 December 1802 when little Luigi was seven years old. Some accounts say he was living in hiding and possibly under an assumed name.

When research was done in Naples in the early 1900s by descendants of the family,[49] an entry was discovered in the register of the parish of SS. Giuseppe Cristoforo, which stated that "on the 8 December 1802, Don Nicola Lablache, husband of Francesca Bietagh Lablache . . . Having partaken of the Holy Sacrament, died in the Communion of S.M.C. and was buried." This document was signed and countersigned by the singer Luigi Lablache.

When King Ferdinand and his court returned, the witch-hunt started all over again. Those who had aided the French were hunted down and either put on trial or banished. The atrocities and executions continued until 1801 when the Reign of Terror finally came to an end. There were many martyrs;

Queen Carolina's fury knew no boundaries, for as soon as Admiral Nelson dropped anchor in the bay, he unleashed his revenge upon those who had aided the French. Five hundred insurgents were banished. Stendhal wrote the following:

> By the hand of the Queen's public executioner, Naples lost almost every single man of distinction among her citizens. The reactionaries experienced a peculiar thrill in the hanging of Eleonora Fonseca, a woman whose genius was as rare as her beauty, she had been editor of the *Il Monitore Repubblicano,* the first newspaper of Naples. Among the aristocracy who met their death were the Duke of Andria, and the Prince of Strongoli and his brother Mario Pignatelli.[50]

Domenico Cimarosa, close friend of Nicola, had displayed his sympathy with republican ideas. He was imprisoned and sentenced to death, but, like many others, he was finally only banished. Going to Venice on his way to Russia, and while working on a new opera *Artemisia*, he suddenly died on 11 January 1801.[51] Florimo continues,

> The Santa Fede Government did not want to recognize Francesca Lablache as a foreigner. She was known to have made the famous flag. She was arrested, and then dragged through the streets of Naples, with San-Felice, the Piemental and others, and then was imprisoned in the Castle of Ischia. In fact, the poor wife of Nicola was almost forgotten ... awaiting a final decision, she spent six long months in the horrid prison. The Tribunal of Monte Ovieveto, unable to find sufficient valid motive to issue a decree of capital punishment, finally ordered her release, and she was free. A fortunate event had saved her life, and the judges were unable to condemn her. One day, her maid who was looking after the house in her absence, saw the rabble of the Sanfedisti approaching. Quickly, thinking they were about to search and plunder, she had the fortunate inspiration to throw the flag into the fireplace. Once the "corpus delict" was destroyed, there was not sufficient evidence to condemn her. During these terrible times, to make things worse, the brother of Nicola, who had not taken part in either of the political movements or the revolution, took advantage of the time when Nicola and Francesca were in prison, and ran off

with the family money.[52] He was never heard of again. The widow Francesca Lablache was left in great poverty: so in order to feed her three little children, she went to work as a housekeeper for the Princess of Avellino.[53]

Whatever happened to Nicola, he was obviously not in a position to do much for his children. He was certainly dead by the time Luigi, who would have hardly remembered him, was seven. Yet Luigi Lablache kept a portrait of his father with him all his life.[54]

Florimo relates, "The widow Lablache was left in great poverty caring for her family which by then consisted of Luigi, a daughter Clelia and another daughter Adelaide. When the French returned for a second time, life improved." Florimo continues:

> So as to feed her three little orphans, the unfortunate widow and mother had to work as a housekeeper for the princess Avellino. When Giuseppe Napoleon reigned in Naples, both the prince and the princess of Avellino decided to recommend the unfortunate family to the King . . . the prince Avellino being the King's steward and the princess being the lady-in-waiting.[55]

The children were then brought up and educated in the Avellino villa. From this, we can infer that Francesca must have maintained good relations with the French probably because of her liberal views and her marriage. It is not unreasonable to assume that she managed to move into high social circles even though she had such a stormy past. And they all apparently flourished in the princess Avellino's household.

Chapter Four

The Young Lablache

1800-1812

Napoleon Bonaparte, the Corsican adventurer, was now emperor of the newly formed French Republic. In four brief years, he had imposed his will on France whose people were now sick of the Revolution and looked toward peace and order under a different rule. Soon, however, Napoleon provoked war, and it was apparent to all that he was bent on conquering most of Europe. Declaring that war was essential to his political purposes, he had mapped the road to his ultimate failure.

The French had taken over Italy, where new dynasties were established and Napoleon elevated his brother to the throne of Naples and Sicily. He declared the Bourbons deposed, and a detachment of troops was sent to occupy Naples. King Ferdinand fled again with his court, returning to Palermo for a second time.[56] Created King of Naples, Joseph Napoleon was the older brother of Napoleon Bonaparte and the first French ruler of the Kingdom of Naples.[57] Florimo continues,

> In 1806, the prince and princess Avellino, through their closeness to the King, were able to help the Lablache family receive some compensation for the misfortunes endured by Luigi Lablache's father. They persuaded the King of Naples to give a free place at the Conservatori della Pietá dei Turchini to little Luigi, and another free place at the Conservatori Gesù Nuovo for his sister Adelaide. Clelia, his other sister, was sent to a German boarding school paid for by princess Avellino. She remained there until she was eighteen. Returning to Naples, Clelia then become a governess to one of the daughters of the Avellino family, the princess of Centola. Now princess of Angri. Clelia then married the Marquis Brayda (a Neapolitan bearing a Spanish title).[58]

17

"Song is a natural expression of musical talent," wrote Florimo, and the little Luigi was able to sing and play the piano long before he was placed in college. And who could explain his peculiar talent for whistling that according to family history "would have put a picolo player to shame"? At the age of nine, Paganini played so miraculously, so well that it moved Rossini to say that he had only wept three times in his life—once when his first opera failed, once when on a boating excursion a turkey stuffed with truffles fell into the water, and once when he first heard Paganini play.

Was Lablache a child prodigy? Yes, most certainly. We know he was a boy soprano and sang in the Cathedral of Naples. Children were admitted to the conservatories of Naples at the ages of seven. Mozart at age six could play the clavier and the violin at five.[59] Schubert was a boy soprano and began composing at age five. At age eleven, Tito Mattei, a child prodigy and pupil of Lablache was created *professore* of the Accademia Nazionale di Santa Cecilia, Rome. From there, he was appointed pianist to the King of Italy.[60]

The Musical World's reporter gave us a good insight into the world of music behind the doors of the conservatory in Naples. His guide was librarian Signor Cavaliere Florimo:

> I asked to be conducted to the librarian of the conservatory, who had been described to me as a Signor Cavaliere Florimo. I found Signor Florimo an agreeable gentleman, who most readily and obligingly showed me the musical library under his care, and furnished me all the information I wished to obtain. I learned the following facts:
>
> The conservatory of music at Naples was one of the finest schools in Europe. The college of Pietà dei Turchini moved to San Sebastino in 1806. It being then that Napoleon combined in one institution the four musical schools existing there (in Naples) at that period. These establishments, whose histories some of which extended back as far as the middle of the 16th century, that is to say over a period of 300 years, were, the Conservatorio della Pietà dei Turchini, the Conservatorio dei Poveri di Jean Christo, the Conservatorio S. Onofrio and the Conservatorio di Maria Loretto. It would appear from the above titles that all the schools of music in Naples in those days were connected with the monasteries of the town. It is very certain that the Italian priesthood took a lively interest in music. The pupils of this long-celebrated school, of whom a hundred were taught free, were bound to this institution

for at least six years. In some cases they remained even longer. In addition to receiving artistic and scientific instruction they were also lodged and boarded free of cost. No pupil was admitted under the age of seven and on the other hand, no one was allowed to attend over the age of twenty-four. The subjects of study included every branch of music, but also an elementary course in geography, history and philosophy.[61]

Thus, the little Lablache would have had a good education in spite of the troubled times that surrounded him. Florimo tells us, on the subject of Luigi's early years, that he studied the elements of music under Gentilli; and while Valesi instructed him in singing, Marcello Perrino taught the young boy the violin, piano, cello, and double bass:

> Although he was showing great aptitude for music, he initially had little or no desire to study it. When the young boy started to study the violin he was very unwilling, but an unforeseen circumstance made him change instruments, and change his attitude. This revealed how strong his natural disposition to music was. A fellow student who was to play double bass at a concert had become ill. Lablache, who had never before played that instrument in public, volunteered to take his place. Three days were enough for him to learn his part and for him to enjoy the difficult new instrument, which, by the way, suited his physique. At that time, he already had a tendency to put on weight and become corpulent. His main passion was singing, at which he excelled. Before reaching puberty, he had a beautiful contralto voice, and sang solos with considerable éclat in the cathedral at Naples. Soon he had earned the reputation as one of the finest boy singers of church music.[62]

In May 1809, Joseph Haydn died in Vienna. The students of the Conservatory performed Mozart's *Requiem Mass* in his honor:

> Young Luigi was entrusted with the alto solos. However, he encountered difficulties. He became hoarse and then could not utter a sound, or reach the final fugue—his voice was breaking. Everyone feared he had badly damaged his vocal cords, and his teacher advised him to rest his voice for several months. Soon however, he acquired a magnificent bass register, with a

phenomenal range of two octaves, from E flat hiqh, and a volume that increased year by year. He was given the opportunity to study with the best singing teacher of the city, Valenti, who instructed him according to the old true technique. A few years later the College built a theatre on the premises, indispensable for the instruction of students. The first opera performance was *La Contadina Bizzarra* by Castignace. Lablache was cast as the part of the Neapolitan comic, which may have been his first stage appearance. He was a huge success and played the part with true gusto.[63]

At last, he must have felt destiny was in the making. He was maturing. Tall (over six foot was most unusual in those days), handsome, and full of natural artistic talent, there was a great future ahead for him as an operatic singer. Florimo continues to tell us about Lablache without giving dates, so we can only guess at when these events happened. At that time, however, he had grown rather impatient with the discipline of the college. When he heard that the manager of a Salerno Theater needed a double bass player, he signed an agreement for a monthly salary of 15 ducats and set off without the permission of the college. He received a month's salary in advance, which he spent before he even got there. As he could not appear decently without luggage, he filled a small trunk with sand and set out. Two days later, the vice president of the conservatory, having notified the authorities, arranged for the pupil deserter to be picked up and returned at once. He was brought back by the carabinieri and placed under arrest for a month. Lablache obediently returned to his duties. The impresario was most put out by all this and upon young Lablache's hasty departure rushed to the young truant's lodgings to see whether he could recoup himself in any way for his losses. Finding to his delight a heavy trunk, he told his man to have it hauled to his quarters. When on the way the man complained of its dead weight, they opened it only to find it was filled with sand.

On another occasion when Lablache became weary of his studies, he engaged himself to an actor manager called Benevola and earned great success in such parts as Otello in one of the small theaters.[64] This time, he was ordered back to his studies by no less a person than Joachim Murat, King of Naples,[65] who this time sent six *sbiri* to make sure that the itinerant musician should return to the conservatory. His employer was in the depths of despair at his departure, but Lablache promised he would never forget his kindness and would make it up to him later. Indeed, he was as good as his word. A quarter of a century later, when he was rich and famous, he discovered that Benevola had fallen on evil days. Lablache sent him 500 lire to come to Paris to hear his great triumph in *Otello* and after the performance presented Benevola with a deed, which ensured for him a pension of 1,200 lire for life.

> Lablache was finally expelled from the college, as he had run away five times. This was meant to be an example to the other students, so they would not try *escapades a la Lablache*. This expression was used on the original ministerial letter preserved in the college. An Act of Law was passed completely new in the history of the college, which forbade any manager of a theatre in the Kingdom of Naples to engage any student of the college, without first having obtained special permission from the local goverment, ratified by ministerial consent. In cases of infringement of these rules, the theatre would be fined 2,000 ducats, and would be closed for 15 days. Poor Lablache was then without food or clothes, and unable to ask his mother for help, as she could hardly take care of herself. He turned to his friends, who were only too happy to help. They formed a collection of 5 ducats, which they gave him and also managed to find clothes here and there. Not long afterwards, his friend, a student by the name of Giovanni Cioffi, took him to live at an Inn called San Camillo. It was located on the via San Bartolomeo, close to the Castel Nuovo, just off the via Medina.[66] Cioffi had a relative who happened to be self-styled manager of a small theatre which was temporarily erected in the refectory of the old conservatory of the Pieta dei Turchini.[67]

In this small theater, Lablache was allowed to sing comic operas in the Neapolitan dialect. Between acts, he could also sing some separate pieces not pertaining to the opera so as to also vary and improve afternoon and evening performances.[68] The modest sum he received for his singing was five *Carlini* per day for both performances. This was enough to pay for his lodgings and enabled him to eat fairly well. Florimo remembers his fast rise to fame, and soon he became a sensation. At first, it was local patrons who came to hear him; but as time went by him, more and more people came from all over the city to enjoy and admire him. The little theater was always packed to the rooftops and became the fashionable place to go.

Lablache felt his vocation was the stage. With a natural talent for buffo Napolitano roles, he buckled down and learned how to be a singing actor and comedian in the rough and ready and often sleazy atmosphere of the minor theaters of Naples. None the worse for his experiences, Lablache emerged streetwise and confident but with a strong provincial accent which still marred his pronunciation.

Moving forward in society, he was patronized by Mme. Méricofre, a banker's wife, who was an admired patron of Neapolitan musical society. Before her marriage, she was known as the beautiful La Coltellini.[69] Lablache had matured into a tall and extremely handsome young man with plenty of charisma, natural wit, and enormous charm; his hair was thick dark and curly, his deep-set eyes were dark and twinkled with fun.[70] Mme. Méricofre was instrumental in pushing him forward, giving him encouragement and counsel. She cautioned him to avoid impresarios who exploited young singers; Lablache had need of such advice.

ଔଔଔ

Chapter Five

Early Successes

1813-1820

This success did not escape the notice of the manager of Naples's Teatro San Carlino. Always looking for new talent and an expert at bringing off a successful deal, he hired the young Lablache to sing many of the comic roles and paid him a relatively good salary of 80 ducats per month, which Lablache accepted with joy and gratitude. He was now nearly eighteen years old.[71]

His official debut was at the little theater San Carlino, in Silvestro Palma's *L'erede senza eredita* although there was some argument that his debut may have been in *La Molinara* by Giovanni Paisiello. Here, however, Florimo wrote, "Cioffi assured us, his debut was not in *La Molinara* as Fetis wrote." Certainly, he sang *La Molinara* there. He also sang Domenico Cimarosa's *Le trame deluse* and Luigi Mosca's *Gli sposi in cimento*.[72]

Apparently while he was there for only a short time, he continued to practice his singing and, despite his inexperience, was a sensation. Lablache was the constant topic of conversation among those who inhabited the small coffee shops and salons of the neighborhood. Almost everybody predicted the glorious future, which indeed he had.

After enjoying this popularity with the local Neapolitans, for only six months, Lablache fell in love with his young singing teacher,[73] Teresa Pinotti. She was the daughter of the celebrated dramatic actor, singer, and comedian Alessandro Pinotti.[74] He and his wife Rosina were well-known singers in Naples and had sung all across Italy. On many occasions, the members of the Pinotti family had performed at the royal theaters Fiorentini, Fondo, Nuovo, and the San Carlo. Elisabetta and Rosina Pinotti were believed to be sisters.[75] During this time, Giovanni Battista Rubini, an unknown young tenor, left his home in Romano, a small town in the province of Bergamo to try his luck in the operatic world of Naples.[76] Rubini first met Lablache in Naples; later they became friends and colleagues.

Several months later, Lablache proposed marriage to Teresa Pinotti, which was accepted. They married in Naples in the little church Giuseppe a Chiaia on 13 October 1814.[77] Lablache found Teresa Pinotti more than just an attractive young lady, and she was well brought up and well-educated by her talented father. Apparently ambitious, she encouraged her young husband by awakening his self-esteem to stop singing in the Neapolitan dialect of which he was very fond and to study "better" Italian. Florimo says the following:

> In una parola, la dolce compagna ch'egli aveva scelta per abbellirgli la vita, sublimo il suo spirito, trasformandolo in un altro uomo . . . "Che poi divenne celebre!"[78]

Conquering the language and dropping the patois would help him become a serious dramatic opera singer. Before long, Teresa transformed him into a different man: a young man interested in fulfilling his destiny as a world figure in grand opera.

Early in the spring of 1815, with the aid of the British, Naples was recaptured by Austrian troops and returned to Bourbon rule. Napoleon Bonaparte escaped from Elba; and Joachim Murat, the emperor's brother-in-law, King of Naples, tried unsuccessfuly to keep a hold on Italy. After a long and trying absence of nine years in exile, the Bourbon king Ferdinand and his court returned.[79] Soon after their return, the Teatro San Carlo celebrated their arrival on 4 October 1815 with a new opera, *Elisabetta regina d'Inghilterra*,[80] written especially for the occasion by a young composer from Pesaro—Gioacchino Rossini. The title role was written for the celebrated prima donna, the beautiful Isabella Colbran,[81] a Spanish soprano and favorite of the king and the Neapolitan public.

Gioacchino Rossini's musical fame was known throughout Italy, and in 1814, he had been engaged by the impresario Domenico Barbaja to compose two operas a year for the royal opera houses of Naples, the Teatro San Carlo, and the Teatro Fondo. Rossini, as musical director, was kept busy; besides writing, he supervised rehearsals. In return, he received a good salary, a share in the gambling profits, plus free lodgings in the impresario's palace at Posillipo, a beautiful coastal suburb overlooking the Bay of Naples.

Rossini was just twenty-three when he arrived in Naples, three years older than Lablache. It is unknown when Lablache met Rossini, but as Lablache was in constant touch with his Pinotti theatrical in-laws, it is possible they met each other that year. Or it may have been through a relative, the contralto

Elisabetta Pinotti (Bettina). She sang Rossini's first Ottone in *Adelaide di Borgogna in Rome* at the Teatro Argentina in 1817. An interesting comment about Elisabetta was written by Alberto Camotti, who wrote a book about the librettist Ferretti. It was quoted by Weinstock in his biography of Rossini:[82]

> The role of Ottone, by one of those strange customs of the time, was sustained by a woman; it was the contralto, also called that of the *primomusico*, a denomination that explains itself when one thinks that the contralto donna had taken the place of the elephant songbirds (castrati) of the seventeen hundreds. The part was interpreted by one of the two Pinotti sisters, Elisabetta, of a robust, wide-ranged voice, who was a little unsteady. The part that Rossini wrote for her rises from a deep B to the high F, and a few times pushes from the deep G to the high B-flat.

Elisabetta Pinotti sang seasons 1807-'09 and 1810-'13 at the San Carlo. She surfaced all over Italy during the beginning of the nineteenth century, proving she occupied a place on the lyric stage for a respectable number of years. Present in Rome and Milan in 1822, she also sang in the well-known performance as Teona in Nicola Manfroce's *Ecuba* a *tragedia* (a three-act Greek tragedy). Following on the heels of Spontini's classical opera *La Vestale*, in 1811, Florimo tells us, this composer was so inspired by this work he wrote *Ecuba*, his second opera.[83]

When it opened on 20 December 1812, everyone in Naples knew the composer Nicola Manfroce had not long to live, so his success was brief; indeed seven months later, he was dead of tuberculosis at age twenty-two. He had been one of Lablache's friends at the Collegio di San Sebastiano.

On 29 August 1815, the young Lablache couple had their first child, a boy. Fredrico Licterius Paul Nicola Augustin Lablache.[84] Frédéric, a carefully educated child, was taught singing by his father and followed in his father's footsteps onto the stage. The couple would then continue to sire a vast family totaling thirteen children in all: seven boys and six girls. Later many of them became singers; some did not survive to adulthood.[85]

The most important and powerful individual in operatic Naples was Domenico Barbaja, the legendary impresario. Notably responsible for shaping the careers of many singers of the time, he served as the director of the Teatro San Carlo and the other royal Neapolitan theaters Nuovo and Fondo. His empire widened later when he returned from Naples to Milan while presiding over the management of Milan's Teatro La Scala and the Teatro della Canobbiana (1826-32). The Kärnthnertor Theater at Vienna also came under his control from 1821-28.[86]

Notably, Barbaja proved himself to be extremely influential in launching Luigi Lablache's career. A self-made millionaire, he had risen from humble beginnings as a waiter and kitchen scullion in Milan. Earlier, he had managed and controlled a successful gambling business. Operating gambling tables in the foyer of the La Scala opera house, he catered to the whims of the rich and famous during the French occupation. Later, he also took credit for introducing the roulette wheel to the Italians.[87]

During October 1809, Barbaja left for Naples where he introduced more gaming tables at the theaters there. Soon his name became a household word for inventing the famous coffee or chocolate with a head of whipped cream named after him—*barbaja*! Often called *granite di caffe* or *cappuccino*. A man of sharp instincts, he was quick to notice talent; mixing in with all classes of people, making deals with princes, musicians, and gamblers, he moved among a cosmopolitan society bent on pleasure and easy gratification. Barbaja was even known to go out scouting the urban coffee houses and country hills for new operatic talent.[88]

The Italians, who had suffered through enough wars and revolutions in the last decade, were now eager to pursue pleasure; what was more pleasurable than opera with a dash of gambling? Domenico Barbaja was to contribute more than any other Italian impresario in furthering the careers of the bel canto composers like Rossini, Bellini, Donizetti, Mercadante, Pacini, and many others. Joining his company assured fame and fortune to many young singers, some of whom have gone down in history as the finest singers of the first half of the nineteenth century. Among those golden voices were Colbran, Ungher, Fodor, Winter, Nozzari, Galli, Dardanelli, David, Donzelli, Ciccimarra, Ambrogi, Garcia, Benedetti, Malibran, Malanotte, Marcolini, Giovanni Battista Rubini called King of Tenors, and Luigi Lablache.

The eighteenth century went out with such an upheaval of violence and bloodshed in Naples that opera suffered and almost came to a halt when the French invaders took control. King Ferdinand and his court had been the mainstay of the operatic world before their forced exit to Palermo. From the chronologies of the San Carlo Theater,[89] there is evidence that seasons were very sparse. Rehashes of inferior or mediocre material seemed to dominate performances in the early years of the French Republic. Change was inevitable, and by the end of the first decade, the French rule was accepted and Naples returned to its former lifestyle. Before Rossini's entrance, Neapolitan opera favored the usual mythological subjects set off in a framework of pageantry. Singers displayed their talents in highly embellished, elaborate arias. There was opera buffa where the recitative was prevalent and the great castrati ruled supreme in *opera seria* in decadent splendor. By the Age of Enlightenment, the memories of the French Revolution had faded, the castrati were vanquished, and the musical world of the early nineteenth century changed. Rossini ushered in the dawning of a dazzling New Age.[90]

> No composer in the first half of the nineteenth century enjoyed the measure of prestige, wealth, more popular acclaim or artistic influence than belonged to Rossini. His contemporaries recognized him as the greatest Italian composer of his time. His achievements cast into oblivion the operatic world of Cimarosa and Paisiello, creating new standards against which other composers were to be judged. That both Bellini and Donizetti carved out personal styles is undeniable but they worked under Rossini's shadow, and their artistic personalities emerged in confrontation with his operas. Not until the advent of Verdi was Rossini replaced at the centre of Italian operatic life.[91]

Rossini composed his operas for a new breed of singers, sopranos, tenors, and basses that were skilled in matching the styles of singing of their eighteenth-century counterparts. While steeped in tradition, sopranos aimed at delivering anything that the great castrati achieved, except now they would abide by the composers' wishes without the usual custom of singing embellishments of their own. A certain amount of this apparently was still tolerated by the composer and expected by the singers and audiences alike. Now singers even learned to channel their emotions into acting instead of standing motionless. Techniques of singing and melodic style altered drastically. The New Age brought an excitement that had not been felt before.

The long traditions of Neapolitan opera can never be ignored. During the early part of the nineteenth century, opera filled an important role in the lives of Italians. Opera houses were the meeting place for all classes of people and the fashionable place to be seen to exchange gossip and gamble. Opera has generally been accepted as an Italian invention even though its origins in earlier dramatic forms have been traced back to the Greeks. Certain Italian opera houses set a new standard during the New Age, and it was in Italy that Italian opera developed into the varied art form it is today.

When the famous composer Giovanni Paisiello died in Naples in June 1816, Lablache was hired to sing the bass part in the *Requiem Mass* by Mozart at the funeral. All of Naples paid respect to the memory of this great Neapolitan opera composer. The sound of Lablache singing Mozart's "Lacrimosa" was so beautiful that many people wept. This did not go unnoticed, for when Lablache left the church, the impresario Domenico Barbaja was waiting outside; he immediately hired Lablache to sing at the new theater San Ferdinando in Palermo.[92]

Lablache in the meantime had been performing also at the theater La Munizione in Messina with his inlaws, Alessandro and Rosa Pinotti, and his wife Teresa. Although records of these early performances are very difficult to find, it is known that Luigi and Teresa Lablache sang in Giovanni de Luca's *L'appuntamento notturna per burla,* and *Il Servo padrone* by Pietro Generali, and *Raul signore di Sequi* by Valentino Fioravanti.

The Pinotti family took many engagements all over Italy; sometimes they sang in the so-called dialect theaters.[93] Rosa Pinotti sang during the carnival period of 1802 in Cimarosa's *Giannina e Bernardone* at the Teatro Nuova in Naples. Singing there until about 1804, she went on later to sing at Teatro Imperiale Turin creating the role of Elgira, in Vincenzo Lavigna's *Hoango.* (Dec 26 1806*).* She surfaced again in Naples in 1812 and in many other cities in Italy, such as Florence, Venice, and Milan in 1814. Often because only the last name is given in theater chronologies, it is hard to recognize which Pinotti is which, making it difficult to trace this early group of singers.[94] Did Elisabetta, the sister of Rosa, sing only in Italy? The impression she leaves behind is unfortunately vague; all we can guess is she must have been younger. Often singers changed their names or got married, but overall not much trace of her can be found. While the family commuted between Naples and Sicily, their performances in Naples are easier to trace.[95]

Meanwhile, in Palermo, the Lablaches became parents again. Francesca Rosa Marie Nicolette Lablache (Cecchina) was born on 3 December 1816.[96] Palermo then became their home for the next five years.[97] They joined many other fellow Neapolitans and foreigners (British and French) who made up a huge part of the community that settled in Palermo. Trevelyan writes:

> Messina was traditionally jealous of Palermo as the capital, there was no doubt that Palermo had the aura of a metropolis. The large foreign community, in more peaceful times, was happy here. Many of the British merchants had originally come during the Napoleonic Wars, and had stayed on. Palermo and Messina were the two main

trading centres. Other, but small, groups of foreigners were to be found at places on the coast such as Syracuse, Catania, Licata and Marsala. 'Few Sicilians' carry on commerce with as much energy, the major part of the profits springing from this activity goes into the hands of the foreigners.'[98]

In honor of King Ferdinand, Palermo built a new grand theater, the San Ferdinando. Before the theater was finished, in the spring of 1815, the royal family suddenly returned to Naples. After his debut, Lablache sang on at the San Ferdinando with Teresa Pinotti; then for five years, he was the reigning *basso cantante* at the Palermo Teatro Carolino.

Some of these theaters specialized in dialect comedies and intimate productions enjoyed by the public. At these performances, there was a warmth that went with the audience participation even when tomatoes and cabbages were thrown, even when the singers did not care to stick to the score, going wild with their own embellishments and often engaged in shouting matches with their audiences. Lablache as a natural comedian fell into these buffo roles easily, and he was content. Teresa, however, was more calculating and ambitious for him. She stepped in to further his career.

Meanwhile, hired for all the leading buffo roles at the new San Ferdinando, Lablache debuted in the title role for the gala performance given for the inauguration of the theater. The chosen work was the popular comic opera by the brilliant composer Stefano Pavesi, *Ser Marcantonio*,[99] and the text was by Angelo Anelli. Did Teresa sing Bettina? It would be most likely. Certainly, Ottavio Tiby listed her as in the performance.[100] Lablache's reputation had preceded him, and he took the city by storm as the opera was repeated on many consecutive evenings. Pavesi's opera *Ser Marcantonio* had "flourished between the decline of Paisiello's productivity and the emergence of Rossini and Gaetano Donizetti." Definitely Pavesi's most popular opera, it was repeated on fifty-four consecutive evenings at La Scala in Milan after its premiere there on 26 September 1810.

Later, in 1843, Giovanni Ruffini and Gaetano Donizetti reworked the score and adapted the libretto for Donizetti's hilarious masterpiece *Don Pasquale* in which Lablache created the title role (Weinstock 399). Without doubt, Lablache contributed to the great success of this opera at the Théâtre-Italien in Paris later that year.

For the rest of the 1816 season in Palermo, he sang *La Calzolaia* (*The Shoemaker*) by Generali and *Il Vascello d'occidente* by Carafa.[101] Tiby tells us that after the season of 1816, while Lablache was only a young man of twenty-two, he was so successful that he was engaged at the theater Carolino for four consecutive years right up till the season of 1821 when he went directly to La Scala.

In the first season at the Carolino, he sang with his father-in-law, Alessandro Pinotti, and Girolamo Dardanelli in *Maria Stuarda,* a drama serio in two acts by Luigi Carlini. In September 1817, this opera opened with Luigi Lablache singing the part of Douglas for the first time with Giovanni David as Ormondo and Luigi Sirletti as the count.[102]

Three Rossini operas made an appearance during the Palermo season of 1817-1818, first *La Pietra del Paragone,* Rossini's first opera commissioned for Milan's La Scala (written in 1812), then *L'Occasione fa il ladro, ossia il cambio della valigia, burletta per musica,* a one-act piece, followed by *Ciro in Babilonia.* Here there are some questions. How many Rossini's operas had Lablache sung before? There was no mention of a debut in 1817 or in 1818. Certainly records here are vague. However, it's possible to guess he had sung most of them either in Palermo or in undocumented performances in theaters elsewhere. On 14 October 1818, he was documented as singing the first performance of Rossini's *Il Barbiere di Siviglia* in Naples at the Teatro Fenice. This performance was reviewed and mentioned in the *Giornale del regno delle due Sicilie* on 13 November 1818.

The same newspaper comments about the first performance that year of *La Pietra del Paragone.* Featuring Lablache, the reviewer seems to be more interested in the way the audience behaved "Prima stagional il 19 giugno 1818, Da *Il Gran Foglio di Sicilia* del 20 giugno 1818":

> Yesterday at the Real Teatro Carolino the *"La Pietra del Paragone"* by Rossini was given—which last year was re presented without success. We did not recognize it in fact; and we heard with pleasure Signori Lablache and Donzelli, and above all Signora Fabre. This clever and pretty actress has a voice that excites the ear and captivates the heart. As she sang her last aria in masculine attire, and with mannerisms, which animate the action, she rightly received the applause of the public. But, in the middle of this, one was aware, of a whistle. At this point the public threw itself into avenging the insult. The applause continued with greater enthusiasm, even wildly. Fabre was called back onto the stage, the aria was repeated and the applause crowned her for the third time. Here was a musical Scaramouch in which all three fighting partners seemed to have won. Signora Fabre must have been content with

the true spirit of the public in her favour; the public was satisfied with their vengeance and had the pleasure of establishing a triumph for someone who in reality did not deserve to be offended. In the end, the "whistler" can give himself the honour of having, like a powerful and unknown genius, with one whistle, succeeded in moving so many hands, exciting so much passion, fermenting so many souls, and producing so many things in one moment, that perhaps it was and could only be the whole object of this bizarre behaviour.[103]

At that time whistling and hissing as well as boos were commonplace at the theaters to show displeasure. Stendhal writes, "Giuseppina Fabre was a French contralto brought up in Milan, born actually within the walls of the Royal Palace."[104] She was supposed to have been the daughter of Beaumarchais's cook.[105] Stendhal, always with an eye for the ladies, noticed her in *La Testa di Bronzo* on the stage of La Scala on the night of 25 September 1816:

The entrancing Mademoiselle Fabre flaunted a cape of sky-blue and silver, with a white plume flown bravely over her shako. The whole stage of La Scala is afire with wealth and magnificence; the crowd of singers and actors rarely numbers less than a hundred. I am in a feverish daze. Her performance is bewitching in certain passages of intense emotion.[106]

Fabre also sang at the San Carlo between 1817 and 1821. While at the Teatro Carolino in Palermo, she distinguished herself there as one of the highest paid artists earning three times what Lablache made.[107]

Lablache was certainly one of the early Rossini interpreters in Sicily. Of interest here, the opera houses there might have been considered off the mainstream of events by later musicologists in general, but Palermo was at the center of events when King Ferdinand I of Naples and his queen held court. The loss of Naples burned deep into the hearts of the Bourbons; revenge became their lives. Paranoia overwhelmed them everywhere even where they had felt safe before; now not even in the theater. "Detachments of soldiers attend all the theatres, and sentinels are placed not only on the stage, but in various parts of the house. Even private families apply for sentinels, when they give large entertainments." Apparently the police were very deficient;[108] secret societies like today's Mafia spread fear, and the royal family feared death also from French assassins. Who knows if Lablache ever felt threatened by such things? His main concern was being not only a fine singer but an actor as well. And it was not always easy for him; still young, we find him getting help from his father-in-law, actor Alessandro Pinotti. In 1817, he was given the title role of a king in Mosca's *Federic II*:

> It was a new opera and Lablache read all he could regarding the King of Prussia . . . trying to imagine himself in the part, by imitating his way of walking, his gestures, his ways, and on the night of the final rehearsal, he consulted his father-in-law about it (Alessandro Pinotti). "It's alright," he replied. "You followed the play . . . you held your head on the side like Federic, you bent your knees like Federic, you even managed to reproduce the expression of Frederico . . . but why did you not take some tobacco? (Snuff). It was one of his habits." "Not taken tobacco! (snuff)," replied Lablache. "I filled the pockets of my jacket with it and I have been taking it all the time." "That is the problem, my boy," his father-in-law replied with a smile, "You took it all the time, but you did not take it at the right moment. There is a perfect situation during the second act, when the wife of the officer guilty of disobedience throws herself at the feet of the king to ask for his pardon. At this moment, everyone is looking at Federic . . . Everyone is asking themselves with anxiety what he will do! If at this moment, before replying, you had taken a pinch of snuff, this (act) would have been sufficient for the whole play. Instead, you took it all the time when no one was looking at you. This was useless. You have reproduced the habits of the King, but you did not make him live." You should have heard Lablache relating this fact, for his ability of story-telling was equal to that of singing.[109]

While well-established in Palermo, Lablache encountered many operas by Rossini during those four years before he was called to Milan in 1821. From 1817 he sang in about a dozen different Rossini operas. In April of 1819, tenor Giovanni Battista Rubini arrived in Palermo. Lablache knew Rubini had already made a deep impression on the public at Rome's Apollo theater in *La Gazza ladra* while he was also singing at all the royal theaters of Naples. They sang together in Palermo in at least two operas—*L'Impostore o il marcotondo* (Mosca) and *Il Rivale de se stesso* (Weigl). Palermo fashioned itself on bringing the leading singers from the mainland, and by 1821, many of Rossini's operas had opened there, including *Mosè in Egitto*. There,

Giuseppina Fabre and Lablache created a lasting impression. Luigi Lablache successfully sang in this opera at the Theatre Carolino on 20 February 1820 with an equally well-known cast. Later, the opera was revised for Paris, but the changes sacrificing drama for special effects weakened it. Lablache sang in *Mosè in Egitto,* again on 6 October 1824 with Fodor-Mainville in Vienna and again on 25 April 1827. Because of the sacred subject matter, the opera was usually shown at Lent. Eight showings for an opera per season was respectable for the San Carlo, and Lablache made a splendid first impression starting on 23 March 1829 in the *nuova versione*. M. Benedetti was still cast in the role of Moses while Lablache sang Faraone. Rossini triumphed in the grand scenes between the prophet and the pharaoh of Egypt. "The scenery and choruses were magnificent," wrote Lady Morgan, who often gave accounts of operatic life in Naples.[110] This opera was featured in Parma in 1829 when Lablache was singing there, but it is not known if Lablache sang *Mosè e Faraone* in the new version there in Italian—Lablache sang the title role on many occasions during his singing career in London and Paris.

Among three other operas written in 1818, Rossini wrote the *Mosè in Egitto* for the San Carlo. On 5 March during Lent, the opera opened with Naples's favorite soprano and leading prima donna, Isabella Colbran, and Benedetti. Historically, he was not overall as famous as Lablache. The voice of Benedetti was described as a true *basso profundo*, or true bass, and the rarest to be found among male singers. They have a darker and heavier tone. "Since the days of Remorini," writes *The Musical World* in 1848, "the opera stage has witnessed no real bass singers, other than Marini. (Ignazio) Marini's voice certainly was the purest and finest specimen of the basso profundo we ever heard, and it is a mistake to call Lablache a basso profundo."[111] Benedetti was very effective as Rossini's Moses. Stendhal tells us:

> Benedetti entered wearing a costume that was sublime in its very simplicity, and had been copied from Michelangelo's statue in the church of San Pietro in Vincoli, in Rome.[112]

Although Rossini's work was a triumph at the San Carlo, Stendhal did not really find *Mosè* to his taste. In fact, in many respects, he found it boring and basically poor theater.[113] Understandably, the incredibly dreadful staging and bad management of the props on the first night brought about this judgment. The action-packed drama suffered a few disasters; the major one came with the parting of the Red Sea. "A real masterpiece in absurdity," wrote Stendhal who attended. The scene did not quite have the desired effect when peals of laughter broke forth from the pit. Perhaps by the time Lablache returned to Naples, this problem had been ironed out. Another well-known bass during that time was Filippo Galli. Born in Rome in 1783, he was older than Lablache. Historically, he too was the major Rossini bass of importance before 1821.[114] Both singers pursued parallel courses, but records prove, though Galli created many Rossini roles, Lablache superseded him and sang "more" overall. He endured longer and was more famous. Lablache encompassed more Rossini roles at the San Carlo than Galli, who hardly ever sang there. For some reason, Galli was employed in the northern cities of Italy.[115] By the time Lablache's career had reached full maturity, Galli's career was on the decline.

The newspaper *Giornale regno dell Due Sicilie* reported Rossini's arrival in Naples without much enthusiasm. Even though Rossini's reputation had preceded him and his operas had proved themselves in other parts of Italy, the insular Neapolitans were not prone to accepting composers born elsewhere, calling them foreigners.

By 1815, Rossini had composed a dozen operas including *La Scala di Seta, L'Inganno Felice, La Pietra Paragone, Tancredi, L'Italiana in Algeri, Il Turco in Italia.* While the premieres of these operas took place in the northern cities of Italy, *Elisabetta regina d'Inghilterra* was Rossini's first Neapolitan work. When King Ferdinand and the royal household attended the world premiere of *Elisabetta regina d'Inghilterra*, Stendhal was also in the audience; he comments, "Fortunate as ever, Rossini made his debut in Naples in the most brilliant manner imaginable."[116]

Creating the role of Elisabeth I, Colbran was particularly admired, especially singing with the great Spanish dramatic tenor Manuel Garcia, father of Malibran, who created Norfolk. The opera ran for fifteen nights with a stellar cast including soprano Girolama Dardanelli cast with the splendid heroic tenor Andrea Nozzari as Leicester. Nozzari was still busy teaching Rubini.[117] That spring, Barbaja launched the young singer onto the stage of the Teatro Fondo for his Neapolitan debut in the *L'Italiana in Algeri*.[118] He also sang at the Teatro Fioravanti. Later, this theater, beside the Fondo, was also used by Rossini to launch many of his other operas. Simultaneously, *Elisabetta regina d'Inghilterra* was shown there as at the San Carlo. Later, Rossini and all the Garcia family left for Rome where he was involved in writing two works, one of which proved later the vehicle upon which Lablache launched his international career and considered historically Rossini's finest comic masterpiece, the popular *Il Barbiere di Siviglia.*

Success was not the only reward Rossini took with him when he left Naples. A ménage à trois, not unlike that of Lord and Lady Emma

Hamilton and Lord Nelson, was to emerge among these opera celebrities. The hot-blooded celebrated prima donna Isabella Colbran, reigning star of the teatro San Carlo and favorite of the King, was also Barbaja's mistress. Rossini, a guest in the Barbaja palace, was commissioned to write operas for the impresario. Difficulties soon arose because Rossini failed to deliver the expected scores on time. Months went by, and Barbaja was in despair and as an extreme measure resorted to locking Rossini in his room while ordering only bowls of plain pasta lowered by a rope-tied basket through the window. He was refused an exit until he had finished the overture to *Otello*. So it was no great surprise to the servants in the household when it was discovered later by Barbaja that Rossini had eloped with Colbran. (In 1822 they married).[119] Unshaken, Barbaja said afterward, "I am revenged."

Not long after the Neapolitan premiere of *Elisabetta,* however, a disastrous event occurred. On 12 February 1816—the great San Carlo theater was destroyed by a fire.

Chapter Six

San Carlo to La Scala

1816-1821

Charles the III of Bourbon built the original Teatro di San Carlo adjoining the royal palace in 1737. Designed by the architect Medrano, King Charles intended it be "stylish and grandiose"; and indeed it was, without question, one of the finest opera houses in Italy. Neapolitans were proud of their operatic tradition going back into the early seventeenth century. Naples was where opera flourished, and it was regarded as the capital of the musical world. All the major Italian composers at one time or another had been represented on the stages of this great historical theater. Now the theater was destroyed. And the Neapolitans blamed it all on the Jacobins.

    King Ferdinand was in despair; wrote Stendhal, "This blow, so they say, affected him more deeply than defeat in a dozen pitched battles or the loss of the whole realm."[120] However, Domenico Barbaja was at hand, and the King gave him the order to build a new theater at once. After all, theaters were always burning down; that was nothing new in the nineteenth century or for that matter in the eighteenth century. The best architect Antonio Nicolini was hired, and the theater was rebuilt up to its former glory in less than a year.[121]

    Theater life in Naples was an institution, and Naples boasted of many theaters. Even after the turmoil of the revolution of 1799 and the departure of the King and his court, the theaters continued entertaining the French. John Black gives us an insight into how many theaters were in operation a few years later during the time of Donizetti in *Donizetti's Operas in Naples 1822-1848*:

> For most of the period 1822-1838, 5 theatres were in regular use for performance of opera: the Teatri S. Carlo, Fondo, Nuovo, Fenice and Partenope. Occasional use was made of the S. Ferdinando

and, rarely, other theatres such as the Grande Arena (presumably out of doors) and the Fosse del Grano. In the average year there would have been over 700 performances of some 150 operas, but some operas, being performed at several theatres during the same year, would appear more than once in the summary. The S. Carlo and the Fondo were never open on the same evening, except for very rare occasions when the S. Carlo mounted a "Gran Festa di Ballo." Certain productions, usually but not always of a serious nature, were played with the same cast at either of these two Royal Theatres, which were, in any case, under the same management. There is evidence of occasional transfer of works from the Nuovo to the S. Carlo for isolated performances, and some suggestion of common repertoire between the Fenice and the Partenope in some years, again because the theatres were under the same management. Each theatre had its own favorite composers and librettists, and there can be no doubt that works in the lighter vein were the most popular. The most frequently performed composers were Vincenzo Fioravanti (notably *Il Ritorno di Pulcinella dagli Studi di Padova*), Pietro Raimondi (in particular, *Il Ventaglio*), Lauro Rossi (for instance, *La Contessa Villana*) and Luigi Ricci, whose *Il Diavola Condannato nel Mondo a Prender Moglia* seems to have been quite indestructible, and probably gives a pretty fair indication of popular taste. Bellini was by far the most frequently performed composer of more serious works, and *La Sonnambula* was the most often performed opera in Naples of the 1830s and 1840s.[122]

Stendhal wrote after the reopening on 12 February 1817: "The long awaited day at last, the gala-opening of the new San Carlo. Farewell sweet reason!"

> There is nothing in all of Europe that in any way approaches this theatre, or indeed even gives the faintest idea of it. I believed I was transported into a Palace of some oriental Emperor of the East. My eyes were dazzled, my soul ravished . . .[123]

Stendhal points out that the teatro San Carlo is as far ahead of La Scala in the brilliance of its orchestral performance as the Neapolitan theater is inferior to the Milanese in the poverty of its decor and the shoddiness of its costumes. Later again on 13 February, he returns:

> Standing once more within the theater, I discovered anew that sense of awe and ecstasy. Search to the farthest boundaries of Europe, you will find nothing to rival it, what am I saying? Nothing to give so much as the haziest glimmering of the meaning of it. This mighty edifice, rebuilt in the space of three hundred days, is nothing less than a *coup d'etat*: it binds the people in fealty and homage to their sovereign far more effectively than any Constitution. From prince to pot-boy, all Naples is drunk with delight . . .[124]

When Charles Burley visited Naples in the 1770s, he was deeply impressed by the San Carlo; he wrote the following:

> It is not easy to imagine or describe the grandeur and magnificence of this spectacle. The court was in grand gala. In front of each box there is a mirror, three or four feet long, by two or three wide, before which are two large wax tapers; these, by reflection, being multiplied, and added to the lights of the stage and those within the boxes, make a splendour too much for the aching sight . . . as a spectacle it surpasses all that poetry and romance have painted.[125]

On 12 January 1817, a birthday gala for King Ferdinand was arranged at the Teatro San Carlo, with a performance of *Il sogno di Partenope* by Mayr, with Isabella Colbran as Partenope, tenor Giovanni Battista Rubini sang Apollo accompanied by Italy's leading singers of the day. Canonici was Minerva, David-Mercurio and Nozzari sang Poliflegonte, and Benedetti was Il Tempo. There were three performances with each performance a ballet. King Ferdinand was fond of ballet.

Long before Lablache's debut at the San Carlo, Lablache sang Figaro in the first Neapolitan performance of the *Il Barbiere di Siviglia* on 14 October 1818 at the Teatro Fenice.[126] The cast that has come down to us: Maria Manzi sang Rosina, and Guiseppe Tavassi sang Bartolo.

The same cast sang with the exception of Rubini in a staggering thirty performances of Rossini's *Otello*. Rossini wrote, "I was forced to compose the overture to *Otello* by Barbaja while locked in a small room in his palace."[127] The overture has been often considered one of Rossini's worst most likely because of Rossini's suffering behind locked doors; it rather spoils the work that is considered to be one of Rossini's finest. Later during the nineteenth century, it unfortunately became overshadowed by Verdi's heavier masterpiece by the same name. Today, Rossini's *Otello* is not given the attention it deserves.

From 1812, Rossini's star was rising over the horizon, and his fame as a composer swept across Italy. Stendhal wrote:

> You have only to pick up any opera by Rossini to find yourself in a new and undiscovered country; the clear, refreshing winds of the high mountains are stirring about you; the air is purer to breathe; you seem to be born again in a new world, and the thirst for genius is upon you.[128]

Clearly, Rossini's style was fresh and new. He boldly brought forth different ideas and themes that eclipsed the mythological subject matter that saturated operas. While before they often idealized royalty, these themes were considered unfashionable by the "new order" and as outmoded as the powdered wig after the French Revolution. Rossini's music was quickly identified with the young people of that age while neoclassical simplicity was the rage in architecture and funiture. Classical lines of Grecian and Roman dress even influenced the styles of fashion: women wore soft, flowing lines and empire dresses of flimsy materials that feature low decollete, and tiny puffed sleeves were in vogue.

From Egypt, where great archaeological discoveries were made, Napoleon hauled off many antiquities to Paris. Fine art collections were taken from Italy, including the famous bronze horses from the cathedral of San Marco in Venice. Some of these treasures were never returned and to this day adorn the finest museums in London and Paris.

Rossini's arrival in Milan came during the final period of the Napoleonic Kingdom of Italy in 1812 before his Neapolitan and Roman successes, *Elisabetta regina d' Inghilterra* and *Il Barbiere di Siviglia*. His reputation was already established in the cities of Venice and Bologna with *Tancredi* and *L'Italiana in Algeri*.

On 26 September 1812, Rossini had launched his first work written especially for La Scala, a buffa in two acts, *La Pietra del Paragone*—libretto by Luigi Romanelli.

Rossini triumphed, and all of Milan was enraptured with this work. Now he was the leading composer of Italy, especially when this opera achieved fifty-three performances, almost as many as *Ser Marcantonio* in 1810. *La Pietra del Paragone* was sung in Palermo a few years later at the Teatro Carolino where Lablache was the leading *basso cantante*. It was an opera with which Lablache was very familiar, and it was part of his regular early repertoire.

Lablache sang *La Pietra del Paragone* at La Scala Milan 15 May 1822.[129] "Only twenty-two years earlier," wrote Stendhal, "Napoleon had stood up in his box there for the first time, while thousands in the theatre acclaimed him madly."[130] Moving to Milan after the defeat of Napoleon, Stendhal had experienced much of the world traveling with Napoleon, including his entrance into Italy and his harrowing retreat from Russia. We owe a debt to him for insight into those times when Rossini was enjoying the first upsurge of popularity.[131]

When Stendhal first came to Milan, he was introduced often to important Milanese, like Count Ludovico di Breme who, when he was under Napoleon, had been almoner to the King of Italy as the biography tells us:[132]

> Naturally Stendhal was introduced to him in someone's box at the Scala. Around him were grouped the already famous poets of young Italy, such as Monti, Silvo, Pellico, Grossi, and Manzoni, who already likened to his great model Byron . . . Little wonder he felt at ease in this circle of young men, as he entertained them with his endless "inside stories" about the court of Napoleon, or tales of his youth as a soldier of the Republic. They liked him because, besides being a romantic poet, they too were devoted Jacobins; they had generous passions, and dreamed of liberating their country from the yoke of foreign conquerors.

"Romanticism is all the rage here," wrote Stendhal to one of his friends in Paris. "I too am a wild romantic, that is to say, I am for Shakespeare against Racine, for Lord Bryon against Boileau."[133]

Here we learn that Stendhal was not wealthy, but he lived well in rooms adjacent to the late Renaissance palaces where dwelt still the descendants of the mighty Sforzas and Viscontes of the quattrocento. Here he gives us a view of life in Milan and at the La Scala:

> The warm-blooded Milanese, despite the distractions of war and revolution, continued to be impassioned music lovers, knowing the scores of the operas of Paisiello and Cimarosa which they heard over and over again, encouraging the actors with shouts or sobs of pleasure, or censuring them angrily . . . Beyle, attending *La Scala* every night, caught their fever for *opera buffa* in earnest,

and remained a musical maniac all his life. The imposing ballet of *La Scala* was also something that endlessly pleased him, the like of which he had never seen. Within the semicircle of that lofty hall, with its five tiers of candle-lit, silk-curtained boxes, he would sit by the hour, lost in a voluptuous and sentimental rapture that the Italian voices never failed to evoke. Soon he noticed that the Scala was the very center of social life, a sort of public salon for all the fashionable world of Milan. No woman who was in vogue would fail to appear there every night, mounting the grand stairway to her private loge in the company of eight or ten admirers and guests, while the town gallants thronged the broad foyer to ogle them. For without waiting to grasp the full import of Revolutionary ideas, the charming ladies of Milan had adopted the republican or "Roman" costumes that so freely revealed their arms and breasts. The full-bosomed Milanese belles seemed, to his eyes, the most beautiful women of the world, and their inviting and facile manners aroused the most pleasurable anticipations. Moreover, it was the young French officers who, by right of conquest, invariably escorted them, sat proudly beside them in carriages, acted as their faithful cavalieri servants. Perhaps the Italian lovers and husbands were vexed; but many, on returning to their homes, found their women in the arms of French officers, who sometimes drew their swords to turn them out of doors. Others shrugged their shoulders and consoled themselves by sharing with wives and sweethearts and sisters the rich trinkets that the French plunderers distributed with prodigal hands. Indeed some of the ladies of Milan, according to one diverting legend, could not quite remember who the fathers of their children had been, but tenderly named them after the French regiments that had been quartered among them. The morals of Milan had long been of the comfortable kind; a lover was expected to show jealousy, but a husband, never![134]

A turning point in the career of Lablache happened early in January 1821, the year the Congress of Laibach in Ljubljana, Yugoslavia opened. Lablache was invited to sing for the attending royalty, heads of state, and dignitaries, including the King of the Two Sicilies, King Ferdinand; Clement Metternich, foreign minister of Austria; Minister Capodistrias; Count Ruffo the Neapolitan ambassador in Vienna; and Czar Alexander I of Russia. Lablache entertained them at the festivities afterward and ended up staying there at least until 1

May. Two of Rossini's recent compositions were mounted.[135] One of the most popular operas sung there was Rossini's brilliant opera buffa *La Cenerentola* with Lablache singing Dandini.[136]

Czar Alexander I congratulated King Ferdinand of Naples on having a subject with such extraordinary talent, and it was then that King Ferdinand appointed him "Singer of the Royal Chamber and Chapel."[137] This was quite an honor: it was more than likely that Barbaja was responsible for arranging for the singer to be with the King on this important occasion. As a result of this congress, Metternich announced that Austria would restore law and order and install an orderly goverment back in the Kingdom of the Two Sicilies. Clearly, it was not surprising that King Ferdinand became afraid to return home; for seven weeks later, the Austrian army was back in control of Naples.[138]

Lablache was just twenty-six years old when he was removed from Palermo by Barbaja to sing at the great theater La Scala in Milan. His debut was in Rossini's *La Cenerentola,* on 15 August 1821.[139]

Leaving Palermo behind for Milan, Lablache had filled much of his early years singing Rossini operas.[140] Certainly by the time Lablache debuted at La Scala, his experience earned from those galley years supported an unsurpassed repertoire for a young man. Behind him a vast repertory had built up; he now had over fifty-five roles at his disposal. His future in opera was assured.

There was no turning back for Lablache when he first set foot on the boards of the most important theater in northern Italy, La Scala of Milan. The public enthusiastically welcomed Lablache's debut there with famed mezzo-soprano Teresa Belloc-Giorgi in August 1821 in *La Cenerentola*.[141] Recognized as a universal success, *La Cenerentola* was held over for a staggering thirty-six performances.

When the world premiere of Mercadante's buffo opera *Eliza e Claudio* opened, it was at the end of October. Lablache created the role of Arnoldo. It was written especially for him by Mercadante. *Elisa e Claudio* clocked up thirty performances the same season with the same cast. *Buonissimo* was written in a special column for ratings inside the theater's chronology, reproduced in Pompeo Cambiasi's book on *La Scala of Milan*.

La Cenerentola was first performed on an extremely stormy night in Rome on 25 January 1817 at the Teatro Valle. This theater was the home of the opera buffa and ready for the carnival season. Gertrude Righetti-Giorgi, who had created Rosina in *Il Barbiere di Siviglia,* was well cast in the leading role of Angiolina (who was Cenerentola), Andrea Verni (Don Magifico), and Giuseppe De Begnis (Dandini). This opera libretto was based on the French story "Cendrillon" by Charles Perrault and on the opera written by Isouard and produced first in Paris in 1810. The text was written by Charles Guillaume Etienna.[142] Jacopo Ferretti was considered one of the finest librettists in Italy, and this opera was one of his triumphs: he not only wrote for Rossini, but also for many other composers including Pacini, Mayr, Donizetti, and Mercadante.

In Milan, we find Lablache as publicly acclaimed King of Basses, and the Italian masses thronged to the theater to hear him, often exclaiming, "That since tobacco had crossed the English channel, there was only one other addiction with Italians . . . that was Lablache!"[143]

He rivaled most other basses now and enjoyed bringing Rossini into the arms of an ever-waiting public, first in Italy and then in Vienna. There he sang the first 1823 Italian performances of *Semiramide*, *Il Barbiere di Siviglia*, *La Cenerentola*, *Zelmira*, and *La Donna del largo*.

Barbaja hired Lablache to sing with his company at all the theaters he owned up and down the Italian peninsula, from the San Carlo in Naples to the Kärntnertor theater in Vienna; and from then on, his future success was assured. What excitement this generated; never before had the charm and the vivacity of Rossini been brought more to the public's attention than through the dazzling interpretation of Lablache. There always was this freshness and rare qualities that Lablache brought to his characters. Lablache was what we would call a *basso cantante*, not a profondo. His tremendous voice boomed through theaters, jarring even the most jaded opera devotee into noticing his existence. They now sat up and turned around in their boxes.

The antics and humor of Lablache so excited the Milanese that in its first season, *La Cenerentola* was a triumph for Rossini and Lablache and for all the members of the cast. Mezzo-soprano Teresa Belloc-Giorgi sang the title role with Lablache's old friend, Domenico Donzelli, who was Don Ramiro, and Nicola De Grecis sang Don Magnifico. The set designer was the brilliant Alessandro Sanquirico, one of the finest in the entire history of Italian opera.[144]

In October, Lablache sang in Morlacchi's *Donna Aurora* and *La Sciocca per Astuzia* with the same cast. Lablache sang there till the end of the 1821 season after which he left for Rome. For the first time in Rome, Lablache sang Figaro in Rossini's masterpiece *Il Barbiere di Siviglia*. Remembered always as Figaro, this was a role with which he was closely associated for most of his life; he carved a career from this role alone, but in later years, he was fondly remembered for his Bartolo.

Chapter Seven

Rome, Rossini and Vienna

1821-23

Rome, the Eternal City, in the early nineteenth century, was not a cosmopolitan city like Naples. Neither did it qualify as a musical center. Though considered picturesque by artists, its former glory was now gone, and many parts of the city were in decay and ruins. Amid filth and sickness, brigands frequented the wide-open spaces between the great ruins of ancient monuments while sheep, pigs, and donkeys freely roamed the dirty mud-filled streets. The French had captured the city under the usual guise of liberating the Romans from the Austrian domination. "We are friends of every nation," Bonaparte lied. Meanwhile, the French looted everywhere, stripping churches, palaces, and galleries of works of art, taking precious stones, gold, tapestries, and antique sculptures (including the famous Belverdere Apollo). According to descriptions of the time, everything was packed up and shipped back to France.[145]

The mostly wooden theaters of Rome were a disgrace; dark, dirty, and gloomy in their decorations; the hallways and entrances literally stank of dampness and decay. The oil lamps hanging down from the ceilings and elsewhere were rarely cleaned, and this presented a fire hazard. The citizens complained, but little was done. Rome boasted of three opera theaters—the Teatro Argentina, the Teatro Valli, and the Apollo. The Apollo was erected in 1671; since then, it had been rebuilt five times. It was there that Niccolo Paganini, the great violin virtuoso, conducted the premiere of Rossini's *Matilde di Shabran* on 24 February 1821 in the carnival season.

Paganini and Rossini moved in high society in Rome. Rossini was invited to sing at one of the Friday receptions of Pauline Bonaparte Borghese; there he sang the famous cavatina from *Il Barbiere di Siviglia,* "Largo al factotum." In the memoirs of Pacini, the composer recalled his wild antics with Rossini dressing up in eighteenth-century clothes; complete with masks and wigs, they walked along the Corso to the Caffe Ruspoli singing the chorus from

Il Pellegrino o Bianco. Still singing, they stopped outside. The place was known for having music, so as soon as a crowd of the curious gathered, a few remarks were made that they were there to ridicule a certain Maestro Grazioli, owner of the establishment. When things started to get a bit heated, they made a fast getaway.[146]

When Rome celebrated the carnival of 1821-22, Luigi Lablache brought in the New Year 1822 for the Roman public at the Apollo theater with the world premieres of two now-long-forgotten operas—*La Capriciosa e il Soldato* by Michael Enrico Carafa and *La Festa del Villaggio,* by Vincenzo Puccitta, both Neapolitans. Nearby at the Teatro Argentina, Domenico Donzelli was singing in the Roman premiere of Gaetano Donizetti's *opera seria Zoraide di Granata* that opened on 28 January 1822. There, it is possible Donizetti met Lablache.

Lablache became a father again that winter in Rome. Nicola Pierre Andre Lablache, who was named after his grandfather, was born there on 5 February 1822. Nicola was the second son of Luigi and Teresa Lablache.[147] Here it is only a guess that he was their second son. Teresa had lost a few children in childbirth. Francesca, their oldest daughter, was named after her grandmother. The day his son was born, Lablache made his Roman debut at the Apollo theater, where he apparently was appreciated as Figaro in the *Il Barbiere*. Elisabeth Pinotti sang in the same performance.[148]

To sing before a Roman audience must have been difficult since the famous world premiere of *Il Barbiere* was written up as a fiasco. Despite this, it was almost immediately recognized as Rossini's comic masterpiece and historically the most outstanding example of early nineteenth-century opera buffa. Lablache's powerful voice and antics succeeded even in Rome, and audiences most likely had enthusiastically applauded his Figaro. Though it is believed he took great liberties with the role, he greatly enriched its style and humor as had no other singer before him, consequently bringing more fame for himself and Rossini.

Lablache later became a favorite interpreter of Figaro when he sang in Milan and later Vienna. *Il Barbiere's* fame spread fast across Italy and soon was heard by many in other opera houses around the world.

The disastrous events at the earlier world premiere of *Il Barbiere di Siviglia* in Rome on 20 February 1816 are well documented, but so amusing that it would not be amiss to repeat the story. Rossini, a man of boundless energy, wrote this opera in an amazing thirteen days, which is a shorter time than most people would take to copy the score by hand. Manuel del Populo Garcia, the Spanish tenor and father of Maria Malibran, sang the part of Count Almaviva (written especially for him). Roman audiences were known to be critical and rowdy, but what happened that night at the Teatro Argentina was most unfortunate. First, a cat appeared from the wings and walked among the singers: after it was chased off by Figaro (Zamboni), it reappeared on the other side of the stage and proceeded to leap onto one of them during a duet, frightening the ladies of the cast. This stirred up the already rowdy audience, who then started to catcall, whistle, and meow. That was not all—one of the members of the cast had the misfortune to fall over the trap door, cutting his nose and scratching his face. The audience again thought this was hilarious and called out for him to do it again! If that was not enough, Garcia, the tenor, was hit in the eye by an orange. All was quiet on the following evenings, and the opera continued without incident.

Lablache left Rome and went straight to Milan for the opening of the season. There he sang through June 1822 with the same cast as the year before. The premiere of the opera buffa *La Dame Locandiera* by Luigi Mosca followed with *Elisa e Claudio, La Pietra del Paragone*, and then the season concluded with *Arrighetto* by Carlo Coccia and *L'Occasione fa il ladro*.[149]

In the autumn of 1822, Lablache was engaged to sing in Turin at the Teatro Carignano. The operas were *Una Casa da Venere* by Turina and *La Cenerentola* and *Agnese* by Fernando Paer.[150]

Then Lablache returned for a brilliant carnival season 1822-1823 in Milan. The great Festa at Verona opened on 24 November 1822 for the Verona Congress—it is possible Lablache sang there. Certainly, he was back in Milan for the 1822-1823 carnival season for the premiere of *Ameleto*, a *melodramma tragico,* based on Shakespeare by Saverio Mercadante and *Medea in Corinto* by Johann Simon Mayr, ending with *L'Esule di Granata* by Giacomo Meyerbeer. The soprano supporting him during his Milan seasons 1821-1828 was usually Belloc-Giorgi, but in the later 1820s, the leading soprano was Méric-Lalande. Most of the time, Monelli sang the tenor roles.[151]

The last Milan season in 1828, Lablache merely repeated his early successes and one world premiere *L'Orfano Della Seva* by Carlo Coccia. By this time, rumors of his leaving Italy were everywhere. He had been invited to sing in Paris and London where many Italian singers already held elevated positions. A glorious future lay ahead of him.

Afterward, Lablache would leave Milan for Vienna to join the brilliant cast from the San Carlo of Naples for the second season of Rossini works at the Vienna Kärnthnertor Theater. The impresario Barbaja's company consisted of Naples's finest: sopranos Isabella Colbran, Joséphine Fodor-Mainville, and Caroline Unger; Domenico Donzelli, tenor; Antonio Ambrogi, bass; Comelli-Rubini, mezzo-soprano and wife of Rubini, with the famous tenor

Giovanni David. No one could wish for a finer group of artists, and all of Vienna was waiting to enjoy more of Rossini.

The opera that the Viennese clammered to hear was *Il Barbiere di Siviglia*, sung in original Italian by an Italian cast. They had only heard it before in German.[152]

Upon their arrival in Vienna, the Italian opera was engaged from April through September. By now, Vienna was steeped in the music of Rossini: the year before, the Kärnthnertor Theater had staged a Rossini festival, which successfully presented a program of Rossini's works to Vienna. Now an international celebrity in the Austrian capital, Rossini enjoyed all the attention. His music, elegant manners, and brilliant conversation made him the favorite of the aristocracy. Crowds followed him, and he and his cast of singers were feted, wined, and dined by the elite: all Vienna was at their feet. Another troupe of principal Italian singers, headed by Lablache, arrived in April 1823 to ride a second wave of popularity. David and Ambrosi stayed, and they all supported Joséphine Fodor-Mainville who replaced Isabella Colbran who left with Rossini.

Barbaja had commissioned composer Franz Schubert to write an opera for the Court theater, but unfortunately, Barbaja, upon reading the score, threw it out because he said the libretto was very bad. There was a lot of resentment among the German composers about the success of the Italian opera. Schubert regularly grumbled about the bad taste of the public and "the wretched Italian music." Count Galenburg, who was the assistant to Barbaja, hearing his remark, said, "I will not contest the view of an authority, but I am indebted to the enterprise of Barbaja for many enjoyable hours." When Rossini called on Ludwig van Beethoven, Beethoven spoke to him in Italian:

> Ah Rossini, you are the composer of *Il Barbiere di Siviglia* I congratulate you; it is an excellent opera buffa; I read it with pleasure and it delights me. It will be played as long as Italian opera exists. Never try to do anything else but opera buffa; wanting to succeed in another genre would be trying to force your destiny.

Beethoven, who had heard the singers including Lablache, asserted that on the whole, the northern Germans know little about music and they will never produce anything higher than *Der Freischutz*. He went on to say:[153]

> And yet I cannot agree with those who reject Italian opera . . . to my mind there are two kinds of opera . . . one setting out from the

> text, the other from the music. The latter is Italian opera. Lablache, and to a degree Fodor, are better actors than the Germans ever had. Perhaps Mozart formed himself on Italian opera.

When the Italian season ended, Schubert said, "Thank God that we have got rid of that Turkish music!"

After the last performance of his opera *Zelmira* (it was previewed in Naples before opening in Vienna), Rossini left Naples, never to return to compose there again. It was reported in the newspapers that after Vienna, he would be visiting Paris and London.

Joining Barbaja in Vienna on 27 March 1822, Rossini was present to hear Weber conduct a performance of *Der Freischutz* at the Kärnthnertor Theater. On the way to Austria, he and Isabella Colbran stopped by Bologna where they were quietly married.

Carl von Weber, the composer of *Der Freischutz,* was full of praise for Rossini. Weber, after having been to the opera, wrote to his wife: "A pair of artists such as Fodor and Lablache have never come my way." After hearing Lablache's rendering of Geronomo in *Il Matrimonio Segreto*, one of Lablache's greatest roles, he confessed:

> I was completely bowled over, and Fodor sang an inserted aria so beautifully that I was convinced that if only she would sing *Euryanthe*, one would go mad.[154]

Weber strode out of the theater overwhelmed by emotion and jealousy after hearing Lablache singing the duet of Dandini and Don Magnifico with Ambrogi in *La Cenerentola*—Weber was totally enchanted by the music of Rossini, but intensely disappointed and angry that it was not German opera that was captivating the city that year.[155]

Ending his first season of 1823, Lablache was the toast of Vienna; the season certainly had been a success and, without doubt, an orgy of opera buffa. Rossini fever was in full swing. *Opera seria* was also well represented, mostly Rossini again; the Viennese could not get enough. Lablache sang with Joséphine Fodor-Mainville and the soprano Caroline Unger, Giovanni David tenor, and with Antonio Ambrogi, bass, in the first representation that season of the *Il Barbiere di Siviglia* and *La Cenerentola,* the *Zelmira*, and *Abufa* by Carafa, then the famous *Il Matrimonio Segreto*, followed by *La Donna del lago.*

On 4 September 1823, that grandest and most majestic essay in *canto fiorito*, the two-act melodramma tragico *Semiramide*, opened in Vienna. Written by Rossini in thirty-three days, it was considered his *opera seria* masterpiece. The libretto was by Gaetano Rossi, and the text was taken from the French author Voltaire's tragedy *Semiramis*. The first performance of this remarkable work took place in Venice at the Teatro Fenice.

Semiramide debuted in Naples on 30 November 1824. A little over a year later, Lablache sang the powerful Assur for twelve performances with Fodor. Soon he was repeating the opera in Vienna.

ತಿತಿತಿ

Chapter Eight

Naples, Vienna and Beethoven

1823-1827

Lablache, with his first international successes under his belt, returned to Naples for his debut at the Teatro San Carlo in the world premiere there of Mercadante's *Constanza ed Almeriska* (23 September 1823). Lablache had the distinction of having his debut recorded in a special column in the chronology of performances at the San Carlo in Francesco Florimo's *La scuola musicale di Napoli*. Later, the renown English opera critic Henry F. Chorley wrote:

> Musical history contains no account of a bass singer so gifted by nature, so accomplished by art, so popular without measure or drawback, as Louis Lablache. For the most part, the lowest voice of the quartette has habitually been considered as useful rather than interesting—at least in serious Italian opera. It is true that Mozart and other Germans have given it prominence—arising from the larqe supply of bass voices in their country, as compared with tenors. It is as true that, in Italian comic operas, the *buffo* has always been the prime favourite: though his occupation is more dependent on lively action and rapid delivery of the words, than on qualities strictly musical. But the fact, so far as Lablache is concerned, remains as I have stated it. Never, at all events, in memory, has the spell of indifference been so completely broken by this wonderful artist. Taking him for "all in all," the most remarkable man whom I have ever seen in Opera.[156]

Singing Figaro at the Teatro Fondo in August, Lablache went on to triumph in the same role for his San Carlo debut of *Il Barbiere di Siviglia*, following with the Naples premieres: *La Fondazione di Partenope* (autori diversi), *Federico II Re di Prussia* (Mosca), and *Sansone* (Basili). Proving his extraordinary dramatic powers, he created a great impression as Assur in the first *Semiramide* at the San Carlo before his fellow citizens. It was acclaimed the most exciting opera of the season, clocking up over a dozen representations. Francesco Florimo wrote in his *La scuola musicale di Napoli*:

> He was excellent, astounding in the part of the leading character fearfully pronouncing in the grand finale "*Oual mesto gemito!*" and in that gloomy calm of the adagio in the second act duet "*Quella ricordati notte di morte.*" From time to time, some inflexions in his voice made one feel that this was not calmness, only apparent and simulated serenity in the cruel Assur. This did not hide the deadly anxiety and terror which troubled the perverse soul of Nino's killer.[157]

The celebrated artist De Marini, who was in Naples at the time acting in the Fiorentini theater, described the great scene of delirium, "I don't think any other dramatic artist could have performed it better." Everyone agreed that Lablache was a superb actor as well as a excellent singer.

One night, the young composer Vincenzo Bellini sat in the audience. He emerged from that extravagant entertainment stupefied and disheartened. Florimo wrote:[158]

> Bellini was so affected after hearing it that, on his way back to the Collegio after the theatre with me and other companions, he gave vent to sad words of discomfort to us as he dawdled near the Porta Alba, because it seemed impossible to him to write good music in the face of that classic music by Rossini.

Another figure was now emerging into the field of Neapolitan opera besides Vincenzo Bellini, the composer Gaetano Donizetti. Donizetti came from the northern city of Bergamo and Bellini from the southern city of Catania in Sicily. Distinctly, the destiny of both composers would be linked to the career of Lablache. Both wrote many roles in their operas for his distinctive voice.

When Donizetti arrived in Naples in February 1822, he had already established himself as a successful composer and had written an opera for the Teatro Argentina in Rome, *Zoraida di Granata*. As a result, the shrewd Barbaja, ever on the lookout for new talent, hired him immediately, offering him a contract to write for the Teatro Nuovo, one of the three Neapolitan theaters he managed. Perhaps Barbaja needed to fill the gap left by Rossini's departure for Paris. Donizetti, like Rossini, a prolific artist, Donzetti wrote two to five operas a year and stayed in Naples till his departure for Paris in 1838.[159]

On 12 May 1822, his first Neapolitan work, *La zingara*, was performed at the Teatro Nuova with great success. No less than twenty-eight of his operas received their first performances in Naples. Most of his lighter operas were successful mainly because Neapolitan audiences enjoyed works that were of a lighter vein while his early more dramatic operas had failed. This pattern would change later with the arrival of his highly successful dramas, *Anna Bolena* and *Lucia di Lammermoor*. Both of these operas were proven successes long before they reached Naples.[160]

All the composers would write for the leading singers of the day. These singers could demand enormous fees; the composers received considerably less. Rossini was paid very little by the impresario Barbaja. Most certainly, Lablache, by this stage of his career, received larger fees; but if we compare charts formulated for the years 1823 to 1838, we find the prima donna's fees triple the amount of the basses. (Malibran and Pasta earned even more.)[161] Certainly, the number of performances Lablache sang would have helped compensate for all the "galley years" in Palermo. Now in his late twenties, his fame was secure in Italy, but he was constantly pursued by offers to sing in London and Paris for better fees. Was he loyal to Barbaja? Most likely a contract held him back. Was he was still reluctant to leave his family and travel there?

Rossini had left for Paris and London intending never to work in Naples again. Singers such as Fodor and Pasta also made their way to the northern cities; there, higher salaries were secure. Paris, London, St. Petersburg, even New York brought unquestionable fame and fortune to Italian singers. Opera flourished everywhere, being the major musical entertainment during the early years of the nineteenth century. Eventually, most singers and composers of any worth would secure a place in such cities. Italians, for the most part, always had a reputation for the art of singing and composing. Naples had always been the cradle of opera civilization, its long tradition rising from when Naples was a colony of the Greeks, and nearly all studies of music begin by stating that the origins of opera are to be found in a Greek drama.

Eighteenth-century Neapolitan composers were often invited to take up posts in foreign courts as directors of court theaters, composing, directing orchestras, and teaching members of the royal household. These duties earned them substantial salaries from the royal courts of Europe—Paisiello and Cimarosa both composed for the Russian court. Alessandro Scarlatti composed several operas for Ferdinando de Medici in Florence. His son,

Domenico Scarlatti, became a composer to Queen Marie Casimire of Poland's court in Rome. Antonio Salieri, another Italian composer, well-known during Mozart's life, enjoyed the post as Kapellmeister at the Viennese court.[162]

Lablache returned to Vienna for the June 1824-25 season. Eclipsing all previous seasons, he opened with the ever-popular *Il Barbiere di Siviglia*. Lablache singing with Fodor-Mainville, Donzelli, Dardanelli, Ungher, and Rubini triumphed in the Italian favorites. He sang in three world premieres, including 2 new roles by Mercadante, and introduced *Elisa e Claudio* to Vienna. In all, he sang in seventeen different operas that season.

Lablache wrote from Vienna on 1 July 1824 to Domenico Barbaja, the impresario of the San Carlo Theatre:

> Dearest Domenico,
>
> I received your appreciated (letter) in which I noted the superb efforts by Sig. Cavaliere Glossop[163] and the honours which ever more he disposes on the Neapolitan public.
>
> I went to Signora Fodor and read to her those parts of the letter which concerned her and I got the impression that both she and her husband are not against giving you displeasure; in fact I found them very attached to Barbaja! In spite of all the troubles, we reached there in eight and a half days, but I found out that the rehearsals for *Elisa e Claudio* had not begun and therefore we would have needed at least fifteen days for my First Night and even more (time) for Fodor (Joséphine Fodor-Mainville); therefore I thought we should go on the stage immediately with Fodor in *Otello*, and after two evenings, in *Il Barbiere*—without however neglecting the rehearsals for *Elisa e Claudio* (as was done), but Fodor did not want to go on first in *Otello* and instead we did *Barbiere*—against our interests in fact, because both Fodor and I went on for one evening only. What can you do! It was better than being twenty days without doing anything.
>
> Now that I am going to relate you everything, please do not read my letter to just anyone—especially in view of what I am about to tell you.
>
> Your presence here is as necessary as that of God! Because I can see clearly and declare that those who should be looking after your interests are the first to go against them, because they have secret ambitions for the current year, and their whole purpose is to show that nothing can be done with Italian opera and that "dancing"

is sufficient to support the Theatre. Oh my dear Domenico, what manoeuvring is going on in such an underhand manner—how dishonest and your Signor Figlio-without reflecting on what he is doing—how well one is being taken by the nose by these "polite" people.

Dear D: Domenico, it is only true friendship which allows me to write to you in this way, for I am sure that no-one would have written to you more sincerely than I and therefore is like a present.

Would you please have the delicacy to deliver this package to my mother,[164] and in case that Tonio[165] does not pay the usual monthly, please can you do so.

Best wishes to all the friends and believe me.

Your friend,
Luigi Lablache[166]

(This letter is unusual for a few reasons and difficult to understand the meaning behind it. Signor Figlio refers to an alais of some kind. Also, it is one of the very few letters to surface where Lablache uses his first name—even when writing to his wife, he signs L. Lablache.)

Six operas of Rossini were presented for the first time in Italian. Saverio Mercadante's first success came in 1821 at La Scala with *Elisa e Claudio*. It was given on thirty successive nights and repeated six months later for a further twenty-eight. With this work, Lablache helped Mercadante establish a good reputation; when it was performed in Vienna, the composer conducted the performances.

Giovanni Battista Rubini, the famous tenor, added his wonderful voice to that of his wife, Comelli-Rubini, who was already with the troupe. This season presented some of the best singers that Italy had to offer. In July, Lablache sang *Semiramide* again with the French soprano Joséphine Fodor-Mainville. However, understandably, after singing an amazing sixty performances of this opera, she was never the same again. For after going to Paris, she lost her voice and retired in 1831 in Naples. Colbran also lost her voice after twenty-eight performances of *Semiramide*.

During that month, Lablache sang briefly with a young German soprano, Henriette Sontag, in Rossini's *La Donna del largo*. Weber signed her up to sing in his opera *Euryanthe*.[167] Sontag was one of the prettiest and talented nightingales to ever grace the German stage. After a short stay in Vienna, she left for Berlin. Singing there in Rossini's *L'Italiana in Algeri,* the Berliners were enchanted by her. Here Karoline Bauer, an actress of the time, gives us an account of her debut (*Nachgelassene Memoiren*):

> Finally there appeared on the deck of the ship a slight, youthful, graceful girl in a sky-blue skirt and a tiny white feathered hat framing a charming, fresh, childlike forget-me-not face with blond curls, bright blue eyes and an enchanting little-girl mouth, whose merry smile disclosed the most beautiful pearly teeth. At rest or in movement, it was a delightful picture of joyous youth and of harmonious charm and grace, but more pretty than beautiful . . . And then she opened that budding little mouth, like a little woodland bird opening its bill, so naturally, so spontaneously, so gayly—and the sweetest, bright bird song echoed jubilantly through the house. The voice was neither full nor strong, but pure as a bell, clear as a pearl, silver-bright, mellifluous, particularly in the middle, flexible, distinctly articulated and of seductive sweetness. And how beautifully she trilled—like the bright jubilation of a soaring lark. Then again there was the brilliance of her singularly high head tones in the most difficult passages and roulades—as precise as a delicate musical clock. Incomparably enchanting was her *sotto voce.* And it all came so easily, so effortlessly from the charming little mouth that the listener had but to relax and enjoy, confident that nothing could go wrong.[168]

The *Manchester Guardian* of 1849 gives us details of the singer Sontag's early days:

> Coming to Vienna the celebrated German prima donna Henriette Sontag (1806-1854) was hired by Barbaja 'who had to overcome her parents' abhorrence of the Italian stage. 'She could sing in Italian, but never set foot in Italy. She made her operatic debut at age 14, in *Jean de Paris* by Boieldieu, in Prague, when the favorite prima donna became sick. The young Sontag was grabbed out of the conservatoire by the desperate manager, then she was supplied with enormous cork heels to make her taller. At first, the audience was most apprehensive but she proved herself so well that the celebrated leading tenor Gerstener became as enamored with her as the audience and he sang better than ever.

Lablache and Sontag were in the spring of their international careers and were destined to sing together again in Paris and London.

Henriette Sontag had the distinction of having been one of the soloists in the first performance of Beethoven's *Ninth Symphony (Symphony in D minor)*, on 7 May 1824 at the Kärnthnertor Theater, together with the *Overture op. 124* and parts of the *Missa solemnis*. All of Vienna was there, and the house was packed. Beethoven attended although he had to be carried in on a sedan chair. Tragically, the composer, who was by then deaf, could not hear the thunderous applause; as he stood turning over the pages of the score, oblivious to the standing ovation, one of the soloists, Caroline Unger, tugged on his sleeve and turned his face to the audience so that he could see his success. Beethoven was full of praise for Lablache and felt he was one of the finest singers he had ever known.[169]

Lablache returned to Vienna on 20 February 1827 after a very successful season at the theaters Fondo and San Carlo in Naples. Launching Pacini with usual Rossini repertory that season might have irritated the sensitive Weber who felt the Italians were invading Vienna. Then he sang for the first time in Vienna Pacini's *Amazilia, Gli Arabi nelle Gallie,* and *L'ultimo giorno di Pompei*. Joining the cast this time was French soprano, the lovely Henriette Méric-Lalande.

On Monday 26 March 1827, Ludwig van Beethoven died at fifty-six years old. The whole world mourned. When his funeral took place on the afternoon of 29 April, on a warm, sunny spring day, over twenty thousand people gathered before the Schwarzspanierhaus, Beethoven's last residence, to pay their last respects. Lablache led the long procession of thirty-two torchbearers who accompanied the coffin to the church. Later, Franz Schubert joined the funeral with many other notables and dignitaries from the artistic, literary, and musical world in the procession to the grave site. From an article "Life of Lablache" in *The Musical World*, August 1838:

> The memorial services were held shortly after one on 3 April in the Church of St. Augustines, where Mozart's *Requiem* was given, and one on 5 April in the St. Charles Church, when Cherubini's *Requiem* was performed. The famous bass Lablache, a man as huge as he was generous . . . sang in the Mozart's *Requiem*. A long-standing ruling by Barbaja forbade any member of his opera troupe to sing outside the Court Opera, under penalty of a fine. Lablache sang, and paid the opera singers fines,(Lablache paid Barbaja 200 gulden) and paid the other singers as well.[170]

Lablache had the extraordinary distinction of having sung Mozart's *Requiem* at not only at Beethoven's memorial mass but before that at a service in Naples in 1909 commemorating Haydn's death and later at Paisiello's funeral. Again at Chopin's funeral, plus Bellini's obsequies in Paris in 1835. Not forgetting Napoleon's interment in Paris. Lablache and the torchbearers surrounded Beethoven's coffin at his interment.[171]

It is presumed that Lablache attended, and bought many manuscripts and important and valuable autographed documents at the auction held after Beethoven's death.

The Viennese were by now full of gratitude and admiration. Wanting to reward him for such outstanding merit, they had a sterling silver medal struck bearing the effigy of Lablache with an inscription in Latin on the coin. Expert Pierre M. Bellemare, PhD, numismatist and historian, describes the medal and the inscription below:

AR medal (SIZE-WEIGHT). Raised and ridged border.
Obverse: ALOYSIO LABLACHE. Bareheaded, bust r.
Reverse: Inscription in field:

ACTIONE*ROSCIO
IOPAE*CANTV*COMPARANDVS
VTRAQVE*LAVRV*CONSERTA
AMBOBVS*MAIOR
VINDOBONAE*MDCCCXXV

He then translates the inscripton above and writes his observations below:

Obverse: (Dedicated to or in Honor of) Luigi Lablache
Reverse: For (his) acting to Roscius, to Iopas for (his) singing he is to be compared, but the laurels of the one and those of the other being united (on his forehead), he is greater than both.
Vienna 1825.

The inscription contains two allusions to Ancient history and literature which does require some explanation. The Roscius to whom Lablache is compared as an actor is Quintus Roscius Gallus, the brightest star of the Roman stage in the last decades of the Republic (died ca 62 BCE). The memory of Roscius' career and immense talent both as a comedian and a tragedian has been preserved by a variety of sources, and especialy the writings of his friend and admirer, and sometime attorney, Marcus Tullius Cicero. The reference to Roscius in the inscription echoes a famous passage from *De Oratore* (1,130), in which Cicero presents him as ultimate standard of perfection in acting:

> Do you not see how he does nothing otherwise than perfectly, nothing without cosummate charm, nothing save in the manner befitting the occasion, and so as to move and enchant everybody? Accordingly he has long ago brought it about that, in whatsoever craft a man excelled, the same was called a Roscius in his own line (E. W. Sutton, Loeb Classicial Library).

As for Iopas, to whom Lablache is compared as a singer, he is not a figure of history, but of fiction, a minstrel and member of Queen Dido's entourage in Virgil's *Aeneid* (I,740 and sqq.), where he performs at the banquet celebrating Aeneas' visit to Carthage. A pure literary invention, that character, mentioned but once in the whole epic, is closely patterned on that of the blind singer Demodocus, who performs for Odysseus at the court of Alcinous, King of the Pheacians, in a parallel episode from the *Odyssey* (VIII.44 and sqq.). The "long haired" Iopas, accompanying himself on the "golden lyre", is presented as a pupil of Atlas and an incomparable performer who receives thunderous applause first from the Carthaginians, and then the Trojans (ingeminant plausu Tyrii, Troesque sequuntur", v,747). Interestingly, this fictional figure was later to gain a second lease on life through opera, when Hector Berlioz chose (1863) to make him a character (a light tenor) in *Troyens a Carthage*, with a small aria to sing ("O blonde Ceres!" Act IV).

Also, it was translated in several different places by the famed translator of Horace in a reading by Marquis Gargallo.

Actione Roscio Ioppe cantu,
Comparandus, ulrique. lauru conserta, ambombus major
Vienna, 1825[172]

When the young Franz Schubert encountered Lablache, he was so enamored by Lablache's singing that he wrote three Italian songs. These were dedicated to Lablache in 1827:[173]

> Schubert is said to have met him at Kiesewetter's, but he also frequented Frau von Laszny's house, where he once took the second bass in the male-voice quartet *The Gondolier* and that of Kajetan Giannatasio del Rio, who had two musical daughters, Fanny (Franziska) and Nanni (Anna), and where *Domestic Warfare* (*Der hausliche Krieg*) was once performed with pianoforte accompaniment.[174]

The *Leipzig Musikalische Zeitung* was generous in its praise.[175] The song titles there were "L'incanto degli occhi," "Il traditor deluso," "Il mondo di prender moglie" (D902) C. opus 83. M.Brown writes, "The title names Metastasio as the author of the three poems, but that of the third song, is not by him, the author is unknown." The celebrated dramatist, Pietro Metastasio, had been a student of the Neapolitan composer Porpora, whose works were admired and played by Lablache. Florimo recalls Lablache enjoyed playing the piano, and his love of early Italian music.[176] Here are the songs from Reed's *The Schubert Song Companion*:[177]

> L'INCANTO DEGLI OCCHI, (The Enchantment of Eyes.) Pietro Metastasio. 1827. C major D902 no.1 Peters VI p.146 GA XX no.579
>
> On you, dear eyes, depends my whole life. You are my gods, and my destiny. At your will my mood changes.
> If you shine with happiness you fill me with daring. When the clouds gather you make me tremble.
> On you, dear eyes, depends my whole life. You are my gods and my destiny. At your will my mood changes.
>
> The text comes from Metastasio's opera *Attilio Regolo,* written in 1740. The song is the first of 'Three Songs for Bass Voice,' announced by Tobias Haslinger in September 1827, and dedicated to Luigi Lablache, the celebrated bass singer of Barbaja's company at the Karntnertortheatre. The songs were written in the Italian style and designed to cash in on the popularity of the Italian opera

in Vienna. See notes on Il Modo di prende moglie and Il Traditor deluso. The three songs were published as op. 83 in three parts, with both Italian and German words. This one is sometimes referred to by its German title, Die Macht der Augen. The autograph fair copy is in London' British Library, together with the first draft of the other two. The catalogue of the Witteczek-Spaun collection gives the date of the songs as 1827. It is to be noted, however, that the preliminary sketches for the melody of this and the companion songs may be much earlier than 1827. See D2 990E and 990F, which leave open the possibility that Schubert worked up the songs from much earlier exercises in the Italian style. It is a proof of the universal nature of Schubert's genius that he could so easily slip into the Italian operatic manner, even in a year which produced Winterreise and the Momens musicals. There is, to be sure, something academic about this song; the melodic line falls into familiar patterns, and the purely supportive accompaniment sounds faintly anachronistic, though not more so than in Der Hirt auf dem Felsen. It is easy to believe that Schubert was fascinated by 'the sweetness and range of Lablache's voice, and the ease with which he could alter his register' (Einstein, 346), for only a singer who aspires to the same strength and flexibility will be able to do justice to this fine song.

IL TRADITOR DELUSO (The Traitor Outwitted), Pietro Metastasio
1827 E minor D902 no.2 Peters VI p.150 GA XX no.580

Recit: Alas, what unknown power inspires these voices? I tremble. A cold sweat breaks out upon my breast. I must flee, but whither? Who will show me the way? Oh God, what do I hear? What has happene? Where am I?
Aria: Ha, the air sparkles and flashes. The earth quakes. Deep night surrounds me with horror. What fearful creatures surround me! What wild terror I feel in my breast!

The text comes from part II of the sacred drama Gioas re di Giuda ('Joab, King of Judah'). The song was published as op. 83 no. 2, with Italian and German words. The manuscript in the British Library contains only the voice line of no.2 with German text. A sketch in Vienna(SB) is fully worked for the first sixty-four bars, thereafter only the voice line in the bass clef, with Italian words. A sketch of the voice line in the treble clef ID2 990PI, formerly in private possession, is missing. This splendid operatic recitative and da capo aria is the most impressive of the three songs of op. 83. The opening recitative is full of dramatic tension, and the aria works with cumulative effect. The unexpected shift from E minor to C minor at bar 60, and from B minor to G minor at bar 78, is a particularly effective, and Schubertian, touch. One is reminded of the tonal juxtapositions at the beginning of the Sanctus in the E flat Mass of 1828.

IL MODO DI PRENDER MOGLIE (The Way to Choose a Wife), Author unknown C major D902 no.3 Peters VI p.157 GA XX no.581

Come on! Let's not think about it. Courage, let's have done with it. If I have to take a wife, I know very well why. I do it for the money, I do it to pay my debts. I don't hesitate to say so, again and again.

Of all the ways of choosing a wife in the world, I don't know a happier one than mine. One marries for love, another out of respect, another takes advice, another from a sense of duty, another for a whim. Isn't that the truth, yes or no?

Well, why shouldn't I take a little wife as a remedy for all my troubles? I say it again. I do it for the money. So many people do it. I do it too.

In September 1827 Tobias Haslinger announced the publication of 'Three Songs for Bass Voice.' The songs were settings of Italian words: with German translations, and the texts were attributed to Metastasio. In fact, however, only the first two are by Metastasio; the author of this third one has never been traced. Schubert dedicated the songs published as op. 83, to the famous bass singer of the Italian opera, Luigi Lablache. Spaun tells (Memoirs pp.135-6) that Schubert was much taken with Lablache, and that the two got on well together. The three songs are all in the Italian operatic style, and it may be that Lablache had a hand in choosing the texts. The autograph fair copy of this song, together with drafts of the other two, is in London British Library. See the following entry. This buffo aria, very much in the Figaro manner, confirms Spaun's statement that Schubert was captivated by Rossini's *Il*

> *Barbiere di Siviglia*. Indeed, there is a suggestion of that about it. Schubert's brilliance as a musical impersonator is astounding; these exercises 'in the Italian style' must have been written about the same time as the Momens musicals and the op. 90. Impromptus. (Capell, 226; Fischer-Dieskau,259).[178]

One week after Beethoven's death, Lablache helped introduce the first Donizetti work to be staged in Vienna—*L'Ajo nell'imbarazzo*, an opera buffa in two acts with libretto by Jacopo Ferretti. Having already sung several Donizetti works at the San Carlo Naples, Lablache had high hopes that this opera would make a lasting impression. William Ashbrook writes:

> This was the first of Donizetti's buffa operas to establish itself; it is much helped by Ferretti's superior libretto which tastefully treats a rather risqué subject. "Here we find Donizetti revealing his talent as a composer of *opera buffa*, leading the way for the writing of his later charming, lighthearted masterpieces, *L'Elisir d'amore* and *Don Pasquale*. Slowly, his unique style was emerging into an opera world now dominated by Rossini.[179]

☙☙☙

Chapter Nine

Fame at the San Carlo

1825-1828

When Lablache opened the season at Naples's San Carlo theater on April 8 of 1825 in Rossini's *Semiramide*, he had another phenomenal season on his hands. On January 5, King Ferdinand of Naples had died. Terrible rumors spread that he had been murdered in his bed. Now all Naples was in mourning. His son Francesco I ascended to the throne, and he was reputed to be more cunning and cruel, if that was possible, than his father.

That season, two of Rossini's dramatic *opera seria*s *Semiramide* and *Bianca e Falliero* were presented among others. In the former, Lablache surely was greatly appreciated again as the wicked Assur. Giuditta Grisi sang Arsace.[180] She was the sister of Giulia Grisi; that season she sang the travesti role of a Venetian general in the Neapolitan premiere of *Bianca e Falliero* while Lablache was cast as the striking character senator Capellio. Set in seventeenth-century Venice, Felice Romani wrote the text.[181]

After that, he continued through the summer with a single performance of Rossini's next-to-last Neapolitan opera *Maometto II*. Featuring Turks and Venetians, it was unsuccessful in Naples even with Lablache in the title role. Rossini later revised the work in 1826 for the Paris opera whereupon it was renamed the *Le Siège de Corinthe*.[182]

Lablache continued the season singing the role of Cabano in the Neapolitan premiere of Pacini's *Amazilia*, and then from 2 June, he sang eight performances of an attractive little one-act farce by Rossini, *L'Inganno Felice*. He terminated the season with a first Neapolitan performance of *Didone Abbandonata* by Saverio Mercadante and on 6 August the ever-favorite opera buffa of the Neapolitans and one of Lablache's memorable roles—the old Don in Domenico Cimarosa's *Il Matrimonio Segreto*. Lablache always played this one up to the hilt, taking liberties that were unbelievable. He must have loved to play decrepit old men as he relished in dressing up and playing these roles.

63

The Secret Marriage, written in 1792, in Vienna was Cimarosa's *chef d'oeuvre*. The most important composer of opera buffa to precede Rossini's operas, "he was," says George Ferris, "the finest example of the school perfected by Piccini and was indeed the link between the old Italian masters and the new development." R. A. Streatfield has written the following:

> His talent is thoroughly Italian, untouched by German influence, and he excels in portraying the gay superficiality of the times without attempting to dive far below the surface.

This delightful work must have been close to Lablache's heart, or was it because of the love the people of the nineteenth century had for it? Certainly Lablache's reputation was closely tied up with this opera; it won him the title of first dramatic *artiste* of his time. So with this *melodramma giocoso*, he captivated audiences in Paris and London in 1830 with his hilarious interpretation of the role of Geronimo. Few could forget his debut there or that name! Cimarosa, a prolific composer who had written over eighty operas became Paisiello's greatest rival. Although he wrote much music in other forms, his real talent lay with opera buffa. Later, Emperor Leopold II of Austria engaged him as court composer where he wrote *Il Matrimonio Segreto*. This opera eclipsed not only his former works but also those of his rivals. So successful was the first performance before the Viennese court that the emperor Leopold had dinner served to the cast while they played it again![183]

Returning to Naples in 1793, the first performance of *Il Matrimonio Segreto* was at the Teatro Fiorentini, with Cimarosa at the cembalo for seven nights. The opera continued on for an unstoppable one hundred continuous performances. The enthusiasm and excitement can hardly be conceived. Giuseppe Farinelli (1769-36), who was generally considered to be Cimarosa's successor and cleverest imitator, somehow inserted a duet into the opera—"No, non credo a quel che dite." For a long time, it was thought to be by Cimarosa. This work fixed the wavering opinions of the Italians, especially the Neapolitan audiences, who although highly cultivated and sophisticated, could be very critical and insular.[184]

Cimarosa was a friend of Lablache's father Nicola. Unfortunately to his detriment, he manifested a fondness for the French. When the French republican troops invaded Naples and sent the Bourbons in flight to Sicily, Cimarosa enthusiastically wrote a political poem in their praise—a Neapolitan carmagnole. When, however, the Bourbons regained power, he was disgraced and narrowly escaped death; after all, they felt he had sold out to the French, and with Lablache's father, he was thrown into prison. His subsequent banishment from the Kingdom of the Two Sciles had a disastrous effect on his health. After some time, he became ill and died in Venice on his way to Russia. Rumors that he had been poisoned on the order of Queen Carolina became so strong that the court was forced to issue an offical denial.[185]

The grandest spectacular of the 1825 winter season was without any doubt Pacini's *L'ultimo giorno di Pompei* on November 19, with the sets by the architect of the San Carlo theater, the illustrious Antonio Niccolini.[186] The librettist was Andrea Leone Tottola:

> The opera ended, with horrendous explosions-thunder and lightning and black smoke arose from the painted cardboard Vesuvius, then an immense quantity of ashes and pumice showered over the stage. The ceiling and walls of the vault caved in, huge pillars fell creating scenes of the great castastrophe in the time of the last days of Pompeii. To top it all, a chariot drawn by four beautiful white horses crossed the stage at full gallop, with many horsemen following behind-in most probably the most dramatic ending of any opera![187]

What is incredible is how the special effects were produced in the days before electricity and gas light. Here, Florimo writes about this great event:

> Lablache was sublime in the part of Sallustio. So much dignity and character in the imposing figure worthy of great Rome! So much enthusiasm appeared in his expression and all the movements of his body, midst the crowd who had acclaimed him victorious, uttering these words: "*Se i Numi fausti sperar mi lice, Ah! sempre rendano Pompei felice, Di più quest'anima bramar non sa!* How much truth, resignation, suffering in the famous duet (one of the most beautiful pieces of the opera) with his wife, Ottavia, when he tries to find her innocent. He was really sublime in these pathetic and loving moments. Those not fortunate enough to see and hear him cannot imagine at all the perfection and ability of this singer.[188]

The whole atmosphere of the Bay of Naples has always been volatile and unstable, so it seems strange that the Neapolitans, living under the constant threat of the real Vesuvius erupting, would enjoy this opera. After all, the volcano had erupted in 1822 and before that in 1794; in fact, the earthquakes and tremors had been very severe as well.[189]

Lablache sang in multiple premieres that season. First, he sang in *Gli L'Italianie Indinai* by Carafa, on the 4 October. Then *L'ultimo giorno di Pompei,* followed by *Ipermestra* by Saverio Mercadante on December 29. Familiar with this composer, Lablache had sung in about a dozen of Mercadante's operas during his early career, six of them were premieres. He had triumphed singing Arnoldo in *Elisa e Claudio* in Milan. Since Lablache arrived back in Naples, *Il Barbiere di Siviglia* was always part of his regular yearly agenda.

Historically, Mercandante's operas, in spite of stellar casts, lacked a certain quality to make them as popular as those of Rossini. At this time, an Englishman and manager for some time of the Royal Colburg Theatre in London (Old Vic), Joseph Glossop took an appointment as temporary manager of the Neapolitan Royal Theatres in 1824. Unmasked later as a shady character, he masqueraded as an English gentleman with means. King Ferdinand and his court were not pleased and soon became somewhat disenchanted with his broken promises of recruiting new singers, and he soon got himself into difficulties over money. On a personal level, he became directly entangled with several singers of the London theater. First, he married soprano Elizabeth Féron; later, he became the husband of Joséphine de Méric, the mother of Emilie de Méric, the daughter-in-law of Lablache.[190]

By Passion Sunday 1825, Glossop's contract was annulled after serving only one year. Not long after Barbaja returned.

One of the most interesting events in the year of 1826 was Vincenzo Bellini's first work for the San Carlo, his second opera, *Bianca e Gernando*, a *melodramma* in two acts, libretto by Domenico Gilardoni. Bellini was still a student at the conservatory when he won the honor to compose a full-length opera *Adelson e Salvini*. This first opera had only been sung by students in the conservatory. Now at twenty-five, intensely ambitious, he was well on the first stepping-stone to a unique and successful career.[191]

Opening again with the dramatic *opera seria*, Rossini's foremost *opera seria* of the decade, *Semiramide*, Lablache took on two more world premieres. After singing in *Il Solitario ed Elodia* by Pavesi, Lablache rehearsed his role of Filippo for the young maestro Bellini's debut—his first opera at the Teatro San Carlo, *Bianca e Gernando*. On the very brink of the gala opening, however, it had the misfortune to be postponed by the new King of the Two Sicilies, Francesco I, when all the cast were well into rehearsal. This made the young composer understandably extremely nervous; five months went by before the final opening on 30 of May 1826 at a grand gala with a new cast. Filippo, as originally intended, was sung superbly by Lablache, joined by tenor Giovanni Battista Rubini and the French soprano Henriette Méric-Lalande as Bianca, one of the most beautiful and talented sopranos of the time; she was only twenty-five years old. *Bianca e Gernando* was received well. Florimo remembers Lablache:

> He was superb in the andante of his aria: *De che tragge i suoi di Carlo sepolto* an original new composition at that time, which the artist interpreted so beautifully and with excellent effect. In the *terzetto* of the first act and in the final arias he showed himself to be absolutely supreme, especially in the scenes with Bianca.[192]

Bellini specially composed and rewrote for the voices of Luigi Lablache and Henriette Méric-Lalande. She soon was replaced with Adelaide Tosi. Like the ailing Joséphine Fodor-Mainville, she also lost her voice after singing too many seasons:

> Bellini was informed that these were the chief singers for whom he was to compose would be Adelaide Tosi, a Milanese and another soprano . . . A gifted tenor Giovanni David, and that physically and artistically tremendous favorite, first in Naples, and then in all Europe, the bass Luigi Lablache.[193]

The tenor Giovanni Battista Rubini sang the title role Gernando. Returning from Milan and Vienna, now though still under contract to Barbaja, he had left Naples in 1825 for a brief and triumphant debut at the Théâtre-Italien in Paris. Repeating "the best of Rossini," he successfully opened the season on 6 October, singing Ramiro in his sensational Paris debut of *La Cenerentola*, and then he sang with Pasta in *Tancredi* and *Otello*.

All Paris was ecstatic about him. Barbaja released him for six months so long as he returned to Italy. Unparalleled most certainly in his time, Rubini, like Lablache, had a huge repertory at his finger tips. Historically a sensational singer, the foremost tenor of his era, contempories named him the King of Tenors. As a leading Rossini interpreter, he sang Rossini roles during and after the well-known tenor Manuel Garcia left the stage and throughout the prime years of Rossini's international successes in Paris, London, and Russia until he retired to Italy in 1842.

Donizetti was in the audience for the opening of *Bianca e Gernando* that night at the San Carlo, and he wrote to Giovanni Simone Mayr, his former teacher, on 30 May the day the opera was performed.

> Our Bellini ... his first production ... beautiful ... beautiful, and especially considering this is the first time he has written an opera.[194] It's all too beautiful, as I will realize when my own opera is given in two weeks time.[195]

At the royal gala on 6 July 1826 for the birthday of Queen Marie Clementina, Lablache now sang in his first Donizetti opera *Elvida* with the same first-rate cast: Henriette Méric-Lalande in the title role, Gaetano Chizzola, Brigitta Lorenzani, Giovanni Battista Rubini as Alfonso. Lablache created the role of Amur, *capo d'una tribù di Mori*. *Elvida* was an *opera seria* in one act with text by Giovanni Schmidt. King Francesco and all the court attended. On the second night, the cast were called out with Donizetti. Weinstock quotes from Pacini's autobiography about royal performances:

> It was court etiquette never to applaud the singers that belonged to the royal '*capella*.' Since Rubini and Lablache were in the category of those that enjoyed that honor, most of the time they remained unapplauded.[196]

The Harmonicon of London reviewed this *Elvida* in January 1827: Teatro S. Carlo. "On the occasion of the birthday of the Queen, a new operetta was produced, entitled *Elvida*, from the pen of Donizetti. It contained several pleasing passages, but as a whole, was meagre, and full of common-place music."

Donizetti was now under contract to Barbaja to compose twelve operas for the Royal Theatres of Naples. A prolific writer, *Alahor in Granata* was his fourteenth work; it had first been sung in Palermo at the Teatro Carolino with Elizabeth Féron. A Londoner, she sang not only at the Teatro Carolino in Palermo but also at the San Carlo and at La Scala from 1822-1825, replacing the void that Isabella Colbran had left when she married Rossini and some of the ailing Fodor's roles. Féron also sang in London and New York and was the grandmother of Sir Augustus Harris, director of Covent Garden Opera,[197] by her second husband Harris. Her first husband was the infamous Joseph Glossop, who then married Joséphine de Méric, a French soprano and mother of Emilie de Méric, a famous contralto and wife of Luigi Labache's son, Nicola Lablache.[198]

Alahor di Granata was staged later that year on 19 July 1826 at the San Carlo, Naples. After a favorable reception in Palermo, *The Harmonicon* reported an equal success in Naples. Lablache took the role of Alahor opposite Henriette Méric-Lalande and his friend tenor Berardo Winter (he sang the tenor roles in both Palermo and Naples). Lablache was constantly occupied with other roles; he did not sing any more Donizetti operas till *L'Esule di Roma* on 1 January 1828.

The premiere of *L'Esule di Roma*—libretti by Domenico Gilardoni—was spectacular. Donizetti's opera is an action drama and takes place in Roman times. Shown first on New Year's Day 1828, it was greeted so enthusiastically at the San Carlo that it was repeated a staggering nineteen times. This was Donizetti's first success with *opera seria* though by no means his first attempt at the genre at which he produced his finest operas, clearly proving that his star was now rising and that the insatiable public of Naples was ready for more Donizetti productions.[199]

Breaking some of the usual traditions, first the opera has no overture, and second the trio which ends the first act was regarded as quite different and special by the public and Rossini alike, who remarked that it was enough to make the composer's reputation. The opera tells of love and treachery in ancient Rome at the climax of which all ends well; the heroine's (Argelia) father (Murena) and lover (Settimo) are rescued from certain death in the Roman arena by the intervention of a friendly lion (Androcles style). The dry *The Harmonicon* of London wrote later in the year: "According to some journals, the music was excellent; while others assure us that it was devoid of merit, and nothing rescued it from destruction but the powerful talents of Tosi and Lablache." They also noted that Donizetti was becoming extraordinarily prolific (August 1828, p.187). Florimo remembers a different occasion and praised Lablache's performance highly:

> For the Gala on the 1st of January, 1828, Lablache was marvellous in the character of Murena; Adelaide Tosi, Berardo Winter and Benedetti all beautifully completed the picture. This was the first step which eventually opened the doors to the Maestro of Bergamo. Lablache contributed greatly to the splendid success of this opera. The trio in the first Act was so marvellous as to drive the public delirious with applause. This *terzetto* above all is one of the spontaneous inspirations of Donizetti. It could not have had a more faithful interpreter than Luigi Lablache. He succeeded in identifying himself so much with the part and with such a fantastic result that no one else can be compared with him.

> He is great in the subdued tones, his agitated and distraught face, untidy and rebellious hair, trembling right hand, stretched towards the betrayed Settimio, the shivering body. It was a manifestation of remorse, repentance, pain in the innermost soul, that whoever heard and saw him was deeply moved, and the memory unforgettable.[200]

In this opera, it is the bass, not the soprano, who has the mad scene (second act). Donizetti showed his appreciation to Lablache by composing for him and dedicating the score to him of a cantata with piano accompaniment with text from the Conte Ugolino episode entitled *Ugolino la tragedia dal XXXIII canto di Dante della Divina Commedia*.[201] Barbaja immediately and enthusiastically signed Donizetti up to write two more operas for the San Carlo at five hundred ducati per opera.

Lablache, already a San Carlo favorite, was in his element; another Donizetti role and his second Donizetti world premiere. It is most likely he believed in the vitality of this man from Bergamo, for like Rossini before him, Lablache recognized his talent would bring fame. It was to be later in Paris where their joint efforts and genius would bring more success and everlasting glory. But for Lablache, it was not the right time yet.

ಌಌಌ

Chapter Ten

Parma

1828-29

Lablache returned to Naples in December 1828 after a long and exhausting season in Milan. Barbaja engaged Donizetti as musical director of the San Carlo in the autumn, filling the post the following year.[202] Donizetti was waiting for Lablache to rehearse for two new operas written especially for the Royal Theatres San Carlo and the Fondo: *Il Paria* and *Il Giovedi grasso*.

Lablache's repertoire had increased in stature from the time of his Neapolitan debut at the San Carlo on 23 September 1823 through the winter of 1827, he appeared in approximately eighty different operas. Most noticeable among these were from the pen of Rossini; in fact, an overwhelming abundance of works were all written by Rossini. Few could distinguish which operas Lablache sang the best; he triumphed in both genres—opera buffa and *opera seria*—gaining admiration and a popularity that eclipsed that of most of his rivals of the day.

Rossini roles were part of Lablache's early repertoire at Messina and Palermo. We note that by the time Lablache left the Teatro Carolino in Palermo in 1819, he had sung approximately eighteen different Rossini roles, perhaps more, as it was well known he often sang two parts in one opera, sometimes even three. As an example of this, while he certainly sang Dandini and Don Magnifico in Rossini's *La Cenerentola,* in *Il Barbiere di Siviglia,* he was a famous Figaro and equally or even more famous Bartolo. During the years from 1817-1828, in just over a decade, Lablache further established his reputation by singing in over fifty Rossini operas. From the chronologies of the Teatro San Carlo for the 1825 season: Lablache sang *Semiramide,* twelve presentations; *Amazilia,* eighteen presentations; *L'Inganno Felice,* eight presentations; Pacini's *L'ultimo giorno di Pompei* and his *Gli Italici e Gli Indianni,* each eighteen presentations.[203] Lablache sang from 8 May to 15

January a total of about eighty-eight performances. By today's standards, that would be judged as incredible. Most certainly, he sang even more because there are some opera houses for which there are no chronologies. Private concerts and other theaters cannot be ruled out. We may be sure he sang in a hundred performances or more per year from Palermo to Vienna, which was an enormous achievement.

For these last two years, Lablache also plowed through a steady diet of operas by Giovanni Pacini at the San Carlo, singing in one Neapolitan favorite after another by this very prolific composer. From the opening of *Niobe* on 19 November 1826, he sang in *Glia Arabe Nelle Gallie, Amazilia*, which were all very warmly received according to Florimo. Then on 19 November in 1827, another historical opera of Pacini's appeared on the boards of the San Carlo, a drama entitled *Margherita Regina d'Inghilterra*. Later, Lablache sang the *L'ultimo giorno di Pompei* in December and in the carnival season, 1 January 1829.

On 12 January 1829, Lablache first sang the role of Zaréte (*padre di Idamore*) at the premiere of Donizetti's *Il Paria*, an *opera seria* in two acts that was not a success. Ashbrook writes, "Although it is the most carefully worked out of all Donizetti's scores up to this time . . . the opera failed to meet the expectations Donizetti had for it."[204] The cast featured the splendid voices of Adelaide Tosi and Giovanni Battista Rubini and Gaetano Chizzola. After six performances, it disappeared, possibly eclipsed by the New Year's Day showing of *L'ultimo giorno di Pompei*.

Then on 27 February, Lablache sang in another world premiere of Donizetti's *Il Giovedi grasso* at the Teatro del Fondo. Donizetti writes an aria for Lablache as Sigismundo in the Neapolitan dialect, *Cola Co non fa zimeo*, which was a very popular tarantella. Then during Lent, Lablache sang the title role in another premiere *Saul,* written by the composer Nicola Vaccai.

In April of that year, he was invited to Parma for the grand gala opening of the Teatro Regio, formerly the Teatro Ducale. The change of name came about at the time of the defeat of Napoleon. The beautiful empress Marie Louise, second wife to Napoleon Bonaparte, had taken up residence there in April 1816 as the Duchess of Parma. Refusing to join Napoleon in exile at St. Helena, she preferred to stay behind in Italy. This decision was most likely dictated by her attachment to her lover, the brave and distinguished Lt. Gen. Adam Count von Neipperg, a dashing cavalryman and diplomat in the Austrian army and later Austrian ambassador to Naples. Survivor and hero of many battles against France, he was known also as a famous lady-killer; even though he had the misfortune to lose an eye in battle, apparently undaunted, he continued to annihilate the French successfully at every opportunity. Mme. Stael remarked that with his one unbandaged eye he could devastate the fair sex in half the time another man could do with two.[205]

Empress Marie Louise became one of Parma's most well-known inhabitants. In 1821, she commissioned architects to rebuild the theater; like La Scala, she redecorated the interior in white, gold, and red velvet. The beautiful ceiling and drop curtain with its allegory of the Triumph of Knowledge were both painted by Gian Battista Borghese. Spike Hughes writes:

> If Marie Louise herself is not represented seated along with *Pallas athene* in the curtain, I think she is to be found in the Borghese's ceiling. If not, she will not be far away for one never has to go far in Parma to find her portrait somewhere.[206]

This magnificent theater opened on 16 May 1829 with Lablache and Henriette Méric-Lalande in Vincenzo Bellini's *Zaira*, an *opera seria*. The libretto by Felice Romani was based on a play by Voltaire. This work, though it had all the ingredients for success, unfortunately failed. However, the season could not have fared too badly with such excellent singers and superb operas by Rossini—*Semiramide*, *Mosè e Farone* (for eight nights), and *Il Barbiere di Siviglia*, terminating with the premiere of Luigi Ricci's *Colombo*. The tenor came from Parma, a certain Timoleone (Timolino) Alexander. He became the second husband to French singer Joséphine Bonnaud de Méric and stepfather to Joséphine's daughter Emilie de Méric-Lablache. The season was somewhat of a fiasco for Bellini:

> Bellini, for his part, took the score of *Zaira* and adapted the best part of it to his Romeo and Juliet opera, *I Capuleti e I Montecchi*, which as we know was played at the La Fenice (Venice) the following year. It was not until five years later, in 1834, that Bellini's reputation was vindicated in Parma by the prodigious success of *Norma*. While Parma missed the chance of introducing Verdi to the world, it lost none in showing its appreciation of the local-born composer when his first success reached the Teatro Regio. *Nabucco* was first performed in Parma on 17 April 1843, and between that date and the 28 May was played no fewer than twenty-two times. Singing the part of Abigail was Giuseppina Strepponi, who had created the part at La Scala, and it is one of the legends of Parma that it was at this time that the friendship of

> Verdi and Giuseppina developed into a life-long love affair as the couple walked in the gardens of the Ducal Palace together. I have never had the heart to question whether or not Marie Louise made a practice of opening the palace gardens to courting couples, even if one of these couples was a famous singer and a young composer, but the thought she did is in keeping with the character of that sympathetic ruler.[207]

Leaving the Duchy of Parma, Lablache returned to his beloved Naples, where he teamed up again for his final season with soprano Adelaide Tosi and his close friend, the tenor Bernardo Winter, before leaving for his first engagements in Paris and London. Usually, alternating between the Royal Theatres Fondo and the San Carlo, Lablache sang *Il Barbiere* for the carnival season of 1 January 1830 with Fodor. Next, he celebrated three world premieres: first, *I Portuguesi in Goa,* a work by Lablache's lifelong British friend Sir Julius Benedict; on 28 January, Lablache sang the role of Idalcan just twice with Tosi and Winter and followed this with two Donizettis, *I Pazzi per progretto* (Lunatics by Design) on 6 February and Donizetti's biblical drama *Il Diluvio universale* on 6 March at the San Carlo—both of these operas featured the singing of Luigia Boccabadati-Gazzuoli.[208]

Donizetti's *I Pazzi per progretto*, a one-act *farca* with a libretto written by Domenico Gilardoni, was first performed at the San Carlo[209] with a very unusual cast: a soprano, a mezzo-soprano, and five basses. Ashbrook remarked that the five basses make the piece rather monotonous because "they adopt the same buffo cliches, and the piece is lacking in those moments of pathos that in his best comedies give Donizetti humor its humanity."[210]

The first performance is described by Donizetti in a letter to his father as "a little comedy-farca," going on to say, "it went off brilliantly: that may be because I am well regarded and everything goes well here with everything I do."[211] Certainly with fine basses like Lablache, Gennaro Luzio, Fiorvanti, and Ambrogini, not too much could go wrong. However, a year later at the Teatro Valle Rome, it was hissed off the stage.[212] London's *The Harmonicon* wrote, "That the two duets between Lablache and Boccabadati and Luzio were much applauded" (July 1830, p.309). Another comment comes from Italy's *Teatri Arti e Letteratura*, Bologna, on April 1, 1830:

> Regarding Sig. Lablache, it has been noted that, like the meeting of the minds between two geniuses, you could not tell if Lablache was born for Donizetti, or Donizetti for Lablache. One thing certain

there is a sympathetic friendship formed, by the greatest stroke of luck between the composer and the interpreter. And here one is left with the bitter thought; that is, the imminent departure of Sig. Lablache from our Italy to London. It is also agreed that not one slightest defect of Sig. Lablache will ever be heard in roles that require sublime acting and dramatic declamation-in the great music of *Semiramide, L'Assedio di Corinto. L'Esule di Roma, Il Paria, Il Diluvio universale.*

Donizetti composed the last opera Lablache sang in Naples that season, *Il Diluvio universale* (the librettos of this and the former operas were written by Domenico Gilardoni). The opera was delayed because Lablache was ill; however, it opened on 6 March and ran through Lent. The reporter for L'Eco of Milan, March 17, 1830 wrote:

Well-received were Mme. Boccabadati's cavatina, which ended the introduction, supported by the always-excellent Lablache and the duet between Signor Winter and Mme. Boccabadati in the second act. Lablache sung with great force and skill, and he deserved all the applause he received as Noah.

A mixed genre, *Il diluvio* was conceived on a grand scale, part oratorio and part opera; it is easy to imagine Lablache as Noè, the title role written by Donizetti especially for him. This opera was entitled a three-act *azione tragica-sacra*. Lablache fell easily into the role of Noè. Godlike, the stereotyped image materializes before our eyes, the white-bearded huge father figure, larger than life, swooping down and rescuing his family and animals from the deluge, gathering them into the ark. The thundering voice of Lablache sang out to an enraptured audience, who must have remembered him singing yet another of these biblical father-figures in Rossini's *Mosè*, not too long before, as well as Saul. In fact, in the subject matter, one cannot fail but notice that here Donizetti follows in the footsteps of Rossini's *opera seria*, reminding us that during the nineteenth-century biblical figures were taken a lot more seriously than they are today. Apparently the dramatic finale was not well-staged, for while the ark floated over the waves, the audience whistled.[213]

Lablache's solemn utterances of Noah gave the opera dignity and meaning, but in spite of the hard work by Donizetti, the work failed to please. Soon afterward, Lablache departed for his first engagements at the

King's Theatre, England, not to return to sing at the San Carlo again till 1832. Florimo writes,

> When Lablache returns to Naples . . . it is like a family party, when the Neapolitan public hear Lablache on the stage of the San Carlo, or at the Fondo, his presence alone produces joy, high spirits and good humour. He thrilled his fellow countrymen, who were delighted to spend a happy evening listening to him, admiring and applauding him as always.

It was common knowledge that the King of Naples, a devout opera goer, would sit in his royal box at the Teatro San Carlo,

> eating spaghetti with his hands, laughing uproariously, speaking loudly, especially at the Neapolitan works . . . he applauds with a ringing voice and beats time vigorously on the ledge of his box; at a performance of *Il Barbiere* he shouted, "*Bravo, lazzarone, bravo Lablache,*" his enthusiasm for Lablache was boundless, when he sang Figaro in *Il Barbiere di Siviglia*. The actor was delighted by the King's exclamation, which he had heard perfectly.[214]

Finally at last, well-established in the operatic world, Lablache moved his family up to Posillipo, the fashionable hillside suburb of Naples.

The Lablache home was well-situated, high above the seaside villa Barbaja had built for himself. The Lablache villa enjoyed an excellent position, perched, overlooking the beautiful bay. Still standing today, from its lower level, one can enjoy a good view of the city of Naples and Vesuvius to the east and to the west a wonderful panorama of the Gulf of Pozzuoli and the Phlegrean Fields; straight ahead lies Capri. Many splendid villas of the rich and famous were surrounded by terraced vineyards, nestled among the scented orange groves and pine trees.

Later, Lablache interested himself in the art of wine growing, his extensive property extending all the way downhill to the shore. It was reported he took a lively interest in the welfare of his product and hired a gardener to cultivate and harvest the grapes.[215]

Nicola Lablache portrait (Balsan collection)

Luigi Lablache portrait (Dr. Stephen Stanley-Little)

Teresa Lablache portrait (Dr. Stephen Stanley-Little)

Compte Falcoz de la Blache portrait (Lablache Archives)

Coat of Arms of Falcoz de la Blache family (Lablache Archives)

Antique postcard of de la Blache chateau at Anjou, France (Lablache Archives)

Modern photo of chateau, Anjou, France 2006
(Simonette de la Fuente) (Lablache Archives)

Modern photo of chateau, Anjou, France 2006
(Simonette de la Fuente) (Lablache Archives)

Bay of Naples antique postcard circa 1902 (Lablache Archives)

Bay of Naples antique postcard circa 1902 (Lablache Archives)

Park on Via Caracciola, Naples, antique postcard (Lablache Archives)

Vesuvius erupting antique lithograph (Lablache Archives)

Gioachino Rossini portrait lithograph (Lablache Archives)

Donizetti Caricature, Charivari (Fulvio Stefano Lo Presti)

Vincenzo Bellini portrait (Andrew S. Pope)

Luigi Lablache with Saverio Mercadante cartoon (Private collection)

Luigi Lablache in Le Cantatrici villane (Don White-Opera Rara)

Amazalia score frontispiece (Jack Rokahr Archives)

Luigi Lablache in Amazalia role (Lablache Archives)

Luigi Lablache as Figaro in Il Barbiere di Siviglia (Lablache Archives)

La Scala Opera house postcard (Lablache Archives)

Giuditta Pasta and Luigi Lablache in La Prova d'un Opera Seria
(Lablache Archives)

Luigi Lablache portrait (La Moda) (Lablache Archives)

Franz Schubert carte de visite (Lablache Archives)

Vienna Karntnertortheater photo (Lablache Archives)

Ludwig von Beethoven engraving (Lablache Archives)

Medal awarded to Luigi Lablache (head-side) in Vienna (Sergio Ragni)

Medal awarded to Luigi Lablache (back-side) in Vienna (Sergio Ragni)

San Carlo Opera Theatre early postcard (Lablache Archives)

San Carlo Opera Theatre interior, early postcard (Lablache Archives)

Domenico Cimarosa (Andrew S. Pope)

Domenico Barbaja
(Museo teatrale alla Scala)

Saverio Mercadante by Vincenzo Roscioni (Sergio Ragni)

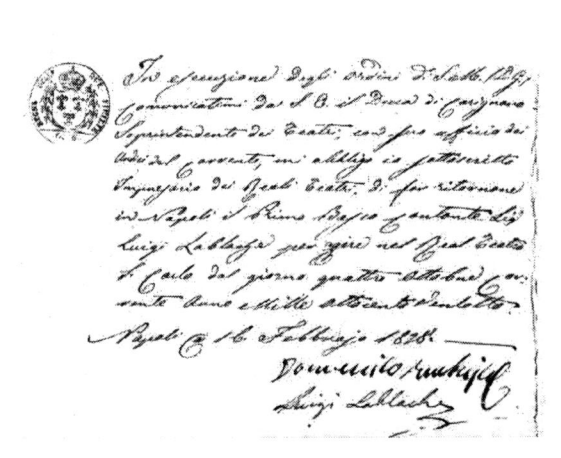

Luigi Lablache contract for San Carlo (Sergio Ragni)

Giovanni Paisiello (Donizetti Society)

L'Ulitimo Giorno Pompeii (Donizetti Society)

Giovanni Pacini (Sergio Ragni)

Joséphine Fodor-Mainvielle (Jacques Gheusi)

Teresa Belloc-Giorgi (Sergio Ragni)

Giuseppina Ronzi de Begnis as Rosina (Sergio Ragni)

Henriette Méric-Lalande as Zobeida in Alahor in Granata
(Conservatore di San Pietro a Majella)

Luigi Lablache as Alahor in Alahor in Granata
(Conservatore di San Pietro a Majella)

Emma Albertazzi as Rosina (Jacques Gheusi)

Henriette Sontag as Rosina (Lablache Archives)

Rubini, Donzelli, and Luigi Lablache (Sergio Ragni)

Domenico Donzelli

Henri Beyle aka Stendhal

Giovanni David (Sergio Ragni)

Giovanni Battista Rubini (Sergio Ragni)

Il Barbiere di Siviglia Playbill (Lablache Archives)

Teresa Lablache and child, oil painting by François Bouchot
(Museo di San Martino, Naples)

Luigi Lablache oil painting by François Bouchot
(Museo di San Martino, Naples)

Gioachino Rossini statue (photo by author Rome) (Lablache Archives)

Gioachino Rossini cartoon by André Gill (Phillip Gossett)

Gioachino Rossini letter (Conservatrice Raccolte Piancastelli in Forli, Italy)

Luigi Lablache as Dandini in La Cenerentola (L'avant Scene Opera)

Book Two

Chapter Eleven

London Debut

1830-1831

After the long spring season of 1830 in Naples was over, Lablache traveled to London, unable to refuse the constant pleas of Pierre Laporte, the manager of the King's Theatre in the Haymarket. This theater had been the exclusive home of Italian opera since 1710. After a fire, a larger new theater replaced the previous one, and it became the largest in England with a capacity of three thousand three hundred seats. Designed by Polish architect Michael Nowosielski, the King's Theatre had first opened on 16 January 1793 with Paisiello's popular *Il Barbiere di Siviglia*.[216]

Lablache's fame had long preceded him. He was engaged to sing Geronimo in *Il Matrimonio Segreto* on Thursday 13 May 1830. There was much excitement and expectancy in and around the theater at that time. *The Morning Post* writes on that morning: "Crowded houses are expected... Lablache and Malibran will sing... attracted by his reputation, a lot of celebrities were at the rehearsal... he appears to combine the excellencies of Morelli, Naldi, Zuchelli, and Ambrogetti." In fact, London had never heard a bass voice such as this before. *The Morning Post* reviews the second performance:

> *Il Matrimonio Segreto* was again presented last night, with the same cast of character that afforded so much delight and satisfaction on the preceding Thursday. The second appearance of Lablache was hailed with continued marks of approbation, which his admirable performance fully justified. Indeed there can be little hesitation in concluding to him the rank of first bass singer of the day, and one of the best comic actors that Italy has ever yet sent beyond the Alps. His beautiful, flexible voice:

> The stream of music pours along
> Deep, majestic, smooth, and strong

> whilst the clearness of his articulation, and the exquisite expression which he gives the melody, excite all those feelings which belong to 'the soul of harmony.' 'His performance is chaste, and at the same time richly humorous; and although the enthusiastic applause and joyous mirth which his performance called forth might lead many an actor to outstep the modesty of nature, his Comedy never verged on caricature, nor went beyond the display necessary to exhibit the singularities of the deaf, old merchant. The part of Geronimo does not afford much scope for the display of science; his voice however, as we have already stated, is a magnificent bass quality. It ranges in this opera from A first space to D above the staff, this later being the note which thunders out with so wonderful a power in the Quartet, *Tu mi dici*. He probably can sing lower than A, and that his falsetto is of great compass, he proves by his imitation of Lalande's voice in one of his arias. That he will continue one of the first favourites of *The Musical World* we unhesitatingly pronounce, and the enthusiastic applause that he won from his audience, who were indeed completely enraptured with him, fully justifies the high opinion we have already pronounced upon his merits.[217]

The supporting cast of Maria Malibran, Henrietta Méric-Lalande, and the great tenor Domenico Donzelli all received praise from the critics: "The house was filled to the roof tops." The *Morning Post* goes on to say, "The boxes displayed as much loveliness and elegance as we ever remember to have graced the King's Theatre," the *Morning Post* quotes on the same page as the review "Lady Jane Walsh's Concert":

> On Friday evening, her Ladyship gave a most delightful concert of vocal music at her house in Berkeley Square, where Lablache was heard for the first time in a private concert. Among the company present were . . ."

Here the newspaper lists all the names of the dignitaries present-Duchesses, Lords and Ladies of the Court, Counts and Countesses etc.[218]

The Italian season had opened without Lablache. In the *London Times*, we find an entry, under the advert for the King's Theatre opera program: "We are expecting Signor Lablache very soon" and "Signor Lablache has arrived in this country" and "he will make his first appearance in a few days."

On the day after his first performance, the very conservative *The London Times* published on the top of the first page: "A review: Kings's Theatre . . . Signor Lablache made his first appearance in this country in the character of Geronimo:"

> He has a bass voice of great depth, power and flexibility. Its intonation is remarkably clear and correct, and his articulation so distinct that each of his words is understood in every part of the house. He is the perfect *buffo* style of the Italian stage-comic without extravagance, and humorous without vulgarity. Almost everything he utters is productive of effect; and his recitative is given in a talking way, which is highly amusing, without ever being at variance with the instrumental modulations that follow him. Signor Lablache was greatly applauded throughout his performance, and altogether met with a reception, on the part of a very crowded audience, of the most flattering kind. The part of Fidelma was again sustained by Marie Malibran, a lady whose versatility of talents will no doubt confer distinction on any character in which she chooses to appear, but did a great deal too much honour to the one in question. Madame Lalande personated Carolina in a very efficient manner. Signor Santini, as the Count, completed the list of *dramatis personae* and played with much humour. The celebrated duet in the opening of the second act, *Se fiste in corpo avete*, between him and Signor Lablache, was given in a style of excellence which elicited an unanimous 'encore' . . . The same compliment was very deservedly paid to the quartette, '*Tu mi dice che del Conte,*' between Mesdames Malibran and Lalande, and Signor Donzelli and Lablache. On the whole, the performance appeared to give great satisfaction, and deserves to be ranked among the best of the season.[219]

London in the thirties was host to some of the finest Italian singers of the first half of the nineteenth century: Pasta, Malibran, Méric-Lalande, Grisi, Davide, Donzelli, Rubini, Tamburini, and Lablache. The later three would be entertaining Londoners for many years to come. These artists had left their native Italy and would now, upon finding adoration befitting their talents and income to match, return to Italy only spasmodically for over the next two decades.

The careers of the tenor Rubini and Lablache had run parallel since the early twenties. Collaborating together, they climbed to dazzling heights of success. Rubini became a multimillonaire and retired to Romano, Italy, in 1842. Close friends, it was Lablache who urged Rubini to break away from his ties in Italy and go to Paris, and finally he could not refuse to follow.

The beautiful prima donna Maria Garcia Malibran (1808-1836) had enjoyed unparalleled successes in London, New York, and many other cities by 1830. She was already very well-known to audiences on the stages of London when she and Lablache appeared together at the King's Theatre that season. Her debut there was on 11 June 1825 in *Il Barbiere di Siviglia*; as the famous tenor Manuel Garcia's daughter, Maria, taught by her father, had been singing since a child; and because of her talent, beauty, and notoriety as a prima donna, she was able to ask for enormous fees and get them. A superstar of her time, she was much sought after, filling the gap between the departure of the great prima donnas Giudetta Pasta and Henriette Méric-Lalande. When Lablache arrived in London, clearly Lalande was in a decline and no rival after Malibran's London debut. Of Lalande, Chorley commented, "She had arrived in England too late . . . and gave little satisfaction."[220] Lablache and Lalande had sung together for many years in great successes like *Semiramide* at the San Carlo and in Vienna, now to be repeated in England. Lalande, however, only thirty-two years old, was fading, eclipsed by Malibran. Losing her voice, she retired in 1836, totally worn out.

Marie Malibran's brief career was glorious; she was described best by that dour London critic Chorley in wonderful and unforgettable terms:

> Of a woman so bright, so kindly, so ill starred, and thence so unequal, as she, it is impossible to think, without a strange and affectionate regret. Of the artist it must be recorded that, boundless as were Malibran's resources, keen as was her intelligence, dazzling as was her genius, she never produced a single type in opera for other women to adopt. She passed over the stage like a meteor, as an apparition of wonder, rather than as one who, on her departure, left her mantle behind her for others to take up and wear.[221]

On 22 May 1830, sang his first *Semiramide* in London with Malibran and Lalande. A critic wrote a negative review:

> Lablache has appeared as a serious character, and since our last Assur in Rossini's magnificent opera *Semiramide,* we have no hesitation in saying he disappointed us, both in his acting and singing, and we find an occasional incorrectness in intonation in his unequalled voice.

On 3 June, he was engaged in another great role, Leporello, in Mozart's *Don Giovanni. The London Times*, on reviewing the opera, wrote,

> We must however say that, ably as Signor Lablache exerted himself as Leporello, his personal appearance was too strikingly at variance with the well-known requisites of that character to reconcile us with this personation.

Later, his would be the definitive interpretation. On 17 June, he sang in *Il Turco in Italia* compressed into one act. Lablache soon was much admired by the British in two totally different roles, first the sinister Assur and then his famous interpretation of Leporello. Both *Semiramide* and *Don Giovanni* were part of the usual bill of fare for the early thirties in London and Paris. *Don Giovanni,* however, would overcome in popularity if one was to compare Mozart overall. On 29 April 1837, the *Observer* remarked, "The house was filled in every part except the subscription boxes, for it is not the fashion to like Mozart; it is, of course, not the fashion to listen to much of his music." Lablache did not follow this fashion, however, and Mozart was a very real part of his concert repertory.

All the Italians from the King's Theatre, plus some English artists, sang at a huge concert there at the King's Theatre arranged on Whitsun-Eve, Saturday, 29 May 1830. The mainly Rossini concert started with a prayer for the recovery of His Majesty George IV.

When the King of England George IV, died on the 26 June, all of England was in mourning. The black-edged newspapers were full of details of his last hours, plus long descriptions of the funeral. All this rather subtracted from all the proceedings at the King's Theatre; concerts at some of the homes of the elite were of course cancelled. The king's brother, the Duke of Clarence, who was next in line, succeeded to the throne. King William IV and Queen

Adelaide were childless, and as the King was sixty-five, it was proclaimed that the little thirteen-year-old princess Victoria, who was next in line to the throne, would become the next queen of England.[222]

☙☙☙

Chapter Twelve

Paris and High Society

1830-31

Fame had long proceeded Lablache to London and Paris. Almost instantly, he became the idol of the Parisians. He had a love affair with the city until the day he died and eventually brought his wife and family to live there in a villa, which he built in the fashionable beautiful suburb of Maisons-Laffitte,[223] where he lived out his remaining years.

Triumphing in his first season in Paris at the Théâtre-Italien, he was immediately dubbed the Napoleon of Bassos by the French. For his debut on 2 November, he sang again in Cimarosa's *Il Matrimonio Segreto*. Undisputably, Rossini's operas were still the rage, and Lablache would soon bring added glory to Rossini, for never before had Paris heard and seen the likes of such an accomplished and skillful artist as Lablache in *Il Barbiere di Siviglia, La Gazza ladra,* and *La Cenerentola*. Mme. Maria Malibran helped complete the delightful picture, appearing with him throughout the season. *La France Musicale* decribes his debut in an article republished in English in *The Musical World,* in December 1839, under the title, *Characteristics of Lablache*:[224]

> Lablache! Here is a name to which the greatest artists do homage, as subjects to royalty. Since Lablache's appearance, the fame of all preceding bassi has been eclipsed, and none have arisen to contest his supremacy. Lablache is, like Rubini, still of an age to derive pleasure and glory from the agitations of professional life.

After writing about his early life, the writer discribes Lablache's successful debut as Geronimo in *Il Matrimonio Segreto.*

> It was in November of the year 1830 that our fat, facetious, and funny friend made his debut in the French capital, in the part of

Geronimo, in the opera *Il Matrimonio Segreto*. His *entrée* was a perfect triumph; he enacted his part with immense superiority of talent, and was immediately recognized as the first *basso cantante*, and *primo buffa* of our era. To form an idea of the power which this actor possesses over a select and intelligent auditory, he should be seen on the Italian stage in a part of some importance. His entrance is attended by a general sensation similar to that produced by a stream of electricity. Figure to yourself an assembly of cold, silent, and abstracted spectators—in an instant every head is raised, every countenance animated, every mouth smiling—Lablache is before them. Survey those fine and noble features, those eyes beaming with genius and frank expression, that stature so colossal yet so dignified! Physically, as well as vocally, Lablache is the perfect type of the true *basso cantante*. He is at home in every character, serious or comic, tragic or sentimental; he seduces and captivates your imagination, and holds you in breathless suspense. He is an absolute PROTEUS; as or Dulcamara, as the father of Desdemona or Don Magnifico, he makes you weep, laugh, or shudder at pleasure, and frequently by a mere look, a gesture, or a simple movement of his body. The compass of Lablache's voice is from G in the bass to E natural, embracing but thirteen notes; but the *timbre*, power, and vibration of his tones are prodigious, taken as they are with unerring precision. Hear him in grand concerted pieces, with all the surrounding voices in full development, and the orchestra putting forth its powers-Lablache surmounts the whole, overpowers both chorus and instruments; and the *éclat* of his bass phrases, streaking the general mass of sound, is never confounded with unisonous accompaniment. It is impossible to describe the effect of his magnificent organ in *morceaux d'ensemble*; it is as a cannon amid a rolling fire of musketry; as thunder amid the tempest. Nevertheless, he is in perfect control over this immense volume of tone, subduing it at pleasure, and endowing it with graces, delicacy, and occasionally even a spice of coquetry. Such are the triumphs of art! Cultivation has perfected nature without trespassing on her primitive beauty . . . Lablache is not a singer in the ordinary sense of the word. Look not at him on every occasion for rapid execution, a profusion of graces, chromatic ascents and descents. He aims not at effect by such trivialities. He attains it by dramatic truth, by accents of real melody, by the intensity of his feelings. Ever awake to a sense of the beautiful, he is as capable of interpreting the *chefs d'oeuvre* of the older masters, as the most finished productions of contemporary art . . . Lablache's great triumph is the *opera buffa*. No actor has ever been so natural in his bye-play, or more comic and diverting in his text illustrations. Few things are more amusing than to see this Rhodian colossus caper and flit about the stage with the elasticity of a sylph, we expect every moment to see him prostrate; but at the instant that a lapse seems inevitable, he is off again like a butterfly—*Mi vedrai farfallone amoroso.*

The knowledge that larger salaries could be made in the northern capitals convinced many singers in the first half of the nineteenth century to leave Italy and pursue opera careers in these more cosmopolitan capitals of Europe, such as Paris, London, Vienna, and Russia's St. Petersburg. There the economy was often more stable even though the threat of revolutions was always present. In Italy, the atmosphere was always volatile.

Since the fame of Rossini swept across Europe, the public had an insatiable hunger for his music. By the 1850's, some operas had run their course and vanished; but Rossini held his own, still popular against the onslaught of many newer composers like Bellini, Donizetti, Mercadante, and Meyerbeer. Never replacing Rossini, they merely added to the rich carpet of varied operas that were available to the public of that time. However later, some of Rossini's operas and those of other bel canto composers were replaced by the popularity of later talent, such as Gounod, Verdi, Wagner, and Meyerbeer.

Il Barbiere di Siviglia, unanimously proclaimed as Rossini's masterpiece, the most popular work in the history of opera, has never left the major repertoire of opera houses. Translated into over seventeen different languages, it is still performed throughout the world with great regularity. Lablache—*the* Figaro of his age—probably sang this work more than any other, certainly without doubt his dazzling interpretation, first as Figaro in his younger thinner days and, just as unforgettable, his brilliant acting as the older character—Bartolo. After many years in this role, the critic of *Musical World* wrote on April 13, 1850:

> The part of Bartolo is essentially the creation of Lablache. Beaumarchais never wrote it; Rossini never composed it; with him it wlll die. Fortunately, it still lives in all its matchless charm, to the delight of the public and the enduring honour of the great Neapolitan whose genius has nobly rescued so many secondary parts from their supressed infernality.

When a friend of his implied that Bartolo was a role, that was inferior to his great talents, Lablache wisely replied, "My friend, to a great singer, there are no small parts; and to a small singer there are no great ones."

Marie Malibran and her lover De Beriot finished their commitments that season before Lablache, leaving London for the provinces in August 1830. Lablache then joined them, and they traveled to Paris from England together as most of their engagements were together. Lablache loved Maria like a daughter, and most probably Lablache knew all the details of Maria's tempestuous marriage and how she wanted a divorce from Malibran, the gentleman she had unfortunately married when she was in New York. Now she was in love with the well-known Belgian violinist, the elegant and handsome Charles de Beriot. Desperate to dissolve her marriage now, the leading diva at the Théâtre-Italien found her personal problems overwhelming. She was demanding enormous fees, and the Italian theaters wanted her back in Italy and were prepared to pay better fees than Paris, but the joint directors of the Théâtre-Italien, Edouard Robert and Carlo Severini, won out by giving in to her demands. Severini wrote, "We urgently need that rapacious blood sucker to get through these hard times."[225] So Marie had her way as usual for she knew she was unequalled.

How did the thirty-five-year-old Lablache feel about singing with Maria Malibran? Now in her prime, she was quite the fearless superstar with all of Paris at her feet and at their performances. Together, they took Paris by storm. Lablache gaily domineering the stage of the Théâtre-Italien as Figaro again and again with La Malibran and Dominico Donzelli in *Il Barbiere di Siviglia,* one of the first operas of the 1830 Paris season.

Domenico Donzelli, a dramatic tenor with a strong baritone quality, had joined Lablache at La Scala when Mercadante wrote the tenor role for him in *Elisa and Claudio.* Born in Bergamo, he first appeared on the operatic stage in 1807 when he was only seventeen as comprimario in Mayr's *Elisa*. Historically later, he was most well known for having created the role of Pollione in Bellini's *Norma* at La Scala in 1831 and sang the role in London with Lablache. His reputation was based on his ability to conquer high-flying tenor roles as in such operas as Rossini's *Otello*; apparently he was remembered for attacking the role of Otello without resorting to the use of falsetto. First appearing in 1815, in *Tancredi* at the La Fenice in Venice, he went on to sing with Lablache in Palermo at the Teatro Carolino. And he was the lead tenor for many seasons again with Lablache in Vienna in the early twenties. Then it wasn't long before he established himself in Paris many years before Lablache and Rubini arrived, singing Rossini roles. Henry Chorley wrote of him in his *Musical Recollections:*

> The volume of Donzelli's rich and sonorous voice was real, not forced. When he gave out his high notes there was no misgiving as to the peril of his blood vessels; and hence his reign on the Italian stage was thrice as long as that of any of the worse-endowered, worse-trained folk, who have since adopted the career of forcible tenors, partly from a wish to split the ears of the groundlings, partly from laziness which together with the increased facilities in gathering gains during modern times has so largely corrupted art.[226]

L'ultimo giorno di Pompei really wasn't so successful in Paris and London as it had been in Naples. *La Cenerentola, La Gazza ladra, La prova di un'opera seria,* and *Don Giovanni* were. Lablache alternated between singing the title role in *Don Giovanni* in London and Paris. Surely, he fitted right into the image of the former role, the huge form, the handsome face, the twinkling eyes, his reputation as having an eye for the ladies and they for him. Noticeably by now, he had become rather plump to say the least. He preferred the role of Don Giovanni's faithful but complaining servant—Leporello—and abandoned the extremely demanding role of the libertine Don Giovanni. Part of his later reputation rested on his hilarious interpretation of Leporello, and it was in this role that he was remembered affectionately by audiences. Especially when he picked up Masseto and tucked him under his arm as he walked off the stage.

Evidently, not long after his arrival (7 January 1831) in the French capital Lablache enters Parisan high society. There he first sang at the fashionable Salon of the Countess Merlin. The countess was a Spanish society lady who, after taking singing lessons from famed singer and teacher Manuel Garcia, befriended his daughter Maria Malibran and Lablache. So smitten by Lablache, it was the Countess Merlin herself who first played an active role in introducing Lablache into established fashionable society as well as the musical and artistic world of Paris. While singing at these fashionable soirées, he first became acquainted with such personages as the beautiful Italian Princess Christina Belgiojoso and Mme. De Girardin, the wife of a newspaper tycoon. Describing the Countess Merlin, her dazzling beauty and charm, the Princess Belgiojoso could have been describing herself; she recalls in her memoirs:

> That memorable contest in which she had as competitors the youthful beauties of three united kingdoms . . . These young ladies had to yield to the dean of beauties whose well-established charms seemed to be consolidated with time . . . every man turned to Countess Merlin as though attracted by a bottle of vintage wine, generous and vermilion . . . placed amid an assortment of insipid syrups.[227]

Born in Havana, Cuba, she came to the French capital as a child.[228] Her fortune was reputed to have come from slave trading in the West Indies. That evening, Rossini played the piano and the countess sang with David, Raimbaux, and Mme. Donzelli. Much in demand, Lablache and La Malibran sang together at many of the most brilliant salons in the French capital with such other artistes as Henriette Méric-Lalande, Nourrit, and Donzelli. They also entertained at the court. At the Palais Royal, most of the concerts featured excerpts from Rossini's *Semiramide*; the famous duet that thrilled audiences was the salon favorite in the spring of 1831 and was repeated again for the concerts of November and December that year, especially when sung by La Malibran. The Countess Merlin describes their first meeting, in her memoirs, when Malibran was still a young unknown singer:

> This interesting young singer, a wanderer from a distant land, presented herself to me. Her dark, silken hair hung in long ringlets on her neck; she was simply attired in a dress of white muslin. Her youth, her beauty, her intelligence, her friendless and destitute condition, all combined to excite my deepest interest. I gazed on her with mingled feelings of sympathy and admiration.[229]

Full of admiration for Malibran that year was the young Frédéric Chopin who had just arrived in Paris. The young Polish composer and brilliant pianist, almost unknown he had just completed a successful series of concerts in Germany on the way to the French capital. There, like so many other musicians before and after him, he found in Paris his second and spiritually final home. His destiny now lay in the arms of France. Handsome, elegant, and of slight build, he spent his first few months absorbing Parisian life. He wrote on 14 December 1831:

> It is only here that one can learn what singing is. I believe that not Pasta, but Malibran Garcia is now the greatest singer in Europe. Prince Valentin Radziwill is quite enraptured by her! And we often wish you were here, for you would be charmed by her singing . . . There are a host of interesting people here belonging to various professions. Three of the orchestras can be called first rate: that of the Academy, the Italian Opera, and the Theatre Feydeau. Rossini is the director of the Italian Opera, which is undoubtedly now the best in Europe. Lablache, Rubini, Santini, Pasta, Malibran, and Schroder-Devrient perform three times a week for the delectation of the elite.[230]

On 6 December Chopin wrote to his friend Titus Woyciechowski:

> As for the Opera, I must say I never heard such a fine performance as last week, when the *Barbiere* was given, with Lablache, Rubini, and Malibran-Garcia. There was too, an excellent rendering of *Otello*, with Rubini, Lablache, and Pasta; also *L'Italiana in Algeri*, Paris has, in this respect, never offered as many attractions as now. You can have no idea of Lablache! They say that Pasta's voice has rather gone off, but I never in my life heard such heavenly singing.[231]

Again he writes to Titus on 25 December:

> There is to be a grand concert today at the Italien opera house, in which Malibran, Rubini, Lablache, Santini, Mad. Raimbaux, Mad. Schröder, Mad. Casadori are to appear; Herz and Beriot, with whom Mad. Malibran is in love, will assist in the instrumental portion.[232]

Chopin's most intimate friends in Paris were Poles. As he entered aristocratic circles, he became very attached to the Countess Delphine Potocka, and it was said that she took as much trouble and pride in giving choice musical entertainments as other people did in giving choice dinners.[233]

In Albert Sowinski's *Musiciens polonais*, we read she had a beautiful soprano voice and occupied the first place among the amateur ladies of Paris:

> A great friend of the illustrious Chopin, she gave formerly splendid concerts at her house with the old company of the Italians, which one shall see no more in Paris. To cite the names of Rubini, Lablache, Tamburini, Malibran, Grisi, Persiani, is to give the highest idea of Italian singing. The Countess Potocka sang herself according to the method of the Italian masters.[234]

Chopin dedicated his D-flat-major (minute) waltz to the countess. This waltz was one of his Trois Valses op. 64. Delphine Pototska was devoted to Chopin.[235] Edmund d'Alton-Shee, a close friend of Emilio Belgiojoso, writes of a new generation in Paris enjoying a brief interlude between revolutions and wars:

> My story, but for a few exceptions, is that of the leisure class of my generation . . . One was in a hurry to live, heedless of ruin and death. Poets, composers, artists came to support our tendencies with an entire literature in our image, amusing, impassioned, evanescent, wafting like the smoke of their beloved cigars, inflaming the imagination like the alcohol they abused. Polish counts, Italian princes, Spanish grandees deprived of their freedom but not their fortunes joined in the ranks of this derailed youth that had retreated from the battlefield to the Cafe de Paris. The jeunesse doree supplied the wine, the artists the entertainment. Hugo, Lamartine, Heine, Musset offered poetry of sensuality and irony; Balzac, Dumas, and Sue brought heroes of infinite vitality and occasional melodrama; Hoffmann added fantasy more real than reality. Rossini contributed his subtle laughter that concealed tears; Bellini, tears of stifled heroism; and Pasta, Malibran, Mario, Rubini, Lablache, Nourrit sang to their golden spell. Rachel, Marie Dorval, Lemaitre rekindled the tragic embers left by Talma and Paganini. Liszt, Thalberg, Chopin provided magical sounds never heard before. There was no energy left for action. The senses reeled from one orgy to another. A new world was born.[236]

Chapter Thirteen

Paganini and Lablache

1831-1832

Niccolo Paganini, the famed violin virtuoso from Italy, swept into London from Paris that summer intending to conquer England. Long before he crossed the channel, his reputation as the world's greatest violinist had preceded him. Londoners, hearing of his triumphs, rushed to the King's Theatre to buy tickets for a series of concerts. There was, however, a problem—the buyers objected to the price of the tickets. Lablache, upon his return to the King's Theatre from Paris that spring, was scheduled to sing at Paganini's first concert on 3 June and his third on 13 June.[237] It is difficult to say if teaming up with Paganini brought Lablache added fame or not.

Although the concerts were soon all sold out, Paganini faced trouble and was directly accused of gross overcharging. The London public became very hostile, grumbling that Pierre Laporte, manager of the King's Theatre, was going to charge much more for all the seats. Directly, the playbills were circulated, posting prices. There was a terrible uproar; the conservative *London Times* wrote a full-length column on the subject, attacking Laporte:

> Laporte's presumption in doubling the prices of admission to the King's Theatre on the first night of Paganini's performance is one of those extravagances which could only have entered the head of a foreigner, who had beforehand arrived at the happy conviction, moreover, of the infinite gullibility of the English.

Then the article continued with a lengthy argument about prices and concluded with the following opinion of the performers:

> We have had enough instances before in this country of extravagant pretension on the part of opera singers, dancers, and others;

> yet none of them in the full zenith of their popularity, with far stronger reasons on their side, ever ventured on such an outrageous proceeding as this. The prices at the King's Theatre are already higher than any others in Europe. They secure, as they are, the most brilliant recompense that can possibly await individual talent . . . There can be nothing in his art, a mere instrumental performer, so great a prodigy, as to deserve such a price. The frequenters of the King's Theatre are frivolous enough, perhaps many of them, to take their estimate of Paganini's concert by the rate of admission which is demanded to it, but the common sense of the great majority of them will, we are persuaded, furnish the best remedy for such extortion, by causing them to absent themselves till Laporte and his foreign idol are brought to their senses.

The *Athenaeum* wrote, "We have no wish to keep up excitement beyond the occasion, and shall therefore only announce that Paganini will appear at the Opera house, early in June . . . at the old prices."[238] All the Paganini reviews were ecstatic about his performance on 3 June at the King's theater. The concert began with orchestra playing Beethoven's Symphony in D, the program followed by Lablache singing the famous cavatina "Largo al factotum." This was encored. Then Paganini played his own composition Grand Concerto in three movements. The first entrance of Paganni, after Lablache finished, was recorded in detail and in length by *The London Times*:[239]

> . . . a breathless silence ensued and every eye was watching the action of this extraordinary violinist. As he glided from the side scenes to the front of the stage an involuntary cheering burst forth from every part of the house, many rising from their seats to view the spectre during the thunder of this unprecedented cheering-his gaunt and extraordinary appearance being more like that of a devotee about to suffer martyrdom, than one to delight you with his art. With the tip of his bow, he sent off the orchestra in a grand military movement with a force and vivacity as surprising as it was new. At the termination of this introduction, he commenced with a soft streaming note of celestial quality, and with three or four whips of his bow elicited points of sound that mounted to the third heaven and as bright as the stars . . .

Before the Paganini concert, Lablache sang *Il Barbiere di Siviglia* and *Il Matrimonio Segreto* at the King's and the first London performance of Pacini's *L'ultimo giorno di Pompei* with an excellent cast including the prima donna assoluta Guiditta Pasta and tenor Rubini. However, like in Paris, Pacini's opera was received coldly. The *London Times* critic pointed out that "at the present moment there is no musical writer in Italy that can outrival or supersede the works of Rossini, if we except Bellini alone; Bellini is yet a young man."[240]

On 12 May, Lablache sang in Simon Mayr's *Medea in Corinto*, supported by Guiditta Pasta and Giovanni Battista Rubini. On 2 June, they joined Lablache in *Semiramide* and Pasta sang the title role. Arzace was sung by Adelaide Comelli-Rubini (Rubini's wife) while Rubini sang Idreno. Rubini had enjoyed enormous successes in Italy, Paris, and Vienna and was referred to as Italy's foremost tenor. The *London Times* in March of that year wrote, "Signor Rubini's performance was a masterpiece of acting" in *L'ultimo giorno di Pompei*, and they compared him to his predecessor David.[241] Signor Rubini sang in Paganini's second concert. On 4 June 1831, another critic wrote,

> Lablache is very loud in this piece—very loud and very fine, but too loud we think, for the women who sing duets with him. He swallows them up like an ogre. The voice is very powerful. The power of this singer seems to come out of a body lined in brass. If one of the giants at the Guildhall were to astonish a city dinner some day by taking part in glee, he would sound like Lablache. Or as a lady whom we had the pleasure of sitting next to observed . . . an elephant might sing like him. We fancy we see the inspired bulk open his mouth, and exhaling the mighty music, the essence of nine trombones.

London and Paris had more opportunities to offer aspiring artists and musicians. Even though the competition was fierce, the rewards were excellent compared to Italy; the northern theaters of Europe such as London's King's and the Théâtre-Italien seasons lasted almost throughout the year. There was a continuous output of northern festivals in England every year and an endless parade of concerts, public and private. The fashionable society hostesses arranged lavish private soirées using the Italian singers to impress their society peers. Although the Italians reigned supreme over the English singers, many fine English voices emerged to sing opera. Often they assumed Italian stage names, for example, Mme. Favanti was an English woman.

Britain was now in the throes of the Industrial Revolution. The manpower required by such productivity unleashed a labor force of great magnitude. A newly prosperous middle class emerged, and the rich Victorian industrialists often supported the arts and enjoyed the great musical festivals that were put on every year in such cities as Norwich, Liverpool, Manchester, Sheffield, and Birmingham. Most of these large cities hosted members of the Italian opera. Groups of Italian singers set up concerts in many of the smaller towns as well from the south of England to northern Scotland and Ireland.

Twenty Paganini concerts were arranged in London, not all at the King's Theatre. Lablache sang the cavatina from *Schiava in Bagdad* at the third Paganini concert, second to Mozart's Symphony no. 3 in G Minor. Part two of the concert featured Lablache and Rubini singing the duetta from *L'Italiana in Algieri.*[242] "This astonishing being," as the newspapers called Paganini, would also appear at Covent Garden in many private homes and concert halls. From Wilhelm Kuhe's *My Musical Recollections*:[243]

> Paganini, I was told, was in the habit, when engaged in conversation, of giving very laconic answers to questions asked, but they were invariably to the point. A lady occupying a considerable position in the social world invited him to a dinner-party, to which men and women distinguished in art and literature were bidden. Rightly or wrongly, she expected that he would consent to play something during the evening. But she reckoned without her guest. When the great man arrived, she discovered that he had not brought his instrument. "Oh, Signor Paganini!" she exclaimed repoachfully, "you have not brought your violin." "No, my Lady—," was the witty answer; "my violin never dines out."

While in Paris, Paganini brought about a change in the life of young pianist Franz Liszt, who after hearing the virtuoso violinist, was never the same again. Alan Walker describes what happened:[244]

> In March 1831 Paganini glided onto the stage of the Paris Opera House and played to a packed audience. Liszt who was there was electrified. He was nineteen years old, and it is not too much to say the experience changed the course of his life. He locked himself away, and practiced for ten, twelve, sometimes fourteen hours a day. His aim was very simple: he wanted to do for the piano what Paganini had done for the violin; he drove himself mercilessly to

conquer the keyboard's last remaining secrets, and he succeeded. When he re-emerged, the term "virtuoso" was no longer adequate to describe what he had become.

Henry W. Goodban writes in his *Journal and Jottings*,[245] "At one of my parties in London, in 1852, on which occasion Camile Sivori, the nephew and pupil of Paganini, played the first violin, Goffrie the second, Tolbecque, *Chef d'attaque* at Her Majesty's Theatre, the alto and myself the violoncello. Tolbecque told us at a merry supper afterwards two stories about Paganini, illustrative of a peculiar character . . . evincing traits of strange antagonism."

> When he first arrived in London he knew scarcely anybody. Signor Lablache, the eminent Italian singer, who he had heard, and had been introduced to him abroad, and was consequently aware of his great genius and executive facility, called upon, welcomed warmly, and invited him to accept his hospitality, telling him he always dined at four o'clock, and there would be a place at his table for him whenever he was disposed to avail himself of it. Paganini appreciated the privilege so highly that he dined nearly every day for a month at the residence of the celebrated and hospitable basso, where the Chef was a Cordon blu, the champagne of the best brand, and the society and welcome, genial and warm. The expiration of this period Paganini's mind evidently began to be uneasy at so constant an attendance at the "Chateau Lablache" at dinner time, so he wrote his esteemed host a note, which he sent by his servant, expressing his feeling of delicacy, enclosing a sum of money at the rate of two shillings and six pence for each meal—begging him to accept it, and requesting an acknowledgment of its receipt. Good-natured Lablache, ever ready at seizing and indulging in the humour of a ridiculous position, was intensely amused; appearing to treat the matter seriously, signed a receipt for the money, and presented it to the servant, who had brought it from his eccentric master, as recompense for the trouble he had had in calling to settle the account.

From June 1831 through to the end of February 1832, Paganini went on a lightning tour of the English provinces including Ireland, performing in an amazing 120 concerts up and down the country, finally leaving only because there was a severe cholera epidemic. His last concerts were at Winchester and Southampton and reported in the *Hampshire Advertiser*. From there, he sailed away, promising to return with possibly the greatest "cache" to be taken in by any instrumentalist of that era.

Lablache had a tremendous program to sing in London that year. Paganini may have gone down as violinist extraordinaire, but after he left, the spotlight fell on Donizetti's first work to be performed in London at the King's Theatre—a new historical opera based on the story of the tragic queen of England Anne Boleyn.

> This work expresses true Romantic feeling and represents both the culmination of Donizetti's earlier experience and the beginning of a highly productive period in which he would create a number of superb romantic tragedies, among them *Torquato Tasso*, *Lucrezia Borgia* and *Lucia di Lammermoor*.[246]

The English premiere of *Anna Bolena* was considered a very important event when it opened on 8 July 1831 at the King's Theatre. In contrast to the heavy subject matter of this opera, Bellini's lighthearted piece, *La Sonnambula*, was to have its first showing at the same theater, on 28 July.

Anna Bolena, an *opera seria*, with a libretti by Romani, had its first performance in Italy at the Teatro Carcano in Milan on 26 December 1830 with Filippo Galli as Henry VIII. The singers Guiditta Pasta (Anna Bolena) and Giovanni Battista Rubini (Percy) were highly acclaimed. The next year brought the same singers together in another world premiere, Bellini's *opera semiseria* La *Sonnambula* at the same theater on 6 March 1831. Audiences were ecstatic; Bellini wrote to Lamperi:

> Here you have the happy news of the uproarious success of opera last evening at the Carcano . . . I assure you that Rubini and Pasta are two angels who enraptured the whole audience to the verge of madness.[247]

In the audience that night was the Russian composer Mikhail Glinka, who later wrote, "In the second act the singers themselves wept and carried the audience along with them."[248]

When *Anna Bolena* reached London in the same year, it became popular with English audiences, not only because of the Elizabethan subject matter but because it was sung by the finest singers of the day. Lablache was Henry VIII,

Rubini as Percy, and Pasta took the role of the tragic queen. Luigi Lablache astonished London audiences with his perfect rendering of the wicked king Henry VIII. Gaetano Donizetti wrote at once to his wife after the premiere:[249]

> My respected and beloved Lady, I am pleased to announce to you that the new opera by your beloved and famous husband has had a reception that could not possibly be improved upon. Success, triumph, delirium; it seemed that the public had gone mad. Everyone says that they cannot remember ever having been present at such a triumph.

William Ashbrook writes of this opera:

> The success of *Anna Bolena* was crucially important to Donizetti's later development because it opened for him the doors of important opera houses, first in northern Italy and then abroad; for these centers which, if they could scarcely be called liberal, were at least less conservative than Naples, he could write works that indulged and developed his taste for the tragic Romantic melodrama.[250]

This opera exemplifies the spirit of the times as England was steeped in the melodramatic romantic novels of Sir Walter Scott; it was the Romantic Age. The role of the tyrant Henry VIII was a demanding one for Lablache; he was not worried how he sang but was more concerned that he "looked" the part. Opera stars of those days were responsible for their own costumes; for *Anna Bolena*, Lablache went to see the royal portraits, probably by Holbein, to have his costumes created in an authentic manner. *The Musical World* writes,[251]

> Lablache never appears in public without much patient and extensive enquiry as to traditionl costume and appearance of the individual to be represented. It may be remembered that in his first appearance in London as Henry VIII in *Anna Bolena*, his resemblance to the historical personage struck the spectators with horror as though the tyrant himself were before them.

Chorley writes many years later on this opera's reception:

> *Anna Bolena*, brought hither under the protection of Madame Pasta's royal robes, was permitted, rather than admitted. Though in this historical English opera might be discerned something of

Donizetti's own; and though three of the characters, those of the Queen (Pasta), Percy (Rubini), and Henry VIII (Lablache), were played to perfection. Donizetti, however, was not an utter stranger. A duet of his *I Messicani* had, a season or two earlier, excited attention. But he was credited with small individuality by those who then ruled public opinion, so it is curious to recollect how Bellini's second opera introduced here (also by Madame Pasta), *La Sonnambula*, was treated on its introduction with contempt; the want of science on the part of the composer dwelt on—and that which is true in expression, and that which has kept the opera alive—utterly overlooked. It may have been that possibly, truth in expression was not that much cared for by those who frequented our Italian opera. The time of Donizetti and Bellini, though at hand, was still to come.[252]

The *London Times* was not over enthusiastic in its first reviews, commenting that, "Lablache looked as if he did not know how to hold a scepter!"[253] However, soon this opera reaped nothing but success for Donizetti. And Lablache was showered with compliments; for obvious reasons the opera was even more successful in London than Paris and in the long run, Lablache was to clock up over seventeen seasons with *Anna Bolena* from the opening performance there on 8 July at the King's Theatre to his last performances there in 1 August 1851. It was featured again at the Royal Italian Theatre at Covent Garden in the fifties.[254] Lablache was the definitive Henry VIII of that era. No one could replace him, and no *Anna Bolena* would have been complete without his rendering of the role. About Rubini's performance, a critic later wrote:

> In *Anna Bolena* and *Lucia,* Rubini was no less admirable than in the operas of Bellini. In the first of these works, in which he created the part of Percy, he sang with profound emotion, the well-known air, *Vivi-tu, te ne scongiuro,* where Donizetti has evidently imitated the melodious manner of his young rival. As for the scene of the malediction, which forms the dramatic climax of the second finale of *Lucia,* no singer has ever been able to imitate the cry of anguish which escaped from Rubini's quivering lips.

The great prima donna Giuditta Pasta's operatic reign was on the decline when Bellini and Donizetti arrived on the operatic scene; Rossini had never created an opera for her nor did he really like her, yet her successes were during his time. She was a legendary figure who created many roles. Yet, was it left for Bellini and Donizetti to bring out her true genius? Here in the role of Anna, she showed her dramatic strength, yet she was best remembered for her Norma. Besides Norma, she created Amina, Beatrice di Tenda, Ugo. Long before Malibran operatic arrival, Pasta's rendering of Rossini's Desdemona sent audiences into raptures. A critic said, "Of Madame Pasta's acting in *Anna Bolena* it is hardly possible to speak in adequate terms. After witnessing her Medea, her Semiramide, her Desdemona, her Maria Stuarta . . . Her vocal powers were historic . . . It would seem that the libretto was written by the author expressly for her."

On 12 May, before the 8 July opening of *Anna Bolena*, Rubini, Pasta, and Lablache sang together at the King's Theatre in Simone Mayr's most celebrated work, *Medea in Corinto*. Lablache then sang with Pasta in *Semiramide, Don Giovanni,* and *Otello*. Afterward, *Anna Bolena, Don Giovanni,* and the above Rossini operas were repeated at the Théâtre-Italien.

From the time of its first performance in Italy, *Anna Bolena* was staged up and down the peninsula and was a triumph for Donizetti, his first international success.

Chopin's first concert In Paris was not to materialize till 26 February 1832 at the Pleyel rooms. Naturally, he visited the theater. Chopin wrote, "Paris offers anything you wish. You can amuse yourself, mope, laugh, weep, in short, do whatever you like; no one notices it, thousands do the same. Everyone goes his own way."[255]

Of the three theaters in Paris, it was the Théâtre-Italien that was the most fashionable in those years and the most popular. Chopin wrote back to his friend in Poland:[256]

> I am happy at what I have found in this city, the finest musicians and the finest opera in the world. I met Rossini, Cherubini, Paer, etc., etc.

The Théâtre-Italien opened early with *Anna Bolena* on 1 September, featuring some of the same cast as in London. Mme. Pasta, Rubini, and Lablache, all the singers were the toast of the town. There was a change in the casts of sopranos. Caradori-Allan, Malibran, Devrient, Tadolini, and Amigo took the place of the previous divas such as Méric-Lalande.

Clearly, at no other time was there such a vast constellation of vocal talent to be found in one place than at the Théâtre-Italien that season. The

Grand Opera House (or less simply, Académie Royale de Musique—the principal opera house), not to be outdone, staged the grand production that winter of Giacomo Meyerbeer's stupendous and flashy French opera in five acts, *Robert le Diable*. The composer Meyerbeer, enamoured of Parisian life, stopped writing Italian operas and, with the collaboration with Eugene Scribe, launched his first work in French.[257]

Chopin visited the Théâtre-Italien that season. Chopin's judgment of the music was impeccable, and as a critic, he was most observant:

> Malibran with her wonderful voice embraces a compass of three octaves; her singing is quite unique . . . enchanting! Rubini, an excellent tenor, makes endless "roulades," often too many "colorature," vibrates and trills continually, for which he is rewarded with the greatest applause. His "mezza-voca" is incomparable. Schroder-Devrient is now making her appearance, but she does not produce such a "furore" here as in Germany. She played the role of Desdemona with Malibran as Otello! (Chopin must have been very amused.) Malibran is petite, and the German prima donna enormous! One thought that Desdemona was going to strangle Otello! It was a very expensive performance; I paid twenty-four francs for my seat, and did so because I wished to see Malibran play the Moor, which she did not do particularly well. The orchestra was excellent, but the "mise en scène" in the Italian Opera is nothing compared with that of the French Académie Royale . . . Madame Cinti-Damoreau sings also very beautifully; I prefer her singing to that of Malibran. The latter astonishes one, but Cinti charms. She sings the chromatic scales and *coloratura* almost more perfectly than the famous flute player Tulou. It is hardly possible to find a more finished execution. In Nourrit, the first tenor of the Grand Opera, one admires the warmth of feeling which speaks out of his singing. (Here he is referring to the singers in *Robert le Diable* at the Opera.)[258]

Lablache passed an exhausting winter in Paris of mostly Rossini's "best" *Otello*, *La Cenerentola*, *La Gazza ladra*, *Barbiere*, also *Don Giovanni*, *Il Matrimonio Segreto*, *Anna Bolena*, and *La prova di un'opera seria*. Lablache then sang Donizetti's *L'Ajo nell'imbarazzo!* the charming *opera buffo* written in 1824 for the first time at the Théâtre-Italien. Not to be forgotten, he created this role for the local premiere in Vienna—the first Donizetti to be heard there.[259]

The following year, 1832, Lablache returned to London in April for a few performances of *Il Barbiere di Siviglia,* one of which he sang on 1 May[260] at the King's Theatre and then immediately left for Naples. Was it the terrible cholera epidemic that drove him away, or had he been under contract to return to Naples? If that was true, why did he sing so briefly in London?

Lablache's fashionable London address in 1832 was now 54 the Quadrant, the curve of white Georgian buildings that became Regents Street. Since he did not return to London that year or the next, did he buy a house there as an investment and possibly move some of his family to London? Eventually, it was in Paris that he would build a home and London where his first son Frédéric would settle. Frédéric was now a young man of seventeen, and his father was very careful to provide him with a fine musical education; in fact, he helped teach his son the fundamentals of singing himself. Frédéric followed in the footsteps of his father and became a professional singer, teacher, and composer. Nicolas and Henri, the two younger sons, sang but without the same success.

Lablache and his entourage travelled many times over the continent to Naples (after passage by boat over the English Channel). In the nineteenth century, traveling by coach across the continent was not easy; Lablache and his entourage often encountered the unimaginable adverse conditions compared with travel today. Trains were not available everywhere until the next decade. After the spring and summer opera seasons in London, beginning in 1834, he would return briefly before the autumn rains and then return to commence the winter seasons in Paris (from October to March). By the midthirties, his family had grown older and his sons began to travel with him. His entourage included servants, a manager, and his doctor, a chef, and bodyguards. The roads between Naples and Rome were notorious for bandits, robbers, and assassins lurking by the wayside and although these highways were patrolled by the military, the soldiers were often recalled by the government and then it was very dangerous to travel.

By the summer of 1831, the dreaded cholera had reached Vienna after its devastating attack on Russia; then by the spring of 1832, it was raging in Paris among the poor and twenty thousand died. Many people left the city for the country. The British Isles for the first time were reporting cases. The scourge of the nineteenth century, cholera would eventually spread to Naples by 1836 and then to Sicily where 136,033 people died.[261] During this time, Maria Malibran's father Manuel Garcia died in Paris.[262]

For these three years, at least Lablache was far away from the oncoming cholera, fulfilling his engagements in Naples. By the middle thirties, he was well-established in Paris and London, and he continued to sing between the two capitals until he left for Russia in 1852.

ఴఴఴ

Chapter Fourteen

Return to Naples

1832

Lablache, recalled to Naples, was still under contract with Barbaja to sing the premiere of *Anna Bolena* at the San Carlo.

Before leaving England, he gave a farewell benefit at the King's Theatre on 1 May. Singing Figaro with Laure Cinti-Damoreau, *Barbiere* was compressed into one act, coupled with one act of *L'esule di Roma* (with Tosi and Berardo Winter); the *London Times* writes, "As originally composed for them in Naples." He then sang in the first act of *Don Giovanni* as the Don with De Begnis as Leporello, followed by the first act of *Il Matrimonio Segreto* on Thursday, 3 May.[263]

Mme. Joséphine de Méric, Lablache's son Nicolas's future mother-in-law, was also singing at the King's that season. In April, she sang in Vaccai's last successful opera *Giulietta e Romeo*. On 31 March, she sang in the first performance of Donizetti's *Olivo e Pasquale* in England at the King's Theatre, with Curioni, Mariani, and Vincenzo Galli, who had sung the opera with Duprez before in Bergamo.[264]

Donizetti was nearly unknown in England before his premiere of *Anna Bolena* in London. Probably Paris brought him international fame; however, it wasn't till after his *Lucia di Lammermoor* and *L'Elisir d'amore* that he won acceptance with northern audiences. Even though his works were flourishing in Italy, especially Naples, some of his other operas had not emerged past the borders of Italy.

L'esule di Roma and *Olivo e Pasquale* were put forward for the first time in England that spring at the King's Theatre; Lablache was familiar with *L'esule di Roma* because he had created the original character of Murena in Naples in 1828. Of his performance at the King's Theatre, the *Court Journal* said, "He exhibited as much purity of taste and depth of expression as he did of comic verve and spirit in Figaro."[265]

Early that spring, two French sopranos Mme. Joséphine Bonnaud de Méric[266] and Mme. Laure Cinti-Damoreau found themselves engaged to sing in London.[267] Both lovely ladies would later carve a place in history for themselves. The first singer, Joséphine de Méric, was from Strasburg and formally married to the esoteric impresario, Joseph Glossip,[268] the Englishman who had taken over management of the San Carlo and La Scala for a few seasons from Barbaja. Mme. de Méric became estranged or separated from this rather shady character, who was not only suspected of bigamy but also filed for bankruptcy. Glossip's first marriage was to the well-known British singer, Elizabeth Féron,[269] producing a son by the name of Augustus Harris (father of the impresario Sir Augustus Harris of Her Majesty's Theatre and friend of the Lablache family).[270] It was uncertain, however, if he was ever formally divorced from Mme. Feron, so his marriage to Joséphine in 1827 would have been in question. Author Dudley Cheke and descendant of the de Meric family [271] produced a copy of Joséphine's marriage certificate to Glossip; however, if Glossip was never divorced from Feron, did that make their famed daughter Emilie de Méric illegitimate?

Elizabeth Féron was a fairly prominent singer in London when she sang in Mozart's *Cosi fan tutte* in the first English production under the title of *Tit for Tat* at the English Opera House (the Lyceum) with Ms. A. Betts and Ms. Cawse (29 July 1828).[272] She possibly was also fleeing from Glossip when she ran off to New York with their son, putting as much distance between them there; she continued to pursue her career successfully.

English singer Ms. Abigail Betts succeeded as a vocalist and stage actress during that period.[273] Family history tells us she was the mistress of the Marquis of Anglesea and never married. Her father, Arthur Betts, was the son of John Betts, a well-known London violin-maker,[274] who was skilled enough to make a violin once for Paganini. As to date, we find her possible London debut in Arnes's *Love in a Village* at the Lyceum on 1 August 1827.[275] Usually singing in English, her playbills indicate how many Mozart and Rossini operas were sung in the British provinces in English. Other so-called patiches and operettas were shown at dozens of the local Theatre Royals from Dublin across northern England, southern England, and into the far reaches of Scotland. In London, she created a name for herself and was very noticable singing with Joséphine de Méric and Maria Malibran through the thirties and forties. Equally at home in Italian opera, she was also cast in many roles that required both singing and acting. Oddly, she never seemed to sing at one theater for long, mostly vacillating between London's Drury Lane and Covent Garden. When she was not on the stage of the Theatre Royal in Dublin,[276] she could be found singing on the boards of all the British Theatre Royals between there and London.[277] Well-remembered as creating the role of the gypsy in Balfe's 1843 *The Bohemian Girl*, she sang in many of his operas, often with Maria Malibran at Drury Lane, *The Siege of Rochelle*, *The Maid of Artois*, and Bellini's *Sonnambula*.

Laure Cinti-Damoreau was another attractive young soprano. Like Josephine de Méric, she also sang at the Théâtre-Italien (debut 1815). Noteworthy in mostly Rossini roles, she sang in *Mosè, L'Assedio di Corinto, Compte Ory*, and later she created Mathilde in the first performance of *Guillaume Tell* (Paris Opera on 3 August 1829). Joséphine de Méric sang Argelia for her London debut of *L'esule di Roma*. *The London Times* noted that she was not to be confused with another singer Mme. Méric-Lalande, also French but no relative. *The Times* recommended de Meric's talents when she sang the heroine in Mercadante's *opera seria Elisa e Claudio* on 29 February:

> We never saw this opera so well presented here, nor has any performance this season proved so entirely successful as on this occasion. The music, though not quite original, is light and agreeable and ably written. The part of Elisa was well-sustained by Madame de Méric, who sang with great taste and dramatic expression. She was applauded wildly throughout the performance, but especialy in the aria "Vado senti" in the second act. After the curtain fell there was a call for Madame Méric, who appeared once more before the curtain.

The event that comes to mind first to any one interested in theater history in 1832 is ballet. All operas at that time were accompanied with a ballet; to have none would be unheard of at the time of our Lablache. And they were plentiful enough. The year of 1832 was marked in history for birth of the first romantic ballet introduced to London, Filippo Taglioni's successful *La Sylphide*. The brilliant choreography by Taglioni showcased the talents of his daughter, Marie Taglioni, who was after all the principle dancer. Floating across the stage by extraordinary means, she was dubbed the high priestess of the *dance d'elevation*.

> *La Sylphide*, the most successful of Taglioni's compositions, and the one with which his daughter's name is inseparably linked, was the first romantic ballet. This work exerted enormous influence, for not only did it abolish the mythological ballet so popular in the

eighteenth century, but it opened the door to a new ballet world and a new conception of ballet. Gods and heroes were replaced by supernatural beings who came from the dark forests and misty pools, or descended from some poetic heaven to bring romance into the lives of some mortals; while the ballet, instead of being a vehicle for voluptuous and provocative poses, was ennobled, spiritualized, elevated almost to the height of religion.[278]

Wagner projects this Romantic feeling also with some of his operas like his *Ring* cycle. Mlle Taglioni made her first appearance before an English audience at the King's Theatre in 1830 in Charles Didilot's *Flore et Zèphire* on 3 June 1830. Lablache was singing Leporello in *Don Giovanni* with tenor Donizelli and Malibran also that evening. Taglioni became the favorite at the King's Theatre, dancing in Auber's *La Bayadere* and *La Noyade* and *Masmaniello*. Marie Taglioni was spoken of all over Paris as Our Sylphide.[279] Taglioni set a new fashion trend with her dresses of white muslin. Maria Malibran, indeed, clearly from her portraits wore such clothes. Ribbons and feathers were in vogue, worn in profusion decking enormous hats. "At London's Theatre Royal Covent Garden on 26 July 1832, the first production of *La Sylphide* was received with thunders of applause," reported *The London Times*. "A most amazing family production, first Filippo Taglioni did the choreography for Marie and Paul Taglioni, including Amalia Galster Taglioni."

Leaving the Jaunay's Hotel in Leicester Square London in May,[280] Lablache traveled south to Italy through Belgium. On the way, he visited for one evening the mansion of Maria Malibran and the violinist Charles Auguste de Beriot. Delighted to see him, Maria and Charles begged him to stay longer with them, but he explained that he was rising at dawn to continue his journey to Italy. This excited Maria who cried out, "We're going with you!" Lablache, not really thinking that they could possibly make arrangements in such a short time, told them to be at his hotel at six in the morning. At five, he was awakened by the sound of horses and a carriage beneath his window. There were Maria and Charles. Within half an hour, they were on their way through France and Switzerland, but when they reached the Italian border, only Lablache had the proper documents: Marie and Charles, in their haste, had forgotten theirs. After a wait of three days, they were allowed to continue to Bologna and then to Rome.[281]

Hearing of her sudden arrival in Italy, the impresarios rushed to engage La Malibran, offering her enormous fees. She at once accepted and was hired to sing in *Otello* at the Teatro Valle in Rome: it was there, while fulfilling her engagement, she learned of the death of her father Manuel Garcia in Paris.[282] This was a terrible blow to her. Lablache continued on to Naples where he opened at the Teatro San Carlo in *Il Barbiere* on 19 June 1832.[283] Charles de Beriot and Malibran hated Rome, so after only six performances, they joined Lablache in Naples.[284]

However, fate decided that on 6 August, Malibran would make her Neapolitan debut as Desdemona at the Teatro Fondo and not at the San Carlo. Malibran's success there assured her appearance at the premiere theater of Naples—the San Carlo—much to the distress of her rival, Giuseppina Ronzi de Begnis, San Carlo's leading soprano and the king's favorite. Donizetti noted that Ronzi was very large and fleshy, yet she still ruled supreme in spite of the Malibran invasion.[285]

Donizetti was preoccupied with writing other operas and, with his usual energy, dashed around attending to his arrangements for their performances in Italy. His thoughts, however, were veering toward Paris from where information filtered back on his overwhelming successes there and in London. Lablache, Pasta, and Rubini were responsible for this musical grand epic—*Anna Bolena*.

All of Naples attended the grand gala of *Anna Bolena* at the San Carlo on 6 July 1832. Giuseppe Mazzini, the great republican leader, wrote after seeing the opera:

> The individuality of the character, so barbarously neglected by the servile imitators of Rossini's lyricism, is painted with rare energy and religiously observed in many of Donizetti's works. Who has not felt in the musical expression of Henry VIII the severe, tyrannical, and artificial language required by the story at that point? And when Luigi Lablache fulminates these words: "U Salira d'Inghilterra sul trono. Altra donna piu degna d'affetto . . ." (There will come to the throne of England another women more worthy of affection). Who has not felt his spirit shrink, who has not understood all of tyranny in that moment, who has not seen the trickery of that Court, which showed that Anne Boleyn will die? And Anne, furthermore, is the chosen victim, whom the libretto, and history too, whatever others may say—depicts, and her song is a swan song that foresees death, the song of a tired person touched by the sweet memory of love.[286]

While Lablache was in Northern Europe, many of the bass baritone roles were taken over by Antonio Tamburini in Italy and later vice versa. When Lablache returned to Italy from Paris and London in 1832, Tamburini went north. After Tamburini and Lablache sang together in Paris on 2 October 1834 in *La Gazza ladra,* they would be inseparable. Tamburini was the most celebrated Italian baritone of that era.[287] Remarkable for his extraordinary flexibility and beauty of tone, he had climbed to the pinnacle of fame by the time he reached Paris after many galley years singing in Italy.

Rossini continued to draw the crowds at the Teatro San Carlo in Naples. Rossini was still at the zenith of his popularity through 1830-32. *Otello, L'Assedio di Corinto,* and *Semiramide* were shown often. Bellini's new opera, *La straniera,* was performed twenty-eight times the first season there; and when the 1832 season opened with *I Capuleti e i Montecchi,* it brought the young Bellini more public recognition. Many remarkable singers congregated together at the Royal Theatres of Naples that year. Most of them arrived from Northern Europe and were not unfamiliar with Naples: Maria Malibran had sung there before, but Teresa Rambeaux had not.

Many singers like Lablache and Malibran had achieved international careers and for Barbaja to have secured Malibran that season was a triumph. The managers in Paris were most put out by this, fearing, so they said, that she might lose her voice in Italy by singing too much. Their sentiments were not really that noble—they wanted her for themselves. Malibran then was waiting for a divorce and vowed she'd never return to Paris "not until I'm married to de Beriot, not because of the public, which is always disposed to pardon those who entertain them, but because of my relatives and friends."[288]

In spite of the tremendous popularity of Malibran that year, *Anna Bolena* and Pacini's *Gli Arabi nella Gallie* clocked more performances than *Otello.*[289] Malibran felt uncomfortable that the applause was withheld. "I need that spark of life," she writes to Countess Merlin.[290] Altogether, seventeen performances were given; *Otello, La Cenenertola,* and *La Gazza ladra* all sold out at double the price. Florimo writes,

> Lablache showed himself sublime in the small part of Desdemona's father, which when he interpreted the role became even greater than Rossini himself had ever imagined. When he is cursing his daughter Desdemona, whoever has not seen or heard Lablache cannot have any idea of the artistic magnitude of this wonderful

performer. In the grand finale, sung by Malibran and Lablache, there lies the indication of the degrees of excellence possible when the performance of a masterpiece is entrusted to artists whose own souls can identify with the composer's feelings.[291]

Cottrau said of the wild scene of uncontrollable enthusiasm that took place upon the last night of the opera *La Gazza ladra*; it was beyond description:[292]

> ... wildest imagination, even considering the decriptions of the Roman Circuses, could not give any idea of the electrifying spectacle which the immense hall of the San Carlo offered, filled up to the roof and resounding with applause, acclamations, stamping and enthusiatic cries. The object of this unanimous rapture, the twenty-five curtain calls during the course of the opera, was called back many times after the curtain fell by an idolatrous multitude unable to bear separation that might be permanent. Malibran could only get out of her costume by throwing kisses ... numerous crowds were at the stage door and they escorted her home to Barbaja's palace, and applauded more as she ascended the steps."[293]

Malibran then left Naples in a blaze of glory to conquer Bologna. Lablache and most of the opera goers felt a light had left their lives and a gloom spread over the rest of the season—an anticlimax.

Her departure did not influence the first performance on 6 November 1932 of Donizetti's latest opera set in Castile Spain in the Middle Ages *Sancia di Castiglia*. Since its birth, it was not one of Donizetti's successes and has never been widely performed. But, on the first night, the newspapers reported,

"It is a decided fanatic success." Donizetti wrote to a friend:

> My *Sancia di Castiglia* was performed marvellously, and the applause was such as to bring out the singers and in company with them the Maestro, among shouts of joy! ... How La Ronzi sang ... how Lablache, and how Basadonna ... oh, my happiness!"[294]

Obviously, however, it was not *Sancia di Castiglia* that would bring Donizetti fame. Clearly, that was reserved for another opera, a work written in two weeks that showed that Donizetti had a stroke of genius. He had already written thirty-five operas when he wrote his charming comic masterpiece *L'Elisir d'amore*.

Undeniably, this opera brought him lasting fame and fortune. A lighthearted work of such irresistible charm and musical grace as to become such a favorite that it would never leave the hearts of opera lovers down through the ages. Herbert Weinstock writes on *L'Elisir d'amore's* humble beginnings:[295]

> The impresario for the rowdy Teatro della Canobbiana in Milan was in a terrible predicament. He needed an opera in fourteen days because another composer had failed to 'deliver', begging Donizetti to help. Donizetti fulfilled his obligation in the record time, with the help of the fast writing of the poet Romani, thus the delightful *opera comica L'Elisir d'amore*, was born! The marvel of opera buffa.[296]

At the premiere, on 12 May 1832, it was recalled that the cast was inferior; apparently the buffo, Giuseppe Frezzolini, had a voice like a goat. Donizetti had written the role of Dr. Dulcamara with Lablache in mind. Lablache sang the role of Dr. Dulcamara in 1834 to great acclaim at the Teatro Fondo for the first time in Naples.

Hector Berlioz was in the audience at the first performance in Milan, and he had to strain to hear the music over the din in the theater and wrote in his memoirs:

> The people talk, gamble, eat and succeed in drowning out the orchestra. Consequently, perceiving it was useless to expect to hear anything of the score, which was new to me, I left. It appears that the Italians do sometimes listen, I have been assured by several people!

We do not know their reaction on that night when Lablache first sang the comical Dr. Dulcamara in Naples; audiences usually split their sides at the sight of him, wearing an old-fashioned red wig and squeezing his huge form into an out-of-date eighteen-century clothing (sometimes topped with a rather loud, jaunty checked waistcoat). In Naples, he was in his element; he was not unknown to take liberties with the language and break into a wild dialect aimed at stirring the audience into a frenzy of delight. Neapolitan audiences who were well known to be critical and, the worst audiences to please, were not past throwing vegetables at singers they did not like. Since Lablache was their favorite, all was well when he returned. He owned his own box at the San Carlo and often attended with his family when he was not singing.

While Lablache was in Naples, many people connected to the Court of Napoleon talked about an amusing happening that took place at a time when Lablache was very friendly with King Ferdinand I of Naples. (Lablache was supposed to have had a head cold.) Florimo recalls the following:[297]

> Can you imagine this event taking place in the Royal Palace of Capodimonte, in fact in a very decorated and gilded room, full of masterpieces, mirrors and glowing lights . . . and a sovereign in flesh and blood . . . who deigns every day to receive one by one a few visitors, previously authorized of course. Sometimes there are petitions that have to be signed, or foreign gentlemen wishing an introduction. The Royal Palace, the year is 1834, and King Ferdinand is giving an audience . . . and one of our favourites is running up and down the halls, holding a very special and flattering invitation. It is our Luigi Lablache! For whom the King of the Two Sicilies has a decided and notorious preference, and with whom he enjoyed exchanging pleasant conversation, sometimes in the vernacular. Having reached the antechamber Lablache realized that there were others waiting, and many persons preceding him. At this he felt disappointed and reluctantly resigned himself, thinking of the inevitable waste of time. The steward who knew quite well who deserved a favour, and was well 'in' with the King, saw to it that our hero did not have to wait for long. Suddenly the door opened and the head steward, having changed the order of the lists, called out aloud "Signor Luigi Lablache!" Surprised by this honour, his face brightened in spite of the hurry, and with a courtly dignified smile he stretches his hand towards the nearest chair picks up a hat which happened to be on it and sets off. Having walked through the door which the footman quickly closed behind him, he appeared bowing before the King. Alas! Seeing the incomparable artist, how did the King respond to his very respectful greeting? With huge, long, and hearty laughter. Poor Lablache did not know what had happened: finding inexplicable gales of laughter, he quickly took a slidelong glance at a nearby mirror on the wall, and as fate would have it, Lablache realized he was guilty of the most

flagrant loss of etiquette . . . on his head he had on his own hat, which he forgot to remove while waiting in the antechamber, and in his hand he was holding another hat, unconsciously taken from one of the privileged people admitted to the audience on that day. "Excuse me Your Majesty," stuttered Lablache, bowing lower than before and stretching out his arms, with a hat in each hand, with an ineffable smile . . . looking funny and penitent . . . "Forgive me if you can," he said stuttering . . . "Even one hat, would be too much for a fellow who has no head!"

ඖඖඖ

Chapter Fifteen

Concerts in Naples

1833-1834

The prima donna Maria Malibran had returned to Naples from London to fulfil engagements for the following season with Lablache. From January 1833, Lablache sang continually through the summer months to November in various Giovanni Pacini operas at the San Carlo: 12 January, *Gli Elvezi*; on 3 February, *Il Contestabile di Chester*; and on 30 May, *Ferdinando Duca di Valenza,* intermingled with the usual fare of other well-known operas. Malibran sang in many successful Bellini presentations—*I Capuleti e i Montecchi, La Sonnambula,* and *Norma*. Because of her tremendous popularity, these operas sustained over a dozen performances. *Norma* and *La Sonnambula* ran sixteen and eighteen performances a piece.[298]

Notably, Lablache sang the title role in the Neapolitan premiere of Rossini's *Guglielmo Tell* at the San Carlo on 7 April with Teresa Raimbaux as Matilda, Nicolas Ivanoff as Arnold, and Ambrogi as Gualtiero. At a later performance, there was an eye witness John Orlando Parry, a young Englishman.

Parry, a baritone-bass and comedian, visited Naples later that year. He records this account of the performance of *Guglielmo Tell* on 27 October, as well as the accounts that follow, in his diaries.[299] (Diaries of John Parry). The cast, according to Parry's description, was slightly different. The theater boasted it had the finest equipment of the day.

> We all adjourned to the Great San Carlo Teatro to see Lablache in Rossini's *Guglielmo Tell (William Tell)*. We were up in the third tier nearly under the proscenium. The house was not very full, but it looked more majestic and imposing from here than any view we had had of it. It was certainly very grand! The piece was (with

147

the exception of Lablache) very badly executed! Horrible dresses, scenery and machinery! I never saw anything so badly done! The band played very well and Sigr' Lablache sung magnificently—such *Cs, Ds, Es!* He also acted very well—but of all horrid things, of all (to me) disagreeable, painful things—Signor David's singing was the most wretched! No voice! No effect! No music! And yet they applauded him to the skies! A Mlle. St Ange (French woman) sung and acted Arnold (sic) (Tell's son) sang very well indeed—but I will not say much of her husband's singing, who played Gesler. *C'est mauvais*!! Really I never saw anything so clumsily, so badly managed as the scenery and machinery! Was horrible! Fancy, William Tell, when he comes on in the last scene, appears in a large boat on the lake with a number of other persons in it. This boat was placed on a little carriage with four very low wheels—and being placed on a large pivot in the centre of the carriage two men in their shirtsleeves tossed it up and down to give the effect of waves. These two men were visible to the whole house and fine laughter they caused—and had not some of the Royal Family been present, they would have been famously hissed as many other things done in the course of the evening ought. The audience broke thro' their own rules, that of not applauding when any of the Royal Family are present; but the celebrated trio in the opera, which was sung by Lablache, Ambroggi and David, was so beautifully and excellently performed that they gave them two rounds, and were obliged to come forward twice at the end of the act (in which the trio is) to receive the plaudits of "discerning public!".

Parry and his friends, while staying in Naples, made the rounds of all the other theaters, small and large. The Carlino, the Fondo, the Fenice, and the Pulcinella theaters were among others. These theaters were often launching grounds for young talent and featured two shows a day. The show started at half past four, the second show at half past eight. Certainly, Parry noted over and over in his diary that he found the females "most charming," and he and his friends returned often. His favorite was the "dear little" Teatro Fenice—part of the Largo del Castello. He found the Carlino "small, neat and clean . . . and a very genteel audience indeed." As for the Pulcinella Theatre, he thought it was a funny little opera house: "You could shake hands with the people in the boxes at the other side of the house." They used a ladder to get to the gallery. Parry describes the Naples Teatro Fenice:

> Made out of a cellar and partly underground! We were surprised to see so large a place, very much like our English Opera House before it was burnt down. They were relighting it and trimming all the lamps . . . And the smell and smoke had not yet subsided from the last scene. In at least half an hour the theatre was crammed full again (Parry, p. 160).

John Orlando Parry was born in London in 1810. He received lessons from Sir George Smart in sacred and classical music and composition and had received singing lessons from Lablache. While in Naples, he became a favorite guest of Charles de Beriot and Maria Malibran. He made his presence felt in the wealthy British circles and became a constant visitor to the Lablache villa.

It was the birthday of the Queen Mother on 19 November 1833, and everyone came into town. From the earliest hours on this day of festivity through to the evening, the celebrations went on. Here, a firsthand report from Parry gives us an idea of how this event unfolded:

> The guns were firing at a very early hour this morning for the King's Mother (an elderly lady, wife to the last King). Mr. Trueman called—we tried over several duets, and then I went on with my Largo al factotuming until dinner time . . . The soldiers were all dressed as on 14 November. Had a very excellent dinner—returned and saw they were getting every thing ready to illumunate the church opposite the Palace as on the Queen's birthday. We were going to the great San Carlo—we were determined we would see this extaordinary show of fireworks tonight, as we missed it on the 14th; accordingly we waited about half an hour, and presently heard a tremendous burst, and before we could almost turn round to see what it was, the whole church and collonade was one blaze of light! I never beheld such a magicical thing! The only thing it was at all like was the last burst of fireworks at Paris on the 29 July this year. There were hundreds of people here, the bands were playing and the cannon firing. After enjoying the animated and interesting scene before us, we returned home and dressed

ourselves in order to go to the great St. Carlo—with the Madame Masi. We arrived at their house by half past seven, and soon after Madame Masi and her husband returned from a visit they had made to the Prince Leopold (Prince of Salerno). In about a quarter of an hour we four adjourned to the San Carlo, it being a Gala night! But what am I to say or how am I to describe with a pen the splendid, matchless sight I saw on entering our box! Twas brilliant and dazzling in the extreme! All gold and chandeliers! The whole house was lit with wax candles of an enormous size—being around the lower circle of boxes, about 5 feet high, and diminishing as they go up. By the following computation, we found the exact number of these light-headed creatures. There were six tiers of boxes—one row of chandeliers between each, making five rows of chandeliers; in each row, thirty of these holding five candles each, which makes altogether seven hundred and fifty of these enormous lights! No one can imagine the coup d'oeuil; and to add to the princely, superb effect of this tremendous house, the pit was nearly filled with officers of different regiments, who were dressed in their most splendid uniforms—and were arranged in rows! All those who had blue uniforms, were placed next to the great orchestra, those in red (of which there were most) in the middle! The boxes were filled with ladies, gentlemen and officers—in the most costly attire like our Opera House on our "Drawing Room" night. The King and all the Royal Family were in their large private box (on the right from the Stage). The Royal State box which is in the centre of the house, although it was most superbly illuminated tonight, is never used by the Royal Family, but, on the first day of the year when they come in State. The Queen Mother was received with great applause on her entry. This was the only applause all night. Everybody seemed in ecstasies with the magnificent sight prepared for them. I never saw anything in a theatre to even approach it. The immensity of the gold lattice work around the boxes added greatly to the effect, we thought when we entered this theatre the first time that it had a heavy appearance, but we find it was done on purpose for splendour when there was a Gala night. The Opera was *La Gazza ladra* in which the divine Malibran performed Ninetta. On her third appearance tonight she was astonishing . . . What a splendid creature she is—what a voice; what a mind in everything she undertakes! It is needless

> to add that every one was in raptures with her. My friend, Signor Lablache, performed the part of Fernando, the father for the first time. He only had two days to study it BUT rather that the public should not be disappointed with the opera through the illness of Reina, the tenor—he undertook it for "this night only", though it does not suit him at all. However, he astonished the house by his excellent acting and singing, making the father a most interesting and feeling performance. All the performers exerted themselves to the utmost. Ambrogi in particular. David played the lover and really, I never in my life heard any thing so horrible, so painful as his attempting to sing. His attitudes, faces, and tomfooleries are, to me, unbearable; and every one that I have yet heard speak of him, are of the same opinion. Singularly enough when there is a Gala night, they never play any overture or introduction, but up goes the curtain all unawares. This is an extremely odd way! The opera was followed by the superb ballet "Barba Blu."

During this time, several private concerts were planned in Naples, but permission had been obtained from the impresario, Domenico Barbaja, for any singer to leave the San Carlo and sing elsewhere. A noble gentleman and friend of Parry, planning a concert, shook to his knees as he approached Barbaja.

> My friend Negri then went forward and said in a very humble tone of voice: "If your Excellency would allow Signor Lablache to sing at a little concert I am giving on Monday evening next." The moment Barbaja heard this he shouted out in his shrill voice . . . "Don't you know Malibran leaves on Monday and I shall want Lablache to play every night to supply the deficiency eh?" . . . pinch of snuff. After this rencontre we stood for some while perfectly silent until Barbaja had finished looking over a playbill. Presently he turned round and, after taking another pinch of snuff, said, "Where's this thing to be, eh?" "At the grand Trattoria House in Strada Nuovo, Signor." "You'll have all the Inglese there I suppose eh?" Upon this he turned, looked at another bill, when suddenly a smile darted over his countenance. He took off his green velvet cap, scratched his head, took an extra extraordinary pinch of snuff (which fell and almost covered his waist-coat), then placing his hands behind him came slowly towards us . . . we were standing like two culprits not knowing what to do or say. After looking at ME for some while he

said "Young man, I'll tell you what I'll do for you! You know my Casina or Villa at Posillipo?" Yes, Sigr' "Well, you shall come with me today to see it. If you like it you shall give your concert there, you shall have the whole house at your disposal—you shall have the gardens and the Theatre open . . . you shall have all the opera singers! You shall have the bills and tickets arranged for you. You shall have the police permission obtained and you shall not have a farthing of expense!!!" Was the like ever heard . . . we thought he was joking. We knew not what to make of it. I was going to make an observation about troubling him when he burst out again, "But why in the devil did you not come to me before! Eh? Ha!"(pinch of snuff) then almost in the same breath he said, "Come here at twelve and I'll take you there in my carriage, Avete Capito! Good morning. Adio." We returned home, but I could not eat or drink and I hardly knew whether I stood on my heels or my head.

Returning, they all went with Barbaja, and he took them in his carriage to Posillipo where his villa is situated beside the water and about half a mile from the end of the Villa Reale. Entering by the gateway, they immediately found themselves going through a tunnel. All this part had been excavated from the solid rock, and there was room here for more than forty carriages. Parry wrote,

> A most wonderful curious place. From here we ascended a kind of broad staircase, a very easy ascent so that a person can go on horseback to his bedroom or drawing room in the house which is over this part! Descending this winding staircase we found ourselves on the ground floor of the house which is immense and most splendidly furnished. Barbaja took us through magnificent apartments full of mirrors, chandeliers, English fire-places of shells, carpets, easy chairs, ottomans and every luxury one can imagine. From these splendid rooms you come into a lovely grotto or cavern, most beautifully fitted up with chandeliers, statues from the antique, also a fountain playing to cool this retreat in summer. The ceiling was arranged most curiously like icicles, and you almost fancied you felt the water dropping. I never saw anything so unique or curious. All this is cut from the solid rock as well. After passing another rock cavern with glasses so placed that you would actually fancy you looked out on the city of Naples. It is impossible

to describe the effect of these. You descend another staircase cut from the rock and paved with lava—lined with statues, stuffed beasts which looked out of caverns on the side, and apparently going to eat you up! This leads you into the theatre. In my life I never saw anything so beautiful or so elegant. This is entirely cut in the solid rock and is capable of holding nearly three hundred people seated! It is lined with white marble and full of statues. The light comes in at one end and sufficient to make it all perfectly light like any other room or hall. The stage is beautifully fitted up, everything complete—scenes, lights, etc. Eight boxes cut into the rock on the side which are very curious. Near the stage is a canopy of blue and gold cords, surrounded by wreaths of roses under which any people of distinction sit when any play or *festa* is going forward! There is an orchestra behind the stage plus a staircase that goes to the top of the hill and commands one of the finest views in the world! Everything about the place is novel and curious. From this lovely little theatre, you enter the garden which is beautifully laid out, and has a fountain of large dimensions playing constantly. In this garden are all kinds of curiosities from Pompeii, and a number of statues from Egypt; ruins of temples placed in the most picturesque spots. The front of the theatre has an elegant garden bordered by two wooden figures, excellently carved, representing two Swiss Guards with real guns. They are as large as life and being painted to have the appearance of living men on duty! From the garden you pass the fountain again and come upon the terrace. The border is lined with exquisite plants, flowers and shrubs and the view from this terrace is most lovely as it commands a view of Naples, Vesuvius, the whole bay and part of the Appenine mountains. He then led us through all kinds of rooms adapted for billiards, games, secretary's rooms, smoking apartments . . . and after passing down some curious stairs of lava in a kind of cavern or grotto cut through the rock we found ourselves opposite where we entered and the carriage waiting for us. We again took our seats and were conducted back to the Toledo (main street of Naples).

Barbaja explained to Parry on their arrival that his motive for the tour was this: he wanted to let his villa for the summer, and as he thought I should have a great many dashing and monied people at my concert, the idea at once struck him that it would be an excellent opportunity for him to light it up and make it look as elegant as possible for his own sake. The date was finally fixed for Saturday the 15 March (p. 205).

> I was running about all this morning telling everybody of my good fortune. We called on Barbaja. I found him, his daughter Calvarola, Lablache, Reina, all sitting together after their dinner. Lablache turned secretary and made a kind of prospectus for the police, naming the singers, this was to obtain the license. We had a great deal of fun in making the play bill out. Lablache is such an exceedingly good-natured man . . . you may do anything with him . . . he is uncommonly kind. Directly we went to Barbaja. He told me he had hired the celebrated buffo of the Court, Calvarola, to play a scene for me at the end and, as he is such a great favourite both with English and Italian, this will of course be a great card for me. He also said he had asked David and his daughter. Barbaja was quite altered, he was quite affable and pleasant and (what's more) very talkative. Every one was wondering how it was I could so get on the right side of such a man as Barbaja. He said he would ask the King and Queen to come of course . . . if His Majesty came, the whole Court must! I fancied I was two inches higher really hearing all kinds of news.

At half past one, the theater was opened by the sound of trumpets! Parry tells us the company then descended the staircase in the rock to the sounds of a military band playing behind the scenes. There were many members of elegant English society. The countess of Arundell, Lady Nightingale, attended. Parry's friend, Lady Drummond, was in the boxes with all of her train. She was delighted with the "elegance of the theatre."

The concert then began. Lablache was as great as ever. Parry said he played the harp "very well indeed—considering the flurry I was in." Reina was particularly good. Lablache was really most admirable, the manner he sang and kissed the hand to Bella Napoli was perfect in "Tis a Neapolitan Song." In the end, he was loudly called forward! The concealed military band played part of *Guillaume Tell* between some of the pieces (p.305).

The first part of the concert was serious, sung by singers from the San Carlo, while the second part was not:

> Lablache gave a burlesque piece based on *Otello*: "He sustained the part of Brabantio, Calvarola, the 'Liston' of Naples, the Moor, and John Parry—Desdemona, Madame Vestris, whom he imitated in the

most pathetic scenes, by singing "Cherry ripe," an effect that gave rise to uproarious merriment. This burlesque was repeated at the San Carlo for the benefit of Sanvarola, and went off with renewed success at this time to comply with Malibran's request (p. 306).

John Parry, plainly quite a comedian, stood up and did imitations of Lablache, Rubini, and lastly Malibran herself in a mock Italian trio. This evidently created such excitement that he was asked to do it again. This time for the King and Queen, who like the rest, were delighted. On another occasion, in the summer of 1833, we hear of another concert reported in the London *Morning Post:*

> There was a large party assembled at a Nobleman's mansion in Naples, where an evening concert was taking place. Lablache and Malibran were enjoying each others' voices around the piano, near the windows that were flung open to let the beautiful summer night air in, but the grinding sounds of a hurdy-gurdy outside, directly below the windows on the street corner, interrupted the recital. A servant was sent outside to persuade him to leave, but he refused to budge, and refused to stop playing. Lablache and Malibran hit on an idea to get rid of him. Malibran turned to Lablache and John Parry and said: We'll drive him away by a hurdy-gurdy of our own. She then requested them to sustain notes forming drone on the common chord, at the same time pinching their noses, whilst she herself gave a wondrous imitation of the sonorous tones of that mellifluous instrument. Amidst the merriment of the company, who split their sides with laughter, the disconcerted itinerant musician, who could not stand the rivalry, was fairly driven off the field.[300]

The lively young Englishman Parry was a constant companion to Malibran and all the Lablaches later on their famous British tours. Parry had received a good musical training from his father, John Parry Sr. a well-known musician, and it was his father who sent him to study singing with Lablache in Naples. He also studied with Sir George Smart and the notorious Nicolas Charles Bochsa. Sadly, his voice did not mature into the greatness that is required to be an operatic star. So he settled for a career of an entertainer and singer of comic pieces and assumed this role with great professionalism.[301]

Lablache, it seems, was drafted that year to perform at most of the premieres, especially those of Pacini. Besides the above operas, Maria

Malibran joined him for yet another Pacini premiere 30 November, *Irene*. Pacini, like Bellini, was from Catania. Born in 1796, he was a well-known and very successful composer of his time and became music director of the San Carlo in 1825. A prolific worker, like most composers of the era, historically he had the misfortune to be overshadowed by the overwhelming successes of Bellini, Rossini, and Donizetti. Although he never won such international acclaim, his operas were performed widely during the mid-nineteen century in Italy. Amongst the Neapolitans, he held his own after a fashion as the favorite son. His place in history is secure as a foremost nineteenth-century opera composer, but his popularity stayed mainly within the borders of Italy.[302]

Pacini also lived in the palace of Barbaja, where Malibran was taking up residence that year. Lablache, acclaimed and admired for his stamina, must have been quite "a war horse," wading through all those premieres of Pacini works only to find that they had been dropped from the repertoire. Pacini was quite taken by Malibran's performance in the title role of *Irene*, and upon hearing her in *La Gazza ladra*, he wrote,[303]

> When I heard her for the first time, they had to drag me out of the San Carlo, because I was giving an additional performance in my box. Never I can say quite honestly have I ever experienced such an emotion in hearing a singer. She was thoroughly extraordinary.

An American who was visiting Naples at the time recalls her:

> There are many doubtless among us who recollect that bright creature, with her attractive person and her acknowledged talents; Madame Malibran was in person a little below middle size, with the just and graceful degree of 'embonpoint;' her hair which, at the time I saw her, she wore smoothly combed over her head, from whence it fell in masses upon her snowy neck, was black and glossy as is the plumage on the raven's wing. Her eyes were those dark, expressive orbs, that we gaze upon as indicating the fatal possession of qenius. Her teeth were beautifuly white and regular, and her whole countenance, with its pensive, and at times melancholy expression, possessed a something of indefinable interest and attraction.[304]

As a true daughter of the Romantic age, she embraced life with a fierce passion that swept away everyone who came in contact with her. She was one of those brilliant women who today would be called a superstar. Opera was the vehicle in which women who wanted to express themselves could in other ways than being wives, mistresses, or courtesans. By the year of 1834, Malibran demanded the highest fees of all her contempories,[305] surpassing even the great prima donna Giudetta Pasta.[306]

Lablache continued to appear on the stages of the theaters Fondo and the San Carlo with Malibran and also with Carolina Unger who had sung with him in Vienna. The singer, however, that was to make an impression on him that season was the beautiful young soprano by the name of Fanny Tacchinardi Persiani, who made her Neapolitan debut with Lablache at the Teatro del Fondo in Fioravanti's *Le cantatrici villane* on 30 March.[307]

Another milestone in his career came on 6 July 1834 when Lablache indroduced Mozart's *Don Giovanni* to Naples. How well Lablache played that great seducer, that disturbingly attractive figure, immortalized by the composer would be hard to imagine. The premiere at the San Carlo was packed to the ceiling.

Apparently, the drama was well recieved! Don Giovanni, sung by Lablache, was recorded as quite legendary. The title role, the central figure, already a bit plump but very energetic, was dashing after the coy Fanny Persiani as Zerlina and other ladies in the cast. It seems strange that Mozart's masterpiece had never been shown at the San Carlo before although it had been seen in 1816 at the Fondo. Was it possible that Lablache had something to do with having it performed? After all, Lablache had sung the roles of both Don Giovanni and Leporello in Paris and London every year since 1830 and would continue to do so for the rest of his life. Was it that the disposition of the Neapolitans, who were known to be so insular, played a part in this? Mozart was not Italian. Nor was he fashionable then. Few performances of Mozart were shown. Understandable perhaps as the mood was anti-Austrian owing to long disputes under Austrian rule.

After fulfilling his engagements in Naples and Livorno, Lablache returned in the autumn of 1834 to Paris, then the musical capital of the world. Embracing his old friend Rossini at the Théâtre-Italien, he plunged once more into the usual Rossini repertory for the first time with a young and beautiful Italian singer Giulia Grisi. Maria Malibran and Charles de Beriot were in the audience that night when they first sang together in *La Gazza ladra* on 24 October 1834. Unknown to them at the time, their lives would become interwoven as they sang together for the next twenty years. Lablache sang *Mosè* for the first time in Paris on November 8. According to the *Gazetta Musicale*, p. 371: "This opera made a phenomenal impression! Lablache outdid himself in an aria by Pacini which he interpolated towards the end of the opera, and which the enthusiastic public encored." He had not sung this opera since Vienna, but he was very familiar with the role. (Lablache always sang at the Théâtre-Italien.) It was not known if it was the new version translated back into Italian from the French or not. Lablache did not sing in the French version in Paris.

Giulia Grisi was born in Milan of a musical family in 1811. Her father, Gaetano, was an Italian officer in the army of Napoleon, and her mother was Giovanna Grassini, sister to the well-known contralto, Josephina Grassini. All the girls in the Grisi family were stagestruck. All were beautiful. First, there was the divine Carlotta Grisi, one of the most enchanting ballet dancers of the era. So smitten by Carlotta, the famous Paris art critic, writer, and jounalist Theophile Gautier wrote the ballet *Giselle* especially for her. Gautier was a brilliant reporter of the varied life of the nineteenth century. A major figure with high principles, he first and above all was a romantic. As a writer, poet, and an art and theater critic, he subscribed to the asthetic movement. Understanding this, Victor Hugo admired Gautier so much that he wrote, "Your criticism has the power of creation." He wrote columns filled with adulation for Carlotta as *Giselle*.[308] "What marvellous dancing! You would think her a rose leaf bourne on the wind," he wrote about her *Spirite* as she floated across the stages of Paris and London with her dancers. Gautier adored the sensual beauty of all the Grisi females. *La Diva*, Giulia did not escape his admiring eye; his admiration for her shines out of the pages of his famous novel *Mademoiselle de Maupin* and the lines of *La Diva*. As fate would have it, this strange artistic and impressive figure settled down for twenty years with the fiery contralto Ernesta Grisi.

Giulia Grisi's debut in Bologna in Rossini's *Zelmira* was in 1828. She had sung all over Italy, finally making her La Scala debut. There, her most famous appearance was on 26 November of 1831 when the new season opened with the premiere of Bellini's *Norma*. Grisi created the role of Adalgisa with the prima donna Guiditta Pasta, the leading soprano of the day, singing the title role. Pasta had just created the title roles in Bellini's *Sonnambula* and Donizetti's *Anna Bolena*. Later, Grisi fled Italy after a contract dispute and arrived in Paris just at the right time. Rossini needed a prima donna for the title role of *Semiramide*. She was hired to replace Malibran who was pregnant and had broken her contract by leaving for Italy.

Grisi was to win praise for her singing at the Théâtre-Italien. From 1832 onward, she became the reigning prima donna of that era, replacing first the beautiful diva Guiditta Pasta and then Maria Malibran after her untimely death. Repeating Rossini's *La Gazza ladra*, *Il Barbiere*, and *Otello* was not a difficult task for Lablache. Rossini was still the toast of Paris that decade. *Anna Bolena* and *La prova di un'opera seria* filled the menu for the rest of the season.

Lablache was so well-known for his portrayal of Figaro that tiny hand-painted plaster statues were sold on the streets while Dantan, the French artist and sculptor, molded a small figure of him as Figaro holding a guitar cast in black bronze. This small statue is about eighteen inches high and is a caricature and one of a series of bronze caricatures of musicians and singers housed in the special Dantan collection in Paris.[309]

There are also rare French porcelain figures of Lablache as Figaro. And in the English Staffordshire series, these rare figures can be seen in private operatic collections. The Staffordshire hand-painted white china Lablache pieces came in different roles or characters: Dr. Dulcamara, Falstaff, Dandini, and Henry VIII with Pasta. Jenny Lind porcelain figures were also represented, plus Jenny Lind with Frédéric Lablache.

A decription of Lablache's activities are written in *De Celebrites de Epoque* with lithographs of all the opera and musical celebrities of the time:

> Again another musical phenomenon! Probably Beaumarchais wasn't thinking of Lablache's stomach while creating the role of the mischievous, versatile, alert Figaro. It is true that contrasts are excellent for the theatre and sat 300 kgs, Figaro is no less amusing than another, more like the jockeys that ride at the *Champs de Mars*. Here! there! we have Figaro . . . Lablache . . . that to please his illustrious master Almavira, sings to the beautiful Rosina under her balcony, and even if this enormous stomach doesn't try very hard to produce it's 'La's,' I can't help but fear for her tutor, Bartolo's windows. As far as I remember, we must agree that the famous Italian singer has no less amplitude in talent than in girth. Few actors are more loved by the Parisian public and we agree that the applause is deserved. Excellent both in serious and comic roles, Lablache, whose powerful and accommodating voice fits all styles, knows how to move, and how to provoke laughter. Even if Lablache had not been given by nature such a notable voice, his acting would have merited him his great reputation. It is not possible to surpass Lablache in comic roles, as in *La Cenerentola, Il Barbiere,* and mostly *La prova di un'opera seria*. Some years ago, during a presentation of *Il Barbiere di Siviglia*, Lablache saw his entry into the theatre marred by a comic incident; coming out

> from behind drapes, he rushes onto the stage with such force that some of the planks gave way under his voluminous weight; so Figaro, trapped, like in a wolf trap, couldn't free himself without the help of ropes and all the machinery that the Italien theatre could muster together.[310]

Lablache did not continue to sing Figaro much past the forties, but still sang the part in concerts. That Lablache excelled in comic roles was common knowledge; plus his reputation for singing Don Bartolo was universally known and enjoyed by all; but overall, he remained however the most celebrated Figaro of the first half of the nineteenth century, and his signature tune was always "Largo al factotum."

How did he tackle those high notes for a bass? He was first a baritone, then a bass. In those days, all the early scores listed Figaro, Dr. Bartolo, and Don Basilio under "bassi." At that time, Figaro was sung in a different key than it is now, according to Henry Pleasants when he explored this subject in an article, "How High Was G?" and came to some interesting conclusions although the final analysis has still to be made. The high Gs in "Largo al factotum" bothered Pleasants:[311]

> Basses were categorized in those days as *basso buffo, basso nobile* and *basso cantante*. The normal range, regardless of category, was the two-octave span from F to F as reflected, with minor exeptions, in the bass parts in Mozart's operas. The G was required occasionally, but never the prevailing high tessitura of Figaro's music. Many basses of the time sang in all three cateqories, including the greatest of them, Luigi Lablache and Antonio Tamburini. Lablache's voice is usually described as having a two-octave range from E to E, while Tamburini's would appear to have been pitched about a tone higher. Since Lablache and Tamburini were celebrated Figaro's, the question arises, what did they do about those Gs? Who were these singers who first took these roles? Were they prodigies or freaks? And what of the poor fellows who took over from them as *Il Barbiere* began its rounds of the European opera houses? An examination of the original casts only adds to the mystery. Luigi Zamboni, the first Figaro, was a buffo MORE celebrated as a comedian than a singer, and in 1816 he was already forty-nine. The first Bartolo was Bartolomeo Botticelli, an obscure buffo characterized by Rossini's biographer

Giuseppe Radiciotti as 'not much above mediocrity,' and Zenobio Vitarrelli, the first Don Basilio, had been dismissed by a Venitian critic in 1809 as "already rather old and listless." There is nothing in the record to support an assumption that Rossini's high tessitura was tailored to the specifications of exceptional voices. As to what happened afterwards in other opera houses everybody transposed. "Largo al factotum" was put down from C to B-flat. Lablache who also sang Bartolo, put *A dottor* down from E flat to D Flat; and *La calunnia* was put down a whole tone and has remained there.

Chapter Sixteen

I Puritani

1835

The year 1835 brought with it one of the most memorable seasons of Luigi Lablache's career, for here his destiny was linked to two new dramatic operas: one by the young composer, Vincenzo Bellini, the other by Gatano Donizetti. Both premieres were scheduled for the spring of 1835 and would open within a short time of one another at the Théâtre-Italien.

I Puritani was Bellini's tenth work, an *opera seria*, in three acts with a libretto by Carlo Pepoli based on a drama *Tete Rondes et Cavaliers* by Jacques-Arsene Ancelot and Joseph-Xavier Boniface Saintine. The opera composed in Paris decribes a romantic melodrama set in 1650 during the civil war in England soon after the execution of Charles I by the Puritans. Bellini, now at the height of his fame, wrote to his uncle, telling him how this opera came about:

> I will relate my actions since I left Italy, and why I am now in Paris. Under contract to London, I went there and directed several operas. On my way through Paris, the director of the Opera asked me to write an opera for him, and I said I would, willingly do so. Five months later I took up the subject but we could come to no agreement. The impresario of the Théâtre Italien made some offers to me, which it suited me to accept, because the payment was better, though not as much as I have had in Italy.[312]

Bellini soon heard that Donizetti was also contracted to write an opera for the Théâtre-Italien; this really set his teeth on edge; he writes again to his uncle:

> I had a fever for three days, understanding that a plot had been hatched against me; and in fact an acquaintance of mine told me

not to hope for a good reception in Paris, and that if there was to be a success, it would be Donizettis' because he had been brought there by Rossini. Then at once I took heart and began to think how to bring about the disappearance of those diabolic intrigues, which would have compromised me before all of Europe. I resolved to take particular care over my new score, even more than usual; then pay court to Rossini and approach and win him over by making it known how much I admired him, and valued his immense talent, and put myself on such an intimate basis, that they would decide to become my protectors instead of my persecutors. This took no special effort, since I have always adored Rossini. Having won Rossini's friendship, I said to myself: now let Donizetti come![313]

The young Bellini is described by Heinrich Heine, in *Musical World*:

Bellini had a tall, up-shooting, slender figure, who always moved gracefully; coquettish, ever looking as though just emerged from a band-box; a regular, but large, delicately rose-tinted face; light almost golden brown hair, worn in waving curls, a high, very high, marble forehead, straight nose, light blue eyes, well-sized mouth, and rounded chin. His features had something vague in them, a want of character, something milk-like; and in this milk-face flitted sometimes a pleasing expression of sorrow. This expression in his face took the place of the fire that was wanting; but it was that of a sorrow without depth; it glanced, but unpoetically, from his eyes and played without passion upon his lips. It was this poutless, shallow sorrow that the young 'Maestro' most willing seemed to represent in his whole appearance. His hair was dressed so fancifully sad; his clothes fitted so languishingly round his delicate body; he carried his cane so idyle-like, that he reminded me of the young shepherds we find in our pastorals, with their crooks decorated with ribbon, and their gaily coloured jackets and pants. And then his walk was so innocent, so airy, so sentimental. The whole man looked like a sigh, in pumps and silk stockings, he has met with much sympathy from women, but I doubt if he has ever produced a strong passion in anyone. To me his appearance always had something ludicrously distasteful . . .

The description of Bellini seems so opposite to the passion that this composer poured into his music. Distasteful would be the last word used to describe Bellini's genius. Audiences the world over are moved by the sheer passion, pathos, and beauty of his operas.

The new glittering Paris production of *I Puritani* was shown alongside Donizetti's new work *Marino Faliero*, the story of an elderly Venetian doge *Marino Faliero*. Both were composed for the unrivalled quartet of the finest voices in the world of opera at that time: Giulia Grisi, Giovanni Battista Rubini, Antonio Tamburini, and Luigi Lablache. Both operas would also be heard the same spring in London.

A romantic wanderer in Italy, Lord Byron wrote pages of poetry about Marino Faliero, the fiery old doge of fourteenth-century Venice. A few years afterward in 1820, the French dramatist M. Casimir Delavigne wrote a very successful play based on the same story. It was from this play that Donizetti composed his tragic melodrama. The title role written especially for Lablache—"the huge bearded figure, in purple robes." Here again, he proves his great acting abilities, for just as in *Anna Bolena*, the unfortunate protagonist, who here happens to be Lablache, ends up in the hands of the executioner—decapitated. *The London Times* wrote later when it was shown in London:

> The stern character of the plot, and the necessity of creating out of its most striking parts situations calculated to keep up the same interest in the lyric adaptation of the drama, have necessarily perserved it pure from many of the trashy frivolities which abound in Italian dramas.

However, it was the preeminently bel canto romantic melodrama, *I Puritani*, not *Marino Faliero,* that took Paris by storm on 24 January 1835 at the Théâtre-Italien. The *Journal des Debats* wrote,

> The curtain fell amid unanimous applause. All were moved, excited, in the stalls, in the boxes; with one accord they called for the composer. The curtain rose again, and Lablache and Tamburini pulled Bellini on to the stage. The young composer was engulfed with applause, received with bravos and greeted by waving handkerchiefs from every part of the hall.[314]

Bellini wrote to Florimo, "The Queen had someone write to me that she will attend the second performance tomorrow. I count upon having the dedication offered to her ... Lablache sang like a God, Grisi like a little angel, Rubini and Tamburini the same."[315] Donizetti was there. What must his thoughts have been? He writes to his librettist Romani:[316]

> Bellini's success has been great despite a mediocre libretto, we are already at the fifth performance and it will be that way to the end of the season ... Today I begin my own rehearsals, and I hope to be able to give the first performance by the end of the month. I don't at all deserve the success of *I Puritani*, but I don't desire not to please.

In fact, when the premiere of *Marino Faliero* took place on 12 March, many celebrated Parisians and Italians attended the brilliant gala performance—Giacomo Meyerbeer, Theophile Gautier, Adolphe Adam. Critics lavished praise on Lablache but were not enthralled with the opera overall. Many arias were encored, and the audience enjoyed the duel scene and the gondolier's barcarolle. Donizetti wrote to a friend:[317]

> Rubini has sung as I've never heard him sing before ... The success of Bellini with his *I Puritani* has made me tremble more than a little, but as we are different in character, therefore we both have obtained good success without displeasing the public.

Here, we see how the two men were each fearful of the other's success. Bellini, however, was never generous toward the kindly Donizetti; he was extremely jealous toward him at all times:

> Bellini, trained in the old Neapolitan traditions, wrote in a distinctive vocal style, that was Romantic, and lyrical ... it was sentimental, and emotional ... through his melodies, he speaks directly to the heart and to the soul. Some of his characters are melancholy and gentle, but this did not mean he was unable to display strong emotions; in music, there is much colour and displays of strength, as in the wonderful uplifting warlike melody, which ends Act II, in *I Puritani* ... a Hymn to Liberty, for baritone and bass, 'Suoni la Tromba,' sung by Tamburini and Lablache. This was the aria Lablache sang with much praise, throughout

his lifetime. At the first performances, *Son vergin* vezzosa and 'Suoni la Tromba' regularly had to be repeated . . . the audiences demanded encores. Here the singers express the poetry, Bellini spoke through poetry, and the tradition of incorporating the ideals of the old Italian bel canto technique, where the singer's recitatives ruled supreme over the orchestra.[318]

During the time that the opera *I Puritani* was being written in 1834, Bellini wrote to Count Carlo Pepoli during the writing of libretto:

> Don't forget to bring with you the libretto . . . so we can finish discussing the first act, which, if you arm yourself with a good dose of monastic patience, will be interesting, magnificent, and proper poetry for music in spite of you and all your absurd rules, which are good subjects for chatter, but never will convince a living soul initiated into the difficult art that *must bring tears through singing*. If my music turns out to be beautiful and the opera pleases, you can write a million letters against composers' abuse of poetry, etc., which will prove nothing. Deeds, not tittle-tattle, that deludes because of a certain polished eloquence; in the face of that fact, everything else becomes *very watery soup*. You can call my reasons all the names you like, but that won't prove a thing. Engrave on your mind in adamantine letters: The *"drama per musica"(i.e., Opera) must make one weep, shudder, die through singing.*[319]

Bellini's success came at last, and all Paris knew he was the handsome Italian protege of the beautiful Princess Christina Belgiojoso. Under her "royal mantle," he became known to the society of Paris. Bellini had first met the princess in Milan when she was a leading Milanese *salonnier*. Now removed to Paris, she set up her salon on the Rue di Montparnasse; there, Paris society flocked to her fashionable soirées and her salon was the habitat of the princess's favorite Italian exiles. Brombert writes: "She received diplomats and poets, historians and novelists, musicians and even conspirators (Count Pepoli), without regard to wealth, rank or even success." It is to her credit that she supported Liszt long before he became an idol and Heine before he became translated into French. Heinrich Heine wrote, "Before knowing you I only imagined that people like you . . . existed only in fairy tales—in a poet's dream." It was there that Bellini met the Count Carlo Pepoli, who wrote the libretto of *I Puritani*.

Princess Christina Belgiojoso was a patron of the arts, and she inspired the writer, Honore de Balzac, to create his heroine Massimilla in her image. In his work *Massimilla Doni*, Capraja, a music lover, authoritatively places music in the required perspective as described by Massimilla: "Music addresses to the heart, while words speak only to the intelligence; music immediately communicates its ideas, in the manner of perfumes."[320]

I *Puritani* was performed seventeen times during its first season at the Théâtre-Italien while *Marino Faliero* sustained only five, totally eclipsed by the popularity of *I Puritani*. No opera could equal its popularity during the decades that followed. Rubini became the first tenor of his time, and his method of singing has been emulated ever since. The genuis of Bellini's music shines through the veil of time and as long as romance flutters in the human heart. Rubini, as he was remembered in the eyes of a Victorian critic of the time, *Rubini, The Musical World* (vol. 32 no. 46),

> It was emphatically in the works of Bellini that he proved himself the grand master of song. It is necessary to have heard him sing the first air in *Il Pirata*, "Nel furor delle tempeste," and especially the second motive, "Come un'angelo celeste"—in which we already find the germ of that short and touching *melopoeia,* constituting the prominent feature of Bellini's genius—to form an idea of the power of emotion possessed by this incomparable artist. He was no less remarkable in the duet in the second act of the same opera, and I can still hear the phrase, "Vieni, cerchiam pe'mare," still re-echoing in the inmost recesses of my heart. It was only surpassed by that which follows, and which was the complement of it:
>
> > Per noi tranquillo un porto
> > L'immenso mar avrà . . .
>
> There was, in Rubini's voice, when he sang this charming and expressive *cantilena*, a kind of melancholy which gradually evaporated into a magic horizon, and impressed you with the sentiment of Immensity. In the part of Elvino, in *La Sonnambula*, Rubini's talent rose with the genius of his favourite composor. Everyone in Paris remembers how he gave phrase, "Prendi, l'anel ti dono," in the duet of the first act, and with what a mixture of grace and naive emotion he sang the pleasing madrigal which forms the subject of the second duet, "Son geloso." In the quartet of the

finale in the first act, Rubini displayed the most sublime pathos when singing the phrase so well-known and so touching:

> Ah! tel mostri s'io t'amai questo
> pianto del mio cor

Who, too, would not give ten five-act operas, as they are performed every day, to hear Rubini sing, only once a week, that cry of despairing love, in the duet in the second act of *La Sonnambula*-

> Pasci il quardo, e appaga l'alma
> Dell' eccesso de' miei mali;
> Il più tristo dei mortali;
> Sono, cruda, e il son per te

In the character of Arturo in *I Puritani*, which was his last creation, Rubini has left us such recollections of emotion and enchantment, that we can only recall them to the mind of those who heard them, without pretending to transmit an idea of them to the generations who were not so fortunate. Let us first quote the phrase of the quartet in the first act:

> Ah te, o cara, amor talora
> Mi guido furtiveo e in pianto,

In which the artist's voice burst forth into bloom like a rose beneath the first beams of a morning in spring; while, to this phrase, serene and *spianata,* he vigorously opposed that accompanying the words, "Tra la gioja e l'esultar," by sending forth from his chest a magniicent *la*, which re-echoed to the clouds, and then bounded back again from the depths of harmony. In the finale of the first act he gave with prodigious power the passage, "Non parlar di Lei ch' adoro," which he made the most bold *point-d'orgue*. Lastly, we may mention the romance of the second act, "A una fonte afflitto e solo," which Rubini only murmured, and allowed to escape from his lips like a sigh. In the duet following this romance, the phrase, full of brilliancy, "Nel mirarti un solo istante," and, finally, the duet between Elvira and Arturo, where Rubini rose to great energy of expression in the memorial passage—

> Non mi sarai rapita
> Fin che ti stringerò.

Marino Faliero was eclipsed by *I Puritani,* there is no doubt. It was unfortunate for Donizetti; however, both Donizetti and Bellini were heroes in Paris that year, and both were created chevalier of the Royal Order of the Legion of Honor and had an audience with King Louis-Philippe and Queen Marie-Amelie, who presented Donizetti with a gold ring with his name picked out in diamonds.[321]

Departing for Naples, via Rome, to rejoin his wife Virginia, Donizetti was soon to start work on his masterpiece *Lucia di Lammermoor.* This opera, based on the novel by Walter Scott, would become one of the most loved and universally popular operas of its day. Like *I Puritani,* the location is set in the British Isles. Italian opera's popularity swept across Europe, and it was not until the entry of Strauss, the Waltz King in 1837, that any other music was allowed to penetrate that bel canto world:

> Of all the foreign nationals, Italians occupied a privileged position. Italophilia was raging throughout Europe, and the highest temperature was recorded in Paris. Barely three years after Beethoven's death, Rossini had all but obliterated his memory. Rossini was probably the best known, most played, and highest paid composer who ever lived. No concert could take place without an overture, aria, duet, quartet, or at least a piano transcription, from one of his operas. Musicians of every kind, pupils or professionals, grabbed up his scores as they were published. Every young lady *comme il faut* had her repertory of Rossini arias. On 9 March 1831, Rossini's genius was sanctified as Italy's genius by Paganini's sublime concert. With all due respect to Newton and Einstein, this event can go down as the revelation of yet another natural force, another new dimension. Paganini's playing was in its way a breaking of the sound barrier. Singers, pianists, string players, all were inspired to go beyond the established capacities of their instruments and reach for new sounds, unexplored textures. July 1833 saw Bellini's arrival in Paris. His *I Puritani*, premiered later, marked an apogee of lyric drama, exalted melody, and vocal style whose marvels of legato and coloratura have never been surpassed. Bel canto moved from the opera house into every area of composition. Chopin was the greatest exponent of the style in non vocal music; Liszt exploited it to near parodistic excess. Fortunately for impecunious Italian exiles everybody wanted to know Italian; many of them in fact

survived by giving language lessons. Musical Italo mania had reached epidemic proportions. Berlioz was among the few to remain immune. Considering Italian music of the day vulgar, he tried to promote a festival of German music—with little success, it should be added. Even a cultivated aristocrat, the poet Terenzio Mamiani found German music 'full of pompous doctrine and over-elaborate counter point.' If this is how Mamiani felt, little wonder that Paris's latter-day music buffs preferred roulades to fugues.[322]

Lablache and his fellow singers, well-known now as the famous Puritani Quartet, moved on immediately for a full season in London. Opening at the King's Theatre in the Haymarket, it was an unusually crowded theater that night for the performance of *La Gazza ladra*. According to the critic of the *The London Times*,

> The opera was given for the purpose of enabling Mademoiselle Giulia Grisi to appear in one of her best Parts—that of Ninetta . . . she was well greeted from all parts of the house, and went with great power and animation through the celebrated cavatina, *Di piacer mi balsa il cuor*. Her voice since we last heard her, has acquired much additional strength, her powers of execution now most decidedly place her in the highest rank of female vocalists of her day.

After praising the performances of Rubini, Tamburini, and Ivanhoff, *The London Times* goes on to say the following:

> But the 'debutant' (for the season) who received the warmest and the most cordial welcome was the old established favourite of the Italian opera, Signor Lablache, who undertook on this occasion the prominent, though not very interesting part of Pondesta. Signor Lablache's powers of voice have no more undergone alteration, since he was last heard some years ago, than if time had remained quite stationary for him. He is precisely as we have seen and heard him so often in his inimitable Geronimo. The personation of the Podesta had never fallen in better hands.[323]

The critic of the *Athenaeum,* Chorley, explains best what happened that season and especially Lablache in the title role of *Marino Faliero*:[324]

> In the year 1835—the return of Lablache to Paris and London, completed that quartet of accomplished singers and artists, which for many following years was to present performances unprecedented in their evenness and finished concord. The admirable union thus made up was improved to its utmost by the Parisian managers . . . always more courageous in catering for novelty than our London ones have been. It was by them that Donizetti's *Marino Faliero* and Bellini's *I Puritani* were commissioned from their composers—Signor Rossini having retired into obstinate silence which no temptation could induce him to break. The production of these two operas in London was the event of the season, on such occasions there is always a successs and a failure. The public will not endure two favourites. In spite of the grandeur of Lablache as the doge of Venice, in spite of the beauty of the duets of the two basses in the first act of *Marino Faliero*, in spite of the second act containing a beautiful moonlight scene with barcarolle sung to perfection by Ivanoff, and one of Rubini's most incomparable and superb vocal displays *Marino Faliero* languished—in part for want of interest in the female character—a fault fatal to an opera's popularity.

In spite of the critics, *Marino Faliero* was not without its admirers. Many beautiful prints were published of the opera sets. There were oil paintings, and Chalon published a lithograph of Lablache in his purple robes. The little princess Victoria drew Lablache again and again in her sketchbook first as Faliero: she boldly portrays Lablache in watercolors, in bold purple robes with red shoes and cap, holding a sword as if in combat. Then she sketches Lablache and Giulia Grisi over and over in different poses from her favorite opera *I Puritani*.[325] She always referred to the opera very affectionately as "Dear *Puritani*". The story is romantic, a Romeo-and-Juliet theme set against a backdrop of Cromwellian England when the Roundheads fought against the Royalists.

The little princess was caught up with more than she knew; for the first time she enjoyed this opera—she was in the company of her cousin Albert whom later she would ask to be her husband.[326] Chorley writes,[327]

On the other hand, from first to last note, "*I Puritani*" was found enchanting. The picture of Grisi leaning against Lablache to listen, in the second scene—the honeyed elegance of Rubini's song of entrance—the bridal *polacca* in the first act—in the second, the mad scene, and the duet between the two basses . . . In the third act, Rubini, who had not appeared since an early stage of the story, sent every one to the seventh heaven by a display of his powers of expression.

*Luigi Lablache as HenryVIII in Anna Bolena,
lithograph by A. Devéria (Lablache Archives)*

Giuditta Pasta lithograph (Lablache Archives)

Staffordshire china figures (Sotherby's)
Luigi Lablache as HenryVIII (Lablache Archives)

Anna Bolena score frontispiece from Paris (Lablache Archives)

Semiramide characters in The Illustrated London News 1847
(Andrew S. Pope)

King's Theatre lithograph (Lablache Archives)

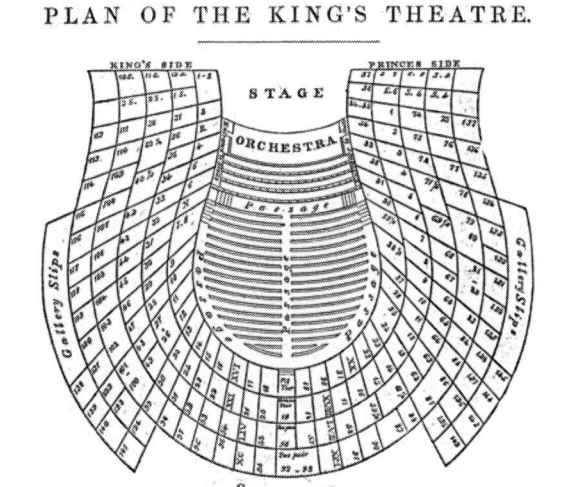

Seating plan King's Theatre from Mirror 1832 (Lablache Archives)

Don Giovanni scene Beauties of the Opera and Ballet (Lablache Archives)

Don Giovanni scene Beauties of the Opera and Ballet (Lablache Archives)

Luigi Lablache as Leporello Don Giovanni (Lablache Archives)

Amadeus Mozart (Lablache Archives)

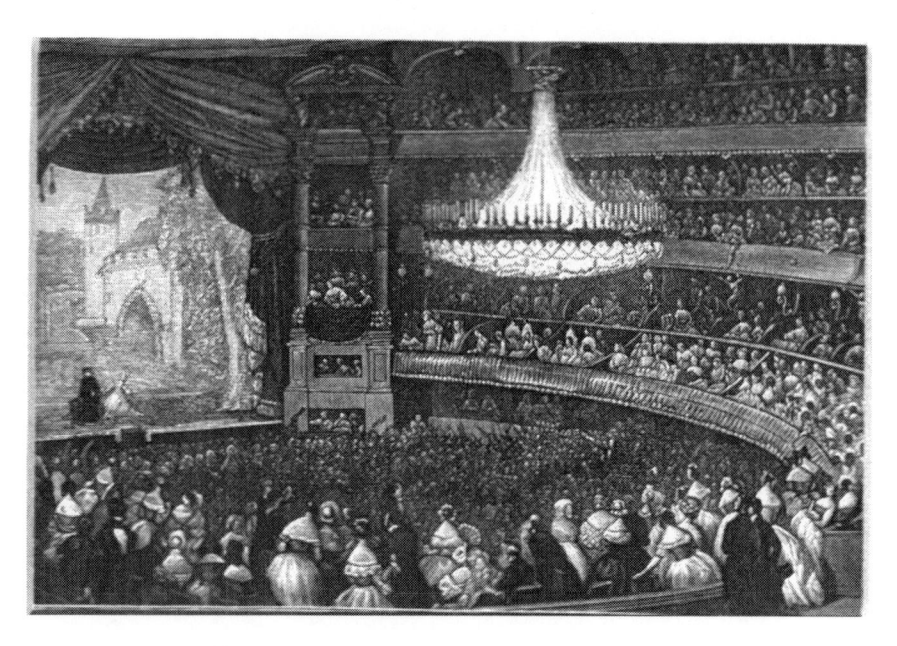

Théâtre Italian steel engraving (Lablache Archives)

Frédéric Chopin (Lablache Archives)

Princess Cristina Belgiojoso portrait by Vincent Vidal c1836 (Private collection)

Nicolo Paganini lithograph 1816 (Lablache Archives)

Paganini silhouette, antique postcard (Lablache Archives)

Luigi Lablache as Otello by A. Lacanchie (Sergio Ragni)

*Luigi Lablache as Figaro lithograph of the statue by
Jean Pierre Dantan (Lablache Archives)*

*Adelaide Comelli-Rubini with Luigi Lablache
by A.E. Chalon (Dr. Richard Copeman)*

HER MAJESTY'S THEATRE.

LE NOZZE DI FIGARO.
LES GRACES.

INCLUDING THE TALENTS OF

Mesdames SONTAG, FIORENTINI, CRUVELLI;
Signori COLETTI, FERRANTI, CASANOVA, MERCURIALI,
AND
LABLACHE;
Mlles. CARLOTTA GRISI, CAROLINA ROSATI, MARIE TAGLIONI, and AMALIA FERRARIS.

SIGNOR PUZZI

Has the honor to announce to the Nobility, Subscribers of the Opera, his Friends and the Public, that his BENEFIT will take place on

THURSDAY, JULY 10, 1851;

On which occasion will be presented, *for the first time this Season*,

INCLUDING THE TALENTS OF

Mesdames SONTAG, FIORENTINI, & CRUVELLI,
MOZART'S CELEBRATED OPERA, LE

NOZZE DI FIGARO,

WITH THE FOLLOWING POWERFUL CAST:

Susanna	Madame SONTAG.
The Countess	Madame FIORENTINI.
Cherubino	Mlle. SOFIE CRUVELLI.
Marcellina	Madame GRIMALDI.
Count Almaviva	Signor COLETTI.
Figaro	Signor FERRANTI.
Basilio	Signor MERCURIALI.
Don Curzio	Signor DAI FIORI.
Antonio	Signor GALLI.
Don Bartolo	Signor LABLACHE.

In the course of the Evening,

Madlle. CARLOTTA GRISI

Will appear in a

FAVORITE PAS.

To conclude with the first Representation of the Reprise of the admired Divertissement,

LES GRACES;

INTRODUCING THE

CELEBRATED PAS DE TROIS.

Euphrosyne	Mlle. CAROLINA ROSATI.
Thalia	Mlle. MARIA TAGLIONI.
Eglaia	Mlle. AMALIA FERRARIS.

ASSISTED BY

Mlles KOHLENBERG, ROSA, ESPER, JULIEN, LAMOUREUX, SOTO, DANTONIE, ESTHER, PASCALES, ALLEGRINI, SOLDANSKY, EMMA, ELIZA, LAVINIA, BEALE, and the Ladies of the Corps de Ballet.

Boxes—Pit Tier, Five Guineas; Grand Tier, Six Guineas; One Pair, Five Guineas and a Half; Two Pair, Four Guineas. Stalls, One Guinea. Pit, Half-a Guinea. Applications for Boxes, Stalls, and Tickets, to be made at Signor PUZZI's, 5 a, Cork Street, Burlington Gardens, and at the Opera Office, Opera Colonnade.
Doors opened at Half-past Seven o'Clock—the Opera to commence at Eight o'Clock.

Playbill Nozze di Figaro (Lablache Archives)

Maria Malibran lithograph by John Hayter 1829 (Lablache Archives)

Laura Cinti-Damoreau steel engraving (Lablache Archives)

Abigail Betts/Harriet Cawse by A.E Chalon (National Portrait Gallery)

Abigail Betts Playbill (Lablache Archives)

Abigail Betts lithograph (Lablache Archives)

Luigi Lablache as Georgio in I Puritani 1835 (Lablache Archives)

Luigi Lablache as Georgio in I Puritani cartoon 1835 (Lablache Archives)

Giovanni Battista Rubini in I Puritani (Sergio Ragni)

Antonio Tambourini in I Puritani (Private collection)

*Guilia Grisi and Luigi Lablache in I Puritani by
A.E. Chalon (Museo teatrale alla Scala)*

Marino Faliero by François Bouchot (Antony de Friston)

Marino Faliero score frontispiece (Jack Rokahr Archives)

*Luigi Lablache as Doge of Venice in Marino Faliero,
lithograph by A. E. Chalon (Lablache Archives)*

Luigi Lablache lithograph by Filippo Caporali (Lablache Archives)

Luigi Lablache lithograph (Sergio Ragni)

Luigi Lablache by Achille Devéria lithograph (Andrew S. Pope)

Luigi Lablache carte de visite (Lablache Archives)

Luigi Lablache as Falstaff photo (Liff Collection)

Luigi Lablache lithograph Galerie Voleur 65 (Lablache Archives)

Luigi Lablache lithograph (Sergio Ragni)

Luigi Lablache lithograph (Lablache Archives)

Luigi Lablache lithograph (Fulvio Stefano Lo Presti)

Luigi Lablache (Andrew S. Pope)

Luigi Lablache letter from Osborne about Queen Victoria in Italian.
(Lablache Archives)

Book Three

Chapter Seventeen

The Princess Victoria and Lablache

1835-36

Chorley writes that all London was steeped in the music of Bellini's masterpiece *I Puritani*:[328]

> The organs ground it—adventurous amateurs dared it—the singers themselves sang it to such satiety as to lose all consciousness of what they were engaged in, and, when once launched, to go on mechanically. I must have heard Mlle. Grisi's Polacca that year alone, if once, one hundred times-to speak without exaggeration.

The young princess Victoria was in the audience for the 23 April production of *Anna Bolena* at the King's Theatre, and from that time on, the young Giulia Grisi became her favorite prima donna. "She is a beautiful singer and actress and is likewise very young and pretty," the young Victoria wrote in her journal. The greatest ensemble of Italian singers were performing in London that season: Grisi, Malibran, Rubini, Tamburini, and Lablache. Clearly, Victoria was stagestruck and visited the theater often. She wrote in her journal and filled her sketchbook with drawings of the plays, ballets, and operas she had seen. Although she idolized Romantic ballet and the famous ballet stars of the time, such as Maria Taglioni and her brother Paul, it was the opera that was closest to her heart. Eventually maturing into a young woman, she was only two years away from becoming the Queen of England.

It was at Kensington Palace, right in the heart of London, that the Duchess of Kent arranged an evening concert on 18 May for her daughter's sixteenth birthday party. All the members of the Italian opera were invited to sing. The program began with Rossini arias from *L'Assedio di Corinto*, *La Donna del largo*, and *Guillaume Tell*. The rest of the concert consisted of a preview of selections from *I Puritani*. Grisi sang "Son vergin vezzosa," then the duet for two basses, "Il rival salvar tu dei," was sung by Lablache and Tamburini. Victoria wrote in her journal, "They sing beautifully together. Lablache's voice is immensely powerful but not too much so (for my taste) even in a room. Tamburini's too is most splendid."

Malibran, back in England from her usual wild adventures in Italy, arrived late; Victoria notes:

> Dressed in white satin with a scarlet hat with feathers . . . Her low notes are beautiful but her high notes are thick and not clear, she's shorter than Grisi and not nearly so pretty . . . I like Grisi far better than her! The concert ended with Rubini singing 'A te o cara.' It was the most delightful concert I ever heard. It was Mamma's birthday present for me . . . I stayed up till 20 minutes past one. I was MOST EXCEEDINGLY DELIGHTED.[329]

Lablache sang *I Puritani* on 21 May for the first time at the King's Theatre. As in Paris, the opera had instant success, unlike the London premiere of Donizetti's *Marino Faliero* on 14 May. For Tamburini's benefit on 11 June, two operas, two acts of *I Puritani*, back-to-back with one act of *La Cenerentola* were staged. Rubini sang the Prince, Tamburini Dandini. Here are *The London Times* comments on Lablache in a rare review, bringing into focus how Lablache sang and looked:

> And Don Magnifico found of course a very proper representation in Signor Lablache. Lablache is certainly the most burlesque Baron di Monte Fiascone that was ever seen on any stage. His portly person and his comic powers qualify him in a peculiar manner for the character. His dress too was so characteristic and droll, that it is difficult to look at him without being provoked to laughter.

Another milestone in the career of Lablache was about to happen. After a long season in London with hardly any rest, he joined the troupe of vocalists to sing at the the Fourth Yorkshire Grand Musical Festival, held at the old York Minster on 6 September and for three more days. This followed the same pattern as another magnificent Royal Musical Festival that had taken place in Westminster Abbey the year before on 24 June 1834. The vocalists according to *The Mirror* were Giulietta Grisi (sister of Giulia Grisi), Antonio Tamburini, Giovanni Battista Rubini, Carlo Zucchelli, Nicolas Ivanoff, Abigail Betts, Clara Novello, Mme. Stockhausen and Mr. Seguin, Mme. Caradori-Allan,

Ms. Sheriff and Mr. John Braham,—all well-known singers of the day and many of them British. The program consisted of the great oratorios of Handel and Haydn: *The Messiah,* the *Creation,* and many selections from *Samson,* Mozart, and Ludwig van Beethoven. From *The Mirror* on Saturday 5 July, 1834, we have an early description of the former event:

> Their Majesties and suite were present at each of the four performances. The Duchess of Kent, and the Princess Victoria were present at the first, third and last. Their Majesties went in state each day with a suite of ten or eleven carriages and a military escort from St. James Palace through the Park by the Horse Guards.

The newspaper, *The Mirror,* describes the young princess in detail, writing that the young princess Victoria was the most interesting object in the royal box:

> There is a tone of character about her that is very delightful . . . with the look and pleasurable expression of a child, she has a sedate aspect which is promising in one who is probably destined to fill a throne. A sweet smile sometimes played over her features, and illumined for a moment the languor they take when they are at rest. Occasionally a charming colour mounted to her cheeks, naturally wan, and flushed them with a glow of sudden delight, then it rapidly subsided, and her fair, round face and her eyes . . . which have the placid beauty of the dove's and her delicately outlined mouth fell into that tranquility which seems to be her natural temperament.

Some of the same performers attended the York festival that year. Lablache who had not been in England since 1832 now joined the vocalists. The vocal groups would remain much the same through the years, give or take a few different singers, for all the music festivals performed in different northern cities in the English provinces: the great industrial cities such as Manchester, Sheffield, Liverpool, Newcastle, and Birmingham. Smaller cathedral towns and cities in between also hosted festivals such as York, Norwich, and Worcester. Other towns and cities too numerous to mention (see concert chronologies) hosted concerts almost continuously around the year, featuring amateurs and professionals alike. The Italian groups from Her Majesty's joined many of these festivals nearly every year in the month of September; and every year they always concluded with a grand ball.

After hearing Lablache and Grisi sing at this festival, the young Princess Victoria wrote, "I am not fond of Handel's music . . . I am a terribly modern person . . . and I must say I prefer the present Italian school such as Rossini, Bellini and Donizetti to anything else." Princess Victoria begged her mother, the duchess of Kent, to be allowed to study singing with the artist and senior member of the *corps opératique* she so admired: Luigi Lablache.[330] This was arranged, and Lablache received an enormous sum per lesson. After the singers left England for Paris, Victoria laments and wrote in her journal on 11 September 1835:[331]

> Alas, it will be sometime before I hear their two fine voices again. But time passes away quickly and April and the dear Opera will soon return. I am to sing next year. Mamma promised I should; and I hope to learn from Lablache. What a delightful master he would be to learn from![332]

The tedium of Kensington was hard on the young girl, and she could not wait for Lablache to return from Paris to give her singing lessons. Kensington Palace was the home of the little princess Victoria. She was born there on 24 May 1819, and with her mother, the duchess of Kent, she continued to reside there after her father's death in 1820. Then when she became queen in 1837, she at once moved to Buckingham Palace. The palace had just been built in St. James's Park. Friedrich von Raumer, a critic of the day, gives this description of the interior in 1835:

> I never saw anything that might be pronounced a more total failure. In every respect, the King is so ill-satisfied with the result, that he has no mind to take up his residence in it when the unhappy edifice shall be finished. For my own part I would not live in it rent free . . . The grand apartments of the principal story are adorned with pillars; but what kind of pillars? Partly red, like raw sausages; partly blue, like starch—bad imitations of marbles . . . in the same apartments fragments of Egypt, Greece, Etruria, Rome, and the Middle Ages, all confusedly mingled together; doors windows and chimney-pieces, in such incorrect proportions, that even the most unpracticed eye must be offended . . . in one room there are three doors of different height and breadth; some apartments, have reliefs and sculptures over the doors in which pygmies and Brobdingnagians are huddled together-people from two to six feet high living in admirable harmony.[333]

The success of Bellini's latest opera, *I Puritani,* was celebrated on both sides of the British channel and proved a great favorite, especially when the famous quartet sang.

On 3 January 1837, the son of Luigi, Frédéric Lablache sang the role of Riccardo Forth in *I Puritani* at the Neapolitan premiere staged at the Teatro San Carlo with Caterina Barili-Patti as Elvira, Giovanni Bassadona was Arturo, and Paolo Barroilhet as Giorgio Valton. Caterina Barili-Patti, the future mother of the great prima donna Adelina Patti, sang with Frédéric Lablache on 19 November 1836 in Donizetti's *L'Assedio di Calais.* Salvatore Patti, Caterina Barili's second husband, also sang that year. It is not known if these operas were the only operas that Frédéric Lablache sang that season. During that time, Giuseppina Demery (Joséphine de Méric) sang Elvira at the Teatro Carolino in Palermo; and another more famous soprano Giuseppina Strepponi, who became the wife of Verdi—sang Elvira first in Venice on 23 April 1836 and then in Trieste.

I Puritani only began to lose its popularity as the nineteenth century waned; the opera was featured constantly most seasons in Paris and London through the fifties. Notably, it was the fourth opera sung during the initial 1883 season of the Metropolitan Opera in New York with Marcella Sembrich as Elvira. Why it disappeared from the Metropolitan's roster for many years afterward is hard to understand.

At London's Covent Garden, Giulia Grisi sang the first Elvira in 1846. The opera stayed in the repertory till 1887. Elvira was sung by many great divas including Angiolina Bosio, Ilma di Murska, Adelina Patti, Emma Albani, and Marcella Sembrich. Suddenly, *I Puritani* vanished from most theatres for a staggering number of years. Returning again in 1964 featuring Joan Sutherland as Elvira, the opera has enjoyed a revival with many wonderful performances world wide.

Unfortunately, Bellini was not to enjoy the fruits of his success. Still in Paris, hoping for work during the summer of 1835, he began to feel unwell; while he was staying with friends in Puteaux, there his condition rapidly deteriorated. An Italian doctor Montallegi was called in by the Princess Belgioioso who worked desperately to save his life, but in vain. Lablache and Bellini's friends were clearly concerned, but too late: Bellini died alone at five o'clock on the morning of 23 September 1835. He was found by composer Michele Carafa "bewildered and frantic, I rushed as fast as possible to Lablache's, Rue des Trois Frères, whence the fatal news spreads through Paris."[334] Bellini died of of a terminal chronic amebiasis flare up.[335]

Rossini took charge of all the funeral arrangements and the proper distribution of his belongings and his estate. Rossini also appointed a commission to raise funds for a monument to his memory.[336] Lablache was also deeply involved in raising funds. The funeral service was held at the Chapel at Les Invalides on 2 October, where all of the musical artists and notables gathered to pay homage:

> The pallbearers were Carafa, Cherubini, Paer and Rossini. After the soft intoning of the Gregorian Requiem, the rest of the Mass was sung by a chorus of three hundred and fifty voices and a quartet of great opera singers: Nicholas Ivanoff, Lablache, Rubini and Tamburini. To the text of the Lacrymosa, the four men (arranged for four voices, by Panseron), sang an adaptation of *Credeasi misera*, Arturo's solo from the final act of *I Puritani*.[337]

So sadly ended the life of Bellini. It had been the best of times—the operatic world had finally recognized his genius, but then it was the worst of times—he would not live to reap his rewards. In the continuous rain, the hearse followed by a procession of eleven black carriages proceeded over the Seine through the Rue Royal up the broad boulevards towards the east of Paris to the gloomy tree-covered cemetery of Pere-Lachaise. All along the boulevards crowds stood in silent farewell. At the burial, Rossini spoke over the coffin,[338] everyone was in deep shock over the loss of one so young and brilliant. Bellini's librettist, Felice Romani, writes the most eloquent tribute:[339]

> The 24th (sic) of September was the last day of an illustrious Italian, and closed, in the Pateaux (sic), near Paris, a brief life of thirty-three years blossoming with and irradiated with Glory Vincenzo Bellini is no more! . . . a tear falls on those words, but I cannot blot them out. Catania where he was born; Naples where he had his schooling; Milan, which produce the beautiful wreath with which his youth was adorned; Paris, which was generous to him with hospitality and glory—every every place in short into which the light of the arts, the flame of talent and the love of the beautiful penetrate—will lament this untimely extinguished torch and weep for the loss of this sublime young man. But no one, perhaps no one so much as I, will be able to measure the emptiness that he leaves, because no one so much as I penetrated into the most hidden recesses of that noble intellect and discerned the source from which emerged the spark that inspired him . . .[340]

During the months afterward, Lablache spent time while he was still in Paris helping Rossini. Rossini appointed a commission of distinguished musical people and then opened a subscription: "Destined for erection of a monument to his memory."[341]

Paris 10 November 1835

My dear Corelli,

With regard to poor Bellini, I inform you that we are making a collection both for the funeral expenses and to erect a monument, and that up until now we have collected 14,000 francs. The monument will be created by the best sculptor existing in France—Mr. Marocchetti, an Italian.

It is impossible to tell you what Rossini is doing for this collection—it is enough to know that two thirds of the amount is due to him, because he continues to go around, almost grabbing hold of people by the throat and obliging them to sign. It is easy for him to do this because in this country he is a big figure. This is the period that Rossini is known as a shameful man—his merits being taken away by those driven by none other than base jealousies. Judge for yourself, my dear Corelli. In this moment, Rossini is Director of the Italian Theatre here—and what does he do. He has Bellini, Donizetti Mercandante and Mariiane engaged—and not only allows them to give their music; he helps them like a father, giving them invaluable advice from which they can obtain advantages. If you had seen him at the moment when they gave him the news of the death of Bellini crying hot tears, you would have said, goodness, so this is the man without a heart—because this is how he is called by his enemies. A hundred times I have had occasion to make collections for those unhappy persons which fill this country, and I have always found Rossini ready and inclined to do good.

Forgive me, dear Corelli, to have insisted on this matter, but I felt the need to tell the truth and to whom better to tell these things but to a friend like you!

Your most affectionate friend,
L. Lablache

(In a letter later with no date, it is pretty certain that this letter is referring to the money to be given to the Bellini family for the funeral. Lablache was always raising funds for operatic unfortunates.)

> My dear Florimo,
>
>> I join my prayers with those of Mr. Dormoy.
>> Whenever you can, and with the greatest tact, please take care of this matter and in case you do not know Bellini's family, you can write to the lawyer, Dr. Canale of Palermo, who, I am sure, can give you all the necessary information, without any trouble,
>
> Your affectionate friend,
> L. Lablache

Paris, saddened by the death of Bellini, welcomed the chance to hear his *I Puritani* again when it opened the Paris season of 1835 on 1 October at the Théâtre-Italien as a tribute to Bellini, only eight days after he died. Bellini's works were not lessened by his death, however; for on 8 December, Paris was to hear for the first time another of his masterpieces—*Norma*.

Superb in the title role of Norma, the druidess, Giulia Grisi made the role her own personal achievement. The success of this marvelous opera depends on the leading prima donna, Norma. Simon Maguire writes in 1987 *Norma and Bel Canto*[342] on the 350th performance of *Norma* at the Royal Opera House Covent Garden:

> Bellini's operas were written after the decline of the castrators, but most of the singers he favoured had been schooled in their techniques: indeed there had been no other school. Giuditta Pasta, for whom he designed the roleof *Norma,* had actually taken on many of the old castrato roles, like Romeo in Zingarelli's *Giulietta e Romeo* written for Girolamo Crescentini in 1776. She was, perhaps, the leading prima donna of her time; and in 1828 a critic wrote that her *bel canto spianato* was 'perfectly adapted to declamation.' It may surprise some that such qualities were generally valued more than sheer beauty of sound (the conventional understanding of *bel canto*), and that Pasta's voice was rarely noted for its evenness or security of tone. The success of the opera depends on

the vividness which Norma's complex character and vicissitudes are portrayed. Bellini both permits and requires a multifaceted display of histrionics and vocal powers through the secretion of his instrumental accompaniments.[343]

Lablache's Oroveso in *Norma* was first heard in Paris at the Théâtre-Italien on 8 December 1835 with Giulia Grisi as Norma and Laura Assandri as Adalgisa, tenor Giovanni Battista Rubini sang Pollione. The bass role is another traditional role for a bel canto bass. Bellini's style, steeped in Romantic warmth and love, also displays a languid eloquence and grace in his characters. Lablache was much admired in this role, clearly recognizable from lithographs of the time, white-bearded and dressed in the druid robes, looms over the others in the cast carrying a wooden staff. Giulia Grisi created the role of Adalgisa when she sang at its premiere in Milan with Pasta as Norma. Now it was her turn to triumph in the role at the Théâtre-Italien. Her appearance was regal and dignified, and she was reputed to be more beautiful than Pasta and Malibran; though she took over the roles that Pasta had made famous, she made them her own and in no way imitated anyone. Proving herself a superb dramatic actress as well as a great singer from that time on and until her death, she reigned supreme as Queen of Song. Grisi depicted the ideal classic beauty of her age.

Princess Victoria thought Norma was Grisi's best role. Often she drew her in the character of Norma with a green wreath around her head, her jet-black hair tied back in a Grecian style, dressed in white Grecian robes, with a dark blue cloak.[344] Victoria adored Grisi and could not hear enough of her. Rowell writes, "As early as 1838 Victoria had asserted—she loved Grisi as Norma; and great and perfect as Grisi *always* is in this character, I never saw her act with so much power, feeling and grandeur or sing so exquisitely or look so beautiful as she did last night."[345]

A Victorian contemporary book: *Beauties of the Opera and Ballet* describes Grisi in the role of Norma:[346]

> Norma approaches, surrounded by her priestesses. And here let the imagination dwell on the perfect beauty of such an impersonation of this fine creation of a poet's fancy, as represented by Giuletta Grisi, who, looking indeed the proud, inspired priestess of Irminsul, walks with an air of high majesty to the altar, dressed in the tasteful costume required, her brows bound with oak-leaves, and carrying the golden sickle in her hand. The pale classic features, the deep

expressive eyes, the intellectual brow, and commanding figure, with the exquisitely turned arms and shoulders, conspire to render Grisi's first appearance as "Norma" the signal for one loud and simultaneous round of enthusiastic applause. Indeed, this part may be considered her greatest triumph; and those who have not been fortunate enough to witness the truth of our assertion cannot be said to have had an opportunity of estimating the wonderful capabilities of this incomparable actress as well as songstress. All here are united. Madame Grisi, as "Norma," most admirably employs her voice, her energy, her beauty, continued rage, sublime violence, threats and tears, love and anger—all are mingled with such artistic skill as to produce a whole unequalled in any histrionic picture afforded by any female tragedian. At length her voice breaks the dead stillness that prevails. "Who is here," she utters, in clear, calm tones, "who here dares presumptuously to seek to penetrate the secrets of destiny, and presage the downfall of Rome?" "Oh! my daughter," replies Oroveso, "too long have our sacred groves and temples been polluted by the presence of the Latin eagles. Should not the sword of Brennus quit its scabbard? Say, is not the hour of just vengeance arrived?" "No," replies the priestess, with commanding majesty; "not yet has the day come. The Roman javelins are far too strong for the hatchets of the Sicumbri. My eyes behold the future—the veil is withdrawn from my vision, and I see that the city of the Caesars must perish, but not by your hand: it will fall by its own vices, worn out by its own excesses. Await the appointed hour, and seek not to accelerate the decrees of mighty Fate. In the name of the Deity by which I am inspired, I command peace; and thus I sever the sacred mistletoe, as a symbol you dare not disobey."

Thus speaking, and raising her beautiful arm, with movement of unapproachable majesty, she cut off a branch of the mysterious plant, which the youthful priestesses received with deep reverence in their sacred vases.

Chapter Eighteen

Victoria's Lessons

1836-1837

Princess Victoria began her first singing lessons on 19 April 1836 at Kensington Palace. They were to continue for over twenty years, and the giant Lablache became as she phrased it "Beloved Master." Looking up to him enraptured, he represented the father figure, the father she had never had. From the beginning, she gives us a glowing report and full description of his looks and behavior. Victoria, for her young years, was a mature and very observant critic; yet when she first met her new music master, she was nervous. Lablache immediately set her at ease. The lesson was successful, and Lablache became one of Princess Victoria's heroes. She wrote in her journal:

> He looks far younger off the stage, extremely gentlemanlike, I sung in fear and trembling . . . *Or che in cielo.* He praised my voice. *Or che in cielo* is the barcarole from Donizetti's opera *Marino Faliero*, an ambitious choice. "You must not be afraid of me . . . *Personne a jamais eu peur de moi,"* which I am sure nobody ever can be who knows him.[347]

The following week, the princess and the Duchess of Kent sang duets together, including two from *Norma*. "Then Mama and I sang *Mira O Norma!* And *Se fine al ore*, both twice over."[348] Lablache accompanied, after which the princess sang duets with Lablache to his accompaniment, which she enjoyed greatly, including "a very pretty little duo from *L'Elisir d'amore* by Donizetti, *Io son ricco e tu sei bella*."[349] Lablache made no attempt to train the princess's voice by imposing the discipline of exercises on her; she sang arias from operas which Lablache transposed and adapted to be within her range, duets with Lablache himself who helped her over the hard bits. The princess had a small but true voice with the same sweetness as her speaking voice. Lessons became one of her greatest pleasures. She admired him wholeheartedly—his wonderful voice, his talent for acting, his patience, his good humor, his kindness; when she went to the opera to hear him she was "in raptures."[350]

On 3 May 1836, the young princess gives a valuable and detailed description of Lablache. She writes in her journal:

> I like Lablache very much, and he is such a nice, good-natured, good-humoured man, and very patient and excellent master; he's so merry too, *en profile* he has a very fine countenance, I think, an aquiline nose, dark arched eyebrows, and fine long eyelashes, and a very clever expression. He has a profusion of hair, which is very grey, and strangely mixed with a few black locks here and there. I sang first the recitative of *Notte d'orrore* from *Marino Faliero* several times over . . . Then with Lablache over . . . Then I sang twice with Lablache *Io son ricco e tu sei bella,* a very pretty duo from *L'Elisir d'amore* by Donizetti. He sang this delightfully, he has such a fine voice and pronounces so distinctly and so well. *En conclusion* I sang *Vivi tu* (*Anna Bolena*) I liked my lesson extremely; I only wish I had one every *day* instead of one *every week.*[351]

In her later entries, Lablache is always referred to as "my dear Master."[352] And he was the first one of the Italians to gain real favor with the young Victoria and to earn that high mark of her attachment;[353] and sometimes, though, she knew she must not be "quite cross" when he could not come![354] She was still studying with him two years before he died in 1858.[355] Sometimes, the three voices—hers, the duchess of Kent's, and Lablache's—would be heard all rambling away together; and it is to be hoped that Victoria and the duchess were more in tune than the year before when they had sung a duet on some country house visit, and Lady Holland had reported afterward that "the singing of mother and daughter was execrably inharmonious, but of course was highly lauded." Later in August of that year, Victoria laments,

> I took leave of IL MOI BUON E CARO MAESTRO with GREAT regret . . . I have had 26 lessons . . . and shall look forward with equal delight to next April . . . . It was such a pleasure to hear his fine voice and to sing with him. Everything is so pleasant,

alas! passes so quickly . . . I was exceedingly delighted with this my LAST lesson; the time seemed to fly even faster than usual, for it appeared to me that these pleasant lessons were over in an instant . . . he was always ready to sing anything I like and stay as long as I liked.[356]

The future queen was not Lablache's only pupil; through the years, he gave lessons to many students, but Victoria was his most famous. His character, fame, and reputation had to have been impeccable to fill such a job. He was her favorite.

When Victoria became queen, in the minds of many, she personified the new spirit of nineteenth-century England. The monarchy had taken on a different look from the time of her uncle George IV, who had been regarded with contempt. Victoria represented a new order of respectability.

Lablache's son, Frédéric, fresh from his French debut in Bellini's *Sonnambula* at the Théâtre-Italien the previous year on 24 October, was now ready to enter into the operatic arena in London. Joining his father at the King's Theatre was his first opportunity to make his name in England. Frédéric, though not as handsome as his father, was well-liked; he had a nice, pleasing face with a profusion of naturally curly dark brown hair. Most of his life, he sported long waxed mustaches; in later life, he wore a large white beard.[357]

Sadly for Maria Malibran, time was running out. Now in Italy, she moved to and fro to avoid the path of the fast-spreading dreaded cholera. While singing in Milan, she heard the unexpected news of Bellini's death.[358] There, she maybe had a premonition; putting her hand to her forehead, she said, "I feel it won't be very long before I follow him."[359] A memorial service was held there for Bellini, and April Fitzlyon wrote, "La Malibran contributed both her voice and her money."[360]

Bellini's operas became more in demand after his death. The spring season at the King's Theatre featured the same cast in *I Puritani*, followed by *Norma*. Frédéric Lablache joined his father at the many private and public concerts during that year; many more were to follow. Frédéric became more confident in himself and got plenty of usage from these musical events. However, the press was always comparing him to Lablache, year after year, which must have been rather trying, as it cannot be denied; overall, he suffered from living in the shadow of his famous father.

Noteworthy events of this season were a performance of Rossini's *Le Siège de Corinthe* (*Maometto II*) and the first showing of Mercadante's *I Brigante,* on 22 March in Paris, then repeated in London on 2 July without any success. This opera was taken from the Schiller's drama *Die Rauber* and portrayed Lablache as the starved old Moor. As soon as Lablache crossed the stage, however, laughter broke out throughout the house; there was no way that audiences could take him seriously since he was quite enormous. The same thing happened with the same role in Verdi's *I Masnadieri* later when the opera premiered in London in 1847.

After a quiet wedding in Paris on 29 March 1836, La Malibran returned to London happily as Mme. Malibran de Bériot, ten months after her divorce became finalized. She continued, however, to use the name of Malibran.

Hired by the impresario Alfred Bunn of the Theatre Royal Drury Lane, Malibran thrilled audiences by singing in English: Michael Balfe's *The Maid of Artois*. She then sang Bellini's *La Sonnambula* followed by Beethoven's *Fidelio,* but it was for *The Maid of Artois* that she received rave reviews and exerted herself to her limits. She assured its place as one of the most successful operas of the season.

Before the opera, Malibran had rehearsals at her house, inviting among other guests Lablache and Templeton. At the conclusion, Malibran served champagne; and as everyone was hot, she proceeded to give their heads a cologne rub to cool them down; but when it was Templeton's turn, it was revealed that he wore a wig which fell to the floor. Amidst much merriment, Malibran dived for it and refused to give it back after rubbing his bald head with cologne; she dropped the hair on backward so the curls hung over his face with the remark, "My dear Mr. T, I'm deceived. I did not think there was anything fake about you."[361]

Most of the prominent vocalists from the Italian Opera, plus local English singers were engaged in almost a daily schedule of concerts in addition to their opera obligations. Fashionable London concerts were scheduled from early April, often earlier, through the month of July, terminating by the conclusion of the London opera season. The international singers left to tour the English provinces or for engagements in Paris and beyond. The locations of these concerts were varied, usually in concert halls and palaces, sometimes in St. James's or Buckingham Palace. The homes of the aristocracy in the London region were used, such as Stafford House now Lancaster House. The public locations were at Her Majesty's Theatre Concert Rooms; Hanover Square Rooms; the Masonic Temple Rooms; Exeter Hall (now the Strand Palace Hotel); the Willis Rooms; and St. James's Hall, Piccadilly. Other smaller and less formal rooms were used such as the Green Man Rooms at Blackfriars and the London Tavern.

During Lablache's time, concert recitals expanded at a tremendous rate, especially in the provinces. Popular opera singers like Lind, Roger, Tamburini,

Rubini, Grisi, and the Lablaches toured England, alongside trios and quartets of instrumental artists such as Listz, Piatti, Old Bull, Chopin, Vieuxtemps, Thalberg, Paganini, and Strauss to name a few.

By the end of the 1840s, however, the concerts took on larger and different dimensions with the onslaught of the so-called musical fetes with huge orchestras, choirs, and military bands, squeezing out the smaller more intimate groups that had sung so successfully before. Fashion in opera embraced different dimensions including monumental stage spectacles, grand opera from France, fantastic Gothic melodramas by Giacomo Meyerbeer. There were such operas as *The Huguenots*, *The Prophet,* and the opera that brought Jenny Lind to the forefront *Robert le Diable* (*Roberto il Diavolo*. Jenny Lind only sang this opera in Italian, though most reviews referred to the French spelling).

On 13 July, there was a dazzling grand reception at Stafford House just across the street from Buckingham Palace. The perfection of the ensemble was beyond comparison; all the members of Italian Opera sang including the famous Puritani Quartet-Grisi, Tamburini, Rubini, and Lablache with Michael Costa conducting. They sung selections from well-known operas of the time by Bellini, Donizetti, and Rossini.

A concert took place on 7 June 1836 for the benefit of pianist Edward Schulz during the last summer of Maria Malibran's life. Singing under her married name at last was very important to her. Details below reported in *The Musical World*:

PART I

OVERTURE (*Midsummer Night's Dream*)	F. M. BARTHOLDY
DUETTO, Signor Tamburini and Signor Lablache, 'Un segreto' (*La Cenerentola*)	ROSSINI
ARIA, Mme Giuletta Grisi, 'Dal asilo'	COSTA
FANTASIA, Pianoforte, Mr. E. Schult, 'Montecchi e Capuletti'(first time of performance)	THALBERG
Air, Signor Ivanoff, 'O care imagine' (*The Magic Flute*)	MOZART
TRIO, Signor Rubini, Signor Tamburini, and Signor Lablache (*Guillaume Tell*)	ROSSINI
SOLO, French Horn, Signor Puzzi (first time of performance)	PUZZI
ARIA, Signor Rubini (*Adelaide*)	BEETHOVEN
POLACCA, Mme Giuletta Grisi, Signor Rubini Signor Tamburini, and Signor Lablache	BELLINI

PART II

TARTINI'S DREAM, for Voice and Violin, Mme Malibran and M. de Bèriot	TARTINI
GRAND DUET for Two Pianofortes, Monsieur Henry Herz and Mr. E. Schulz	HERZ
ARIA, Madame Malibran de Beriot, 'La tremenda ultrice spada' (*Capuletti*)	BELLINI
DUETTO, Signor Ivanoff and Mr. Balfe, 'La Marinari'	ROSSINI
SOLO VIOLIN, Monsieur de Bèriot	DE BERIOT
ARIA, Signor Tambunni, 'Vi ravviso,' (*La Sonnambula*)	BELLINI
TARANTELLA, Signor Lablache (La Dansa)[362]	ROSSINI
OVERTURE (*Fidelio*)	BEETHOVEN

Leader, Mr. Monri. Conductor, Signor Costa

Lablache finished a full season at the King's Theatre, interlaced with the usual concerts. The operas he sang in that season were *La Gazza ladra, Mosè, Norma, Otello, I Puritani, Marino Faliero, Anna Bolena*, and *Don Giovanni*. The performance of *Marino Faliero* was enjoyed by Princess Victoria and her cousins, Ernest and Albert, from Germany. Prince Albert later would marry Princess Victoria.[363] Giving an excellent write-up, the *London Times* reviewed the last opera performance on 6 August 1836:

> The close of the season at the King's theatre last Saturday evening, was in all respects, a brilliant one. The audience was the most numerous and fashionable collected on any night during its continuance, and all seemed determined to enjoy the gratifications from which, for a few months, they were about to part. *I Puritani* was the established favourite of the season, and if the supposition did not seem extravagant that the new impressions could be given after such frequent repetitions, we should say that Bellini's opera, in the hands of the "incomparable four," disclosed beauties which, if not absolutely new, had all the effect of novelty in the excitement they produced. All were in excellent voice, but particularly Grisi and Rubini, and tasked themselves to the utmost finish and refinement, as if resolved to be remembered long after they have quitted us. In this combination has lain the great strength

of Lamport's present campaign, and it has given vigor to all his operations, amidst great neglect to those other attractions of new and good operas on which managers generally depend. Panegyric has been nearly exhausted on this splendid quartet, but it has not yet been remarked, as a source of its beauty and perfection, how admirable the quality of each voice assimilates to the rest, so that the notes are carried down in one uniform graduation, from the extreme compass of Grisi's soprano to the depths, the deep beyond the "lowest deep," of Lablache's bass. No more perfect means have existed in the art of producing the highest effect of which vocal music is susceptible.

Sometime during the successes of Lablache at the King's Theatre, Lablache wrote to a Mr. Sequin, one of the under managers at the King's Theatre. The letter has no date and written in Italian; obviously, it was not the first time Lablache had to put his foot down:

Dear Mr. Sequin,

It seems to me Mr Lamporte either does not understand, or does not want to understand that I cannot do two operas of the stature of Puritani and of Prova . . . (unreadable) Therefore I declare once and for all that I do not intend to do so as I am not obliged to sing more than one opera. Please inform Mr. Laporte so and I beg you not to put up posters because you could find yourself in an embarrassing situation. I warned you about this some time ago.

Yours sincerely, your friend,
L. Lablache

After finishing his London engagements, Lablache headed north by carriage to Manchester for the music festival. But on the way, unfortunately, his carriage broke down. It was reported first in *The Morning Post,* under the heading Miscellaneous Coach Accident and retold by *The Musical World.* The reporter gives us this amusing little tidbit about the trip:

A carriage, which was conveying Mori and Lablache to Leicester, broke down close to an Inn. The first who made his debut out of the broken vehicle was Ivanoff, then followed Madame Assandri and her daughter and last, though not least, out crept Lablache . . . on seeing his mighty bulk the crowd laughed right out, in which the basso joined in, with his accustomed good humour. The Duke of Brunswick was passing through Leicester on his way to the Manchester Festival and offered a seat in his carriage to Lablache. When they got to Derby, a crowd gathered round to have a peak at the Duke; a lady, upon seeing Lablache said, "Aye, aye, no wonder the bloomin' coach broke down with such a tremendous bulk piece of goods."

Manchester hosted many singers for the festival that year. It was a magnificent and sumptuous affair, and special buildings were set up from the Theatre Royal to the assembly rooms—one was a magnificent gigantic Turkish pavilion, which extended on one side into a vista of considerable length, supported by pillars around a stage draped in red and white. *The Times* reports on the food served:

> The refreshment room was 200 feet by 28 feet wide, and was hung with draperies of amber and white in the same manner as the other apartments. The ceiling was arched, and from it hung a succession of elegant chandeliers served to shed light on the beautiful and gorgeous scene, in addition to which 16 bronze pillars, each bearing three branches with gas light, were placed along the tables. The bill of fare for supper being rather a curiosity . . . we submit for inspection . . . 2,000 veal pies, 2,000 sandwiches, 500lbs of grapes, 65 pineapples, 25 bushels of plums, apples and pears, 65 pieces of montes, 250 quarts of jellies and creams, 200 quarts of ices, 200 dishes of pastry, 50 dishes of savory cakes, 2 hogs head of sherry, 2 hogshead of port, and 16 hogshead of negus. This was all followed by a grand fancy dress ball.

The singers from the Italian Opera consisted of Luigi Lablache, Maria Malibran de Bèriot, and Nicolas Ivanoff. The English singers were Ms. Clara Novello; Mrs. Shaw; Mme. Caradori Allan; Mrs. K. Knyvett; and Mrs. H. R. Bishop—all well-known singers of the time joined by the English gentlemen Messrs. Bennett, Braham, and Phillips while the instrumentalists were supported by a huge chorus.

When the Bèriots arrived at the festival on the 11 September, La Malibran was far from well. There had been rumors she would not attend but she was engaged to sing at Norwich, Worcester, and Liverpool, and later in Dublin. These northern audiences were unaware she was pregnant and worn out from her extensive engagements in London. That year, while riding in Regents Park, she fell from her horse and while entangled in the reins was dragged by the animal quite a way. She suffered severe injuries to the head, which with other complications unfortunately led to her tragic and premature death some time later in Manchester. In spite of all this, with great strength of purpose, she continued singing, often with blinding headaches.

On 13 September, a Tuesday, the festival opened at the Collegiate Church (Manchester Cathedral); the *London Times* reported the morning program:

> The performance commenced with the overture and Dead March in Saul, Lablache sang in Handel's quartetto, *"Tu di Grazia."* Malibran sang "Sing to the Lord" with great pathos. Sung in the evening at the Theatre Royal, the theatre was filled to the roof tops . . . Malibran sang the duetto with Madame Cadori Allan from *Andronico*, by Mercadante . . . in this, Cadori shone out with surpassing brilliancy, and in the concluding portion of the duetto, the notes of Malibran were showered forth in gorgeous profusion. A complete storm of applause testified the enthusiasm of the audience, and the rapturous 'encore' which succeeded it was instantly responded to. Here beauty followed beauty and the repetition was followed with equal enthusiasm. Lablache sang in Rossini's beautiful quintet, *"Oh guardante che accidente"* from *Il Turco in Italia*, with Madame Cadori Allan, Mademoiselle Assandri, Signor Ivanoff and Mr. H. Phillips. The second part of the concert was ushered in with the ever popular *William Tell* overture, then Lablache was greatly applauded in Mozart's aria from *Le Nozze di Figaro*, *"Non piu andrai farfalione amoroso"* . . . reported to be a real treat!

But a disappointment was in store for the audience. Malibran was to sing the quintet from Mozart's *Cosi fan tutte,* but as *The Times* reported, she was taken ill again and could not continue. Backstage, she collapsed. The doctors wanted to bleed her. Lablache was opposed to this-he believed in homoeopathic medicine which was against bloodletting—and tried in vain to stop the doctors who bled Maria's arm while the concert continued. The audience were unaware of what was happening, and in fact, Lablache brought the house down with his comic duet from *Il Matrimonio Segreto*. Charles de

Bèriot played a concerto at the end of the concert and was also unaware of what was going on; even when Lablache tried to attract his attention from the wings, he even went on to play an encore.

The program for the next day of the festival consisted of Beethoven's oratorio, *The Mount of Olives*, and Handel's Hallelujah chorus. Martin Luther's *Hymn* was sung by Braham with Harpers's trumpet obligato and an accompaniment on the organ. Haydn's "Qui tollis peccata mundi" was sung by Lablache with violoncello obligato by Mr. Lindley. Bishop conducted his own cantata based on Milton's *Paradise Lost*, finishing with *The Last Judgement* by Spohr. This was not relished by the audience, nor was the very noticeable absence of the beautiful Maria Malibran. On Saturday, 17 September 1836, *The London Times* covered the story in great detail and with three columns reported:

> The indisposition of Madame Malibran has increased, and she is considered to be in great danger, being far advanced in pregnancy, a premature delivery is anticipated . . . her husband De Beriot is constant in his attention to her and is in great anxiety for her safety. It is supposed that she has injured herself by over-exertion.

Maria Malibran lingered painfully for days. The doctors could do nothing to save her. She finally died. Her husband's reaction was violent as to be expected: he was so distressed that the doctors advised him to leave England and go back to Belgium to his family. This he did, leaving the funeral arrangements in the hands of others.

The news quickly spread through Europe. Lablache had left for the Norwich Festival and while Beriot wrote to Lablache that she had improved after Malibran's homoeopathic doctor, Dr. Joseph Belluomini, had arrived from London, he did not know she suffered a terrible further setback. Lingering in terrible pain before she died, she was able to talk just a few words about Beroit and Lablache: "I love very few persons," she said, "but those I do love, I love."[364] Lablache, like Beroit, was shattered when the news reached him. Queen Victoria commented in her diary on 30 September:

> It is the most melancholy end that could be imagined! To come to an inn in a foreign land with nobody to nurse her, and die there! What a sad and tragic end to her bright career![365]

La Malibran died on the 23 of September, exactly a year to the day after Bellini. Another death was to follow on 12 October—that of Maria's former husband, Eugene Malibran.[366] Two days after the Norwich Festival opened, her friends Lablache, Caradori Allan, and Ivanoff continued on, singing with heavy hearts. The *London Times* reviewed it thus:

> With Beethoven's magnificent sinfonia in C minor, which was received with more enthusiasm than we had anticipated. Ivanoff and Lablache sang the well-known duet from *William Tell* with great effect. Every seat was filled with the respectable inhabitants of the ancient city. Madame Cadori Allan and Miss Rainforth sang from *Sonnambula* and *Der Freishutz*. The Festival concluded with Handel's unrivalled *Israel in Egypt*.

Cholera now swept across most of Europe, reaching down into France and southern Italy, from Naples to Palermo. The Italians suffered tremendously from the attack of this deadly disease, and thirteen thousand eight hundred people died of the cholera in that year alone. After the Northern Festivals, Lablache did not return to Italy as usual but left for the Paris season, opening there just a week after the death of Maria Malibran. The *Gazette Musicale* reported in 1837, page 179:

> Those of our readers who have applauded the talents that Lablache displays as a singer and actor will doubtless be curious to aquaint themselves with his talent as a poet. Here are some of the verses last year after a concert given by the Italian artists at Norwich. Lablache went to visit Warwich Castle. Named the 'King Maker' on 3 of September, he writes in his poem that "the towers, gardens, halls all are handsome, I thought I was carried back to the Middle Ages." There are found hundreds of Italian paintings, but he writes that he soon forgot the towers and the gardens in an instant, but he could never forget the greatest of all wonders, the angel in a painting by Raphael:
>
> > Del fattor di re il gran castello
> > Il tre settembre a visitar son stato.
> > E torri, e parchi, e sale tutto e bello;
> > E fui ne' bassi tempi trasportanto.
> > Vi son teli dipinte a centro a centro
> > Di nostri grand' Italian pittori,

> Vi son dei grandi fiamminghi; ma no mento,
> All'italo penello I primi onori
> Le torri e i parchi scorda sul momento,
> Appena son sortito dal costello.
> Ma non s'obblia giammai il gran portento
> L'angel della pittura, Raffaello.

Frédéric Lablache, Luigi's oldest son, returned to Naples for the San Carlo premiere, on 19 November 1836, of a new *Dramma lirico* in three acts by Donizetti *L'Assedio di Calais* (*The Siege of Calais*). Frédéric Lablache created the role of Edoardo III, King of England in 1347, and the subject matter is a famous incident in the Hundred Years' War. Joining him on stage that night were Almerinda Manzocchi, Catherina Barili-Patti, and Paul Barroilhet.[367] The libretto was by Salvatore Cammarano. The opera was a success, and Donizetti, who was present, was called before the curtain six times. The occasion was a birthday gala performance for the Queen Mother, Maria Isabella of Naples. Afterward, Donizetti wrote to his publisher Ricordi, "It is my most carefully worked-out score . . . but the cholera keeps everyone in the country."[368] In a letter to Gilbert-Louis Duprez in Paris of 12 May 1837, Donizetti writes:

> Having given it in November, they are still performing it, especially at every gala, as the best! and it's billed for 6 July (the Queen's birthday).

Outside Naples, the opera did not do so well, a typical fate of some operas. Donizetti's operas *Betly, O La Capanna svizzera* (*The Swiss chalet*) and *Il Campanello di notte* (*The Night Bell*) were performed at the Theatre Nuovo; the former on 6 June, the latter on 24 August.[369] Frédéric may have seen these operas: we do know he had knowledge of them, and he would later sing them successfully in the London and Dublin premieres.[370]

Cholera was still present in parts of northern Italy in 1837. Paganini's brother died from the disease, and it was feared that Paganini had caught it too. Paganini gave a concert on 9 July 1837 when he was gravely ill. Unable to speak, he was diagnosed as having tuberculosis of the larynx. He only had a few years to live.

Naples, laboring under a terrible cholera epidemic, was not a desirable place to be. The streets were deserted, and coffins lay outside everywhere waiting for burial crews. These years were filled with doom for Donizetti. Upon leaving for Venice in December of 1836, he heard that the La Fenice Theatre had been burnt down and that his opera would have to be transferred to another theater.[371] Other personal tragedies soon would follow him.

Frédéric Lablache returned to England and continued to sing concerts at the King's Theatre, and being single, he plainly fell under the wing of his father who pushed his son's career through the connections he had established by that time. On 1 October, the Théâtre-Italien opened with the perfect ensemble, the Puritani Quartet in *I Puritani*. All Paris was eager to hear it again and again with the right cast, and the group was eager to oblige. Lablache also sang his usual repertoire: *La Cenerentola, Norma, Il Matrimonio Segreto, Anna Bolena, La Gazza ladra, IL Barbiere, Otello, La prova di un'opera seria*.

In the early months of 1837, Rubini, Lablache, and Grisi introduced two new operas about the Crusaders to Paris—*Malek Adel* by Michael Costa and *Il Degona* by Marco Marliani. Emma Albertazzi, an English soprano, sang the trouser role of the crusader with Rubini in the title role of Malek Adel. Albertazzi was much admired and drawn by Princess Victoria in her sketchbook. "A voice of great compass," she wrote of her after seeing her at the London premiere on 18 May 1837.[372] "Three quarto albums in the Royal library at Windsor record the Princess's impressions: Volume I is inscribed: *Souvenirs de L'Opéra, Sketches from Recollection,* Mlle Giulietta Grisi and by P.V. 1835, 1836."[373]

The season in Paris at the Théâtre-Italien finished after beginning on 12 March with Rossini's *Mosè*. Lablache slipped over to the Academie Royale de Musique from 27 March. There, the Parisians no doubt enjoyed another one of his unrivalled interpretations of Gnecco's ever-popular *La prova di un'opera seria* with Grisi and Ivanoff.

Under the title Chit Chat from the Continent, here is a review from *The Musical World's* Paris correspondent:

> Signor Costa's new opera, *Malek Adel* in 3 acts, was represented for the first time in Paris on 14 January. The theatre was crowded, and the piece went off amid acclamations of applause. The story is taken from Madame Cottin's *Malek Adel;* the opera was brought out with abundance of cost and painstaking trouble. The performers were Grisi, Amigo and Albertazzi, the new contralto, who has "reaped" golden opinions for her performance and singing upon the occasion, Rubini, Ivanoff, Tamburini, and Lablache. Rubini sang as he always sings, like a great artist who disdains to truckle to the commonality, and performed with unusual pathos. Rubini gave himself wholly to the expression, not the ornamenting, of his music. His delivery of a solo in the last act was so extraordinary an effort of art that it will form the subject of conversation in the musical circles here for a long time.

Italian composer Luigi Ricci's two-act opera *Un'avventura di Scaramuccia* was staged for the first London performance at the new Theatre Royal Lyceum—also called the home of Italian opera buffa. The date was 29 December 1836 and featured Elizabeth Féron's daughter Ms. Glossip. The following evening, this singer was replaced by a young contralto, an English woman of Scottish descent and graduate of the Royal Academy of Music—Ms. Fanny Wyndham. Using her stage name (her real name was Frances Wilton), Ms. Fanny Wyndham filled the trouser role of Count de Pontigny to perfection. Wearing a beautiful seventeenth-century-style costume dripping with lace, ribbons, and tassels over velvet, she was portrayed by the famous artist Chalon, looking very dashing, sporting a small false mustache and brandishing a sword. She wore high boots, and from under her broad feathered hat, a multitude of black curls cascaded to her shoulders.

On 25 January 1837, the London Lyceum announced in *The London Times* that Fanny Wyndham would appear again, this time in Luigi Ricci's first performance in London of *Chiara di Rosenberg* as Princess Euphemia.[374] Catone and Wyndham's pleasing solo by Benedict, *Ah la trista rimembranza*, with clarinet was encored. This opera reportedly had been plagiarized by Balfe for his opera, *The Siege of Rochelle,* from the overture to the finale.[375]

From the time of her debut at Covent Garden the year before on 4 February in *Quasimodo*,[376] she clearly drew attention to herself performing there as Ursula in *Carmelites*. Not only did she sing and act, but she danced as well.[377] Her repertory included *The Bronze Horse, Guy Mannering, John Bull, Steel Pavilion, Hunchback, Zazezizozo* (Queen of the Dominoes) *Assurance Co. Macbeth, Hamlet*, and the *Provok'd Husband*. On 5 April, she played Virginia in *Virginius*. She remained for more plays and operas up to October 1836.

Certainly, by then, she had enjoyed great success as a singer and actress of worth. However, the critic of *The Musical World* wrote after the end of the Lyceum opera season with *Le nozze di Figaro* in which Ms. F. Wyndham had played Cherubino:

> It is evident the other evening that her knowledge of Mozart is very moderate, and more shame to the Directors of the Academy where she was educated. "Miss Wyndham should become more intimate with the music of Handel and Mozart, as she now is with Bellini and Donizetti.[378]

Ms. Wyndham's debut at the King's Theatre took place 4 March 1837 in Rossini's *La donna del largo*. She sang with the tenor Catone. During April,

Wyndham sang the part of Peppo in *La Gazza ladra* with Grisi as Ninetta. The newspapers reported that she "distinguished herself as usual throughout the piece." Not to slight tenor Ivanoff, Lablache as Podesta and Tamburini as Fernando, "they were a strong cast," wrote the *London Times* on 17 April. Michael Costa conducted.

On 24 April 1837, Ms. Wyndham sang in concert with Clara Novello at the Hanover Square Rooms.[379] Clearly, she was beginning to create a success for herself at Covent Garden where she appeared in many plays, operas, and operettas.

While singing at Drury Lane and at Her Majesty's Theatre through the 1830s she met the young Frédéric Lablache, most probably at the Lyceum or at the many concerts in which they participated together in London and in the provinces. They were married in the summer of 1839.[380]

☙☙☙

Chapter Nineteen

Frédéric and Fanny

1837-1838

The season at the King's Theatre had opened again with the usual *I Puritani* on 8 April with Grisi, Rubini, Tamburini, and Lablache. On 24 May, Princess Victoria wrote in her journal:

> Today is my 18th birthday! How old! and yet how far am I from being what I should be. I shall from this day take the firm resolution to study with renewed assiduity, to keep my attention always well fixed on whatever I am about, and to strive to become every day less trifling and more fit for what, if Heaven wills it, I'm some day to be! . . . At half past three we drove out . . . The demonstrations of locality and affection from all the people were highly gratifying. The parks and streets were thronged and everything looked like a Gala day. Numbers of people put down their names and amongst others . . . good old Lablache inscribed his . . . We went to the ball at St. James's Palace. The Courtyard and the streets were crammed . . . and the anxiety of the people to see poor stupid me was very great, and I must say I am quite touched by it, and feel proud which I always have done of my country and of the English nation.[381]

Malek Adel by Costa was sung again by Lablache, and then he sang in *Romeo e Giulietta* by Nicola Zingarelli. *I Puritani* passed into its third year of overwhelming popularity, and young Fanny Wyndham sang Enrichetta, the small role of the hapless queen of England, wife of the martyred Charles I. Meanwhile, a proper royal box now was being constructed at the English Opera House, Lyceum for the royal family. Wyndham sung Cherubino at the Lyceum in *Le nozze de Figaro*.

Lablache continued to teach Victoria. On 15 June 1837, Princess Victoria writes,

> The news of the King (William IV) are so very bad that all my lessons save the Dean's (her principal Master, Dean of Chester) are put off, including Lablache's . . . and we see nobody. I regret rather my singing-lesson, though it is only for a short period, but duty and proper feelings go before all pleasures . . . I just hear that the Doctors think my poor Uncle the King cannot last more than 48 hours.[382]

Soon the King's condition became worse, and Princess Victoria, calm and collected, prepared for the event that would surely follow her ascent to the throne of England as crown head of the British Empire.

On the next day, 20 June, she was awakened by her mother who told her that the archbishop of Canterbury and Lord Conyngham were waiting to see her. She wrote in her journal:

> I got out of bed and went into the sittingroom (only in my dressing gown), and alone, and saw them. Lord Conynham then acquainted me that my poor Uncle, the King, was no more . . . and consequently that I am Queen. Lord Conynham knelt down and kissed my hand. Since it has pleased Providence to place me in this station, I shall do my utmost to fulfil my duty towards my country: I am very young and perhaps in many, though not in all things inexperienced, but I am sure that very few have more real good will and more real desire to do what is fit and right than I have.[383]

Victoria was not only Queen of the United Kingdom of Great Britain and Ireland, but she was also Empress of India. During the Victorian era, England controlled more of the earth than had any country in history. Lord Macaulay, historian and essayist, put it this way:

> The English had become the greatest and most highly civilized people that ever the world saw; they have spread their dominion over every quarter of the globe . . . have created a maritime power which would annihilate in a quarter of an hour the navies of Tyre, Athens, Carthage, Venice and Genoa together, have carried the

> science of healing, the means of locomotion and correspondence, every mechanical art, every manufacture, every thing that promotes the convenience of life, to a perfection which our ancestors would have thought magical.[384]

That summer on 28 July 1837, the Queen gave a concert at Buckingham Palace. It was the first concert given there since her accession to the throne as she was not formally crowned till 1838. The usual members of the Italian Opera sang—Lablache, Grisi, Tamburini, Rubini, and, making an appearance after many years, Giuditta Pasta, who returned to sing that season at the King's Theatre, now renamed Her Majesty's. Lablache sang, "Oh! Guardate che igura!" from *La prova di un'opera seria* with Grisi. Grisi sang the aria "l'Ah! si fugga" from *Il Degonda*. On 1 August, Queen Victoria wrote to her uncle King Leopold:

> I have resumed my singing lessons with Lablache twice a week, which form an agreeable recreation in the midst of all the business I have to do. He is such a good old soul, and greatly pleased to go on with him. I admire the music of *the Huguenots* very much, but I do not sing it, as I prefer Italian to French for singing greatly. I have learned in the beginning of the season many of your old favorites, which I hope to sing with you when we meet.[385]

The Queen had a very busy schedule that year; however, she was never too busy not to attend the theater.

The elegant, gaslit new Theatre Royal Lyceum opened on 16 November with Frédéric Lablache in Donizetti's *L'Elisir d'amore* singing Dr. Dulcamara; he was very successful. This famous theater, situated just off the Strand—also called the English Opera House—was rebuilt on the site of the old Lyceum that had burned down in 1834.[386] Many famous actors and actresses have contributed to the glory of the Lyceum: the most well known in the early years were Mme. Ristori, Mme. Vestris, Mary Keeley, John Braham, the tenor, Fanny Kelly, C. J. Mathews and in later years, Henry Irving, Ellen Terry, Sarah Bernhardt, Forbes Robinson, William Terriss, George Alexander, Charles Santley, Kate Terry, Charles Fechter, and William Harrison to name a few.

The Lyceum later was better known for plays, but on many occasions, the house was used for opera. *The London Times* writes of Frédéric's voice:

F. Lablache was very good as Dulcamara; his voice is not powerful, but he uses it with good judgement, and went through his comic scene with great spirit and humour. He avoids the wretched practice of speaking instead of singing, which is so common among Italian buffo singers.

On 23 November 1837 and 20 January 1838, the young Queen attended the Italian buffa opera at the Lyceum. Those nights, young Frédéric Lablache sang, according to the *Times*. In November 1837, he sang in Donizetti's *L'Elisir d'amore*, *Il Campanello* (The Bell), coupled with Rossini's *Il Inganno Felice* (called an incident rather than a story). The *Times* reviewed the performance of *Le nozze di Figaro:* "Young Lablache is a judicious singer . . . the house was very well attended." He continued to sing through the winter season. The Queen returned for *Un'avventura di Scaramuccia* on 23 December and 23 January 1838. The following is another *Times* review:

Young Frédéric Lablache sang the title role of Scaramuche—or rather Scaramuccia—with taste and expression. With Miss Fanny Wyndham, who sang the trouser role of the Count Pontigny, a role she has had great success with. The prima donna Mad. Scheroni sang Sadrina. The part of Lelio was well sung by Catoni. Bellini sang Tomasso . . . it is one of the best things of the extravagant buffo school. Miss Wyndham looked well . . . but sang the gay air of the Don Juan cast in the tone of a solemn chant!

The Paris season went well for Luigi Lablache, singing the same operas as the year before. Two hours after a performance of *Don Giovanni*, in the early morning of 15 January 1838, a terrible fire broke out at the Salle Favart, home of the Théâtre-Italien. From *The Musical World*, "We hear of a sad event at the Theatre Italian":

On the 14th instant, the *Don Giovanni*, was performed with the strong cast Grisi, Persiani, Albertazzi, Tamburini, Rubini, and Lablache. About an hour after the doors had closed, the Opera-house was discovered to be on fire, and was very shortly reduced to a heap of ruins. The prevalent belief is that the accident arose from some of the fireworks used in the infernal gulf into which *Commandatore* so righteously hurls the incorrigible libertine. The managers were MM. Severini and Roberts. The former leaped from a window at nearly the top of the building, and was instantaneously killed; the latter saved himself by means of a ladder and rope. The justice of the remark that fires are coincidental has this winter been verified to a melancholy extent. London deplores the destruction of her noble Exchange, St. Petersburg of the largest palace in Europe, capable, it is said, of accommodating 12,000 persons. This accident happened whilst the Emperor and Empress were at the theatre witnessing the performances of Mdle. Taglioni. The losses sustained by several individuals are irreparable. In Paris Rossini had an apartment in the theatre, and the whole of his musical library, which is said to be valued at upwards of 200,000 fx., is entirely destroyed, besides many rare and invaluable manuscripts. The library of M. Kalaproth, the musical repertory of the director, and his furniture, have been saved. We are enabled to contradict the report that all the scores belonging to the theatre are lost. A great quantity of old music has been more than half burnt, but we are assured that the scores of the new pieces are all safe, having been placed in a part of the building which the flames did not reach. It is understood that M. Lablache has sustained an immense and irreparable loss by the death of M. Severini, who acted as his agent in the investments of his savings, and in whose hands were all the documents by which was secured the accumulated property derived from twenty years arduous exertions in his profession. If this be so, M.Lablache and his numerous family will be totally ruined.

Later, however, this report of Lablache losing his savings was found to be erroneous. The Italien was moved to the Salle Ventadour and later to the Odeon. Another fire had claimed the famous Venetian Theatre La Fenice on 12 December 1836; however, like a true phoenix, it rose rapidly from its ashes and reopened on the 26 December 1837.[387]

In the autumn of 1837 in Paris, Donizetti had revealed again his great dramatic powers with another *opera seria* in three acts, the historical masterpiece, *Lucia di Lammermoor*, based on Sir Walter Scott's melodramatic story "The Bride of Lammermoor." A Gothic piece full of gore and frustrated love set in the Scottish Highlands, the opera opened for the first time on 26 September 1835 in Naples (Teatro San Carlo). The title role of the doomed heroine, who goes mad and stabs her bridegroom, was very successfully executed by the beautiful coloratura soprano Fanny Tacchinardi Persiani.

The Neapolitan librettist Salvatore Cammarano claimed international fame after this opera soon became an all-time tremendous favorite. A master of melodrama and stories of unfrequented love and romance, his works fitted the Romantic ideal of the age. Author of thirty-six libretti, one of his most famous compositions was Giuseppe Verdi's *Il Trovatore*.

Lucia was followed by another new Donizetti production, *Parisina,* on 24 February 1838. An *opera seria* taken from a poem by Lord Byron (text by Felice Romani) was sung in Paris by Luigi Lablache, Giulia Grisi, Rubini, and Tamburini.

Later that year, both operas were shown in London. *Lucia di Lammermoor* would triumph over *Parisina*. The more popular *Lucia* would enter the international circuit, traveling with worldwide success. With this opera, Donizetti became established as a foremost composer of Italian opera during that decade.

These years, however, had brought deep personal tragedy to Donizetti—first the death of his parents and then the death of his beloved wife Virginia in 1837 and their newborn son. In great pain, he writes to Antonio Vasselli on 12 August: "Without a father, without a mother, without a wife, without children . . . Why do I labor on?" But he labored on; his *Roberto Devereux* opened at the San Carlo on 29 October 1837. Afterward, he spent New Year's alone in Venice, awaiting the opening of *Maria di Rudenz* at the new theater La Fenice. The opera was a failure, mostly attributed to the very gloomy state of mind and deep sorrow he was suffering.[388]

By the end of February, the Theatre Royal, Dublin, Ireland, welcomed Mr. Mitchell's Italian Opera Company straight from London's Royal Lyceum theater in the Strand. They proudly announced:

> Mr. Mitchell, Manager of the Opera Buffa London . . . begs respectfully to announce that he has made arrangements with Mr. Caleraft for a series of twelve representations, at this theatre, of the most popular Italian Operas recently performed in London. Accordingly, on Tuesday 27 February 1838, was produced for the first time in Dublin Donizetti's, *Opera Buffa—L'Elisir d'amore*. Nemorino—Signor Catone, Belcore—Signor Bellini; Dr. Dulcamara—Signor Frédéric Lablache; Adena was sung by Madame Franceschini. The conductor Signor Nergi. The selections from the following operas: Donizetti's *L'Elisir d'amore, Elisa e Claudio* by Mercadante; *Le Nozze di Figaro*, Mozart, *L'Italiana in Algieri*, Rossini, *Betly, Il Campanelli*, Donizetti. *Nina, Pazza per Amore,* Copola; *Un Avventura di Scaramuccia*, by Luigi Ricci. A more perfect quartet of voices has seldom come together.

All the details of the season were carefully recorded in the *Annals of Theatre Royal*:[389]

> Here, the praise goes to Catone... Some old opera goers will remember the lovely pure tenor Catone, his delivery of *Una futiva Lagrima* really enchanted his listeners; in fact, all through the work he carried the audience by storm. It may be safely recorded that, with the exception of Mario, Rubini and Giuglini, no tenor ever created such an effect as Catone on the Dublin stage. Unfortunately, this was his first and last engagement in Dublin; he was killed by a fall from a window in Naples. Frédéric Lablache, son of the giant (in talent and person) of the same name, happily is well-known as a first-rate artist and musician. Signor Bellini, an artist of perhaps the highest quality, completed the excellent quartet.[390]

Through March, the company featured *Un'avventura di Scaramuccia* with Frédéric as Scaramuccia. On 3 April, for his benefit, *Elisa e Claudio* was performed with some detached pieces, which included the Moor's melody:

> The beautiful *Oft in the Stilly Night*, sung by Signor Frédéric Lablache and Signor Catone, as a duet, received a tremendous encore. The voices blended exquisitely, and the slightly broken English seemed to lend additional interest to the music.[391]

Mr. Mitchell and company, by popular request, were asked to stay for four more nights. Frédéric Lablache among other operas sang the title role of Donizetti's *Torquato Tasso*. Afterward, they all left for Belfast and Edinburgh. On 12 May, *The Musical World* printed a review of Ms. Wyndham:[392]

> The Italian Opera at Edinburgh... The performances of the Italian company give universal satisfaction. The house was crowded on Thursday night, when the entertainments were Ricci's opera *Un Avventura di Scaramuccia*. The scene where Tomaso the peasant intrudes among the band of players, and is, after much uproar, taken to the guard house, was highly ludicrous and the animation and activity of Bellini and the comic effect was all together admirable. The subsequent scene, in which Lablache, Catone and Sanquirico appear as Scaramuccia, Lelio and Dominico... and Miss Fanny Wyndham made her debut in Scotland in the part of

the Count of Pontigny . . . her graceful and imposing presence, joined to her vocal talents produced a deep impression on the audience. Her voice is a contralto of the richest and most melodious quality, flexible and of surpassing sweetness, though by no means powerful. Her lowest notes are exceedly beautiful and the compass is considerable for a voice of this kind. Her articulation of notes is distinct, and she sings with perfect ease, and with exquisite taste and expression. Her mellifluous notes captivated every ear, while her whole demeanour is marked by an ease and finished grace that gives fine effect to her other talents. With what softness and beauty and appropriate expression did she sing the first air which introduced her to her admiring audience, *Mi fa Lelio brutto muso;* and when Scaramuccia asks her, in the character of the Count, if she has decided to marry Elena, and hints at the reproaching voice of the world, what a fine expression she gave to the words . . . *Il mondo, o babbuino, il mondo ridera.*[393] To the song "Le piu leggiadre e amabili," she imparted unspeakable softness and beauty. Lablache fully sustained his part in this scene; and to the song, *Deh! Prego, lasciatela partire innocente*, he gave an express of tenderness that was truly touching. (*Edinburgh Courant*, 12 May 1838).

Mr. Mitchell's Italian Opera Company did not return to Dublin again. The singers of the opera buffa dispersed to join other companies most probably because of the death of the tenor Catone. Fanny Wyndham later appeared at Covent Garden and sang alongside Frédéric Lablache at Her Majesty's. Not until 1841 did they reappear again in Dublin. The season opened with *I Puritani* that proved to be a remarkable one.

Unforgettable in the entire history of the Theatre Royal was the debut of the new tenor Mario from Italy. Joining the two Lablaches were Mme. Giulia Grisi and her cousin soprano Ernesta Grisi.

After that triumph, Luigi and Frédéric returned to the London arena for a tremendous schedule of concerts planned for the coronation of Queen Victoria. Frédéric's horizons now had expanded with his London winter season of 1837-38 and his highly successful tour with Mr. Mitchell's Italian opera buffa.

Chapter Twenty

Coronation Year

1838-1839

Johann Strauss and his famous orchestra, of some twenty-six players, swept into London on 12 April 1838. They were engaged to play at Buckingham Palace on 10 May for an important state ball. For this grand occasion,[394] Strauss dedicated his waltz *Hommage a la Reine d'Angleterre* to Her Majesty Queen Victoria. The coronation was not only an important world event, but it heralded in a new era and the beginning of a time of great historical achievement.

Great honors had been bestowed on Strauss by the French, and before long, his enchanting Viennese waltzes were played in all the fashionable salons of London and Paris. Strauss's greatest triumph came after five concerts at the Willis Rooms when he was to be asked to play at Buckingham Palace. Creating entertainment and pleasure for the coronation became Strauss's chief task, and the orchestra provided the best entertainment for all these celebrations. Prior to the coronation, there was a frenzy of balls, concerts, and garden parties. The baroness Rothschild even had a small hall built on her estate for one of his concerts.[395]

All of Strauss's triumphs came to a climax in the early summer 1838 when he took over London society's events. Having given 86 concerts in Paris, Strauss and his orchestra now gave 72 concerts in England in 120 days.[396] Lablache sang at Buckingham Palace on 18 May and 22 June. Strauss played at the Hanover Square Rooms (18 April); the *London Times* tells us:

> The pieces performed were chiefly his own waltzes, but they were done in a manner most extraordinary . . . The most eccentric instruments such as bells, castanets, cracking whips etc., are occasionally introduced . . .

Victoria wrote to her uncle: "I have been dancing till past four o'clock this morning; we have had a charming ball . . ."[397] Recognized everywhere as the Waltz King, Strauss's music became the craze of young Victorians. Evidently, it became known that Lablache was a great dancer; he was certainly involved everywhere in the celebrations. A small note about him was written up in *The Musical World* under the heading "Lablache and the Duchess":

> At a fete given by the Duchess of St. Alban's at Holly Lodge, in the year of 1835, Signor Lablache was frequently observed as one of the most . . . prominent, and indeed inveterate—dancers of the evening. When about to take his leave of the hospitable hostess, her Grace remarked that Signor Lablache looked very overheated by his recent exertions on the "liqht fantastic toe" and kindly asked if he was provided with a cloak. Being informed that he was not furnished with one, and fearing he might catch a cold, she called one of the household who was desired to see the 'primo basso' was attended to. In a few minutes afterwards Lablache was seen seated in one of her Grace's carriages, tastefully enveloped in the ample folds of a very large blanket! Looking rather pleased with himself no doubt.

The young Clara Anastasia Novello was a close friend of Lablache; she was also dubbed "the greatest English soprano of her time."[398] Well-known, she had sung with Malibran at the festivals.

> Like Clara, Maria Felicita loved dancing and was celebrated, too, for her Tarantella. One winter's day Clara met Lablache proudly wrapped in what was quite obviously large Witney blanket, and to her mirthful inquiries, answered that at a party given by a Duchess . . . he and Malibran had been persuaded to dance the Tarantella and got so hot that the Duchess, alarmed, had presented them each with one of her specially woven blankets in which to return home.[399]

Lablache would entertain Clara and her vast family by placing two lighted candles either side of his face on a table; there he held them spellbound while he acted a thunderstorm. "He left an indelible picture on Clara's young impressionable mind surpassed only by Paganini playing *The Witches'*

Dance from Weber's *Freischutz*," writes Mackenzie-Grieve, Novello's biographer.[400]

Clara Novello was a member of the Royal Society of Female Musicians established in 1839. Other members were Frances Lablache (Fanny) and Miss. Betts. The society patronesses were Queen Victoria, the Queen Dowager, and the Duchess of Kent. The society of a modest forty odd female members was created to give assistance to destitute female musicians.[401]

A sad event in May was to personally mar the celebrations that year for the Lablache family. A short notice was posted in *The Musical World*:

> M. Lablache we regret to learn, has recently lost his third daughter, an amiable and highly accomplished young lady who was on the eve of being united in marriage to M. Gauterau the celebrated artist. She fell victim to that insidious disease, consumption, which ever seems to mark its victims the fairest, and those most distinguished for great natural endowments.(This daughter was Rosina).[402]
> *I Puritani*, has consequently, been postponed until Saturday.[403]

The Coronation of Victoria took place at Westminster Abbey on Thursday, 28 June 1838. The opera was cancelled that night because of all the people celebrating on the streets. During the Coronation, the Strauss orchestra played "God Save the Queen" outside on the street while the church bells all rang and the cannons fired.[404] A special concert was held later on 2 July at the abbey. All the Italian singers took part. Queen Victoria continued to be a enthusiastic opera fan, visiting Her Majesty's Theatre (renamed in her honor) at least thirty-six times.[405]

An important Irish composer of the time was Michael Balfe, a close friend of Lablache. A baritone, he studied singing under Filippo Galli in Milan and sang in Italy before coming to London. Embarking on a successful career as a composer, he wrote *The Siege of La Rochelle* for Drury Lane in 1835 and launched Maria Malibran shortly before her death in his opera *The Maid of Artois*.

For the Coronation year, Balfe wrote a new Italian opera for Her Majesty's Theatre, *Falstaff,* the first Italian opera written for the theatre since Arne's *Olimpiade*. Lablache proudly sang Shakespeare's famous protagonist Sir John Falstaff without, however, the usual costume adjustments, such as padded stomach enlargers! Of course he was *en naturel* and needed no help. He sang the the role admirably with a supporting cast of Grisi as Mistress Ford, Rubini as Fenton, and Tamburini as Master Ford. While the cast could not have been finer, the critics such as Chorley gave it terrible reviews. The opera did not survive. Yet the review from *The Musical World* was positive:[406]

> On the second night its success was unquestionable according to the numerous and fashionable company, including the presence of Her Majesty Queen Victoria, the Duchess of Kent and many distinguished foreigners.

"*Falstaff*, regarded as a comic opera, is a failure," wrote another critic, going on to slaughter Balfe. "The overture is feeble . . . he would succeed better in English than in the Italian libretto, he can't seem to decide what school of music he is following or what composer he was imitating." The basis of the nasty review—it was a sort of patchwork of everything is as follows:

> Here was a good opportunity for Mr. Balfe to have introduced a *scena* for his hero . . . something for Lablache, descriptive of his mishaps in the buck basket; and we think this great singer rather scurvily treated . . . for in fact Lablache has not a good line of music to take care of anything! Mr Balfe has been lucky in having such artists for his opera. Lablache's acting was inimitable. Such a protagonist would have made Shakespeare's heart leap for joy to look upon. His walk, swagger, wink and leer were worth all the notes he had to sing. Rubini looked like the Flying Dutchman, and the old English costume did not even sit well on Tamburini. We doubt that either liked his part . . . Grisi exerted herself strenuously, and sang with grace and vigour. The most amusing part of this national opera was the a la Swiss scenery . . . this is BUFFA with a vengeance.

Frances Rogers clearly didn't know about Lablache's earlier trials when he wrote, "If he had been born forty years later, what a Hans Sachs, what a Wotan and what a Falstaff he would have made."[407] Another critic who didn't know about Lablache's earlier trials either, wrote,

> Lablache died too soon to sing Verdi's *Falstaff*. This deprives the world of what unquestionably would have been one of the most perfect impersonations in all operatic history!

Verdi admired Lablache tremendously and had him in mind for the role of King Lear, but the opera never materialized.[408]

The Strauss band continued to tour England. Strauss realized as much as two hundred pounds a night. Touring the provinces and Ireland before returning to France left him totally exhausted, minus some of his musicians. Relentless, Strauss envisioned more tours before allowing his band to return to Vienna, and it was not until Strauss himself became deathly ill that he consented to return home.[409]

In Rossini's *Otello,* or *The Moor of Venice,* the role of the father of Desdemona was a part that Queen Victoria much admired. Lablache sang the role of Elmiro (Brambatito in Shakespeare's play) through 1831-52 in London and in Paris. *Otello,* one of Rossini's *opera seria* masterpieces, is an unusual piece because Otello, Iago, Rodrigo are all tenors. It had been a showcase for the great tenor Manuel Garcia, father of Maria Malibran, and another great Italian tenor Andrea Nozzari. Both singers had sung the lead role for over a decade, and their voices were the voices that Rossini had in mind when he wrote the opera. Did Lablache insert extra arias to enlarge his role? Most of the reviews during *Otello's* popularity in London write of the voice of Lablache far more favorably than other members of the cast and often at length.

> The Doge (Elmiro) denunciating his daughter (Desdemona) is perhaps, as treated by Lablache and Grisi, the most splendid lyric-tragic passage in the opera ever seen on any stage. The prostration of Grisi before the lightning blast of Lablache's malediction is truly awful. We thought we almost heard the dreadful lines from "Troilus and Cressida" issue from the angry father's lips: "Now Hell's bluest plagues receive her quick, with all her crimes upon her let her sink spotted down; let the dark Host make room, and point, and hiss her as she goes. Let the most branded Ghosts of all her sex rejoice and cry. Here comes a blacker Fiend!"
>
> The terrible fierceness of Lablache is in those lines. Mario as the Moor serves but as an accessory to the picture; he cannot stand out in any great prominence against the other mighty portraits. Garcia was the only Otello who could have withstood Lablache's Elimiro; but still Mario is very charming in the part and sings its music beautifully.

Remember, Isabel Colbran had created the role of Desdemona in the first 1816 *Otello* performance at the Fondo in Naples: it was also Pasta,

Malibran, and later Viardot who were all great interpreters of the heroic role of Desdemona. Now the mantle was passed down to Giulia Grisi, who rose to match the exploits of her predecessors before her and held her own as she emerged to become the most prominent soprano of her time. Brilliant in both serious and comic roles from the 1820s to the 1860s, she reigned supreme and endured much longer than her other rivals, Jenny Lind and Henrietta Sontag.

Maria Malibran was considered extraordinary in her time even though the voice was uneven and often erratic. Queen Victoria, however, preferred and even adored the beautiful Grisi. Grisi was her favorite. She was delighted when she saw the singer out riding in the park and wrote in her journal:[410]

> She's so pale off stage, but has not at all a delicate appearance. On the contrary she has a very slight pinkish hue over her face. She looks very pretty and mild . . . I know no singer I like as well as Grisi . . . She is perfection (to my feeling), she is VERY PRETTY and an EXQUISITE and CHARMING actress! . . . Such a lovely mild expression . . . such beautiful dark eyes with fine long eyelashes . . . her beautiful dark hair . . . She is quiet, ladylike and unaffected in her manners.

The fatherless Victoria drew Lablache and Grisi over and over from the scene in *Otello* in which Desdemona finds that everyone, even her father, has lost faith in her:

> The member of the quartet (Puritani Quartet) whom Victoria came to know the best was Luigi Lablache, the monumental basso. Lablache had a genius for *opera buffa* roles, to which his great size and nimbleness suited him, as well as for *opera seria*, in which, as the Druid in *Norma* or the leading Roundhead in *I Puritani*, he dominated majestically. She drew him more often than any figure. One particular scene . . . Lablache towering over the little Grisi as Desdemona as she pleads for understanding from her father Elmiro '*Se il padre m'abbandona, da chi sperar pieta?* ('If my father abandons me from whom else can I hope for pity?') was a line carved deep in Victoria's memory.[411]

She also discovered that Lablache did not share her own high opinion of Grisi, but criticized the singer's way of swallowing before a roulade—"a habit she has contracted from fear of failing . . . I do not think he quite likes her." "But even Lablache's reservations did not dim her attraction for Victoria," writes Warner.[412] On another occasion that year, a reviewer in The *Musical World* wrote:

> We never admired Grisi's singing of 'Let the bright seraphim.' She cannot understand nor execute the Handel divisions, and the air therefore becomes a mere Italian b*ravura* by her style of execution. She sings out of tune, arising probably from the feeling of her own incompetency.

Here, the composer Balfe gives his impressions to a friend of Grisi's debut: "If I could have seen an angel from heaven, I could never have dreamed I should have seen one so beautiful." Of Lablache, in *Otello* on 23 April 1838, we again feel the strength and expression from this review in the *London Times*:

> Grisi's performance is too well-known to require any Notice . . . it was perfect in all respects as it has always been . . . Lablache was surprisingly fine . . . there was true grandeur in the words "*Empia ti malidicto*" when he discovers that Desdemona had pledged herself to Otello, and the uttermost pathos in the look that followed . . . the painful reflection that his curse had fallen upon the being whom on earth he most loved. His indignation at the discovery afterwards was in no degree less powerful. There is no concealing the fact that Lablache in tragic or in comic effect is among the fortunate few doomed to be equally great, and attain in both the highest range in his art.[413]

Donizetti's *Matilda di Shabran* was not well-received when it was shown on 7 June, and the production according to the *Times* had no merit. On 21 August 1838, a small column appeared in *The Musical World* headed "Naples Extract from a Letter," dated 6 August:

> The Queen of Naples and the mountain were both delivered on Wednesday last, August 1st, the former a male child, the latter a very magnificent eruption. On Wednesday at midday three streams of lava flowed down over the old pathway up. On Thursday at midday a fresh flow of lava took place over the same ground.

> On Thursday night I went up close to the crater to view the fires coming from two mouths (situated very close to each other), then rocks were hurtled all over, and the roaring was louder than I had ever heard it, except from the eruption on the 1st of April 1835. On Saturday it began to decrease, and yesterday the lava no longer flowed. Today there is not much smoke from the mouths. As if to prove me a liar at this moment looking up from my paper, the mountain gave a great heave, and the action started again. Now it is over; perhaps tonight there will be a relapse.

London's Vauxhall Garden rotunda announced that for a Signor Venafra's benefit 21 August 1838 in addition to the usual entertainments, Mme. Grisi, Mme. Persiani, Mme. Caramoli, Signore Lablache, Rubini, Ivanhoff, etc., "would lend their services." Again *The Musical World* writes:

> The opera corps arrived very late at the rotunda because the artists were detained by another concert at Drury Lane. However, the company waited with the greatest of patience and were amused in the interim by the vaudeville and other entertainments . . . the singing was first class . . . and the entertainments of the evening concluded with a brilliant display of fireworks.

Lablache opened in Paris in *Otello* on 2 October 1838. Donizetti arrived on 21 October. Lablache first concluded the usual annual concert tours of the English provinces. Now trains were linking up with the major northern cities; it was easier for the singers to travel. People in the provinces eagerly waited for the Italian Opera tours.

Donizetti's successful *Lucia di Lammermoor* premiered in Paris on 12 December 1837 with the original Lucia, Fanny Tacchinardi Persiani who created *Lucia* in Naples and sang the role in Venice and Vienna. The opera was first heard in London on 5 April 1838 at Her Majesty's. Persiani sang Lucia for six seasons at Her Majesty's and a dozen seasons at the Théâtre-Italien.

Donizetti's obligations in Naples were over. He set sail for Marseilles and Paris where he started rehearsals for his new opera *Roberto Devereux*. On his departure from Naples, Donizetti clearly had high expectations of fame and greater financial rewards in Paris. With his agent Accursi, he secured contracts, and at last he was on his way to introduce his *Roberto Devereux* and his comic opera *L'Elisir d'amore*. Lablache's heavy agenda that season consisted of eight operas, including *La Gazza ladra*, *Norma*, and *Don*

Giovanni. He sang Dr. Dulcamara in *L'Elisir d'amore* on 17 January 1839 for the first time in the French capital.

Donizetti wrote the role of Dr. Dulcamara with Lablache in mind; it proved over time to be one of his greatest comic roles. Unfortunately, we have no reviews of Lablache singing *L'Elisir d'amore* in Naples at the Teatro Fondo on 13 April 1834, and then later again on 17 August 1834, at Teatro San Carlo, again with Fanny Persiani.

Weinstock tells us, "In June of 1834 after the seasonal closing of the Italien, Rossini left for Italy in the company of manager Robert and director Severini, who went in search of new operas and new singers. Rossini was welcomed like a homecoming conqueror on 15 June, when he reached Bologna." Lablache wrote to Severini who was the director of the Théâtre-Italien maybe during the summer of 1834 (but there is no date on the letter),

> Dear Severini,
>
> I hear with pleasure that you have arrived in Bologna with our good Rossini because I am absolutely sure that the air of his birthland will contribute very much to the perfect greatness of that extraordinary man.
>
> Regarding *L'Elisir d'amore*, I do not have any difficulty in `doing it'—but never for a debut because it is a very cold (sic) work, even more so in Paris where they know it with a better libretto.
>
> I ask you to think about my debut in something sure. I shall be in Paris in the first days of September. Embrace dear Rossini a thousand, and then another thousand, times. Regards to Robert and Anna.
>
> Il tuo L. Lablache
> P.S. Ricordi asks me to send you his regards[414]

Before his triumphs with *Anna Bolena* and *Lucia di Lammermoor*, Donizetti clocked up more successes with his buffa operas than his *opera seria in Naples*; at first, his lighter works were popular, but his serious works were not. This all changed with the onslaught of *Anna Bolena* and *Lucia*. The Neapolitan librettist Salvadore Cammarano had a lot to do with this opera's rapid establishment in the international repertoire. Clearly, it had been difficult for Donizetti to work in Naples; although he had succeeded there, he was looking forward to go and leave the tiresome and constant conflict with petty managers.

Difficulties always arose because of the very complicated arrangements and politics in Naples for lending out singers for a certain length of time and withdrawing them. The battles behind the scenes were as dramatic as any onstage and sometimes worse. The managers were often trying to treat the singers shabbily, and there were times they even took advantage of Lablache's good nature. This anecdote was titled "Lablache Furibondo."[415]

> Lablache storms into the theatre to berate another of those scurvy impresarios. What is it this time? Back salary still outstanding after three weeks patient waiting? Lablache's name placed a bit too discreetly on the posters? Whatever the cause the bass is in thunder . . . and, remember, that's six feet plus and some two hundred pounds of him. But the impresario knows his man . . . "My dear Lablache?" he says. "You're too good natured to feel this way by yourself, so your wife has loyally puffed you up and sent you down here to press me for payment." "Unfair!" cries Lablache . . . "I have come here to have a row, and you disarm me with your pleasantry!" "My dear fellow, you were not made to have rows. Go home and tell your wife I said so." They shake hands on it, and Lablache starts out, at the door he pauses . . . "No . . . I think I shall tell her you weren't in."

L'Elisir d'amore, Donizetti's romantic opera buffa, became an instant success story, beloved since it was first performed. William Ashbrook points out the differences between *Il Barbiere di Siviglia* and *L'Elisir d'amore*:[416]

> To contrast Rossini's *Il Barbiere* with *L'Elisir d'amore* on the level of sentiment is to see that *Il Barbiere* contains so much whirling wit and ingenuity, such sheer exuberance, that one scarcely notices that it characteristically defines situations in terms of external description. For all its masterful comedy, *Il Barbiere* stems from a style and approach that takes matters of the heart for granted and wastes little time evoking them. *L'Elisir d'amore,* on the other hand, is a romantic opera buffa, wherein the conflict is ultimately resolved, not through trickery or any outward circumstance, but through Adina's coming to appreciate the true value of Nemorino's constancy.

Lablache, in the role of the rollicking jovial quack Dr. Dulcamara, the charlatan with a heart, must have been very enjoyable to hear, the huge figure towering pleasantly over a cast of gullible countryfolk bumpkins. Lablache played the role to perfection as it was one of his most successful comic roles in Paris, then afterward, he continued singing in the opera's debut at Her Majesty's. Mario took over the role of Nemorino in Paris and London for the following seasons through 1843. The *Athenaeum* gives a review of the first performance of *L'Elisir d'amore* at her Majesty's Theatre on 13 June 1839:

> We can hardly call to mind an opera so exquisitely cast as *L'Elisir d'amore*, which was given for here. Barring a slight meagerness of voice, especially conspicuous in her wonderful final bravura, Madame Persiani entirely fills our idea of Adina, while Signor Mario, with his exquisitely musical tones and prepossessing face and figure, neither of which have been trained so as to tell upon the stage in more heroic parts, is, because of that very simplicity and slight awkwardness, so exact a representive of the innocent peasant Nemorino, that we found ourselves forgetting the stage lights and shabby old trees of the back scene, and feeling a gentle concern and interest as in the real story. It is superfluous to say of Lablache—who is always the best singer, the best actor, and the best dresser of his company—that in Dulcamara, the quack, he added another capital and mirth-provoking figure to his long and singularly varied gallery of wonderful characters. Tamburini's Belcore too is the best of his comic parts—impudent, vulgar, and always the soldier's impudence and vulgarity. Add to this, that there are no second rates to spoil such an assemblage of talent by their inferiority—that the music is Donizetti's very best; melodious, sprightly, and sometimes, if not always, new—and we may then well express our wonder that the opera has been so coldly received by an audience which last year applauded the dismal *Parisina* and which this year tolerates the yet more dismal *Lucrezia Borgia*. The only cause for this indifference must be, that *L'Elisir d'amore* is on too small a scale for the great stage and orchestra of the Haymarket, and that the palates of "the subscribers and general public" are so habituated to the instruments so imposingly announced by Lablache in *La prova di un'opera seria*, to wit, the "long drum" and others of its noisy family, that no composition, unless dressed up with such fierce and exaggerated condiment, is any longer tasted with relish.

Lablache and Fanny Persiani continued to sing in this opera together through the 1840s. Then, both sang *L'Elisir d'amore* in St. Petersburg on separate occasions, but never sang together there. Lablache sang with her for the last time in 1850 in *Don Pasquale* in Paris.

A month before *L'Elisir d'amore's* debut in Paris, on 1 December 1838, a young tenor Giovanni Matteo de Candia, later known simply as Mario, entered the operatic scene singing in *Robert le Diable* at the Paris Grand Opera. His destiny would be to replace Rubini as leading tenor of the era.

Mario was not at all like Rubini. His figure was slim, his demeanor elegant and refined, and unlike Rubini, he came from an aristocratic family. His father was a general in the Piedmontese Army and later appointed governor of Nice. Giovanni Matteo Cavaliere di Candia was born in Cagliari, Sardinia, on 18 October 1810.[417] Leaving his family, he chose to abandon a military life and become a singer. Coming to Paris in 1836, he signed himself simply as Mario, and within four years, he was already singing at the Paris Opera. He first appeared in London at Her Majesty's Theatre on 6 June 1839 in *Lucrezia Borgia* with Giulia Grisi, Tamburini, Ernesta Grisi, and Lablache. He sang opposite Rubini in the same season when Rubini sang *Sonnambula*, with Frédéric Lablache and Persiani at Mario's benefit on 25 July. Critic Chorley writes:

> Signor Mario was a Hyperion born, who had only to be seen and heard, and the enchantment was complete . . . The new Romeo of the Italian stage . . . possessing a handsome presence and a delicious voice . . . his success is complete but he must work hard to make it lasting.[418]

Mario's natural elegance and sweet style of singing was very different to the voice and style of Rubini. Mario was thrust into a difficult position—to follow and replace the King of Tenors whose wonderful voice had dominated the stages of Europe and thrilled audiences for so many years. With next to no musical training, he was at first classified by some as an amateur (Chorley), and indeed it was true, but what he lacked in training he made up with his youthful voice, appearance, and romantic charm. Chorley writes,

> There have been better singers—there have been better Musicians—there may have been better voices—than Signor Mario. There has been no more favorite artist on the stage, in the memory of man

or women than he. It was not, however, till the season of 1846 that he took the place of which no wear and tear of Time has been able to deprive him.[419]

Only twenty-eight at his debut (late for a newcomer), with the natural ease of a born aristocrat, he asserted himself and started at the top and continued to stay there conquering audiences at all the most important opera houses in Europe. Mario himself said, "I was not considered a success at any rate; and, in fact, my career did not begin until 1842, when I sang in Dublin with Tamburini, Grisi and Lablache, and Benedict as conductor. After that I returned to Paris and sang 'Rubini Repertoire,' in which I was most fortunate."[420] Chorley later remembers the following:

> In one point the career of Signor Mario has been Peculiar—it might be said unique. He will live in the world's memory as the best Opera lover ever seen: as one who in a range of parts, always difficult, often times insipid, never failed to give a charm and probability to the scene.[421]

Arriving at the scene just a few years before Rubini's retirement, after singing Meyerbeer's *Robert le Diable* and Donizetti's *Lucrezia Borgia* in London, he then debuted at Théâtre-Italien in *L'Elisir d'amore*. Clearly, operatic roles must have fallen into his hands easily for in less than four years he had sung in over a dozen parts: *Robert le Diable, Lucrezia Borgia, Norma, Le Comte Ory, L'Elisir d'amore, La Donna del lago, Il Barbiere di Siviglia, I Puritani, Lucia di Lammermoor, Beatrice di Tenda,* and *Sonnambula*.

Climbing to the top of his profession for Mario had apparently been fairly easy, and certainly, he deserved to be named Prince of Tenors and a very romantic one too. "Strange as it may be," said Mario, "I have never sung in Italy." Rogers writes:

> He was matchless too as a stage lover and a drawing room singer. His personality and voice were disquieting to the peace of mind of unattached ladies. It is related that once he was singing in a salon in Paris. The last line of his song was "Come with me to the woods." As he uttered the final syllables a young woman, who had been listening in a state of semi-hypnosis, rose to her feet and tottered towards him, murmuring, "I'm coming."[422]

Soon, Mario's romantic stage life became a reality when he fell in love with his leading lady, the beautiful Giulia Grisi. They were to become the most famous operatic couple of the mid-nineteenth century. Walter Mayard recollects:

> They were an incomparable pair; more liberally endowed by nature with every attribute of personal beauty, vocal power, and dramatic genius, than any of their rivals. Their union an inestimable gain to art, and their attachment to one another as romantic and devoted as that of any hero and heroine they ever impersonated. It was, at once, passionate and faithful; it was hallowed by their mutual pursuit in life; it sanctified their home; it gave incessantly renewed fire and zest to their representations upon the lyric stage.[423]

Mario and Grisi's lives were closely intertwined with that of Lablache as almost every season they were all together. Like a close family, the unrivalled Puritani Quartet continued under that title after Rubini retired. Tamburini still sang with them fairly often into the fifties until Lablache and Tamburini lost their health, diminished by the terrible winter seasons in St. Petersburg.

Mario and Grisi toured Russia (1849) and the United States of America (1854) and sang long past their prime, long past the time where good sense should have told them to retire. Rubini died after a short retirement at the Rubini Palace near Romano, between Milan and Verona.[424] He too had been lured by Russia's siren call of huge salaries. There he amassed a fortune, but he would pay the price. After his last trip to Russia in 1844, the cold climate seriously affected his voice, and he returned to Italy where he died in 1854.

Chapter Twenty-One

William Tell in London

1839

To the continued delight of Parisian audiences at the Théâtre-Italien, the singers Grisi, Tadolini, Persiani, Rubini, Ivanoff, Duprez, Tamburini, and Lablache staged a concert conducted by Donizetti at the Paris *Salle-Hertz* on 17 March. Wrapping up the season with *I Puritani*, Lablache returned to England to open another London season there on 9 April, featuring the same popular opera.[425]

The Queen attended; she was devoted to this opera. She adored Bellini and over a period of twenty years heard *Norma*, *I Puritani*, and *Sonnambula* often. Bellini was considered modern by Queen Victoria even though he incorporated the singing traditions of the old Italian bel canto method into his operas. When Bellini composed, he paid close attention to the poetry and the dramatic content, using Felice Romani as his major librettist, with exception of course being the libretti for *Puritani*.[426]

The method that Bellini learnt at the Naples Conservatory could be described as a style of writing in which the singer's delivery and musical expression of the poetry is prevalent over the orchestra, which was restrained. Composers of that time wrote for the particular skills of the singers who were hired for the production. The vocal score could be adapted and revised if need be, and nothing was regarded as unalterable. Bellini's operas faded in popularity toward the end of the nineteenth century with the onset of German Romantic opera and other changes in operatic trends. This shows a radical switch from poetic to musical domination.[427] By the beginning of the twentieth century, some of his operas disappeared and were rarely heard. Composers of the early nineteenth century wrote for singers agile enough to conquer the difficult high tessitura required by the bel canto roles.

In the 1950s, some of these operas were rediscovered with the arrival of such sopranos as Maria Callas and Joan Sutherland who made successful recordings and were able to sing in the florid style known as *canto spianato*, so characteristic of the melodies of Bellini. Sopranos today may take on Bellini, but there are few who can sing with required style and passion. Queen Victoria was indeed fortunate to hear *I Puritani* every season.

During the first part of the nineteenth century, after the social upheavals of the Napoleonic Wars had ended and before the period of Giuseppe Verdi, Giacomo Meyerbeer, and Richard Wagner's popularity, it was mainly the works of Rossini, Donizetti, and Bellini that flourished. Rossini, emulated by his contempories, was the foremost Italian composer of his time. While some opera composers fell short of Rossini's immediate European successes, many excelled in their own countries: Michael Balfe in England; Hector Berlioz and Giacomo Meyerbeer in France; Carl Von Weber's in the German-speaking countries and composer of *Der Freischutz*, a celebrated favorite during the 1830s. Though some Italian composers never succeeded abroad, some eventually became the established backbone of operatic entertainment worldwide. Major entertainment tastes quickly changed during the 1840s and continued through the rest of the century. French opera repertoire became fashionable intermingled with German opera, bringing out new and different composers' works to the forefront. These often were larger productions, featuring larger orchestras, presenting longer, dramatic, and heavier representations, such as the operas of Verdi, Meyerbeer, and Wagner. French composers emerging then were Charles Gounod, Auber, Halvey, etc., followed by Georges Bizet, composer of *Carmen*—one of the world's favorite operas. Most of these works surfaced after the death of Luigi Lablache.

Lablache's grandson and namesake, Luigi Frederick Lablache, a lead actor on the London stage during the last quarter of the nineteenth century, toured America successfully with the play *Carmen,* among other plays.[428]

Donizetti's operas were favorites with Queen Victoria; records indicate that by 1838 she had heard approximately fourteen Donizetti operas—all were widely represented at Her Majesty's. The Queen enjoyed the lighter works of Donizetti's *La Fille du régiment* and *L'Elisir d'amore,* as well as *Lucia di Lammermoor*.[429]

Another newcomer to Her Majesty's was Donizetti's *Lucrezia Borgia*, featuring Lablache, Grisi, and the tenor Mario. The premiere was on 6 June, 1839. First composed for La Scala of Milan, the opera, in two acts, is based on a drama by Victor Hugo.

The *Athenaeum* writes, "Its reception was rather cool at first with the critics. Soon however, it was accepted wholeheartedly." Giulia Grisi triumphed in the role of the wicked protagonist and now emerged as the reigning prima *Donna* of the era. The title role became one of Grisi's favorites. Joined by Mario and Lablache together, they repeated the opera almost every year at Her Majesty's—from June 1839 through June 1846. Lablache sang Alfonso for nine seasons.

Victorian audiences, fond of Romantic melodramas dripping with doom and gloom, did not mind whether the period depicted was medieval or Tudor, or chosen authors like Shakespeare, Victor Hugo or Walter Scott, all were popular. But they were quite critical of the music. Donizetti certainly pleased Victorian audiences with his melodramatic themes. Victoria attended *Lucrezia Borgia* many times that season to hear her favorites Giulia Grisi and Lablache. Grisi ruled supreme and not only in the mind of Victoria. *Lucrezia Borgia* would prove to be one of her best roles.[430] Victoria specially noticed the debut of the newcomer, the young Italian Mario. "A beautiful opera," she writes. "Grisi, Mario, Tamburini and Lablache sang beautifully!" Of Mario, she writes, "He is tall, young and handsome."[431]

Queen Victoria that year had a passion for the circus as well as the opera, and this well-known appetite was fulfilled by her enthusiastic attendance nearly every time the circus was in town. The Queen was fascinated by wild animals and as an animal lover, her state of mind and excitement would have been different to ours for in Victorian times, people had very little exposure to live animals from Africa and India. The royal family enjoyed animals—the palace was home to many pets, mostly dogs of all sizes and breeds:[432]

> Her life long devotion to circus dates from at least 1833, when a visit to Astley's Amphitheater to see Ducrow, most dashing of riders, as St. George and the Dragon . . . sent her hurrying for her sketchbook to record her impressions. The Drury Lane pantomime for Christmas of 1838 was Harlequin and Jack Frost, and included among its 'turns' Van Amburgh's lions. The Queen set out for the performance on the 10th of January 1839 with no great expectations, for the pantomime was 'noisy and nonsensical as usual.' But in the eleventh scene noise and nonsense were forgotten: 'The lions repaid all.' Although no Adonis ('He is a very strong man and has an awful squint in his eyes.') Van Amburgh fascinated the Queen by his mastery of the menagerie, which included lions, lionesses, tigers, cheetahs, and leopards: 'They all seem actuated by the most awful fear of him . . . he takes them by their paws, throws them down, makes them roar, and lies upon them after enraging them. It's quite beautiful to see, and makes me wish I could do the same!'[433]

Here, Rowell comments, "The notion of the Queen of England as a lady lion tamer defies rational thought; nevertheless, it suggests her growing appetite for authority . . . Van Amburgh lent his support to various operas (at Drury Lane Theatre) and the Queen had sat impatiently through Rossini's *William Tell*, and Balfe's *Maid of Artois* for 'what was worth *more* than *all* the rest.'"[434]

Here she may have also dismissed Lablache when he sang *Guglielmo Tell* (*William Tell*), except the version at Her Majesty's was in Italian and did not open till July. Macready, the famous actor, it seems was a bit jealous because she visited more "lion" performances than his *King Lear* performances at Covent Garden. He confided morosely to his diary: "Heard that the Queen was going to pay her third visit to Drury Lane Theatre to see the lions."[435] Actually, according to Rowell, Queen Victoria visited Drury Lane six times. The Queen was "unrepentant," writes Rowell; when she patronized Covent Garden to see the *Lady of Lyons* again with Rob Roy, she noted, "I was much more amused at Drury Lane, though I liked *The Lady of Lyons* . . . but those lions beat Rob Roy and everything else of that sort to the ground."

The conductor and musical director for Her Majesty's Theatre from 1833-46 was Sir Michael Costa. One of the most enduring Italian conductors of the Victorian era, he composed many operas besides *Makel Adel* and was appointed director of the Royal Italian Opera at Covent Garden from 1847-67. *Makel Adel* was a flop in the eyes of many critics—even with Lablache.

That season Frédéric Lablache joined his father for at least ten concerts in London. Beside him, singing at these events was his future wife Frances Wilton, (stage name Fanny Wyndham). They continued to sing together through the '40s and the first half of the '50s. Later, Fanny Lablache retired from the operatic stage to care for their three children—Therese, Fanny, and Luigi. She still sang in concerts and continued her teaching. She possibly preferred teaching singing, than stage appearances. Like Frédéric, she obtained a degree to teach from the Royal Academy of Music in London. Mme. Lablache was also a talented composer like her husband and was well known in London musical circles. In addition to writing many charming arias and pieces for the piano (that have survived her), Mme. Lablache was a charming hostess, and the home of the Lablaches on Albany Street (London) was a gathering place for notable musicians. Frédéric, like his father, found English food much too plain and enjoyed rich gourmet food, especially French and Italian. Moreover, many notable foreigners, exiled from their native countries, were welcomed at Frédéric's table; most notable later were the Prince of Rohan, the Prince of Syracuse, and Louis Napoleon—afterward Napoleon III.

During May 1839, Frédéric and Luigi Lablache were scheduled to sing the usual rounds of fashionable London concerts, including concerts at Her Majesty's Theatre in the mornings and afternoons. Subjected to two concerts a day, their obligations often concluded with private concerts in the evening or an opera. Many concert occasions brought the Italian singers and English singers together often at the famed Hanover Square Rooms, a crowded hall holding about six hundred people. A good description is given to us from an article in *Leisure Hour,* 1876, by Dr. Rimbault:

> Nearly every famous singer and instrumentalist in Europe, for a period of all but a century, has sung or played at the Hanover Square Rooms. On that well remembered platform have walked Catalani, Billington, and Storace. There John Braham, Rubini, Lablache, and Tamburini—names which may have little significance at present, but which, in bygone times, stirred the hearts of the lovers of music as briskly as the names of Adelina Patti and Sims Reeves do now. There Marie Malibran de Beriot has gladdened the ears of a bygone generation with the incomparable sweetness, melody, and pathos of her vocalization; there the terrible, weird man, Paganini, with his flashing eyes, his long hair streaming over his shoulders, his cadaverous face and gaunt limbs, has, with his bony, lissome fingers, extorted such exquisitely beautiful, such passionate, such eloquent yet such wild and half-distraught strains £rom his violin, then, hearing him, you might have imagined him as one struggling with an evil spirit, whom he had imprisoned in his instrument, and who was frantically striving to burst his bonds. The Hanover Square Rooms also have heard Dragonetti, simplest, severest, grandest of double bass players; the dexterous Thalberg, the melodious Pleyel, and the famous Liszt, about whom connoisseurs, could never make up their mind whether the mysterious pianist was a prophet or a pretender. The history of these rooms, indeed, between 1810 and the present era, is virtually the history of the lyrical art, not only English, but Italian, French, German, and in the truest sense of the term, cosmopolitan. Every *prima donna,* every *primo tenore,* every bass and baritone and contralto of repute, has in turn sung at the Queen's Concert Rooms, Hanover Square. Every world-renowned pianist, harpist, or master of instruments stringed or instruments windy, has been heard on that platform.[436]

Buckingham Palace was a delightful place in 1839 (June 13, 14) for a summer concert, especially with the singers all London nobility enjoyed to hear. During this first concert, Giulia Grisi sang "Con pazienza" from *Il fanatico per la musica* by Fioravanti with Lablache. Rubini sang "Un tenero core," from *Roberto Devereux*. "A te o cara" was sung from *I Puritani* with Rubini, Tamburini, and Lablache. "*L'amor suo mi fe beato,*" *Roberto Devereux*, and "*Sappi che un rio dovere*" from *Bianca e Falliero* followed, and sung by the younger sister of Malibran—Pauline Garcia—later Mme. Viardot. Here, a young women of energy and genius made her opera debut in *Otello* at Her Majesty's on 9 May just three years after her sister's tragic death. The Queen attended all four performances. Sometime during this period, a newspaper reported the following:

> Lablache, great in stature, is greater as a vocalist, and no less formidable as a champion of the dignity of art. On one occasion, entering the music room at a certain great house in London, he observed the usual rope separating musicians and company laid down in front of him when he came along to sing in a duet. He quietly stooped and threw it aside. It was never replaced.

Strangely, Pauline Garcia-Viardot's London opera stage debut was as Desdemona—the same role that her sister Maria Malibran had reaped fame from in Rossini's *Otello*. Pauline was the younger sister of Malibran, so audiences expected much from her. Critic Chorley commented that she was an accomplished musician and a unique artiste. She proved herself successful in *Otello* when she sang with Lablache later on 8 October again in Paris at the Théâtre-Italien. April Fitzlyon writes (*The Price of Genius*):

> As the performance continued, it became clear to everyone in the audience that they were witnessing the birth of a genius, the applause was great; Pauline was recalled at the end of every act; and the audience was touched by the sight of Lablache, the bass, embracing the young debutante in a paternal way at the end of the performance. 'Oh, cunning Lablache,' commented Gautier, 'who pretends to be fat and grey-haired in order to kiss pretty women!'[437]

Here, *The Musical World* reports that on 22 May 1839, the great concert room at Her Majesty's was filled for the first public concert appearance of Pauline Garcia:

> Signor Costa conducted Miss Pauline Garcia and the splendid voices of Lablache, F. Lablache, Miss F. Wyndham (later Mad. F. Lablache) Rubini, Tamburini, Miss Birch, Albertazzi, Grisi, Persiani, Balfe and Madame Balfe, Madame Stockhausen, Misses De Riviere Monanni and Bilstien. The instrumental performers were: M. Dohler, M. Benedict, on the piano forte, M. A. Batta on the violoncello, M. David, Blagrove and Mori on the violin. Puzzi played on the French horn. *The Athenaeum* wrote: Grisi, Persiani, Albertazzi sang their very best, each one was resolved to lose no part of her hold upon the good graces of the public, now that a dangerous rival has appeared in Pauline Garcia. Her share of the concert, Costa's *Suon profondo* and Rossini's *Lasciami* sung with Persiani, was the most extraordinary musical exhibition we can recollect.

Rossini's chef d'oeuvre *Gugliemo Tell* was first shown at Her Majesty's in London on 11 July 1839 in Italian, with Luigi Lablache in the title role, ten years after the premiere at the Academie Royale de Musique in Paris on 3 August 1829. Rossini's last opera has been judged by musical historians to be his greatest *opera seria* achievement. It was composed in French with text in four acts by Etienne de Jouy, Florent Bis, and Armand Marast after Friedrich von Schiller's drama *Guillaume Tell*. Of the huge original French cast, Laure Cinti-Damoreau sang Mathilde, Louise-Zulm Dabadie was Jemmy, Henry Bernard Dabadie sang Guillaume Tell, and French tenor Adolphe Nourrit sang Arnold.

Guillaume Tell is a unique opera and a remarkable piece of drama. Rossini changes his style, pointing the way to a different and more experimental work. Clearly, the opera was years ahead of its time and forewarns of the operas that would follow. Written about freedom, based on a legend, the spirit of the opera represents the quest for freedom from tyranny, a very popular theme in grand opera, both in the collective sense and in personal drama. In all operas, there must always be conflict; Giuseppe Verdi's operas are prime examples of heartrending operatic conflicts, *Nabucco, Attila, Aida, Vespri, Il Trovatore, La Traviata, Rigoletto* to name a few. On 10 July, *The London Times* announced the usual events:

> Her Majesty's Theatre . . . Mr Laporte has the honour to acquaint Nobility subscribers to the opera, and the public, that his benefit will take place tomorrow, July 11th, Rossini's grand opera of *Guglielmo Tell*. The principal characters by Madame Persiani, Madame Bellini, and Madlle E. Grisi, Signori Rubini, Tati, F. Lablache, Morelli, Giubilei, and Signor Lablache. In order to give the fullest effect, the choruses have been greatly increased. In the second act of the opera, Madlle Taglioni will introduce the celebrated Tyrollienne, with Bellon and Guerra(the ballet).

The Queen attended 13 July. On hearing Lablache singing the title role, she writes on 18 July, "Lablache's acting and singing as Guglielmo were very, VERY fine; he looked so well, too." She did not think, however, it was an interesting opera, though she acknowledged, "It is splendidly and beautifully composed."[438]

However, the Queen visited Her Majesty's again on 16 July and again on 3 August and the sixth. She had also seen another production at Drury Lane that year on 4 February.

Drury Lane had also launched a huge production of the opera on 3 December 1838, the first time in England. The playbill states, "By more than 100 voices, the WHOLE of the music—first time in this country in English." The famous English cast at Drury Lane were: tenor John Braham (whose voice had darkened to sing bass roles) sang William Tell, Abigail Betts sang the role of Martha and Miss Romer sang Matilda.[439]

After the magnificent production was mounted at Her Majesty's Theatre on 11 July 1839, the *Athenaeum* praised Rossini's work and Lablache's singing: "We hope that the public will recognize the pains which have been taken, on the present occasion, to represent one of the noblest lyric dramas in a fitting manner." A July review in *The Times* describes the first performance with Lablache at some length:

> The announcement of *Guglielmo Tell* raised the highest of expectations, and immediately after the opening of the doors last night every seat in the pit was occupied, such occupation having been preceeded by a terrific struggle at the entrance. Public expectations were not only equalled, but surpassed: for whether we regard the cast of the principal characters, the perfect organization of the chorus, or the beauty of the scenery, and the general attention

paid to the picturesque effect, a more complete production is, perhaps, unrecorded in the annals of the drama. The assemblage of the inhabitants of Switz, Uri, and Unterwalden, at the end of the second act, the entrance from every part of the mountains, the scene in the back ground with dramatic effect of the moon on the waters, the union and precision of the immense body of voices, produced a sensation that cannot be described. Lablache as Guglielmo maintained the whole dramatic weight of the drama, and no Atlas could have supported it better. He completely conceived the part, his very look stamped him as leader of his countrymen. His words in the second act,

> Trova aicura guida L uom che nel
> eielo interamento affida,

were uttered with calm dignity which electrified the house. He embraced his son before placing the apple on his head, was exquisitely pathetic, and his manning himself with the words "Io son Guglielmo Tell," produced an effect only to be equalled by his terrific "Io ti maledieo" in *Otello*. Matilda and Arnoldo were beautifully sustained by Persiani and Rubini, their scenes stand apart from the bustling part of the drama, and had the effect of a delightful calm between the storms of the rest. Their duet in the second act went off with loud applause not withstanding, it was unpleasantly interrupted by a vain attempt to encore a passage in the middle of it, and further by the fainting of a lady in the pit. The opera may be pronounced the most successful production of the season; the audiences went with it . . . CON AMORE, and, at the fall of the curtain, their enthusiasm knew no bounds. It should be mentioned that the most rival parts were respectably filled; F. Lablache, Tati, Guibilei and Morelli being when in a suitable position, all calculated to add to the general strength. (These singers were all leading talents as well.) Nor must the exertions of Messrs. Grieve be passed over in silence; their three scenes, two mountain views, and the third Gessler's Castle, were masterpieces of their art. In the third act, Taglioni danced her Tyrolienne, aided by Bellon and Guerra, amid loud approbation. At the end of the opera ballet, dancer Fanny Elsler and her sister made their debut for the season, therefore obliging the lovers of the early hours. They went through an eccentric pleasing *pas de deux* with great applause, and were followed by Taglioni, who gave her celebrated Spanish dance. This was rapturously encored, then all the dancers were called and came on to the stage for the agreeable purpose of picking up certain garlands that were flung to them. Pauline Garcia appeared, and sang with Grisi; after all this, the evening ended very late.

Here, the *Athenaeum* continues to describe the singers:

Lablache . . . how are we to speak of him in terms of praise which shall not appear hyperbolical? . . . he was so impressive . . . amounting almost to sublime. But of a still higher excellence was the great scene with his son.

Guillaume Tell is mentioned by Rossini when he comments about his future and his operas:

"My immortality?" Rossini replied, "do you know what will survive me? (*sais-tu ce que restera apres moi?*) the third act of *Tell*, the second act of *Otello,* and *Il Barbiere di Siviglia* from one end to the other."[440]

While *Guglielmo Tell* was making its entrance on the stages of London, Rossini was in Italy. His health since 1833 had deteriorated. His father Giuseppe Rossini had just died at the age of eighty, and this may have been one of the causes of Rossini's bouts of depression. In the summer of 1839, he visited Naples. There he relaxed in the company of his old friend, impresario Domenico Barbaja.[441]

Donizetti's operas now occupied theaters all over Europe. Lablache filled the role of Donizetti's foremost bass interpreter from the time he sang his first Donizetti opera in Naples *Elvida* until his death. Lablache's repertory consisted of approximately twenty-three different Donizetti roles. He created ten world premieres, including the revised version of *Linda di Chamounix* for Paris. Clearly, many of the twenty-two roles that Lablache had actively sung earlier never entered the so-called international circuit and were rarely performed outside of Italy. Of all of Donizetti's operas, only a small group enjoyed overwhelming success in the Northern European cities. The group of Donizetti operas that Lablache sang most often after 1830 in Paris, London, and St. Petersburg were *Anna Bolena, Lucrezia Borgia, L'Elisir d'amore*, and

Don Pasquale. Now and then, he sang *L'Ajo nell'imbarazzo*, *La Favorita*, and *Linda*. He rarely sang La *Figlia del reggimento*. *Marino Faliero* languished after the first few years and was only sung occasionally again in Lablache's lifetime.

Lablache was fondly remembered for his comic performances in the sentimental *L'Elisir d'amore* and the uproarious *Don Pasquale*. Frédéric Lablache made the role of Sergeant Sulpice his own in the successful lighthearted *La Fille du régiment*. The hit of the late forties, he sang Sulpice often alongside Ms. Jenny Lind.

Ms. Fanny Wyndham sang from February through June that year in various concerts at the Hanover Square Rooms, Her Majesty's Theatre, and later at Mori's morning Drury Lane concerts. The singers that participated were mostly Italians.

In August of 1839, Frédéric Lablache and Ms. Frances Wilton became husband and wife as described in a brief notice in *The Musical World,* under the heading Miscellaneous.

> We prefer giving the following announcement from *La France Musicale*, to saying the same thing in polite English, on account of the tournure of the paragraph: "F. Lablache, *fils du tout-puissant Lablacho, vient d'epouser Miss Fanny* Wyndham, jeune et jolie cantatrice Anglaise non sans quelque celebrite."[442]

Beneath this article in *The Musical World*, on the same page, there was another announcement:

> Among the honorary members of the Musical Academy of St. Cecilia at Rome, we find . . . Mesdames Catalani, Pasta, Judith et Julia Grisi, Cherubini, Caraffa, Onslow, Berton, Auber, Adams, Donizetti, Mercadante, Neukomn, Pixis, Labarre, Thalberg, Liszt, Rubini, Lablache, Tamburini, Crescentini, Mayseder, Baillot, De Beriot.

Another young debutante, the new Romeo of the Italian stage, Mario, sang that season in *Norma*. Queen Victoria enjoyed Mario's singing of Pollione, she wrote:

> . . . Again *Norma* . . . and oh! more splendid than before. Grisi was perfection, it is really a treat to see and hear her; Mario too is so delightful; alas! his and *Norma's* last night, for he's away to Paris, and this charming opera can't be performed any more.[443]

Mario returned to the Paris Opera for *Robert le Diable*, *Le Comte Ory*, and his debut in *L'Elisir d'amore* with the same London cast. Pauline Garcia was now engaged by the new manager of the Théâtre-Italien, Louis Viardot, to sing in her debut there.

In Paris that summer, Chopin had settled down at Nohant; though physically not strong, he continued to compose his finest works before his tragic and early death from tuberculosis. To one of his pupils, he said, "How I envy strong people who have robust health and nothing to do! I am very irritated. I have no time in which to be sick."

After a heavy season of concerts, three of which were at Buckingham Palace, Her Majesty's closed. Many singers headed north to Manchester. Lablache and Grisi, Rubini and Tamburini all sang together on 12 August and 13, bringing *Anna Bolena* and *I Puritani* to the Theatre Royal Manchester for the first time.

Lablache then returned to Paris for the winter season of 1839. The composer Richard Wagner, who was at that time trying to break into the musical world, came to his house in an attempt to persuade the great bass to introduce a Wagnerian grand bass aria with chorus a la Bellini as an extra aria for Oroveso when Lablache sang *Norma*.

Lablache diplomatically declined. Wagner gives the details of what happened:

> I next stumbled on the idea of writing a grand bass aria with chorus, for Lablache to introduce into his part of Oroveso in Bellini's *Norma*. Lehrs had to hunt up an Italian political refugee to get the text out of him; this was done, and I produced an effective composition a la Bellini (which still exists among my manuscripts), and went off to offer it to Lablache. The friendly Moor, who received me in the great singer's anteroom, insisted upon admitting me straight into his master's presence without announcing me.
>
> As I anticipated some difficulty in getting near such a celebrity, I had written my request, as I thought this would be simpler than explaining verbally. The black servant's pleasant manner made me feel very uncomfortable; I entrusted my score and letter to him to give to Lablache, without taking any notice of his kindly astonishment at my refusal of his repeated invitation to go into his master's room. I left hurriedly, to return in a few days. When I came back Lablache received me most kindly, and assured me that my aria was excellent, though it was impossible

to introduce it into Bellini's opera after the latter had already been performed so often. My relapse into the domain of Bellini's style, of which I had been guilty through writing this aria, was therefore useless to me, and I soon became convinced of the fruitlessness of my efforts in that direction. I saw that I should need personal introductions to various singers in order to ensure the production of one of my compositions.[444]

Wagner was very disturbed by the fact that Liszt was such a slave to his public and "making millions banging on the piano" while he, the German idealist, was starving and could hardly play the piano; and although he had many letters of introduction, he was not selling anything other than a few songs. His "Trois Melodies" was published in 1840 and dedicated to the future mother-in-law of Lablache's daughter, the well-known Marie-Baroness de Caters.[445]

After writing *Guillaume Tell*, Rossini abandoned his career as an opera composer. He lived on till 1868 as a semi-invalid but continued to enjoy life, occasionally composing music. Living in a fashionable suburb of Passy near Paris with his devoted mistress Olympe Pelissier. After the death of his ex-wife, Isabella Colbran, Rossini had married Olympe.

At Passy, he would hold his famous soirées, always surrounded by friends and admirers whom he would dazzle with his sparkling conversation and would say of him, "What an abundance of memories, what a profusion of original ideas . . . What a picturesque way of speaking . . ." Rossini loved to tell this anecdote about Lablache over and over again.[446] It was also remembered by Florimo in an article under the title: "*Lablache scambiato per un celebre nano, Le general Tom Ponce*:"[447]

Once, Lablache was staying in the same apartment house in Paris, no. 16 Rue Taitbout, on the first floor, as the P.T. Barnum's famous attraction General Tom Thumb. Billed as "the smallest man in the world. "One of the General's fans, an Englishman, sought an audience with this curious celebrity, and made the mistake of asking Berlioz for assistance. Offended that the Briton assumed there was some sort confraternity of musicians and freaks, Berlioz gave the man the address of Lablache's suite. When the giant Lablache opened the door, his visitor was so startled he could hardly speak. "I . . . I was calling on . . . Le General Tom Thumb.

Monsieur Berlioz sent me here." "Yes," said Lablache calmly, "Yes, I am Tom Thumb," he replied poker faced and smiling. "But . . . excuse me . . . Tom Thumb is the smallest man in the world!" "Yes," agreed Lablache, "in public, of course. But. you should know Monsieur! when I'm at home, I make myself comfortable."

In February 1845, the famous American Tom Thumb visited Paris where he was received by Louis Philippe and the royal family, afterward making a tour of France and Belguim. Subsequently, he appeared before the Spanish Court. A notice in the London newspapers on 9 May 1846 wrote: "General Tom Thumb has gone to the city of London Theatre, and plays nightly, to the wonder of the east-enders, in his burlesque of 'Hop o' My Thumb.'" The *Manchester Guardian* gives full details of his size: he was twenty-five inches high. And it was the truth, many carte de visites of him still exist. The event of the year 1844 was the triumphal visit of Gen. Tom Thumb to London. Queen Victoria was most amused by him; the journal *Punch* dared to critize—they thought it absurd that the Queen asked him to appear at Buckingham Palace and Windsor Castle by royal command.[448] After his engagements, ten thousand people sent him off from the docks back to New York.

Chapter Twenty-Two

Thalberg and Napoleon's Funeral

1839-40

All through the autumn of 1839, Queen Victoria confided to her journal her thoughts about marrying Prince Albert of Saxe-Coburg. At first, she was against an early wedding, even against marriage. But slowly she changed her mind, for after being with the young prince Albert on a few occasions, she decided he was to be her husband.[449] Thus it was on 15 October, the young queen asked him to marry her and he accepted. The wedding took place on 10 February 1840 at the Chapel Royal, St. James.[450]

Albert and Victoria had one thing in common more perhaps than anything else, and that was music. Lablache continued his usual practice of teaching Victoria singing lessons at Buckingham Palace and at Osborne House if she so desired. Prince Albert was not above joining in with Victoria, and they all happily sang together, continuing this way until Lablache's death in 1858.

Frédéric and Fanny Lablache sang at the Theatre Royal in Manchester on 14 January 1840. Returning to sing at the Hanover Rooms in London on 7 February, they would participate in concerts again throughout the summer in London, joining their father, Luigi Lablache, at Her Majesty's Theatre concerts at least once a week.

By 1835, the Italian opera singers firmly believed that with their major success of *I Puritani* and the fame of the so-called Puritani Quartet, it was in their interest to form a *vieille garde*. This tight little circle could put pressure on the managers, who were according to Lablache of questionable repute. Now, instead of being treated shabbily as they were earlier in their careers, the singers clearly added market power to their popular appeal. Benjamin Lumley, manager of Her Majesty's, in his *Reminiscences of the Opera* accused the beautiful prima donna Grisi of being the leader of the *vieille garde*. He later wrote of "their determination to resist every effort of the director to vary the composition of the phalanx, by declaring that not one of them would engage singly." They would sing together or not at all. In 1840, the manager Laporte decided to test this arrangement with disastrous results, amounted to the famous Tamburini riots.

The performance of *I Puritani* in which Lablache sang on 25 April took place at Her Majesty's under near riot conditions, when a member of the Puritani Quartet, Tamburini, had been replaced by another singer, Coletti. The *Times* reported that the so-called "omnibus," a party of noblemen representing the feelings of the house, were so furious that they shouted and hissed and stopped the ballet going on at the end of the performance, therefore depriving the house of their usual entertainment. *The Musical World* wrote,

> Again and again Laporte came forward and tried to bring things to a settlement, at the same time compromising himself as little as possible, declaring since he was the manager he had the right to engage performers according to his own discretion—an assertion which only poured oil on the flame. The managerial party was chiefly in the pit, and raised a counter-cry of "Shame!" "No Tamburini." "No intimidation," while a gentleman from a box shouted "Turn the omnibus out". Laporte came out again and talked on engaging Tamburini on conditions; this word "conditions" upset all, and the Tamburinists asked, "Will you engage him yes or no?!" Laporte said he would make proposals, and if those proposals, etc.—This would not do; "Yes or no?!" said his supporters. He began talking terms; "Same terms as last year," shouted all the omnibus.

By then, the audience was getting tired: the supporters of Tamburini stormed the stage and took possession, waving their hats triumphantly as the curtain fell.

Frédéric Lablache made his debut at Her Majesty's on 14 March 1839 singing the Victorian favorite, Bellini's *Sonnambula* with Fanny Persiani and Rubini. Frédéric was familiar with the role of the Count; in fact, he made quite a career out of it since his French debut in the same role at the Théâtre-Italien.

Persiani, who had sung in *Sonnambula* often in Vienna, Paris, and Italy was known as an accomplished Amina. Still only twenty-five, the young Frédéric had sung in Naples and Paris before. His Paris debut was in the same opera in 1835. In London, he had participated in concerts since 1836, many at the King's Theatre, Hanover Rooms, and elsewhere, not forgetting his performances with the opera buffa at London's Lyceum theater. His entree into the operatic world and later development was made easier by his father's constant guidance. Frédéric sometime ran into such difficulties that he had to be bailed out by his father.

Opening the new London season of 1840, Luigi Lablache sang alongside Fanny Persiani, Tamburini, Rubini, Grisi, and Mario in *Don Giovanni, Le nozze di Figaro, Norma, L'Elisir d'amore*, and *Il Matrimonio Segreto* to name a few. Standing out among these operas was the first showing in London of Giuseppe Persiani's opera *Inez de Castro*, on 30 May, a grand Spanish story and "lyrical tragedy". Queen Victoria and the Queen Dowager attended. From the letters of Maria Malibran, we learn the following:[451]

> The opera's first performance, at the San Carlo theatre in Naples, was said to have quaked from explosions of applause that surpassed Vesuvius' strongest eruptions, and when the hapless Ines was led to the block singing "Io non moro, vado in ciel i miei figli a ritrovar" (I will not die, I go to heaven, my sons to find), people sobbed audibly, and several women were carried out fainting. Upon these words, sung by Maria Malibran, Maria was considered "superhuman," and before the evening ended, she was responsible for a new law . . . only one curtain call per artist.

In London, this review appeared in the *Athenaeum*:

> Her Majesty's Theatre—an opera with one duet, magnificently performed and agreeably composed, and with Lablache in the costume of a Spanish king, so filling the stage by his gorgeous presence as to give the mind through the eye, a pleasure which there is little chance of its receiving through the ear from "Il Maestro" Persiani's music—such, at best, is *Inez de Castro*. The force and the passion of the well-known historical passage having, according to custom, been tamed out of the libretto, the latter is as weak and hackneyed in its structure as the musician would not desire; and, but for the energetic acting of Lablache, and—wonderful to add . . . of Rubini in the duet above mentioned, the audience would have been unmoved in mood as if a lecture had been read, in the place of a tragedy presented. As regards to the composition, from the first foolish bars of the overture, to "dying

fall" of the prima donna's mad scene . . . not all the admirable singing of Persiani and Rubini, who, indeed, outdid themselves in delicacy, finish, and brilliancy to the audacious point-the former touching E flat *altissimo*, the latter a high soprano note, which we will not name, lest our ears have deceived us—could hide us from the truth, that the work is utterly barren, poor, and common place. A week ago, we should have thought it impossible that we could think wistfully of Donizetti; yet we did, while suffering our first weariness under the infliction of *Inez de Castro*. Are there no operas by Pacini, to go back futher back-which, if revived, would be more agreeable to the ear than this hackneyed and ungracious music?

In fact, critic Chorley remarked, "Save for an old memoranda, I recollect nothing." The musical news of 1840 was full of the arrival of Franz Liszt and the death of Nicola Paganini. Paganini became a legend in his own lifetime. Lablache knew Paganini well; according to family tradition, they had been friends. Little information survives to indicate how close they were. Paganini got involved in many unsavory scandals that tainted his reputation. One can only surmise that Lablache might have not exactly welcomed to be associated with him. However, on one occasion, we find them together as recorded in *Dwight's Journal of Music* "Anecdote of Paganini's Heir":[452]

Paganini has left only one son, Achilles, a fortune of two millions of francs and the title of nobility. An anecdote of Monsieur Achilles shows that the proverb: "What fathers add, the sons subtract," will not be likely to apply to him. While yet a boy, Achilles was one evening present with a couple of gentlemen at the house of the famous singer Lablache. Four candles were burning on the table. This luxury of lights troubled the boy's feeling; after a little while he silently got up, crept on tiptoe to the first light and, while the gentlemen were eagerly engaged in conversation, blew it out. Lablache winked at him and let it go on. Thinking himself unobserved, he presently blew out a second and then a third light. But as he was about to pursue the same process with the fourth, Lablache said to him in a friendly way: "Child, if you blow out that light we shall be unable to see." "We don't need light to talk by!" was the answer of the boy, now the possessor of two millions.

> Paganini amassed a huge fortune. Unfortunately, he was deprived of its enjoyment by his sudden death. He was already wasting away from tuberculosis of the larynx when Liszt first heard him, and

of course, there was then no cure. By his last concert, on 9 July 1837, he could no longer speak other than in a whisper; and after the closing of his Casino Paganini, in Paris, his life ebbed away. He was in dispute with everybody, dragged into court often for no good cause and hounded everywhere he went with his young son as his only spokesman. Even when he died in Nice, he was denied a Christian burial because of his reputation of being in league with the devil. These stories were often born of rumors; his reputation for "playing like a devil" was capitalized on by his promoters, no doubt to sell more tickets. This impression was abetted by his appearance which in later years had become grotesque, his face a macabre mask, death-white complexion, with two piercing black eyes and a hank of long, greasy black hair. Wearing black tails he would slither onto the stage, a nineteenth-century equivalent of some rock stars, except with a violin instead of a guitar. His appearance never, at any point, took anything away from his performance for he was, without doubt, the greatest violin virtuoso of his age indeed of all time.

Earlier that year, on 31 January, a concert took place in Paris at the home of the Duke of Orleans. It was reported by *The Musical World*:

> It was attended by the (French) Royal family and an immense crowd of the highest rank. The singers were confined to the artists of the Italian opera, with the celebrated Puzzi, who accompanied Rubini on the horn solo, in an air of Tadolini's with wonderful effect. A duo from *Il Fanatico*, by Madame Grisi and Lablache, one from *Tancredi*, by Mme Persiani and Pauline Garcia.

In London, on Whitsunday at the Sardinian Chapel, a mass was held. The principal singers were Persiani, Rubini, Tamburini, and Lablache. The mass consisted of the following:

Veni Sancti Spiritus (Lablache) . . . . Neukomm Alma
Virgo (Persiani) . . . . Hummel
Tantum Ergo (Tamburini). . . . . De Angioli
The Quoniam (Rubini)

On 8 June 1840, a grand concert drew much attention at Her Majesty's. The advert read:

> The vocalists: Grisi, Persiani, Dorus Gras, Stockhausen, Tosi; Rubini, Tamburini, Lablache, John Parry, Frédéric Lablache. At the pianoforte, Mme. Ducken, M. Franz Liszt and Hertz, who will perform a trio for three pianofortes. Violin Old Bull, French horn, Puzzi, conductor Sir G. Smart.

One of the towering personalities of music in the Romantic age was pianist and composer Franz Liszt. In 1840 he decided to slip into London while his rival Sigismund Thalberg was elsewhere and show off his talent. Thalberg, the celebrated virtuoso, was just as famous a figure of the times as Franz Liszt. Liszt was not a stranger to London. He had played there as a boy. His performances were always brilliant, and he was as well received as he had been in Paris. After a successful English visit, he left to tour Belgium, Germany, and Russia. The *Gazette Musicale* of March 1837 gives an amusing description of Liszt: "The piano vibrated under Liszt's fingers like the voice of Lablache." Another opinion was from the front page of *The Musical World*, 11 June 1840, after hearing his concert:

> Liszt made a tremendous impression, he was a little short of a miracle... words alone cannot describe the power which he possesses dividing himself as it were into two, or sometimes even three performers; feathery delicacy of his touch at one moment, and its enormous forte at another... he even transcends Thalberg.

History has not been kind to Sigismund Thalberg. Overshadowed by negative comments in biographies of Liszt over many years, he became unjustly considered inferior by later music commentators, who asserted that Liszt was the greater of the two pianists. It was found that Thalberg's playing was just as brilliant; he composed well and was just as handsome as Liszt though his lifestyle in public was not as flamboyant. The first occasion Thalberg became known to Europe was in 1835 at a soirée of Count Apponyi's, then at the Austrian ambassador's in Paris. Thalberg was just twenty-three years old of an extremely agreeable, aristocratic appearance, refined manners, and very witty. Engel tells us:[453]

> ... he was kindhearted and uncommonly careful not to say an incautious word against anybody or ever to hurt any man's feelings. He became at once the ladies' pet, and what that means in Paris to those who know French society will not undervalue ... Among great pianists, it should be said of him as Catalani said of Sontag: 'His *genre* was not great, but he was great in his *genre*.' Thalberg was amiable, both as a man and a performer.

Like Liszt and Paganini, Thalberg's life concealed many scandals and secrets, but the rumors only served to strengthen his sex appeal. Liszt said of him, "Thalberg est le seul pianiste qui joue du violin sur le clavier." (Thalberg is the only pianist I know who can play the violin on the piano.)[454]

Thalberg traveled on an endless circuit of concert tours throughout the British Isles and was more popular in England than Liszt in the early years. Many times, Liszt was targeted as being too flamboyant, an egomaniac: there was something of the showman about him that the British found a bit hard to take—the wild gestures, the thumps on the piano, the ladies falling all over him, some fainting with excitement upon attending his concerts, which were often called "weird affairs" by the press.

Sigismund Thalberg was an extraordinary virtuoso. He was born near Geneva on 8 January 1812, the natural son of Prince Franz Josef Dietrichstein (who had many mistresses) and the Baroness von Wetzlar. Educated in Vienna at his father's palace by the best teachers, he was destined to become a diplomat; but later, he showed a strong aptitude for music. His father gave up an ambassador's appointment to devote all his time to the education of Sigi (nickname). An early public success came in 1826, when he was only fourteen years old, then he played before Prince Klemins von Metternich, the great Austrian diplomat. By 1829, he was playing in public in Vienna; and from there he embarked on a concert tour of Germany and Austria. Engel wrote, "Thalberg and Mario were, to my mind, the BEAU IDEAL of cultivated, polished musicians."[455] Both gentlemen by birth and education possessed refined and elegant manners, and they both were handsome men. No wonder that they were adored by the female sex; for in addition to their virtues and attractions, they carried about with them the inexpressible charm and magnetism of artistic superiority. "When we hear Thalberg play," said Schumann, "we wonder from whence he gets all his fingers."[456]

By the age of twenty-seven, he had composed thirty original works, chiefly of the class calculated to display his own unique style and execution;

but many were of a different type and proved that Thalberg was capable of writing wonderful concertos and sonatas on the lines of the great masters.

Thalberg's piano pieces reached a wide audience through his sheet music; they sold by the thousands across Europe and in the United States. While he was in vogue, fashionable ladies across several continents were busy thumping out his opera fantasies and other piano pieces. His arrangement of *Home Sweet Home* was one of the most popular.

Although pianists, professional and amateur, have practiced Thalberg's pieces until both their fingers and heads have ached hopelessly, some of his works are fiendishly difficult. He complained in his time of having many imitators; many tried unsuccessfully to copy him, all fell short of the mark. Thalberg spent most of his life touring Europe and the British provinces, Russia, South America, and the United States. He had entertained across three continents before retiring in 1858 to Posillipo near Naples Italy.

In July 1843, he married the eldest daughter of Luigi Lablache, Francesca, at the well-known church of St. James in Piccadily, London. Lablache signed the register.[457] Francesca was the recent young widow of the famed French artist of the Romantic school and portrait painter Francois Bouchot who died in 1842. Commissioned by the opera singers of the day, including Lablache, his wife and daughters were all his subjects. Others were Malibran, Grisi, and Balzac. A Bouchot painting exists of his young wife, Francesca: "One of the toasts of Naples in her day," La Cecchina enjoyed a flaming reputation as a beautiful wild dancer and singer, "she was always known in the theatrical world . . . for her impetuous and fantastic character,"[458] Francesca posed for her portrait in Neapolitan costume.[459] Bouchot paintings reflected a true romantic temperament and sadly remembered for signing "Mary Magdalene Witness to the death of Christ: 'Bouchot jam moriens pinxit' Bouchot already dying, painted it."

During the last years of the thirties, Lablache averaged over a dozen different operas per London season. At the Théâtre-Italien, he sang a little less. By 1840, he sang in fourteen different operas at Her Majesty's. Total performances of each opera varied. The season opened in the spring, often finishing by the end of July; but as the benefit performances increased, the opera season stretched well into August. Daily concerts were heavily scattered throughout London in season. While "off season" concerts were customary, they were not as frequent nor did they feature the Italians; mostly the artists were local British or German. From the thirties, the Italian singers began to engage in tours of the provinces during the gaps falling between the start of the Paris season. A great many of these autumn tours took the singers all over Britain.

Musical activity in London was rich in variety and was plentiful enough to provide entertainment throughout the winter months. Theatrical attractions at many different London theaters had a lot to offer. Besides plays, there was the circus and Christmas programs, such as the pantomime.

Not all the Italian opera singers left for the Birmingham Festival in 1840. Grisi sang there the year before to everyone's satisfaction, and now the *Birmingham Journal* did not approve of the choice: "Their sins of omission (speaking for the committee) is the non-engagement of certain Italians (Grisi etc.)." Luigi Lablache left for the provinces and sang at the Birmingham Festival with Frédéric Lablache, Dorus Gras, Caradori, Brahm, and a Ms. Birch. On the first night, *The Musical World* reports the following:

> Mendelssohn's "Lobgesang" or "Hymn of Praise," which he composed for the Birmingham Festival, was performed. On the second night the selections from operas were performed. Rossini's *Gazza Ladra* (compressed into one act) followed by Gnecco's *La prova di un'opera seria*. Mr. Loder led the band. Between pieces Mendelssohn performed a concerto on the grand pianoforte.

The Birmingham Festival wrote to the editor of *The Musical World* on 8 September 1840:

> With varied attractions . . . and the newly-opened railways, it is no unreasonable hope to indulge that Birmingham will be honoured by the presence of a brilliant and distinguished crowd of visitors and that the noble charity, the General Hospital, on whose behalf the festival is given, will receive an effective acquisition to its diminished funds . . .

Rubini and Persiani gave a concert at Cheltenham Rotunda:

> Rubini was as great as ever . . . eliciting unanimous encores in the melodia "La Potenza d'Amore" accompanied by Puzzi on the horn; and in Pacini's aria, "I tuoi froquenti palpiti" (*Musical World*).

That cold December, the remains of Napoleon I were brought back from St. Helena by ship and ceremonially reinterred in Paris beneath the dome of Les Invalides. There, the dark plum red marble catafalque is enshrined to this day. Berlioz was there and Kern Holoman describes the event in his biography of Berlioz:[460]

> Tuesday, 15th December, a frigid day, saw the slow procession of the rococo catafalque from the docks in Courbevoie to the Invalides. Berlioz had imagined a splendid national event, with cannonades of five hundred rounds and majestic funeral marches by grand ensembles. What he witnessed was pale and prosaic. He could hear only disjunct snatches of the music as the bands passed by, and Requiem as played in the church seemed anything but Napoleonic, unsuited even to the scale of the coffin, let alone to the magnitude of the myth. He wept at the ceremony for "our sublime emperor" and felt his tears freeze—not from the cold, he thought, but from the shame.

Lablache was sent a letter from the director summoning him to sing the bass role in Mozart's Requiem. The *London Musical World* gives us an account of the day:[461]

> The choir engaged for the requiem, at the Chapel of *Les Invalides*, surpasses that of any previous celebration. In addition to the choristers of the various episcopal establishments of Paris, and the chorus singers of the Academie Royale, Opera Italien, and Salle Favart, the following principal vocalists give their Soprani-Grisi, Persiani, Cinti-Damoreau, Dorus Gras, Contralti-Garcia Viardot, Eugenie Garcia, Albertazzi, and Stoltz. Tenori-Rubini, Duprez, Alexis Dupont, and Bassi, Lablache, Tamburini, Lavasseur and Alizard. This, a very strong list, together with the orchestras of three lyric theatres, form a constellation not easily equalled in Europe, and worthy to participate in the most solemn ceremonial of modern times:
>
> NAPOLEON FUNERAL—(from our own correspondent.)—A trial was made on Sunday (December 13th) at the Paris Conservatoire, of the new trumpets, thirty in number, constructed by Schiltz on a novel model of extraordinary dimensions and power, expressly for the solemn pageant and interment of Napoleon's remains. The instruments were found to possess very great capabilities

of expression and compass, and the effect produced by them surpassed the expectations of the numerous professors and amateurs assembled on the occasion. Halévy has been engaged to compose a Funeral March, to be executed by a hundred and fifty performers who will accompany the pageant up the river Seine, from Rouen to Courbevoie; there, a new band of two hundred performers, with a solemn March by Auber, will accompany the procession to the capital. Berlioz's *Dirge*, executed by the united bands of the several regiments of the line, and the National Guards of Paris, amounting, perhaps two or three hundred instruments, will conduct the *cortege* to the chapel of the Invalides, where a new Requiem, by the veteran Cherubini, supported by the band and chorus of the Academy Royal, in addition to the choirs of Notre Dame and various other churches, will consign the honoured remains to their very appropriate resting place, and conclude the interesting ceremonial. This as it should be; it is the just homage of art to him, who, amidst all the cravings of his own ambition and the bustle of his own glory, found yet sufficient leisure and inclination to foster the arts and elevate their professors, feeling, justly enough, that ambition and glory reached a higher and more refined character by such means. The French Government has awarded most liberal remunerations to several composers and artists engaged, and the whole affair promises to be at once a national tribute and a national honour. (The below letter was handwritten in French, with Lablache's name on the lower left side, the date was printed as was the address on the top).

Ministry of the Interior, Paris
184
Fine Arts Department,
Office of theatres.

Emperor s Funeral, Presention
Mozart's Requieum by the Lyric
Theatre First Fellows.

> Sir, its my honour to inform you that, concurring on the choosing of First fellows (Premiere subjects) of the Lyric theatre for the presentation of Mozarts Requiem to be sung

at the funeral ceremonies for Napoleon in the church of the Invalides. I have assigned you to participate on that occasion. I'll congratulate myself for using this opportunity to show my appreciation for your talents. Mr. Habeneck, in charge of the direction of the orchestra, will coordinate with you the details of this presentation.

Accept, Sir, my most devoted consideration.

In representation of the Minister by the authority of Master of Petitions. Director of Fine Arts and theatres.

Signed. Cave (Signature unclear)[462]

Lablache (name on right corner)

(This letter was translated from the French by Jack Rohkar). The correspondent from *Musical World* goes on to complain that the English don't seem to do honor to their national heros, even Shakespeare:

> Shall we ever see such patriotic doings in England? Bacon and the Black Prince are yet unmonumentated, their memories being left to slumber in the bosoms of the grateful few, their high deserts unrevealed to the admiration and for the advantage of the illiterate many. The "poet of all time"—the reverence in every land, has gained no national tribute, during two centuries, from his countrymen; yet, if these stars of our isle were to be publicly celebrated in London, fashion would collect together the choristers of the Italian and German operas, and Royalty itself would probably select the music of Bellini and Strauss as alone fit and tolerable for the occasion, while native artists would be expelled from participation, or, at best, condemned to endure the double discords of alien lips and inferior talents.

Chapter Twenty-Three

Dublin

1841-42

Throughout the eighteenth century, opera had been a most important part of life in Dublin. The nineteenth century was no different, and Italian opera at the Theatre Royal was extremely popular. Great prima donnas such as Billington, Catalani, and Pasta visited the capital. Later in the nineteenth century, many touring companies from London were heard there regularly. These companies brought the finest productions and outstanding international artists.

During the 1820s and early '30s, Rossini's operas swept across Europe and opera lovers in Ireland were not left out although Rossini was pretty much the sole bill of fare with *Il Barbiere, Tancredi, Otello,* and *Semiramide.* All Dublin remembered the wonderful 1829 performance of Signor de Begnis when he sang Figaro's aria "Largo al factotum." Signor Giuseppe de Begnis was remembered not only for being a remarkable singer and impresario, but also for bringing about the first properly organized Italian opera company in Dublin[463] and also for creating the first Georgio in *I Puritani* in Dublin (4 February 1837).[464]

> When he sang the well-known duet,'Suoni la Tromba,' then heard for the first time on this stage, he created quite a sensation. De Begnis' voice was sufficiently heavy; that of Berrettoni still more so, and when they both joined in unison, the *fortissimo* was indeed tremendous—the brassy tone of two trumpets playing the melody added much to the effect.[465]

A leading bass baritone of his day, he created the role of Dandini in the premiere of Rossini's *La Cenerentola* in 1817. His wife Giuseppina Ronzi sang with Lablache in countless operas in Naples; the most noteworthy to some was Donizetti's *Anna Bolena* in the seasons of 1832-34.

An Italian opera company, under the management of Mr Mitchell, comenced an engagement anounced thus; Mr. Michell, Of the Opera buffa, London, begs respectfully to annouce that he has made arrangementswith Mr. Calcraft for a series of twelve representations. At this theatre, of the most popular italian operas recently performed in London.

Among the opera chosen were Donizetti's *L'Elisir d'amore* and heard for the first time in Dublin on 27 February 1838. There, Frédéric Lablache created the role of Dr. Dulcamara among others so-called most popular operas from London:

"Signor F. Lablache, son to the giant (in talent and person) of the same name, was, and happily is well known as a first-rate vocalist and musician," wrote the *Annals of the Theatre Royal Dublin*. Among the operas sung there were Donizetti's *Betly, Il Campanello, Torquato Tasso*. Also Copola's *Nina, Pazza per Amore* and Mozart's *Nozze de Figaro; Rossini's L'Italiana in Algeri, Il Barbiere di Siviglia, Mercadante's Eliza a Claudio*, and Ricci's *Avventura di Scaramuccia*. How many of these roles were sung by Frédéric Lablache is not certain, but it was stated, in the *Annals*, that he sang Torquato Tasso, Count Arnaldo, Count Almaviva among other roles. Afterward the whole company left for Belfast.[466]

In 1839, there were no performances of the Italian opera in Dublin. Sigismund Thalberg performed at the Theatre Royal with Michael Balfe in concert, and in 1840, Tamburini and Grisi made their first visit there singing in *Semiramide* and *Anna Bolena*.

Lablache's engagements for the London season of 1841 finished with Rossini's *La Gazza ladra*. Then Lablache, Mario, Grisi, and F. Lablache left for the northern cities of Manchester and Liverpool. On 20 August, they sang *I Puritani* and *La Sonnambula* at Liverpool. The latter was repeated in Manchester. Julius Benedict conducted, and he continued to conduct through the rest of the time in Dublin.

Luigi Lablache managed that year to fulfill the Theatre Royal's request to come to Dublin. Frédéric Lablache had created quite a furor after his debut there. Clearly, he was pretty well established now in his own right. Immediately, he paved the way for his father's debut, and a season was promised far superior to any which had been attempted before:

> The Company includes the following artistes, indeed a stellar cast if there was to be one! Madame Grisi, Signor Lablache (far-famed bass singer, his first appearance here) Signor Mario (first tenor of the Queens Theatre the undoubted successor of Rubini), Signor

Frédéric Lablache, Signora Ernesta Grisi, and Signor Puzzi (horn player). Conductor, Mons. Benedict; Leader. Mr. Levey. A stellar cast for the grand opening performance of *I Puritani*, on Monday, August 30th 1841. Of course. Sir. George, Signor Lablache;, Lord Talbot, Signor Mario; Sir Richard Forth, Signor F. Lablache Henrietta, Signora Ernesta Grisi; Elvira, Madame Grisi (*Annals of Theatre Royal*).

Basically, the so-called Puritani Quartet was well known as a team of four Italian singers—Rubini, Grisi, Tamburini, and Lablache, Mario replacing Rubini in the tenor roles, and here F. Lablache replacing Tamburini. Lablache encouraged his son into as many roles as he could handle as fast as possible, often pleading and putting pressure on the managers to give him a chance to sing. Frédéric often resented this push and pull between managers on his account. The *Annals* continues:

This should be a memorable date in our musical annals the first appearance of perhaps the greatest tenor the world has ever seen or heard, 'undoubted successor of Rubini.' Mario, in some points alike, possessed qualities in many respects superior. It would require a musical Plutarch to find a parallel description of the two wonders. Rubini, as before alluded to, possessed a marvellous range of voice, without a break, making constant use of what Italian singing-masters term the *Voce il testa* . . . the head voice. In the 'Ah perche' in *Sonnambula,* he reached F sharp in alt with great ease, singing the scena in D natural as written by Bellini. The voice was also capable of much dramatic power; indeed the general impression prevailed that Rubini was matchless, and that years might elapse before another could approach him. The star, however, appeared, and only those who then heard of Mario, and witnessed the occasion could judge the effect. There is possibly no position in the lyric world of which requires so many qualities combined in a single individual as a perfect Italian tenor. Of course the same will apply to an English artiste; but it cannot be denied that the language of Italy is peculiarly adapted to musical sounds. Well all the various talents necessary to make perfection were concentrated on Mario, with one trifling exception (which he always tried to overcome by high-heeled boots), he was slightly below the standard in stature. In every other respect perfection is not too strong a word to apply to him. With the most manly beauty, he possessed a grace of form and a fascination of manner which made him the 'observed of all observers.' An artist as well as a nobleman by nature, he studied costume to a degree, (like Lablache) and in all his characters was most exact in this particular, to the very 'buckle of his shoe.' The sound of his marvellous voice (he used the chest voice more than Rubini) still lingers in our ears. The quality, the high training, the exquisite TIMBRE—shall we ever hear the like again? And as an actor, fortunately many well remember his Raoul in *The Huguenots* in which it would be difficult to say which was better, the acting or the singing. Few are aware that he performed (once only) in Dublin in Rossini's Otello, which was independent of the vocalism, a magnificent display of histrionic power, and parts of which were compared with the impersonation of the great Edmund Kean. In 1841, the date of this engagement, Mario was in his zenith; it will therefore be understood that his very appearance at the end of the first Act of I Puritani created a sensation; but when the first liquid notes of the 'A te o cara' commenced, a death-like stillness (without the slightest exaggeration) prevailed, and at the conclusion of the movement there was "shout" of delight, the like has never been heard outside of Dublin. No words can give an adequate idea of his "Crede a misera", in which he reached the F in alt, thus equalling his great predecessors in range of voice, while exceeding him in power. the duet, also 'Vieni' with Grisi in the third Act, enraptured the audience. Thus commenced the Grisi and Mario era of Opera in Dublin, which continued for many years to the delight of the Dublin public. Well might Sheridan's beautiful words from the "Duenna" be applied to the two;

"Ah, sure a pair were never seen
So justly formed to meet by nature."

This also was the first appearance of Lablache, enormous in size as in talent. His voice came forth "as from a mountain." The death of this wonderful artiste left a gap that has never been filled up. Although of such immense dimensions, his every movement was a model for students of the art. He was an exception to the general rule of Italian Vocalists, who for the most part devote (perhaps wisely) their whole time and attention to the cultivation of the voice, without giving, much trouble to the study of music to a science. Lablache was an excellent musician, a good double bass player, and would sometimes for a change come into the orchestra and take the part on that instrument. So consummate an artiste was Lablache on the stage that his performance of even a second-rate part (to which he sometimes descended) would make it unusually prominent and important, as all who remember his "Doctor Bartolo" will bear witness to. He also "essayed" Figaro, a grand performance, in which he danced about the stage as lightly as a gossamer, although his reputed weight was twenty-five stone. Lablache indeed "astonished the natives" with his wonderous combined powers. When the voice rolled out in the "Suoni la Tromba," the comparatively weak organ of his son Fred, even combined with the whole power of the orchestra, was "nowhere!" The same effect is recorded of one of the musical festivals of England, in which, during the combined efforts of an enormous chorus and a band of perhaps 1,000 performers, Lablache's D thundered prominently over all. This artiste's face was, as it were, "chiselled" in the highest classic form, and is said to have been taken as a model by several great sculptors. In social life he sometimes delighted his friends by kneeling at the end of the table, placing his head between two lights, and depicting the passions—rage, envy, despair, love, revenge, pity, etc . . . a really magnificent exhibition of facial expression and refined art.[467]

It was only ten years before that Bellini had written his masterpiece *Norma*. There was great excitement in Dublin, and the opera opened on 31 August 1841. Lablache sung Oroveso with Grisi many times at the Théâtre-Italien from 1835-1840. Rubini had sung Pollione there in 1835 and 1836. For some reason, he later refused to sing it.

The *Dublin Annals* wrote, "Now we must turn to hear the praises of the Diva . . . Giulia Grisi." This was Grisi's first appearance in Dublin in this great role, (she sang in Dublin in 1840) and it was at this wonderful performance that the Irish bestowed upon her the title of "Queen of Song."[468]

> Her majestic form and commanding expression of feature were sufficiently impressive as she entered, with measured and dignified step to which we became well accustomed. The recitative "Seditiose Voci, voci di guerras" followed, and the long-sustained

A flat on the first syllable of the last word "micto"(which appeared endless), the house, of course, "came down." Her delivery of "Oh non tremare" was fittingly described as "awesome" by a listener in the pit. It was supposed that *Norma* would die with Grisi.[469]

Certainly, Grisi was unrivalled in this role and many others.

Norma opens with Lablache as Oroveso, the Archdruid, standing in the sacred forest of the druids. The druidical soldiers and priests await the rising of the moon. At that mystic hour, Norma, the daughter of Oroveso, who is a high priestess, will perform a sacred rite. The chorus sings of vengeance against their Roman oppressors. Again, praise for Lablache:

> He was simply grand. In the third bar of the opening recitative—"Ite sul colle o Druid" ... he had the chance of thundering out that wonderful D of his; also in the "Si parlera" and "Tremendo," the last word was, indeed appropriate to the tremendous tone of the voice. A "roaring" encore was the result, which rarely occurs with the opening chorus of *Norma*.[470]

Florimo writes about how he remembers Lablache singing the role at the San Carlo in Naples:

> Lablache was stupendous in *Norma* as Oroveso, when he appeared in his striking priest's robes, with the anger of an overpowered and oppressed nation in his heart. He was outstanding when he stirs up the Druids singing a powerful war hymn, in the prophetic words of the prelude "Si, parlera terribile da queste quercie antiche." And in the finale scene when touched by his daughter's tears, he forgives her, after she confesses in fear and terror that she is a mother, here he was at his very best, and the whole audience shared his emotions. He possessed a tremendous dramatic feeling and strength, and something else which few privileged beings have received from God, "Il grido del cuore" (cry from the heart).[471]

Florimo continues praising Lablache:

> Geniuses cannot be taken as models, whoever understands them does not imitate them. They understand and perform beautifully, often though they do not know what they are doing, because

they are guided by a superior power, which enters into them, and dominates their minds. They make nature sublime, because they raise up to that happy world of images and impressions, which constitute the soul and fantasy of the artist. In those perfect moments of inspiration they give back to us the echo of a superior virtue, something which comes to us from heaven and therefore transports us from beyond our world. If one can define enthusiasm, rapture, then one has defined genius, the artist's work. To understand genius, reason does not count, and even less so rules. Heart and fantasy instead count a lot. Sometimes it's better to admire and keep silent. Rossini often used to say, "many singers in my day have been great artists, others have been sublime in their individual specialties, but the true geniuses are only three: *il Papa Lablache;* il prediletto filio,(beloved son) il vero *Rubino del canto,* il caro *Don Giovanni Battista;* e quell' *enfant gâté della natura*—(Child of nature) *Maria Felicita Malibran*."[472]

The Dublin season continued with *Sonnambula* with Frédéric as the Count Rodolpho, Mario as Elvino, Grisi as Amina; the reviews were superb by *The Musical World*:

The best operatic Company that ever graced our boards of our theatre have just taken their departure. The article goes on. Long before the time appointed crowds of persons, anxious to enjoy the so rich a treat, besieged the doors, although the prices of admission had doubled. Of Mario's debut, they were ecstatic. "Signor Mario made his first bow as Arturo in *I Puritani*, and all of Dublin was at his feet, after singing "A te o cara." At once established him as their favorite tenor. What could be more beautiful than Madame Grisi's warbling of the polacca, "Son vergin vezzosa" and Lablache's rich undercurrent melody? She also gave the beautiful air "Qui la voca" In the celebrated trumpet duet the great Lablache's sonorous voice (audible far above the entire orchestra) fairly astonished his auditors. In *Norma* Madame Grisi had room to display her powers as an actress. In the scene where she accuses her lover, she actually electrified the audience; the duet "Si, fino all'ore estreme," was charmingly given by her and her cousin, Ernesta Grisi. Bellini's *Sonnambula* was next performed, and anything like the enthusiasm evinced was never witnessed. Mario was very successful in the part of Elvino . . . Madame Grisi gave with exquisite tenderness "Come per me", but the delightful way. She warbled the beautiful final baffles description; the wreaths of flowers which covered the stage on its third repetition showed how it was felt by the audience.

Il Barbiere next performed for Lablache's benefit. A mercurial spirit seemed to pervade the whole, and Lablache alternately amused and astonished the audience; the trio "Zitti,Zitti," between Mario, Grisi, and F, Lablache, was beautifully given. Madame Grisi introduced the Rodes' air with variations. Continuing with Lablache singing his usual excellent and amusing representation of Campanone, in the old favorite *Il Prova d'un Opera seria*.

The operatic season closed with a performance of *I Puritani*, and the whole troupe left for Glasgow Scotland. Needless to say they were invited back to Ireland the next year.[473]

On 15 September, the Scottish newspapers stated that there was great interest in hearing that the group had come from Ireland (passing on their way to Paris via a few towns in the provinces). Lablache and the others sang before a very fashionable audience that had been waiting in great expectation for the Italian singers. According to *The Musical World*,

> Lablache sang Mozart's 'Non piu andrai' . . . it is one of those gems that no succeeding composer has approached; and in spite of the absence of a full band which would have completely exhibited the intentions and merits of the author, Lablache's splendid singing of it made it forgotten and that such accessories were ever employed. Next to Mozart, Rossini claims notice: "there is in all his operas a brilliancy which dazzles the imagination; his melodies are so graceful, and the accomplishments so exciting that the attention is agreeably arrested at once, and the pleasure prolonged to the end of each piece." During the concerts there were several pieces from *Il Barbiere* and other operas. Cimarosa's magnificent duet from *Il Matrimonio Segreto* and Rossini's duet from *La Cenerentola* "Un Segreto d'importanza" are compositions of first rate excellence; Luigi Lablache and Frédéric Lablache (father and son) imparted to them a musical-like finish which went far to compensate the imperfection we have alluded to. But of all music which was performed, the selection from *I Puritani* was that most generally admired. Bellini's fame seems to rest on this foundation and a

goodly fabric it is, supported by such pillars of strength as Grisi and Lablache. Another variety was the buffo duets, by Madame Grisi and Signor Lablache, "Oh guardate che figura" and the singing lesson from the opera *Il Fanatico Per La Musica.*

This concert was performed at the Glasgow assembly rooms and then again at the Theatre Royal.

Afterward, they headed up to Edinburgh for two concerts at the Waterloo rooms on September 17-18 (returning to London after a concert at Newcastle on the twentieth.) Here again, a very fashionable assembly gathered to hear the singers. This was not however the first visit to this city. The newspapers wrote how Edinburgh received the Italians:

> The second concert given by Madame Grisi and Signor Lablache was given in the Waterloo Rooms on Saturday morning. Shortly after the doors were opened the rooms were crowded in every part with an assembly of the first elegance and fashion. The reception of the performers was enthusiastic. Standing as they do at the summit of their profession, and having received the homage of the first musical circles in Europe, the audience had no choice but to be enraptured, or sacrifice all pretention to taste or critical acumen. At the same time it must be confessed that a concert room with a meager pianoforte accompaniment is not the place best fitted for the display of operatic talent. The selections were chiefly from Mozart, Donizetti, Bellini and Rossini, and it is hardly an exaggeration to say that the concert was performed twice over, almost every piece encored. Among the most striking efforts were: "Deh Calma" and "Una voce poco fa" by Madame Grisi; "Una furtiva lagrima," by Signor Mario; and the buffo duet, "Con pazienza" by Grisi and Lablache; all of which were rapturously encored. Lablache's voice is, the most wonderful in the world; and excited the amazement of all present by its prodigious strength and compass. F. Lablache has improved since his last visit to this city, and evinces a good deal of humour for which his father is remarkable. Signora Ernesta Grisi promises well, but beside her accomplished relative she appears to some disadvantage. The only instrumental performers were Signor Puzzi, on the French horn, and Monsieur Benedict, on the pianoforte; the former a master of his very difficult instrument, and the latter a pianist of considerable merit.[474]

Giulia Grisi by then was without rival. Her beauty of voice and classic looks were without equal; she personified the Victorian ideal prima donna. The entrance of Jenny Lind to the opera world was far away to present any challenge. Lind, a star of magnitude in her own country Sweden, left to sing in Berlin and Vienna. Soon, she encountered difficulties with her singing and sought help in Paris from the skilled teacher Manuel Garcia, brother of Maria Malibran. He told her that she was about to lose her voice and only rest and proper training would bring it back.[475]

During the summer of 1841, the adventuresome oldest daughter of Luigi Lablache, Francesca (La Cecchina), a young widow and former wife of painter Francois Bouchot, arrived at Civitavecchia, Italy. There she wanted to spend time at the seaside away from Paris and to take the waters at a nearby spa. She was properly provisioned with a letter of introduction to the French consul.[476]

A tall, slim Italian beauty, she soon attracted the attention of the little French colony and especially the French consul there, Henry Beyle. Beyle, widely known as the famous author Stendhal, had a reputation as a notorious womanizer, and Mme. Bouchot was referred to in books by Stendhal and others at that time under a thinly disguised name, Mme. Bonola or Mme. Os.[477] Beyle was in Civitavecchia recovering slowly from a stroke and other various ailments, one of which was gout.[478] Mme. Bouchot was there apparently to rendezvous with her lover, German painter Henri Lehmann.

Here, there are conflicting stories for sure. Reports explain Beyle first met Cecchina in Cititavecchia; however, the author Matthew Josephson writes that Beyle knew Cecchina long before in Naples[479] and while returning from Rome, he visited Florence in July, and feeling lonely and bored one evening, he went to the Theatre Leopold (25 July). There, he was very surprised and pleased to behold the delightful chanteuse La Cecchina on the stage of the opera before him in Bellini's *Beatrice di Tenda*. Josephson writes, "Cecchina, was a dark and passionate beauty . . . he called on her several times." There, they were supposed to have had an affair. Evidence points to the couple having spent the nights of 13 August and 14 together at the Hotel de la Porta Rossa. It seems after encountering each other by accident in Florence in July, La Cecchina continued to travel to Civitavecchia. Beyle writes, "The accommodating Madame Francesca Bouchot was an 'oasis in the desert' of his life in Civitavecchia."[480] In early August, the twenty-seven-year-old painter Henri Lehmann showed up there, drawing a pencil sketch of the decaying Beyle, the last portrait made of him.

> For a moment, however, she was a lovely young woman alone in a dull seaside town, and she needed some amusement. She and Beyle spent hours of conversation through July, he gave her *Chartreuse*[481] to read, and she returned the compliment with teasing signs of sexual invitation. "*Great faus-two and tenth August 1841,*" he wrote in English in a marginalium. "*Perhaps the last of his life.*"[482]

Stendhal died shortly later in Paris on the 23 March[483] 1842.

ଔଔଔ

Chapter Twenty-Four

Stabat Mater

1841-42

The Puritani Quartet were back that season in Paris, plus Frédéric Lablache with the usual favorites—*L'Elisir d'amore, I Puritani, La Cenerentola, Norma, Il Turco, Il Barbiere, Lucrezia Borgia, Don Giovanni*, supplemented by the first performance of Rossini's *Stabat Mater*.

On the 19 October 1841, quite suddenly, impresario Domenico Barbaja died at his villa home in Posillipo of a stroke. The news would have not improved Rossini's mood, already fearful of his own mortality and as, at that time, he was fighting all manner of ailments, real and imaginary. Pierre Laporte, the manager of Her Majesty's Theatre also passed away the same year. Benjamin Lumley took over his position.

Rossini's *Stabat Mater* was first sung in a private home in Paris, then again for a rehearsal on 31 October 1841 attended by journalists and critics. On 7 January 1842, *Stabat Mater* was performed before a immense throng and was acclaimed by all as the most outstanding event of the year at the Théâtre-Italien.[484]

From there on, the work was heard throughout the world. In Italy, Donizetti left Milan after a successful premiere at La Scala of his opera *Maria Padilla* on 28 December 1841. He had been asked by Rossini to go to Bologna and conduct the *Stabat Mater*, which to him was a great honor. Rossini was still not at all well, but the performances of 18 March, 19, and 20 succeeded as scheduled before an enormous throng of enthusiastic supporters at the Archiginnasio, directed by Donizetti. After it was all over, the sick Rossini managed to get up on to the platform, and there he embraced and kissed Donizetti, saying, "You are the only *maestro* who knows how to conduct my Stabat as I wish it."[485] Donizetti recollects the event and Rossini: "If you could see how he wept on leaving me!"[486]

In June 1842, Rossini was knighted in Italy; and during that year, the composer Verdi visited him. Then upon writing to a friend, Verdi states that it must be great to be Rossini—is there a touch of envy here when he writes? "When I think that the reputation alive throughout the world is Rossini, I could kill myself, and with me, all the imbeciles. Oh it is a great thing to be Rossini!"

Donizetti left Bologna for Vienna with a letter of introduction from Rossini to Prince Clemens von Metternich, Austrian minister of foreign affairs, a man very well-known to Rossini. Donizetti started his rehearsals for his *Linda Di Chamounix* there. Ill health continued to plague Rossini, and on 27 May 1843,[487] Rossini and Olympe returned to Paris where Rossini would receive further treatments from French doctors.

Queen Victoria still expressed a keen interest in opera, and her visits to Her Majesty's were just as frequent as before, often about two to three times a week. Albert joined her there and was just as much a devotee as the Queen, and it has been suggested that was all they had in common. Husband and wife liked nothing better than to spend their evenings together playing and singing at the piano.

One of the Italian baritones to debut that year at Her Majesty's was Giorgio Ronconi. Like Lablache, he came from a musical family; his father Domenico was from Milan and an artiste of great eminence in his time and was first tenor to Alexander the emperor of Russia, Francesco I of Austria, and Maximilian of Prussia. Giorgio Ronconi's debut came at the age of eighteen in Bellini's *La straniera* where he sang before the composer himself. Donizetti wrote his opera *Torquato Tasso* especially for Ronconi, and he sang it in Rome with great success. He also created roles in many other Donizetti operas. Chorley wrote of him:

> He possessed such wonderful dramatic powers, that one virtually forgot his vocal limitations, a compass of barely more than one octave, inferior in quality, weak and habitually out of tune.

Ronconi sang at the San Carlo in the late thirties where he was reputed to have sung "no less that 282 times"(*Musical World*). When former manager for Her Majesty's Laporte discovered Ronconi singing in Italy, he was so delighted with his talent that he immediately arranged for him to sing in England. Mme.Ronconi was also included in the engagement. However, when they arrived in London, it was a bit of a shock to find Laporte had died. However, manager Benjamin Lumley honored their engagement that season. Afterward, Ronconi even took a tour of the provinces accompanied by Sigismund Thalberg, Mme. Ronconi, and John Parry.

During the summer opera season of 1842 at Her Majesty's, Lablache was engaged to sing Rossini's *Stabat Mater* on 6 July. He was also signed up for an enormous agenda of different operas, *Torquato Tasso, L'Elisir d'amore, Lucrezia Borgia, Le cantatrici villane, Barbiere, Don Giovanni, Puritani, Mosè, Anna Bolena, Il Matrimonio Segreto, Cosi fan tutte*, and on 11 August, *Otello*.

The Illustrated London News started publishing that year and did not leave out Lablache:[488] "Lablache who is marvelous in sacred music will sing in Rossini's *Stabat Mater* on 6 July." Later in October under the heading of "Theatre All Over the Country": "Lablache has just undergone an operation at the jawbone which produced a favourable effect."

The Illustrated London News on 9 July 1842 writes under the title "Rossini's *Stabat Mater*":[489]

> At this present moment Rossini's sacred production, *Stabat Mater*, is creating as great a sensation as any of his dramatic works; and the splendid scale on which it has been produced during the past week at Her Majesty's Theatre will tend to give it an enduring place in public estimation, as well as to swell the measure of Rossini's fame. The whole glorious production was brought out on Wednesday morning. The following 'artistes' assisting on the occasion—Signore Lablache, F. Lablache, G. Ronconi, Poggi, Guasco, Rubini, and Mesdames Persiani, Moltini, Graziani, and Grammaglia. The choruses were sung by upwards of a hundred voices, and the orchestra was composed of all the instrumentalists or Her Majesty's Theatre. The whole under the direction of Signor Costa, who conducted the performance. The *Stabat Mater* went off with the greatest success nearly one half of the pieces being enthusiastically encored; Signor Rubini gave the air "Cujus animam" in his best style, and was honoured with an enthusiastic encore. Signor Lablache was encored in the recitative (with chorus) "Eia Mater;" his powerful voice and correct judgement render him, of course, fully equal to sustain the most difficult portion of a sacred performance, and on this occasion he was eminently successful; we wish he had also been selected to sing the beautiful solo "Pro Peccatis" Madame Persiani thrilled the audience by her very exquisite execution of the grand aria (with

chorus), "Inflammatus et accensus"; this air and chorus were loudly encored, as was the quartet "Quando Corpus," sung by Persiani, Grammaglia, Rubini and Lablache.

Rubini's voice was admired above all tenors of the nineteenth century. His voice even endured longer than some; that year, he left England for Russia and then retired from the stage. Family tradition recounts this anecdote:

> Signor Frédéric Lablache once told a friend that when singing on one occasion with Rubini in the *Matrimonio Segreto,* he held the great tenor's hand in his own, during a passage in the famous duet, and at the same time, looked him full in the face, without being able to detect the act of breathing in the least degree. This wonderful power of concealment led the vulgar to believe that Rubini could sing only during the act of inspiration! Of course, it was simply the triumph of his consummate art, misunderstood only by those who were ignorant of the first principles of singing.

Don Giovanni was sung on 16 June. Lablache was an expert on Mozart, and he was known to be at his best and the most comfortable singing Mozart. His rendering of Leporello was the "definitive one" while he was alive, never failing to leave the audience roaring with laughter while producing a new twist to the role as he took greater and greater liberties while he was frolicking about. Sometimes, he came down to the audience. The humor came about especially when in the last act, he tries to crawl under the table; being so large, he finds that the table is on his back and now he's stuck with all the dishes and plates rattling, the candles swaying. He maintained his position, quietly for a moment while the audience roared, the music came to a halt, and Lablache became unstuck. Sometimes he put on huge carpet slippers. Alfredo Piatti remembers an incident:

> The gentleman who held the post of prompter at Covent Garden was Signor Monterasi, a native of Bergamo, and as big a man as Lablache. In the supper scene of *Don Giovanni,* Lablache, in the part of Leporello, moved about the stage trembling and carrying a lighted tallow candle. He always contrived to pour plenty of tallow over Signor Monterasi who in the narrow limits of the prompter box was unable to escape it.[490]

Queen Victoria did not attend *Cosi fan tutte*. She had strong opinions about Mozart as he had a reputation of being immoral to the proper Victorians. The characters in *Cosi fan tutte* scheme and deceive. The Queen also dismisses *The Magic Flute* and writes, "The music of the immoral Mozart is so fine, but the story is too simple, trivial and rather absurd for our times." Of *La Clemenza di Tito*: "The music is very fine, but remarkably dull and heavy. We went away in the second act." She was not keen on *Le nozze di Figaro* and found *Cosi fan tutte* "much too long and the story much too uninteresting and absurd."[491] Again, she uses the word *absurd*. Which reminds one of her earlier statement that she was a thoughly "modern person" who preferred the works of Rossini, Donizetti, and Bellini to Mozart. While *Don Giovanni* was shown more or less annually at Her Majesty's, *Cosi fan tutte* was not. The opera was shown again in 1845, and then the Queen wrote that she preferred the ballet. Strangely the now mature queen did enjoy *Don Giovanni,* the story of the famed seducer Don Juan, whose morals had much to be desired. "The more I see *Don Giovanni*, the more I admire it . . . the music is so splendid."[492] In fact to any woman, it is the Don, that libertine Don Giovanni, who is so overwhelmingly appealing and fascinating. Queen Victoria was overcome too.

At the end of August, Giulia Grisi, Mario, Lablache, F. Lablache, E. Grisi, and conductor and musical director of Her Majesty's Theatre Michael Costa left for Dublin via Manchester, Liverpool, and Edinburgh. On 22 August and 24 August, they were in Manchester and sang a program of concerts including selections from *Mosè, Malek Abel, Stabat Mater*, and *Elisa e Claudio*. Then they sang at the Theatre Royal Liverpool. The playbill reads "A Grand concert, an Italian concert, consisting of selections from popular Italian operas . . . *La Cenerentola, Flauto Magico, Norma, Malek Abel, Guillaume Tell, Sonnambula, Il fanatico, Aureliano, Stabat Mater.*" Mme. Grisi sang "Casta Diva." The two Lablaches sang a duet "Un Segreto d'importanza" from Rossini's *La Cenerentola*. Afterward, they left for Edinburgh Scotland, singing there at the Assembly Rooms. Later arriving in Dublin, there the season opened with *I Puritani* on 5 September at the Theatre Royal. After *I Puritani*, they sang Bellini's *Norma*.

When Donizetti's *Anna Bolena* opened on 14 September, it was Mario who sang the poetic "Vivi tu" and it was Mario's turn to become *primo tenore*, taking over the mantle of fame now discarded by Rubini. Just like the romantic roles he played before to the footlights, he had not only grabbed the title of first tenor of his time but also the hand of the most beautiful leading prima donna of the day, Giulia Grisi. This was quite an achievement to be proud of, considering his climb to fame had only taken four years. Unfortunately, Grisi could never marry Mario as she was married already; though separated, she had no grounds for divorce.

Lablache was a sensation as Henry VIII with Mario in *Anna Bolena,* his first interpretation there; the *Dublin Theatre Annals* wrote:

> Lablache's representation of the King Henry was quite in keeping when undertaken by that consummate artiste. Grisi was suffering a cold, and was unable to sing for four or five days; concerts were inserted instead, but this was a terrible blow to the management. Madame Grisi, now in her prime was the major attraction; all Dublin wanted to see and hear her.

Her looks personified the classic Greek or Italian beauty. The Victorian ideal woman was modelled on the beauty of the Venus de Milo, with the classic features, the high brow, the large eyes and roman nose, all these features Grisi possessed, thus in the Romantic age, Victorians found their ideals in Classical times.

After the French Revolution, the time of Napoleon brought in an age where fashion and style were in sharp contrast to the overdecorated decor and fashion of the previous century. Grisi was a modern woman of her age, like Malibran before her. Both her statuesque beauty and her genius were displayed best in lyric tragedy. Her most famous role, first and foremost and without any doubt, was *Norma.* With *Norma,* she took over where the great Pasta left off and was her equal. Mythical roles and heroines from the Middle Ages were her forte, thus she was a great *Semiramide. Lucrezia Borgia* gave large scope to Grisi's powers, and it was with these roles she would electrify audiences. Overall, she now eclipsed most of her rivals, and for years, it remained that way. The *Annals of the Theatre Royal* wrote, "Grisi was sick most of the week . . . this caused the loss of thousands of pounds in receipts." The next year, the Italian opera in Dublin was abandoned; it was announced there had been too many difficulties. Luigi Lablache never sang in Dublin again, but Frédéric Lablache returned in 1844 with Grisi, successfully introducing *Don Pasquale* to Dublin.

That year, the King of Tenors, Giovanni Battista Rubini, planned to retire. The public still would not let him leave the stage. *The Illustrated London News* comments 1 June 1842:

> Rubini, 'the first tenor of his age' ... in spite of all the reports of his intention to absent himself is still among us and has been crowned with a triple crown of popularity for his acceptance of an engagement in England after he had refused all the other major capitals of the world. His reception at Her Majesty's Theatre on Saturday night was enthusiastic in the extreme. Every part of the theatre was crowded to excess and the boxes presented one of the most brilliant assemblages of rank and fashion that have ever been seen with in its walls. Her Majesty was present. The opera was *Sonnambula* and he was singing with the beautiful Fanny Persiani, second only to Grisi, and Frédéric Lablache as the Count. This was his last season. Flowers and bouquets were thrown after a thunderous applause upon his entrance as the opera villager ...

In September after singing in the London summer season of 1842, he gave a farewell tour around the southern counties singing in Plymouth, Brighton, Exeter, and Torquay. After returning to London, immediately he left for engagements in Berlin, Moscow, and St. Petersburg. So successful was he there that *The Musical World* wrote in 1845:[493]

> Among one of the souvenirs Rubini carries away with him from St. Petersburg is a crown of massive gold, inlaid with brilliants of great value. What an earth can Rubini do with this crown? We know that German Kingdoms are going very cheap, maybe he'll buy one, and retire on a cheap throne!

Rubini retired to his huge palace in Italy near Milan—still standing today. There he lived out his remaining days. In 1847, Rubini visited Donizetti in Bergamo on his deathbed and sang "Verrano a Te," from *Lucia di Lammermoor*, in a vain attempt to revive him from the grip of death.

ჱჱჱ

Chapter Twenty Five

Don Pasquale

1843-44

When Donizetti was commissioned to write *Don Pasquale* for the Théâtre-Italien, he was unaware that this work would be his last comic opera. Italian opera buffa had always had a place in the theater since the eighteenth century, and it remained a most important part of society of that era, especially now that Rossini had stopped composing operas. New lighter works were needed, and *Don Pasquale* filled that gap. It had been a few decades since Rossini's *Il Barbiere di Siviglia* was written, and the time was ripe to bring a new comic work into the repertoire.

Donizetti's new opera buffa *Don Pasquale* was based on Angelo Anelli's libretto of Stefano Pavesi's *Ser Marcantonio,* put together from a story by Ben Johnson, *The Silent Women.*[494] This successful work surfaced in Paris in 1811 and had held its own against Rossini's comedies. And the brilliant first performance, at La Scala in 1810, was repeated fifty-four times. Lablache also had great success singing this work for its first performance at the newly inaugurated Teatro San Ferdinando in Palermo in 1816.[495] Donizetti may have noticed too that it was shown in Vienna when he was there in 1842. William Ashbrook notes,

> Hoping to repeat his success he had with *L'Elisir d'amore* Donizetti hired the librettist Giovanni Ruffini to adapt the text, expressly for the talents of Grisi, Mario, Tamburini and Lablache.[496]

When Donizetti wrote the title role for Lablache, the success of the opera was then regarded as a foregone conclusion as Lablache had proved himself from his youth opera buffa's most famous exponent. In 1842, Donizetti's operas were the toast of Paris. The season opened on 1 October with *Lucia di Lammermoor* starring beautiful Fanny Persiani and a stellar cast. Persiani again starred in the Paris premiere of *Linda di Chamounix* on 17 November. Donizetti had revised it, adding quite a few arias and a new cabaletta written especially for Lablache. Also in the cast were Mario, Tamburini, F. Lablache, and soprano Marietta Brambilla. *Linda's* overwhelming success in Vienna[497] did not happen in Paris at first; it was received rather coldly, but later found a following.[498]

Meanwhile, Donizetti was writing *Don Pasquale* to a text adapted by the Italian exile Giovanni Ruffini. In an amazing eleven days, Donizetti completed the piano vocal score in even fewer days than Rossini was reputed to have written the *Barbiere*. The truth in Donizetti's case was a bit dramatized. Ashbrook writes, "It would be more realistic to say that Donizetti worked on the opera for three months."[499] Certainly he did write *Don Pasquale* in a hurry, but he did not sacrifice any of the quality although many changes were made, changes that drove his librettist mad. The managers Vatel and Dormoy had doubts about its success, but Donizetti was the picture of self-confidence. "Have no fear for me," he told Leon Escudier. "My work will be a success."[500] The timeless tenor aria written for Mario in the last act. "Com'e Gentile" was reputed to have been added at the last minute. The scenario of creating this opera took on the appearance of an opera buffa in itself. There was also some trouble when Tamburini complained that Lablache's role was better than his and threatened to walk out unless this was corrected.[501] In fact, so many changes were made to the score that eventually Ruffini declined to put his name to it. He explained to his mother:

> I have not put my name to it, be it understood, because, it having been written in such haste and my freedom of action having in a certain sense been paralyzed by the maestro, I don't recognize it as mine.[502]

Clearly, Donizetti did not write this opera as a period piece as the settings and costumes were modern. Yet even that was argued over. Lablache agreed with Donizetti that the music did not permit period costumes, and he won out. In the first performance as one can see clearly from the drawings, Lablache towers over the other singers in the quartet. The glass plates for this picture belong to the descendants of the family and are in Paris.[503]

Don Pasquale opened at the Théâtre-Italien on 3 January 1843 and immediately became an overwhelming success. Clearly now Lablache proved himself the greatest basso of the Italian repertory of all time. Donizetti received a flood of praises from audiences and critics alike, pleased that he had written a witty and comic masterpiece possibly equal in popularity to *L'Elisir d'amore*. Donizetti was delighted; it helped heal the wounds of *Marino Faliero* for both Lablache and Donizetti.[504] The title role of the portly old uncle, most usually called an old flop trying to play a gallant suitor, was played to perfection by Luigi Lablache. The other members of the cast were Grisi as Norina, Tamburini as Dr. Malatesta, and Mario as Ernesto. Frédéric Lablache sang the small role of Notario. Donizetti describes the evening in a letter to Matteo Salvi:

> The reception was most cheering. The *adagio* of the finale to Act 2 was repeated. The *stretta* of the duet between Lablache and Grisi was repeated. I was called out at the close of the second and third acts. There was not one piece, from the overture on, that was not more or less applauded. I am very happy.[505]

All Paris was enjoying the antics of the great singer. In another letter to Ricordi, he reported that Lablache was the "pivot of the new work."[506] The following is from a review:

> The entire weight of the drama may be stated to fall on Don Pasquale. It is one of the most admirable assumptions of Lablache; he is comic to the fingers' ends: if he had never been the great bass he is, he would have gained glory as a consummate comedian. His making up as a 'young flop' to be introduced to the presumed novice, was admirable. His 'indescribables' were a gigantic check and striped pattern, with an inflammatory 'toupet' and a party coloured cravat to correspond. The audience were convulsed with laughter at his strange antics, his eccentric action, and his inimitable byplay.[507]

Théophile Gautier's review also describes Lablache:

> The uncle played by Lablache, wearing a house coat of white dimity, nankeen trousers and in a black silk bonnet, is like all uncles everywhere, is very displeased with his nephew. Following ancient and solemn precedent he seeks to disinherit him . . . Don Pasquale, despite his sixty-eight years and that he has gout, finds himself a bold fellow (gaillard) still green enough to make heirs less collateral than M. Ernest. He consults with Dr Malatesta on this

> delicate point . . . The doctor returns with a young women wearing a dress of the most virginal carmelite and a black veil that hardly lets one suspect her pretty face. To receive this angel of youth and beauty, Don Pasquale makes a most extravagant toilette: a superb wig the colour of mahogany with too many curls; a green tailcoat with engraved gold buttons, which he could never fasten because of the enormous rotundity of his figure. All of this gives him a look of a monstrous beetle that wants to open his wings and fly and cannot succeed. With the most gallant air he advances with popping eyes, his mouth heart shaped, to take the girls hand. she emits a cry as though she was bitten by a viper.[508]

The *Don Pasquale* sheet music sold well. On the cover was the huge lithograph of Lablache with *Don Pasquale* written across his stomach with words Valse de Don Pasquale, arrange pour piano par Labarre, 3 F. The words Opera de Donizetti appears in small letters on a camellia in Lablache's lapel buttonhole. Underneath appear the publishers, Vienne Diabelli in France, Addison and Beale in London, and Ricordi in Milan. In the London version, some things were the same, but a different head was interposed on the same figure. The suit he wears is the same and he wears the same camellia, but the artist has copied the drawing; two shillings has now replaced three francs and on the scroll is written London. Cramer, Addison, and Beale, 201 Regent Street.[509]

Donizetti now left for Vienna. When he returned, his health had taken a definite turn for the worse. *Don Pasquale* is reviewed by Théophile Gautier who praises Lablache as thus:

> Neither the black spleen of the London fogs, nor the ennui and disillusion of Paris, could resist Lablache in the title role. This Titanic prophet of woe, this gigantic jester with the brow of Jupiter, is always immensely effective. In the theatre actors who play ridiculous parts are usually pathetic . . . Lablache, on the other hand, has only to remove his grotesque makeup and burnt cork wrinkles, to thunder forth the sublime curse of Brabantio (*Otello*), or the crushing imprecation of Oroveso (*Norma*), now (*Don Pasquale*) Tomorrow he will fulminate in the duet "Suoni la Tromba" (*I Puritani*) and certainly no more terrible and majestic figure can be imagined. One can therefore surrender entirely to the hilarity he provokes; there is nothing degrading about it, one is not laughing at an infirmity or a misfortune.'

Leon Escudier wrote of Lablache: "When he came on, with his bright face, advancing timidly with svelte air, and weighed down despite himself by his gigantic corpulence, laughter broke out throughout the house."[510] The audiences couldn't get enough of Lablache, and the theatre was sold out every night. It almost seemed that Donizetti was overwhelmed by his success; he wrote to Tommaso Persico from Vienna on 2 January:

> Even today I received eight papers from Paris talking about *Don Pasquale*. I myself am stupefied, but that's the way it is: nineteen thousand francs in eleven days! A stroke of fortune. Voila tout. Un imprudence . . .[511]

For the production, Lablache always wore a white camellia in his buttonhole. The gardener in charge of the Marquis Alexandre-Marie Aguado's famous greenhouses[512] arrived each day just before the performance with a single camellia for him. Wearing this flower every day was his trademark. Florimo remembers another story behind this daily event:

> The first time one of the pearls of Donizetti was performed in Paris, *Don Pasquale*, we have Lablache with his "new-market," blond hair, shiny boots, a camellia in his buttonhole, with his usual wit and his famous voice, heard shouts and cheers coming from the beautiful ladies mouths and saw snow-white hands clapping. The most beautiful ladies were competing amongst themselves for the pleasure of providing a camellia for the buttonhole of the great artiste. One particular evening, a well turned out gentleman approached the commissioner of the Italien theatre, and left a box for Lablache. This box was sealed at each end with wax seals, representing a camellia with the crown of a Count on tho top of it. Lablache opened the box; there beautifully arranged he saw in it a camellia resting on a bed of cotton wool. This was a flower of extraordinary beauty: an artificial stem substituted the real one, it was exquisitely made of gold; the leaves were of velvet, but so well made that art was superior to nature. From then on every night he received a similar camellia. Naturally such persistence aroused the curiosity of Lablache. Determined to find out the truth, he bought a lorgnette. This amused the public no end, but nobody knew that it was an expedient used by Lablache to find out who was the unknown lady that sent him the precious with such

regularity. (Sometimes the flower was just a single fresh white camellia.) No 15, on the first row of boxes was occupied every evening by a young lady, with curled blond hair, blue eyes, always dressed in white. Convinced the flowers came from the same lady he persuaded himself that that was the case. In vain he tried to see if the flowers she was resting every night on the parapet of her box contained camellias. In fact a fabulous camellia he received every night, christened by the botanists "La Grand Federica", as maybe it was a clue to her name. But the favourite bouquet, resting on the ledge of the blond beauty's box, consisted always of roses, and dawn coloured violets. Then Lablache questioned the messenger, trying to get him to talk, but every evening there was a different person who professed ignorance to all his questions. One evening he appeared on the stage without the usual flower: everyone noticed his concern although he tried to appear as happy as ever. But the matter became even more complicated, not only because they thought he had lost the flower and were sharing in his unhappiness but also because nephew Ernesto (Mario) came on the stage sporting the camellia in his buttonhole, the same one that adorned Lablache "The new market" of his uncle Don Pasquale did not know what to do, he almost lost his voice! . . . but God did not allow such a nasty accident to perturb the career of this eminent singer. In spite of his emotion Lablache continued to sing as normal. At the same time he was questioning with his eyes . . . Mario, promising to himself to challenge him later. When the artists returned back stage, Lablache firmly asked for his camellia. "Your camellia" replied the tenor, "is mine. Your beautiful unknown lady has finally done justice to the tenors and it was high time too, because we have fallen into disrepute thanks to the preference for basses. Here is the sacred box and here is my name written by the same hand which once wrote yours."

Lablache remained speechless, astounded at the sight of his rival's name, but Ernesto, afraid of a jealous disagreement between the two of them, removed the flower, placing in to Lablache's buttonhole. Lablache returned to the stage.

The audience is mystified as to what happened, now Don Pasquale has a camellia, and Ernesto is without, this gave rise to a lot of gossip, on stage and off. This is what really happened. A certain Countess M. felt particular affection for the greatest genius of the Italian theatre. As a token of her secret admiration she devised to send him a flower every evening, a finishing touch for the part he performed so well. For the first seven performances the camellia was religiously handed to him, but on the eighth it had ended up on another suit. Should the Countess be accused of inconsistency? On the contrary. The maid, a quick-witted brunette, who had to find a messenger either rather silly or rather faithful to keep the important secret. One evening the maid thought the Countess had done enough for Lablache, and that she was unjust towards Mario. The vivacious and rather giddy brunette went to the theatre with the same dedication as her mistress, who was obviously far above her socially, and the very handsome Mario had made her head swim. Without saying a word to anyone, she substituted Mario's name for Lablache's, so our tenor Mario received the flower.[513]

One rather wonders if this deliberate mistake was not perhaps an opportunity for Mario to have some fun at Lablache's expense.

After the end of the season, the group all left for London, minus Pauline Viardot and Tamburini. Tamburini, after singing briefly in Marseilles, joined Rubini in St. Petersburg at the Imperial Theatre. Viardot proceeded to Russia via Vienna. Tamburini, who had not been treated well by the management of Her Majesty's Theatre, did not sing in London again till 1847 and then only for the opening season of the new Royal Italian house at Covent Garden when it became a permanent opera house. Here, Lablache answers a letter from Rubini who was obviously triumphant in Russia:

> My Dear Friend, Rogna,
>
> I cannot tell you how grateful I would have been to see you in your roles, and how much pain I felt at the same time, not be being able to accept your beautiful proposition. But you know I have, and will always be, a blockhead. After all the dirt I got from all the impresarios in Paris, I should not have engaged myself with them, but they have totally so annoyed and fatigued me that I had to sign a new contract. And, to my great torment, all this a few days before the arrival of your letter. Dear God! Why did you not write something to me before His Majesty the Emperor's decision?

I could have been again in your company, and in a land that rouses my curiosity. Patience. I was destined otherwise.

I have not failed to answer General Guedeonoff expressing all my pain for not having been able to accept a similar offer. It is futile to tell you, dear Rogna, how much-I enjoyed to hear about your triumphs, and your earnings, because you know how much I always praised your talents in unity with all my family—and, thank God! I was never envious of you. Always good health, followed by good into better for the Glory of our poor Italy.

I salute cordially thy good Adelaide, and remember sometimes your Scalandrone that names you a thousand times in one season.

Adieu. Good health.

L. Lablache

P.S. Teresa entrusts me to salute your Adelaide in friend ship, and she asked me, also, to beg you for our son, Federico. "You know him, dear Rubini. If you think you could do something, and put in a good word for him, you would be doing your old comrade a great service."

We, send to you all the gratitude from our family, and to everyone close to you, for Eternity.[514]

Russia welcomed back Pauline Viardot; after successes in London and Paris, she had many admirers waiting for her. She also wrote from Russia to Lablache calling him, "Caro Papa Lablache," telling him how she is (1/2/43).[515] There she joined Rubini and Tamburini at St. Petersburg and at the Bolshoi in Moscow. The Imperial Theatre there needed plenty of singers to fill the roles as they had split into two companies. In the autumn season, Rubini and Viardot sang together in *Il Barbiere di Siviglia*, *Otello*, *La Sonnambula*, and *Lucia*. Tamburini sang in all these operas and many others with Viardot, and to the delight of the Russian audiences, on 30 November 1844, Viardot sang Norma. While she lacked the charisma and dramatic looks of Grisi, she sang her way into the hearts of the Russians, and they welcomed her enthusiastically. Russia treated Pauline Viardot like the prima donna assoluta she was without the overwhelming competition of Grisi.

Many Italian singers braved the icy journey to Russia. Like America, Australia, and South America, these operatic frontiers were waiting to be conquered. Lured by the promise of fame, riches, and other rewards that had eluded them perhaps in the competitive operatic marketplace of Paris and London, sopranos and tenors, unable to squeeze into the major operatic stream there, struck out on their own and secured better roles across the Atlantic and in Russia. After Jenny Lind's success in America, Sontag followed and many others like Grisi and Mario, Elena D'Angri, Emilie de Méric, Parodi, Viardot, Bosio secured greater fame in Russia. With the invention of the great railways, now cutting across continents, a way opened up for more and more operatic touring companies to bring talent to wider audiences. In America, Mapleson soon blazed the trail across the states with one of the most famous companies of all time—Her Majesty's Opera.

Frédéric, and Fanny Lablache became parents of a baby girl that year. Fanny Rose Louise was born in Paris on 2 February 1843, and baptized at the Church of St. Roch on 13 March. This baby was Luigi Lablache's second granddaughter. Fanny Therese, their oldest child, was born in 1840 in London at the Lablache home on Albany Street. Another child, a girl also named Fanny died at birth on 2 October 1841.

In July, a family wedding took place. The famous pianist Sigismund Thalberg married Lablache's oldest daughter Francesca known as Cecchina[516] in London's St. James Church, Piccadilly, on 22 July 1843. Francesca Lablache (1816-1895) was the lovely widow of the French artist Francois Bouchot who died only the year before. *The Musical World* reported, "From which on his *sorte* the eminent pianist was *radiant* with happiness."[517] Not long afterward, the Thalbergs left for Brussels and Naples. In Naples, Thalberg and his wife gave a concert for the poor in November of that year.[518]

Don Pasquale now opened in London on 29 June, 1843. Her Majesty attended the 8 July performance and again later on 22 July.[519] Chorley writes in his *Thirty Years of Musical Recollections*, a most admirable and much quoted review of *Don Pasquale:*

> I have already spoken, as the last, and not the least blithe, of comic operas. The perfection with which its comedy was rendered, by Madame Grisi, Signor Mario, and Lablache will not, it may be feared, be presently seen again. They reveled in the easy music . . . and Lablache seemed especially to court favour, by presenting the farce of fatness trying to make itself seductive. It used to be said, in Paris, that the BOUQUET which the dear silly hero of the farce wore in the coat which stuck to him with as terrible a closeness, as the outside garment of a sausage does to the contents within . . .

was offered night after night, by anonymous admirers... But, throughout the entire farce of Lablache's performances, nothing was more admirable than his entire avoidance of grossness, or coarse intimation. There was with him that security, the highest power of expressing comedy, tragedy, or grotesque, because it belongs to one who will risk nothing hazardous, one who is not afraid of daring anything extraordinary. When I hear of this person's style, and that person's high note, and when I think of Lablache, I am tempted to feel as if I had parted company with real comic genius on the musical stage for ever.[520]

The *London Times* review gives a long interesting synopsis, including comments on the clothes, which is rare in opera reviews. Here, again, as in the Paris production, it is obvious that they were wearing modern clothes (see chromolithographic prints of the Don Pasquale published then), and music covers. It is reviewed here in *The Illustrated London News*:

Donizetti's *Don Pasquale* was produced last night, on the occasion of Lablache's benefit. Having been one of the most successful pieces played by the Italian company in Paris, a brilliant reputation had preceded its performance here, the house was more than usually crowded, and that by an audience, whose expectations were raised to a high pitch. The ascent of the curtain, after a very pleasing overture, formed of the principal melodies of the opera, at once introduces our hero. Lablache, in the person of Don Pasquale, a warm old bachelor, with sleek countenance, basking in the luxuries of an exceedingly easy dressing gown, loose nankeens, and a velvet cap, is before us. "He looks the personification of good-humour, but he is not as good-humoured as he looks."

The *London Times* again comments that the arias heard in the first Act are of far more than ordinary merit and the promise is great, then goes on to describe how Lablache is dressed. As the plot thickens he finds out that he is being deceived:[521]

Don Pasquale's troubles begin in the second act... Radiant with felicity, his dressing gown exchanged for a blue coat and a magnificent striped waistcoat buttoned over his ample chest... Lablache and Grisi completely act up to each other, he 'broadly comic' with his old fashioned gallantry, she, very humourous with her 'affected bashfulness.' Concluding with a very pretty finale solo part sung by Grisi. Comic opera appears to be the forte of Donizetti, and *Don Pasquale* is studded with more musical beauties, and bears more marks of originality, than the generality of his works, while it is decidedly inferior to his *L'Elisir d'amore.*

"History has ranked it otherwise: while the earlier opera has more delicate pathos, *Don Pasquale*, rather than *L'Elisir d'amore* (its only rival in popular esteem), should emerge as Donizetti's comic masterpiece and is at first sight rather hard to understand," writes Julian Budden. He explains that Donizetti had grown as a musician:

> Ultimately the reason for Don Pasquale's superiority lies in the musical progress accomplished by the composer over the ten years that separates it from the earlier piece.

Professor Philip Gossett points out, "Characters that rise above their *commedia dell'arte* ancestors, a buffo style laced with sentiment and tender feeling, a constant freshness of invention within the framework of Italian opera: *Don Pasquale* is a comedy of age and experience." Here, reference from the third volume of *"Miei Ricordi"* of Leone Escudier; Florimo takes another interesting anecdote:[522]

> From his aristocratic relationships, Lablache had acquired the tastes of that world that he frequented. Having been received privately by the family Aguado,[523] he had become an intimate friend of M. Aguado, Marquis de las Marismas; (Alejandro Marismas was a naturalized Frenchman of Spanish birth, and was a man of great wealth and a very generous patron of Rossini).[524] There weren't weddings or banquets without the cheerful Lablache. Everywhere, he was in great demand and flattered. He loved to lead a life of luxury. He was a real sybarite of the nineteen-century. After having sung at these parties with his usual splendid artistic ability and his famous bass voice, expressing his tender, ardent and joyous feelings, Lablache became man of the world and with his humour rectitude and exquisite tact, he could face the most intrepid speakers. The anecdotes followed each other with constant interest. People would have willingly applauded him. Using a proverb in

its true meaning, one could say of him, "When he spoke, it was as if he were singing." Lablache's evenings were very sought after. He used to entertain only a few intimate friends and his fellow artists of the Italian theatre. They did not play much music but on the other hand they danced parenthetically. The ladies Grisi, Persiani, Albertazzi and Viardot-Garcia were always present at these gatherings. Tamburini, Mario, Thalberg, the son-in-law and the daughter of Lablache, Donizetti, Fiorentino, Vatel and Dormoy, two associates of the same theatre, came regularly to these family parties which Lablache called "macaroni parties" and for this reason.

At midnight, all dances ceased and everybody went into the dining room. There it appeared in all its glory, an enormous cauldron. It contained the traditional macaroni which Lablache offered to his guests. Each one received his portion. The master of the house was present at the meal and was content with watching. But as soon as his guests had finished, he sat down alone at the table with a large table napkin tucked round his neck and covering his chest; and without a word, he ate his favourite dish with indescribable pleasure.

One evening Donizetti, who felt for the macaroni the same enthusiasm as Lablache, arrived too late and nothing was left.

"You will be given some", said Lablache, "on one condition. Here is an album sent by Countess Merlin. Sit down and write two pages of music. While you'll be writing your impromptu there'll be silence around and whoever will utter a word will be penalized and I'll condemn the culprit."

"Agreed" replied Donizetti. He took his pen and started writing. As soon as he had drawn two lines, a voice let out a few words. It was Mrs. Persiani who was telling Mario: "I bet he's composing a cavatina. "And Mario imprudently replied: "If this cavatina were for me, I would be delighted."

Thalberg also was caught out and Lablache with his powerful voice called to order the three of them.

"A forfeit for Mrs. Persiani, for Mario and Thalberg."

"I have finished," exclaimed Donizetti.

In twenty-two minutes he had covered with notes (musical) two pages. Lablache offered him his arm and led him to the dining room, where shortly after a second cauldron of macaroni was brought in. The Maestro sat down very seriously and began to eat a gargantuan meal while Lablache was passing sentence on the three culprits. Mrs. Persiani and Mario were obliged to sing a duet from *L'Elisir d'amore*, accompanied by Thalberg. It was a beautiful sight. The composer was called with loud shouts and Donizetti arrived with a large table napkin hanging from his front row of buttons and greeted them bursting with laughter.

The article tells us: "Two days later, Donizetti asked Lablache for the album where he had written his notes. He improvised a few words and those two pages became the choir of the servants in the *Don Pasquale*; a beautiful waltz which two months later was arranged to be played as a piano piece."[525] Sadly, when Donizetti's illness overtook him within a few years, Donizetti could not even remember how to play the piano and sat aimlessly banging on the keys at Lablache's home.

ಜಜಜ

Chapter Twenty-Six

Concerns and Concerns

1845

It was about this time that Queen Victoria, now the mother of young children, found the three palaces, Windsor Castle, Buckingham Palace, and the Royal Pavilion in Brighton, unsuitable for family life. The Queen and her consort were looking for a quiet place to retreat to in the country. Victoria had always loved the Isle of Wight, and she wrote to her uncle Leopold on 25 March 1845:

> We have succeeded in purchasing Osborne House on the Isle of Wight, and if we can manage it we shall probably run down there before we return to town. It sounds so snug and nice to have a place of one's own, quiet and retired.[526] . . . It's impossible to imagine a prettier spot . . . valleys and woods which would be beautiful anywhere; but all this near the sea is quite perfection; we have this charming beach all to ourselves. The sea was so blue and calm that the Prince said it was like Naples, and then we can walk about anywhere by ourselves without being followed and mobbed.[527]

The young queen expressed her delight to her former prime minister Lord Melbourne and present prime minister Sir Robert Peel. She writes a little later to Peel: "We are more and more delighted with this lovely spot, the air is so pure and fresh, and in spite of the hottest sun which oppresses one so dreadfully in London and Windsor . . . the purest air . . . for us . . . a perfect little Paradise."[528]

Soon they settled in, and it was not long before Her Majesty felt the need to put on a few concerts, and then Lablache began to visit her, sailing from Portsmouth on the packet boat.[529] Other Italian singers would also join him, such as Mario and Grisi. On their way to sing at Osborne House, they would fulfill some engagements at the Royal Victoria Spa and Assembly Rooms in Southampton. Named on the occasion of a visit by the then princess Victoria in 1830, they were located close to the sea, ideally situated and a very fashionable meeting place for residents and visitors. According to the nineteenth-century local artist Philip Brannon who published a steel engraving of the spa, "The Victorian Rooms are the most handsome and fashionable built, and fitted up in a chaste and elegant style." The steel engraving portrays the spa with fountains outside, a Regency-style house surrounded by trees. It supplied chalybeate water reputed to be the finest in the land.[530]

Frédéric Lablache and his wife sang there in November 1840. Often, Piatti would tour with the Lablaches on their provincial tours; he tells an amusing anecdote about Frédéric Lablache and the well-known baritone Giovanni Belletti:

> Belletti was an excellent vocalist, but he was not of a literary turn of mind. At Stratford-on-Avon the party went to see Shakespeares's house. A women opened the door and Belletti asked who she was. Frédéric Lablache, who was full of fun, said, "Oh, don't you know? That's Shakespeare's nurse." Belletti's admiration of the old women was immense.[531]

Lablache was now getting older and was fondly referred to by Queen Victoria, as by his many children and later grandchildren, as Papa Lablache. While his hair was still thick and curly, it was snow-white as he approached fifty years old. Ever more corpulent, this condition would seriously affect his health in later years and contribute to his death. Florimo tells us a story about Lablache's collection of snuffboxes—*Le Tabacchiere*:

> At the close of one of her singing lessons, Queen Victoria once inquired of Lablache concerning his collection of snuff-boxes, which was so unique that the fame of it had reached our late sovereign's ears. The great basso told her Majesty that he had "three hundred and sixty-five," one for every day of the year. "Ah, then, Signor Lablache, your collection is not complete," answered the royal lady. At the close of the following lesson the Queen presented Lablache with a finely wrought gold box: "Now, Signor Lablache, your collection will really be complete. Accept this box as a specimen for leap year.[532]

Luigi Lablache, as everybody knew, had a great passion for snuffboxes that could have been called a mania. Some he received as gifts from kings, high-ranking people, and friends and some he had bought himself. One of these a very beautiful one was bought in Russia for 15,OOO francs. Now this number had reached 366 with the gift from the Queen, and he took great pleasure in using one every day and showing them off to his friends. Being an amusing talker, he was not lacking in interesting comments regarding their origin and value. He always concluded by saying that he used the best for special days of the year and for the galas at court. Florimo tells us that the collection was well known and unusual and was sold after his death and that as his heirs were numerous, nobody wanted to accept the collection as it was considered fruitless and dead capital. However, his sons kept the most beautiful as objets d'art as mementos to remember their beloved father. The remains of this collection can be seen in the Wallace Museum collection in London.[533]

One silver engraved snuffbox remains in the family: inside there is a dry red rose. The rose has been intact since the great-grandson of Lablache could remember—that has been over one hundred years.

Rossini, still in bad health, returned to Paris where his doctors were able to accomplish a temporary relief for his ills. Chopin had reached the zenith of his musical powers as a composer in the forties, but sadly now his strength was ebbing away by the slow encroachment of tuberculosis.

Donizetti returned to Paris after visiting Vienna a dying man. On 30 August 1845, doctors in Paris prescribed many treatments, but they were fighting a losing battle; for he was stricken with venereal disease, which manifested itself in a type of insanity. Soon, he lost his mental abilities and became slowly incapable of taking care of himself. After living for some time in a mental institution near Paris, he was removed by relatives to his birthplace Bergamo, Italy. From there on, his illness was not hidden from the media. All the newspapers including *The Manchester Guardian* reported Donizetti's condition quite openly in the spring of 1847. Bergamo became his last resting place; there surrounded by a loving family, he lingered on for some time and finally died on 8 April 1848.[534]

Frédéric Lablache sang alongside his father from the time of his debut. He had been singing since the young age of twenty in most seasons through the years to 1845. His successes in Dublin and the provinces helped further his career, and he returned there often. Fanny Lablache often accompanied him.

On 2 May 1845, all the singers were invited to Buckingham Palace for a program entirely consisting of music by Prince Albert. The singers chosen for this exclusive concert were Lablache, Grisi, Mario, Staudigl. Taking part for the first time was Jeanne Castellan the French soprano; this was her first season at Her Majesty's, singing with great tenor Napoleone Moriani. This tenor later sang the part of Pollione with Grisi in *Norma*. *The Musical World* wrote,

> Lablache's Figaro that season is the "greatest" ever witnessed, but we prefer him as Bartolo. F. Lablache deserves much praise for his quaint interpretation of Basilio and his singing is still worthy of consideration. Lablache is without doubt the greatest comic actor the lyric stage has ever seen.[535]

The Musical World's opinion on Rossini's *Otello* on 19 June. Lablache sang the ever popular role of Desdemona's father:

> *Otello* possesses several morceaux which have obtained the award of popularity, but on the whole the music is too intense to stir the groundlings, and unfortunately these groundlings will ever be the arbiters of dramatic success. That this opera commanded so much applause on Thursday and Saturday nights we attribute more to Grisi's splendid acting than the appreciation of its music. To us the music of *Otello* is a rare intellectual feast, but it is evidently *Caviare* to the multitude. The drama too is utterly lost in the opera. Not merely its poetical essence is ventilated in the transcript, but the grandeur of its passion, its heart-rending pathos, its grace and captivation, all evaporate. We have a skeleton of the play—but not even a natural skeleton—it is anatomical preparation made of gums, and wires, and varnish in conjunction with the original bones. *Otello* retains hidden fire and none of his dignity; and the "gentle Desdemona" modulates into a second-Medea or a Norma furens. It is thus that the Desdemona of this opera suits Grisi so admirably; she cannot "play calm content and die dumb and unreproving" rage and wrong speak aloud, enforcing redress, and "passion topmost high takes opposition by the crest overpowering all."[536]

Here, *The Musical World* continues to tell us about the audience of Thursday night and tell us that it was for Grisi's benefit:

> We were taken by storm, and the lovely beneficiaries (would we could coin an English word) was summoned before the curtain to meet the vociferate cheers of three thousand voices. After the last

act she was called out a second time and in an instant the stage was covered with bouquets. *Otello's* music is quite unsuited to Mario. It was written for Nozzari, a tenore serio, and is altogether unadapted to the high tenor singing of the modern school. After Nozzari, Garcia and Donzelli alone found it adequate to their voices. Even Rubini, with all his art could not make it effective, and was forced to transpose it in several instances. The part is one requiring great 'physique' and energy, in both of which Signor Mario is deficient. Fornasari was respectable as Iago. There is, however, too much fineness of discrimination and deep subtlety demanded in the evolution of the character to fit itself to this clever artist's powers. His forte lies in strong and energetic passions, where the ruggedness of his style and want of finish are rather favourable than adverse to his embodiment. Lablache elevates the inferior part of the father to dignity and importance. He has little to do throughout the opera, yet that little in Lablache's hands makes us sorry the composer had not done more with the character. His imprecation on his daughter in the second act is one of the most terrible outbursts of frenzy we have ever witnessed on the lyric stage.[537]

After 20 August 1845, Grisi, Mario, Parry, Lablache, Frédéric Lablache, and Julius Benedict set out on a grand tour of the provinces, visiting over twenty different cities (see chronology), giving a concert in each city. Much credit should be given to the extraordinary stamina of the singers at that time. The concerts were much longer than they are today, and often, every aria or song was encored enthusiastically by Victorian audiences. From Manchester, 17 September 1845,[538]

> We had the best concert ever given in Manchester, on Thursday last—The two Lablaches, Grisi, and Mario, form such a quartet as all Europe cannot surpass—they never were in better voice or better spirits. The consequence was the encores were numerous, and although readily responded to, the singers frequently with the greatest of good nature and with exquisite taste, gave something else as a substitute; as for instance, the *La Cenerentola* duet, "Un segreto d'importanza," was encored, and instead of repeating it, the Lablaches gave "Se Fiato in corpo avete," from *Matrimonio*. When Mario was called forth for the second time in the "Tu

> vedrai," he substituted "Come e gentil," from Pasquale, with Grisi and Lablache vamping the chorus to it. Amongst the other encores were Mario's "Bella adorata," Grisi's "Que la voca," and the "Suoni la Tromba" duet, etc, etc—all were excellent. Mario is greatly improved and has become a prodigious favorite here. F. Lablache is improved too—and old Lablache! Great and glorious as he always is—he never exhibited more innate drollery off the stage; yet not a note of his music did he sacrifice to his fun—always correctly in tune—although, at times he had his audience in roars of laughter. Grisi wears well—she sang the Polacca, "Son vergine vezzosa," and her part in the "A te o cara" quartet, from *Puritani*, as brilliantly as ever; and her humour and Lablache's together caused the *"Prova" duet, "Oh guardate che figura,"* to be encored.

Among so many concerts, we find another long review of interest from the *Staffordshire Advertiser* titled "Grand Concert" at Newcastle Theatre. The same group sung much the same repertory and were greeted with enthusiastic applause. However, the praise for Lablache even topped Grisi who had encountered rapturous plaudits when she first appeared, but the reviewer thought she was not in such good voice as last year. Since the debut of Lablache, it has been almost impossible to find a bad review. Did he ever have an off day? He was rarely ill until the year before his death.[539]

> But the lion of the evening was Lablache—the great Lablache in more senses than one. He is a mountain of a man; and he occasionally contrives to pour forth a volume of sound, that one could fancy as proceeding from the depths of a volcano, rather than a human frame. His singing of "Non piu andrai," was the finest specimen of vocal power we ever heard. He kindly acceded to the wish of the audience, and sang the piece again. To trace him through all his numerous engagements, would only be to record a succession of triumphs, as he united in a supreme degree, all the qualities necessary to constitute a good actor and first-rate singer, a combination so rarely to be met with, as to render it necessary to witness the performance of Lablache to understand and appreciate.[540]

The major singers were back at the Théâtre-Italien Paris for the opening of *I Puritani* on 2 October 1845.

Isabella Colbran, Rossini's first wife, died on 7 October 1845; Rossini had rushed to her side when he heard she was ill and remained with her till the end. Separated, and later divorced from Colbran for many years, Rossini lived with the courtesan Olympe Pelissier.

In the issue of *The Musical World* of September 1845, there is an interesting description of a private concert in London. It details an event that happened earlier than 1845, most likely in the early forties before Rubini retired. The article is taken from another publication *Willis's Loiterings of Travel* under the title "A Musical Supper Party":[541]

> I was at one of those private concerts given at enormous expense during the opera season, at which "assisted" Giulia Grisi, Rubini, Lablache, Tamburini, and Ivanoff. Grisi came in the carriage of a foreign lady of rank, who dined with her, and she walked into the room like an empress. She was dressed in the plainest white, with her glossy hair put smooth from her brow, and a single white japonica dropped over one of her temples. The lady who brought her chaperoned her during the evening, as if she had been her own daughter. Supported by the kindness of her friend, she sang with rapture and a 'fresh glory' which set all hearts on fire. She surpassed her most applauded hour on the stage. The audience was composed almost exclusively of those who are not only cultivated judges, but who sometimes repay delight with a present of diamonds. Lablache shook the house to its foundations in his turn; Rubini ran through his miraculous compass with ease, truth and melody for which his singing is surpassed; Tamburini poured his rich and even fullness on the ear; and Russian Ivanhoff sang his fine and spiritual notes. The concert was over by twelve, the gold and silver paper bills of the performance were turned into fans, and every one was waiting till supper should be announced—the *Prima Donna* still sitting by her friend, but surrounded by foreign attaches, and in the highest elation of her own success.
>
> The doors to an inner-suite of rooms were thrown open at last, and Grisi's 'cordon' of admirers prepared to follow her in, and wait on her at supper. At this moment one of the powdered menials of the house stepped up and informed her very respectfully that supper was prepared in a separate room for the singers! Medea, in her most tragic hour, never stood so absolutely the picture of hate, as did Grisi for a single instant, in the centre of that aristocratic crowd.

Her chest swelled and rose, her lips closed over her snowy teeth, and compressed till the blood left them, and for myself, I looked unconsciously to see where she would strike. I knew, then, that there was more than fancy, there was nature and capability of the real in the imaginary passions she played so powerfully. A laugh of extreme amusement at the scene from the highborn women who had accompanied her suddenly turned her humour, and she stopped in the midst of a muttering of Italian, in which I could distinguish only the terminations, and with a sort of theatrical quickness of transition, joined heartily in her mirth. It was immediately proposed by this lady, however, that herself and her particular circle should join the insulted *Prima Donna* at the lower table, and they succeeded by this manoeuvre in retaining Rubini and the others, who were leaving the house in a most unequivocal Italian fury. I had been fortunate enough to be included in the invitation, and, with one or two foreign diplomatic men, I followed Grisi and her amused friend to a small room on a lower floor, that seemed to be the housekeepers parlour. Here supper was set for six (including the pianist) and on the side table stood every variety of wine and fruit, and there was nothing in the supper at least to make us regret the table we had left. With a most imperative gesture, and rather an amusing attempt at English, Grisi ordered the servants out of the room, and locked the door, and from that moment the conversation commenced and continued in their own musical, passionate, and energetic Italian. Finding the room too cold after the heat of the concert, some put on their cloaks and hats as a safeguard to their lungs (more valuable to them than others), and as most of the cloaks were the worst for travel, and the hats, opera hats with two corners, the grotesque contrast with diamonds of one lady and the radiant beauty of the other, may easily be imagined. Singing should be hungry work, by knife and fork they played; and between the excavations of truffle pies, and the bumpers of champagne and burgundy, the words were few. Lablache appeared to be an established droll, and every syllable he found time to utter was received with the most unbounded laughter. Rubini could not recover from the slight he conceived put upon him and his profession by the separate table; and he continually reminded Grisi, who by this time had quite recovered her good humour, that the night before, supping at Devonshire House, the Duke of

Wellington had held her gloves on one side, while his grace, their host, attended to her on the other. 'E vero!' said Ivanhoff, with a look of modest admiration at the *Prima Donna*. 'E vero. e bravo!' called out Tamburini, with his sepulchral talking tone, much deeper than his singing. 'Si, si, si, bravo!' echoed all the company; and the haughty and happy actress nodded all round with a radiant smile, and repeated, in her silver tones,

'Grazie! cari amici! grazie!' As the servants had been turned out the removal of the first course was managed picnic fashion; and when the fruit and wine were set upon the table by the attaches and younger gentlemen, the health of the princess who honoured them by her presence was proposed in that language which, it seems to me, is more capable than all others of expressing affectionate and respectful devotion. All uncovered Grisi stood up, and with tears in her eyes, kissed the hand of her benefactress and drank her health in silence. It is a polite and common accomplishment in Italy to improvise in verse, and the lady I speak of is well known among her immediate friends for a singular facility in this beautiful art. She reflected a moment or two with the moisture in her eyes, and then commenced, low and soft, a poem, of which it would be difficult, nay impossible, to convey in English, an idea of its music and beauty. It took us back to Italy, to its heavenly climate, its glorious arts, its beauty, and its ruins, and concluded with a line of which I remember the sentiment to have been 'out of Italy every land is exile!' The glasses were raised as she ceased, and one repeated after, 'Fuori d'Italia tutto e esilio!' 'Ma!' cried out the fat Lablache, holding up his glass of champagne, and looking through it with one eye, 'siamo ben esiliati qua!'('but we are well exiled here!') and with a word of drollery, the party recovered its gayer tone, and wit and humour flowed on brilliantly as before. The house had been long still, and the last carriage belonging to the company above stairs had rolled from the door. Suddenly Grisi began to sing, remembering a bird that she lately bought, of which she proceeded to give us a description that probably penetrated to every corner of the silent mansion. It was a mocking bird, that had been kept two years in the opera house.

How much of embellishment there was in her imitations of her treasure I do not know; but certainly the whole power of her wondrous voice, passion, and knowledge of music, seemed drunk up at once in the wild, various, difficult, and rapid mixture of the capricious melody she undertook. Soon the others following by singing "Suoni la Tromba intrepida," the tremendous duet in the *Puritani* between Tamburini and Lablache filled the room. Up to the sky, and down to the earth again-away with a note of the wildest gladness, and back upon a note of the most touching melancholy. If the bird half equals the imitation of his mistress, he was worth the jewel in a sultan's turban. 'Giulia! Giuletta! Giulettina!' cried out one and another, as she ceased, expressing, in their Italian diminutives, the love and delight she had inspired by her incomparable execution. The stillness of the house in the occasional pauses of conversation reminded the gay party, at last, that it was late. The door was unlocked, and the half-dozen sleepy footmen hanging about the hall were despatched for the cloaks and carriages; the drowsy porter was roused, and opened the door, and broad upon the street lay the cold gray light of a summer's morning.

It is of little consolation to us and for all of us who wonder what those voices of the early and mid-nineteenth century sounded like before the invention of the gramophone. Even through the reports of the newspapers and journals and memoirs of the time, we somehow feel left out of that world of long ago. We must content ourselves with yet another review from word of mouth. During the period immediately following the death of Lablache, there were many complaints from people that the Golden Age of opera had passed.

To those who wonder what Lablache sounded like, we sadly will never know. Frances Rogers writes in 1914:[542]

> Singers, like actors, of the 19th century, and unlike painters and sculptors, left no records of their art behind them. Their song must have lingered a while in the memory of their hearers, but it is after all only a memory pretty sure sooner or later to fade into oblivion. 'How can we know all the qualities of the singers voice and art?' the personal magnetism and the thousand subtleties that are the secret and essence great singer's power over his audience. The only knowledge or opinion we can have of a voice that we have never heard is from hearsay, and it has all the vagueness and unreliability that is characteristic of hearsay. Of all the singers of the 19th century however, none has left behind such a fragrant

and delightful memory as has Luigi Lablache. Big in voice, stature, mind and heart, rich in musical and historic talent, he was the dominating personality whenever and wherever he sang. To hear him was to provide one's self with a never-fading memory of complete musical satisfaction; to know him personally was to love and admire him.

Lablache retained his voice, practically unimpaired till his death, and few reviews have surfaced to the contrary although he grew so corpulent as to become toward the end almost immovable. Looking back to the year of 1844, it had passed with only a few memorable events to speak of; Lumley wrote, "Lablache, the Magnificent, was at his accustomed post in the opera hemisphere, the brilliant planet, accompanied by the revolving satellite, his son." Lumley remembers, "That year one of the chief public events was the visit of Her Majesty to the opera, accompanied by the late Emperor of the Russias and the King of Saxony":

> I may now confess that the pleasure derived from the honour of this visit was somewhat mitigated by apprehension as to its possible consequences. The Emperor Nicholas was known to be an object of almost fanatical hatred to the Polish refugees who find their home in London, and an attempt at assassination was certainly an event probable enough to justify strong precautionary measures. Special care was taken to ascertain who was likely to occupy the boxes opposite to the Royal one, and a sort of surveillance was exercised generally . . . The opera was the "Barbiere." The Emperor was delighted with Lablache, and laughing heartily at his drolleries, especially when this "spoiled child" of the public introduced his English or made allusions to the Royal visit; and I was requested to convey to Lablache the Emperor's satisfaction with his performance. Shortly afterwards overtures were made to the great artist for a season at St.Petersburg, which, after some hesitation, he accepted. It has been remarked that on state occasions it is always judicious to select an *opera buffa*.[543]

This year, a few new operas were produced for Her Majesty's Theatre. These included Herold's *Zampa*, *Corrado d'Altamura* by Federico Ricci, and the world premiere of Michael Costa's *Don Carlos* on June 20, 1844. These operas failed in spite of excellent casts. *Corrado D'Altamura* had first been presented at the Théâtre-Italien with Grisi, Mario, and Giorgio Ronconi. *Don Carlos* in London with Grisi, Lablache, Mario, and Fornasari. Chorley found it gloomy. Lablache looked magnificent in his costume though, but Lumley wrote that Mario and Lablache were both hoarse from long rehearsals even before the opening night. They complained that the tessitura was too high for them. "It survived but a few nights, and then, like *Malek Adel*, sank into the vast 'limbo' of forgotten works."[544] When *Zampa* also fell by the wayside, Fanny Persiani sat down on a chair in the middle of the performance sighing with the appearance of giving up the entire matter as hopeless while the hisses from the audience came wafting across the footlights in waves.[545] In any event, that was the last season for her at Her Majesty's Theatre; after singing *Lucia* in June, she left for Paris and Vienna, only to return to London briefly in the 1850s. She continued singing in St. Petersburg, Germany, and France. Retiring in Paris, she led a quiet life, sometimes teaching until her death in 1867.[546]

Frédéric Lablache packed quite a few operas roles under his belt in the 1844 season; he sang in *Don Giovanni, Zampa, Il Matrimonio Segreto*, and *Il Barbiere* at Her Majesty's. Instead of going to Paris, he joined Grisi and Mario in Dublin. There, the Italians appeared at the Theatre Royal for ten nights starting on September 9. On the opening night, Frédéric sang the count in *Sonnambula*, followed by Malatesta in the first performance of *Don Pasquale*. Then *Semiramide*, and after a performance of Rossini's *Stabat Mater* on September 13, he joined Mario on the stage in a great rendering of Rossini's *Otello*.[547] Here, we are told it was the only time that Mario ever sang the title role; it seems it would have been a difficult undertaking for him, but the *Dublin Theatre Annals* were wrong for sure—Mario had sung Otello in Paris and London.[548] Afterward, Frédéric Lablache sang Don Magnifico with the new English soprano Favanti, who was a friend of the family and took London by storm earlier that season.

Frédéric Lablache did not return to Dublin in 1845, nor did Grisi or Mario. Back at Her Majesty's on April 4, 1845, Frédéric sang with Mario and Castellan in *Sonnambula*. This was his tenth year singing the role of the Count Rodolfo, one of the few roles that Luigi Lablache was not known to have ever sung. The Queen attended and noted in her journal that Mario's voice was "splendid and if possible it seems to have improved," and she noted, "Madame Castellan has the loveliest, purest, freshest voice."[549] She had been brought in to replace Mme. Persiani, but her voice was in no way comparable; it was said of her by Chorley, "A character made up of negatives; though she was always courteously received, she never excited the slightest enthusiasm."[550]

The highlight of the season was Verdi's *Ernani*, first heard in London and produced for Her Majesty's; but strangely, the cast chosen were unremarkable and failed to excite. The French newspapers had gotten hold of a rumor that Mario had been killed in a duel. The *Morning Post* had fun with this:[551]

> If Signor Mario be really dead, we are right happy he has been considerate enough to leave his ghost behind—a right hearty ghost who last night looked most carnally . . . the very incarnation of the Caballero and the Hidalgo of those augustan days when Spain could boast of real cavaliers and nobles in bearing as well as lineage.[552]

But later Mario, while singing in *Il Barbiere,* did lose his voice; the Queen wrote in her journal (26th of April):

> He tried to sing but could not: he then bowed and said . . . "e impossible, non posso", and left the stage. Upon this Lablache made such a funny charming face, rolling his eyes with a shoulder shrug, that the whole audience laughed.[553]

That night, however, the house was not amused and a near riot broke out when Almaviva reappeared again and tried to sing; Lumley tells us, "The indignant tenor left the stage, to return no more that evening. The inimitable humour of Lablache, expressed at this sudden flight, restored the audience to good temper by its irresistible comicality."[554] Grisi even stopped singing and gave the audience a terrible glare, a haughty glare that only she could give. Mario had nothing to worry about he was now the one and only tenor that could enrapture audiences. In Paris, the *Journal des Debat* wrote of him: "His voice so fresh and pure, becomes more agile every day." Impresario Lumley attempted to return some order to Her Majesty's Theatre; in spite of having some of the world's finest singers, the theater was losing money.

After 1845, all the singers followed Michael Costa over to the rival theater at Covent Garden. Lablache was the only big name who refused to desert and remained behind at Her Majesty's, where he urged Lumley to secure a certain Swedish singer by the name of Jenny Lind at any cost to save the theater, pointing out, she would be an enormous office draw as her success elsewhere had proved.

Lablache had not heard Lind sing, but he had heard a good deal about her and knew what a tremendous drawing card she would be for the theater.

He was also impressed by reports of her good character. The three years she spent studying with Manuel Garcia in Paris had brought good results and improved her technique. In 1844, she sang *Norma* in Berlin, which led to successful appearances all over Europe. Yet she still refused all offers that Lumley made to persuade her to sing in England. Lumley writes to Lablache for help.[555]

☙☙☙

Chapter Twenty-Seven

Difficulty at Her Majesty's

1846-47

Historically, the event that took place at La Scala in Milan on 9 March 1842 was paramount . . . the first production of Giuseppe Verdi's opera *Nabucco*. "With this opera it is fair to say my artistic career began," Verdi wrote, "and in spite of the difficulties I had to contend with, *Nabucco* was born under a lucky star."[556]

For Italian audiences of the time, still under the control of Austria, its celebrated chorus with the unforgettable soaring melody, "Va, Pensiero, sull'ali dorate"(Fly, Thought, on Wings of Gold), sunk deep into their hearts. "Oh my country so lovely and lost! Oh, remembrance so dear and so fraught with despair" was a reminder that Italy was not free. For Verdi, this was a turning point; a cloud had hung over him ever since his second opera *Un giorno di regno* had failed, and personal tragedy had followed him when his wife and children had died within two years. Like Donizetti, who had almost the same personal experience, he was flung into deep depression. "With a mind tormented by my domestic misfortunes," he wrote, "embittered by failure of my work . . . I decided never to compose again." Luckily for all of us, this did not happen—Verdi, more than a great musician and a great man, became a legend in his own time. With *Nabucco*, his fame as a composer was realized not just in Italy but throughout the world.

In London, *Nabucco* was first heard at Her Majesty's Theatre under the name *Nino, Re d' Assyra* because the British censorship forbade biblical subjects on the stage. Another premiere that season was Donizetti's opera buffa *L'Ajo nell' imbarazzo* (The tutor embarrassed) brought in at the end of the season. Lablache was very familiar with this opera, which he had introduced to Vienna in 1827 just before Beethoven's death.

Chorley later remarked about Verdi's *Nabucco*—first seen in London at Her Majesty's on 8 March 1845—"It was the only novelty attempted that season and Signor Verdi, by this time, was an Italian celebrity who could no longer be overlooked." (It was just a year after its Italian premiere at La Fenice Venice on 9 March 1844.) However, Chorley named 1846 "a season of confusion . . . the principal event of which was a forcible attempt to give Signor Verdi that place he already held in the opera houses of Italy." Of his first three operas—*Ernanni, Lombardi*, and *Nino*—Lablache would not sing in any of them. Artists that did were mediocre. Chorley continued that "1846 was not the best year for Her Majesty's Theatre," and that was an understatement. The *Athenaeum* added a few jibes, pointing out that Lumley's management was deteriorating, and that some casts of singers at Her Majesty's were not of the highest calibre. However, the critic of the *Illustrated London News* wrote on 18 July 1846: "*Anna Bolena* had a superb cast with Grisi, Mario and Lablache":

> Lablache as Henry the VIII, was marvellous. Mario was Percy with Brambilla and Corbari. The first glance shows us that all remembrance of our joyous, witty, favourite is banished. His face assumes an expression of hardened brutality, in which no trace of the real man is to be discerned. The light coloured false hair which he wears gives him an appearance of a much younger man, renders his opulence of person even more remarkable.

The critic Chorley, ever disagreeable, accused Mario of trying to sing like Rubini because of his increased use of falsetto. But he was the favorite tenor, and he delighted his public with his rendering of "Vivi tu." Chorley, in later years, wrote, "As a singer of Romances, he has never been exceeded; rarely equalled," and he goes on about his taste in dress under the page title Personal Embellishment.[557]

> Few who have trod the stage have dressed to such perfection as Signor Mario. The painter's eye, as well as the lover's honeyed tongue, have had no small part in the success of the charming tenor. His characters recur to us as do the happiest portraits of Veronese, or Tintoretto, or Bronzino, which grow into the mind, as so many faces and figures recollected by their beauty, well set off by a waving or floating feather. There is more in this than the stage-tailors's craft, a touch of poetry, never to be undervalued, whatever the form taken by it. Those who sneer at taste in dress-harmony, in colour, proportion of form might as well disparage

perfume; or speak ill of a pleasant chord of music . . . but love of Beauty is distinct from, and above, all that is temporary and trumpery; and, above all men, the man who presents himself on the stage, must be encouraged to understand and to consider this as a part of his art, and of his intercourse with the public. I have seen this by no men so well comprehended as by Signor Lablache and Signor Mario.

On 22 August 1846, the *Illustrated London News* writes under the title "Her Majesty's—A Retrospect of the Season":

We have now witnessed the closing of this great establishment, which, during the last nights, was filled by an audience more numerous and more aristocratic than we ever remember to have seen remaining in London so late in the season. *I Puritani* and *The Last Judgement of Paris* terminated the subscription nights. Grisi, Castellan, Lablache, Mario, Fornasari, Tadlioni, Grahn and Cerito (latter three dancers) and other numerous stars, too many to mention, received the enthusiastic parting homage.

Then in praise of the unequalled splendor of the previous season the critic gives a list of the so-called first-class lyrical works given over the past season. Turning to the performers, he praises the voices of Fornasari, Castellan, Brambilla, then the Lablaches:

Lablache is always the same—unapproached and unapproachable in all the parts he undertakes, whether tragic or comic. In the character of the brutal tyrant Henry VIII in *Anna Bolena*, and in that of the duped old beau in *Don Pasquale*, we are equally convinced that we shall never look upon his like again. We must not omit to mention his son, F. Lablache—an artist who is always zealous, always useful; and who unites to these qualities no small portion of his father's talents, without the addition of that extraordinary physical power, which renders the latter one of the most remarkable artists of our day.

Hundreds had been turned away disappointed earlier that May when the Philharmonic Society put on a grand concert featuring the first English performance of Beethoven's *Missa solemnis* in D; it had been played in

Germany, the previous year and billed as Beethoven's mightiest inspiration. Costa was the conductor. Also on the program were Mozart's *Sinfonia in G Minor,* Beethoven's *Choral Fantasy,* a violoncello caprice, and a vocal quintet from Rossini's *Zelmira.* Frédéric Lablache sang among many others.[558]

Soon the new rival Royal Italian Opera was established at Covent Garden. The *Illustrated London News* writes:

> The house is to be fitted up and decorated in the most costly and luxuriant style and the stage arrangements and mounting of the operas will be an expenditure.

Billed always as London's Greatest Opera House, Her Majesty's never really recovered from this shock. First, Lumley's dispute with Signor Costa ended with Costa leaving for the rival opera house, followed by his orchestra. Worst, Grisi, Mario, and Tamburini1 also left. No other than Giuseppe and Mme. Persiani had purchased the lease where they thought a better future for themselves would materialize. It didn't.

Lablache, however, was faithful to the old theater where he had been a favorite and stayed on with Lumley. In fact, he helped him recruit a new batch of sopranos, the most attractive of which was the now famous Swedish prima donna Jenny Lind.

Letters began to pour in from all over begging Jenny Lind to come to England. She was enjoying enormous successes on the continent, but had not been engaged to sing as yet at any of the leading London theaters. Lumley and Chorley both went to Germany in the hope of engaging her, but she refused to come, even when her close friend Felix Mendelssohn-Bartholdy tried to persuade her. Manager Lumley was desperate after losing Her Majesty's superstars, Grisi and Mario. He thought hiring Lind as a new and vital prima donna would save the theater! Lablache, whose judgment was not to be despised, had strongly urged the management to engage Lind and had addressed the following letter on the subject to Lumley:

> Naples, October 12, 1846
>
> Dear Mr. Lumley,
>
> I learn, with much regret, from your last letter, that Mdlle. Lind finds some difficulty in coming to London. It is a great misfortune that this exceptional *artiste* neither knows London, nor

the exceptional position of your theatre for the coming year; for, she will never find a more favourable moment for her interests, or her reputation. Try, then, to decide her; and make her understand that she will find herself surrounded by brothers and friends, and not by intriguing *artistes*, as is, unfortunately, too often the case. Her success is certain. I answer to you for it; and you, who know me, will understand all that I am prepared to do, myself, to aid it. It is not only her immense reputation as an *artiste*, that gives me this conviction; but, the good that is said of her, as a woman. I tell you, frankly, that I have been, as you know, the friend of Pasta, and the friend of Malibran; and, that I shall be very proud to be able to say: 'I am the friend of Lind.' If you think it necessary, I will write a letter to her, myself; and, if she knows me, she cannot fail to put faith in my words. Forgive me, my dear Mr. Lumley, if I meddle with your affairs; but, you know my device: 'Art, before all things.' Do not forget me; and remember that you have ever in me,

Your wholly devoted,
L. Lablache*

* The original letter, written in French, was sent to Mdlle. Lind by Mr. Lumley, who also forwarded a copy of it to Mendelssohn.[559]

Much has been written about Lind's short singing career partly because she came to the United States, possibly because she was an actress who knew how to sell her image. Grisi towered over her historically; Grisi wore the crown of the greatest diva, and, after Pasta, was the greatest prima donna of the first half of the ottocento. (Malibran might have been had she not died young.) Grisi's long career continued after Lablache died. Wearing the so-called royal mantle passed down by Pasta, her predecessor, she was dedicated and experienced at following in the strict traditions of bel canto while Jenny Lind flashed by and was gone. Jenny Lind fever came and went, and she sustained a comparatively short time in the limelight. Continually insisting that her voice should be employed in singing music of a higher calibre than opera, she became tiresome, incessantly implying she was too pure and good for this life, constantly threatening retirement as a ploy to sell more tickets. Grisi sustained her position and her dignity, and even while Lind mania swept across London, her position was never threatened.

Lumley was confident of an overwhelming sellout at the box office at Her Majesty's if he could obtain Lind. Jenny Lind, the simple little Swedish girl, is well-described by Henry Pleasants:

> The role of the simple little Swedish girl, a Hans Christian Anderson "Ugly Duckling," the insignificant, snub-nosed, plain, simple dressed, hesitant, unassuming poor-little-me, pining for the northern homeland, pure of heart and noble of thought, was the greatest of her roles. The legendary Jenny Lind was her own masterpiece. As a historic accomplishment it had only one flaw. It lacked the true artist's detachment. The public were taken in, and so were most of her friends and acquaintances; but so, also, was she.[560]

Late in the season of 1846, Donizetti's opera buffa *L'Ajo nell' imbarazzo, O Don Gregorio* was introduced and given under the latter title on 28 July 1846 at Her Majesty's with Lablache in the title role. Here, the work was presented as a pastiche with singers introducing their own chosen arias. *The Musical World* writes:

> There are scenes in the libretto that are laughable: Frédéric Lablache in his infantile costume, his father portrayed the character of the unfortunate scape goat. The duet was comic to the extreme, Lablache's impersonation is a masterpiece. *Don Gregorio's* chief attraction lies in the drollery of the libretto.

"Useless," commented Chorley. "It's not one of his happy comic operas," saying nothing about the music.[561] But the audiences enjoyed it. Elizabeth Forbes remarks in her *Grisi and Mario*: "Only Lablache as the embarrassed tutor, Don Gregorio, saved the evening from disaster."[562]

That August, after completing his engagements in London, Luigi Lablache left for his home in Naples. There the weather was so hot, reported *The London Times*, that animals were dying in the fields for lack of water. Lablache did not return to sing in Paris that autumn. He wrote in French twice at least to Mr. Natali from Naples on October 8 1846:

> Both in your interest and in mine I am asking you to lengthen my leave for a month. My health needs it and I hope you won't have difficulties in helping me. I shall be in Paris for the 1st of January.

> The doctors think I should stay here as long as possible to breath the pure air of Naples. I am waiting anxiously for your reply, which I hope will be favourable. Goodbye, Mr. Natali—remember me to your friends.
>
> Yours sincerely, L. Lablache

Another letter follows to Natali on October 10, 1846:

> I hasten to write to you to say that neither the journey or the stay in Naples has brought about the big change that we were hoping for in Paris. If you can give me a month more I shall be very grateful, and it must be remembered that this measure is as much in your interests as mine.
> Please can you send your reply via Marseilles.
>
> Yours sincerely, L. Lablache

Frédéric Lablache, Mario, and Grisi toured the provinces with the comedian, John Parry, and their conductor Julius Benedict, a close friend of Frédéric. The English singer, Ms. Maria Hawes, and Herr Staudigl joined them. Starting in Birmingham on 26 August, they toured for over a month, visiting most of the major cities in the provinces. Mario and Grisi were back at the Théâtre-Italien in Paris for *Semiramide* on 8 October. A correspondent from a Birmingham newspaper reports on Saturday, 5 October 1846:

> The Birmingham Festival was not merely instituted that only one work should be considered in four days performance, (Only *Elijah* was given). Why should the *Messiah* have been overlooked? Why should *Mount of Olives* be shown of its beams, and its lights diffused through a lessening medium? Why should the *Miscellaneous Concerts* be ill-arranged, the music wretchedly selected, and the vocalists allowed to choose their own pieces? Who's fault was all that? Take the performance of *Elijah* away, and it cannot for one moment be denied that the Birmingham festival of 1846 was a lamentable failure. We have listened to complaints on all sides, and among others we heard strong remarks about the undue partiality shown to foreigners and men of no name to the

rejection of native artists and sound musicians in the selection of members forming the corps management. Where was Sir Henry Bishop, or Sterndale Bennett, or George Alexander Macfarren, or Lucas.[563]

The Birmingham Festival over, another correspondent thought it was capital entertainment and finished at least with good spirit. On 26, 27 August, the Italian singers sang a program, the selections of which were as follows:

Programme:

First part:
Mario: A te fra tante affanni (*Davide Penitente*-Mozart)
Grisi: Ah parlate (*Il sacrificio d'Abramo*-Cimarosa)
Grisi: Qui la voce (*I Puritani*) Grisi: Lascia ch'io piangi (*Rinaldo*)
Grisi: e Con pazienza (*Il Fanatico per la Musica*) con F. Lablache
Mario: Il mio tesoro (*Don Giovanni*)
Mario: e Dove son (*Cosi fan tutte*) con Caradori Allan, Bassano, Williams e F. Lablache

Second part:
Grisi: Non fu sogno (*I Lombardi*),
Grisi: Oh guardate che figura (*La prova di un'opera seria*) con F. Lablache
Mario: Pria che spunti in ciel l'aurora (*Il Matrimonio Segreto*)
Mario e Grisi: Solingo, errante e misero (*Ernani*) con F. Lablache.

The *London Times* wrote on Thursday, 3 September, "There is not a town in England where music is cultivated with more assiduity than at Manchester." It continues:

Their first attempt in 1843, was *the Messiah,* for which the most eminent London vocalists, with band and chorus of upward to 300, were engaged. Their success was unprecedented. In 1844 the experiment was repeated, with the *Creation.* Emboldened by their success, in addition to the usual band and chorus, they have engaged Madame Grisi, Miss Hawes, Signor Mario, Signor F. Lablache, and Herr Staudigl (main artists) and the conductor Mr.

Benedict. With these extraordinary forces, they ventured upon two grand concerts. The Free Trade Hall is an enormous and ungainly edifice . . . capable of holding 3,700 auditors, comfortably seated. Packed together, standing, it will accommodate very nearly 10,000. As the building was not originally intended for a music hall, it would scarcely be fair to rate the musical inhabitants of Manchester on the unparalleled bad taste that distinguishes the decoration of the interior, no less than the form of the exterior. The Italian party continued on to Liverpool where the performances were given at the Royal Amphitheater which was crowded by an elegant audience. John Parry joined the party here and produced the *furore* which never fails to attend his efforts. The pianist here was a local resident, Mr. Isaac, formally a pupil of the Royal Academy.

The Grisi and Mario party left for Buxton where they gave an afternoon concert, another at Macclesfield in the evening. The next day, they left for Leeds, thence Newcastle-under-Lyme. From there, they continued on for another month.(The *Times*) At Shrewsbury:

> . . . their programme was pretty nigh the same as at Manchester and Liverpool, it is only necessary to say, that they passed off with great éclat, encores being frequent and applause incessant. Shrewsbury Choral Society built a magnificent music-hall in the market place, capable of accommodating nearly one thousand persons. The appearance at the music hall at an evening dress concert was exceedingly brilliant. Such a bevy of lovely women, perhaps, could not be mustered in any other town of England. They came in swarms to the artist's room, between the parts, to have a look at the handsome Mario.

Mario was in his prime in 1846: he would go on singing for many more years and would be much loved by the public. Chorley describes him here eloquently:

> There have been better singers—there have been better Musicians—there have been better voices than Mario. There has been no more favourite artist on the stage, in memory of man or of women, than he. It was not, however, till the season of 1846 that he took the place of which no wear and tear of Time has been able to deprive

him. The admiration is easy to explain referable, as it has been, to Nature and circumstance rather than to artistic perfection.[564]

When on 17 October, Lumley finally signed Ms. Lind to sing at Her Majesty's, he wrote joyfully to Mendelssohn, who had also written to persuade her to come to London. "I'm delighted to tell you that your letter has had its effect and the lady has signed the engagement." Lablache had never heard Jenny Lind sing, but knew of her reputation through his connection in Paris, her teacher Manuel Garcia. Lumley hoped engaging Lind would save his theater; clearly, his difficulties were not over after all the trouble he had to obtain her.

ಌಌಌ

Chapter Twenty-Eight

Jenny Lind and Lablache

1847-1848

The long-awaited Swedish Nightingale Jenny Lind finally arrived in London on 17 April 1847 and that very night was whisked off to attend a performance of *I Puritani* at Her Majesty's. Lablache, Coletti, Gardoni, and Mme. Castellan were already onstage when there was a stir of excitement in the house as people began to notice Jenny Lind was present. Lablache and Mr. Lumley stopped by her box between acts to pay their respects. All eyes in the theater were directed toward where she sat—number 48 on the grand tier.

After the performance, Jenny Lind gave a small supper party and among the guests were Lablache, Felix Mendelssohn, and Lumley. Mendelssohn was in London to conduct performances of his oratorio, *Elijah*, at Exeter Hall, London, and in Birmingham:

> As soon as Mendelssohn started to play, everyone gathered round the piano. Mendelssohn asked Jenny to sing his *On Wings of Song*, but no sooner had she started to sing than she broke down, unable to continue, just as she had done when she sang for Manuel Garcia. Lablache, seeing her difficulty, overcame the awkward moment with some Neapolitan songs. Calming down, she recovered her composure and delighted everyone with her Swedish songs, and enchanted the group.[565]

Lablache was very taken by her, and when he spoke of her voice to Grisi, he said, "Every note is a pearl." Jenny Lind for her part, when speaking of Lablache, said (she was not too charitable toward her fellow singers), "Lablache is a genius—and what a voice! Oh, God in heaven! And the most perfect actor you could ever see."[566]

"Papa Lablache," always kind and understanding, a family man who could be counted on to understand the difficulties of young singers, is remembered here by Wilhelm Kuhe in his *Musical Recollections*:[567]

> Lablache was singularly fascinating, full of wit and *bonhomie*, and always cheery and good-humoured. He would talk for hours in a bright, amusing vein, and I cannot recall ever having seen him ruffled. I forgot, in writing of Lablache's artistic gifts, that his singing of buffo songs was absolutely different from anything of the kind one hears nowadays, either in this country or abroad. Indeed, that style of singing, as exemplified by Lablache's unique rendering of Rossini's *Tarantella*, may almost be said to have become obsolete.

When Rossini wrote *Soirées Musicales de Rossini* in 1834, the *Tarantella*, better known as *La Danza,* became the favorite of the fashionable soirées and concerts in England. These soirées musicales were sung all over the world and played by Ferruccio Busoni, Liszt, and Thalberg on the piano. Liszt completed arrangements of all twelve of the songs while he was in Milan in 1839. Rossini wrote *La Danza* for Lablache:

> Written for the great basso, Lablache, it became so popular at Naples, his birth place, that its strains must have sounded out all over the town, as did *Funiculi-Funicula* when the author remembers Naples. In fact, *La Danza* became entirely identified with that city and was perpetually sung to the tinkling mandoline, below the windows of the hotels along the Chiaia, on gaily lit barges in the bay, and in front of every celebrated view of Vesuvius. Yet *La Danza* had completely faded out of existence when Diaghilev revived it, for the Tarantella in *La Boutique Fantasque.*[568]

Rossini songs, ever popular in the concert repertory, paled beside the music of grand opera. Lind's debut at Her Majesty's was on 4 May 1847 as Alice in Meyerbeer's *Robert le Diable* (*Robert the Devil*) in Italian; her last performance two years later was in the same opera. This opera had created a sensation in Paris bordering on hysteria, and Lind repeated its success in London, creating a furor never before seen in the history of opera. Gladys Shultz in her book *Jenny Lind* gives some idea of the pandemonium:

As it had happened so many times before, Jenny's fears proved to be completely unjustified, the very delays and rumors and counter-rumors had only heightened the public's interest in her. By the night of her debut, it had reached fever pitch.

The *Encyclopaedia Britannica,* a publication not given to hyperbole, said in its 1910-1911 edition that the furor she created "exceeded everything of the kind . . . in London or anywhere else; the sufferings and struggles of her well-dressed admirers, who had to stand for hours to get into the pit, have become historic." The elaborate costumes of the ladies were severely crumpled and in several cases torn off altogether. The surging mob picked many people off their feet, and H. S. Holland related that he was thrown to the ground by the rush when the doors were opened and believed he would have been trampled to death if a friendly giant had not held the crowd back and helped him up. On the dot of eight o'clock, Queen Victoria and Prince Albert, the Queen Dowager, and the Duchess of Kent entered the royal boxes at the left of the stage. Mendelssohn and Mr. Grote sat together in the stalls, having surrendered their places in the Grote box to Fanny Kemble and Sir Charles Lemon, who had been unable to get tickets.

H. S. Holland recorded that when the curtain rose, "The excitement was indescribable." When Jenny made her entrance, being dragged onto the stage in her pilgrim's dress, the audience rose and applauded her. This was entirely contrary to continental custom and disconcerted her further. Her opening recitative could scarcely be heard. But quiet was restored by the time she had reached the passage in which Alice tells the prince of his mother's death, and the audience decided then and there that its historic sufferings had been worthwhile.[569]

Lablache attended the performance and was the first to shout out from his box, brava, after her first aria. The audience was wildly enthusiastic, and Queen Victoria and Albert were "very much amused."[570]

The Queen and Prince Albert enthusiastically attended all sixteen performances, seeing her five times in *Robert le Diable* and *Sonnambula* and three times in *La Fille du régiment* (in Italian). The Queen attended over thirty operas that year, mostly at Her Majesty's, Covent Garden, and St. James Theatre.[571]

The Royal Italian Opera House at Covent Garden was now bankrupt. Persiani and his wife fled the country, and Salvi the tenor also was missing, leaving behind debts of over three million francs. He showed up later in America.[572]

Her Majesty's Theatre planned a new opera by Verdi, *I Masnadieri,* to showcase Jenny Lind. Lablache would support her performance. Written especially for that theater, Verdi would conduct the royal gala performance on 22 July 1847. The Queen, Prince Albert, and all the royal family and high society of London would be there; expectations ran very high.

When Verdi finally arrived in foggy London for the first time, Frank Walker tells us that he found the weather very different from sunny Italy: "I hate the smoke . . . and this smell of coal . . . its like being on a steam boat." Emmanuele Muzio, Verdi's amanuensis, describes everything in length about Verdi's short stay in London. Though the Maestro Verdi had many invitations, Muzio writes, he refused most of them: "He even rejected an invitation, sent through Lablache, to meet the Queen . . . he can't eat those foods full of drugs and pepper, and all those cold dishes, and wine so strong that its like rum." Muzio describes life at that time:[573]

> Milan is nothing, Paris *something* in comparison with London; but London is a city unique in all the world; it suffices to consider that there are almost two million inhabitants. Then one can imagine what an immense city it is. It's a mistake to think the English don't love music . . . a mistake that the French have spread around and the Italians adopted it because it was a French idea. I say that no man pays for things he doesn't like and which don't give him pleasure. The English have never hissed a masterpiece. They have never received with indifference an *Il Barbere di Seville*, as Rome has, or a *William Tell*, as Paris has, and they never hissed an *Otello*, as Naples did on its first appearance.[574]

It had been early in January when Frédéric's wife Fanny Lablache joined her husband in concert with Mme. Bishop at the Beaumont Institution. Singing together in twelve concerts in London tired Fanny Lablache, so she declined to go with her husband on the huge provincial tour of England in 1846 with Mario and Grisi. Frédéric sang quite often at Her Majesty's, usually cast as the count in Bellini's *Sonnambula*. On 22 April, he sang in *L'Elisir d'amore* with his father and soprano Castellan. The review in the *Illustrated London*

News in June reads, "The veteran Lablache was in full force; his gigantic 'Pirouettes' were received with shouts of laughter."[575]

Frédéric Lablache sang the count in *Sonnambula* with Lind on 13 May, and together they sang in the London premiere of *La Fille du régiment* on 27 May (sung in Italian).

Luigi Lablache, Grisi, Lind, Mario, Alboni, and Tamburini all sang at Buckingham Palace for the Queen. The first concert on 3 May was without Lind and on 28 May with Lind. Next, Mme. Fanny Lablache joined her husband Frédéric and her father-in-law for more concerts in town before her husband left with Jenny Lind for Liverpool.

Her Majesty's Theatre, in addition to Verdi's four operas—*Ernanni, I due Foscari, I Lombardi, I Masnadieri*—the theater introduced two of Donizetti's French operas: *La Favorita* and the opera comique *La Fille du régiment*. Both of them were very successful, but it was the latter opera that became the rage the next two years. It was one of Jenny Lind's greatest triumphs. And Frédéric supported her antics as Maria, cavorting gaily with her; yet historically, he is hardly mentioned—Ms. Lind captures all the glory. Both operas have had their premieres in Paris in 1840, sung in both French and Italian.

A splendid cast was assembled for the gala first night of *I Masnadieri* (*The Robbers*). Set in four acts, the opera is based on a drama by Schiller, *Die Rauber*. Luigi Lablache played the Massimilian, a count, supported by Lind as Amalia. The cast included Gardoni, Coletti, Corelli, and Bouche. Muzio writes a description of the event:

> The opera aroused a furore. From the overture to the finale there was nothing but applause, recalls and encores. As soon as Verdi appeared in the orchestra pit, applause broke out and continued for a quarter of an hour. Before it had finished, the Queen and Prince Albert, the Queen Mother and the Duke of Cambridge, uncle of the Queen, the Prince of Wales, son of the Queen, and all the royal family and a countless number of lords and dukes arrived. The Maestro himself conducted, seated on a chair higher than the others, baton in hand. As soon as he appeared in the orchestra pit there was continuous applause, which lasted a quarter of an hour. At the end the Maestro was cheered and called on the stage, alone, and then with the other singers, flowers were thrown to him, and nothing was heard but 'Viva Verdi.'[576]

The critics had a field day with the ludicrous casting of the mountainous Lablache portraying an aged man in the last throes of starvation! Lumley said of Lablache: "He had to do about the only thing he could not do to perfection . . . represent a man who nearly starved to death." Lablache, of course, did his best with the role. Throughout the history of opera, huge, and often ungainly prima donnas have sung roles better suited to young sylphs. Grisi herself became humungous in later years, and a long line of celebrated heavy sopranos followed her, from Titiens to Callas. The Victorian and Edwardian aristocracy and middle class were gargantuan eaters. They were proud of their wealth, and it was proper to show one's opulence. Everything then was on a grand scale. The nobility and the prosperous middle classes lived in mansions and large semidetached houses in which their large families were waited on hand and foot by armies of live-in servants. Here, the *Ilustrated London News* reviewed the opera *I Masnadieri*:

> The duet between Gardoni and Lablache, which is beautiful and beautifully performed, many may consider the gem of the opera, voices such as Lind and Lablache, completely fill the ear with their beauty and fullness and leave an impression hard to be forgotten. Lablache, as the old Bohemian noble, is splendid as he always is. Both for his majestic appearance, his glorious voice, and his noble acting . . . innumerable bouquets were thrown.

Poor Lablache seemed to always be doomed to be the star of premieres that had grand galas and great openings, where praise was lavished upon him, but the end result was the same—the opera would sink into obscurity. In these operas, few could match his performance. There was Balfe's *Falstaff*—Persiani's *Inez de Castro* and then *I Masnadieri*. Public opinion felt the opera was unsuccessful partly because of its gloomy subject matter. Verdi conducted twice more before leaving for Paris with Muzio.

Lind and Lablache sang in concert at Buckingham Palace by command of the Queen on 28 May 1847 and at Marlborough House on 9 June. Jenny Lind then went down to Osborne House in August with Lablache just after singing again at Buckingham Palace. Queen Victoria's family residence—Osborne House—is situated on the north coast of the beautiful Isle of Wight. The diamond-shaped island lies off the south coast of England, facing the port of Southampton. The Italian-style house was built overlooking the sea and was at that time an estate of some one thousand acres. Lablache writes to his nephew in Naples during his stay at Osborne.[577]

August 3rd. 1847.
Dear Tony,

I spent a few days on the Isle of Wight with Her Majesty the Queen. Upon my return, I found your letter in which you informed me that Eric and Domenico[578] have been registered for conscription and that it would be necessary to pay 43 or 45 ducats—I do not remember exactly—then nine ducats per month; but you do not tell me the most essential thing which is for how long it is necessary to pay the nine ducats per month—which is what I would like to know immediately.

Eric and Domenico, benefiting from my status as a Frenchman (according to the law), were naturalized French, and Domenico is already serving in a dragoon regiment; if this reason is sufficient then so much the better, but if it could lead to trouble I prefer to pay. So ask the advice of Mr. Lucio and do what he recommends you to do.

It has not been possible for me to obtain permission to come to Naples this year, so I must postpone that pleasure until next year. Do not say anything yet so that everything is good at your end, and I ask you to inform me about what has happened there and what will happen. For the love of God write me more often about what you are doing.

I would like to hope that the wine was closely managed by Nicolas, putting the brandies in on time and changing the bottles in due course. I beg you to have it put in good old order and send me some of it in Paris.

I am still waiting anxiously for the drawing of the garden, which you promised me, and I hope it will not be delayed. Let me know if Lucio has done anything with Mr. Nicolino—in short, everything that interests me.

Remember that after the end of the work on the Pizzofalcone house,[579] it is necessary to have the billiard room built in the garden so that it can dry out before being lived in.

Teresa sends her best wishes to you, as also to the whole family and to the Doctor.

Give news of us to Maria Maddalina and tell her that as soon as I arrive in Paris where I will be a little more free, I shall write to her at length.

Goodbye, dear Tony. Best wishes to Lucio, Pandolfelli, Coltran, Mucricoffre and all those who remember us.

From your affectionate,
L. Lablache

Has Peter paid his debt? If he has not done so, it would be time to make him pay.

It is a strange fact that Luigi Lablache always signed L. Lablache even to his wife. Only in one early letter of his have we found that he signed his complete name.

I Masnadieri was replaced by Mozart's *Le Nozze di Figaro*, once more showcasing Jenny Lind whose passion for Mozart was quite well-known. She continued the season with *La Sonnambula* and by then another universal favorite—Donizetti's delightful *La Figlia del reggimento*, a good addition to the narrowing repertory shown at Her Majesty's Theatre. In the ensuing months, these two operas alone brought her staggering popularity unsurpassed that year by another soprano. At the end of the season, a tour of the provinces was a necessity as the public was clamoring to hear her. She left at once for an extensive grand whirlwind tour of the provinces, visiting over a dozen cities from Brighton to Edinburgh.

All England demanded to hear her, and with the railway now reaching many of the main cities, she left with the support of Frédéric Lablache, Gardoni, and Solari. Even Mme. Lablache joined them for part of the way. They appeared first at the fashionable seaside town of Brighton on 23 August and then continued north to Liverpool.

In Dublin, receipts from the nights in which Jenny Lind sang in *Sonnambula, Lucia, La Figlia del reggimento* were never equalled before or since in the history of the Theatre Royal. The question has often been asked, "Was Jenny Lind so great?" The simple answer is yes, recalls the *Annals of the Theatre Royal* Dublin. But not everyone was of the same view:

Bristol, October 1847 (from a correspondent)

The fact that Jenny Lind's appearances at Bath and Bristol would be her last in England added no small impetus to the excitement which engagements originated. The prices of admissions were increased almost sevenfold, yet the theatres of Bath and Bristol were crowded on the first evening of the two, almost to suffocation. At the concert on Monday evening at the Bristol Theatre, an apology was made for Madame Solari and Madame F. Lablache on the score of illness, but nothing was considered, or cared about save the *Swedish Nightingale* and so she could sing; the audience cared not one rush if the orchestra, accompanist, and the pianoforte were labouring under an indisposition.

The reception of Jenny Lind was of course tremendous, and her singing excited various sentiments among the listeners, the majority being certainly among her admirers. I, for one, felt quite charmed, and though I would not rank her with such vocalists as Grisi, or even Alboni, I must say she is a very superior artiste. The quality of her voice is, I think, overrated. There is an unpleasant guttural sound in her singing which I have never heard in the Italians. I take it her ART is her all in all. Her execution is sometimes surprising and pleases me as quite as well as Persiani's, though it may not have her astonishing flights of fancy, or self-dependencies which seem to make Persiani's singing so spontaneous. I was disappointed, I must confess, with Jenny Lind's "Casta Diva." Comparisons naturally suggested themselves, and I could not help the feeling that the *Swedish Nightingale* had not the power to usurp the throne of *La Diva*. In the *buffo* duet from the *Il Fanatico per Musica* with F. Lablache, she was much happier, her singing being characterized by great beauty and expression. In the final aria from *Sonnambula* she was also excellent, and vocalized with great precision. The throatiness of her voice, just mentioned, injured occasionally, the effect of this very brilliant display. The air was heard amid a tumult of acclamations, in the "Ouando lascia la Normandia," from *Robert le Diable*, and in a canzonet of Haydn's, with German words, she sang with great purity and taste. Her greatest impression of the evening was the Swedish melodies. In these and like national airs which require purity of tone, and facility of execution, I do not think she can be surpassed. Mr. Balfe deserves the highest possible praise for the masterly manner in which he officiated at the piano and conducted. Mr. Balfe at the piano is really an orchestra in himself.[580]

Donizetti's operas became increasingly popular in England by the 1840s, and his popularity now became worldwide. During 1838, Donizetti left Naples for Paris. Here, Dr. John Black explains how Donizetti's operas had been received in Naples:

Donizetti was by far the most frequently performed composer, and most of his operas were seen on the stage during these years (1828-1838), 51 in all. In the earlier years it was mostly the comic operas which predominated, but as the 1830's wore on, the great tragic works ushered in by *Anna Bolena* (which were first given in Naples in 1832) gradually took over. The period reached its peak in the late 1830's with *Lucia di Lammermoor* (1835) and *Roberto Devereux* (1837), though the evergreen lighthearted favorites, *L'Ajo nell'imbarazzo*, *L'Elisir d'amore* and *Il furioso* were never displaced. The popularity of his operas in the 1840's, after he had left Naples, was sustained by two highly successful works, *La Fille du régiment* (from Paris) and *Linda di Chamounix* (from Vienna). The proportion of his performances given in the Royal Theatres, 40 or so, was the same as for Bellini. His lighter works were particularly suited to the small theatres, and it is not surprising to find that many of his operas were given there. The evidence is that his popularity was consistent, with a strong base in each group of theatres. If Donizetti never had occasion to complain about lack of performances of his work, he certainly complained often enough of the pirated versions current, scores orchestrated by unknown hands from vocal scores filched from other theatres, but his principal difficulty in establishing his deeply personal tragic style lay with the censors and the regime in which he had to work, and this does not show up in the statistics.

By 1847, Donizetti was in the last stages of a fatal illness that he first contracted in Paris. From 1845 on, his health was deteriorating at an ever-increasing rate; he was no longer in his right mind and would suffer from incurable mental paralysis, finally sinking into a permanent coma. The Donizetti family brought him back to his birthplace in Bergamo, Italy, where he spent his final days with his family. Donizetti died on 8 April 1848—a terrible loss to the world of opera.

Chapter Twenty-Nine

More Concerts and Chopin's Death

1848-49

The death of Donizetti echoed through *The Musical World*, bringing back memories of the earlier loss of Bellini. Rossini's health remained for many years uncertain, and the hope he could be persuaded to compose again had been abandoned. Who then would fill the gap? Verdi's star was rising, but it was not till later years that he came into his own and made an impression in England. Other composers died young; Mendelssohn passed away on 4 November 1847 during the height of Lind's success, shortly followed by the tragic death of Frédéric Chopin in 1849.

While Liszt and Thalberg continued to compose, neither were of the same caliber as the above. Liszt, exhausted by eight years as a travelling virtuoso, abandoned his career and took up residence in Weimar. Thalberg's cool, brilliant playing did not tire him. His fantasies on the piano shimmered with lasting light and elegance while Liszt's wild playing burned out. Always regarded as the epitome of cool, finished accomplishment in piano playing, he appealed to the elegant salon crowd; he pursued that life with his usual refined manner relentlessly into the fifties, successfully conquering musical soirées first across Europe and later in America.

Donizetti's premature death left a decided void. His popularity in England had reached its zenith in the forties, and briefly, he even supplanted that of Rossini. From 1830 to 1845, before the Verdi era, Rossini always dominated the selections at Her Majesty's. However, by 1845, the Royal Theatre featured more Donizetti operas. Early in 1848, the Lablaches were involved in many fashionable concerts mostly intermixed with operas through August.

Another revolution broke out in Paris during February of 1848. Louis-Philippe abdicated and a new French Republic was formed. This had a considerable negative effect on the singers; while they enjoyed life in Paris, London had a much more stable environment. For Mario and Grisi, it was the last time either one of them sang in Paris for five years and for Lablache, who was now an honorary French citizen, things were still more uncertain.

Only Lablache returned to Her Majesty's. Mario and Grisi were now singing at Covent Garden. Frédéric Lablache was engaged to accompany Jenny Lind on another tour of the provinces of England in the autumn. While Lind enjoyed so much popularity, she briefly eclipsed most of the other sopranos. However, during this time, many other fine sopranos were being lured by impresarios to sing in Russia. Therefore, she filled a gap. They had been forced out to choose that path because of unstable management at the British theaters in those years.

When the ailing Frédéric Chopin arrived in London on 21 April in '48, the *Athenaeum* announced his arrival: "M. Chopin's visit is an event for which we most heartily thank the French Republic." During May, he met Jenny Lind and Lablache and two days later, on 15 May, he played at Stafford House (now Lancaster House), the beautiful home of the Duke and Duchess of Sutherland before a glittering audience of high society, including Queen Victoria, Prince Albert, and the Duke of Wellington. Chopin played his mazurkas, op. 7, no. 2, and op. 7, no. 1. (1832). Between Chopin's brilliant piano pieces, Lablache, Tamburini, and Mario obliged by singing, among other arias, the trio, "Quand l'Helvetie est un champ de supplices" from *Guillaume Tell*. The concert celebrated the christening of the duchess's new infant (Lady Alexandrina Leuson-Gower) and was held in the magnificent State Drawing Room. Chopin wrote, "The season is almost over; I have not yet played at the Queen's palace, though I have played before them."[581]

The Queen left for Scotland after attending the premiere of Meyerbeer's *Les Huguenots* at the Royal Italian Opera at Covent Garden. The Royal Command Performance showcased Pauline Viardot as Valentine and Mario sang Raoul. The opera was highly successful, and the Queen and Prince Albert enjoyed their first visit to the newly decorated theater. That season was noted for the debut of the fine French tenor, Gustave Roger, who filled in for Mario at Covent Garden when he was sick. Singing Raul in French, Roger created John of Leyden in *Le Prophète*. He returned to England later to tour the provinces with Lind. On 11 May that year, Chopin writes,

> I have just returned from the Italian Theatre. Jenny Lind sang for the first time this year, and the Queen showed herself for the first time since the Chartists. Both produced great effect—and, on me, so did old Wellington, who sat beneath the Queen's box

like an old monarchical dog in his kennel under his crowned Lady. I have met J. Lind, and she very graciously sent me a most excellent stall with her card . . . She is a typical Swede, not in an ordinary light, but in some sort of polar dawn. She is tremendously effective in *Sonnambula*. She sings with extreme purity and certainty, and her soft notes are steady and as even as her hair.[582]

France was not the only country touched by waves of unrest; Italy, Germany, and Ireland were all affected. Ireland had suffered the great potato crop famine, and people were starving to death. England remained undisturbed. Cecil Woodham-Smith writes,

By the spring of 1849 the wave of liberalism which resulted in the revolutions of 1848 had receded. The tangible result was small, the intangible result important. The tangible result was that Metternich had gone, and without his genius and his cunning, Austria never regained the reactionary domination of Europe; the intangible result was the revelation of an unsuspected strength of liberal opinion in every country in Europe. All absolute rulers were given food for reflection. Of the great powers, Britain alone remained undisturbed in spite of the strongest social reasons for revolution; the appalling poverty of the mass of the population in both rural and urban areas, and the appalling conditions of the industrial workers contrasted with the splendour and wealth of the upper classes, and the comfort enjoyed by the middle ranks of society. Visitors from the continent were astonished by the contrast.[583]

Donizetti's life was over, but like many musical geniuses, their works reach even greater heights after death. That year at Her Majesty's, Frédéric Lablache and his father began the season on 13 April 1848, Lablache sang in *Lucrezia Borgia* with Cruvelli, then on 20 May for the first time that season, *Linda Di Chamounix* followed by *L'Elisir d'amore* and *Don Pasquale*. A periodical of the time praises Lablache: "He is a comic to his finger ends." He sang with Eugene Tadolini in *Linda* and *Don* Pasquale. Jenny Lind joined him in *L'Elisir d'amore* and later in *Le nozze di Figaro*, and on 29 July, the season finished up with *I Puritani*. Lablache, Viardot, Alboni, and Castellan left for the provinces. Here, the *Illustrated London News* reported on the Worcester Musical Festival on 9 September:

> Worcester is well situated for such a gathering of the three Cathedral towns. On the banks of the Severn river in the sight of the Malvern hills . . . it is in the center of a large and populous district—in its approximation to Cheltenham, Birmingham, and Bristol, by the railroad . . . the first part of the Festival took place at the Cathedral where Mendelssohn's composition *Elijah* was sung.

Lablache sang at the College Hall situated to the south of the cloister, singing with Alboni and Castellan in the first concert of the evening, and the above newspaper writes that Lablache was much cheered as he entered the orchestra and was encored when he sang *Non piu andrai*. He sang also with Mme. Castellan the comic duo from *L'Elisir d'amore,* "Quanto amore." While Mr. John Sims Reeves, first English tenor of the day, joined them to sing selections from *Lucia* and Beethoven's *Adelaide*. Alboni was in great voice and sang Rossini's "Una Voca," among other arias.

The *Illustrated London News* on 14 October reported that Lablache visited Naples prior to his season in Paris and on another page of the same newspaper: "Lablache is expected to return in December." Under the title "Italian Opera in St. Petersburg," the same newspaper lists all the names of the principal singers engaged for St. Petersburg.

The winter season of 1848-1849 began 1 October and terminated 27 February 1849. Interestingly, a singer who had taken over management of the Royal Italian Opera at Covent Garden, the tenor Salvi, was on the list. He was joined by Frezzolini, Cobari, D'Angri (a Greek contralto), Gardoni, Tamburini, Coletti, Tagliafico, Rossi, and Demis. Music director was Baven.

Frédéric Lablache finished the London season with Lind after singing in *Figlia del reggimento* and *I Puritani* with Luigi Lablache. Then the full orchestra of Her Majesty's Theatre were off again on tour of the English provinces, leaving on 4 September. Jenny Lind was the main attraction, supported strongly by the finest singers of the day—French tenor Gustave Roger, Belletti, Frédéric Lablache, and conductor Michael Balfe. (Roger made his London debut in June of 1847.) Reviews of the *Times* praise him highly:

> Roger's voice is exquisitely pure, mostly proceeding from the chest, and rings like a silver bell. He is entirely free from that nasality

of tone which is so much injurious to the singing of the French school. His style simple and chaste, and his method of vocalization irreproachable. Roger produced an immense sensation.

After the Midlands, they continued to Edinburgh and Glasgow where Chopin was also an attraction. Another newspaper reported "Chopin in Edinburgh":

> This eminent pianist's concert in the Hopetown Rooms drew a large audience, despite the late attractive performances of Grisi, Alboni and Lind at the museum and the Theatre. There he performed some of his studies, the Andante and Largo, introduced some Polish melodies and mazurkas. His finished execution and poetic touch quite enraptured the auditory.

Chopin had many invitations from all over England, which his health would not permit him to accept for he was now in the advanced stages of consumption.

After the Midlands, the group from Her Majesty's featuring Lind moved on to Ireland. In their program of concerts, they usually sang arias from operas by Donizetti and Bellini and all the other music most associated with Lind. The *Illustrated London News* reports "The Whereabouts of Jenny Lind":

> This famed vocalist quitted Glasgow on Saturday for Dublin by sea, taking the Belfast steamer, accompanied by Mr. Lumley. Balfe, Roger, Belletti, and F. Lablache, not liking the long sea voyage, took the Liverpool route. The operatic performances in Glasgow were well attended. Mdlle. Lind sang in the La *Sonnambula* and *La Figlia del reggimento*. Roger's Elvino was much applauded. The tour terminated at Glasgow, with a concert on the 6th at the Town-Hall.(the British tour only).

By the end of October, they were back in Brighton at the Theatre Royal; and on 2 November, the *Brighton Gazette* reported,

> A concert at 2 o'clock on Monday a huge crowd assembled outside the Town Hall (as there was no more room inside). After the overture to *Der Freishutz*, conducted by Balfe, Monsieur Roger, and Signor F. Lablache sang first a duet. Then Jenny Lind, dressed

in a pink water-silk dress, sang first from Mozart: "Dove Sono," "La ci damen" with Belletti, "Casa Diva," from *Norma*. "Quando lascian," from *Roberto de Diablo*, and "Ah, non giunge" from *Sonnambula*. Roger sang, "Quel plaisir d'etre soldat," Balfe sang from his own opera the *Bohemian Girl* . . . "Then you'll remember me." Piatti played, with M. Lavigne on the oboe, and E. Belletti on the clarionetti.

After also singing in the provinces, the elder Lablache left for Naples, but later when he returned to Paris after "travelling day and night" from his villa in Naples to commence his duties, he found the Italian Theatre closed (*Illustrated London News*).

On 8 November, the former group performed en route back to the west coast in the old town of Southampton, famous seaport and the gateway to England. They were much appreciated when they sang at the Royal Victorian Spa and Assembly Rooms. We read of a most interesting program, a potpourri of delightful arias, sung in one of the most elegant establishments on the south coast of England. The spa was situated by the River Itchen and was then surrounded by lawns and trees, giving the place a delightful look. The program was printed in the *Hampshire Advertiser,* a newspaper that covered most of Hampshire including Winchester, the county town. Travelling west after Southampton, they gave concerts in Bath, Clifton, and Cheltenham, ending up in Birmingham on 28 December 1848.

Returning to Paris to the Théâtre-Italien on 6 January 1849, Luigi Lablache sang with great success in *La Cenerentola*. *Le Messager*, writing about Alboni, also gives us a good review of Lablache, this time singing Don Magnifico, included *The Musical World* comments on the Paris performance:

> Lablache's reception was immense, one word more about so superb a performance as his Don Magnifico would be superogatory. It is incomparable, both as a piece of acting and a piece of singing. The duet with Ronconi in the second act created a furore.

Back at London's Exeter Hall a month later, Frédéric Lablache joined his father and Jenny Lind for a grand concert on 29 January 1849, the conductor being Balfe. Jenny Lind sang again with Frédéric and his wife at Mme. Dulcken's concert at the Hanover Rooms on 21 February. That year, Mme. Frédéric Lablache joined her husband for a number of London concerts before Luigi Lablache arrived back from Paris.

Luigi opened the London season with *Norma* on 10 April. The Queen was present for the 21 April performance. The royal party was also present on 26 April for *La Sonnambula* and then on the 28 for *Lucia*.[584]

A new soprano, T. Parodi, joined Lablache on 12 April. Mozart's *Magic Flute* was sung in concert at Her Majesty's when he was supported by Frédéric Lablache and Jenny Lind. The Queen did not attend; as she had stated in her journal, she was not fond of the opera: "The music by the immortal Mozart is fine, but the story is too simple, trivial and rather absurd for our times."[585] Lablache performed in about thirteen operas that season, singing mostly Donizetti, Mozart, and Rossini. Frédéric Lablache and M. Alboni joined the cast.

By this time, Jenny Lind declined to sing at Her Majesty's again and was replaced by Henrietta Sontag. Lablache and Sontag had briefly sung with each other in Vienna in 1825 at the Karntnertortheater in *Le cantatrici villane*. Sontag, Germany's leading prima donna, had retired from the operatic stage at twenty-four to marry a Count Rossi. Unfortunately, the count had become a victim of political upheavals; and since they were living on a reduced income, the Countess Rossi was toying with the idea of returning to the stage to make ends meet.

Lumley had known of this situation. Fearful that some other impresario would reach her first and engage her, he sent a personal envoy, the virtuoso Sigismund Thalberg, who knew the Rossis in Berlin, to try to persuade her to come to Her Majesty's. Thalberg pointed out to Sontag that unlike Italy at that time, England was a stable country and remained untouched by revolution.[586] Sontag had to obtain permission from the king of Italy to lift his ban on her stage career. (No diplomat or military man could have a wife on the stage.) The King suggested a separation, which Rossi refused angrily and immediately resigned his post. Courageously then, Sontag clearly reached out to resume her title as the prima donna assoluta. Arriving after a long absence in London, Sontag returned to the scene of her former triumphs, this time, however, with dependent husband and children in tow.

Audiences everywhere in Northern Europe fondly remembered the beautiful, gracious lady from her early singing career. This situation was to Lumley's advantage as he was now desperate for a lead soprano after Lind's departure midseason following her performance of Alice in *Robert le Diable* on 10 May. Deserting opera for the concert hall, Lind said, was for religious reasons; most likely after her bumper concert tours, she could well afford to do so.

Lind was leaving later for New York after only two seasons in England; she had put in more time on her tours than she did singing opera at Her Majesty's. Often prima donnas left just as quickly as they came at Her Majesty's.

Sontag's return was greeted with enthusiastic applause at the opening of Donizetti's *Linda di Chamounix* at Her Majesty's Theatre on Saturday night 7 July 1849. Londoners, in fact, welcomed her back with a furor: (from the *London Times*:

> The greeting with which Madame Sontag was received on her first entrance was most enthusiastic, and lasted some minutes. This was the cheer of welcome to the long-established favourite. Then came the anxious pause of curiosity as to whether the fame of former days would be maintained . . . the question of the voice was decided at once by the first few notes of the recitative; not a particle of the original charm and freshness was lost. Then came the cavatina, "O luce di quest anima," sung with such a profusion of vocal brilliancy, and at the same time with such exquisite taste, that the hearers were completely taken by surprise . . . An execution facile to the last degree, the most unerring certainty of intonation, a management of the "sotto voce" passages, so give the greatest variety of colouring while retaining the full quality of every note, and above all, a certain sweetness in the voice, which went at once to the hearts of the audience. All these qualities exhibited in one sparkling little cavatina created an universal rapture, which few artists indeed succeed in producing. The repetition of this cavatina was loudly demanded.

Lumley was overjoyed, and he was firmly convinced that this lovely lady had saved his company and "joined in the chorus of her devoted admirers, adding his praise to the general homage."[587]

The rest of the season was a busy one for the two Lablaches at Her Majesty's Theater. Luigi Lablache teamed up with Sontag first in Rossini's *Otello* on 25 July, then *Le nozze di Figaro* and *Il Barbiere di Siviglia* on 4 August. "Sontag returned in her famous role: Rosina," wrote her biographer Frank Russell. "She was showered with applause and flowers after 'Una voce poco fa.' Sontag never looked back but constantly forged ahead with all the enthusiastic determination of a debutante."[588]

Another change came that season; the *Times* announced that Fanny Persiani was to retire. She sang at Her Majesty's for the last time in *Le nozze di Figaro*. The newspaper writes:

> She was in good voice and sung throughout with great brilliancy. When she reappeared at the end of the opera, accompanied by Grisi, D'Angri, Tamburini, Mariani and other principal artists, bouquets and wreaths were being thrown from every part of the house. Madame Persiani's retirement will be a great loss to the lyric stage. She is still in the zenith of her powers, and in certain parts can, with difficulty, be replaced. As mistress of florid vocalization she has had few equals even among the Italians, who excel all others in elaborate and ornamental style of singing, whether from natural aptitude or superiority of method it is not easy to decide upon perhaps from both.

Mme. Persiani must have had a change of heart, however, because she left almost at once for Paris and sang a whole season there before leaving for Russia, where she sang for two more seasons. Then she still continued to sing in Germany and Holland; retiring from the stage in 1859, she taught singing in Paris till her death there in 1867.

Singers from London's leading opera houses took part in a grand concert in Liverpool to celebrate the opening of the new Philharmonic Hall. In August, the London season of 1849 had finished. Then the two Lablaches, father and son; Mme. Sontag; tenor Calzolari; Belletti; the pianist Sigismund Thalberg; and conductor Michael Balfe left to tour the northern provinces of England. After a pretty full program of operas, such as *I Puritani, Don Pasquale*, and *Otello* in Manchester, they left for Liverpool, joining Grisi, Mario, Hayes, Alboni, Viardot, and others to sing *Elijah*, *The Messiah,* and the *Stabat Mater,* finishing with a fancy dress ball on 31 August.

Luigi and Frédéric Lablache, instead of returning to France, spent the autumn touring England with Sontag, Calzolari, Belletti, and Thalberg.

After the Birmingham Music Festival, they went south to Southampton. The *Hampshire Advertiser* and *Salisbury Guardian* announced a grand morning concert to be held at the beautiful Royal Victoria Assembly Rooms there for which the tickets were ten shillings and sixpence, about the same price as a return trip to Waterloo by train. Most likely, they stayed at the Drummund Arms on the old High Street below the ancient Bargate, a short distance from the Assembly Rooms.

We are well-informed that when such artists as John Parry and Liszt visited Southampton, they included Romsey, Winchester, Blandford, and Weymouth in their tours. We wondered if the Lablache group did the same, but we have no evidence to support it. It is most likely they included some of those places.

From there, they went on to the Isle of Wight and gave another morning concert, this time at the Town Hall in Ryde on Tuesday, 25 September. (Most concert artists stayed at the Star Hotel.) Through October, the Lablache group continued on their tour to many places such as Bristol, Bath, and Exeter; at Plymouth, it was believed they sung at Mount Edgecumbe's stately home before returning to the north again.

No exact date was given as to when this group arrived in Bury St. Edmunds.[589]

> At half past one, five hundred ladies and gentlemen were assembled at the Bury Assembly Rooms, Angel Hill, "the largest attendance of the nobility and gentry of this town and neighbourhood we ever saw assembled on any similar occasion."

Sometime during the tour, they visited Salisbury (the exact dates are unknown). However, it was remembered by the Lablache family as being one of the highlights of that trip. Here, it was mentioned that they sung at the home of a noble family. Did they sing at Wilton House for a private party there? The group had not seen Stonehenge, so one moonlit night, they jumped into their carriages, followed by the locals of the region, and rode out across the Salisbury plain to Stonehenge.

What a thrilling experience it must have been for those who were there, hearing Sontag standing in the moonlight, her crystal clear voice piercing the silence of the night singing "Casta Diva." There they listened to her under the stars surrounded by the circles of Druid stones overlooking the windswept valleys and dark tree-covered hills, hills that conceal the remains of the ancient Britons. Did Lablache sing Oroveso's aria? One wonders what he sang, perhaps something sacred. One can easily imagine his rich voice thundering out into the blackness of the night.

Lablache could not have failed to notice all the upheavals at Her Majesty's and the steady departure of his colleagues for Russia. He had turned down offers to sing there many times, and his agents tried to persuade him that Russia had a lot to offer—even better earnings, more glory. The knowledge that Italian singers secured larger salaries there and in the United States were well known. But Lablache, now in his middle fifties, could not be lured by money; he was wealthy enough. Nor was the closure of Her Majesty's a factor. He still sang in Paris, and the Royal Italian Opera wanted him. However, the additions pressures of the planned departure of his daughter, Marie, and Emilie de Méric and family whom he knew well overcame him. So before the autumn of 1852, Lablache reluctantly relented. He had long ignored the open invitation that Czar Nicholas I had extended to him many years before. Most of the Italian singers, more zealous than Lablache and a good deal younger, naturally welcomed Russia as a challenge and a new operatic frontier to conquer. For Lablache, that was all behind him. Lablache remained adamant; he could not be persuaded. It was known, too, that Lablache never overstepped his boundaries or demanded larger fees, unlike many of the prima donnas of the day:

> From 1828 Lablache's terms for four months of operatic singing were including 40,000 francs (perhaps equivalent to 6,250 pounds), free lodgings, an expense-free benefit night, and the choice both of the first opera in which he was to appear and that for his benefit.[590]

Mario and Grisi were engaged to sing in Russia at the St. Petersburg's Imperial Theatre. Since the beginnings of their long careers in England and France, they sang yearly with Lablache at the numerous British concerts and operas together. As an Italian "quartet" they reaped success for all of them. After Rubini retired, Mario took over most leading tenor roles then the four singers continued till Tamburini and Lablache ended their singing careers.

Arriving from Paris that season was Emilie de Meric, the young daughter of Joséphine de Méric, the celebrated French singer from Strasburg. Only nineteen and a novice to the stage, contralto Mlle. Emilie de Méric teamed up with another newcomer, the Irish soprano Catherine Hayes, to make their debuts that year at the Royal Italian Opera in London. Catherine Hayes sang the title role in Donizetti's *Linda di Chamounix*. Mlle de Méric sang Pierotto for the first time there.[591] She was acknowledged to show promise, and was invited to sing the following year. Emilie and Catherine Hayes sang together in many concerts that season. In September, Emilie joined Lablache, Grisi, Mario, and Frédéric Lablache at the Grand Festival Concerts given in the Birmingham Town Hall. It was a four-day event.

The *Times* wrote about how the program included such major works as Mendelssohn's *Elijah,* which had been composed for the 1846 festival,

Athaliah, the *Messiah,* and part of *Israel in Egypt.* Beethoven's *Pastoral Symphony* and the appearance of Mme. Sontag were looked forward to with eager and general expectation. Emilie de Meric sang *Deh non voler* from *Anna Bolena.* The local *Gazette* said that she had interpreted this with great taste, displaying a voice of considerable extent, power, and sweetness.

>The orchestra was conducted by Michael Costa. He had made his debut as a singer at the Birmingham Festival in 1829. In one of Costa's own quartets, *Ecco quel fiero istante,* Emilie sang with Madame Castellan, Mario and Frédéric Lablache, the bass who was to become her brother-in-law. This had been much and deservedly applauded.
>
>Although evidently suffering from nervousness, Emilie had given Cherubini's beautiful sacred number, *O Salutaris Hostia,* in a highly artistic manner. She had joined Jetty de Treffz, Mario and Machior in Mozart's *Ave Verum.*
>
>On that Thursday, the Hall had been crowded to suffocation with 2,433 people present. *The Times* wrote that: "A feature of general interest . . . was a grand chorus, interspersed with solos, *L'Invocazione all'Armonia,* the composition of His Royal Highness Prince Albert . . . The music is highly creditable to the illustrious amateur. The chorus in C Major, which forms the burden of the *morceau, is* rhythmical and animated, and the solos are melodious and effectively written for voices. The execution was admirable and the encore unanimous. Mme. Castellan, Mlle. de Méric, Mario and Lablache, sang the solo voice parts with great care and effect. Emilie had sung the duet *Lasciami,* from *Tancredi,* with Mme. Castellan. This had been very pleasing. Then a notice was circulated asking for no encores, so that the performance could be over by 11 o'clock. This had little effect, however. Mendelssohn's *First Walpurgis Nacht* did not come on till 11:30. Mozart's *Splendente te* had been very well executed, the solo parts having been sustained with great ability by Mlle. de Treffz, Mlle. de Méric, Mr. Sims Reeves and Herr Pischek. One of the gems of the evening had been the *Benedictus* from Mozart's *Requiem,* in which Emilie de Méric had sung with Castellan, Sim Reeves and Frédéric Lablache.[592]

Then Emilie de Méric rushed off to join the Russian opera with Mario and Grisi. There she earned herself the title of Russian Court Singer. The *Revue et Gazette Musicale de Paris* wrote, "St. Petersburg has the finest singers in the world."[593] And there was little doubt when she returned to London the following year, the Royal Italian Opera House bent in her direction to give her juicier roles, but the Russians paid her better and treated her more favorably.

During the early years in St. Petersburg, she came into closer contact with Nicolas Lablache, the second son of Luigi Lablache, who traveled there with his father. They had met sometime before in Paris. Later in 1854, they were married at Maisons-Laffitte. In 1849, she began her English career at the Royal Italian Opera House at Covent Garden. *The Musical World* writes of her debut and of Elena D'Angri:

> Mlle de Méric is not English, nor can she speak a word of the language. Joining the other debutantes that year was a Greek soprano, Elena D'Angri, who also showed great promise at her debut on 17 April. Her voice was a contralto of remarkable quality, even, easy, hollow, without lusciousness and of remarkable volume. She had a good stage presence, but there seemed to be about her something uncouth and wild which got between herself and her English audiences.

While Queen Victoria and Prince Albert leisurely cruised off the Isle of Wight in their royal yacht that hot summer, the cholera broke out and spread up and down England. The *Times* reported daily about the number of deaths and grimly described the horrible living conditions of the victims and how fast they died. England was powerless in the face of cholera; there was no cure then. No attention was paid to a German who was expelled from Prussia and slipped into London by the name of Karl Marx. Soon, on 11 July 1849, the *Times* wrote that a cholera epidemic had broken out in Paris.

All of Paris suffered a torturous heat wave during the summer of 1849. While the cholera swept through the city, Chopin's condition steadily worsened and now he could no longer compose and was too sick to take in students. Mme. Catalani fell victim to the epidemic of cholera in Paris.

Moving to the country, Chopin found peace. There he rested and received many visitors, such as Jenny Lind who came and sang to him. Paris became more and more deserted; finally, the dread cholera receded. But time had run out for Chopin, for it was not cholera that would take his life but tuberculosis. Returning to Paris in September, he slowly worsened; and on 17 October, he died.

A huge funeral was arranged at the famous Church of the Madeleine. Here again, Lablache sang the bass part in Mozart's solemn Requiem Mass. Here, a firsthand account from Paris printed in a newspaper of the day:

> After the coffin was laid in its place, the sounds of the chanting gradually died away, and then after a pause, sweet music began to float about us. The music deepened on and on . . . then suddenly the waves divided before a mighty voice—a voice which rose and rose, louder and more loud, full, rich, more clear than the ring of trumpets, more sweet and deep than the tones of an organ—the wonderful voice of Lablache! My anticipations of this voice were more than fulfilled. Hardly could I persuade myself that it came from human lips. In all its power faultlessly sweet, it overwhelmed my senses in its flood of melody. This was Lablache. Of the rest, to say that my ignorance has no words to describe the progress of the Requiem, is to say little. Even God's vocabulary might fail him here.

Another full report of the musical part of the service we find in a letter from the Paris correspondent of *The Musical World* (10 November 1849):

> The ceremony, which took place on Tuesday (the 30th ult.), in the church of the Madeleine, was one of the most imposing we ever remember to have witnessed. The great door of the church was hung with black curtains, with the initials of the deceased, "F.C." emblazoned in silver. On our entry we found the vast area of the modern Parthenon entirely crowded. Nave, aisles, galleries, were alive with human beings who had come to see the last of Frédéric Chopin . . . At noon, the service began. The orchestra and chorus (both from the Conservatoire, with M. Girard as conductor) and the principal singers Madame Viardot-Garcia, Madame Castellan, Signor Lablache, and M. Alexis Dupont were placed at the extreme end of the church, a black drapery concealing them from view. When the service commenced the drapery was partially withdrawn and exposed the male executents to view, concealing the women, whose presence, being uncanonical, was being felt, not seen. A solemn march was then struck up by the band, during the performance of which the coffin containing the body of the deceased was slowly carried up the middle of the nave. As soon as

the coffin was placed in the mausoleum, Mozart's Requiem was begun. The march that accompanied the body to the mausoleum was Chopin's own composition from his first piano forte sonata, instrumented for the orchestra by M. Henri Reber. During the ceremony M. Lefebure-Wely, organist of the Madeleine, performed two of Chopin's preludes upon the organ . . . The coffin was then carried from the church, all along the Boulevards, to the cemetery of Pere-Lachaise—a distance of three miles at least. Meyerbeer and the other chief mourners, who held the cords, walking on foot, bareheaded. A vast number of carriages followed . . . At Pere-Lachaise, in one of the most secluded spots, near the tombs of Habeneck and Maria Milanollo, the coffin was deposited in a newly-made grave. The friends and admirers took a last look, ladies in deep mourning threw garlands and flowers upon the coffin, and then the gravedigger resumed his work . . . The ceremony was performed in silence.

Meanwhile, back in England, the blazing summer heat had given way to a severe winter, bringing the cholera outbreak to an end, which was the only consolation. Lumley arranged another winter tour for Sontag and Frédéric Lablache. After the successful Jenny Lind tours of the years before, Lumley was hoped to bolster his shaky financial situation with the charms of Ms. Sontag. However, he was too hasty. Few people outside of London had heard of her, and it was hard to erase the memory of Lind in their minds. After their autumn tour of southern England, Luigi left for France some time after singing in Liverpool on 10 October. Frédéric Lablache, Sontag, Count Rossi, her husband, continued on to Scotland. Besides the wretched weather, cholera had taken many lives in the provinces and kept many people away. Real tragedy hit them in December when they were deep in the north of Scotland. Caught in a major snowstorm, and stuck in their carriage on route for days, they nearly all lost their lives before they were rescued.[594]

ଔଔଔ

Chapter Thirty

La Tempesta

1850-51

Queen Victoria's attendance at Her Majesty's Theatre dropped noticeably in 1850, and although Lablache sang in at least ten operas there, she only visited the theater a few times. This was in sharp contrast to her attendance record for 1849 and 1851. She even missed the debuts at Her Majesty's in April of two well-known British singers Sims Reeves and Catherine Hayes in *Lucia di Lammermoor*. The reason for this absence was clear, for on 1 May, there was another new addition to the royal couple, a baby boy Arthur. *The Musical World* writes about *Lucia*:

> They were recalled and encored unanimously, on several occasions. Their acquisition to the Lumley establishment cannot be too highly estimated—Frédéric Lablache and Belletti were all that could be desired.

However, the lead singers were not Italians, and the reputation of Her Majesty's was at stake. Chorley wrote that the public did NOT appreciate the new singers and that they failed to excite. Everyone from Balfe to Lablache wanted to leave in spite of newspaper reports of new successes. Eventually, the theater got into difficulties and was eclipsed by the Royal Italian Opera (Covent Garden).

Attending *Il Barbiere di Siviglia* and *Don Pasquale* that season the critic for *The Musical World* mentioned:[595]

> Lablache sang in the *Barbiere* and 'it was a fine house.' Among the audience were Her Majesty Queen Victoria, Prince Albert and a brace of royal infants . . . Lablache's Dr. Bartolo has lost none of its unctuous and irresistible humour and his 'cavatina' in the lesson

scene was as inimitably lackadaisical as ever. *Don Pasquale* also sparkled . . . The *Don Pasquale* of Lablache is a miracle of racy humour. No description can do it justice, and as we are not inclined to profess, much less exhibit, incompetency where mere words and phrases are concerned; we shall not attempt to describe what, in the spirit of candour, we have pronounced as in describable. The only piece of "gag" in this enormous piece of comedy is when Lablache picks up the letter, with help of a chair and a toasting fork, and after having accomplished his aim, throws himself into that attitude which painters and sculptors, from time immemorial, have assigned to the more mischievous and frolicsome moods of the small god Cupid. To see this was worth an entire pantomime, and would have turned the melancholy grimace of Heraclitus the crying philosopher into a broad grin . . . The fact is Lablache can do as he pleases with the public, whom he has held by the coat button for nearly thirty years. In the 'finale' the voice of Lablache comes out with all its early thunder; and an audience of deaf men might hear without their trumpets, and be edified.

Lablache sometimes sang in small parts, recorded under the title of "Lablache Sententioso" by Florimo:

Despite his quite literally towering prominence, Lablache often sang parts of smallish importance in between his Leporellos and Pasquales, for the repertory offered few genuine leads for basses. When a colleague commiserated on Lablache's being wasted as Don Basilio in *Barbiere*, Lablache said "My friends, to a great singer there are no small parts. And to a small singer there are no great ones."

Here is another review of *Don Pasquale* from the *Morning Herald*:

The occasion was further distinguished by the reappearance of the elder Lablache. The matchless buffo was warmly welcomed. The addition of twelve months to his age does not seem to have affected him in the least; neither has he diminished an inch in bulk. He is as potential in voice and as unctuous in humour as ever; and this involves everything that need to be said, for who is there that is not familiar with his diverting vanities—his cruel perplexities? His acting in this character is a sublime tidbit of comedy; and when he retires—Don Pasquale will retire too.[596]

The three Lablaches—Luigi, Frédéric, and Fanny (father, son, and now daughter-in-law)—sang in concerts together throughout the year, mostly in England. When Luigi left for Russia in 1852, Frédéric and Fanny continued on without him. Later, Fanny took on concerts only in London and Paris because of her family obligations. The Frédéric Lablache family now consisted of two little girls. The oldest, Thérèse Frances was named after her grandmother Teresa (Pinotti) and her mother Frances. The second daughter, Fanny Rose Louise, was born in Paris on 6 February 1843. On the 27 January 1850, Frédéric and Fanny became the proud parents of a boy. Named Luigi Frederick, after his grandfather Luigi, the child was born at St. Pancras, a part of central London.

Mme. Lablache was soon back singing first at the Princess Rooms, 10 May, then at the Hanover Square Rooms on 15 May. A grand extra night was packed with double entertainment at Her Majesty's on 18 April. With not only *Le nozze di Figaro*, with Lablache and Sontag, Parodi, Hayes, Calzolari, but the last act of *Lucia di Lammermoor*, Frédéric Lablache sang Enrico and Bide the Bent with Sims Reeves as Edgardo and Catherine Hayes as Lucia. Maria Taglioni and Carlotta Grisi were engaged to dance that evening.[597]

Later in the year, Frédéric Lablache returned as Sergente Sulpice, singing along this time with Henrietta Sontag, who had returned to London. While Lind was the Swedish Nightingale, the British newspapers named the principal star of the season, Mme. Sontag, "the drawing-room thrush," when she sang Marie in *La Figlia del reggimento* for the first time on 18 July. *The Musical World* wrote, "It was a decided success . . . the acting of F. Lablache was incomparable, his humour and tact in this opera should not pass unrecorded."

Luigi Lablache followed this by singing Campanone in *Prova di un'opera seria*. In the course of the evening, Donna Maria Loreto Martinez, billed as the Black Malibran, entertained with Spanish Aires from Cuba. Between acts, Carlotta Grisi and Petit danced. Stephan and Amalla Ferraris also entertained.[598]

Queen Victoria and Prince Albert visited the Royal Italian Opera at Covent Garden for the first time after the Queen's confinement for Meyerbeer's *Le Prophète* on 25 June.[599] Victoria wrote that she thought it "quite beautiful."

Mario sang John of Leyden with Pauline Viardot. They were delighted with the production. Mme. Grisi and Mario sang mostly Meyerbeer at the Royal Italian that year and the latter was highly praised by the Queen: "He improves every year, and I think his voice is the finest tenor I ever heard, and he sings and acts with such intense feeling." While she heard *Les Huguenots* on 29 July, there is no record of her seeing *La Juive* till 1852.[600] But she heard *Robert le Diable* and *Les Huguenots* many times. These operas in fact were the royal favorites in the 1850s. Rowell points out that Ms. Lind may have even converted the Queen to Meyerbeer.[601]

Queen Victoria had a harrowing experience that year. On 27 June, she was viciously attacked while leaving Cambridge House. A man leaped up on the carriage and proceeded to beat the frightened queen over the head with a brass-headed cane. It happened in front of her shocked children and a crowd of onlookers who all came to her rescue. Having been knocked to the floor, she bravely got up after receiving many severe blows. The culprit was captured on the spot, and the Queen recovered; however, it was the second attack on her person within a month.[602]

Opera house managers heavily depend on their prima donnas for success; Her Majesty's was no different. Lumley was desperate as he continued to have difficulties hiring exciting new talent to compete with the Royal Italian house. Clearly, the managers of most opera houses had little control over the movements of the temperamental divas in those days. Her Majesty's Theatre needed to reinstate artists of quality. Many of the desirable singers, who were stars during the golden years, had deserted to Covent Garden, such as Grisi and Mario, Tamburini and Ronconi; even conductor Michael Costa now ruled supreme there as field marshal of the orchestra. Even Lablache, who represented everything that was stable and reliable, was forced to leave in 1852, dissatisfied.

The Countess Rossi (Henrietta Sontag) remained with Lumley at least through Britain's great Exhibition year 1851; however, as the Count Rossi's debts were still outstanding, she left for a whirlwind tour of America and Mexico in pursuit of more money. Her Majesty's survived only through 1852. Harold Rosenthal in his *Two Centuries of Covent Garden* explains,

> The public lost all faith in the management and by the end of the season, Lumley was virtually bankrupt. There was to be no opera at Her Majesty's for the next three summers.[603]

The historic Her Majesty's Theatre had survived many a crisis during its long and varied history as a leading opera establishment in London. The 1850 season appeared to be no different; but behind the scenes, acid-tongued critic Henry Chorley had noted a downward course that became more and more evident. The newly formed rival house, the Royal Italian Opera at Covent Garden, had scored many big successes by adopting French repertoire. Especially by the midforties, patrons in both houses were exposed to the attractions of French opera. Tiring of just Italian works, the English were interested in seeing what novelty these operas from Paris could offer. It was said that the insatiable British audiences during that time would not be satisfied even if Da Ponte or Metastasio appeared before them and composed.

A generation of unequaled composers like Rossini, Donizetti, and Meyerbeer had taken up residence in Paris to compose for the French theaters. French composers Auber and Halévy wrote for the stages of the Opera Comique, L' Opéra of Paris, and other establishments.

Soon the orchestra and chorus of the Royal Italian Opera House were pronounced the best in Europe; the previous year had chalked up impressive triumphs with a full program of just opera, increasing prestige for their establishment. Starting with Auber's *Masaniello* (adapted to the Italian stage), this opera drew immense crowds for several successive nights with the tenor, Mario. It continued with Meyerbeer's *Les Huguenots* and the first *Prophète* (1849) starring Malibran's famous sister Pauline Viardot as Rachel, with Hayes and Mario. Chorley even went as far as to say, "Covent Garden keeps its promise and has the OPERA."

These were the significant successes that Her Majesty's Theatre needed to match. First and foremost, the prima donnas from the previous decade might have suffered from overexposure, but they were still up there in the limelight at Covent Garden. Remembering that Jenny Lind was a fresh new face on the British scene in 1847, Lind's Alice in Meyerbeer's *Robert le Diable* at Her Majesty's started the Lind fever that swept through Britain for two years. By the time Lind left for America, she was a legend. Her Majesty's theatre had to fend for itself after that in the soprano department, a hard blow to overcome as there were few major names left; only Catherine Hayes and Lablache were such artists, as Fezzolini and Parodi were hardly major. The press wrote:

> Since the days of the great impresario, Barbaja, when composers and artists of genius were as numerous as they are now rare, the lyrical stage has yearly become more needy in its repertoire.

The popular Lablache, while certainly no youngster and was still not past his prime at fifty-five, carried on uncomfortably. Not wishing to desert his friend Lumley, he was tied into helping the impresario behind closed doors. The press reported:

England lavished more money on the lyrical stage than any other country, owing to prosperous times, her affluent society, and the rapid rise of the new middle class through the Industrial Revolution. Entertainment became more varied and competitive. Hence, while manager Lumley had captured the Swedish Nightingale, Jenny Lind, for a few seasons and reaped plenty from her successes, Her Majesty's failed to secure her forever, leaving the rival Covent Garden to hope that with her departure it would leave them in undisputed possession of the field. Both theaters suffered from financial trouble, but for Her Majesty's, Lumley immediately sought out and engaged the celebrated and still beautiful Henrietta Sontag (Countess Rossi) as a replacement for Lind. Immediately after her debut, she became the mainstay of Lumley's theater for the season of 1850—another glorious windfall for the lessee of Her Majesty's Theatre, another triumph for diplomacy. Triumphant by the end of her first season, she displayed rare talent, and her Susannah was written up as warmly received. Soon, the shadow of Lind was dispelled forever—Sontag held her own. Before long, she was to assume the character that all Jenny Lind lovers all over the British Isles took to their heart—Marie in *La Fille du régiment*. At the Royal Italian Opera, the same week, audiences were enthralled by Meyerbeer's *Les Huguenots*. Packed audiences filled the theater to overflowing on every occasion. The ecstatic enthusiasm with which the third act that contained the "Benediction of the Poignards" and duo of Grisi and Mario was received made it a good year for Meyerbeer again. Sontag's entrance to the operatic scene caused little notice among Grisi's fans; Grisi was still Queen of the Opera and was reported in "splendid voice" later that week as Norma.

Fromental Halévy's grand opera *La Juive* in five acts in collaboration with Eugene Scribe had been a spectacular success at its debut at Academie de Musique, Paris (1835). The opera soon appeared as a new central piece in the operatic repertoire throughout Europe, alongside Meyerbeer's works. Covent Garden took the lead in 1850, producing the premiere London performance of *La Juive* at Covent Garden in French, plus three of Meyerbeer's operas. The *Illustrated London News* wrote a glowing report:

> On Thursday, for the extra night, the long promised *La Juive* of Scribe and Halévy was produced, and beyond all comparison, with the most gorgeous "mise en scene" ever known on the continent. Produced twice in English before at Drury Lane, the English version

in 1835 (another version in 1846), was adapted by Planche, and reduced to two acts, nearly omitting all of the music; but so powerful was Scribe's drama, that even with this musical mutilation it ran eighty-four nights with Ellen Tree, Ford, Messrs Cooper, Warde, Giubilei, E. Seguin, and Vanenhoff sustaining the principle parts.

In 1850, a new Halévy opera *La tempesta* was introduced at Her Majesty's. Especially written in Italian, it was shown alongside Verdi's *Nino, Ernani, I Lombardi*, none of which created much of an impression at that time. Lumley needed another big draw like a Meyerbeer opera to keep his theater afloat. Lablache refused to sing Verdi but agreed to take the lead in *La tempesta*. By May 18, 1850 the team of Halévy and Scribe arrived in London for the final rehearsals. *La Tempesta* was another Halévy-Scribe collaboration, based on William Shakespeare's play, categorically a French work in spite of the Italian libretto, it was conceived against a "dream fantasy background," with choruses of elves, dancing fairies and flying figures. It opened at Her Majesty's on 8 June. Chorley called it "pantomimic music." There had to have been a pantomime atmosphere and he wrote:[604]

> Produced under all these conditions, I have always felt that *La Tempesta* has more real merit than the world agreed to award it ... what musical talent Halévy possessed was exclusively Parisian. Anywhere else, save in the capital of France, I have never heard his stage-works without a feeling of short-coming and weariness. The very peculiarities of his style and extreme illustration of that musical suspense in which the French delight; calling the same "distinction" demand French text, French actors, French audiences. I recollect the man in both capitals, as tenfold more frank and attractive than his music. The best singers in the company were assembled to give every possible strength and spirit to the drama. The Caliban of Lablache was remarkable piece of impersonation and good taste. Had it not been so, the very hazardous scenes of the Monster's persecution of *Miranda* could not have been allowed on the stage. In these, too Madame Sontag's delicacy and reserve stood the drama in good stead. The rest of the company had worked good with no less goodwill; the music had been studied to a nicety rarely attained since Signor Costa had left the theatre. There was rich and tasteful scenery. But *La tempesta* could not live. It was given with less favour when it was subsequently given at the Italian Opera

house in Paris, though there (by way of improvement) the last act was entirely omitted. In England, as yet, Halévy has no public.

The disheartening lethargy which, in spite of every attempt to force applause, and to counterfeit the appearance of success, was creeping over the old Opera house, and got hold of the ballet too. It seemed totally impossible to excite any interest or curiosity. But we still read, morning after morning, of triumph after triumph; of enormous gains and successes; and the farce, melancholy as it was, was kept up for still a year or two longer, as bravely as if the end had not been from the first to be clearly foreseen.

Chorley reported truthfully. By 1852, all the lead artists had left Her Majesty's for better offers elsewhere. Hayes was gone; Sontag left for America; and Luigi Lablache left in the fall of 1852 for Russia, never to return to the theater to which he had given so much of his life.

In spite of Chorley's negative recollections about *La tempesta*, there were other reviews to consider. These were good and in some cases ecstatic; so in fact, it was popular with the general public. The *Illustrated News* reported, "Such a truly artistic work has seldom been seen on any stage; it is full of charming contrasts, employs every resource of modern art, and is free from all that is meretricious, glaring, and noisy." It seemed the whole production hinged on the graceful dancing of Carlotta Grisi as Ariel, and though the performances could have been extended, she was engaged to go to Russia so the opera was terminated after six performances in spite of a great public interest. *La tempesta* has never been staged again in this century or the last as far as we know. Below is a review in 1850 that gives us a little idea of a rather confusing story and roles of the cast:

Alfonso	Signor Lorenzo
Prospero	Signor Colletti
Antonio	Signor F. Lablache
Ferdinand	Signor Baucarde
Trinculo	Signor Ferrari
Stephano	Mdlle. Parodi
Sycorax	Mdlle. Bertrand
Spirit of Air	Madame Giuliani
Ariel	Mdlle. Carlotta Grisi
Caliban	Signor Lablache
Miranda	Madame Sontag

The opera is written in three acts with a prologue by the most rising composer of the age, having written an opera expressly for such performers as Sontag, Parodi, F. Lablache, Giuliani, Baucarde, Coletti, and Lablache; the smaller parts are executed by artists of merit. The *Illustrated London News* writes:

> And the spiriting of Carlotta Grisi (the famous sister of Giulia Grisi) with a select bevy of danseuses, is interwoven, like a thread of gold through the whole opera. Carlotta makes her *entre* so lightly tripping to the tune of "Where the bee sucks," that she appears to be using her wings not her feet. One of the essential differences betwixt Shakespeare and Scribe's plot is, that the English *Tempest* (except in a passing description) is without a tempest . . . the most important subject for the composer to treat! The tempest in the opera forms the prologue . . . *La tempesta* has been given with unabated success. Indeed every fresh representation proves its intrinsic worth. The Miranda of Sontag, the Caliban of Lablache, and the Ariel of Carlotta Grisi.
>
> With the second act, the interest, both musical as well as dramatic, increases tenfold. Here the artistic magnificence of this opera in all respects is demonstrated to the most ordinary observers's comprehension. Lablache appeared as Caliban wearing a hilarious fur suit with long fingernails and toenails. Caliban, wandering near a rock where Sycorax is imprisoned, is told by his mother where three flowers grow, each of which will afford him the accomplishment of a wish. Caliban's triumph, first over Ariel, whom he imprisons in a tree, and next to Miranda, the object of his brutal love, affords the composer and Lablache the opportunity of displaying all the treasures of their respective arts. Lablache's interpretation of the character of Caliban, in this second act, exceeds all praise; he has realized all Shakespeare dreamt of, and makes the spectators feel astonished. Sontag, representing Miranda, indignant innocence in the power of brute force, displays likewise the most delicate traits of dramatic feeling. The struggle of contending passions expressed by composer and vocalist, in the duet, "Pure mi scuota," was truly beyond all ordinary commendation. The delight of the audience is further increased in the next scene when the (hairy) Caliban, carrying away Miranda, encounts the crew of the ship. Calibans's drunken song, "Se tutto giba," with a broken curious rhythm, to

which he dances to the audience's delight. The act ends with the fallen Miranda struck motionless by the means of the talisman she has purloined, curtain falls.

One discovers one of the most beautiful specimens of scene-painting that can be imagined. A gorgeous vessel under full sail is seen advancing to the shore, while the chorus sang, once more, the tune "Where the bee sucks" a most happy idea of the composer who deserves no less praise for the manner in which it was introduced than for the admirable relief given to it by the instrumentation. At the close of this magnificent display, the curtain falls as the vessel reaches the shore. The artists, composer, author, conductor, and impresario were all called forward.[605]

Chorley mentioned, "All was done to produce *La tempesta* worthily and well that Her Majesty's Theatre could do. Another opera with a spectacular opening, but was the music strong enough to remain attractive after repeated hearings? A true test of a great opera."[606]

The season continued with the usual concerts at Her Majesty's Theatre, the Royal Italian Opera House, and many at smaller establishments too numerous to mention. Lablache also sang on July 1 at Buckingham Palace. Most of the best concerts were scheduled before the Queen, and her court left for the summer recess at the end of July.

It was not unusual to find Lablache part of the entertainment during the times when Queen and Prince Albert were at Osborne House. This proved to be one of the favorite homes of Queen Victoria, just built on the Isle of Wight. Queen Victoria wrote in her journal that "Lablache and his son came by royal packet boat"[607] so that Queen Victoria could continue her lessons there as well. Dr. Meyer, the prince's librarian, noted, "They both spoke perfect English with the Queen and perfect Neapolitan Italian with each other."[608] Lablache usually sang at the private concerts that took place in the Council Room beginning a little before ten o'clock,[609] entertaining the royal family and guests in the evening after dinner. Another time, Lablache, Castellan, Costa, Mario, and party would arrive from Portsmouth by Her Majesty's post office steam packet boats. *Portsmouth Portsea and Gosport Herald* describe a similar crossing:

> The beach at Ryde sloped very gently, and so it advertised that the passengers would be landed at Ryde Pier (half a mile long, and begun in 1817) without the inconvenience of ferrying the passengers

in rowing-boats. The packet left Portsmouth each morning at nine, arriving at quarter-past eleven . . . the best aft cabins were two shillings each, with a stewardess to attend upon the ladies.

When Lablache crossed this particular strait, however, on few occasions, the weather would turn nasty and everyone would violently get sick including our illustrious singer.

A concert was held there on 5 August 1850; Queen Victoria wrote in her journal that Mario, Lablache, and Castellan sang with Costa at the piano, "which was a real treat."[610]

Lablache continued to teach Queen Victoria and Prince Albert until he left for Russia. Here, family history passes down a story that was top secret and was very embarrassing for Lablache and naturally could not be told to anyone at that time:

> One evening a concert was held at Buckingham palace with all the Italian singers, when the interval took place Lablache slipped on his overcoat and took a stroll outside in the garden. Retreating inside again, he flopped down heavily, all two hundred and sixty pounds of him, into the nearest overstuffed chair in a quiet corner of the palace. There he dosed off for a few minutes. Imagine his horror upon getting up, he sees the lifeless form of one of the Queen's many little dogs. A dog lover himself at first he didn't know what to do. Terrified he would be discovered, without a word, he slipped the tiny corpse into one of the huge grecian vases in the gardens, before returning to sing.[611]

One of the great events of the nineteenth century in 1851 was the Great Exhibition held in Hyde Park that year. Prince Albert himself had put considerable effort into organizing the Great Exhibition hall, a monumental steel and glass structure in the shape of a cross. The Crystal Palace held all latest modern mechanical inventions and foreign exhibits, including the latest works of the artistic community, from oil painting to sculptures.

Visitors from all over the British Isles and other countries flocked to attend. Encouraging free trade was the main motive for the exhibition as it encouraged people to visit London. Her Majesty's Theatre extended its season as to stay open longer than usual.

The Royal Italian Opera House at Covent Garden closed in August when principal singers Grisi and Mario left for Russia.

Her Majesty's spring season for 1851 featured all the best roles for Lablache. On 8 May, straight from the Théâtre-Italien in Paris, where the world premiere was held, came a show stopper for that season—a new sparkling opera *Le Tre Nozze* composed by Guilio Aláry.(1814-1891). An opera not heard anymore, in 1851 Sontag and the tenor Gardoni supported Lablache who sang the role of Il Barone d'Acetoza. Although the opera was written and sung in Italian, Lablache sang some of it in English: "My pretty little love I die for you," and on the first night, the Italian born composer was led on the stage by the singers. The hit of the opera was the "polka duet" or "Sontag polka" sung by Sontag and Lablache and that sent the London public into ecstasies. "Madame Sontag was irresistible and perfect as ever,"[612] Benjamin Lumley wrote,[613]

> The polka sung by Luigi Lablache and Henrietta Sontag caught every ear, was hummed by every amateur, was copied on every hand—organ, was sought for eagerly at every music shop; it has remained a favourite to this very day . . . His efforts to learn courtly manners, as a shy and embarrassed provincial nobleman . . . his attempts to follow his inamorata in the hurried "mazes of the dance," his awkward experiments at lovemaking, whilst they suggested the gambols of a young hippopotamus, never overstepped the modesty of nature.

Praise was piled on him as usual. Lablache sang with Sontag, sopranos Caroline Duprez and Sophie Cruvelli; he then sang with the singer that Chorley had described as true contralto—Marietta Alboni. This fine singer emerged in 1847 when she was engaged to sing Arsace with Grisi in *Semiramide* at the Royal Italian Opera House. Alboni made a great contribution to the world of opera till she retired in 1863. Perhaps she set a trend for physically larger sopranos who emerged to take over the roles in the fifties. Rossini admired her voice very much but called her "the elephant that swallowed a nightingale," like the bulky Teresa Tietjens and Grisi, who later joined the overweight group. There was no way that these ladies could have caught up with Lablache, who became steadily obese. Everybody, however, pointed out that his bulk never diminished his performance as we shall read from these reviews of *L'Elisir d'amore* in the April issue of *The Musical World:*

> The after easter season brought back Lablache in his great part, Dulcamara, in Donizetti's charming opera, *L'Elisir d' Amore*, and Tuesday night was, in consequence, a carnival with subscribers and

habitues of Her Majesty's Theatre. Lablache's mirth is, as it were, a
Niagara, whose torrent produces an incessant roar . . . a Nile, which
in the season of rains, overflows its banks and inundates the plains.
The great basso has long been one of the principal favourites of
the opera with the London public, and is always welcomed back
with the heartiest applause. His entre in the car was the signal for
a general shout from all parts of the house which made the walls
reverberate. Lablache's voice is as grand and powerful as ever, and
his acting as unctuous and rich. As a piece of eccentric comedy his
rendering of Bartolo is the "ne plus ultra" of humourous acting.

The singer Mlle. Duprez was the daughter of the famous French tenor Gilbert-Louis Duprez, who created the role of Edgardo in Donizetti's *Lucia di Lammermoor*.

Mademoiselle Caroline Duprez was Adina, and a more "naive
et piquante" village coquette could hardly be imagined.
The youthful cantatrice already exhibits a decided talent for
comedy . . . her humour is genial and natural, and her animal
spirits overflowing.

That year, two operas were brought before the British public by the French composer Daniel Auber—*Gustave III* and *La muette de Portici*. Frédéric Lablache, in the former opera "gave unusual weight and excellence to the *morceaux d'ensemble*," wrote critic Lumley.[614] Frédéric, in a minor part, supported soprano Fiorentini, tenor Calzolari as Gustavus, and young Caroline Duprez as the sprightly page. *Gustave III* was the "talk of the town," said Lumley.[615]

Reporting on 15 May, *The Musical World* gives an insight into the Victorians' feelings about Mozart. Clearly, of all Mozart's operas, *Don Giovanni* was the favorite:

Mozart's incomparable work has never failed, for the last quarter
of a century, and upwards, to prove one of the principal attractions
of the season. Despite the love of novelty and the thirst for strange
excitement, in defiance of new stars, new operas, new prejudices,
and changes, *Don Giovanni* still upholds its power over the musical
public, and still asserts its influence, is still the beacon of glory
that, fixed upon the rock of endurance, stands unscathed amid the

waters of all time, to point, to dazzle, and allure. The impetuous crowds who besieged the doors of Her Majesty's Theatre on Thursday evening is a sign of the public taste that is well worth the consideration of the director. Some of the attraction must doubtless be attributed to the union of names brought together in the opera. Nevertheless, we insist that Mozart's name is a tower of strength, even in these days when Meyerbeer and French Opera seem to be the rage. The performance was, in general, admirable. Sontag, Fiorentini and Lablache are entitled to unqualified praise. The music of Zerlina suits Sontag wonderfully well. The "Batti batti" and "l'Vedrai Carino" were never rendered with more exquisite finish and purity. The delicious coquetry and winning simplicity of the former were inimitable, while the tenderness and devotion infused into the "Vedrai Carino" was sufficient to have touched any heart. No freedom was taken with Mozart. The music stood forth unadorned simplicity, and, from the effect produced, proved satisfactorily that it is dangerous to meddle with it. Nor did Madame Sontag have recourse to the usual, and perhaps pardonable custom of dwelling on the last note, or the penultimate, or anti-penultimate, in the two songs. She finished simply as she begun, without effort, or desire to add to Mozart. Madame Sontag's graceful and exquisite singing was conspicuous in the duet with Don Giovanni, which was encored, although not so enthusiastically as her unassisted efforts. In her acting, the great artist betokened a thorough conception of the charming character of Zelina, and supported the peasant girl with irresistible 'verve' and animation. Lablache's Leporello, as everybody knows, is a masterpiece of comic acting and singing. To praise Lablache in Leporello would be to devote our pens to truisms, a practice from which we are decidedly averse. Wherefore, we shall leave Lablache "alone in his glory," a glory which years have not tarnished, and which rivalry has not touched. Lablache and Leporello are synonymous—at least they are alliterative—and may we continue to call them so for a thousand years.[616]

The same critic remarked that Signor Calzolari as Octavio pleased them, "but he would have pleased them more if he adhered to the text. Had Signor Calzolari sung "Il tesoro" as it was written, he would not have escaped the encore usually awarded to it." After his debut, Enrico Calzolari matured later into a fine tenor, leaving Her Majesty's after four years for Russia at the same time as Lablache. Here, the critic goes on to say, "We must pronounce a strong word of praise to F. Lablache who played Masetto and sang the music of the part excellently. He looked the character to the life."[617]

Florinda, written by Sigismund Thalberg, was produced that season for the first time. The premiere was on 3 July with Lablache as the count; Sophie Cruvelli as his daughter Florinda, Coletti, and Sims Reeves, the famed English tenor. Chorley was not enamored by it nor was the public. Chorley points out that when pianists set their mind to writing operas, something happens even to the most brilliant of them, and Thalberg certainly was of that category, but somehow this opera was of small interest. "Everyone, however, concerned in the matter, fought their best for it's success—in particular, Lablache, who was doing his utmost for his son-in-law."[618]

On 26 August, in Donizetti's *Anna Bolena*, Lablache's performance must have been good, for *The Musical World*[619] remarked, "Lablache as Henry VIII looked like a page torn from the history of England"—a rather amusing compliment, considering he did not have a drop of English blood in him. In another comment, his costumer complains thus: "the recent sameness in dress of the great basso, as much as the 'Gros de Naples' requires a great mixture of 'BROAD' cloth."[620]

Donizetti's *Anna Bolena*, featuring Lablache, never failed to be successful in England. Performed more often in England than in Paris, by 1844, the opera had spread throughout the world. Lablache had continued singing in this opera annually since its London and Paris premieres. However, there was a gap of five years since he sang the role at Her Majesty's. In the last performance that season of *La prova di un'opera seria*, Lablache helped out by conducting the overture. It was not unheard for him to do this and then turn around and sing in the same opera.

In the winter of 1851, Lablache returned to Paris, singing just a few operas at the Théâtre-Italien, *Il Barbiere* and *La Cenerentola*, and then again in the following spring before returning to London. The year 1852 was a rather uneventful season for Lablache, singing all the favorites with whatever sopranos were available to the failing theater in the Haymarket—Her Majesty's. Some of these prima donnas, like the Greek soprano Elena D'Angri, Sophie Cruvelli, and Anna de la Grange, went on to have fine careers.

In September Lablache returned to Paris. Frédéric Lablache, Grisi, Mario, Susini, and Bernardi left for a bumper tour of the provinces. They started in Manchester and Liverpool and then went to Ireland, first Cork and Wexford including performances at the Theatre Royal in Dublin, before returning via

Belfast, Glasgow, and Edinburgh. Far earlier, it was reported that the Czar, Nicholas I, had wanted Lablache to come to Russia, but Lablache had flatly refused. Dudley Cheke gives us some details here:

> The Czar, Nicolas I, took the greatest personal interest in opera and did not stand on his dignity with the artistes. He himself, acting as Director of the *Théâtre Italien de St. Pétersbourg*, sent a trusted envoy to Paris in 1850 to recruit the most famous performers. This envoy offered Luigi Lablache every possible inducement to go to Russia, but Lablache could not be persuaded. First, he excused himself on the ground of his age and the severity of the Russian winter. Then he confessed that he did not dare to risk facing an audience which had never seen him before. The envoy laughed this off, adding that in a Russian Theatre no one would dare to hiss without His Majesty's authorization and Lablache would be applauded by Imperial Decree. When Lablache remained adamant, he was assured that the Czar would be going to Paris in the following Spring to hear him. Subsequently, Lablache relented and was in the Russian capital for the 1852-1853 season.[621]

Afterward, it was reported in the Paris newspapers that on the Wednesday before, 18 September, Lablache had left for Russia with his sons Nicolas and Henri and his daughter Marie.[622] (How many were in the party is not certain.) They all began the long and tiring trip by train to Russia (via Stettin) for the first time.

※※※

Victoria and Albert and Royal Family at Windsor Castle (Lablache Archives)

Buckingham Palace antique postcard (Lablache Archives)

Royal Box The Illustrated London News (Lablache Archives)

Lancaster House The Illustrated London News (Lablache Archives)

*Norma with Luigi Lablache Beauties of the
Opera and Ballet (Lablache Archives)*

*Norma with Luigi Lablache Beauties of the Opera and Ballet
(Lablache Archives)*

Guilia Grisi as Norma Beauties of the Opera and Ballet (Lablache Archives)

Frederic Lablache (Andrew S. Pope)

Fanny Wyndham (Mme.F.Lablache) in costume lithograph by A.E. Chalon (Lablache Archives)

Fanny Persiani as Rosina Beauties of the Opera and Ballet
(Lablache Archives)

Maria Malibran lithograph (Lablache Archives)

Luigi Lablache as Falstaff Staffordshire china figure
(Lablache Archives)

Luigi Lablache as William Tell, The Illustrated London News
(Lablache Archives)

Luigi Lablache as *Falstaff, lithograph by F. Salabert (Lablache Archives)*

Luigi Lablache and Mario in L'elisir d'amore lithograph (Museo della Scala)

Luigi Lablache as Dulcamara in L'elisir d'amore (Lablache Archives)

Luigi Lablache in L'elisir d'amore statue (Anthony de Friston)

Maria Malibran playbill (Lablache Archives)

Luigi Lablache in Ines de Castro (Don White Opera Rara)

Mario carte de visite (Lablache Archives)

Giulia Grisi lithograph by F. Courtin (Sergio Ragni)

Johann Strauss early postcard (Lablache Archives)

Hector Berlioz early postcard (Lablache Archives)

Franz Liszt carte de visite (Lablache Archives)

Request Letter to Lablache to sing at Napoleon's Funeral (Lablache Archives)

Luigi Lablache on bench by Constantin Guys (Lablache Archives)

Sigismund Thalberg statue
(The Royal College of Music, London)

Francesca Thalberg carte de visite
(Lablache Archives)

Piano of Sigismund Thalberg
(Princess di Strongoli Donna Francesca Pignatelli)

Dominique Lablache standing in uniform, carte de visite (Lablache Archives)

Francesca Thalberg in Neapolitan costume painting (Lablache Archives)

Dominique Lablache sitting in uniform, carte de visite (Lablache Archives)

Luigi Lablache lithograph by Frederick Tatham (Lablache Archives)

Don Pasquale record cover (Lablache Archives)

Don Pasquale stage set (Balsan)

Don Pasquale cartoon lithograph (Lablache Archives)

Don Pasquale garden scene (Andrew S. Pope)

Jenny Lind and Frederic Lablache lithograph (Lablache Archives)

Jenny Lind and Luigi Lablache in I Masnadieri,
The Illustrated London News (Lablache Archives)

Jenny Lind music cover (Lablache Archives)

Giuseppe Verdi (Lablache Archives)

Jenny Lind singing in concert, The Illustrated London News (Lablache Archives)

Jenny Lind portrait lithograph 1847 (Lablache Archives)

*Carlotta Grisi ballerina, Beauties of the Opera and Ballet
(Lablache Archives)*

Marie Taglioni ballerina (Lablache Archives)

Southampton Concert Room by Brannon (Lablache Archives)

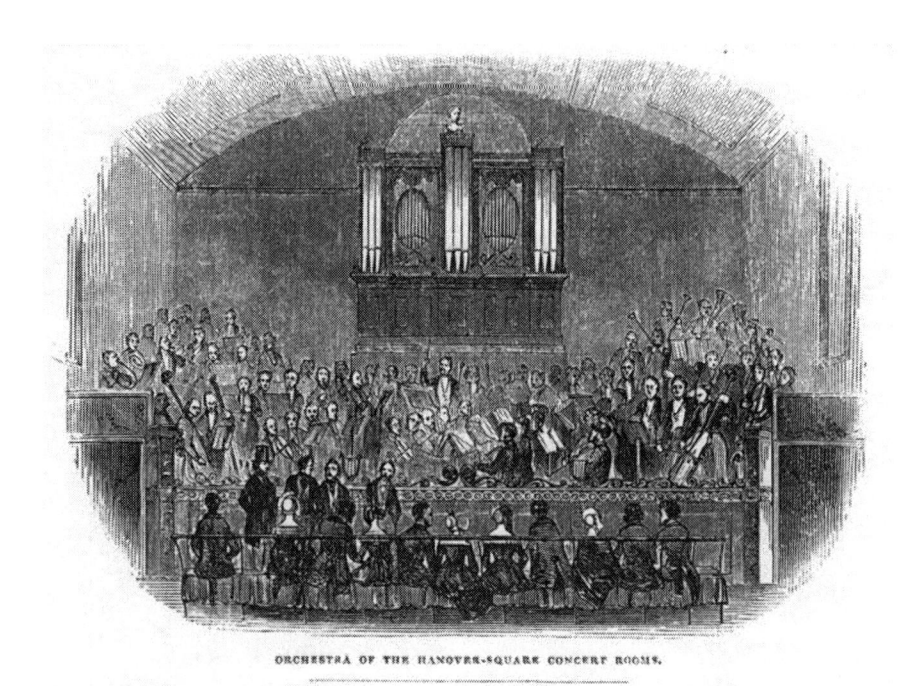

Hanover Square Concert Rooms The Illustrated London News
(Lablache Archives)

*Luigi Lablache and Henrietta Sontag, The Sontag Polka music cover
(Lablache Archives)*

Osborne House (rear view) Nelson's Handbook of the Isle of Wight (Lablache Archives)

Prince Albert carte de visite (Lablache Archives)

Queen Victoria carte de visite (Lablache Archives)

HER MAJESTY'S THEATRE.
SIGNOR PUZZI

Has the honour to announce to the Nobility, Subscribers, his Friends, and the Public, that

HIS BENEFIT

Will take place on

THURSDAY NEXT, JULY 4TH, 1850,

Combining the talents of

MESDAMES SONTAG, PARODI, GIULIANI,
AND
FREZZOLINI.

SIGNORI GARDONI, CALZOLARI, F. LABLACHE, COLETTI, AND LABLACHE.

MADLLE. AMALIA FERRARIS.

On which occasion will be presented, *for the first time this season*, CIMAROSA's admired Opera, entitled

IL MATRIMONIO SEGRETO.

Carolina	Madame SONTAG.
Fidalma	Madlle. PARODI.
	AND
Elisetta	Madame FREZZOLINI.
Paolina	Signor CALZOLARI.
Count Robinson	Signor F. LABLACHE.
	AND
Geronimo	Signor LABLACHE.

After which

A DIVERTISSEMENT,

IN WHICH

Mademoiselle AMALIA FERRARIS
AND
M. CHARLES,
will appear.

To be followed by the GRAND SCENA from VERDI's Opera,

I DUE FOSCARI.

Lucrezia	Madlle. GIULIANI.
The Doge	Signor COLETTI.

TO WHICH WILL BE ADDED

A DIVERTISSEMENT,

IN WHICH,

MADEMOISELLE AMALIA FERRARIS,
MESDAMES ROSA, JULIEN, LAMOREUX, AND AUSSANDON
WILL APPEAR.

After which, the First Act of BELLINI's celebrated Opera

I CAPULETTI ED I'MONTECCHI

Romeo	Madlle. PARODI.
Tebaldo	Signor GARDONI.
Capello	Signor BELLETTI.
Lorenzo	Signor LORENZO.
	AND
Guilliette	Madlle. FREZZOLINI.

To conclude with the admired ICE BALLET, by M. P. TAGLIONI, entitled

LES PLAISIRS DE L'HIVER;
OU, LES PATINEURS.

Applications for Boxes, Stalls, and Pit Tickets, to be made at the Box-Office of the Theatre, and at SIG. PUZZI's Residence, 5A, Cork Street, Burlington Gardens.

Il Matrimonio Segreto playbill (Lablache Archives)

Lablache and Santi drawing by A.E. Chalon (Lablache Archives)

Teaching Lesson for Bass Voice by Luigi Lablache, book cover (Lablache Archives)

La Tempesta review, The Illustrated London News (Lablache Archives)

Opera staircase Paris, early postcard (Lablache Archives)

Book Four

Chapter Thirty-One

Russia

1852-53

Lablache would never have wanted to retire. The idea would have been totally against his nature. He was a vital energetic man who always gave his all, not only to the theater but to his compatriots as well. Having accumulated a vast fortune, it was not in his nature to lie back; singing was his whole existence.

The season of 1852 was the the last for Her Majesty's Theatre, and the last season for Lablache. The theatre closed its doors at the end of the summer and did not open again for three years. Lablache, always on close terms with Lumley, knew that Her Majesty's was failing though it hung on a bit longer trying to recover its losses.

Traveling to Russia was a great undertaking for a man of Lablache's age. First, the climate was not beneficial to the delicate throats of singers, let alone those of a man nearly sixty. Second, though still energetic and in the best voice, his weight must have encumbered him more than a little. Here, on the eve of his trip to Russia, he writes to his old friend, Domenico Donzelli, in Bologna:

> My Dear Dear, Donzelli,   September 18, 1852   Paris
>
> This evening I leave for the polar regions, Teresa cannot accompany me because the doctors do not allow it. She will spend the winter in Nice. Excuse this bad letter, but my mind is not ruling me, because Teresa's state of health grips me in an unspeakable way which finally wears down my patience a lot. Let us always hope in divine Providence.

> Goodbye, my dear Donzelli. Teresa and all my family request me to say so much affectionate things to your Antoinette, to whom you must give a big kiss for me.
>
> Love at your service, love as you are loved,
>
> > your old and affectionate friend,
> > Lablache
>
> P.S. Look at the seal with which this letter is closed and you will remember our happy times in Vienna.[623]

Most likely Teresa spent the winter months at Dr. Maroncelli's house in Nice. Dr. Maroncelli was a family friend and often traveled with Lablache on his tours. Lablache writes to his wife from Russia, often worried about her health, and later at Maisons-Laffitte. He hoped that Frédéric and his family would come from England and be "there" for Teresa.[624] But as far as we can see, Frédéric curtailed none of his engagements. He was off again on a grand opera concert tour to the north of Britain via Manchester, Liverpool, and all the cities from Edinburgh to Dublin with Grisi and Mario.

From Dublin, playbills advertised the so-called first of the last appearances of Mme. Grisi. Describing this event, the *Annals of the Theatre Royal* recall the following:

> This was the first engagement of the Italian Opera under the management of Mr. Harris, and proved a great success . . . and was remarkable for the earliest announcement of the LAST appearance of Grisi. Several others of the same effect subsequently took place; however, at last repeated too often for the fame of the then-acknowledged Queen of Song.[625]

For just six nights, the Harris company played Dublin. Frédéric was cast as the libertine, Don Giovanni, on a Friday evening 24 September 1852. On 17 September, Frédéric sang Alfonzo in *Lucrezia Borgia*; Riccardo Forth, in *I Puritani*; and Malatesta on 21 September in *Don Pasquale*. Later, they agreed to perform for another three nights, adding *Norma*, *L'Elisir d'amore*, and *Sonnambula* to the roster starting on 4 October.[626] Grisi and Mario returned in 1855 for another farewell tour, but Frédéric did not. From January onward, Frédéric and his wife Fanny maintained a tight schedule of concert appearances through 1854.

It was with much regret and worry that Lablache left his wife behind in Paris and, with his sons Nicola and Henri, set out for Russia. Teresa was awaiting the building of the new house.

The house was built in the charming and fashionable suburb of Maison-sur-Seine, west of Paris halfway down the Rue Albine, looking toward the famous chateau of Maisons-Laffitte. According to local history, Lablache became aware earlier of property for sale in that part of the country. The magnificent chateau of Maisons was built by Mausart between 1634-1646, and by 1658, it was surrounded by a large walled park. This we understand from research at the Bibliothèque Municipale at Maisons-Laffitte:

> In 1818 the banker and politician Jacques Laffette bought the estate. In 1833 financial troubles forced him to split up the park into "une colonie, une ville composee de maison de campagne."

In 1847, the railway station opened—the first one outside of Paris; they called the station Maisons-Laffitte. In 1882, the name of the commune was changed to Maisons-Laffitte. Lablache may have bought the land for his house in 1850 when the trains started. Writes Leon Salichet *Histoire de Maisons-Laffitte* (1892),

> During the reign of Napoleon III Maisons-Laffitte was the haunt of the most famous magistrates, financiers, artistes and writers. The train that left Paris at half past midnight was so full of artistes that it was called "le train des theatres." He writes "Lablache habitait, avenue Albine, une fort belle propriete . . . quand Lablache etait en villegiature a Maison il etait impossible aux autres habitanti, de se procurer du ris de veau, par gont, caprice, fraitement medical on adjuvant vocal ce canteur a la mode retenait, en les payant quatre fois leur valeur, tons les ris de veau que ponvaient debiter les bonchets de Maisons-Laffitte.

Lablache built his house a magnificent *maison de campo* on the main avenue of the park facing the chateau of Maisons. There he became a leading member of the fashionable community.

> Lablache built his house in 1853, beginning in August. In addition, at the corner of the avenues Albine and Buffon there were two stables, a large storage place, a gardener's house, and, on the first floor, four guest rooms. In the main house was the wine cellar,

cellar for barrels, coal storage room, heating plant, kitchen, office and a dining room for servants nest to the (dumb waiters). On the ground floor (raised up a little) around hall and stairwell are a large salon, dining room, billiard room, an office and toilets. On the first floor, 5 rooms, 3 toilets and wc's. On the second floor, a linen room, a room for the master, and four servants' rooms. Construction was quick, and was completed in 1854. Name of architect unknown at this time.[627]

In the autumn of 1852 reports of Lablache's successes in Russia began to reach Paris. Lablache's *Don Pasquale* debut 20 October at the Imperial Theatre, Bolshoi, St. Petersburg, *was* reported in the Russian daily newspaper *Severnaya Pehela* of St. Petersburg, October 1852. In December, he sang *Il Barbiere di Siviglia* like never before. He also sang *La Cenerentola, I Puritani,* and *La prova di un'opera seria.* Here is the review of 13 December 1852 by a certain FB.[628]

> The audience had not expected what they were to witness that night under the erroneous impression that Lablache had not preserved his voice "until now." But he is an actor such as I've seen very few in my life . . . a kind of Talma. He made the empty part of Dr. Bartolo into the most important person in the opera. He plays his comic part in a way that is both noble and extremely funny. His voice is a real double-bass sonorous and unbelievably strong . . . . He is the pivot around which the whole opera moves.

Later on 6 February 1853, the same newspaper commented,

> We recommend to all hypochondriacs who see life through jaundiced eyes to take Lablache as Bartolo or Don Magnifico in ultra-allopathic doses.

On 15 November, 1852 the above newspaper featured an advertisement: "Lablache's portrait from life. Lithographs on sale." Of the Italian singers in Russia, most were principal singers from London and Paris, his old compatriots, such as Mario, Viardot, Joséphine and Emilie de Méric and Ronconi among others, like tenors Calzolari and Tamberlic. During those winter months in Russia, Lablache writes to Rubini:

St. Pietroburgo 14. Nov. 1852.

Dear Rubini,

First of all I will tell you that the moment I received your letter I went to see S. E. Il Generale Doubelt, who told me to send his most distinguished regards, and that everything has been done and that today I wrote to Rossini that the order for his passport has been given to Paris.

You are calling me the "Great Lablache;" oh my dear Rubini if that was true, what would one call you?

Lablache would be replaced tomorrow by the first to come. But Rubini, you have given me so many years of your experience that I will never be able to thank you enough. I know that you are happy and loved and may God keep you for many years to come. If I ever should be able to come and visit you it will be a great day of festivity and joy for me. Remember me to your dear Adelaide and,

love always your old comrade,
L. Lablache
alias Scalandrone[629]

Grisi and Mario were touring the British provinces and Dublin with Frédéric Lablache. Grisi, due to another pregnancy, was forced to cancel all her performances in Russia. Mario, however, did not and appeared at the Imperial Theatre at St. Petersburg on 29 November in *I Puritani* with Lablache. After the russian season, he returned to London to be with Grisi at the birth of their child in May. Lablache stayed in Russia as far as we know through the winter and into the spring of 1853.

Lablache's young and beautiful daughter Marie Lablache's debut was a society occasion, and Luigi was a proud father. A mezzo-soprano, she sang at St. Petersburg's magnificent Hermitage Palace in *La Figlia del reggimento* with her father as Ortensio and with Mario and Ronconi. Fully reported upon by the *Gazzetta Musicale de Napoli* on 19 March 1853, the same event was covered by *The Musical World* and[630] (translated from the *Le Menestrel*):

We have received a letter from St. Petersburg, bearing date February 24th, from which we supply the following extracts:

Yesterday there took place at the Palace of the Hermitage, in presence of his Majesty and all the Court, en gala, the most extraordinary representation which those walls have witnessed since the days of the Great Catherine. It was on the occasion of the debut of Mademoiselle Marie Lablache, the youngest daughter of the illustrious *basso cantante* of the Italian Theatre. This young person, remarkable for her beauty, had already sung in many private salons with immense success, when his Imperial Majesty, who heard her for the first time at one of the concerts of the Grand Duchess Helena, and who was charmed with her new and brilliant talent, testified to M. Lablache his lively desire to see his daughter on the stage. The great basso refused as long a time as possible, never having had the intention of exposing his child to a career, strewn with flowers, it is true, but as often replete with vicissitudes and disappointments. Finally, it was agreed that the essay should be made in presence of a select audience—and such an audience! There were present, in addition to the Imperial family—who were all at St. Petersburg—all that Russia can boast of great and illustrious, the diplomatic corps, and, to conclude, that swarm of beautiful and graceful women, who render the Court at St. Petersburg, the most brilliant and richest in Europe. The opera, selected by his Majesty, was *La Figlia del reggimento*. The artists were Mademoiselle Marie Lablache, Mario, Ronconi, Tagliafico, and Lablache himself, who, to assist at the debut of his daughter, undertook the small part of Ortensio. The general expectation was surpassed, and never a debut, if any debut, ever took place under similar circumstances, was so happy, so triumphant. The voice of Mademoiselle Lablache is a mezzo-soprano of the utmost wealth of resources, and of the greatest range, with high tones and a silvery sonority, with chest notes, which recall Mademoiselle Alboni, although we have not heard here that artist before her great success. What shall I tell you of her method? She is her father's daughter, brought up in the school of Grisi, Persiani, Jenny Lind, and Sontag. Is that enough? His Imperial Majesty has been happy in his coup d'essai, and we proclaim him now the most intelligent, as he has already proved himself the nicest and most magnificent of *improsarij*. In the midst of that jewelbox, which is called the Hermitage, in the light of a thousand lustres sparkling in uniforms of gold and silver, and on the necks and shoulders of ladies scintillating with flowers and diamonds, you would nevertheless have imagined yourself in a popular Theatre, only to hear the fracas of applause and the bravi of the clacque-Mon dieu! and what a chef-de-clacque! Mdle. Lablache has then entirely succeeded, and, if her vocation carries her off, she will be one of the most brilliant stars in the Ansonian Heaven. Her Majesty has made her come into the middle of the Court, where she has received the compliments of illustrious dilettanti; each artist has found under his napkin a present of his Majesty as his Majesty knows how to make them.

Sometime during the season of 1852-1853 Marie was courted by Baron Ernest de Caters, a Belgian from Antwerp who lived in Paris. They were later married, but not before Lablache had a few words with Marie's prospective father-in-law. At this point, apparently Lablache wrote a very haughty letter to Ernest de Caters dated 29 August 1853 to the effect and written in French that Ernest's father had asked Luigi to give details of his wealth in view of the possible marriage. Luigi gives a list of his considerable possessions and income, mentions his villa in Posillipo, and says he is at present building a house at Maisons-Laffitte. He concludes by saying that "if Ernest's father attaches such importance to material possessions it would be better to forget about the wedding!" However, they were married in Paris on 24 September 1853. Frédéric, Nicolas, Henri, and Dominique signed the contract as witnesses, and a speech was given by a certain L'Abbe Le Dreuille (most likely the family priest). On 29 July 1854, a girl christened Marie was born, followed later by two more children.[631]

Luigi writes from St. Petersburg on 8 November 1853 to his wife:

My Dear Teresa,

Another good letter—the one of 30 October which I received yesterday evening. I am sorry to hear that Frédéric wants to leave you, but I hope that at this time he is still at Maisons because in my last letter I requested him not to leave you so soon. On the 15 of this month I will receive the first 12000 francs and will send you 10,000 of them immediately keeping 2000 of them for myself. Regarding Lucio, I have already written to him, but you have forgotten that there are the expenses for redoing the cases and for redoing the second floor. It makes me very pleased to hear that everything is going well—the house, the garden, the ponds and above all your vegetable garden but what gives me great relief is to hear that you are in good health—and I do not care about the manner in which you write it—that your mind is at ease, that you are in a good mood and very busy. It follows always that I do not fail to pray to God that it should so continue for a hundred years.

Poor Luigi has been in bed for several days with a very strong inflammation of the eyes. They have applied twelve leeches to his temples and they give him Emetic of Tartar every day. Yesterday evening they bled him and put a blistering ointment on the nape of his neck which made him suffer all the night, and there is only the slightest improvement.

Imagine therefore what a good situation we are in. The only person who dresses is Muscirh, a most dear boy who tries to do whatever he can. His name is Theodore and Juliette knows him because last year he stayed with the master of the house and came to clean the apartment, but this year he is in my service. Our lunch is reduced to a cup of tea with a piece of toast and at 4 o'clock we go to dinner at the de Mérics who send you their regards, both the mother and the daughter. At this moment they are in very great distress because Timolino (Joséphine de Méric's husband),[632] is gravely ill and the doctors say that it is very serious. The poor daughter and wife help him like two angels but God knows what will happen. At 8 o'clock we are back home in front of the table containing Nicola's cigarettes and my snuff-box, playing 10 to 15 rounds of Pique. At 11:30 we go to bed. However do not think that we are unhappy, no! We take the situation philosophically and pray God that our condition may improve.

What's more I have had my very own 10-day diarrhoea which has reduced my stomach and given me two little legs that are so slim that if I were at Maisons I would like to dance a polka with Madame Vatel and a waltz with Madame Commas. It is a pity that electricity is not yet sufficiently advanced to allow me to do that at Maisons from St. Petersburg.

I am also deprived of letters from Marie. I think that the horse riding and hunting are amusing her because otherwise she would already have written to me.

The weather is still good here and indeed there is no sign of winter—which surprises everybody and nobody remembers it happening before.

The debut of Rachel took place yesterday evening. Opinions are mixed. But do not speak about it to anybody because I do not wish to be quoted.

De la Grange has much success and when she wanted to do a lot I came, before *Il Barbiere*.

I hope that you will send me the speech made at the wedding of Marie. It only remains for me to greet dearly all our dear neighbors, to kiss all the family one by one and to give you a thousand kisses.

Your affectionate husband,
L. Lablache[633]

Since the year of 1848, when Russia was devastated by the most terrible epidemic of cholera of the nineteenth century, times had improved and prosperity had returned. Educated society and the aristocracy, ever fearful of revolution, felt secure. There were fewer uprisings and the peasant masses presented no threat. Czar Nicolas I ruled supreme as emperor and autocrat. Like his brother before him, the emperor Alexander I, Nicolas was a great opera lover. Under Alexander's rule, censorship had been lifted and there was renewed interest. Nicolas ruled with a firmer hand, but also was resposible for the great shift from Russian to Italian opera. Lablache also knew Czar Nicolas I as he had met him on more than one occasion, in Paris, and when the Czar visited England in June of 1844.

St. Petersburg was renowned for its beauty; spacious and well-planned, the city glittered with an aura few could resist. It was a center where the Russian aristocracy and educated upper classes ruled supreme. Living comfortably, among surroundings inherited from the centuries before, they enjoyed the seasons of opera and ballet and were as demonstrative, if not more than the audiences of London and Paris. Luckily, unlike the French, they had not gone through a revolution, so they never lost their way of life or the structure and perfect harmony of their relationships. Csar Nicolas I established a permanent Italian opera in St. Petersburg equal to Paris and London and the Italian theatre became unmatched anywhere for its opulance and prestige.

To the Russians, the Italian singers and dancers brought glamor and excitement that intensified their enjoyment of the arts and fulfilled their needs to enjoy and belong to the international society; for what was current in the capitals, like Paris and London, was in vogue all over the world. The Italian troupe, adored and appreciated by society, were overwhelmed by their reception.

This treatment was something that the Italians needed; there came a freshness that was perhaps lacking after singing to the same audience in France and England. Gone were the backstage bickering and fighting with managers and petty jealousies that had become tiring, and all these things had taken their toll. *The Musical World* wrote:

> All this was swept away in Russia—Lablache took over the artistic direction of the Imperial Theatre at St. Petersburg from Tamburini, and remained the head of the administration for five years. It would have been well for the art if neither Tamburini nor Lablache had ever been tempted to the city of snows.(6 February 1858.)

M.Ivanov in his *History of the Italian Theatre in St. Petersburg in the nineteen century: The Second Decade, 1853-1863* says,

> The second decade of the St. Petersburg Italian Theatre began under the cloud of some bad omens. The Crimean War was approaching and with it a difficult time for Russia. War had not yet been declared, the fleets had not yet entered the Dardanelles, but our troops had already taken the Dunai principality, had led the seige of Silistria and the tense situation which had taken hold in Europe was also being felt here.
>
> However, as was also to happen later in 1878 under similar circumstances, the political situation did not noticeably affect the theatrical affairs or the capital and the theatres were well-patronized, as the records of audience attendance testify. Theatre critics of the time, e.g. M A Zagulyaev, testify that before the war and in the first war period even more people than usual visited the Theatre as they feared that both the French and Italian theatres would be closed. This in fact did not happen and French artistes remained with us for the whole duration of the Crimean campaign, despite our war with France. As for the Italians, Italy did not then exist as a political entity and there were always very few Sardinians in our troupe. The affairs of foreign theatres, therefore, carried on as normal. If audiences fluctuated, then no more than usual.

They rose and fell as a result of the repertoire and the cast, not of political events. St. Petersburg residents were as zealous as ever for the Theatre, regardless of the fact that many families had loved ones in the ranks of the army. However, the really testing times had not yet arrived and, despite war losses, the value of the ruble stayed high (in the winter of 1853 it fluctuated between 383-393 cents per ruble) as did the economic credit of Russia. There was no shortage of money, no one lost heart, the majority firmly believed in a Russian victory and only the more farsighted looked into the future with dread.

As a result of this increased attendance at the beginning of the Crimean War, the deficit of the Italian Theatre disappeared.[634]

The Musical World reports on operatic life in Russia in 1854:

> The Italian Opera House, "Bolshoy Teatro," or Great Theatre, as it is called, stands in the centre of a large square. The site is excellent, but the effect of what might have been a handsome pile of masonry, is ruined by bald, stucco-daubed sides, with green verandas, under which carriages take up and set down, and a paltry portico in front. That theatres need not be eyesores may be learnt at Dresden, Berlin, and Hanover, but in this instance it may have been thought desirable to erect a pendant to some of the other hideous public buildings that disfigure St. Petersburg—which has obtained an architectural reputation to which it has no claim, and which has been entirely created by the convulsive admiration of its own orthodox population, or the speculative laudations of distant authors.
>
> The *salle* is not more imposing than the exterior, being large and ugly, while the decorations and fittings are ineffective and tasteless. The door of the pit slopes steeply up from the orchestra, so that the view from the front seats is not limited, as with us, to occasional glimpses of the heads of the taller performers. At Covent Garden and the Haymarket, an opera-box is admirably adapted to the exclusion of air and sound, and, by the ingenious device of a partition wall, the view of the house is so completely blocked out, that only two persons can see what is passing on the stage, of whom one always gets a stiff neck in the attempt, while the rest of the party, who cannot see through the wall, now and

then hear a fragment of some very noisy chorus, provided they are not suffocated before the end of the overture. At St. Petersburg, the divisions between the different boxes reach no higher than the backs of the occupants' chairs. There is no attempt in this Theatre, as in those at Berlin, Dresden, etc., to invoke the assistance of statutory, or other ornamental forms, in piling the successive tiers one above another, the supports are mere carpentry, and not architecture. But the boxes can both hear and see, and people are not stifled.

A box at the opera at St. Petersburg is, in fact, a pleasant luxury, and not, as in some places, a dismal dungeon. We have hurried through the entrance hall and lobbies, because they are best left as quickly as possible. A European visitor is astounded when he mounts the staircase, and walks round the box doors. The steps and floors swarm with servants in squatting or sleeping attitudes, many taking a quiet nap, with their heads comfortably pillowed on *schubes* of the richest fur. The scene is picturesque, for the flunkies of the grandees are dressed in brilliant liveries; but, delightful thought! the soft skins of the squirrel, the fox, the raccoon, the sable, and other sleek beasts, in which these men are rolling, have just been thrown off by their masters and mistresses, by whom, after the opera, they will be resumed. The European lady would perhaps object to this arrangement, and might even doubt whether such practices be really tolerated anywhere except at Khiva and Bekhara; but when we add that the same servants will, at twelve p.m., compose themselves to rest on the drawing room sofas, we anticipate further skepticism.

As the odour in the lobbies is not altogether satisfactory, we shall adjourn to the *salle*, premising that the price of places, though rather cheaper than with us, is not regulated according to the low scale prevalent in most of the continental theatres. In the centre of the grand tier or *bel etage,* is the imperial box, with a private chandelier, a private curtain of red velvet, a private gilt split crow (or double-headed eagle) above, and at the door two grenadiers from some regiment that ends in "off," who keep going through the beyond exercise as vigorously as if they were inflicting a "correction" on the enemies of the orthodox faith. The Emperor and his family seldom, if ever, exhibit their august persons beneath the official canopy, but prefer to be near the stage, and His Imperial

Majesty usually sits in an omnibus box, a position not without its advantage, especially on ballet nights, when His Majesty's opera glass is always actively employed. Those who seeks for good looks on the grand tier will not find them, but, en reranche, the toilettes are ravishing, and the arrangement of the hair and the combination of brilliant colours, leave nothing to be desired by the most refined taste.

We much doubt whether there is a single *dame* or *demoiselle d'honneur* of the imperial court whose toilette be fairly criticized above once a year, and we can only express the immeasurable inferiority in the . . . of our own wives, sisters, daughters, and promises, to those of our enemies, by saying that Russian women dress, and that the English wear clothes. We must add, on the other hand, that if a solitary beauty should appear in the house, she is certain to be a foreigner and that any face of surpassing loveliness is sure to be coloured by Anglo-Saxon blood.[635]

Lablache sang *Il Barbiere* 15 October for the first time that season and sang with his usual vigor throughout 1853. It was a long time for him to spend away from his home, and it is unknown if he returned home during the break in between the Russian seasons during 1853. Hired to sing in London for the first time at the Royal Italian Opera at Covent Garden was sometime away.

Like Her Majesty's, this theater was having difficulties. For three years, the quality of the singers was inferior, even in the Great Exhibition year of 1851: except for Grisi and Mario, there wasn't anybody too exciting to attract the public. Fortunately, after some changes of management, there were some new productions. We can only guess what Lablache's frame of mind was at this time. He naturally worried about the Crimean War; after all, his son was part of it and Teresa's health. Could he have had enough of Russia? What of his health? Split between his feelings for his family, who were so far away, and the uncertainty of the times, whatever fears he had were mounting daily and so he decided that he would return to London. He writes to his old friend Michael Costa—the letter has no date, most likely written in the winter of 1853:

My dear Costa,

Knowing you to be capable of guarding, or rather (to put aside Frenchisms), of keeping a secret, and on account of our old friendship, I tell you that I should like to come to London next season for two or three months. See if there is anything to be done in this matter, but let it be as you had thought of it and do not mention that I have written concerning this matter at all. If you find it possible I shall be eternally grateful, and kindly keep me informed one way or another. Excuse me troubling you but who can I turn to about such a delicate matter—I repeat I know you.

I can trust you have good health, also your brother Raffael. We have had no winter this year. At the moment I write the Neva is not yet frozen, and last year at this time it was frozen already six weeks. You will have heard of Mimi's marriage—here is a prima donna just shooting up (fresh)—and lost to the stage. She is lucky and fortunate! The Queen ordered someone to write and ask me news about my health—I received two or three such letters—also a photo of the Prince (a lithographic photo). The Queen always treats me with the same great kindness. I trust you will answer this letter of mine, and I therefore give you my address:

L. Lablache
Maison Tchapplin au Coin de
la Grand Moskaye

Goodbye dear Costa—in any case I trust to see you next season, and believe in my lively friendship.

L. Lablache

Whatever the answer from Costa was, we can only guess. On 23 January 1854, Lablache writes back to him again:

Dearest Costa,

First of all, I must thank you for the kind interest you take in me—which I could never doubt, for an instant. I received an engagement form from Mr. Gye, but unfortunately I could make no arrangement with him and had to refuse . . . you remember in my letter to you, I said I could come for two or three months, but not for the whole season. Also, were I to leave St. Petersburg the 9th or the 10th of March, it would be impossible to be in London on the 21st of the same month and therefore I would have no time to take any rest at all after such a long and painful journey. Mr. Gye offered me an arrangement for 5 months more than I have had in London before for 400 pounds less than I ever accept . . . 12,000 instead of 1600 pounds. For all these reasons I have to refuse . . . and I have sent the contract back to Federico, to have it returned to Mr. Gye. I am delighted to hear that you are in good health with the exception of a little cold which will make you lose your voice.

I must tell an anecdote:

Lately, a poor singer was most severely criticized by the public—in fact—he was hissed from the beginning of the opera till the end. After the performance a compatriot of his went to see the poor man in his room and found the poor devil in an inexpressible state of excitement, he gave the most awful thumps on the table with his fist, and walked up and down the room taking huge strides and saying "How infamous to treat me like this," "Bye Heaven, I was in very good voice and I sang very well and I swear I shall sing like this till I die." His friend answered coldly: "Yes my friend, in your own house and if you pay the rent."

Perhaps you know that my poor Teresa nearly died just a short time ago, I suffered so much, being far away . . . now however, thank God, I hear that she is better and better each day, and I therefore feel more hopeful and peaceful.

Goodbye dear Michael, continue distributing macaroni and vermicilli round about you, I do likewise from my quarter. Salute your brother and if you get the chance, present homage and my profound respect to Her Majesty the Queen and also to His Royal Highness Prince Albert.

Always love, your old friend,
L. Lablache[636]

Now Lablache was much loved in Russia, writes Palombi, and the Czar (Nicolas I) treated him as a personal friend:

One day the Czar was taking a solitary walk through the streets of St. Petersburg (at that time still possible) followed at a discreet distance by two *moujiks* ready to arrest anyone who spoke a single word to the monarch. Seeing Lablache, the Czar motioned for him to approach, and conversed amiably for several minutes. As soon as Lablache moved away, the *moujiks* came over and put him under arrest. The same evening, His Majesty became annoyed and impatient because the curtain at the Opera House was delayed. He called *the Intendant*, General Gedonoff, and asked the reason for the delay. "Sir, Lablache is not here." "Is he perhaps ill?" "No, he is well." The Czar was at a loss, saying "He certainly has not left, as I spoke with him just a few hours ago, "Precisely, Your Majesty, for that reason . . ." The Czar immediately understood, and ordered Lablache to be freed at once. Ten minutes later, Lablache was in the Theatre, singing in the *Barber of Seville*. When the curtain fell, the Czar had Lablache come to his box and asked how he could make amends for the ill treatment he had been subjected to. Lablache, jokingly said, "Very simple, your Majesty, next time you see me on the street just do not recognize me." However, the Czar thought this inadequate and gave him a handsome present.[637]

On another occasion, this time in London, he accidentally again met royalty—Queen Victoria—but not with the same results as in Russia. During this time, Lablache showed a great interest in plants and trees. The beautiful house he built at Maisons-Laffitte was a gracious country house very like Rossini's house in Passy in design. Lablache paid the same careful attention to the buying of plants, scrubs, and trees as he did to the choosing of costumes that he wore on the stage. Strolling in the gardens of London was a habit that he enjoyed, and ideas flowed into his head while staring at various plants and trees. Lablache built a Swiss-style cottage adjacent to his house, ajoining the stables flanked by two huge Italian-style fountains. Attached to this cottage various greenhouse structures made of glass were designed to hold collections of plants of all varieties. Located in the area to the front of the cottage was a special vegetable garden, where Teresa grew her Italian spices. Florimo writes,

> It was late summer in 1854 and Lablache had terminated his season at the Queen's theatre. As usual, he had performed his favourite operas and with many other basses he sang the part of Baldassare in the *La Favorita*—How awful! Today basses refuse to sing it. He didn't want to follow his companions in their peregrinations throughout the provinces, as it is customary. He went instead to

Chelsea, to the very rich Botanical gardens of the Pharmaceutical Society of London. There are grown the rarest plants of warmer climates and the most exquisite fruits. Lablache remained there for a time in pleasant idleness.

It was on that day, while walking, he noticed in the distance, a very elegant coach coming towards him, but he did not take much notice and carried on. Shortly after, he was greatly surprised when the coach stopped for a while and inside he saw the Queen who beckoned to him. She expressed her surprise in seeing him there and asked him if he had decided to stay in London. He frankly replied that all the beauties of that place couldn't make him forget his enchanting and delightful Naples and he had no other ambition but to end his days in his country.[638]

Chapter Thirty-Two

London Debut at Covent Garden

1854-55

Lablache, having endured two long Russian winters, returned to London for his debut at the Royal Italian Theatre, Covent Garden, on 9 May 1854.[639] It was spring, and all Europe was concerned about Britain declaring war on Russia. France, Turkey, and Sardinia were now allies of England, and the French fought bravely alongside the British in what was called "undoubtedly the worst managed war of the century"—the Crimean War.[640] Fortunately Lablache left Russia for Paris with his gold. (Before the exchange deteriorated)[641] *The Musical World* reveals under the title, "Lablache and Russian gold":

> The consequences of the prohibition of gold from Russia are very serious indeed to foreigners residing there. The case of a French actress (Rachael) is mentioned, who lately remitted 60,000f. to Paris, and, being compelled to send it in Russian paper, received only 45,000f. Lablache had the good luck to leave the day before the new currency was issued, and brought away with him a handsome sum in gold.

Among many notable French soldiers involved in the Crimea was Dominique Lablache (1826-1914), the son of Lablache. As *commandant d'arme,* not only did he receive the title of *Chevalier Legend de Honneur,* but he was also promoted to captain.[642] Though born in Naples, he had, like his father, become a French national, then a professional soldier. He was well-decorated and received many medals and honors, which adorned his uniform.[643]

After making very satisfactory arrangements with Gye, Luigi Lablache appeared on the London stage that season twenty-one times. One must admire the fortitude of the man yet continue to wonder how he did it at his age. We do know one thing, Lablache was often allowed to sit in a chair, the only singer in nineteenth-century history granted that privilege. *The Musical World* commented that the "habitues" of the Covent Garden establishment will not be sorry to have such a "large addition" to their enjoyment!

> —we may look forward to the revival of the *Barbiere*. To say revival advisedly, since we consider Doctor Bartolo an important figure he can only be played by Lablache. Tagliafico, in his own line is one of the best artists on the stage, is altogether out of it in Dr. Bartolo. The humour of that personage is not his humour; or, rather, Tagliafico's humour is the French and not the Italian humour of the character; and Lablache, by his exquisite buffoneria has succeeded in fixing the latter in the mind of the French, no less the English public, as the true "humour of it."

Joseph Tagliafico, a French bass and pupil of Lablache, was born in Toulon in 1821, his debut was in 1844. Highly successful he sang in many operas alongside Lablache in London, Paris and St. Petersburg.

Lablache's success was calculated to please; his debut and his return his London engagements did not go without notice. Queen Victoria and Prince Albert attended the opera. Here, *The Musical World* comments,

> It was a great night for the Royal Italian Opera. Lablache sang one of his most renowned impersonations, Dr. Bartolo, in *Il Barbiere di Siviglia*. Mario sang Almaviva. For her debut, the young Angiolina Bosio sang Rosina and Ronconi was Figaro.[644]

Again *The Musical World* comments on the reappearance of Lablache after the 11 May performance of *Don Giovanni*: "Signor Lablache showed no diminution of his powers as Leporello." The great tenor, Enrico Tamberlik, sang for the first time with Lablache that season as Don Giovanni. Tamberlik also sang with Lablache in *Norma* and *Otello*. Lablache sang in Donizetti's *La Favorita*, the newspapers said, "His singing and acting were grand and impressive." Filling in one evening for Tagliafico in Rossini's *Otello,* Lablache sang the role of Elmiro just the same way as everyone remembered him in the past with great gusto. *The Musical World* reports the following:

> Sig. Lablache was magnificent in the malediction scene, and awed the whole house by the reality and power of his acting, and the grandeur of his voice. He had little to do in the other parts of the

opera. Madame Viardot sang Desdemona which was one of the first roles she appeared in before the public. It was felt she was better as Fidea or Valentine. Her conception, however, of the gentle Desdemona displays the highest intelligence.

Victoria and Albert attended again for *I Puritani* on 18 May, but the opera failed to get good reviews owing to Bosio's rendering of Elvira; apparently, she lacked passion in the mad scene. "The extraordinary 'fact' of the evening was, that the loud duet, 'Suoni la Tromba,' failed to elicit an encore," wrote *The Musical World*.[645] But it was a different story later in July; the critic continues:

> The performance of *Don Pasquale* was worthy of the best days of Her Majesty's Theatre. More finished or more exhilarating comic acting could hardly be witnessed at the best French theatres; while the singing could not be equalled on any stage in the world. The music of *Don Pasquale* is not so difficult for the voice as that of *L'Elisir d'amore*; but requires more *finesse,* more refinement and greater elevation of style. Madame Grisi's Norina must stand among her finest and most vividly realized conceptions. In its way it is as true as Norma, Lucrezia Borgia or Ninetta. The great artiste acted and sang as in her best days when Norma took the town by storm, and *Don Pasquale* was the opera "in vogue." The Don Pasquale of Lablache is inapproachable, irresistible, indescribable. It is the incarnation of mirth, simplicity, and folly; and constitutes a glorious companion to Doctor Bartolo, another transcendent portrait of the immense basso. To do justice to Sig. Lablache's acting and singing in *Don Pasquale* is hardly possible for the critic, criticize he never so wisely. Nor is it necessary, since everybody has seen the performance or heard of its merits and peculiarities. Perhaps on no former occasion did Sig. Lablache obtain more applause, or was his performance better relished. The audience was in ecstacies throughout. The famous "gag" with the letter and the chair, in the second act, was as perfectly managed as ever, and the whole performance was prodigious. The opera passed off with the greatest éclat, and created a regular *furore.*[646]

La Favorita was brought back on 13 July with Lablache, Grisi, and Mario. Lablache had sung Baldassare during the season of 1849. Here, we have the main character of the opera, appearing in the opening scene, final scene, and all the grand finales. Indeed, Baldassare is a central character who moves the action, a devout cleric who leads the monks in prayer, also father's children, and is the pope's emissary in the Betic dominions. King Alfonso himself, victor over the Moors, is terrified of him. He fulminates, dishes out excommunications, and ushers the other characters into and out of monasteries and nunneries. Lablache played the part to the hilt. Mario sang the famous aria "Spirito gentil" (plus an encore). The *Morning Post* reported that both Mario and Grisi were "a little out of voice." Queen Victoria and Prince Albert attended the opera.

The next morning, Lablache showed up to a rather hostile audience at Covent Garden—Mario had failed to show up, and Grisi was unable to attend because of a sudden indisposition. He sang excerpts from Rossini's *Stabat Mater* (*Videt suum dulcem natum*) (Forbes, p. 127).

It was a successful season, but that year, two events were to bring sadness to the operatic world. First, from Italy that spring came the sad news of Rubini's death, then later, in the summer came the sudden and shocking news of Sontag's death in Mexico.

Lablache must have been shattered by the loss of his lifelong friend and comrade, Rubini. Giovanni Battista Rubini, in his later years, had been engaged as artistic director for the Imperial opera in St. Petersburg. There, his success was prodigious and his earnings enormous. The Czar had created at that time a permanent Italian opera troupe under Rubini's direction. In 1842 at the height of his fame and at the zenith of his powers, Rubini visited London and Paris for the last time. Later, after saying farewell to Russia, he retired to his birthplace Romano de Lombardi,[647] near Milan in northern Italy. There, he happily resided with his family in a huge palazzo he had built, where he kept a stud of horses.

Pauline Viardot's return to the Royal Italian Opera in *Le Prophète* was a huge plus for the establishment. However, Mario and Grisi left for the United States after several benefit concerts. Mme. Sontag had been there since Her Majesty's closed in 1851, replacing Jenny Lind, who was returning from her successful tours; and in turn, Alboni followed Sontag over there. Unfortunately, Sontag contracted cholera in Mexico.

For the delicate Sontag, life in America was somewhat harsh in contrast to her style of living as a countess. After a most exhausting tour of the States—(New York debut on 27 September 1852)—she finally arrived in New Orleans at the St. Charles Theatre. She dazzled the natives with her famous rendering of Marie in *La Fille du régiment,* then *Lucia,* and *Sonnambula,* finishing up with a concert at the Armory Hall and Meyerbeer's *Le Prophète* at the Orleans Theatre. Ignoring repeated warnings not to go to Mexico because of the cholera outbreak, she left for Mexico City. There, almost immediately, she was struck down by the dread disease and died in June 1854, a tragic end for one of the leading prima donnas of the nineteenth century.[648] Another young Italian tenor by the name of Pozzolini also lost his life from cholera there.[649]

The tragic events of that year were a prelude to other events that would not only touch Lablache personally but would affect the whole world. Turkey and Russia were at war since October of 1853, and on 27 March 1854, the French and the British formally entered into a state of war against Russia. As early as September of that year, and long before the famous battle of Balaclava and the terrible winter of 1854, the Crimean War already proved to be the "disaster of the decade."[650]

One very happy event took place that year in France at the little church at Maisons-Laffitte, Paris—Lablache's son Nicolas married Emilie Glossip de Méric on September 5, 1854.[651]

Professionally known now as Mme. de Méric-Lablache, Emilie and her new husband returned to Russia in the company of Luigi Lablache for the opening of the twelfth Italian season at St. Petersburg lasting from 20 September 1854 to 8 February 1855. In spite of fears of closure due to the war, the theaters remained open and were well patronized.[652]

Donizetti was as well-represented again that season; however, his *Poliuto* and *Il Campanello* were not well-liked. Russian critic Alexander Serov was completely contemptuous of *Poliuto*, considering that Donizetti "should stick to writing comic operas." And going on to say that in this instance, inspiration has completely failed the composer, who is operating out of his sphere of ability. "Not so with Verdi's music, where great talent is evident with each step," he continued. "The opera had a bad reception and the public was disappointed, but even with Pacini's music (*Saffo* was shown that season), this opera should not appear, and should not be put on the same level."[653]

M. Ivanov, writing in his book *History of the Italian Theatre in St. Petersburg in the 19th Century*, said, "Verdi was very well-received, and with the opera *Macbeth* and *Rigoletto*, he secured his position in the hearts of the Russians." There were twenty-one performances of *Macbeth*. In *Rigoletto*, Mme. Emilie de Méric-Lablache sang Magdelina with Tamberlik as the Duke. Ronconi sang the title role with Mlle. Marai as Gilda. With *Macbeth*, Serov's view of Verdi began to change; before he had not been well-disposed toward the composer despite the fact that *Rigoletto* had been appearing in St. Petersburg for several years already. He stopped attacking Verdi for "distorting

Shakespeare," and he started to find in his music a great dramatic and vibrant talent. Ivanov writes about the December 11 1854 opening of Weber's *Der Freischutz* in Italian:[654]

> As for *Der Freischutz*, the critics did not react well to the Italian's performance considering that they should not undertake to perform German operas which are alien to their character . . . We, however, consider Serov's view that German music should be alien to Italians to be completely paradoxical. How many times have we heard the Italian artistes give a wonderful performance of the most diverse music, including Weber's. However, we will admit that the artistes of that time did not completely enter into the spirit of Weber and were more concerned with their own personal effects than with the intentions of the composer. Nevertheless, Serov remarks that all the parts were performed as written, without embellishment, and only Tamberlik added a cadenza to Max's aria (in the first act). The cast for *Der Freischutz* was: La Grange-Agatha, de Méric-Anneta (the part was transposed for her, as it was originally written for a soprano and she was a contralto), Tamberlik-Max, Dido-Caspar and Lablache—the hermit. "What a voice," exclaims Serov. "Remember that the role of the hermit is very small, but Lablache's voice, as always, is completely captivating!" Like a dense but clear bell covering all other noise on the streets of a populous town, such was the effect of the voice of this old master in the finale of *Der Freischutz*. This last peaceful scene surprisingly crowns the play, harmonizing all the discord of the previous sounds. And the voice of Lablache is as if created for this conciliatory, pacifying harmony. Lablache turns everything he touches to gold. This is how Serov defines the nature of his talent, announcing that "similar artistes (e.g., Viardot) can dispel all the chasms separating different schools of music." *Der Freischutz* was performed 33 times on the St. Petersburg Italian stage.

Cheke writes about the Italians in Russia that winter:[655]

> This was the winter when the terrible events in the Crimea were filling all Russia with desperation. When a Concert Patriotique for the widows and orphans of the soldiers killed at Sebastopol was given in the Hall of the Nobles in December, all the artistes from the Italian Company took part. The concert ended with the

Russian National Anthem, sung by the Italians. There was a strong feeling in Russia against what was considered to be an unholy alliance between the British and French to join with the Turks in fighting against their fellow Christians, the Russians. Nevertheless, the attitude towards non-combatant enemy nationals remained very civilized. Emilie was Anglo-French and her brother-in-law, Dominique Lablache, was in the French Army in the Crimea, but there is no reason to believe that this in any way affected her in St Petersburg. The Anthem 'had made all Russian hearts quiver with enthusiasm': *God the Omnipotent, mighty Avenger. Watching invisible, judging unheard. Doom us not now in the day of our danger, grant to us peace, O most merciful Lord.*

That year, to add to the miseries Russia experienced one of the harshest winters of the century, and it was a devastating one for the brave soldiers fighting in the Crimea. During that time, two letters were written on behalf of Queen Victoria to Luigi in Maisons-Laffitte inquiring about the health of Dominique at the Crimea (dated 23 and 27 of June, but no year).

Lablache returned to the autumn opera 1854 scene opening on 4 October in St. Petersburg with *Il Barbiere di Siviglia*, followed by *L'Elisir d'amore, Don Pasquale*, and *I Puritani* for the first time on 10 December.

Nicola Lablache and Emilie de Méric-Lablache left for further commitments in Vienna in early 1855. In spite of the obvious fact that Emilie was over six months pregnant, she sang on 12 April in Verdi's *Rigoletto*, in *Il Trovatore* on 14 April, and she is listed as singing in Donizetti's *Linda* on 21 April. Emilie repeated all her successes from the year before, and in 1856 she was back in Vienna again.

Here, a letter to Luigi from Vienna on the 18 of June 1855, an excited letter, stated that Nicola and Emilie have a newborn girl named after Luigi, of course—Louise:[656]

Dearest Papa,

I am scribbling these few lines to you above all to wish you, on behalf of Emilie and myself, a thousand happinesses, many, many years to come, and that you have on hand everything that you desire. We are sorry to be far from you on the occasion of your Saint's Day but we are saying prayers for your precious conservation from afar, as we would from close by.

My good Emilie is well—relatively—after the birth. Mam'zelle Louise enjoys perfect health so far and at this moment is besieging a fortress of a German wet-nurse who possesses two "mamelons" which would make the mouth of a Guards corporal water.

This escapade of Emilie's will make us remain in Vienna more than we thought but one must be patient. It is never possible to have complete happiness in this world. I cannot say what emotion I experience when I hear another voice in the house-when I say "voice" I am mistaken, I should say "crying," shrieks which nevertheless scratch on my ears sweetly. It is true however that sometimes, especially at night time, this scratching becomes a demanding disturbance. But I am a father and because of that I consent to suffer a thousand times more, because God accords me the grace to look after a daughter.

You know (I think I mentioned it) that Emilie gave birth at least 20 days before term but I am informed by the doctors and the midwife that this happens almost always with first births. Give us your news, dear Papa, because we are very anxious to hear from you. Embrace Frédéric, Fanny and the children also on behalf of my wife. A thousand good wishes and a thousand kisses from your son,

Nicola

After the Russian season ended in 1855, Lablache returned to London's Covent Garden via Paris. He now rarely changed his repertory there as most audiences wanted to hear him in the favorite roles. The playbills announced his return in only five operas that season, and for the first time, a change in his voice was noticed. It is likely he was still tired, having just returned from Russia, and the opera was postponed on his account (*L'Elisir d'amore*).

On 5 May 1855, the newspaper reported, "Lablache is back! as grandiloquent, pompous, oily, and stolid as the ever imprudent quack doctor."[657] On 12 May 1855, it was reported in the *Illustrated London News*:

Lablache has reappeared at the Royal Italian Opera Covent Garden, in *L'Elisir d'amore*, with Angiolina Bosio. He was welcomed on Saturday evening last by a crowded audience with every demonstration of the most cordial interest. The Queen and Prince Albert were present, and the Royal pair were observed to join warmly in the general applause. Her Majesty has always shown much regard for the illustrious veteran, to whose instructions she owes much proficiency in music and her taste and skill as a vocal performer. He appeared in his old and favourite character of Dr. Dulcamara, the quack doctor, in *L'Elisir d'amore,* in which he used of yore to shake the sides of the audiences at Her Majesty's Theatre. This was his first appearance on the boards of the Royal Italian Opera; the Dulcamara of this Theatre having been Ronconi, who has not come to England this season. Nothing can be more unlike than the readings of the character as given by these two celebrated artists, and yet both are admirable. Ronconi's quack seems a literal copy of the quack of ordinary life; he is the very vagabond shabby, sharp, cunning, and impudent—whom we can see gulling the bumpkins out of their pence at any English country fair. Lablache's charlatan is more of a ideal personage, and of a much more pleasant and genial description. We are intended by the dramatist; for Dr. Dulcamara is not a mere strolling knave—he is respectable in his way—a man of substance, looked up to by the vulgar with respect due to his station and magnificence, and admitted to the intimate society and confidence of the principal persons of the drama, who are guided and controlled by his influence. There is scarcely upon the stage a bit of more truthful and genuine comedy than Lablaches's Dulcamara. On Saturday night he acted the part with all his usual good-humoured gaiety; but there was an evident falling off in his vocal power, which it pained us to observe. His magnificent organ had lost much of its resonance and volume, and he brought out his high notes with visible effort. We trust, however, that this was only the temporary effect of the ungenial weather; and this seems the more likely from the circumstance that, on Tuesday, when he was to have repeated the part, he was unable to sing, owing to hoarseness. After the heavy losses our musical stage has suffered, we cannot too lose Lablache also; and we cling to the belief that he will yet be spared to us for a good long time to come. The *L'Elisir d'amore* is admirably cast this season; with Bosio as Adina, Gardoni as Nemorino, Graziani as Belcore, and Lablache as Dulcamara, it forms as gay and delightful an entertainment as the Italian comic stage can possibly afford.

On December 8 1855, *The Musical World* published a short interview with Rossini titled: "A Conversation with Rossini" by Ferdinand Hiller.

> "What a pity it is that Italians have so completely turned their backs on Italian opera buffa, in which they were so admirable," said I. "The Neapolitans especialy," replied Rossini, "possessed a peculiar talent for it. This kind of opera requires, perhaps a lively feeling for the essential attributes of the stage, rather than great musical powers. At present however, the singers for it are, also, wanting. The everyday p oniard-business rendering them quite incapable of moving with lightness and grace."

The premiere of Meyerbeer's opera *L'Étoile du Nord (Northern Star)* on 19 July 1855, was sung in Italian; and was the most interesting event to take place at Covent Garden that season, and a brillant success. Lablache sang the role of Gritzenko, a Cossack, with his usual authority. The press coverage for this opera was enormous compared to the few words about the London premiere of Verdi's seventeenth opera *Il Trovatore,* proving the public had not been won over yet by the composer. In fact, Lablache had not been at all pleased with Verdi's operas. Rev. Cox wrote, "Lablache as Gritzenko stole the honours among the men, displaying a refreshing voice." It was agreed there was few weak points in the whole production; and the general excution of one of the most difficult operas ever written was admirable. Michael Costa and the orchestra were a *tours de force*, notwithstanding the elaborate chorus and scenary. Meyerbeer was brought out on stage to take a bow, and according to the press received tremendous applause. The respectable cast were Bosio, Marai, Gardoni, Formes, and Rudersdorff. The work ran for nine performances, then faded into obscurity. Lablache left for the Birmingham Festival rehearsals, before the end of *L'Étoile du Nord*. All the Italian singers from the opera house of Covent garden, plus a large group of English singers. The program was huge consisting of choral works like *Elijah, Mount of Olives, Israel in Egypt, Requiem* by Mozart. Several grand concerts were included in the program that lasted over a week, finishing up with a grand ball. Then we persume Lablache left via Paris for the start of the 1855 Russian season.

Lablache sang the role again in Russia and again back-to-back with *Il Trovatore.*

Soon, however, *Il Trovatore* triumphed as one of the most enduring operas of the last century and in fact of all time. The playbill announced the first night, Thursday, 10 May 1855, in huge red letters—"TROVATORE with new scenery, dresses, and appointments." The first London cast was a good one: Mme. Viardot (Azucena), Mlle. Jenny Ney (Lenora), Signor Graziani (Conte di Luna), and Manrico the hero was sung by the impressive dramatic tenor Signor Enrico Tamberlik. A Roman, Tamberlik's strong viril voice and great dramatic stage presence broke away from the usual accepted tenor mold of that time, and soon he was accepted among a public that we must remember adored the lyric sweet voice of Mario. A Russian by the name of N. Raevsky gives us a vivid impression of his voice in Ivanov's book:[658]

> He had a strong voice, with metallic high notes, passionate singing, and an unusual clarity of pronunciation which drew attention to him. He nearly eclipsed Mario in the part of leader of the Scots in *La Donna del lago* in London, and then he had audiences bowled over by his execution of Arnold in *William Tell*, and in his duet with Iago in *Otello*, and his Di quella pira, in *Il Trovatore*. Tamberlik was an artiste to his very soul and this showed always and in everything. His acting was basically very uniform with the occasional flashes of energy. He excelled in recitative, which he pronounced better than anyone else. These recitatives were as precious stones in parts such as Arnold, which together with the part of Otello, were his best parts from his wide repertoire.[659]

Tamberlik's voice contributed to Verdi's huge successes from London to St. Petersburg. He toured both North and South America. His greatest Verdi roles were the Duke in *Rigoletto*, Manrico in *Il Trovatore*, Don Alvaro in *La forza del destino,* and the title role in *Ernani*. While in St. Petersburg, he sang in Rossini's *La Cenerentola* with Lablache on 7 November 1852. Then during the next season there, Tamberlik joined Lablache again in Ricci's *Il Marito e l'Amante* with Emilie de Méric-Lablache and Medori and was Don Ottavio with Lablache and the same cast in *Don Giovanni* on 22 December there. Tamberlik succeeded in Russia, and he was there when Lablache arrived. Enrico Calzolari was his only rival; Nauden was very unpopular and was hissed many times when he sang in *Lucrezia* and *Rigoletto*. The refined Enrico Calzolari was the exact opposite to Tamberlik. The public especially liked him in *I Puritani* with Lablache and *Il Barbiere*. Serov also rated Calzolari highly. He considered him to be the "last of the Mohicans among Italian fioriture tenors—he acts so well," continues Serov in Ivanov:[660]

> The public judged him to be a serious artiste and valued him highly, making him a favourite equal to Tamberlik. Of course he did not ignite them to the extent of Tamberlik, in his ecstatic moments he did not have the fire of the latter and he was less good at lyrical than dramatic parts as he could not touch the heart of his listener so strongly. However, if Tamberlik had more inspiration, Calzolari had incomparably more ability and understanding. His school was the genuine "vero canto italiano" school . . . Calzolari never sang for effect, never allowing himself to sacrifice the beauty of the whole for success in certain parts. His training was remarkable . . . his repertoire was vast. His voice, which was not particularly strong, was remarkable for its delightful timbre, soft, velvety and pouring out from the soul; it was a voice of sweet words, tender outpourings and sadness.

Mario had left the stage open for Calzolari. He had sung in all the major capitals of Europe over a period of eight years when he first arrived in St. Petersburg. M. Ivanov states that "Europe, however, did not see the fully-developed talent of this splendid singer who reached perfection only on our stage." Calzolari remained in Russia for eighteen years and was much beloved by the public. Lablache must have known him well; they first sang together in London in 1849.[661]

The golden voices of Grisi, Mario, Tamburini, and Lablache—the famous Puritani Quartet, sometimes called the famous *vieille garde*—were heard together for the last time at Covent Garden that season in the roles that they had sung together so wonderfully earlier on the stages of London and Paris.

Again, singing in *Don Pasquale*, no one could doubt their voices might have shown some wear. Lablache's, we read, was as refreshing as ever that season despite his age. Of Tamburini, the critics were bold enough to say he had lost his voice. Some said he was just a shadow of his old self. While Grisi had announced her retirement again at the end of the year, she in actuality did not retire but sang on till 1866 with tremendous gusto. Mario, who was younger, was still in perfect form.

Sadly, for London's music lovers, Lablache and the Italian singers would never return to historic Covent Garden again. Early in the morning of 5 March 1856, while a masked ball was winding down, the second Royal Italian Opera House caught fire and was burnt down to the ground. Queen Victoria viewed the still-smoldering ruins the next day. Among the ashes, someone picked up a medal belonging to Lablache.[662] Mr. Gye was shattered. However, plans were drawn up immediately for a new theater. The company moved to another theater. Sometime after the end of the Russian season of 1855 to 1856 season ended Lablache must have returned to Paris. We do not know if he had any contract for Covent Garden that year. Manager Gye later in June, requested Lablache to sign up for another season; it was just a month before Teresa Lablache died—here is Lablache's reply:

Maisons-sur-Seine
27 June 1856

Dear Mr. Gye,

    I appreciate very much the kind offer you made in your letter of the 23 June but, unfortunately, my health is still the same and my greatest desire is to get better. I cannot, therefore, I regret to say, sign the contract for three years—which I am returning to you because an acceptance at this moment would not be approbate.*
    Let us look into this project later which otherwise I would have accepted with pleasure.

With best wishes
L. Lablache

*(Sin of presumption, are the exact words in French.)[663]

That summer of 1856, doctors ordered Rossini to take a trip to the healing baths of Wildbad, Kissinger, and Baden.[664] His health had been bad since he left Florence in April of 1855. Italy never saw him again.[665] He returned to Paris an entirely different man, feeling much better. Lablache too was not in the best of health. Family history and photos that cannot lie reveal Lablache had now become not just overweight but dangerously obese; his condition was out of control. Frédéric and Fanny Lablache arranged to have a special cut out in the huge dining room table—a flap on hinges that folded up and down so Papa Lablache could get closer to the food.

Frédéric, a well-known gourmand, entertained lavishly at his London home on Albany Street. The house was a rendezvous for musicians and composers living in London; moreover, it was a meeting place for many notable foreigners, and exiles from Italy and France were welcomed by Frédéric. The Prince Louis Napoleon—afterward Napoleon III—the Prince of Syracuse, and the Prince de Rohan all visited. The Lablaches were close friends with Sir Julius Benedict and the conductors Michael Costa and Michael Balfe. In the Sir Julius Benedict diaries (private diaries of his descendant), the Lablache family is mentioned over and over. "The Lablaches are coming to tea."[666] Other people that were friends and compatriots are featured in the large Lablache family photo albums. They are Roger, Carl Rosa, Auber, Brignoli, Lind, Patti (Patti's wedding), Mario, and Grisi, and Belletti. On the back of the photo of Carl Rosa's wife, "To my dear friends Madame Lablache et famille" from Euphrosyne Parepa Caroulle. Thalberg writes, "To dear little Fanny," the daughter of Frédéric.

Dr. William Spark mentions an incident that happened near the end of Lablache's life in London:

> On one occasion a rehearsal at Her Majesty's Theatre being over sooner than he expected, and before the arrival of his brougham, Lablache sent his servant for a cab; and when the driver saw the great singer, he said, despairingly, "He'll never, never get in, sir!" The cab door was opened: wide-sideways, frontways, headways, backways, the ponderous singer always failing to effect an entrance; at last with the united efforts of some strong bystanders, Lablache got inside, puffing and groaning from his exertions: but he soon got from bad to worse, for wishing to change his position—he had inadvertently sat down with his back to the horse—the whole of his prodigious weight was, when he rose, upon the few slender boards forming the floor of the cab. The driver, Lablache, and a large crowd which had been attracted by the terrible struggle which was going on, were still more astonished when the boards gave way, and his feet and legs were seen standing in the road! The cabby swore, Lablache grinned, the crowd roared. No scene in pantomime was ever more ludicrous. Fortunately, the weighty basso sustained no injury. If the horse had moved, the consequences would doubtless have been serious. To get him out, greater efforts were necessary than at first. The door was torn from its hinges, and the previously good-conditioned cab had become a complete wreck. The driver uttered some very strong language, very; but, on being assured that the damage would be made good, and that he would be remunerated for his loss of time, he became pacified. After this pretty little experience and unpleasant *fiasco,* Lablache did not attempt to ride in another hack cab.

As usual, with anecdotes on Lablache, the stories are often warped by time and translation. There are always several versions; is this a version of the story above? or is it a different story entirely? as told by W. Kuhe in his *Musical Recollections*:

> Apropos of the singer's extraordinary corpulence, I remember an amusing thing happening. On one occasion, driving to Her Majesty's Theatre in a rickety and prehistoric-looking cab, the licensing of which constituted a disgrace to the authorities, the bottom of the vehicle gave way, and poor Lablache, his feet dangling above the ground, had to run some little distance before the driver of the cab, a patriarchal 'growler,' hearing the unlucky occupant's cries for assistance, became alive to the situation and pulled up. The victim afterwards narrated this accident to me with great gusto, turning the joke against himself, and indulging in no anathema at the expense of the Jehu, whose property had 'gone under' at so unpropitious a moment.

ଔଔଔ

Chapter Thirty-Three

The End of the Career

1856-57

Lablache did not return to London for the next season as he had been invited to participate in the festivities celebrating the coronation of the new Russian Czar, Alexander II. The previous Czar Nicolas I had died in early 1855. After the summer season of 1855 at Covent Garden, Lablache returned to Russia via Paris for the winter season at St. Petersburg. Arriving there for the performance of *L'Elisir d'amore* on 22 October, followed by *I Puritani, Don Pasquale,* and *Il Barbiere,* he sang the former opera with soprano Marai, the later-soprano roles were sung by the young Italian Angiolina Bosio.

Bosio's London Royal Italian Opera debut came about in 1853. Since her debut at La Scala when she was only fifteen in Verdi's *I due Foscari* (in 1844), she had enjoyed a rapid climb to success in the United States. Returning to Europe, she was London's favorite young prima donna during the time Lablache first set foot on the boards of Covent Garden in 1854. The *Times* wrote that she was considered the most accomplished soprano of her day. There she sang Rosina, Elvira, and Gilda opposite Mario. Mario did not sing again in Russia till the late 1860s.

St. Petersburg did not suffer from the loss of Mario. Although there was some grumbling, the tenor roles were filled by two of the finest singers of the day, Calzolari and Tamberlik. The heavier roles were sung by the baritone, Ronconi and De Bassini. Calzolari sang alongside Lablache from the time of Her Majesty's and sang most of the principle tenor roles while Lablache sang in Russia.

Notably on 26 January 1856, Lablache introduced Meyerbeer's *L'Étoile du Nord* (*Northern Star*) alongside the first Russian performance of Verdi's *Il Trovatore,* both operas featuring Bosio. Usually, her voice would be classified as a lyrical soprano, but she also was able to sing dramatic roles, like Leonora; and with this opera, she was a success and critics in St. Petersburg unanimously agreed that it would be unthinkable to cast this opera with anyone else.[667] Lablache writes to Baron Ernest de Caters and Marie that they are fine and "Nicolas embraces you."

Becoming one of Russia's favorite singers, Bosio created the first Violetta in Russia in Verdi's *La Traviata*. Tragically, she died in Russia on March of 1859, at only twenty-nine, a victim of pleurisy and infected lungs. Here, Emilie de Méric felt remorse owing to the fact that shortly before her death, while sitting together in a carriage, they had quarreled; Bosio had fled into the freezing weather and to an unheated carriage. Here, Russia's deadly weather took the life of yet another opera artiste.[668]

Meyerbeer's *L'Étoile du Nord's* first showing in Russia with Lablache was cast with excellent singers: Bosio, Marai, tenor Calzolari, Bettini and de Bassini. The opera had a certain success and was continued on for a total of eight performances. The public gave it their approval, but its sheer length of four hours gave it an oppressive feel as it did subsequently when the opera was renewed for Ms. Sembrich in the 1880s. As for the critic Serov, who was going through an anti-Meyerbeer phase (he had just begun his acquaintance with Wagners's ideas), Meyerbeer came in for some scathing criticism from him:[669]

> Who is reigning now on the operatic stage? He exclaims, Verdi or Meyerbeer?—neither of them is capable of genuine, refined melody. Because of this (in their different ways) coerce both the orchestra and the singers; they make them shriek, wail, drum, etc. For their wild combinations, prompted by a murky fantasy, à la Victor Hugo. What is the result of such an elegant direction? A terrible fortune of singers' throats causing them soon to lose their voices, a greater and greater decline in the art of singing, a growing destruction of all the riches, all the artistry of performance, a terrible damage to the musical taste of virtuoso performers and—no less important—the public. Finally, a complete lack of all true poetry on the operatic stage. What is this if not a general collapse of art? It is especially interesting to read these prophecies in our time and see to what extent they have proven to be true.[670]

Emilie de Méric-Lablache returned to Vienna for the 1856 spring season. Emilie appeared in a successful revival of *Il Trovatore* and in three other operas: *Rigoletto, Zelmira,* and a work by the Chevalier Tommasi called *Guido e Ginevra*, which was being given its Viennese premiere. In all, Emilie sang twenty-two times in May;[671] it was announced from St. Petersburg that three first-class singers from the Italian Opera in Vienna—Jeremiah Bettini, De

Bassini, and Mme. de Méric-Lablache—had been invited to sing during the ceremonies for the coronation in Moscow of the Czar Alexander II.[672]

Teresa Lablache, the beloved wife of Luigi, lived only two years after their house was completed in Maisons-Laffitte. On 26 July 1856, she died and was buried in the little gravel-strewn churchyard of Maisons-Laffitte in a huge neoclassic-style mausoleum built by Lablache in 1838 for his daughter Rosina (we can only presume). Above the door deeply carved into the stone masonry are the words Familie Lablache. Interned to this day here lie many members of the family that lived in France. Teresa Lablache must have borne the difficulties of operatic life like a saint. Mother of thirteen children, she died before knowing all her grandchildren (cause of death not known). The size of her husband's voice became difficult to live with at times. She told of being awakened one night by what she took to be the sounds of a fire tocsin; it was only her husband uttering in his sleep the staccato notes in a duet from *I Puritani*, which he had been singing with Grisi that same night.[673]

Not feeling in the best of health, Lablache, now brokenhearted, reluctantly returned again to Russia in August of 1856 to fulfill his commitments. All the great festivities had begun for the crowning of a new Romanov Czar—Alexander II, the son of Nicholas I, who died of a cold in the winter of 1855. The opera season promised a program like never before.

> The fourteenth Italian season in Russia opened in auspicious circumstances. In March the Crimean War had been brought to an end. The new Czar was to be crowned on 26th August (1856) and he had decided to include in the coronation festivities both the Italian Opera and the Theatre Francais. Festivities began before the artistes even landed in Russia. In Stettin, on a fine Summer day (16 August), the Russian steamer *Vladimir* took on board a party for St. Petersburg which included not only companies of foreign singers and actors but Russian princes, German barons, diplomatic attaches and newspaper correspondents from several countries. Suddenly, the following evening, word went round that there was to be a concert on deck. A milling crowd assembled. Then, spectacle case in hand, Lablache gave the signal for the music to begin: it was the Italian Opera, performing above the placid sea—Mesdames Bosio, Lotti, Marai and de Méric-Lablache, with Signori Lablache, Bettini and Tagliafico. They opened with Rossini's *Carnaval*, followed by the prayer from *Le Comte Ory*. A trio by Martini led to a canon by Salieri and then to the finale of *Il Barbiere*. The enthusiasm was boundless

and the demands for encores were not brought to an end until Mme. Tagliafico went round to make a collection for the benefit of the crew (*Le Menestrel*).[674]

In Moscow, preparations had begun on a lavish scale. The singers in the Italian Company were given free accommodation in the premises at the Imperial Court, and court vehicles were placed at their disposal (*The Musical World*).

> The old Bolshoi Theatre had been burnt out in 1853 and a vast new edifice had replaced it. Resplendent in red, white and gold, it defied all description. It could seat 2,500 and was far higher than the San Carlo in Naples. The cost of a box for six was a "fabulous" twenty-five rubles and four hundred rubles was the price for the eighteen performances which were promised. In the summer of 1856, the talk in Moscow and St. Petersburg was of nothing but the Coronation and the attendant festivities. These were organized for notables and public alike. At the Opera in Moscow, the great gala performance was on 30 August when Lablache appeared in *L'Elisir d'amore* and Ceritto danced in the ballet. Emilie de Méric Lablache's Moscow debut was on the following evening in *Il Trovatore*, the opera which proved to be the most successful of all (*La France Musicale*). Critics went so far as to say that Bettini was even better than Tamberlik as Manrico. The singers in *Lucrezia Borgia* were given a great ovation and Emilie's Brindisi was encored. Emilie also sang in *Rigoletto*, but not in the Russian premiere of *La Traviata*.

On 1 September 1856, Lablache sang *I Puritani* with Mme. Bosio, Calzolari, and the baritone A. de Bassini. On 8 September, he sang the title role of *Don Pasquale* for the first time at the Moscow Bolshoi Theatre with soprano F. Marai and Calzolari. Then on 17 September, he continued the season with *L'Elisir d'amore*, again with the popular soprano Bosio. During this special Moscow season, the concerts included a notable one given on 12 and 24 September by the Grand Duchess Helene in which Emilie played a prominent part. Her solo aria was from *Le Prophète*, and she sang in concerted pieces from *Maria Stuarda* (Niedermeyer), Alla Trinita beata, *Cosi fan tutte*, and *Il Trovatore*. All the artists received rich presents from both the Czar and the Grand Duchess.

On 5 September, Luigi wrote from Moscow to his daughter Marie de Caters describing the entrance of the Czar into Moscow and marveling at the splendor of the uniforms and dresses. He asked Marie to have a mass said for his late wife at the church at Maisons. (Luigi was still unwell but had nevertheless managed to make the journey to Russia.)[675]

After singing in Moscow, Lablache and the other Italian singers returned to St. Petersburg, joining up with the Czar and Czarina in October to a tumultuous reception. The opera season had opened with Verdi's *Macbeth*, followed by *Ernani*, *Il Trovatore*, and *Rigoletto*. This explains the overwhelming enthusiasm for Verdi which suddenly gripped Russian audiences at the time. Above all, the public loved *Il Trovatore*. Maurice Rappaport, director of the *Journal des Theatres et de Musique* at St. Petersburg, as quoted in *La France Musicale,* had this to say about Emilie de Meric Lablache's performance as Azucena:

> The enormous success of the *Il Trovatore* with us (in Russia) is due in great part to Madame de Méric. I have observed that several foreign journals failed to mention Mme. Emilie de Méric in their reports on the performances of the *Il Trovatore* in Moscow. We must acknowledge, in all fairness, that it is she who has created the difficult role of the gypsy. She has proved that she is not only an excellent singer, but a remarkable actress as well. In her acting there is so much truth that the very sight of the sinister gypsy sends a cold shiver down the spine of everyone in the audience. In the *Trovatore*, she shares the ovations which the public unfailingly bestow on Mme. Bosio and that says all.

Azucena became the signature role for Emilie de Meric for the rest of her singing career. On 11 November Lablache writes from St. Petersburg in Italian. "From the last letter I received from Nicolas I knew you had returned to Maisons—a kiss to Louise, also on behalf of Nicolas and Emilie who embrace you."[676] It would seem that Nicolas and Emilie had left baby Louise at home in Maison Laffette while they were in Russia.

Sometime during this season, Lablache's health began to fail again. Then on 3 January 1857, in *L'Italiana in Algeri*, he sang *Mustifa* with his daughter-in-law, Emilie de Méric-Lablache. Was Lablache's health fading then? If he did sing *L'elisir* in January 1857, where was he after that. And yet all during this time, we understand he had considered accepting Gye's engagement in London, but there had also been some difficulty over taxes; here, family history remains unclear. Wilhelm Kuhe's sheds some light on this in his book *My Musical Recollections*:

> Apropos of the last of the great buffos, I remember an amusing story. One year (I forgot which) the Income Tax Commissioners

sent to the Italian Opera House 'demand' papers to be filled in by all the principal artists engaged for the season. Never before had foreign singers, who were only on a few weeks visit to this country, been so importuned in this fashion; nor, to my knowledge, has the experiment been repeated. It so happened that Lablache had quitted London at the time that these precious documents were left in the Theatre, and his papers only reached him some months later in Paris, at the very moment when he was on the point of starting for England. At first, he was completely mystified by the terms of the official blue paper, but when, at length, he had mastered its contents, he was so indignant that he forthwith abandoned his projected journey, and, what is more, he has never been seen or heard in England since. That Income Tax paper was too much for him.[677]

Clearly, however in the spring, Luigi Lablache was back in Maisons-Laffitte. During the summer of 1857, Lablache wrote from there that Dr. Francois Marconcelli and his other doctors had ordered him to take the waters of a well-known spa at Kissingen and then go to Naples for the sunshine and fresh air. This he did, and for the first time, he shows up in Germany. There, an incident took place:

> Lablache was queuing with others in his coach waiting for his turn to enter the hydro (bathing establishment). Emperor Alexander II, who was walking nearby, approached him and graciously saluted him. Immediately, Lablache made as if to get off the coach and go towards him, but the Sovereign, knowing how ill and suffering he was, obliged him not to move. Leaning on the coach door, he stopped for a long time talking to Lablache and chatting very pleasantly. All the passersby stopped to look at them with pleasure, commenting on the fact that also crowned heads pay homage to a great genius.

After Kissingen, on 18 August, he left for the French Riviera and for some time stayed at Dr. Marconcelli's house in Nice; there, the climate bothered his condition and he was advised to go to Naples.

Luigi's oldest daughter Cecchina (Francesca) enjoyed a very close relationship with her father and wanted to have him home, hoping to nurse him and restore his health. She spent a great deal of time alone at the family villa, and family tradition recalls her as rather an overbearing woman, apparently very eccentric; here, there is some evidence that her husband Thalberg's excessive piano tours kept him busy and away from her. Luigi's sister, the Abbess of Sessa, was also devoted to her brother so in Naples, he would have had good care. A London newspaper (*Chronicle*) on 10 August 1857 wrote:

> The Emperor of Russia, on learning that the elder Lablache was ordered, on account of his health, not to think of again appearing on the stage, has sent the great artiste his nomination to the dignity of "His Majesty's singer," accompanied with a gold medal enriched by diamonds, bearing the inscription "Pour distinction," the medal to be suspended from the neck by the blue ribbon of the Order of St. Andrew. Lablache says he is so much improved in health that we understand it is not all improbable he will return to the Italian opera during the approaching season in Paris.

But another report tells us that Lablache, on receiving the medal, remarked sadly, "This will do, to decorate my coffin." The *London Times* wrote:

> Signor Lablache has been so far convalescent, indeed his name was advertised in the prospectus of the French Italian Theatre for the actual season; the aid of his colossal talent was confidently anticipated by the conductors of the Royal Italian opera, for the opening of the new opera Theatre on Bow Street.(*Zampa*)

On 24 October 1857, *The Musical World* reports from the French newspaper *L'Union*:

> Lablache, that eminent artist, whose reputation is a European one, has been residing at his charming villa of Pausilippe, for the month that has elapsed since his return among us. His most ardent desire is to live a life of repose at present, having renounced all sorts of magnificent engagements abroad; unfortunately, he has just had a paralytic attack, which, for some days has inspired his numerous friends, and the no less numerous admirers of his fine talent, with a great deal of uneasiness; his last journeys to Russia and the cold climate of that country have greatly weakened the celebrated singer. There is every day a pilgrimage of visits paid by all our notabilities to the Villa Lablache, to inquire after the health of our excellent buffo, whose place, like that of Rubini and Tamburini, his old companions in success and triumph, will not be filled up on the stage for a long time. The traditions of

Rossini's music, of which the above three celebrated artistes were the sublime interpreters, have now completely disappeared from Italy. The doctors say the illustrious artist will never be able to reappear on the stage. This is a loss which will be vividly felt in *The Musical World*, where Lablache obtained such a large share of public sympathy . . . we know the success he achieved in St. Petersburg, and the kind of marks of esteem he recently received from the Emperor Alexander. But he has bought his glory and his honors with his health. Heaven grant that science may not yet have done its utmost; Heaven grant it may, by skill and care, preserve for us an inimitable artist and a man universally loved.

Later, the *Philadelphia Bulletin* remarked:[678]

Of the singers in the 'Puritani Quartet,' Lablache had the best preserved voice of all, and though some of its volume may have been lost with advancing years and with increasing obesity, it was 'still' regarded as the finest bass voice in Europe.

Reports in encyclopedias, dictionaries, books, and journals falsely state that Lablache retired in 1856 or 1857. In the spring of 1858, Lablache's name appeared in a huge full-page advertisement in *The Musical World*:[679] "Signor Lablache will re-delight his old admirers this season at the Royal Italian Opera. Among other operas he will appear in Herold's *Zampa*, which is to be produced for Mario." On February 14 that year, Mme. Frédéric Lablache sang a new ballad by Balfe, "The Arrow," with "great effect" in Mme. Oury's musicale matinee. The conductor was Balfe and Signor Piatti played.

ধধধ

Czar Nicolas I of Russia, steel engraving
Beauties of the Opera and Ballet (Lablache Archives)

St. Petersburg Opera House (Lablache Archives)

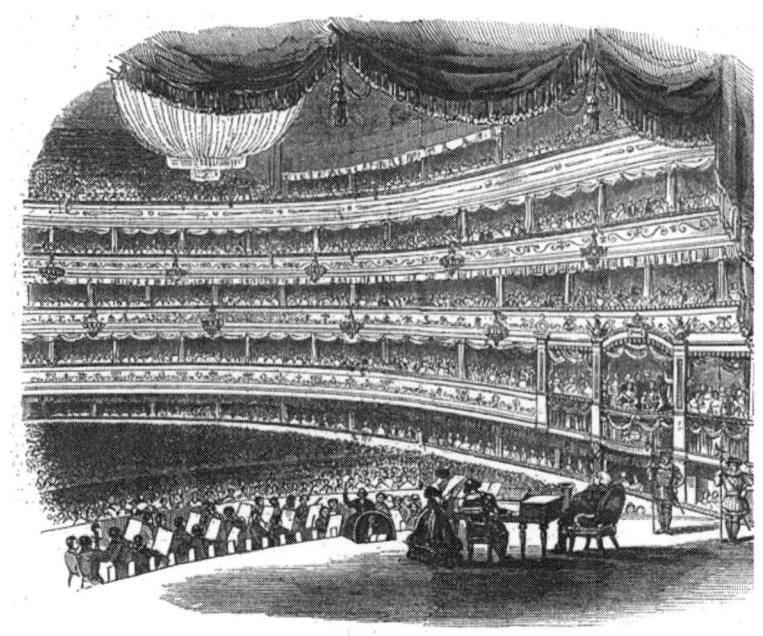

Covent Garden-Luigi Lablache sitting on stage
The Illustrated London News (Lablache Archives)

Covent Garden exterior, wood engraving (Lablache Archives)

Luigi Lablache oil portrait by Franz Xaver Winterhalter
(The Royal CollectionTrust)

"Colonel" James Mapeleson, impresario

Frederick Gye, impresario

Michael Balfe, conductor (Basil Walsh)

Benjamin Lumley, impresario

Michael Costa, conductor carte de visite (Lablache Archives)

OPERA cover 1966 Lablache portrait by Antoine Jean Gros.
(Museo teatrale alla Scala)

Façade d'entrée - Photographiéeen 1897 par A. GODEFROY
(Collection Mme SAUBIE)

The Lablache House, Maison Laffitte Paris, old photo (Monique Saubié)

The Lablache House, Maison Laffitte and author photo (Lablache Archives)

The Lablache House, Maison Laffitte front, author photo (Lablache Archives)

The Lablache House, Maison Laffitte back, author photo (Lablache Archives)

Don Giovanni playbill, 1845.
(Lablache Archives)

Falstaff playbill, 1838 (Lablache Archives)

Don Carlos playbill, 1844. (Lablache Archives)

I Puritani playbill, 1842. (Lablache Archives)

Gaetano Donizetti, antique postcard. (Lablache Archives)

Giuseppe Verdi carte de visite (Lablache Archives)

Wolfgang Amadeus Mozart, steel engraving. (Sergio Ragni)

Henrietta Meric-Lalande (Sergio Ragni)

Bernardo Winter—Father Calveri (Sergio Ragni)

LABLACHE A PARIGI

Lablache in Paris by G. Gatti (Sergio Ragni)

Book Five

Chapter Thirty-Four

Final Days

1858

Lablache lay dying in Naples. At his bedside, he was surrounded by loving friends, his favorite daughter Francesca, and his sister Madelena—the Abbess of Sessa. Florimo writes that while Lablache's success was international and he had received worldwide acclaim, it was to his beloved Naples that he always returned; perhaps his soul yearned to be in the place of his birth, the sunny climate, the warm sea breezes, and the friendly Neapolitans. Florimo was there and described the last hours in a letter to Dominique, his son, who had just been made a captain of the French army. Dominique wrote to a relative about how sad he felt that now his father would never know of his success.

He describes the death scene:[680]

> The giant figure, now smitten, lay still, but not quiet . . . Unmovable, his huge bulk heaved as he laboured to breath, his body racked by pain. Francesca wiped his dripping brow, . . . his white curly hair strewn across the lace pillow.

Visitors came as he lay there. A steady stream of faithful, bowing, whispering humanity filed by. Was this the scene that Florimo found? Surrounded by fussing and whispering Italian females, falling over one another to make him comfortable, where he lay prone and broken like the statues of crumbling old Roman gods, still faintly smiling. This was the Italian way of death.

Florimo remembers how, when the opportunity arose, he used to sing those lovely and popular songs, particularly the aria of (Valentino) Fioravanti in *Camilla*, which begins with the words:

479

> Quando ti vedo, Napoli,
>> Un grido vo' mandar;
> Ed un baciozzo a pizzico;
>> Ti voglio poi donar!

> When I see you, Naples,
>> I want to utter a cry;
> And a big kiss and a pinch;
>> I then want to give this to you!

Just a few days before Lablache's death, Florimo wrote that he went to visit him and found him completely resigned to the approaching end. He remembers these very moving words as his eyes filled with tears:[681]

> God has given me a numerous family and I was always happy when I was with them. Once I lost my wife, my good star started to go the wrong way . . . now death would be less hard and bitter if I could, together with my Francesca, bless all my children and give them my eternal good-bye . . . I am not allowed to have so much joy . . . let's resign ourselves to this!! Very unhappy vicissitudes of life!

The *Athenaeum*, 6 March 1858, extracted a few notes beside a short biography from an article that appeared by M. d'Ortigue in the *Journal des Debats*:

> "To his last hour," adds M. d'Ortigue, "Lablache cherished recollections and thoughts of his art. Feeling his voice expire, and unable any longer to emit any sounds save the weakest possible ones, he called his daughter and said to her, *"Cecchina, non ho piu voce: moro."* On the point of death he repeated the first two verses of Manzoni's *"Cinque Maggio,"* a spasm compelled him to stop. He then tried to sing an English ballad of which he was very fond, "Home Sweet Home"((the tune, is a Sicilian one, and used by Donizetti in his *Anna Bolena*).

Henri Lablache wrote a letter to his sister, Marie, giving the details of the agony of Luigi based on a letter written by Theodore Coltran from Naples to his brother Felix in Paris one hour before the death. The letter mentions that photos were taken of the body before a death mask was made. The body was embalmed and placed in the family crypt at Camposanto, the old cemetery in the northern part of the city of Naples (Balsan collection).

The *Athenaeum* writes,[682]

> Private letters from Naples are full of regret for Lablache whose death may (like Garrick's) be said in some sense—"to have eclipsed the gaiety of nations." They contain a detail or two which complete the record of his last days. He seems to have enjoyed life to the last, in spite of cruel physical suffering—to have kept house and heart open to old friends; not altogether aware that "the narrow house was so near,"—to have been cheered by expressions of sympathy from his distant pupil (among whom was our Sovereign),—never to have relinquished the prospect of returning to England—and, like the real artist he was, to have maintained his voice in working order to the end. "You cannot imagine," writes a correspondent, how beautiful and majestic he looked when he was dead—Lablache's funeral in Naples was merely provisional—attended by as many of his comrades . . . as much state as royal caution permits—the artists being prohibited, by telegraph, from attending the body. His remains, which for the present, are deposited in the Camposanto, will shortly be removed to Paris to be interred besides those of his wife . . . (details of Paris funeral). Our correspondent adds that Lablache is understood to have died in opulence; leaving behind him a fortune upward of L. 60,000.

Here from Naples comes the fullest details of his death and funeral there. From the *Gazzetta Musicale di Napoli*, 28 Gennaio 1858, Anno VII numero. 4, "The Death of Luigi Lablache":

> The sublime interpreter of the music of Rossini, Bellini and Donizetti, the illustrious singer who, with Rossini and Paganini, constituted the famous musical triad that will mark out our century: Luigi Lablache passed away on 23rd Saturday January at a quarter to three in the afternoon. The news of this saddest of events was officially announced by Francesca Thalberg, nee(born) Lablache, to all the friends of the deceased and in the name of his entire scattered family, inviting all to take part in a funeral procession that accompanied our sorely missed citizen on Tuesday 26th of this month to Campo Santo di Poggioreale.

The most gentle and ever flowing comforts of religion rendered tranquil the last moments of this man who united urbane and artistic talents with the purist Christian piety.

His Reverence Father Calveri-Winter (Berardo Winter, ex-singer) of the Dominican order who, through one of those mysterious but admirable designs of Providence, moved from the lyric Theatre to the Church and was Luigi Lablache's companion for many years, having assiduously attended upon him in the course of the long illness, gave the dying man all the pious comforts of his sacred ministry. Thus it was that our virtuous fellow citizen fell asleep in the Lord, with the consolation of Religion and the comforts of friendship.

We, who at every gathering have reported the successes of the famous artist, consider it a duty to dedicate our words to him, associating our sorrow with that of the public.

The account of Signor Tommaso Vernicchi, professor of medicine:

It was five months ago that the famous Luigi Lablache, a man most dear to whomsoever held in high regard the sweetest art of Song, returned here to Naples to seek a cure for some sores which had made their appearance on his legs.

At the beginning, Lablache's disease proceeded fairly smoothly. Unfortunately, however, on the night of the 22nd day of the following month, the illness took a different course, since he suffered greatly from prostration, sleeplessness and breathing difficulties. Towards the early hours of the morning, while the same troublesome symptoms persisted, he was struck by nervous shocks in different limbs and for brief moments also fell into delirium. By the evening of the same day his condition remained much the same such that the patient was troubled by mild breathlessness, coughing, agitation and unspeakable prostration. Not so much through obstinacy as in obedience to his usual habits, the famous patient wished to go through to another room, unwisely relying upon his depleted strength. How ever much his friends and relatives fervently implored him not to move a step, each one considering that any movement could turn out harmful to him, he was unwilling to give in. While the one part of his passage proved truly difficult and laborious, the other he was unable to complete, as he was so lacking in strength that he threw himself breathless and like a corpse into his chair. In this terrible moment he experienced an awful sensation of lifelessness, which he announced in a faint voice, much afraid. One could see this in his frowning eyes, the dark shadows beneath them, his facial muscles partly contorted and partly (in convellimento), his pulse feeble to the touch—his carotid pulse beating with little force and very slowly, his breathing was laboured. This frightful state lasted for a few minutes, then unfortunately repeated itself a few times, each time with less intensity. This state was finally brought to an end in a certain calmness broken from time to time by tremors, strong muscular contractions and tightness of breath. But this was only an apparent calm, false and deceptive, because his heart continued to beat slowly and irregularly, and breathing remained difficult. Every remedy known to science was adopted to stave off this state, most distressing to him and all those who loved him, but despite this, throughout the night the patient was troubled by sleeplessness, difficulties in breathing, by painful expectoration, agitation and by prostration of the limbs and circulation.

So far as it is reported, it is quite apparent that the illness of the day before had progressed and that one was dealing with a mechanical obstruction to the circulation arising from blood pooling in the base of the lungs.

Towards one o'clock in the afternoon of the 23rd, Professors Vernicchi, Prudente, de Rensis and Lanza held a consultation. These learned professors made a careful examination of the state of the patient and ordered all those remedies that might save him. But the hopes and wishes of the doctors, of his relatives and friends came to nothing, when a sudden lapse of consciousness and an unexpected movement, at around 2.45 p.m., brought the sad scene to an end without the patient being aware of his closeness to death.

Thus was extinguished a life most useful and dear to his family, to art, to his friends! His life was no more, but no force could extinguish a famous name and such unique virtues. The history of art will record elsewhere the name of Luigi Lablache. And everyone will mourn in him the loss of an illustrious Neapolitan artist, of a man of such generosity and talent! (The report continues): From the morning of the 26th of this month an extraordinary gathering of people came together around the mortuary house situated in the Strada Egiziaca at Pizzafalcone No.59, and this crowd, growing ever larger, flowed back along the streets through which the procession was to pass, while a gathering of men of science and letters, journalists and artists of every description and noble personages came together in the rooms of the deceased. There, before the body received its parochial blessing, two speeches were given, one by Theodore Cottrau, the other by Mons. Ferdinando Taglioni, and these we report here:

There follow two funeral orations, both flowery and ornate but of no particular interest, apart from the first, which states that Lablache was "the tender father of seven children" (of his thirteen children, the rest had died), and "it was the death of his wife a year and a half previously which so depressed him. He left the Seine, the Thames and the Neva to return to his native Siren((Naples))," and the second which mentions his modesty despite the honors, which were heaped upon him:

> Including that most solemn honour with which the Autocrat of Russia last July, in conferring upon him the title of Court Singer, had sent him a golden medallion, encrusted with splendid diamonds, the same one that you see shining upon his breast worn around his neck with the ribbon of the Order of St. Andrew.

Then follows a description of the funeral procession of monks and more than a thousand people dressed in mourning:

> Preceded by the sorrowing nephew Lucio Della Marra, other notables including the choreographer Salvatore Taglioni, the singers Antonucci, Coliva, Montanaro and composor Vincenzo Fioravanti. More than forty carriages completed the lengthy funeral procession . . . the cortege followed the body to Camposanto from where it was taken to the Capella for the solemn funeral service. Here the coffin was opened for the last blessing upon the body: and while the friars intoned the Libera the lips of the deceased fell open, as a result of the movement caused by the carrying of the coffin up the steps, as if he had wished to let forth a last song; those standing around were all most impressed by such a strange incident and burst into copious tears in saying their last farewells

to the friend whom they would see no more. A rain of flowers inundated the coffin and our own illustrious Mercadante (and this is the greatest honour done to the deceased) placed upon his head a wreath of myrtle . . . it was arranged that they should take a photographic image of him and from it make a death mask to provide a true likeness of the deceased for the worthy scalpel of the honoured Cavaliere Angelini, who will execute a bust to be placed upon his monument at the Camposanto in Naples.

Finally, they announced that the Royal College of Music, etc., will prepare a performance of Mozart's Requiem in Lablache's honor. We cannot close this account of his death without bringing back the following verses dictated by the maestro Vincenzo Fioravanti. Lablache as singer and Fioravanti as composer made their debut in the same opera. The notes of the *Bella Molinara* were the first written by Fioravanti and the first sung by Lablache. Now the composer celebrates in verse the death of the singer. There follows two verses of the song:

> Treme la morte al venerrando aspetto
> Del gran cantor cho tutti vinse in arte:
> Ritrasse il colpe dall'erculeo pette,
> E iacerta dell'oprar, stette in disparte
> E fra se disse da terror eolpita:
> Come! . . . troncar degg'io si bella vita!
>
> Ma l'Angelo di Dio ver lei si mosso,
> Eh stolta, disse, il colpc a che rattieni?
> Troppo la terra un tanto onor riscosse
> In Cielo ei goda giorni piu sereni,
> Morie vibro la cruda falce, e intanto
> Noi non possiam, che tributargli il pianto.

Dr. Camillo Golia remarked during the commemorative eulogy:

> The man we lost belongs to musical history, and all practitioners of the Art know what a void has been left upon his departure. The pages of honours and the praise are not negated today, nor will they be in the future years, as long as the splendor of Italian melody survives, like the rays of sunlight will warm the innermost fibers of our being.

On the 13 February, *L'Illustration Journal Universel* of Paris wrote an obituary on Lablache; here, Marc-Monnier gives us a firsthand report from Naples written on the 30 January. It is much the same as the other reports, but we find a few more names of interest from Naples: "La biere fut portee a bras, de la chambre au char funebre, par les premiers artists de Naples: le sculpteur Angelini, les peintres Smargiassi et d'Auria, le chanteur Coletti, le comedien Majeroni." Later from Paris on 20 February 1858, on page 187 from the *Illustrated London News*, comes the news of the Paris funeral:

> Today the remains of Lablache are consigned to the tomb. The funeral takes place in Paris, the body, after having been embalmed has been brought back in order to be laid in the family vault at Maisons-sur-Seine (Maisons-Laffitte) which he had built for his wife. The interment is to be preceded by a great funeral service in the church of the Madeleine, attended by the chief literary and artistic celebrities in Paris. His eldest son Frédéric Lablache, who has been for some time in Paris returns immediately to England after the funeral. Her Majesty has shown her regards for the memory of her old vocal instructor by kind expressions of regret and condolences to the family. (Letter from Mme Balsan).

The foreign and colonial news on 27 February 1858 in *Illustrated London News* (page 202). From Paris, Thursday, the newspaper reported that on Saturday, the funeral of Lablache took place at the Madeleine. "It was attended by a crowd of people of all descriptions, among others, Rossini, to whom Lablache had sent a case of macaroni a few days before his death . . . The *Requiem Mass* of Mozart was indifferently sung by the artistes of the Italian opera." Another newspaper gives us much more details about his last hours and burial:

> He died of a bronchitis, contracted in Russia during his last engagement. He was attended in his last illness by an old comrade he found in Naples, under the habit of a Dominican friar (Berardo Winter). This opera singer, who had sung frequently with Lablache, quitted the world in despair upon losing his whole family in a few days time by the cholera. During the last hour Lablache found his voice suddenly fail him. He called his daughter Francesca to him and said: "Cecchina, my voice is gone, I'm dying." He was soon afterwards a corpse. The artists of Naples bore his coffin from the

chamber to the hearse, and from the hearse to the vault where it was temporarily placed, that no mercenary hands might touch it. The coffin was opened at the grave yard, and remained open while the last offices of the Church were performed. Just before it was placed in the vault, Mercadante laid a crown of amaranths upon it. Lablache, whose remains were brought to Paris from Naples, was buried February 20th. A grand funeral service was performed at the Madeleine, which was entirely filled with mourners and spectators. Rossini was present. The *Requiem* of Mozart was performed in accordance with the wish expressed by Lablache shortly before he died—a wish recorded, it is said, in his will. The orchestra and chorus of the Italian Opera, reinforced by a number of choristers from the Grand Opera, under the direction of M. Dietsch, had assembled to perform the master piece of the immortal German. The *soli* were sung by Mario, Tamburini, Angelini, Belart, and Mesdames Giulia Grisi, Alboni, Nantier-Didiee and Wilhorst. It was remarked that the *Requiem* of Mozart had not been performed in Paris since the day of the obsequies of Chopin, the celebrated pianist, were performed, in the same church, in November, of 1849, on which occasion Lablache sang, for the last time, the part of basso-solo. M. l'Abbe Deguerry alluded to this circumstance in the funeral oration which he pronounced over the remains of the lamented singer, adding the following interesting particulars: The *Requiem* sung on that occasion (the funeral of Chopin) impressed me far more than it had ever done before; never had my heart felt so intensely the touching melancholy of that exquisite funeral prayer. I learned afterwards that the singer was Lablache, and I could not refrain from expressing to him my warm admiration and the more than usually great impression the *Requiem* had made on me. "Perhaps those you had hitherto heard sing it lacked a quality I am happy to say I possess," said Lablache, 'and that is Faith! faith, which I beg you to believe, M. Le Cure, I possess." I have nothing to add to such a declaration,' said the orator. The chief reason of Lablache's request to have the *Requiem* performed at his funeral is said to have proceeded from a feeling of grateful reminiscence. It was in 1816 that Paisiello died in Naples, and, to honour his memory, the artists of the Theatre of San Carlo performed the *Requiem* of Mozart at his funeral. Lablache, who had hitherto remained unknown to fame, took a part in the celebration, and in the *Tuba Mirum* his magnificent voice obtained the most complete success—a success that decided his prosperity for life. As he left the church, he was engaged by the judicious impresario Barbaja, and from that day *the basso cantante*, of one-and-twenty, had but Galli and Remorini as rivals throughout Italy.

Indeed, it could be noted that Lablache had sung Mozart's Requiem Mass for the funerals and memorial services of six of the world's greatest men of the last century: Haydn's memorial service in Naples; Paisiello in Naples; Beethoven in Vienna; Bellini in Paris; Napoleon's reburial in Paris; and last but not least, for Chopin's funeral. Lablache loved Mozart and held the *Requiem* close to his heart. Was the *Requiem* performed at his wife or his daughter's funeral? On 27 February 1858, *The Musical World* quoted from the Paris based *La France Musical* in which the title is "Funeral Service of Lablache":

The church of the Madeleine was opened this day (Sunday) for a sad and pious ceremony. Vast as it was, it was filled in every part. Dead or living, Lablache had the power to attract a crowd; living his admirers congregated to applaud his exceptional talent; dead, his compatriots and friends united to render the last honors to him. It was because his moral qualities rivalled his merits as an artist, and would have eclipsed them if his merits had not been immense; his heart was equal to his brain; the man marched on a par with the musician.

French by descent, born at Naples, Lablache met his death in the city where he first saw the light, and where he commenced very modestly that career soon to become so brilliant. He returned thither to recruit his strength in the pure and balmy air of those benignant shores where the same sun makes the rose and the citron bloom. Alas, it was too late. The land which gave him his cradle, and which had been the Theatre of his first, his most splendid triumphs, offered this time to the illustrious emigrant a tomb only! . . . I am wrong—it offered him also a treasure of the dearest and most moving recollections; they encountered him on his arrival, as the friends of his infancy; recollections and friends pressed in crowds upon his heart, and seemed to say to him:—We knew well that you would return! Why did you ever leave us? Could you have been more loved and admired elsewhere than here? Have you, in your numerous peregrinations, beheld a more beautiful county, a sky more azure, an air more pure and healthy? You quitted us in the pride and power of manhood, and return to us overcome, worn out, and suffering! And Lablache smiled sadly at these remembrances, so dear at the time, and so poignant, and pressed with tenderness the hands which for so long a time awaited his grasp. But he did not forget, when dying, what a part of himself was here; that he had made a promise to his family; to his children, to return; that here, at some leagues from Paris, slept under a cluster of willows, the sweet companion of his life—a wife with the heart of an angel, who had always blended into one sentiment friendship, devotion, and love. He expressed then the desire, the wish rather, to come and repose beside that excellent wife, that affectionate mother, in the same vault, under the same stone—under the same willows which let fall their nightly tears. Naples was stricken with grief at the cruel loss. She bestowed on Lablache the most solemn obsequies. She put on, as it were, a national mourning. All that the city could boast of artist, musicians, poets, men of heart and talent—with which it is so richly furnished—assembled round his bier. Discourses were pronounced over him which sounded like sobs. We sadly envied the city its doleful privileges; but when we learned the last wish of the celebrated artist—when we were told that we, in our turn, would be permitted to surround his bier, to scatter, likewise, flowers upon his tomb, a sentiment of finer satisfaction was mingled with our sorrow. All the lyric artists of Paris eagerly responded to the appeal made to their affection in the name of their ancient and illustrious comrade. All the managers of the musical theatres consented to allow their artists to pay a last adieu to Lablache. If one exception had been found, the singers would have braved the strange prohibition, enforced by a high and powerful will. Five hundred executants, vocalists, and instrumentalists assisted. After the mass, they performed Mozart's beautiful *Requiem*, that sad and fatal hymn so mysteriously connected with the death and immortality of the young German composer. We name no artist; we speak of all; there may be hierarchies for talent; there are none for the heart; and all fulfilled with their hearts the pious duty.

The ceremony finished, the body of Lablache was transported to Maisons-Laffitte, to be interred in the family vault. An immense crowd followed. The cords of the pall were held by the Prince

Poniatowski and M. San Giacomo, M. the Baron Taylor, and M. the Commander Carafa. We have lost in Lablache the master, the artist, the friend.

What is unclear in these articles is exactly what Lablache died of as they tend to contradict each other. Most often it was considered indelicate to mention the cause of death in the newspapers, but the fact that Lablache was so famous, several causes were given owing to great public interest. Here, we have a professional diagnosis, which can only be based on the sketchy information from the newspaper reports (Dr. Stephen Stanley-Little):

> Allowing for the old-fashioned medical terminology and descriptions, which are a bit impressionistic in the article (Naples obituary) that he died of heart failure (dropsy in old-fashioned terms) brought on by a combination of bronchitis and obesity. His terminal symptoms of acute breathlessness and panic, plus irregular slow pulse are highly characteristic of that condition. It is less clear what the cause of the leg ulcers (sores) would be—but they are very common with varicose veins, and also with chronic edema (swelling of the legs) which may result in heart failure—but gross obesity would very much contribute to varicosities and poor circulation.

As yet we don't have his death certificate. In the first reports of his ill health while in Russia, the newspapers wrote that he had had an "attack of paralysis," which more than often has been known to describe a stroke or would describe a condition closely associated with a stroke. So it was generally thought he had suffered a stroke, but it also could have been a heart attack. The *Athenaeum* writes on 6 March: only two of Lablache's old comrades are left to sing Mozart's *Requiem* for him at the solemn service the other day performed at La Madeleine, these being Mme. Grisi and Signor Tamburini; the other artists were Mmes. Alboni, Saint-Urban, Nantier-Didiee, Signore Mario, Angelini and Graziani.

From *The Musical World* on the death of Lablache February 1858:

> Another of the demigods has passed away; another genuine artistic glory is extinct. On Saturday the patriarch of the Italian stage—"notre pere a tou," as his compatriots reverently styled

him—died of dropsy, at Naples. Lablache has gone to join Rachel in a better world. The death of a great dramatic artist, whose genius and physiognomy have long been familiar to the public, leaves a void that cannot be filled up during the lifetime of the actual generation. He may be replaced by another in his best parts, and even efficiently replaced; but it is not enough for those who, accustomed to the first model, have become past worshippers out of pure affection. Which among ourselves could tolerate another Dr. Bartolo, another Don Pasquale, another Don Magnifico, after having seen Lablache, who identified himself with these characters and made them his own! What other face, what other figure, what other voice, what other talent, would be accepted by the present race of opera frequenters? Or would substitute, for his? Nor is there anything unnatural or unjust in this predilection for long established types; on the contrary, it is honourable to humanity, since it represents gratitude for favors conferred, and shows that the public, after all, is not so unfeeling and utterly heartless an animal as certain persons have endeavored to paint it.

Of all the lyrics artists that ever came from Italy to England, Lablache was, beyond comparison, the most popular. We make no exception. By popular, of course we do not intend the most "attractive," even the uninitiated being aware that a bass, no matter what his merits, can never by any chance expect to rival a soprano or a tenor in the eyes of managers of Italian theatres, or in direct influence upon the paying public. As in a novel, or a play, so in an opera—the hero and heroine are the personages that absorb the greatest amount of interest; and the hero and heroine being, in most operatic representations, impersonated by the tenor and soprano, it is not at all surprising that they should bear away the palm in the estimation of the crowd. An indigent parent, a deep scheming villain, a deposed monarch, a rabid priest, a besotted magistrate, an eccentric charlatan, has no chance, in the long run, against the Romeo or the Juliet of the stereotyped lyric drama. And this is quite independent of the peculiar spell which the highest voices, both in the male and female register, have exercised, exercise, and must always exercise, upon the sympathy of the masses—just as, without knowing why, nine persons out of ten, who listen to a quartet for string instruments, will award all, or nearly all, the merit of the execution to the first fiddle. The popularity which—in common with all who have watched the progress of Italian opera in this country, during the last quarter of a century—we have adjudged to Lablache is, therefore, apart from such considerations. He was a man of such genuis, thoroughly original, a consummate artist, and endowed with an idiosyncracy, both personal and mental, that separated him from his compeers, and enabled him to set his mark upon everything he took in hand. Early familiarity with the public grew at length into a sort of intimate confidence between the actor and his patrons; and this reached such a point, that, instead of undergoing the ordeal of criticism, in common with his fellow artists, Lablache was accepted by the opera patrons as a sort of brother Aristarchus before the footlights, sharing with them whatever opinions, favorable or hostile, the performance might elicit. If Grisi, Sontag, or Jenny Lind sang well, Lablache and the audience would simultaneously declare their approval; if things went slovenly or ill, Lablache (invariably, and seldom otherwise than deservedly, held blameless) would convey—by a shrug, or a wink, both eloquent and unmistakable—how entirely he coincided with the audience in their smothered or openly manifested expressions of dissent.

No actor "filled the stage" more entirely than Lablache; and this not so much because his frame was colossal, as because he was born an actor, and the stage was his element. How dignified his deportment in tragedy—how easy and graceful in comedy—how unrestrained, intensely humorous (and, even when most exaggerated, never verging on licentiousness) in farce!

This poem's original is written in Italian and belongs to the late Mme. Balsan's heirs in Paris.

> Lablache. vous etiez le dieu de l'harmonie; Vous avez sur le front le signe du genie; Vous n'avez un contre, ni rivaux, ni jaloux, Devant votre aureole et durant trente annees Les gloires d'ici-bas, les tetes couronnees Ont fait avec amour cortege autour de vous.

> Par l'esprit ou le gout, la parole ou la lyre, Partout ou vous etiez s'imposait votre empire; Vous aviez la puissance et vous aviez la Foi! De l'humaine raison vous etiez le grand livre; Dan vos rayonnements chacun eut aime vivre, Le chant vous faisait Dieu, l'Esprit vous faisait Roi!

One of Lablache's sisters, abbess of a covent at Sessa, survives him.[683] Florimo writes Michele Baldacchini dedicated this lovely *epigrafe*:

> *Luigi Lablache sommo nell'arte del canto e nelle sceniche imitazione delizio con la sua voce l'europa interpetrando egregiamente I modi de' solenni maestri e dilatando in piu ampio gio la gloria musicale d'italia aggirantesi nelle corti e nelle aule de' grandi fu de' miseri soccoritore pietoso caro a' parenti e agli amici d' indole conversevole bel parlatore morte di sessantatre+ anni la sua perdita fu reputata acerba per l'arte irreparabile da tutti compianta spargete di fiore il tumole dell' ottimo artista benefico.*[684]

༄༄༄

Chapter Thirty-Five

Remembrance

Luigi Lablache received many honors, medals, and diplomas from all the Musical Academies of Europe. Florimo writes, "He wrote several instructional books about singing, *Metodo di canto.*" (Method of Singing). Some were put together and coauthored in different languages. The French copy, *Méthode compléte de chant,* possibly was the first to emerge; however, all continue to bear the name of Lablache.

The *Méthode* sold well in England, America, France, Germany, and Italy (Milan). Several American editions were published in New York, Boston, and Chicago. There were many translations and publications after Lablache died. The first publication in French is dated 1841, another in 1844 (published again in 1850, 1859, 1860, 1869). There were also *Exercises*, translated from the French, a complete method of singing with examples for illustration and progressive vocalizing exercises by Louis Lablache (O. Ditson 1850, p. 102). Of these many versions that exist, some have been shortened and revised. Other lessons have been added to some versions, and some have been written for not only the bass voice but for soprano and tenor. Florimo may have been confused since there seem to be at least two or more totally different publications of the *Méthode compléte de chant.*[685] In 1843, we find another: Lablache's *Singing Tutor, for a Bass Voice* published by Chappell. This is a review from *The Musical World*:

> The name of the author is enough for this treatise, and it by no means discredits its august paternity. Lablache's *Singing Tutor* in all respects is the best *Singing Tutor* that ever came under our notice—the most complete, the most simple, the most clear, and, at the same time, the most comprehensive . . . Whatever Lablache attempts, he effects well, and he has effected *nothing* better than this.[686]

An incomplete listing of Lablache's lessons and exercises was published by F. Pazdirek, publications 1900-1910 (see appendix).[687]

Lablache taught singing whenever he could fit in students and always took a lively interest in his pupils and in turn never forgot to visit his teachers at the college in Naples. His sons Frédéric and Nicola, both were professors of music. His daughter-in-law Frances (Fanny) Lablache, and later his daughter, Marie de Caters, became the singing teacher of Queen Victoria's daughter Beatrice. (it is unknown if she had a degree.) Florimo often related the following:

> Lablache enjoyed telling his students how he was taught, and how one should always follow the old techniques handed down from the old masters. He advised people to: "Sol-fa (*solfeggiare*), sol-fa and always sol-fa." In fact under the direction of this conscientious and expert artist he obtained splendid results.

The young Neapolitan Tito Mattei was an amazing pianist and a pupil of Lablache and Sigismund Thalberg. He gave his first concert in Naples in 1846 when he was only five. At age eleven, in 1852, he was give the honor of *professore* of the Accademia Nazionale di Santa Cecilia, Rome.

> One day Tito Mattei was being shown off before Lablache, who had just come to settle in Naples, in 1846. Tito was about five at the time. Suddenly the great basso turned to him, and carelessly booming a note from his huge chest, asked, "What note is that, Tito?" "It is out of tune," the child answered, "it is neither A flat nor A natural." Lablache crossed the room to where the grand piano stood. He softly played A flat and A natural. The note he had sung was between the two. Taking the child on his knee, he embraced him, saying, "Tito, you are my master."

Later, Mattei was appointed pianist to the king of Italy.[688] Apparently, there was another singer who was not as talented as Tito—he was a cook who fancied he could sing:[689]

> The Countess of Cannazaro's cook was a worthy man, and probably far better chéf. He could not free himself, however, from the belief that he was a singer of the highest order, and that he

only needed a patron to enable him to gain high distinction in *the musical world*. Rubini heard of this, and, assisted by Lablache, arranged a meeting, so that the cook's singing powers might be fairly tested. No stone was left upturned which might conduce to the chéf's success. For accompanists, the leaders in the opera band were secured, and Costa even gave his services as conductor. It was a comical scene. There stood the neglected vocalist full of confidence, and in real earnest, but totally unconscious of the feelings of those around him, some of whom, like Lablache, were evidently splitting with suppressed humor. The result was just what was expected—a ridiculous failure; whereupon M. Le Chéf-de-cuisine was sent back to his kitchen with the advice to give up the idea of becoming a singer, and to devote himself instead to the greatest and most mysterious of all the arts—the art of cookery! It is a pity a good many more singers do not desert the stage for the kitchen, where a good "hash" might win them fame!

Florimo here continues,

When Lablache returned to Naples, often on the following day, he used to go to the College to visit the teacher, Perrella, as a sign of gratitude, and enjoyed repeating in front of the students who surrounded him (once I also was one of them!) the joke of Salerno and the famous carabineers, who although not very pleasant or amusing fellow travellers at the time, still remembered his famous escapade. On another occasion he visited a friend, Cioffi, an unfortunate musician who became a copyist because of necessity and used to cling to him all day long, receiving help, in many ways. One day Cioffi took out a snuff box to take out a pinch of tobacco. Lablache asked for it, went into another room and after his return gave it back to Cioffi warning him not to lose it. Cioffi did not understand anything and put it back in his pocket. Later after he returned home, one could imagine his surprise when opening the snuff box he found it full of gold coins. I heard him repeat this story often with tears of gratitude in his eyes for Luigi who was always ready to help.

The Musical World brings us under the title *Anecdotes of Madame Malibran*, Lablache and Malibran's charity from her *Memoirs* by the Countess de Merlin.

> One day a poor Italian refugee came to Lablache for assistance. He had received permission to return home, but, he was destitute. The next day at the rehearsal, Lablache broached the subject of the refugees' distress, and proposed a subscription. Madame Lablache, Donzelli and several others gave each two guineas. "And you, Marie," said Lablache, turning to Maria Malibran, "what will you give?" "The same as the rest," she answered carelessly, and went on practicing her part. With this money the charitable and kindhearted Lablache flew to secure his unfortunate countryman. The next morning Maria took an opportunity to speak to him alone. "Here's ten pounds more for your poor friend," said she, slipping a note into his hands; "I would not give more than the others yesterday, fearing they might think me ostentatious. Take it to him, but do not say a word about it to any one." Lablache joyfully hastened to the lodgings of the Italian refugee, but he had left. Undaunted, Lablache proceeded to the Tower-stairs. The vessel had pulled away, with his friend on board. He hailed a boat, and offered the boatman a large reward, if he would row after the vessel, and overtake her. He succeeded in doing so. Lablache went on board, and presented the welcome donation to the refugee, who, falling on his knees, poured forth a heartfelt prayer to Lablache and Malibran.

Florimo relates, "An adventure as later described by our witty poet Giulio Genoino and written in the splendid Neapolitan vernacular octaves, under the title: 'Ottavario ncoppa a na careta pe museca' and printed in the *Poliorama Pittoresco*." Lablache had a very benevolent disposition according to Florimo. The anecdotes about his generosity are abundant: *Il Cieco sonator di violino*.[690]

> During one of his many visits to Paris, he happened to see a poor old blind man, led by a little girl dressed in rags. The old man was attempting to scrape some harsh cords on a violin, the notes were badly out of tune, and at the same time he was singing with a feeble

voice, in order to earn some money to keep himself from starving. Once his song came to an end and his hat had gone round for alms he saw as usual all the audience slowly disappear and he managed to collect only a few cents. Lablache feeling very sorry for this poor wretch, with his usual compassionate nature, approached the blind man, gently removing from his hands the violin and started playing it. Who did not know Lablache in Paris? Everything changed. The crowd, including some very distinguished people, quickly gathered round him asking each other: "Is that Lablache playing?" The rumour spread like lightning throughout the near by streets, carriages stopped one after the other so that at the crossroads of four streets the traffic came to a standstill. When Lablache saw all this, he started singing Neapolitan songs; the cheers, the applause, the happy shouts rose to the sky. He himself deeply moved, took the blind man's hat and started going round asking politely, and graciously for help in favour of the poor man. Not one showed himself reluctant and they all put a coin in the hat. The takings were considerable and the newspapers said that the total amounted to several hundred francs. Lablache was above all others in his art. His noble face, his height in a certain way covered up his corpulence. Mother nature had been very generous with him: beautiful voice, relaxed, strong, flexible, capable of the most powerful effects, perfect talent and exquisite taste . . . Moreover the quality of his mind, his good education, his deep knowledge of music, finally his association with distinguished and elegant society produced one of the most satisfactory associations that one can find on the stage: As a man, he was very respectable, extremely honest both in his social relationships and in his affection for the arts. He was equally highly esteemed in his private life and in the Theatre. All these natural gifts made him unique and he was truly unique. As Ariosto used to say: "As soon as nature produces somebody out of the ordinary. the cast is destroyed."

One day, while I was in Paris, I went to visit Lablache. It was eleven in the morning and his servant, who knew me quite well, let me enter into the drawing room without announcing me. There I found Lablache seated at the piano singing the "recitatives" of Porpora. Seeing me, he said, "You have arrived just at the right time, dear Florimo. Come and listen to the miracles of art produced by our great *Maestros* who are nowadays profanely called old fogeys by the 'vandals' of music." He asked me to sit down and started to sing those recitatives which will always be the true models of great artistic value while music will last in the world. To hear Lablache sing Porpora's recitatives was really amazing both for the expression and the dramatic strength of the words. He transported people back to the purity of the old school when those masterpieces were created and with his inimitable art, he made people appreciate them more than any modern aria. Sung and recited by him, as a true jewel of elegance, wit and indescribable effect, because nature had endowed him with so much talent and good taste. His spontaneity and versatility for all types of music made him not only excellent in *opera seria* but equally good in *opera buffo*. In the latter he was unbeatable. He introduced pleasant jokes and used them with great effect. He understood the real character required by a performance of this kind, which may be very gay and full of verve, but its main purpose is not the ridicule and scurrility of clowns. With him, people listened to the *parlanti,* talking melodies, while the orchestra plays with the motives. And when he used a spontaneous sing song he did with great ability and love—nobody could forget a comic performance of that kind. Together with the famous Giulietta Pasta and the talented Malibran, he was the first in Italy to connect together the art of the singer and that of the actor. Lablache was, besides, one of the first innovators of the lyric opera. His listeners loved him because, in this form of art, nobody could match him. It was an influence so perfect and great that it spread from the banks of the Tiber to the Arno and Po. Amongst his many merits he could declaim the recitatives so that the well-known arias of many operas were very moving—these recitatives could be cited as noble examples of whoever composed and performed them. Whoever will read the pages of Scudo, Blaze, Fetis and Berlioz will see the neatly described nature and qualities of Lablache's musical genius. He was a rare man and three factors will send his name to posterity: the musical science, versatility and flexibility of talent and goodness of heart—these three qualities together contributed to his fame.

Florimo writes, "In this biography several facts that differ from others reported on Lablache."

> I advise you that whatever is narrated here is authentic and confirmed by many conversations I had with the singer. As I could not remember everything, I approached one of his daughters, Signora Francesca Lablache, the widow of Sigismund Thalberg, living in Naples who very kindly has helped me. Further information was very graciously given to me by highly esteemed people, belonging to the high nobility, many still living.

Finally, he availed himself of a collection of prose and poems entitled, "Onori alla memoria di Luigi Lablache."

Here, we look into what happened to the huge estate of Luigi Lablache. At first guessing that Lablache might have died intestate, Brian Meringo comments,[691] "Under French law the estate must be divided up between the children and other family members in given proportions. It is not the eldest son who inherits, as in England. This would make an auction necessary to be able to divide the money in the legal proportions." The catalog of the Paris auction held at Salle Dronot on May 1, 3, 4, and 5, 1858, is among the belongings of the Balsan family in Neuilly near Paris. Not known if there was a will without costly research in Paris, we have a few facts.

On these dates, 352 items of the huge estate of Luigi Lablache were put up for auction. This may have been according to his directions in a will. No will has been seen at this date. But mention of a will was referred to on more than one occasion. The estate was under the supervision of the family *notaire* Roquebert, and the lengthy records have all been kept to the present day in the Library National in Paris.[692] At this auction, item after item was catalogued and described in detail, listed under each room, going from the lower to upper part of the house including the attics. The famous collection of over 350 snuffboxes and a Veronese painting *Jesus an banquet du pharisien* were sold. A good many, if not all, of the snuffboxes turned up later in the Wallace museum collection of London.[693]

> Catalogue de belles tabatieres, brillants, argenterie anglaise et objects de curiosite, matieres premieres, bronzes d'art, porcelaines anciennes, de Sevres, de Saxe, de Chine et du Japon montees et non-montees. Bronzes meublantes, membles anciens et modernes.

Today, the house looks much the same as in the last century though rather neglected. Facing Rue Albine, No. 39 lies concealed behind a facade of huge horse-chestnut trees and two heavy rusty iron gates. Flacked by large houses on either side, Rue Abine leads straight up to the old chateau of Maisons Laffette and is part of the huge estate of "parc Maisons Laffette." Tall and imposing with a dusty circular carriageway sweeping past the front entrance, the facade faintly resembles Rossini's house at Passy. All the French windows have peeling shutters, but the statues, either side of the front entrance, give a friendly welcome; and we enter into a tiled vestibule with a large staircase on the left. Before us, through heavy wood-paneled double doors is the main salon, or *salle*, to the center of the house, featuring double glass french doors that open onto a wonderful rear garden flanked either side with massive trees. Among the central group, a beech tree with red leaves shimmers in the sunlight. Inside the main rooms, the paint is peeling off the walls and the parquet floors sadly need a stain. Adjacent to the lovely central salon, double doors open into two side salons, exposing light-filled airy rooms, each with its own fireplace. Down a spiral staircase, we reach a subterranean level. Here, the kitchens look much the same as in the 1850s: huge iron lids cover log-burning stoves that were manned by servants. To the right of the kitchen, wood was stored (wood is still there). A coal storage room for the furnace, a servants' dining room, larders, storage rooms, and lavish wine cellars. On the next level above the grand salon is the grand master bedroom, and what a size it is! The archive must have housed a massive four-poster bed; the massive Lablache would have looked straight out through the french windows onto a beautiful garden. Three large side bedrooms and two dressing rooms are adjacent to the master bedroom. A huge broken-down bathroom lurks, decayed and unused behind locked doors. High up above are considerable attics where the servants were quartered. Ample linen closets line the ironing room, the present owner explained.

Mme. Lablache's vegetable garden lies to the front of the large Swiss cottage, about a two hundred feet from the main house. Behind are stables and a small orchard. On both sides of the cottage, climbing grapevines cascade through the broken panes of glass that once housed luscious tropical plants encased in an opulent greenhouse. Facing high surrounding hedges and chestnut trees is a rock fountain of huge proportions and a fishpond.[694] (The Maisons Laffette house has been listed In "Inscrit aux monuments Historique." French Ministry of Culture).

ಆಆಆ

Chapter Thirty-six

The Thalbergs

At the time of Lablache's death, the family estate consisted of at least four different addresses. Besides the newly built mansion at Maisons-Laffitte and his apartment in central Paris (where Dominique lived), there was his house in London, 51 Albany Street, and a town house in Naples in the Pizzafalcone neighborhood. The house was on the Riviera di Chiaia, near where he was born, and most likely still belonged to the family. The large villa outside of Naples at Posillipo near Capo di Posillipo on the Via Posillipo was outside the city and became his country home.

Precariously perched on the crest of a hill, the villa overlooks the whole gulf of Naples. Facing the island of Capri and Sorrento to the south and Naples and Mount Vesuvius to the east (left), the view to the west is no less spectacular, the view of Pozzuoli. Pozzuoli lies in the gateway to the Phlegraean Fields (*porta dei Campi flegrei*), a district to the west of Posillipo known from time immemorial as the scene of tremendous volcanic activity.[695]

Francesca and Sigismund Thalberg continued to live on at the Lablache villa (now the villa Thalberg) after Lablache's death. Francesca may have resented her husband's career as it took him away from her so much. Why did she not go with him? Did she become lonely without children in the huge Italian villa by herself? In the late spring of 1858 she followed him all the way to New York demanding to see him. Upon hearing from her, he canceled his concert tours and rushed to her side. Rumors spread like wildfire. Did she accuse him of having an affair? Was it the daughter of Elena D'Angri? It looked that way. Some said it was Mme. D'Angri, also married at that time.

Still a mystery, family history records that Thalberg had an affair with one of the daughters of his touring companion, beautiful Greek soprano Elena D'Angri. Later, in 1875, a young soprano surfaces in London at Covent Garden. Her stage name, Zaré Thalberg, was derived from her given name, Nazarena McKenzie. Her mother was Mme. Mathilde McKenzie, the daughter of Elena D'Angri.[696]

The London Graphic, on April 10, 1875, reveals:

> She was born in New York on the 16th of April 1858 . . . the young lady was carefully educated by Madame Elena D'Angri and her husband Signor Pedro de Abella from Spain. Madame D'Angri was singing in *Il Trovatore* on 6 January, at the New York Academy's Gala night and sang at Niblo's salon in a grand concert on the 5 January 1858, while Thalberg played at the New York Academy.

Zaré Thalberg grew up to be a charming young lady and chose London to launch her operatic career. Hired by Gye, she was greeted with great admiration upon her Covent Garden debut in April 1875 as Zerlina in *Don Giovanni.* One of the most authoritative accounts of Thalberg's career and life was written by Louis Engel in his book *From Mozart to Mario*; there, he mentions Zaré:

> He left a daughter by Italian singer, Mlle D'Angri, who resembled him, and who broke what seemed to be a promising career as a prima donna by singing too early and straining her voice in parts too high for her tessitura, both common faults with Victorian singers, who were always too anxious to reap before they had sown, and fancied that screaming high notes to elicit injudicious applause was all that was required to make them famous.

Did she change her name? Another dictionary writes, "She was a pupil of Thalberg's who took his name is entirely false."[697] After leaving Covent Garden, she joined her grandmother, Mme. D'Angri, in Spain. Mme. D'Angri sings again *Il Trovatore* in Madrid shortly afterward she retired. From there on, we lose sight of her, yet the beauty of her face haunts one's memory—her sweet image smiles from the pages of the *Graphic* and her photo has stayed in its place next to Thalberg's in the tattered old Lablache family photo album ever since the 1870s over a hundred years ago. Zazarena Mckenzie married into nobility and had five children in Naples. Renato, her son, was father to Nobili Francesca Pulci-Dora, who married Don Vincenzo Ferrara Pignatelli, Prince di Strongoli. The actual piano Thalberg played still belongs to the princess. And is proudly displayed in her home. She was kind enough to show it to the author and various other guests.

There is a question about Thalberg's other children. Around 1840, before Thalberg married Francesca he intimates in letters written to conductor Julius

Benedict (Collection Daniel L. Hitchcock) that he has fathered at least two illegitimate children in Paris, one he identifies as "my boy" . . . and then hints about his various affairs before marriage.

Apparently, shortly after Thalberg's last American tour in 1858, he retired with his wife to the Lablache villa near Posillipo, there to enjoy a happy existence in seclusion, pursuing the career of a gentleman winegrower like Lablache. Vincenzo Vitale writes about life then in Posillipo in *Sigismundo Thalberg a Posillipo.*[698]

> Posillipo—a hill by the sea, praised in poetry and song, where Vedio Pollone and Lucullus, wealthy bourgeois Neapolitans, maintained splendid homes among the rich greenery of the parks, the orangeries and the pine groves. Posillipo, the Grecian Pausiliplon (the place where pain is suspended) has almost disappeared nowadays under squalid boxes called townhouses, themselves dwarfed in turn by enormous 'falansteri,' so-called buildings for civilian homes. Even today, however, in certain corners which have survived the general desolation of the area, one can evoke the memory of what was one of the most famous and delightful places in the world.
>
> Among the surviving houses, there is one which beautifully resists the pressure of construction companies, even if now it is being threatened by support walls and cooperative housing (the so-called little palaces, with the grotesque use of the diminutive): the house which was first owned by Luigi Lablache and then by Thalberg. Luigi Lablache had lived there during brief holidays, and when—stricken by a serious illness—he was obliged to leave Paris. This also was not a very long visit. Settled in his town house on the Riviera di Chiaia,[699] (very close to the Piazza Principe di Napoli), he died there in 1858.
>
> The Posillipo house, put up for sale in the same year,[700] was bought (in auction) by Sigismund Thalberg.[701] He married Lablache's daughter Francesca in London, widow of the well-known painter Francois Bouchot. Both of them wanted the house to stay in the family, since it had been a place close to the heart of "Papa Lablache."
>
> Here Thalberg found a relaxing pause from the intensity of concert life. A keen winegrower, Posillipo was for him a perfect testing ground. The grapevines which enhanced the slopes around

the house attracted him in more ways than one judging by the description that Lablache, also a winegrower, gave him in Rossini's house at Passy. He had brought with him from France a few vine-cuttings, certain that they would do well in the Neapolitan sunshine. He looked after them with loving care, creating a magnificent vineyard and, after several years, even exquisite wine. Introducing it to Paris in 1867, he apparently won prizes there.[702] He left the house only for a few months to give concerts in London, Paris and Brazil, always returning to it with joy, and when his career required him unavoidably to go elsewhere, he tried to stay away as little as possible from his family and his favourite pastime—taking care of the vineyard.

This villa is on the hilltop, and occupies a splendid position overlooking the gulf, on a promontory which even today is called "Thalberg Heights." (Before Lablache bought the villa from French painter Anton Charles Horace Vernet 1789-1835). Here, as well as in the rooms where he had assembled the trophies of his successful concert tours, he gave receptions for Neapolitan celebrities from culture and the arts. In Naples, the exciting musical evenings of Paris blossomed once more, during which (in Zimmerman's drawingroom of all places) Thalberg aroused the unbounded admiration of those who heard his *Fantasy on a Theme from Mosè in Egitto*, Op. 33. And if this were not enough, he demonstrated his artistic accomplishments by performing sonatas by Mozart, Clementi and Beethoven, as well as his own compositions, the Pensees musicales and *Les soirées de Pausilippe* . . . and in the meantime he happened to establish his reputation and justify himself in Neapolitan eyes by bringing out two of his scholarly editions: Bach's *Well-Tempered Clavier*, and the *Gradus ad Parnassum* by Fux, published by Giraud's Partenopeo musicale, which would already be a sufficient reason to rectify the criticism of his taste, his limitations, and the scarcity of his historical knowledge.

Among the more frequent visitors to the Thalberg home was the Marquis Domenico Tupputi, a gentleman who cultivated music and organized artistic events. He wanted to increase the prestige of the piano school at the Conservatory San Pietro di Majella through the presence of the great Genevan virtuoso on the faculty of that institute. He consequently became the secret promoter of a plan to have the Royal Musical College extend an invitation to Sigismund Thalberg. but on the official resolution of the teaching staff this proposal was turned down. A directive in the school regulations forbade access to the "sancta sanctorum" conservatory by foreign musicians . . ." Other deeper reasons prevented the great Thalberg from becoming a part of the teaching faculty at San Pietro a Majella. Those reasons, as is human, were jealousy and envy. But the name of Thalberg remained "above the crowd," even if it was never seen in the register of teachers. And he who accepted gifts from sovereigns and princes—turquoise, amethysts, diamonds, rings, carpets, slippers from the harem, golden hand-wrought cups, tobacco boxs, brooches covered with diamonds—he refused the gift which the Conservatory decided to give him in 1865, offering him a position which they previously denied him.

While cultivating the tiered vineyards where Lablache once wandered, he had time enough to enlarge the cellars.

Occasionally, he could be persuaded to come out of retirement to play, but he had made all the money he could ever spend and by then, he didn't even play in public anymore. Wilhelm Kuhe once asked Thalberg why he stopped composing. "Alas!" said Thalberg. "My imitators have made me impossible."[703] The critic from *La Revue et Gazette Musicale* writes about Thalberg's last solo concert in London, translated for *Dwight's Journal of Music,* Boston:[704]

> We all knew that he could not grow any further, but he remains as he was—and this is good enough—the incomparable pianist, who first lent a voice to the keys, who has discovered in the piano effects unknown before him; the artist who has revealed a new law, who has been imitated in a hundred fashions, equalled in none. Nobody, in fact, has been so much imitated; his manner has been parodied, exaggerated, twisted tortured, and it may have happened more than once to all of us to curse this Thalbergian school, which overwhelmed us with such an avalanche of notes and arpeggios above and below, with commonly not the least particle of song in the middle. The apostles have altered the word of the master. But when one comes back to the source he is reconciled and prostrates himself anew, as he did twenty years ago, in the time of youth and enthusiasm. Besides, how admirably the external advantages of

Thalberg suit the taste of good English society! That self-possessed and easy attitude, that air *de bon ton*, that Olympian calmness, that benevolent physiognomy, joined to a tranquility of head and body which makes you doubt if it be really his own fingers that execute these prodigies! It would be difficult to say which of the pieces was the most applauded. Among the new compositions it was perhaps the *Ballade*, a piece entirely Thalbergian, a ravishing *bijou*, yet not more ravishing than the old pieces of the great pianist. The fact is, Thalberg is the chief of a school, a seeker, but one who at the first stroke has attained perfection; and his *Etude* in A, his *Tremolo*, his Fantasia on *Moïse* and on *Don Juan* will eternally remain models of their kind, just as the first products of the art of printing are to this day the most precious. Among the old pieces, next to the *Don Juan* fantasia, "Home, Sweet Home" seems to have most transported the audience.

Vicenzo Vitale describes his end: "A lung disease which affected Thalberg over a period of weeks led to his death on 27 April 1871. The honors that were paid him will remain among the most imaginable in the golden century funeral rhetoric." However, strange events preceded the actual burial in the cemetery of Naples.

After he died, he continued to make a strange appearances every evening at the villa Thalberg, but without the same applause. His wife had him embalmed and stuffed and placed in a glass coffin propped up against the wall in the drawing room. Before dinner was served, he was carefully removed, resplendent in full evening attire, including his diamond studs, cufflinks, and white gloves and placed sitting upright in his usual place at the head of the table to the displeasure of her guests. For how long this continued was anyone's guess. Eventually, this behavior came to the attention of the Naples police. They called on Mme. Thalberg and very firmly told her that her husband must be buried properly forthwith:[705]

Naples.—The body of Thalberg has been restored to the deseased's widow, by professor Efisio Marini, who was charged with the task of embalming it, and who has been wonderfully successful. "There is," we are told, "nothing of the mummy about the body, while there is a great deal of the living individual. The tissues are intact; the flexibility of the limbs has been preserved; the fat has not disappeared; the hands look alive; the face has a stony appearance, but is instantly recognizable, the rest of the body resembles leather in substance, in colour, it is like the flesh of a fowl, when the bird has been killed an hour or so." We agree with the *Gazetta di Milano* that the journal whence this account was taken might have found some other comparison not quite so faithful as the concluding one.[706]

Another source says that Thalberg was kept in a barrel of alcohol before the embalming. One tends to wonder if he had a funeral. Was this common behavior in the nineteenth century? Thalberg's burial mausoleum was on a huge scale and would have taken months to build. When the Italian Princess Christina Belgiojoso departed for Asia Minor, a sensational discovery was made by the Austrian police at her villa. Tucked away in a wardrobe in her private apartments, they found the fully clothed embalmed corpse of a young man dressed in black. This gruesome affair created a scandal that was transmitted from Milan to the salons of Paris, and one could readily imagine that the lurid details of this discovery became the topic of many conversations. Her biographer Barbiera tells us some details:[707]

> The body was immediately recognized as that of one Gaetano Stelzi, a young collaborator of the Princess's on her periodical, the *Crociato,* and as such, a frequent visitor at her house both in Milan and in the country. But according to the parish registers, Stelzi was buried in the churchyard of Locate, where he had been laid to rest in the presence of numerous witnesses on June 19, 1848! Yet there was no mistaking the identity of the corpse which confronted the terrified spectators, for it was carefully embalmed and in perfect preservation. An immediate investigation of the grave disclosed the fact that the coffin buried there contained only a heavy log of wood . . . the mystery attached to the secret transfer of the corpse to a cupboard in her villa, and to the sham funeral services held over a bit of timber, has never been solved. Barbiera evokes the memory of Spanish "Crazy Jane," who kept ever with her the remains of her well-beloved Philippe le Bel.[708]

Then comes to mind the case of Lord Nelson's body: he was shipped home to England "wearing a nightcap, and sealed in a lead coffin filled with brandy and this laid in the coffin made from the mast of *L'Orient*."[709]

Francesca Thalberg lived on till 1895; when she died, her will was contested by the family and the case occupied the courts of Naples for a long time.[710]

Louis Engel writes that Thalberg's collection of autographs was of extraordinary interest and value. *The Musical World* reported on 26 October 1872 under the title "Occasional Notes":

> The *Choir* draws attention to the forthcoming sale of musical MSS. belonging to the late M. Thalberg, and urges the desirableness of purchasing them for the nation. It appears that the collection is indeed one of rare value, comprising of the autograph of Beethovens's *First Mass, Moonlight Sonata. Chorus of Dervishes (Ruins of Athen)*, the string trio in E flat, and an unpublished song. There are also included in it the MS. of a new ending for an air in Gluck's *Alceste,* a Cantata for solo voice and orchestra by Handel; a song, with quartet accompaniment by Mozart; and an original quartet of Mendelssohn's, besides a host of relics of great musicians. With reference to this priceless collection our contemporary remarks: "That these MSS, the majority of which were inherited by the great pianist[711] and some few acquired by him personally, should be allowed to fall into the hands of any other country than our own would be a national disgrace."

ଛଛଛ

Chapter Thirty-Seven

The Estate

As the estate of Lablache was divided, it was documented that his second son Nicolas and his wife Emilie de Méric bought the magnificent house at Maisons-Laffitte near Paris at the auction of Lablache's property.[712] From the time young Emilie de Méric-Lablache entered the operatic life of Paris on Saturday 25 November 1848 in Donizetti's *Maria di Rohan*, her career had carried her through many exhausting seasons in London, Vienna, and St. Petersburg.

On 22 August 1858, before her return to Russia, Emilie's *rentrée* in Paris as Azucena was this time at the Opéra, not at the Théâtre-Italien. Paris's famous first tenor Gustave Roger and close friend of the Lablache family sang with her in *Il Trovatore* before a glittering audience.

After another year in Russia, she continued to have a busy career till the birth of her son on the 15 March 1860. Henri Louis Lablache was the first Lablache to be born at the lovely house on Rue Albine in the park of Maisons-Laffitte.[713]

Henri Louis's father, Nicolas Lablache, a shadowy figure at best, never seemed to have had much success as a singer that we know of, even though a newspaper review from Manchester suggests he had plenty of talent. We can only guess and imagine, for his changeable career has been almost impossible to trace. A little advertisement in *The Musical World*[714] states, "Professor Nicolas Lablache, now returned from Cairo, will take students." Sometimes, he is referred to as a landowner or manager. Professor of music, but where? Well, he was reputed to have taught at the Paris Conservatoire, and he also taught many private students in Paris. Emilie soon afterward, in 1862, left Paris in September to sing in Madrid. There Anna was born, their third child.

That year, Covent Garden presented a fresh young French soprano, Marie Battu. A pupil of Gilbert-Louis Duprez, her singing reputation was helped due to her father, the conductor Pantaleon Battu. Her brother, Leon

Battu, was a well-known dramatist who wrote for composers Offenbach and Adam. For two years, she sang mostly the Italian repertory with Mario on the stage of the Théâtre-Italien in such operas as *Lucia, Rigoletto, Un Ballo, Don Giovanni,* and *Cosi fan tutte.* The date of her Paris birth is uncertain but around 1836. Her debut was in Paris in *La Sonnambula* at the Theatre Italien on 12 January 1860. She made her London debut on the 17 June 1862 as Gilda in Verdi's *Rigoletto.* It is not known exactly when she married Dominique Lablache (Luigi's son), who was many years her senior, but it is known that they were married by 1884. There may be several factors which caused them to wait so long to marry. The French military did not allow soldiers to marry anyone who was in the theater. Marie Battu may have retired by 1884, so this prohibition was no longer applicable.

Successful in many French operas, beside many Italian roles, she sang Meyerbeer's popular *Robert le Diable, L'Africaine, Les Huguenots,* and Auber's *La muette de Portici.* The Theater Baden-Baden Kursaal heard her sing in *Trovatore, Rigoletto, and Ballo* in 1863. In 1864, she sang Adalgisa rather indifferently in *Norma* at the Théâtre-Italien, and at Covent Garden with Emilie Lagrua. A week before she also sang in Rossini's *Moïse* at the Grand Opera Paris. The opera was cut short because of Mdlle engagement at Covent Garden. "Mdlle. Marie Battu," writes *The Musical World,* "was not allowed to depart without a demonstration and a magnificent crown of flowers." The *Review Gazetta Musicale* tells its readers, "she was presented the flowers by two members of the company in the name of their comrades and the audience gave her a huge send off." Marie Battu sang Mathilda in Rossini's five hundredth performance of *Guillaume Tell* at the Paris Academie Royale. Her name appears on many concert programs that were all part of Rossini's 1868 birthday celebrations. Battu, was very active through the 1860s to the 1880s, then she ended her career possibly in Brussels. She was still singing there at the Theatre Monnaie in 1877 in *Faust* and *Les Huguenots,* but it was noted that "her voice is now worn, nor has she any particular dramatic ability to compensate for the fatigued condition of her vocal powers."[715] Yet, her career was considerable, most likely she sang for twenty years. From 1877 she sang concerts across France till about 1880.

It would seem by this family there were no heirs, so the Lablache name died with them.

Emilie de Méric-Lablache had a very different career. Long and varied, her whole life was spent singing between opera houses. After singing in London, Vienna, Paris, St. Petersburg, Barcelona, and Germany, Emilie swept back to London and Ireland by 1865 for her part in tours of the British provinces, joining Mario in the great surge of Verdi's popular *Rigoletto* and *Il Trovatore*, plus Donizetti's *Lucrezia Borgia*.

Sailing from Queenstown Ireland on 25 September 1878, for New York, Emilie became the first member of the Lablache family to tour the United States with Her Majesty's Opera Company under the direction of the famous impresario Col. J. H. Mapleson. The conductor of this group was Luigi Arditi. Known as a contralto, she sang mostly mezzo-soprano roles, Emilie often filled in as an understudy for singers who were sick on tour of the states. Luigi Arditi conducted Mapleson's first season at the New York Academy of Music in 1878. Opening with *La Traviata,* Emilie sang with all the great singers of the period—Sembrich, Del Puente, Capoul, Gerster, Hauk, Campanini, Sinco, Nilsson, Scalchi, Trebelli, and Stagno.

When her daughters Louise and Nina were old enough they became singers. Louise was a contralto like her mother, Nina or Anna was a light soprano. Both daughters joined their Mother Emilie de Meric Lablache in De Beauplan's Opera Company in New Orleans together. This successful company specialed in French opera, but made the mistake of leaving New Orleans to go on tour. Not everyone was so keen on French opera and the company went bankrupt leaving the Lablache ladies were without work. Emilie returned to Europe in 1881, and Louise went off to sing in South America. They all regrouped in New York later. Louise Lablache was very young when she was pushed on the stage and sang in the inauguration performance of *Faust* at the opening of the Metropolitan Opera in 1883 in New York.

On the heels of the De Meric-Lablaches arrived Luigi F. Lablache, Frédéric's son and grandson of the great Lablache, a noted British lead actor who was on his first tour of America with his actress wife Jane (Jennie). Lablache had been hired as a Shakespearean actor by Mrs. Scott Siddon's well-known theatrical company to tour the United States.

In the spring of 1880, the *New York Times* reported that M. Lablache (Nicolas), a professor of music at the Paris Conservatoire, had come to New York to give singing lessons. The Boston newspapers also reported this, noting he had been the director of the following opera houses: Cairo Opera house, Havanna, and St. Petersburg. Certainly, he had been in Cairo in 1871, for it was under his direction that *Aïda* was produced. Both Emilie and Louise continued singing in various companies all over the United States and Europe up till 1889. Then Emilie took up teaching in New York briefly, but she still continued to make appearences in London. She was last seen at Mapelson's funeral at Highgate Cemetery London in 1901. (Cheke page 407)Yet to be discovered is where the Nicola and Emilie retired or died. Possibly in the United States.

Of their two daughters Louise and Anna (Nina), Louise Emilie married twice. Her first husband was James Hamilton Colby, her second husband Roumanian tenor Jean (Ion) Dimitresco.(1860-1913). Their daughter Louise Emilie Colby also married twice. Her second husband was William James Parkinson Smith (married 1910), the father of Norman Parkinson, the famed Vogue fashion photographer, society personality and photographer to Queen Elizabeth II.

So the year of 1880-81 brought six Lablaches all touring in the United States; surely, their paths crossed. To make things more confusing, another Lablache, possibly of the same family, made an appearance in New York and Boston that year—the young Bianca La Blanche. She sang with Max Strakosch's Grand Italian Opera and was billed singing Amina in *La Sonnambula* at Booth's theater on 29 January 1880. Her review stated, "She was disappointing."

Of Lablache's four sons, very little is known about the life of Henri Lablache. Born in Naples Italy 7 July 1825 he died in Criel near Dieppe, Normandy, on 27 July 1887. As is so often the case in theatrical families, relationships are often difficult to untangle. From Paris records he was reputed to have fathered several children possibly out of wedlock, then he married 3 April 1884 to a Felicite Caron. Records found by Brian Meringo show on 31 May 1884 he legally recognized a daughter of the above F. Caron, born in 17 August 1854, a Jeanne Felicite Leontine Caron. In 1858 another daughter was legally recognized, the daughter of Victoria Eliza Mace, a Marie Theresa Mace was born 12 August 1856.[716]

All Lablache's daughters, and granddaughters, were extremely lovely with attractive dark Italian looks clearly inherited from their father's side of the family—Teresa, their mother, looked rather plain in her portraits. They possessed, like all well-brought-up ladies of their time, musical talent and were accomplished singers. It was remembered in the family that they reaped enormous praise from their admirers when they sang at the fashionable soirées of the French and Russian courts.

Of the three surviving daughters, two became professional singers as far as we know. Of Francesca—La Cecchina, none of her performances are known to have surfaced. Did she sing or dance under another name?

Court singer Marie (Mimi) de Caters, the wife of Baron Ernest de Caters, abandoned her operatic career after she married but continued later. Known as a talented singer, she sang in private concerts in London and Paris. Marianna

(Anna) Lablache married Henry Singer, and both sisters were ladies-in-waiting at the court of the empress Eugénie and Napoleon III in Paris.

Baronne Marie de Caters sang for Queen Victoria at Windsor on the evening 18 May 1879, and the Queen recorded in her journal.[717]

> Through reverses of fortune, she has had to take up singing again. She is very tall, and large, and is wonderfully like her father, handsome, dark, and between 40 and 50. She is very ladylike and pleasing, her voice is magnificent. It is a full rich mezzo soprano and she manages it beautifully, having perfect 'méthode.'

On that occasion, she sang Gordigiani's "Santa Maria," songs by Gumbert and Pergolese, a hymn from Gounod's *Polyeucte* and his "Le Soir," three comic Neapolitan songs (which the Queen noted her father used to sing), and "Vedrrai Carino" from *Don Giovanni*.

Baroness Marie Isabelle de Caters became the teacher of Princess Beatrice at Windsor Castle from 1879-1881 till her sudden death, not long after the state concert on the 18 May 1881 at Buckingham Palace, which was attended by the Princess of Wales. Participating in this concert were some of the best operatic singers of that time; Christine Nilsson, Zilia Trebelli and Emma Albani among others. Marie de Caters sang "Inflammatus" from *Stabat Mater*, and the duo "Canta a serina" from Boito's *Mefistofile*. Just over a month later (the archivist at the Royal Archives notes) on the 24 June the Queen wrote in her journal: "Greatly shocked and grieved to hear that Madame de Caters Lablache, whom Beatrice was expecting to have a singing lesson from today, was very ill with congestion of the brain."[718] The Queen also noted her death on the 26 of June, and her funeral in Paris on the 30 June.

Repeating the role of teaching royalty like her father, the French composer Camille Saint-Saens gives some insight into musical life then at Windsor castle. James Harding writes about his reception:[719]

> It was rather a special occasion that he travelled to Windsor on the 8 July 1880 and was received by Queen Victoria. At the station he was met by the Baronne Maria de Caters, a daughter of the great bass Lablache, who at that time was teaching the Princess Beatrice to sing. "I had been somewhat intimidated by stories told of the coldness Her Majesty affected at this sort of audience. Imagine my surprise when she arrived, stretched out both her hands to take mine, and talked to me with great cordiality. She was very fond

of the Baronne de Caters and that was the secret of her welcome which immediately put me at ease. Her Majesty wished to hear me play the organ (there is an excellent one in the Chapel at Windsor) and then the piano. Finally I had the honour of accompanying the Princess in an aria from *Etienne Marcel* which she sang with great purity of style and diction. It was the first time Her Royal Highness had sung in front of her august mother and she was dying of fright. The Queen was so charmed that several days later, without telling me anything about it, she summoned to Windsor the wife of the director of Covent Garden—none other than Madame Albani—and asked to have *Ètienne Marcel* performed at the opera house. The Queen's wish was never fulfilled." At the end of the day Queen Victoria noted in her diary: 'Heard Mr. Saint-Saëns play very beautifully on the organ, in the Chapel, and Mme. de Caters Lablache sang to it. He also played some of his compositions on the piano and plays and composes beautifully.' Her daughter's performance was royally ignored.

This was not the only time Marie de Caters sang with San Saens nor the only time she sang for the Queen. She sang on many other occasions at court. Her pupil Princess Beatrice married Prince Henry of Battenburg in 1885, and the wedding was held at Osborne.[720]

At the Paris funeral of Henry Singer in 1884, we get a last view of some of the Lablache family together. The Singer family included Lablache's daughter Marianna, who is the presumed widow. The memorial program (Lablache Archives) bordered in black, included the following names:

Madame Henry Singer, Monsieur George Singer, S. Lieutenant au 6e Cuirassiers, Monsieur Jules Goüin, Chevalier de la Legion d'honneur, et Madame Jules Goüin, Monsieurs Edward Gaston et Ernest Goüin, Mademoiselle Anna Goüin, Madame Alexandre Singer, Monsieur Frédéric Lablache, Monsieur et Madame Nicole Lablache, Monsieur et Madame Henri Lablache, Monsieur Dominique Lablache, Chevalier de la Legion d'honneur et Madame Dominique Lablache, Monsieur Eugene Mira, Percepteur a Corbeil, Monsieur et Madame Louis Singer et leur enfants, Monsieur et Madame Rokitansky et leur enfants, Mademoiselle Fanny Lablache, Monsieur et Madame Luigi Lablache et leur enfants, Monsieur Louis Lablache, Mademoiselle Marie de

Caters, Monsieur Louis de Caters, Mademoiselle Therese de Caters, Madame Wallerstein, et ses enfants, Monsieur Charles Haas, Monsieur et Madame Gaston Mourgues de Carrere et leur enfants.

Ont l'honneur de vous faire part de la perte douloureuse qu'il viennent de faire en la personne de:

Monsieur Henry SINGER

leur epoux, pere, grand pere, beau frere, oncle et cousin, decede le 30 Decembre 1884, a l'age de 65 ans, rue de Clichy, 59, muni des Sacrements de l'Eglise.

Priez pou lui!

Luigi Lablache's other daughter was noticeably absent: Signora Francesca Lablache (Mme. Thalberg). The Dominique Lablache family were there and the parents of Dominique's wife Marie Battu. The Battu family are all buried in the Pierre Lachaise cemetery in Paris.[721]

Frédéric Lablache and Fanny continued to live in London till their death. Their address at 51 Albany Street was in the fashionable West End near the theaters and just behind Regents Park. Fanny no longer sang at Covent Garden. She had graduated from the Royal Academy of music and now qualified as a professor of music (18 July 1857).[722]

Frédéric Lablache taught at the Royal Academy of Music. This famous establishment was hidden away in a quiet corner of London at 4 Tenterden Street, Hanover Square. This magnificent five-story edifice was historically important. It had been Lord Carnarvon's town house. The facade was flanked by Corinthian pillars, and it was just a stone's throw from Oxford Circus.

"The Academy laboured to educate and improve the musical taste of the country, and at regular periods has set the result of its labours without comment before the world," wrote its principal, Dr. A. C. Mackenzie in 1895.[723] Under the patronage of the king, it was founded in 1822 with twenty-five influential noblemen for directors. This school is shrouded in mystery, perhaps, because of confused reporting, but were the London Academy of Music and the Royal Academy of Music the same? Here, there is some confusion for sure; the establishment known as the London Academy of Music was only instituted in 1861, and it mentions in print professor Signori Lablache on the staff. As there are few records of the Royal Academy. Are they one and the same academy? Why signori? Was Nicolas on the staff too? Maybe they referred to Fanny?

"The offices of the London Academy were at St. George's Hall, Lanham Place, Regent Street," writes *The Musical World* on 12 June 1875.[724]

Long before Luigi Lablache left for Russia, Frédéric retired from the operatic stage but continued to sing with his wife as professional concert artist and continued to teach. The Lablaches sang together in hundreds of concerts well into the sixties. Like most well-to-do Victorians, they entertained lavishly, and their dinner parties and soirées were attended by a strange mixture of musicians of all kinds—foreign royalty, Italian and French exiles, actors, relatives, singers, conductors such as Michael Costa and Julien Benedict, Sir Charles Hallé, and Luigi Arditi. Signor Luigi Arditi, Italian composer and conductor, lived only a few doors away at 41 Albany Street and a close friend; and like the Lablaches, he and his wife entertained often.

On June 29 1863, a huge red-and-cream playbill announces, "Madame F. Lablache and Signor F. Lablache in the last one of their final grand musicale matinees. "Mme. Lind Goldschmidt has consented to sing written above her name. (Jenny Lind) Herr Reichart joins them and—virtuosi Sigismund Thalberg and cellist Alfredo Piatti were the distinguished musicians brought together by the conductors Signor Li Calsi and Lindsay Sloper. On the billboard under the name Thalberg, we read "Most positively his last concert in London."

After that, the Frédéric Lablaches seem to have faded into operatic obscurity and we hear little more of them singing in public. During the sixties and seventies, they were frequent visitors to Paris and Boulogne-sur-Mer in the north of France, participating in family affairs. Then from Boulogne came the news that Fanny was knocked down by a wave, and we can only guess that her injuries must have been severe for on the 7 August 1865, she made a will. Eventually, she died ten years later at the Hotel Louvre in Paris.

A long time later, in 1879, in the *Athenaeum*, we find a small mention of Frédéric's music being performed at a concert in London, and we wonder if he sang or was at the piano.[725]

> The appearance of Signor F. Lablache as a composer for the pianoforte will perhaps surprise the opera goers who can recall the days when he was a baritone-bass, singing on the lyric stage of Her Majesty's Theatre, with his celebrated father. Signor Lablache became a professor of singing after his marriage with the contralto, the late Madame F. Lablache, who, as Miss Fanny Wyndham, made her *début* at the Lyceum Theatre in 1836, during the Italian Opera-buffa management of the late John Mitchell.

> Signor F. Lablache's pianoforte pro diction is entitled, *Moments de Loisir,* and there are eight *Pensées Caractéristiques* in the selection, each having a designation according to the period, and, as usual, much must be left to the imagination if the application of the respective prefixes is to be realized. Apart, however, from this technical objection, there is a display of fancy and feeling in the compositions, one or two of which will suggest reminiscences of Thalberg's style, the pianist had been the brother-in-law of Signor Lablache. Of the eight numbers the *Danse Iroquoise,* No. 2, the Nocturne, No 3, and the *Sterienne, No 6,* are the most attractive . . . it need scarcely be added that the composer is gifted with tune.[726]

Another mention of Frédéric's composing comes later in Walter Macfarren in his *Memories: An Autobiography.*[727]

> I refer to a performance of Frédéric Lablache's little *Requiem Mass,* composed on the occasion of the death of his daughter Fanny Rose, it is not on the account of the merit of the work, which was simple and unpretentious, but to record my regard for an excellent professor and estimable gentleman, a worthy son of his great father.[728]

Queen Victoria asked him to write a processional march for her Jubilee, but before he could complete the work, he died in 1887 because of the stress brought on by the untimely death of his favorite daughter, Fanny Rose.[729] The family saga continues into the next generation with Frédéric's children.

ღღღ

Chapter Thirty-Eight

The Descendants

The fashionable place to be married was Westminster Abbey in the sixties, and it was there that Frédéric Lablache's daughter Thérèse, walked down the aisle with Czech operatic bass, Baron Johann von Rokitansky (Hans), from Vienna.[730] Educated in Italy, he was extremely well-connected as his father was a famous professor of pathology and a baron as well. "Herr Karl Rokitansky is a *Hofrath* (Court Councillor) and very celebrated Professor of Medicine in Vienna," wrote *The Musical World*.

> Karl Rokitansky (1804-78). Rokitansky was a Czech who studied philosophy at the University of Prague and later moved to Vienna to study medicine. He was one of the greatest of the gross descriptive pathologists and was able to base his lifelong study of disease on more than 30,000 necropsies personally performed over 40 years. Rokitansky was professor of pathology in Vienna for 30 years from 1844 and was one of the chief founders of the new Vienna School. His Handbuch der pathologischen Anatomie (1842-46) was based on many thousands of necropsies. Among his special contributions were treatise on diseases of the arteries and defects of the heart. He was the first to detect bacteria in the lesions of malignant endocarditis. Acute yellow atrophy of the liver is also known as Rokitansky's disease.
>
> He was a genial and witty man. Of his four sons, two became physicians and the other two concert singers which led him to remark that they were of two classes, the healers and howlers: Die Einen heilen, die Anderen heulen. He was honoured in the set of stamps issued by Austria in 1937 showing great doctors (Stanley Gibbons 817, Scott B158).[731]

Victor von Rokitansky, the younger brother of Johann, sang and studied in Italy under Francesco Lamperti, and later taught singing at the conservatory of music in Vienna. One of his most famous pupils was Marcelina Sembrich-Kochanska, a Polish soprano who studied under him for twelve months before going to Milan for further study with the son of the distinguished teacher of operatic stars at that time—Lamperti.[732]

The young Johann Rokitansky couple were married in the French chapel of Westminster Abbey on 8 November 1865; the witnesses were Sir Julius Benedict; Emilie de Méric-Lablache; Virginia Arditi, the wife of conductor Luigi Arditi; and Ciabatta. The wedding party included many people from the operatic world. A fine bass, Rokitansky sang the first Leporello at the gala opening of the new Vienna Opera House on 25 May 1869. A glittering audience attended, including the Emperor Franz Joseph and the King of Hanover. Thérèse joined her husband to live in Vienna.

In 1866, Herr Rokitansky came to sing the leading role (Falstaff) in Otto Nicolai's opera *Merry Wives of Windsor* at Her Majesty's Theatre. *The Musical World* wrote:

> Mr. Mapelson has secured the services of three excellent contraltos—Mdme. de Méric Lablache, Mdme. Bettelheim, and Mdlle. Trebelli. Mdme. de Méric Lablache is a debutante as far as Her Majesty's Theatre is concerned; but she has had plenty of experience and much success at several of the principal theatres of Europe.[733] The same journal writes on 6 April 1867: "It was only necessary to recall the success which Sig. Rokitansky achieved last season, as Marcel in the *Les Huguenots* and Osmin in the *Seraglio*, to account for his re-engagement."

Rokitansky was engaged to sing in London's event of the year, the first showing of Verdi's *La forza del destino*, 22 June. *The London Times* wrote that it was well-received; afterward, Rokitansky sang the role of Falstaff again. Joining him, Emilie de Méric Lablache sang the part of Mrs. Page with Tietjens as Mrs. Ford. He was also praised by *The London Times* for his performance in *Gli Ugonotti*:

> It would hardly be possible now-a-days to find a better Marcel than Herr Rokitansky, who exults in one of those noble and deep-toned bass voices in which Germany has always been so rich.(Rokitansky was not German, but Czech-Austrian).

When Colonel Mapleson revived Weber's *Oberon* in London, Emilie was a delightful Puck. There she also sang Azucena, Orsini, and Urbano.

Herr Rokitansky sang again with Emilie in a grand concert at London's Crystal Palace on 17 July 1867, joined by a bevy of the most well-known singers of the day: Trebelli-Bettini, Tietjens, Nilsson, Sinico, Baumeister, Foli, Mongini, Hohler, Santley, Pandolfini, Gardoni, and Gassier. The concert terminated with the overture from *Zampa*, one of the most popular overtures in that era and for many decades to come.

However, he was not invited to sing with Emilie at Buckingham Palace. That concert featured a galaxy of artists including Mario, Adelina Patti, and Paolina Lucca. Emilie left for Dublin in September returning to Her Majesty's for the November season. Apparently, Rokitansky had been recalled to Vienna for what was to be the last great event at the old Imperial opera house, Charles Gounod's *Romeo und Juliet*. It was sung in German. *The Musical World* in 1868 reports the following:

> The excitement in musical circles was something quite unusual, and, by the time Monsieur Gounod, who had arrived here about a week previously, made his appearance, and, with the order of Guadeloupe, and the cross of the Legion of Honour on his breast, took his place in the orchestra, that excitement had gone considerably above boiling heat. The opera was favourably received . . . but the enthusiasm of a first night is not a gauge of permanent success, and though *Romeo and Juliet* will maintain an honourable place in the repertory, it will never rank as high as *Faust* in the estimation of the Viennese, whatever it may do elsewhere.

The critic found Mlle. Von Murska a bit overpowering as Juliet and her "Romeo (Herr Walter) sang indifferently, Herr Rokitansky's Lorenzo was impressive." *The Musical World* wrote, "His basso profundo was produced with superb artisty and concentrated on the musical side of the role, he became less static as an actor. He had sung with the Vienna State opera for 30 years."

Rokitansky returned to Her Majesty's in time to sing in the first performance of Richard Wagner's *Lohengrin.* Teresa Tietjens sang Elsa, and the robust tenor Signor Mongini sang the title role. Rokitansky sang Enrico. Rokitansky then sang in *Fidelio* and *Don Giovanni* and was highly praised for his Marcel in *Les Huguenots.*

In 1876, he returned to Her Majesty's after five years[734] to sing Bertram in *Robert le Diable*, followed by *Les Huguenots,* (Marcello) *Der Freischutz,* and *Il Barbiere di Siviglia,* sharing the spotlight with fine artists such as Mlle. Trebelli-Bettini; Mlle. Christine Nilsson; tenor Signor Stagno, who was billed as principal tenor of the Italian opera of Madrid, St. Petersburg, and Moscow. Signor Campanini and Mlle. Tietjens, M. Faure, and Signor del Puente are all noted opera singers of their time.

That year, 1868, prima donna Adelina Patti was married and her wedding was the event of the year. Several of the Lablaches attended, and Patti's wedding photo was featured in the family photo album.

The Paris Opera took the opportunity to celebrate Rossini's seventy-sixth birthday that leap year with *Guillaume Tell*. A gala five-hundredth performance was held among many festivities. Marie Battu-Lablache, a favorite of Rossini, sang Matilda. Sadly, that February 29th was his last birthday for on 13 November 1868, the news was spread throughout the world, from a hospital in Paris, that Rossini had died. Like Lablache, the huge funeral was to be held at the Madeleine, but the church was not large enough to hold five thousand people, so the funeral service was held at La Trinité. All the singers from the Théâtre-Italien and the Opera and the Opera-Comique sang with the students of the conservatoire. Later, a huge throng of people followed his coffin to Pére-Lachaise.

Rossinian performances were given at three different theaters that week: at the Théâtre-Italien, *Stabat Mater*; at the L'Opéra, *Guillaume Tell*; and at the Theatre-Lyrique, *Il Barbiere de Siviglia*. Later, in 1868, Sir Michael Costa would direct a concert of seven hundred performers and three thousand instrumentalists in the huge Crystal Palace to commemorate the passing of Maestro Rossini. Eighteen thousand five hundred people attended including the Queen.[735]

Later, in May 1887, Rossini's remains were removed from Paris and brought back to Italy to the Cathedral of Santa Croce in Florence.[736]

Grisi was staying with her daughters in her villa in Florence when they heard the news of Rossini's death. All Italy mourned his passing. Singing in a memorial service at Florence's Santa Croce, Grisi felt the loss deeply and was unaware that her performance in the *Stabat Mater* would be her last public appearance.[737] Grisi and Mario spent a last summer vacation together in Italy before they left by train for St. Petersburg via Berlin on 25 October 1869. Surviving a nasty train accident, Grisi became ill. By the time they reached Berlin, removed to the Hotel du Nord, Unter den Linden, Grisi's condition worsened and she suddenly had a stroke. Soon after, she died in the arms of her daughters, but sadly without Mario who had rushed to Russia ahead of them.[738] *The Musical World* published a rather rapid obituary on 4 December 1869.[739]

Another not-so-young singer and a Lablache, Emilie de Méric-Lablache with her daughters, Nina and Louise Lablache, survived the first great tour of the United States with Colonel Mapleson. Mapleson in turn brought many singers to London's Her Majesty's Theatre for the first time, including

Gerster, Di Murska, Nordica, Scalchi, Trebelli, Hauk, Nilsson and Campanini, Francelli, Ravelli, De Reszke, Pandolfini, and the favorite, Del Puente.

Notably, most of these singers and many more were included in the so-called golden age of opera tours. They endured incredibly harsh weather and often extreme hardships, not only touring the English provinces, but traveling from city to city across the vast stretches of United States. Emilie de Méric sang not only for Mapleson in the States but was engaged by other impresarios as well.

The first grandson of the great Lablache was born on 27 January 1850 to Frédéric and Fanny, and, in true Italian fashion, named after his grandfather Luigi and his father Frédéric. Luigi Frédéric Lablache was the proud bearer of the Lablache name and of the family's dark Italian good looks. James Stanley-Little, his son-in-law, gives us a good description of him:

> Luigi Lablache, the elder, was a man of generous instincts, and it may be noted in passing that everyone who knew his grandson, Luigi Frederic Lablache, was made conscious at once of the spaciousness of his character and its essential rectitude. Modest and unassuming, the insignia of his birthright has made itself felt the moment one came into his presence. Possessing a rare sense of humour and a large charity of judgement, he was *persona gratissima* wherever he found himself. (Romance of the Lablaches).[740]

He was destined for a life in the army, but apparently, ill health intervened. Eventually, young Luigi became an actor. T. C. Stanley-Little, his grandson, continues:

> My grandfather . . . for some years devoted himself to the study of drawing and painting, first in London and afterwards at Paris under Cabanel. At one time he had a mind to follow the career of his father and grandfather, and with this ambition in view, he asked his father to try his voice. But he was sternly reproved. "No, no, my son," was the characteristic answer, "abandon the idea. My career suffered from my father's distinction, and you are less able to excel than I was.

Luigi pursued his career in theater relentlessly, and by the time he was only twenty-five, he displayed a natural talent, accepting lead-actor roles across London and in the provinces as well. Clearly, discrimination still played a role in the lives of Italians during the Victorian times, but in spite of it, he succeeded and managed to overcome this because his grandfather's name was still fresh in the audiences' memories. When in 1874 he asked actress Jane Clementine Breadon (stage name Jane Emmerson), the pretty stepdaughter of John Mill, Judge Advocate of Bombay, to marry him, she was in the employment of the famous British actor, Henry Irving. Here, his grandson, James Stewart Lablache (Stewart Granger)—the actor and movie star—retells what happened in his autobiography of 1980, *Sparks Fly Upward*. On informing the snobby Mr. Irving that she was marrying young Lablache, he replied, "If you marry that bloody foreigner, you'll never work for me again." "Well, she did, and she didn't."[741]

Luigi was a highly polished actor, who passed his life in what today would be called the golden age of the theater, an era of glory that flourished between the 1860s onward into the nineteenth century, but slowly declined at the onset of World War I and was partially eclipsed by the entrance of a new medium—the movies.

It was a time when Sarah Bernhart ruled supreme and the London stages echoed with the sound of the voices of the actors Henry Irving, Ellen Terry, Sir Herbert Beerbohm Tree, Max Beerbohm, Forbes Robinson. Lablache knew them all, but as well as actors and actresses, he knew the writers of the time, like Oscar Wilde, the young Winston Churchill, George Bernard Shaw, painters like Whistler, Ruskin, Burne Jones. The writers like Frank Harris he met through his son-in-law, James Stanley-Little, who was a journalist and writer and moved in such aesthetic circles and who was friendly with Walter Crane, Rider Haggard, Rudyard Kipling, Lady Wilde, and Conan Doyle.

Both Luigi and Jane, or Jennie as he liked to call her, had long stage careers. Often, their engagements took them far away from each other. Their letters complain bitterly about their separations and loneliness. Devoted to each other, they were devastated when they were apart, yet half of their lives were separated. There were, of course, the good times when they toured together in the English provinces and America.

Lablache's debut came when he was just twenty-four at the London Gaiety Theatre in *The Hunchback* on 13 June 1874. After nine different other plays in London's West End, between 1874-1880, it was *Proof* and Dion Boucicault's *The Shaughraun* that clocked up the longest runs. "*Proof* ran for 247 performances since last Easter uninterrupted at the Adelphi" (Era: 19 January 1879).

The inauguration of the Shakespeare Memorial Theatre at Stratford-upon-Avon on 23 April 1879 was historically an important event, featuring the talents of the great Irish Shakespearian actor, Barry Sullivan. Luigi Lablache and his wife starred in *Much Ado about Nothing*; first, Luigi played Don Pedro with Sullivan and Helen Faucit then Luigi played Horatio in *Hamlet. As You Like It* completed the trio. This engagement came to the attention of Mrs. Scott Siddens, who was "the pride of theatrical representation" and, looking for good actors, signed Lablache up immediately to tour America with her in the 1880s, actually a few years before Henry Irving made his Shakespearian debut. Eager for culture from the "old country," Mrs. Siddons satisfied that hunger by bringing Shakespeare to the States, adding to the British flavor in the 1880s when everyone was steeped in the operettas of Gilbert and Sullivan.

Not long afterward, Oscar Wilde introduced himself and swept across America and, in spite of his unusual notoriety, was a huge success. With the States conquered, he was asked by customs if he had anything to declare. "Only my genius," answered Wilde.

Subjected to the leading male roles in late Victorian melodramas, Lablache reaped many successes in the provinces, but the actors and actresses who toured the northern counties often were subjected to some unpleasant experiences. Enduring undesirable hotels, they complained the theaters were often rough, noisy places filled with smoke and the smell of rank liquor. Six nights per city was the usual time for a play to stay if it wasn't held over. Plays were often held over in such large industrial cities like Liverpool, Glasgow, Nottingham, Manchester, West Hartlepool, and Birmingham to name a few. The demand was enormous for all kinds of entertainment and especially melodrama. After a successful tour put on by F. B. Chatterton's Company from Drury Lane—*Peep o'Day* with Jane Emmerson in 1879 and a short run of *Nicholas Nickleby* at the London Adelphi—both Luigi and Jane sailed for America.

Lablache returned triumphant to London's Haymarket in 1881 for *The Queen and the Cardinal;* he left afterward again with Mrs. Scott Siddens Shakespeare tour of England, visiting at least a dozen cities.

Lablache continued touring with the successful *Romany Rye* in 1882-1883 for nearly a year. Opening at the Grand Theatre Glasgow, the *Era* reports on 4 November 1882: "For the first time in Scotland, the hero Jack Hearne in *Romany Rye* was played in fine manly style by Mr. L. Lablache, who at once, stepped into favour." In a word, the whole performance was excellent. Later, the *Era* reviewed the Theatre Royal Hull production:[742]

> The success attending *Romany Rye* is without parallel at this or any other theatre in the provinces; crowded houses are the rule nightly, and popularity not only continues but increases until one is inclined to think like Tennyson's "Brook," it can go on forever.

Again, on 14 April, the *Era*: "Mr G. R. Sim's sensational drama *Romany Rye*, is held over in Birmingham. Mr. Lablache as a gentleman gypsy in the play, is an immense favorite with the audiences . . . the piece is staged in lavish style." The *Era* reported good reviews from Manchester to Edinburgh. After the play closed, Lablache acted in *Proof, Romeo,* and *Captain Hawksley*.

From 6 August 1883 to May of 1885, Lablache accepted another role that would prove tremendously successful, that of the lead role of Wilfred Denver in Henry A. Jones and Henry Herman's five-act play with an unheard of seventeen scenes—*The Silver King.* With this melodrama, Jones established his success. A contempary of Arthur Pinero, John Galsworthy, and Bernard Shaw, Henry Arthur Jones was one of the most considerable playwrights of the period.

Strongly influenced by the great Norwegian playwright Henrik Ibsen, Jones wrote dramas of social and moral criticism. Author of over 60 plays, of which *The Middleman* (1889), *Michael and His Lost Angel* (1896), *The Liars* (1897), and *Mrs. Dane's Defense* (1900) are among the most important.

The play ran for a record of five hundred successful performances with Lablache in the title role. A playbill from Oldam dated 31 March 1894 writes, "The event of the season is the *The Silver King."* The play was produced by the well-known actor Wilson Barrett, who played the original role on the London stage. A review from the *Leicester Post* on 29 September 1883:

> Mr Luigi Lablache in the role of Denver in *The Silver King* presented a historic study worthy of the highest commendation and his admirable acting contributed to the success of the piece.

Ms. Lilla Wilde played his wife, Nellie Denver, in the early performances. Jane Emmerson took over later. The Jones' publishers stated in 1925 that the play had been performed every weeknight somewhere ever since its first production and the play was enormously successful all over the world (Hudson, Lynton).

When Jane Lablache joined the production with her husband of *The Galley Slave,* the reviews were good. Here, we find one of the few reviews of Jane Lablache on 8 September 1885; the *Nottingham Daily Guardian* wrote, "Jane Emmerson as Cicely Blaine in *The Galley Slave* showed distinct genius." And in another article in the same journal, "She has good stage presence and a sympathetic and flexible voice . . . she was admirable and for a first performance it was remarkably perfect."

After three years touring successfuly with *The Galley Slave, Old Love and the New,* and *Blind Justice,* Lablache returned to London in 1888 to star in the period drama, *The Armada,* at the Drury Lane, *King Richard III* (Globe), *The Royal Oak* (Drury Lane), *The Hunchback* (Adelphi), *Pedigree* (Tooles), *Monte Cristo* (Avenue), *Released* (Comedy), as well as many other plays.

In September of 1895, Lablache and his wife Jane (stage name Jane Emmerson) left for America with English actress Olga Nethersole's company to tour the East Coast of the States, Chicago, the Midwest, and most of the cities on the route. Ms. Olga Nethersole was born in London, but was of Spanish descent on her mother's side. She made her stage debut in Brighton in 1887. Lablache kept a "day-to-day" small pocket diary of his entire trip to America.

The dramas that Ms. Nethersole put before the public were quite daring for the times, judging from the reviews. The plays were *Carman, Camille, Denise*, and *Frou Frou. Denise* was written by the son of Alexander Dumas. They opened at the National Theatre in Washington DC on Wednesday, 13 November 1895. "Washington is a beautiful city," wrote Lablache, "lovely buildings . . . all but one or two are painted white—a slight mixture of Paris and Vienna. There are many black people . . . they give a distinctive look to the place with the cars (trams) rushing along ringing their bells. Everyone is in a hurry, no peace to the ear or to the eye." The Lablaches stayed at the Riggs Hotel Washington; the rates were $1.50 for two per day!

Nethersole and her cast brought such an emotionally charged performance to the audience that the *Washington Post* wrote, "Any one who says that women can't act is a blanket idiot," said a big man, coming out of the National last night. "Why, she made me cry—a thing I haven't done in thirty years—and its a play too!" He was not the only man in the large audience last night who wiped his eyes furtively during the second act of *Denise,* and as for the women, they fairly gave way and wept unrestrainedly. The reviews followed, "Miss Emmerson proved herself a splendid character actress . . . the part of Thaurenin was played admirably by Luigi Lablache." Afterward, they presented *Frou Frou* and then *Carmen.*

Lablache writes in his diary: "*Romeo and Juliet* tonight. It is so funny to see Jennie at the dinner table. She smiles at the black waiter as she pops a macaroon or two! or three! into her pocket, or pulls out her flask and pours her coffee or mine into it. They're all very polite to her—women rule the roost here, and she sees that I'm properly looked after. We leave for Boston, a 13-hour journey!!" They did not like Boston; Lablache commented angrily, "This town is called the 'Hub of Civilization'—well, I pity the civilization!"

Emilie de Méric-Lablache and her daughter had been there, touring all the cities that her nephew had yet to see. The young Louise Lablache made her Metropolitan debut in *Faust* at the opening of the Metropolitan Opera House on 22 October 1883, singing Marthe with her mother Emilie coaching her from the wings. Emilie was forbidden to sing there by Mapleson because of an injuncution. Christine Nilsson sang Marguerite with Campanini as Faust.

Ms. Olga Nethersole's Company returned to New York for the opening on Broadway on 2 December 1895. Lablache and his wife were excited to find themselves at the fashionable Empire Theatre at 1430 Broadway and Fortieth Street, where owner Charles Frohman first put on the lavish production of *The Girl I Left Behind Me* in January 1893.

"An actor's life in the United States in those times could be summed up in three words: 'Theatre, railroad, hotel,'" said actor Tommaso Salvini after returning from a sensational tour a few years before. The Nethersole tour was almost as long, excluding New Orleans and the southern states. Their tour took them by rail to Washington, Baltimore, New York, Brooklyn, Hartford, New Haven, Wilmington, Providence, Syracuse, Rochester, Albany, Utica, Buffalo, Chicago, St. Louis, Pittsburg, Cleveland, Kansas City, Cincinnati, Philadelphia, Troy, Hartford, Stamford, Trenton, and Boston.

Lablache continued his diary the whole tour, commenting on everything. The weather was constantly changing from subzero temperatures to spells of warm weather in the spring. However, it would seem their main interests were food and drink, drink being the alcoholic kind.

When Luigi and Jennie first arrived in New York on 7 October 1895, they paid $3.00 for a room. The French brandy was $4.00 a bottle while American whiskey cost only $1.25. Sometimes they dined for $1.00 at Tony Pastori's. Describing the meals became a pastime; Luigi writes about the Manhattan Chop House, a resturant in New York:

> I had today at the Manhattan a portion of oysters-cape cods, huge fellows, 25 cents a portion and a real English pork chop. What a size! 30 cents, splendid food. We had Welsh rabbit tonight—Ye Gods! What dreams will come! There is nothing to write about . . . life is so much the same day after day. No inclination or time or strength to go anywhere but food and the theatre.

This was understandable as they often gave eight performances a week including the Saturday matinee. Lablache wrote about the Saturday matinee on 4 January 1896:

> Good audiences—and at the night show of *Carmen*. It was the biggest house that has ever been at the Empire . . . We were all taken over in carriages to the Broadway Theatre to entertain at a benifit for American actors—Damm them!—The 4th Act of *Camille*. All the theatrical world was there; we spoke to Irving and Ellen Terry, John Drew, Maud Adams, Elaine Terris, to name a few.

On another occasion, the cast were invited to a formal dinner with champagne at the Savoy Hotel with Marcus Mayer, David Belasco, Daniel Frohman, and Clyde Fitch—the author of *Beau Brummell* and *Sapho*. Lablache wrote, I sang to the company: "I'll sing you the songs of Araby." "We spent New Year 1895 at the Manhatten—where we had to wait for our table to eat our usual oysters and beer."

Lablache wrote, "We stayed another week before going on to Brooklyn. Miss Nethersole is chewing garlic to give *Carmen* a Spanish atmosphere! In America she was supposed to have shocked the puritans by her intense and realistic portrayals of fallen women."

The *New York Times* had a different opinion; its first review appeared under the title, "Carmen as Melodrama." "Olga Nethersole acts the wicked gypsy coquette with superfluous energy. The play is rather heavy and lurid, and the last half is exceedingly coarse." Her notoriously passionate "Nethersole kiss" was not admired by the *New York Times* either. "Her kissing became comic. The seductive dance was the reverse of fascinating. It was vulgarly suggestive and grotesque. Her natural vivacity, quick changes of temper, and her beauty would be very effective if she could free herself of illusion destroying exaggeration." Lablache wrote,

> New York, it's all nothing but noise! The cars (tramcars) are overcrowded, overheated and the company! . . . one car had at least 60 people in it at one time . . . indicated that 36 only had paid! Down near the battery we saw one immense white stone building 20 stories high! There are heaps of 15 to 16 stories. Fancy five times as high as 51 Albany Street!! Not counting the basement and each floor as high if not higher than ours. And they are not even houses but flats. Fancy living on the 19th or 20th floor.

At the Players Club, Lablache chatted with David Frohman, the dandy John Drew, and little Bogey Andrews, whom he had not seen for five years. The Lablaches enjoyed sitting in on a few plays in town. "After a good dinner we went to see Frank Mayo in *Pudding Head Wilson* at the Herald Square Theatre. Frank Mayo was most admirable. Enjoyed this performance immensely! I saw him for 5 minutes in his dressing room after." The last time they met, he writes, was in 1880 when Lablache played *Macbeth*. They were very disappointed with *The Prisoner of Zenda* and Nat Goodwin in *Davy Garrick*—BAD! As for E. Sothern, Lablache wrote, "A sheep-like actor, speaks under his breath then shouts . . . but his face never changes from the stolid sheep-like look, yet the house is crowded 9 times a week, with 3 matinees." Mr. Sothern was well known for the play *Our American Cousin* in which he played the role of Lord Dundreary at least eight hundred times.

> The notices in the theatres are very funny at Baltimore, there was a notice hanging up in the wings. "Do not spit on this wing." You might evidently spit anywhere else except those two wings! Here they say: "Do not spit on the stage. Do not sit on the stairs. Smoking absolutely forbidden."—and they smoke and spit and sit all over the place. We find in all the theatres, the lightning, the orchestra attendance (no fees anymore) are far better than in London, and the general performances of the plays better. Here the star does not hold the centre of the stage. All is done for the advantage of the play, and THE PLAY'S THE THING after all.

Before leaving for Hartford, they took the elevated railway at Forty-second and Sixth to the Battery. "We saw the Statue of Liberty in the distance. Lovely swell to the sea . . . took the tram to Brooklyn bridge, crossed the bridge, 5 cents for two. Thought nothing of it. The high level of Newcastle for height and the Forth Bridge (Scotland) for length and strength beat it hollow!"

They left for Syracuse. Lablache wrote, "The most interesting thing about Syracuse is that all the trains pass through the main street . . . a man walks in front waving a flag. They steam along ringing a huge bell. Carts and people all have to stop till the train goes through."

After Rochester, Troy, Utica, Albany, New York, and Baltimore, they returned to New York. "Frohman and the manager Williams said they have never seen such a performance of *Frou Frou*. Very satisfactory," wrote Lablache. "Henri de Satorys is my best part."

At Philadelphia, they had tremendous houses, but fire broke out on the upper floors of the Layffette Hotel where some of the company were staying. Luckily, no one was hurt, but the ladies lost all their dresses and jewels. Arriving in Chicago in subzero weather, they had time to notice a great improvement in the hotels, theaters, streets, and the stores since they were there in 1880-'81. "Fine theatres," wrote Lablache. "We had dressing rooms all to ourselves, so did the small fry." The lake was frozen as far as they could see. "Neither of us well! Too much steam and hot water heat. BEASTLY place Chicago—NASTY MUDDY HOLE." And to add insult to injury, they ran into the slab-faced actor Henry Irving again, this time in the hotel elevator. On 24 February, they left for Cleveland, again they were not pleased. "A smokey place, full of soot one can't keep clean. Milwakee, Cincianiti was not any better. Nasty depressing dirty places," wrote Lablache. The theaters there were fine, they noted however. "Fine theatres here, we went last night to the Bijou to see *20th Century Girl,* a burlesque."

Returning to Chicago for March 1896, they left to tour Kansas City on 6 April and St. Louis on the 12 April—"VERY hot, eighty-six degrees in the shade." By the time they reached Pittsburgh, they were both totally exhausted. Jennie suffered from a sore throat for two months. "We left Pittsburgh ill and arrived back in New York well. This is no exaggeration." On Sunday, 26 April, Lablache wrote, "I was very nervous and exhausted . . . feeling very sick . . . I took my curtain call with the 'Bitch.' She has not spoken to me since except to say, 'We wanted more rehearsals.'" "I suppose I was too good for her," wrote Luigi. And of course, there was the famous occasion during the trip (told over and over by Luigi to all generations who would listen!), when Ms. Nethersole, draped in furs and dressed in the finest, low cut evening gown New York had to offer, leaned seductively over her champagne glass and, looking like Eve from the Garden of Eden, drawled melodramatically, "Mr. Lablache, there is one word in the dictionary you don't understand and that is 'opportunity.'"

They sailed out of New York at 10:00 a.m. on 29 April on the American line—a U.S. mail steamer—the *St. Louis.* Lablache wrote, "Horrible cabin! right under where they shoot the cinders and ashes, very small too!—It's a good boat, GOOD FOOD." Interestingly, besides Ms. Olga Nethersole and her company, Lablache wrote, "The two Frohmans are aboard and the two De Reszkes, Jean and Édouard, Emma Calvé and a heap of singers." They were in good company in spite of a rough passage back in England. They were, however, in for a surprise.

Leaving behind their two young beautiful daughters, Fanny and Freddy—Francis Maud Therese[743] and Elizabeth Frederica Charlotte Lablache[744]—in the care of a loving family housekeeper Susan Dyer, it was rather a shock to discover upon their return that Fanny, who was only eighteen, had eloped with a man the same age as her father, James Stanley-Little, a rather eccentric journalist and author of endless books on the British Empire. Their other daughter, equally unhappy at home alone with servants, soon followed her sister's example and also eloped, but not with the same results. Here, Stewart Granger tells what happened to his mother Frederica:

> Mother fell in love with a young man Honourable Fritz Herbert or was it William, I can never remember which. They eloped and lived in Monte Carlo where they were very social, going to parties

every night, although my mother knew her husband was very ill. She would beg him to rest but he just wouldn't listen and a year later he died in her arms of tuberculosis, so poor Mummy had to come crawling back to my grandmother who was an absolute bitch and made her life hell. So here was my beautiful mother, dying to get away from home and here was my poor bachelor father (James Stewart). They met and that was it. After a brief courtship they were married. My father was the happiest man in the world and my mother was able to leave home.[745]

Lablache crossed the Atlantic again in 1898-'99 to star again on Broadway and another tour. Charles Frohman lost his life on the ill-fated *Lusitania* when it sank in 1915. His Empire theater was torn down in 1953. Between touring America, Lablache acted in *Carmen* again in London in 1896 at the Gaiety. Next, he joined the Adelphi company in *Boys Together*, *Black-eyed Susan*, *Charlotte Corday*, and *the Lady of Lyons*.

Creating General Burgoyne in the original production of George Bernard Shaw's *The Devil's Disciple* at the Kennington in 1899, Lablache continued to act in many plays, the most notable were *Mice and Men* with Forbes Robinson in 1902 at the Lyric, *The Prodical Son* and *Trial by Dury* at Drury Lane 1905, 1906. He ended his career with *The Philanderer* (1907), *The Devil's Disciple* (1907), *Strife* (1909), and *The Brass Bottle* (1909).[746]

By 1902, Luigi and Jane had two grandchildren—Lois and Colyer. Their parents, James and Francis Maud Stanley-Little, lived comfortably in London. Frederica married a second time to James Stewart; their children were James Lablache Stewart—stage name Stewart Granger—and Iris Stewart.

Luigi Lablache died quietly at home age sixty-four in a wicker chair on 18 December 1914. Jennie lived out the rest of her life alone at their old house at 51 Albany Street. She was the last Lablache to carry the family surname in England.[747]

Stewart Granger was the last of the Lablaches to occupy a place on the stage. Born James Lablache Stewart on 6 May 1913, he writes, "As a child I had Latin good looks and a strong character, meaning I had black hair and a hell of a temper."[748] His good looks brought him fame on the stage and in the films. Later, he changed his name so not to be confused with the Hollywood actor, Jimmy Stewart. However, he was always called Jimmy by friends and family alike. Granger's first stage appearance was as Captain Hamilton in *The Sun Never Sets* at the Drury Lane Theatre London in 1938, and the following year, he joined the Old Vic Company. Starting in the theater, he was coached by George Bernard Shaw and, like his grandfather before him, took a role in *The Devil's Disciple*. He entered the world of films in England in 1933, and after serving in the Black Watch, he continued in films achieving immediate success during World War II. Granger's incredible good looks earned him the title of Britain's "leading romantic hero." Tall, athletic, and handsome like his grandfather before him, women from all over the world were thrilled by his portrayal of a romantic hero.

His seventh film brought him his first success in the 1943 production of *The Man in Grey* with James Mason, Margaret Lockwood, and Phillis Calvett; in his own words, "It was a smash hit and I became a star overnight," holding his own against leading actors of the day like Douglas Fairbanks, Robert Taylor, Allan Ladd, Tyrone Power, Errol Flynn to name a few. He also starred in such hits as *Fanny by Gaslight, Waterloo Road, Madonna of the Seven Moons, Caesar and Cleopatra, Caravan, Blanche Fury*.

After leaving the Rank Organization, he made films for many companies; the most well known were filmed in color by MGM, EMI Films and Twentieth Century Fox. *Saraband for Dead Lovers, Adam and Evelyne, King Solomon's Mines, Scaramouche, Young Bess, The Prisoner of Zenda, Footsteps in the Fog, Magic Bow, Beau Brummell, Green Fire, Bhowani Junction,* and *Harry Black and the Tiger* were among the best known. And there were many others made in Italy and Germany. Established first as a leading romantic actor, he became even better known after *Scaramouche* and *The Prisoner of Zenda* when he was cast in dashing swashbuckling roles one after another on the big screen.[749]

After his three marriages had failed, he retired to Spain where, after losing a small fortune in investments, he returned to Hollywood. There, in 1981, he wrote a successful autobiography, *Sparks Fly Upward*.[750] Satisfied with appearing in a TV series and occasional TV movie, he was persuaded to come out of retirement in his late seventies to star on Broadway in Somerset Maugham's *The Circle* with British actors Rex Harrison and Glynis Johns. After its New York success, he returned to England, touring with the play.

Acting was in his blood, and he bravely continued to appear on the stage like the heroes of his films, his last stage performance was at the Henry Fonda Theatre in the heart of Hollywood, at the age of seventy-nine, in *Don Juan in Hell* by George Bernard Shaw, costaring with Ricardo Montalban, David Carradine, and Lynn Redgrave. Stewart Granger still displayed his skill as an actor with great dignity in spite of the ravages of a fatal illness.[751] A year later, Granger died in Santa Monica California, shortly after his eightieth birthday, on 16 August 1993. He left a son and three daughters.[752]

Jane Lablache never returned to the stage after Luigi died. Living out her life comfortably at 51 Albany Street in London, the family home for over a hundred years, she was persuaded to sell the house and move to Bournemouth to be near her daughter's family. Enduring her life as a theatrical widow, she loved being close to her theatrical cronies and often talked to her grandson, Thomas Colyer, about her days spent on the stage. Rambling on about her youth, she remembered bygone Edwardian days when she was part of those exciting circles among Victorian and Edwardian actresses, such as Ellen Terry, Olga Nethersole, Lilly Lantry, Mrs. Scott Siddens, and many more graceful Edwardian beauties with hourglass figures, huge hats and flowing long dresses.

When the house was sold, her grandson recalled the scene. Large paintings of the family members were taken down, dust sheets were thrown over the piano on which Luigi, Frédéric and Fanny Lablache, and Jenny Lind played in bygone days, and the huge mahogany table with the cutout for the great Lablache's stomach was pushed out to be sold. Echoes of the past haunted the empty house. Here, she is remembered by her grandson T. C. Stanley-Little (author's father):

> Just a faint glimpse of her comes to my mind . . . hovering in the gloom, I remember a frail bent-over figure of Jane—Great Granny, in a silk dressing gown trimmed with wild pink ostrich feathers, her hair a mass of grey frizzy curls, her voice often sharp and dramatic, sometimes sadly moaning incessantly as she looks over her mementos from the past—occasionally it was a familiar little chipped plaster figure of Dr. Dulcamara sitting forlornly on the sideboard among a mass of half-drunk wine glasses and dirty liquor bottles. Does a faint smile cross her face? Dressed in a red coat and boots, he holds up his tiny bottle of love potion, and we imagine we hear faintly in the distant shadows the rich velvet tones of the great Lablache singing.

THE END

☙☙☙

Luigi Lablache carte de visite 1850s (Lablache Archives)

The Madeleine, Paris, photo (Lablache Archives)

IN MEMORIAM.

REQUIEM

Composed by

FRÉDÉRIC LABLACHE.

Ent. Sta. Hall. Price Paper Cover 3/-
Paper Boards 3/6

London & New York
NOVELLO, EWER & Cº

*Requiem Mass frontispiece by Frederic Lablache composer
(Lablache Archives)*

Luigi Lablache's mausoleum Maison Laffitte,
author photo (Lablache Archives)

Emily de Meric Lablache carte de visite (Lablache Archives)

Sigismund Thalberg's Home Sweet Home frontispiece (Lablache Archives)

Sigismund Thalberg by John Frederick Herring (Lablache Archives)

*Sigismund Thalberg mausoleum in Naples,
author photo (Lablache Archives)*

*Francesca Thalberg mausoleum in Naples,
author photo (Lablache Archives)*

Sigismund Thalberg statue in Naples (Francesco Nicolosi)

*Sigismund Thalberg/Lablache villa Posillipo nr. Naples,
author photo (Lablache Archives)*

*Sigismund Thalberg/Lablache villa Posillipo nr.
Naples, author photo (Lablache Archives)*

*Sigismund Thalberg/Lablache villa Posillipo nr. Naples,
author photo (Lablache Archives)*

Queen Victoria and Princess Beatrice carte de visite (Lablache Archives)

Maria de Cater carte de visite
(Lablache Archives)

Ernest de Cater carte de visite
(Lablache Archives)

Zara Thalberg (aka Nazarina McKenzie)
The Graphic (Lablache Archives)

Luigi Lablache Naples bust,
photo by Prince Francesco de Avalos (Lablache Archives)

Luigi Lablache Naples bust,
photo by Prince Francesco de Avalos (Lablache Archives)

Marie Battu (aka Mme. Dominique Lablache) (Lablache Archives)

Marie Battu as Isabelle in Robert le Diable (Lablache Archives)

Baron Johann von Rokitansky carte de visite 1860s (Lablache Archives)

Therese Lablache Rokitansky carte de visite 1860s (Lablache Archives)

Emilie de Meric Lablache (Lablache Archives)

Nina de Meric (Lablache Archives)

Met playbill Faust 1883

Charles Gounod, composer, early postcard (Lablache Archives)

Louise Lablache (Harvard Theatre Collection)

Frederic Lablache carte de visite 1850s (Lablache Archives)

Dominique Lablache carte de visite 1850s (Lablache Archives)

Fanny Wyndham (Mme. F. Lablache) carte de visite 1860s (Lablache Archives)

Henri Lablache or Nicolas Lablache carte de visite (Lablache Archives)

Luigi Frederic Lablache (Lablache Archives)

Jane Emmerson (aka Jane Lablache) photo (Lablache Archives)

Luigi Frederic Lablache actor-grandson 1880s (Lablache Archives)

LYRIC THEATRE.

Lessee .. Mr. William Greet.

BY ARRANGEMENT WITH MR. TOM B. DAVIS.

Mr. Forbes Robertson's Season.

MONDAY, JANUARY 27th, 1902,

AND EVERY EVENING AT 8.15.

MATINEES each SATURDAY at 2.30

A New Play in Four Acts, by Madeleine Lucette Ryley, entitled,

"MICE AND MEN"

"The best-laid schemes o' Mice an' Men gang aft a-gley."—*Burns.*

Mark Embury	Mr. Forbes Robertson
(Scholar, Scientist and Philanthropist)	
Roger Goodlake	Mr. Luigi Lablache
(his Friend and Neighbour)	
Captain George Lovell ...	Mr. Ben Webster
(Embury's Nephew)	
Sir Harry Trimblestone ...	Mr. Leon Quartermaine
Kit Barniger	Mr. J. H. Ryley
(a Fiddler and Professor of Deportment)	
Peter (Embury's Servant)	Mr. William Farren Junr.
Beadle of the Foundling Hospital	Mr. Ernest Cosham
Joanna Goodlake	Miss Alice De Winton
(Wife of Goodlake)	
Mrs. Deborah	Miss Carlingford
(Emburys Housekeeper)	
Matron of the Foundling Hospital	Miss Minnie Griffin
Molly (a Kitchen Maid) ...	Miss Edith Fenchester
Peggy ("Little Britain")...	Miss Gertrude Elliott

PLACE - OLD HAMPSTEAD - PERIOD about 1786.

Mice and Men playbill Lyric Theatre London 1902 (Lablache Archives)

*Luigi Frederic Lablache in Mice and Men costume,
signed postcard 1903 (Lablache Archives)*

Olga Nethersole early postcard 1905
(Lablache Archives)

Olga Nethersole early postcard 1905
(Lablache Archives)

EMPIRE THEATRE
1430 Broadway at Fortieth Street

Empire Theatre Broadway New York (Lablache Archives)

GAIETY THEATRE.

LESSEE AND MANAGER
GEORGE EDWARDS.

OLGA NETHERSOLE'S SEASON.

Management of DANIEL and CHARLES FROHMAN.

Saturday, June 6th, and Every Evening at 8,

A Dramatic Version of PROSPER MÉRIMÉE'S Novel, entitled

CARMEN

By HENRY HAMILTON

Don José	...	Mr. CHARLES DALTON
Don Lucas Lucenda	...	Mr. THOMAS KINGSTON
Lucas Mendez	...	Mr. LUIGI LABLACHE
Serral D'Alfa	(Corporal)	Mr. J. R. CRAUFORD
Pepe	(Muleteer and Toreador)	Mr. ACTON BOND
Pastia Diaz	(Lance-Corporal)	Mr. GEORGE HUMPHREY
Dancaire	...	Mr. G. R. FOSS
Little Paulo	...	Mr. GRAEME GORING
Sebastian	(Sergeant)	Mr. ALBERT SIMS
Pablo	...	Mr. I. CHADWICK
Pepe	...	Mr. LINGSTWELL
Pedro	(Smugglers)	Mr. EVA WILLIAMS
Abbès	...	Miss HELENA DACRE
Teresa	...	Miss ALEXIS LEIGHTON
Jose	...	Miss MAY MERSHALL
		Miss MADGE MEADOWS
Carmen	...	Miss OLGA NETHERSOLE

Soldiers, Smugglers, Bull-Fighters, Factory Girls, Populace.

ACTS

Act I. — A Square in Seville.
Act II. — Tableau I. — The City Wall, Seville. Tableau II. — Patio of Lillas Pastia's Wine Shop.
     NOTE. — Between Tableau I. and II. the Curtain will be lowered for a few minutes.
Act III. — A Ravine in the Bull Ring at Cordova.
Act IV. — Exterior of the Bull Ring at Cordova.

The Principals of the Gaiety Theatre Orchestra will play the following Programme during the Evening under the direction of Mr. J. H. KÖNIG.

1. PRELUDE   "Carmen"   Bizet
2. OVERTURE   "Lily of Lucelle"   Corelli
3. (a) Cèlébre Gavotte   4. INTERMEZZO   "The Shepherd's Call"   Herbert Ewing
   (b) Aubade   5. VALSE CAPRICCIOSO   ... J. König
                         à l'Espagne

The Scenery has been Painted by Mr. W. T. HEMSLEY. The Dramatic Music arranged from the score of Bizet's Opera, "Carmen" by permission of Mr. FRANK A. HOWSON of the Lyceum Theatre, New York. Miss OLGA NETHERSOLE'S Dresses by All Round Carmel. The Spanish Dances arranged by Señor KEPPOCHER. Miss OLGA NETHERSOLE'S Costumes by Mrs. NETTLESHIP of Wigmore St. All other Costumes by Messrs. L & H NATHAN. Wigs by CLARKSON.

The Play Produced under the Stage Direction of Mr. THOMAS A. HALL and Miss OLGA NETHERSOLE.

Business Manager ... ... Mr. THOMAS A. HALL (Assistant Stage Manager ... Mr. LOUIS F. NETHERSOLE
Stage Manager ...
Musical Director ... ... Mr. J. H. KÖNIG   Mr. W. POSTANCE

PRICES OF ADMISSION — Private Boxes, £1 1s to £4 Guineas; Orchestra Stalls, 10s. 6d.; Balcony Stalls, 7s. and 5s.; Dress Circle (Cushioned and Reserved) 4s.; Pit, 2s. 6d.; Gallery, 1s. 3rd and 4th Rows, 6d.; Upper Boxes (Cushioned and Reserved) 4s.; Pit, 2s. 6d.; Gallery, 1s.
                   Carriages at 11.
Doors open at 7.30.   Commence at 8.

Box Office open daily from 10 to 6, under the Direction A. P. OXLEY.
St. Michaelangel & Co., Printers, Royal Street (late Hart Street), Covent Garden.

Carmen program Gaiety Theatre London 1896 (Lablache Archives)

Drury Lane, London wood engraving (Lablache Archives)

The Armada program (Lablache Archives)

Luigi Frederic Lablache in The Armada costume photo 1888
(Lablache Archives)

Prodigal Son program Drury Lane Theatre 1905 (Lablache Archives)

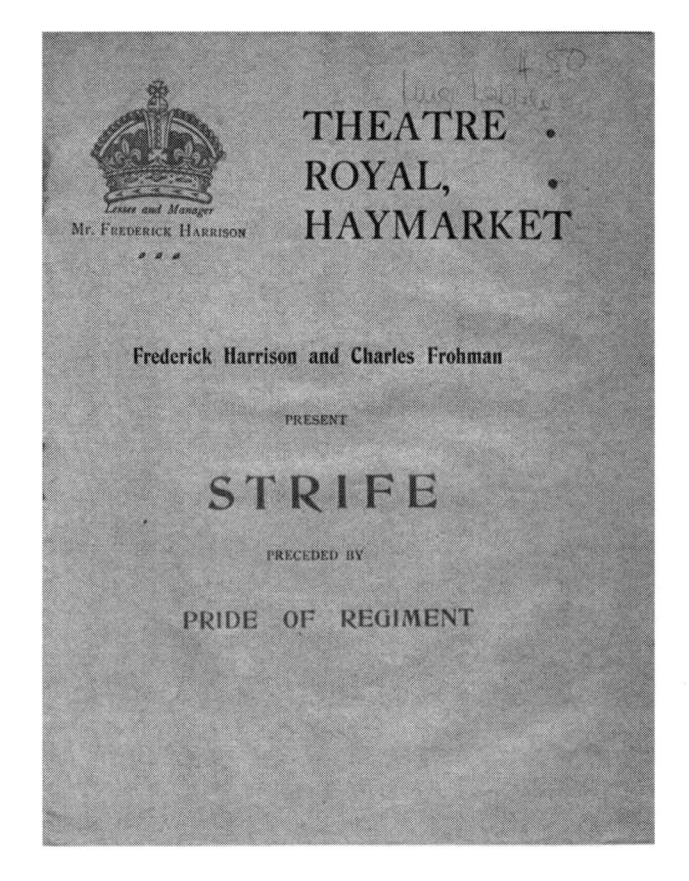

Strife program Haymarket Theatre London 1909 (Lablache Archives)

James Stanley-Little pencil drawing by Leon Little (Lablache Archives)

T.C. (Thomas Colyer) Stanley-Little, photo (Lablache Archives)

Fanny Maud Lablache Stanley-Little, photo (Lablache Archives)

Norman Parkinson Vogue and Queen's photographer newspaper clipping (Lablache Archives)

*Family photo Author's Club with
Sir Arthur Conan Doyle, 1905 (Lablache Archives)*

Close-up of family at club (Lablache Archives)

Stewart Granger photo 1970s (Lablache Archives)

Stewart Granger poster Scaramouche 1952 (Lablache Archives)

Eugene Galvin
Bass-Baritone
Mary Lou McDonald Galvin
Piano

LUIGI LABLACHE

First Bass

8:00 PM Friday, October 14, 1994
Homer Ulrich Recital Hall
University of Maryland College Park

Presented in Partial Fulfillment of the Doctor of Musical Arts Degree
Mr. Galvin is a student of Dominic Cossa

Luigi Lablache concert cover, Washington DC, 1994.

Appendix A

Compositions by Luigi Lablache

Published material of Louis Lablache.*

Papuccie (Cavatina Cantata) ad Published by Antonio Pacini Price F4,50
Nouveaux airs et duos chante lian 1830 Published by Anton
Exercices (Extr. Méthode)p.S ou T, MS ou contralto-
Litolff, un. ed Peters, ed 2.75, Scholt.ND
Esereizi per Basso. 5.50 Ricordi. 4.25 Schott ND
*Flight is vain. (Fuggi in van)*Bass clef 1/—Augener ND
Gesangsubungen. h,m,a,1-Breitkopf ND
Instructions on singing, On a entirely new System. Chappell.ND
Le Petit Frere-50 Schott ND
Method of Singing 1.50, abr. 1.25 Ditson ND
Méthode de chant moderne 11.50 Schott. ND
Metodo di Canto Published. Ricordi, Cotteau, Russian Jurgenson Swedish ND
Ottavio di Torquanto Tasso, piata an bacca-50 Schott. ND
Progressive solfeggi. 2/6 Chappel. ND
Saggiosull'artedi far variazioni. 1.75 Ricordi ND
Singers Daily Practice 2/—Chappel. ND
Solfeggi elementari. Ricordi ND.
Solfeggi facili. 1/50 Cottrau. ND
Vocal exercises, a collection of scales for daily practice which no singer, even when arrived at perfection should ever dispense. 2/6 Chappel. ND
12 Vocals. Ricordi
14 Vocalizes. Brainard
Vocalizzi facili. (estratti dal metodo) 1.50 Cottrau 3.50 Ricordi
Vocalizzi piu difficelli, 1.50 Contrau Ricordi
*Metodo completo di canto. Complete Singing Method.
Facsimile of the 1842 edition.* Published by Ricordi 1997 *

• Lablache Archives. Listed in F. Pazdirek

Appendix B

Lablache Family Musical Compositions

Written by Frédéric Lablache, Mme. F. Lablache, and Mlle. Fanny Lablache

A Simple Country girl. Published by J. B. Cramer.
The Buccaneer. Published by Augener. N.D.
The Buccaneer. Song in English, composed expressly for and sung by Mr. Santley. Words by Henry Farnie. Pub. Cramer and Wood. London. Aurographed. N.D.
Ce que je veux. Published by Ashdown. London. N.D.
Requiem Mass, Voc. score 8vo paper cover. Pub by Novello.
Souvenies d'automn. Silhouettes Musicales pour piano: Pub. by Enoch and Sons.
The Vision. Song, words by Mad. F. Lablache. Pub. J. B. Cramer. London. N.D.
L'incontro, romanza. Pub. Cramer Wood. London. Autographed
Waltz. Unpublished. English Italian. Autographed.
Espère, Romance. Parole de Adolphe de leuven. Dec.
Dediee Miss Novello. Pub. Lamborn Cock. London. Autographed-front N.D.
The Voice of Hope, Song Pub. Lamborn Cock.
M'ami? Si t'amo. Duettino.
Il nome Suo. Canzone, Pub. Cramer(Limited)London. Words by Fanny Lablache. Autographed
Tu del cielo e della Terra, Preghiera. Parole del Sig. Giannone. Cramer, Beale and Co. London. Autographed
The Parting Look. Song. Written by George Linley. Pub. Ashdown and Parry. London. N.D.
Love's Sigh, Song. Words by Miss Lablache. Pub. Hutchings and Romer. London. Autographed-front. N.D.
Six. Morceaux de chant. Le Petite Frere. Songs in French and English.
Le Petite Frere, Songs. Set of six. Londres chez Cramer, Beale et Co. London. N.D
Momens de Loisir. Pour piano. 8 Pieces. *Pensees*

Cararteristiques, pour piano. Pub. J.B. Cramer & Co London, N.D.

1) *Le Colombier.*
2) *Danse iroquoise.*
3) *Nocturne.*
4) *Souvenir du Bal.*
5) *Sur le lac.*
6) *Styrienne.*
7) *Bon Soir.*
8) *Bon Jour.*

Souvenirs d' automn
Tis I ! Song. Words by Miss Fanny Lablache. Music by Ciro Pinsuti. J.B. Cramer & Co. London. N.D.(Signed).

Appendix C

Luigi Lablache Images in Objets d'art

Oil Paintings of Lablache

Portrait. Franz Xaver Winterhalter. Oval. 1852. Royal Archives, England.
Portrait. Friedrich Lieder. Oval Sq. Frame. 1823. Dr. Stephen Stanley-Little, England.
Portrait. Antoine Jean Gros. La Scala Museum, Milan.
Mini portraits of Luigi and Teresa. Black Frame. 1820s. Dr. Stephen Stanley-Little, England.
Painting by F. Tatham. Location unknown. Lithograph of painting. Lablache Archives.
Head to waist in costume by Franz Xaver Winterhalter. Oval. Simonette Lablache de la Fuente, Italy.
Portrait head to waist. François Bouchot. Museo d' S. Martino, Naples.
Marino Faliero, Lablache and Grisi. Oil painting. Jo Waters collection, London.
Portrait Teresa Lablache by François Bouchot. Museo d' S. Martino, Naples.
L'Elisir d'amore, Dulcamara. Full figure holding bottle. La Scala Museum, Milan.

Lithographs, engravings and drawings of Lablache

Anna Bolena, Henry VIII. Devéria. Litho. Lablache Archives.
Portrait head. Litho. G. Brown, F. Tatham. Lablache Archives.
Polka with Sontag Music Cover. Lablache Archives.
Portrait. *La Moda Milan*. Litho. Lablache Archives.
Portrait. P. Fontana. Litho. Ricordi. Lablache Archives.
Portrait. F. Artardo. Litho. Lablache Archives.
Portrait. F. Croll. Lemercier. Litho. Andrew S. Pope.
Figaro. Litho. Caricature from Dantan. Lablache Archives.
Otello. Litho. Sergio Ragni collection, Naples.
Portrait. Litho. Sergio Ragni collection, Naples.

Inez de Castro. Litho. Opera Rara collection, London.
Il prova di opera seria with Pasta. Litho. Opera Rara collection, London.
Cenerentola, Dandini. A. E. Chalon. Litho. 1831. Victoria and Albert Museum, London.
La Tempesta, Caliban. *Illustrated London News*. Lablache Archives.
Don Giovanni, Leporello. Drawing. Lablache Archives.
Falstaff. Full figure. P. Salabert. Litho. Lablache Archives.
Marino Faliero. A. E. Chalon. Litho. Lablache Archives.
Portrait. Devéria. Litho. 1830. Coll. Jacques Gheusi, Paris.
Portrait head from *Marino Faliero*. François Bouchot. Litho. Dominique de Friston, England.
I Puritani Caricature. Pantheon Charivarique. Litho. Lablache Archives.
I Puritani, Grisi & Lablache. Gravure de Pedretta d'apres Verardi. Litho. BO.*
I Puritani, Grisi & Lablache with castle. BO.*
Anna Bolena, Henry VIII. *Illustrated London News*. 1842. Lablache Archives.
Lucrezia Borgia w Grisi. *London Illustrated News*. 1845. Donizetti Society, London.
Portrait. A. Kneisel. Litho. Fulvio Stefano Lo Presti collection, Brussels.
Portrait. Cover of *London Journal*. 1845. Lablache Archives.
Valse *Don Pasquale*. Music Cover. London. Lablache Archives.
Don Pasquale. Whole stage print. Lablache Archives.
Lablache and friends. Constantin Guys. Drawing. Baron Christien de Caters collection, Paris.
Lablache and Madame Rubini. A.E. Chalon. Litho. Dr. R. Copeman collection.
I Masnadieri w Lind. *Illustrated London News*. 1847. Lablache Archives.
I Masnadieri w Lind. *Illustrated London News*. 1847. Lablache Archives.
I Puritani w Jenny Lind. *Illustrated London News*.
I Puritani w Jenny Lind. *Illustrated London News*.
I Puritani w Fornasari. *Illustrated London News*. 1845. Lablache Archives.
Otello w Grisi and Mario. *Illustrated London News*. Enthoven collection.
I Puritani. Costume Figure. French Theatre Italien. Lablache Archives.
Lablache w Santini. A.E Chalon. Drawing. Lablache Archives.
Don Pasquale Garden Scene w Grisi. *Illustrated London News*. Lablache Archives.
Don Pasquale Garden Scene. *Illustrated London News*.
Don Pasquale Garden w flashlight & Grisi. Music Cover. ROH.**
Don Pasquale w plaid pants w La Grange. Enthoven collection.
Portrait. Ridolphi. Litho. Lablache Archives.
Portrait, older Lablache. P. Salabert. 1856. Lablache Archives.
Norma, Oroverso w Jenny Lind. 1847. Clipping.

Norma, Oroverso w Grisi. Illustration-Beauties of Ballet & Opera. 1845. Lablache Archives.
Norma. Oroveso w Grisi. Stonehenge, Conti. Litho Music sheet cover. Unknown location.
Nozze di Figaro. Illustration—Beauties of Ballet & Opera. 1845. Lablache Archives.
Portrait. Julien. Artistes du Italien. Lablache Archives.
I Puritani Lablache and Grisi. A.E Chalon. La Scala Museum, Milan.
I Puritani. Lind. *Illustrated London News.* 1848.
Le Cantatrici Villane w Luzio. Opera Rara collection.
Portrait. Lieder. Litho. Lablache Archives.
Caricature Lablache and Mercadante. Unknown location.
L'Elisir d'amore, Dulcamara Full figure. J. Brandard. Litho. Lablache Archives.
L'Elisir d'amore. Dulcamara w Mario. Jacque Gheusi collection, Paris.
L'Elisir d'amore. Dulcamara w crowd. ROH.**
L'Elisir d'amore. Dulcamara on one knee. ROH.**
Il Matrimonio Segreto. Illustrated London News. Lablache Archives.
Portrait. *Il Matrimonio Segreto,* Geronimo. Litho. Lablache Archives.
Lablache sitting at Covent Garden. *Illustrated London News.*
Portrait, Half figure-older Lablache. Litho. Lablache Archives.
Portrait head. Giovanni Bernadoni. Litho. Sergio Ragni collection, Naples.
Forty drawings of Lablache by Queen Victoria. Windsor Castle, England.
Cartoon P.68. Petite Encyclopédie illustrée de L'Opéra de Paris. Location unknown.
Lablache plays violin in Paris. Giovanni Battista Gatti. Sergio Ragni collection, Naples.
Portrait. Joseph Kriehuber. 1827. Sergio Ragni collection, Naples.

Statues and Staffordshire Figures

Dulcamara, small colored statue. Dominique de Friston. England.
Falstaff, Staffordshire china. Lablache Archives.
Dandini, Staffordshire china. Lablache Archives.
Figaro, French china figure. Baron Christien de Caters collection, Paris.
Large Lablache bust. Conservatorio di San Pietro a Majella, Naples.
Henry VIII, Staffordshire china group w Pasta. Stuart-Liff collection, Isle of Man.
Figaro, bronze statue. Jean Bruson's Dantan collection. Museé Carnavalet, Paris.

Lablache Record Covers

The covers depict full images of Lablache.

Don Pasquale. EMI 0233 Digtal. Lablache Archives.
The Elixir of Love. Stereo. Lablache Archives.
I Puritani. Melodrama DP Made in Italy. Lablache Archives.
I Puritani. London frr.Mono A 4373. Lablache Archives.

- BO = Bibliothèque de L'Opéra, Paris
** ROH = Royal Opera House

Appendix D

Lablache on English Music

Musical World—November 24, 1837

This article was communicated by Luigi Lablache to a Paris paper, *Le Monde Parisien,* from which we have slightly abridged it.) *Morning Post. Musical World.* November 24,1837 Page 166.

The reputation of England, as far as music is concerned, is not yet established in Europe. The exalted position which Great Britain occupies in a commercial point of view, the immense progress which that country has made in the useful arts, the ardour with which she advances on the road of material improvement, have led to the adoption of the opinion that there can be little room in English heads for any thought about the fine arts.

This opinion, which has been gradually disseminated, has now acquired all the strength of a confirmed prejudice, and it seems to be taken for granted that the only kind of harmony understood in England is the shrill scream of a Manchester steam engine, or the heavy fall of the hammers that beat time in the forges of Birmingham.

There is in this preconceived notion an evident exaggeration. God has, more or less, developed the sentiment in every human heart, and could not, therefore, have created a whole nation of individuals thus disinherited of one of their senses. The present inferiority of England is a geographical question rather than one of organization. It has always been observed, that islanders have been apt to impel other nations to improvement, but to be slow in receiving a similar impulse from without. Moreover, at the period when the musical evolution broke out in Italy, England was busily engaged in the accomplishment of a social revolution; she was organizing her political unity, and it is not during such struggles that nations are found disposed to receive the fruitful seeds of letters and the arts.

With all nations a poetical is inseparable from a musical feeling; and if so, the past of the three kingdoms is a sufficient pledge for the future. The country which in recent times has produced a Walter Scott and a Byron, will have its great composers as it had its great poets. The upper classes long since gave the musical impulse, and are now as passionately fond of their concerts as of their ancient fox-chases. The middle-classes obey this useful impulse, and England, which had so long enjoyed the privilege of furnishing excellent pianos to other nations, now sees her own citizens actively encourage this branch of industry. The old family bible is no longer the only article of furniture in an English house; the piano now divides with it the honours of domestic patronage, and the execution of fashionable music occupies a portion of the evening, formerly consecrated to the perusal of pious tracts distributed by religious associations.

Three principal points cannot fail to strike any person desirous of inquiring into the present state of music in England; firstly, the festivals, and public and private concerts; secondly, the orchestras of the theatres and the stage singing; thirdly, the method of teaching, public as well as private.

The proof of musical progress is found in the state of instrumental execution; and this department of the art is constituting itself in England more and more every day. Much may be said on the intelligent efforts made to ameliorate the theatrical orchestras and the establishments for singing, to which it is my intention to return.

In instrumental music great efforts have been made in a few years. Societies have been formed in London for the regular performance of concerts, nearly on the same plan as the *Societe des Concerts du Conservatoire.* These societies, as in Paris, are extremely difficult in the admission of professional members. The first of these establishments is directed by Moscheles, Cramer, and Sir George Smart, who do every thing in their power to make the *ensemble* complete and the execution perfect. The efforts of these able professors are worthily recompensed.

Surrounded by the most celebrated instrumental performers of England, their results are of the happiest and they sufficiently prove what effects may be hereafter produced in the cause of music, under the direction and councils of men of real talent. These concerts, established by an association of English artists, are called the concerts of the Philharmonic Society.

The second association for the execution of instrumental music is called Societa Armonica. It has not yet attained the perfection of the Philharmonic but all its efforts are to equal it. The names of the distinguished artists who have united for the attainment of so noble an end are a sufficient pledge for the success of this useful institution.

An establishment of a less modem origin, but quite as useful in its object, excites at London the particular attention of artists and of the friends of the muscial art: I mean the Ancient Concerts—the only institution of the kind in Europe, either as respects the statutes by which it is governed, or the number of noblemen and artists of high reputation who have combined in spreading its fame.

The most probable version of the origin of the Ancient Concerts is the following: George the Third, in early youth, became acquainted with Handel, then approaching the end of his career; the severe and commanding compositions of the great German master struck the young prince with admiration. He set aside certain evenings for performances at Court, on which occasions Handel's music alone was executed. At times, the King even performed his part in these private concerts, to which none but persons of the highest distinction were ever admitted.

Whether from real enthusiasm for the *chefs-d'oeuvre* of the German master in some, or courtier-like flattery in others, Handel became the favourite composer of the upper classes. They assembled in the apartments of the aristocracy to hear the performance of an oration with more eagerness than they would have joined in a vall; the 'Messiah', and the 'Israelites in Egypt', were the most powerful attraction of the time; the music of Handel excited complete fanaticism, or, to speak more forcibly, it became the fashion. This decided taste for the partitions of Handel, instead of growing weaker, spread more and more, so that in a short time there was formed in London, a society of noblemen for the execution of his music, and that of the celebrated composers who had preceded him. Hence the establishment of the Ancient Concerts.

Lord Sandwich was the founder of the Ancient Concerts, the first performance of which took place about the beginning of the year 1776. In the managing committee, composed of eight members, I find the names of the Earl of Sandwich, the Earl of Exeter, Lord Dudley, the Bishop of Durham, Lord Paget (the father of the present Marquis of Anglesea), etc. The concert was especially consecrated to the execution of ancient music, and to preserve this original character the statutes formally enact that no music shall be executed but that of composers who have been dead at least twenty years. This clause has at all times been strictly observed.

This establishment, already so highly favoured, received further distinctions in 1785. The King and the royal family determined to be present every evening, and the name of Ancient Concerts was dropped, the society being authorized to substitute that of King's Concerts. The King's private band and the chorus of the chapel were ordered to join the musicians of the royal concert, and appeared on each occasion in the uniform of the royal household. This custom continued to prevail until the last illness of George the Third.

The most distinguished artists were at all times called on to give their services to the Ancient Concerts. The celebrated Rubinelli, in 1787, assisted by Mrs. Billington, was warmly applauded in the *'Stabat mater'* of Pergolesi, which he afterwards repeated with equal success with Mme. Storace.

The next year Marchesi made a brilliant debut in Handel's aria, 'Ah! non voler, ben mio!' In 1797, the tenor Viganoni sung with Madame Banti, Handel's beautiful duo *'False imagini,'* from Otho, an opera then in great vogue.

Thus from year to year all the reputations of Europe brought the tribute of their talents to this remarkable institution. I will here mention only the names Champness, Naldi, Porto, Tamburini, Phillips, Clark, Crivelli, Garcia, Donzelli, Rubini, Mesdames Grassini, Catalani, Mainvielle, Fodor, Malibran, Grisi, Knyvett, and Bishop.

The solicitude of the members of the committee to seek the most sonorous and the best-situated room has occasioned the Ancient Concerts frequently to change the place of their performance. In 1794 they removed from Tottenham Street to the King's Theatre, now her Majesty's Theatre, and in 1804 they went to the Hanover Square Rooms, the most favourable for music, and the best arranged for acoustic effect. At the latter place, their musical meetings still continue to be held. Every year the number increases of the wealthy amateurs who encourage this national establishment; in 1783 the members amounted only to four hundred; at present there are twelve hundred subscribers.

I have said that there exists no similar institution in Europe—a fact much to be regretted, for the sake of musical instruction; the execution by a full orchestra of the *chefs d'oeuvre of* the great masters, is the most useful and the most energetic method of teaching: I have always been surprised that France, having derived such great advantages from the establishment of the concerts of the Conservatoire, should not also have had an Ancient Concert, destined to revive so many forgotten master pieces, so necessary as these are to the serious instruction of the artist.

Italy is also without an institution of the kind, but fortunately the Popes have not given up the Sistine Chapel, in which the simple but instructive music of Palestrina, Carissimi, Jomelli, and Pergolesi, continues to be executed.

Germany would also be without the advantages of such an institution if a learned *dilettante* had not felt the importance of reproducing the works of the ancient masters, so little known at present. Mr. Kiesewetter unites at his house in Berlin, the most distinguished artists, and there, nearly every Friday, a selected circle is admitted, to salute the genius of those admirable composers who have done so much for their art, and to whom we too rarely accord a token of our gratitude or recollection.

There is no doubt that every man may have the partitions of Handel or Pergolesi, and study them in private; but how vast the difference between such a private study, and a public performance! What delight, what magic ecstacy do we not experience from this divine music, when executed by a numerous orchestra!

The first time in my life that I ever felt the full effect of one of Handel's *chefs d'oeuvre,* or became satisfied how beneficial it must be to a young musician, was at the great York Festival in 1835, when, in the immense cathedral, a thousand musicians, directed by Knyvett, performed the oratorio of the 'Messiah'. I became speechless with admiration and surprise; it was as though I had seen a colossus of Michael Angelo advancing upon me!

LABLACHE.

Appendix E

Queen Victoria's Gift to the Lablache Family

The Musical World—April 21, 1860 page 252

Since the death of Signor Lablache deep regret is still vividly felt in reference to his memory, and all that relates to an artist so highly esteemed is received with the most lively of interest. We are sure it will afford universal gratification in annoucing that Her Majesty has been pleased to present a copy of the portrait of Sig. Lablache, executed for Her Majesty, by Franz Winterhalter, to the surviving relatives; a compliment no less gratifying to the family than indictive of Her Majesty's appreciation of worth and excellence. With becoming consideration the gift is accompanied with explicit suggestions—from such a distinguished quarter, almost amounting to commands—that the charge of the picture be entrusted, during his lifetime, to Sig. Frederick Lablache; and at his decease, to be transferred in succession to any of his sisters or brothers, children of the late Sig. Lablache—thus providing that the picture should remain a heirloom to the family. A communication embodying such instruction accompanied the gift, which, in accordance with Her Majesty's commands, has been recently delivered to Signor Frederick Lablache, as the eldest member of the family.

This was followed in the Musical World by a copy of the Queen's letter to Frederic Lablache with instructions by a lawyer and the last words of the lengthy letter: in the event of the decease of all the children of Signor Lablache, this portrait should be disposable by you; by bequest in your will to any member of the Lablache family. The lawyer added, "I have directed a copy of this letter to be sent to Madame Thalberg, as Her Majesty wishes this arrangement, to be finally decided upon."

Appendix F
LABLACHE FAMILY TREE

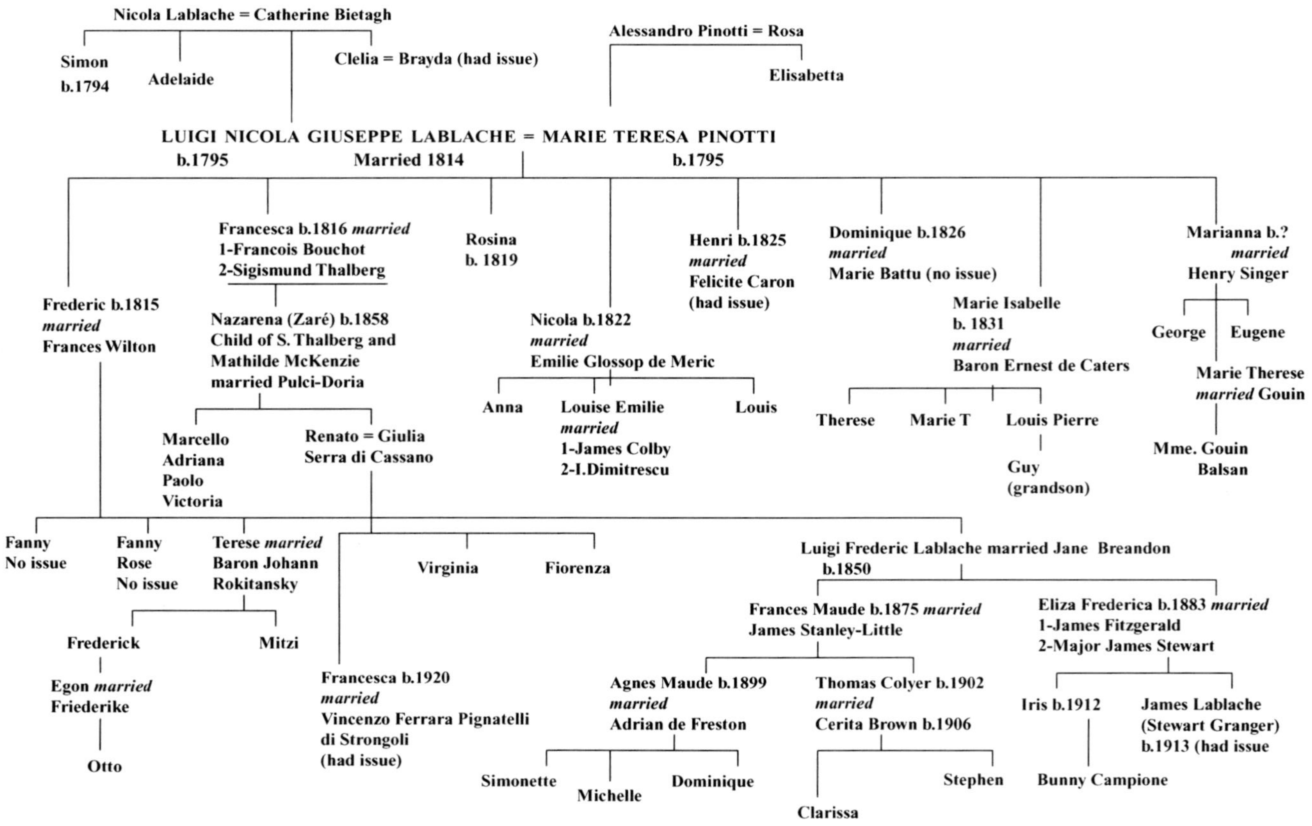

Nicola Lablache = Catherine Bietagh
- Simon b.1794
- Adelaide

Clelia = Brayda (had issue)

Alessandro Pinotti = Rosa
- Elisabetta

LUIGI NICOLA GIUSEPPE LABLACHE b.1795 = MARIE TERESA PINOTTI b.1795
Married 1814

Children of Luigi and Marie Teresa:

Frederic b.1815 married Frances Wilton
- Fanny — No issue
- Fanny Rose — No issue
- Frederick
- Egon married Friederike
  - Otto
- Terese married Baron Johann Rokitansky
  - Mitzi

Francesca b.1816 married 1-Francois Bouchot; 2-Sigismund Thalberg

Rosina b.1819

Nicola b.1822 married Emilie Glossop de Meric
- Anna
- Louise Emilie married 1-James Colby; 2-I. Dimitrescu
- Louis

Henri b.1825 married Félicite Caron (had issue)

Dominique b.1826 married Marie Battu (no issue)

Marie Isabelle b.1831 married Baron Ernest de Caters
- Therese
- Marie T
- Louis Pierre
  - Guy (grandson)

Marianna b.? married Henry Singer
- George
- Eugene
- Marie Therese married Gouin
  - Mme. Gouin Balsan

Nazarena (Zaré) b.1858 — Child of S. Thalberg and Mathilde McKenzie, married Pulci-Doria
- Marcello
- Adriana
- Paolo
- Victoria
- Renato = Giulia Serra di Cassano
  - Francesca b.1920 married Vincenzo Ferrara Pignatelli di Strongoli (had issue)
    - Virginia
    - Fiorenza

Luigi Frederic Lablache b.1850 married Jane Breandon

Frances Maude b.1875 married James Stanley-Little
- Thomas Colyer b.1902 married Cerita Brown b.1906
  - Clarissa
  - Stephen

Agnes Maude b.1899 married Adrian de Freston
- Simonette
- Michelle
- Dominique

Eliza Frederica b.1883 married 1-James Fitzgerald; 2-Major James Stewart
- Iris b.1912
- James Lablache (Stewart Granger) b.1913 (had issue)
  - Bunny Campione

582

CHRONOLOGY A
LUIGI LABLACHE'S OPERA APPEARANCES WITH CASTS.

This chronology is arranged by season rather than by calender year. Only the dates of the first performance per season are provided. To list full casts would have made this chronology unwhieldy and overlong. Early in Lablache's career he sang in opera houses and theaters where there was no published documentation. Lablache created many roles, premieres are shown as follows: ** world premieres. * Confirmed local premieres. A chronology of this kind will never be complete, there are many places where Lablache sang and no information has been found. I take full responsibility for any errors. This chronology would not be possible without the help of Tom Kaufman.

1812 NAPLES-TEATRO SAN CARLINO
    L'erede senza credita (S. Palma)
    La Molinara (V. Fioravanti)
    Gli Sposi in Cimento (L. Mosca)
    Le Trame deluse (Cimarosa)

1815-1816 MESSINA-TEATRO LA MUNIZIONE
    L'Appuntamento Notturna per burla (De Luca)
    Il Servo Padrone (Paisello?)
    Raul, Signor di Sequi (V. Fioravanti)

1816 PALERMO-TEATRO SAN FERDINANDO
    Ser Marcantonio (Pavesi)Gala opening   T. Pinotti s.
    La Calzolaia (Generali)
    Il Vascello d'occidente (Carafa)

1817-1818 SEASON PALERMO-TEATRO CAROLINO
    La Pietra del Paragone
    Il ritorno di Serse? (Portogallo)
    Agnese? (Paer)
    Federico II (G. Mosca)
    Leonora? (Paer)
    Ginevra degli Almieri (Farinelli)
    Camilla (Paer)
Sep.1817   **Maria Stuarda* (Carlini)   R. Pinotti s. L.Sirletti t.
    Cora. (Mayr)   G. David t. G. Dardanelli s.
    Misantropla e Pentimento? (G.Ricci)

La Giovantu d'Enrico V (G. Mosca)
Castore e Polluce (Radicati)
Il cambio della valigia? (Rossini)
I Baccanati di Roma? (Generali)
Ciro in Babilonia? (Rossini) — G. David? t.
La Morte di Adelaide (V. Fioravanti)

1818-1819 SEASON PALERMO-TEATRO CAROLINO

Jan. 12	*Una Lezione ai Giovanni* (?Mosca)	D. Donzelli t. V. Lenzi
		G. Bottari G. Dardanelli s.
Feb 12	**La cenerentola* (Dandini)	D. Donzelli t.
	L'Italiana in Algeri?	
	*Gli Sposi in Cimento? (L. Mosca)	
Jul. 19	*La Pietra del paragone* (Asdrubale)	G. Fabre ms. T. Spada s.
		D. Donzelli t. P. Botticelli
		G. Chambran bs. R. Bonetti
Jul.	**Torvaldo e Dorliska* (Rossini)	G. Fabri s. T.Spada s. R. Bonetti
		D. Donzelli t. V.Camola bs(Farone)
		D. Donizelli t. V.Botticelli
	*Zilia? (C.Mellara)	
	*Clotilde? (C.Coccia)	
	*Amalia e Carlo? (P.C.Guglielmi)	
Oct. 04	**Quinto Fabio?*	
	(Nicolini)	
	*Demetrio e Polibio? (Rossini)	
	*La gazza ladra	
	La Morte di Adelaide? (Fiorvanti)	

1818. NAPLES-TEATRO FENICE

Oct. 14	*Il Barbiere di Seviglia*	M. Manzi s. G. Tavassi bs

1819-1820 SEASON PALERMO-TEATRO CAROLINO

Apr. 19	**Il Trionfo di Giulio Cesare?*	G. B Rubini? t.
	(Niccolini?)	
	L'Impostore o il Marcotondo	T. Spada s. G. B. Rubini t.
	(L. Mosca)	A. Piermarini s. G. Chambran bs
		G. Canonici s. F. Piermarini t Apr.
	Il matrimonio segreto	G. B. Rubini t.

Oct.	*Il Rivale di se Stesso* (J.Weigl)	M. Briga ms. G. B. Rubini t.
	Lablache (Pasquale)	G. Chambran bs. T. Spada s.
		A. Piermarini s. V. Camola bs.
		F. Piermarini t.
	L'amore Intraprendente	M. Briga s. F. Piermarini t.
	(R.Orgitano)	D. Donizelli t. G. Chambran bs.
		T. Spada s.
	Il Barbiere di Siviglia?	
	La gazza ladra?	
	*L'Inganno felice	M. Brida s D. Donzelli t.
		F. Piermarini t. C. Gobbi
		A. Piermarini s. M. Benedetti bs.
	Il matrimonio Segreto?	
	La cenerentola?	
Feb. 20	* *Mosè in Egitto* (Lablache Moses)	T. Spada s. G. Fabre s.
		D. Donzelli t. V.Camola bs(Farone)
		M.Benedetti bs
		F. Piermarini t.
		A. Piermarini s
	La Morte di Adelaide?	T. Spada s. C. Pelralia G.Spech
	La principessa di Navarra	F. Piermarini t. G. Chambran bs
		M. Benedetti bs. O. Fei ms.

1820-1821 SEASON PALERMO-TEATRO CAROLINO

	Ifigenia in Tauride (Mayr)	
May 22	**Violenza e Costanza*	G. Dardanelli s. A. Piermarini s. M. Addati
	(Mercadante)	G. David t. V. Camola bs. G. Chambran bs
Aug.	**Tancredi*	G. Dardanelli s. R. Pisaroni ms G. David t.
Aug. 30	**La donna del lago*	G. Dardanelli s A. Piermarini s. F. Piermarini.
		M. Addati cond. G. Mosca
Jan. 12	**La Rosa Bianca La Rosa*	G. Dardanelli s. R. Pisaroni ms. G.David t.
	1821 Rossa? (Mayr)	
Feb.1821	***Adriano in Siria*	G. Dardanelli s. F. Piermarini t.
	(Pietro Airoldi)	A. Piermarini s. G. Chambran bs.
	Zaira? Oratorio	R. Benedetti. O. Fei ms.
	(V. Federici)	

SUMMER AND AUTUMN 1821 MILAN-TEATRO ALLA SCALA

Aug. 15	*La Cenerentola*	T. Belloc-Giorgi s. C. Sivelli s. G.Donizelli t
		N. De Grecis bs. C. Poggiali bs
		A. Moscheni s.
Oct. 02	*Donna Aurora* (Morlacchi)	T. Belloc-Giorgi s. M. Schira ms.
		D. Donzelli t. N. De Grecis bs. C. Sivelli s.
		A. Cassago s. G. Beretti P. Vasoli.
Oct. 10	*La sciocca per astuzia*	T. Belloc-Giorgi s. D. Donzelli t.
	G. Mosca)	N. De Grecis bs.
Oct. 30	**Elisa e Claudio*	T. Belloc-Giorgi s. M. Schira ms. D.Donzelli t.
	(Mercadante)	N. De Grecis bs. C. Poggiali bs. C. Sivelli s

CARNIVAL 1821-22 ROME-TEATRO APOLLO

Dec. 26	**La Capriciosa e il*	C. Lipparini s. S. Monelli t. N. Tacci bs
	Soldato (Carafa)	C. Bastianelli bs. N.Tacci bs
		C. Smitt s. A. Loyselet s G. Mariani bs
Jan. 26	**La Festa del Villaggio*	C. Lipparini s. S. Monelli t.
	(Puccitta)	C. Bastianelli bs. N. Tacci bs.
Feb. 05	*Il Barbiere di Siviglia*	C. Lipparini s. S. Monelli t.
		C. Bastianelli bs. N. Tacci bs.

SPRING 1822 MILAN-TEATRO ALLA SCALA

Mar. 12	**L'Esule di Granata*	R. Pisaroni s. C. Siber A. Tosi s.
	(Meyerbeer)	B. Winter t. L. Biondini bs. C. Sivelli s.
		F. Fabbri s. G. Gavioli s. G.C.Beretta
Apr. 08	**La Dama Locandiera*	T. Belloc-Giorgi s. A. Galeazzi ms.
		C. Sevelli s. L. Sirletti t. C. Poggialli bs.
		N. De Grecis bs. G. Corbetta L. Biondini bs.
		P. Vasoli A. Cassago s
Apr. 13	*Elisa e Claudio*	T. Belloc-Giorgi s. A. Galeazzi ms.
		L. Sirletti t. N. De Grecis bs.
May 15	*La Pietra del Paragone*	T. Belloc-Giorgi s. A. Galeazzi ms.
		L. Sirletti t. N. De Grecis bs.C.Poggiali bs
		P. Rossignoli A. Cassago s. L. Biondini bs
		P. Vasoli L. Sirletti t.
Jun. 08	*Arrighetto* (Coccia)	T. Belloc-Giorgi s. C. Sevelli s. L.Sirletti t.
		N. De Grecis bs. L. Biondini bs. C.Poggiali bs.
Jun. 19	*L'occasione fa il Ladro*	T. Belloc-Giorgi s. L. Sirletti t.
	(Don Parmenione)	N. De Grecis bs. L. Biondini bs. C. Sivelli
		C. Poggiali bs

AUTUMN 1822 TURIN-TEATRO CARIGNANO

Una Casa da vendere (Turina)   E. Monbelli s. G. B. Verger t. G. Cavalli bs.

La Cenerentola   E. Monbelli s. G. B. Verger t. G. Cavalli bs.
A. Cattenacci F.Settari G. Gherardini

Agnece (Paer)   E. Monbelli s. G. B. Verger t. G. Cavalli bs.

CARNIVAL 1822-23 MILAN-TEATRO ALLA SCALA

Dec. 26	**Amleto* (Mercadante)	T. Belloc-Giorgi s. I. Fabbrica ms. S.Monelli t C. Poggiali bs. G. Rovetta s.
Jan. 07	*Il Barbiere di Siviglia*	T. Belloc-Giorgi s. S. Monelli t. F. Vasoli bs.
	(Figaro)That year Lablache sang both Bartolo and Basilio)	
Feb. 06	**La Vestale* (Pacini)	T. Belloc-Giorgi s. I. Fabbrica ms. S. Monelli t. G. Rovetta A. M. Silvestri Bertozzi s. C. Dona G. Beretta P. Vasoli bs
Mar. 08	*Medea in Corinto* (Mayr)	T. Belloc-Giorgi s. A. Galeazzi ms. L. Sirletti t. Binaghi t. A.M. Silvestri Bertozzi s. C.Dona C. Poggiali bs.

SPRING AND SUMMER 1823 VIENNA-KARNTNERTORTHEATER

Apr. 14	*Il Barbiere di Siviglia*	J. Fodor-Mainvielle s. C. Ungher s. D. Donzelli t. A. Ambrogi bs.
May 17	*La Cenerentola*	A. Comelli-Rubini ms. G. David t. A. Ambrogi bs Bondra.C.Sieber
Jun. 02	*Zelmira*	J. Fodor-Mainvielle s. C. Ungher s. D. Donzelli t. G. David t.
Jun. 28	*Abufar* (Carafa)	J. Fodor-Mainvielle s. C. Ungher s. D. Donzelli t. G. David t.
Jul. 14	*Il matrimonio segreto*	J. Fodor-Mainvielle s. C. Ungher s. ? Lablache ms. G. David t. A. Ambrogi bs.
Jul. 23	*La Donna del lago*	H. Sontag s. Comelli-Rubini ms. G. David t. D. Donzelli t.

AUTUMN AND WINTER 1823-24 NAPLES-TEATRO DEL FONDO
(Concurrent with season at the San Carlo)

Oct. 31	*La Cenerentola*	A. Comelli-Rubini ms. G. B. Rubini t. A. Ambrogi bs.
Nov. 17	*Il matrimonio segreto*	J. Fodor-Mainvielle s. A. Comelli-Rubini G. B. Rubini t. A. Ambrogi bs. G. Dardanelli s.
Jan. 15	*Il Barbiere di Siviglia*	G. B. Rubini t.

AUTUMN AND WINTER 1823-24 NAPLES-TEATRO SAN CARLO - G.Festa Conductor.

Sep. 04	Semiramide?	
Sep. 23	**Costanza ed Almeriska (Mercadante)	J. Fodor-Mainvielle s. F. Eckerlin ms. G. David t. G. Chizzola E. Orlandini Gorini De Bernardis
Oct. 30	Il Barbiere di Siviglia	J. Fodor-Mainvielle s. D. Donzelli t. A. Ambrogi bs.De Franco
Nov. 07	La Cenerentola	A. Comelli-Rubini ms. G. B. Rubini t. A. Ambrogi bs.
Nov. 30	*Semiramide	J. Fodor-Mainvielle s. A. Comelli-Rubini s M. Manzocchi s G. Ciccimarra t. M.Benedetti E. Orlandini s. G. Chizzola bs.
Jan. 12	La Fondazione Partenope (Autori diversi)	J. Fodor-Mainvielle s. E. Ferron s. A. Comelli-Rubini ms. F. Eckerlin s. G. Canonici G. David t. G. B. Rubini t. A. Nozzari t. Dardanelli Ferlotti s. A. Ambrogi bs. De Franco G. Chizzola G. Botticelli E. Orlandini Fontemaggi Gorini Pace Sparano Bolognesi T. Cecconi M. Benedetti bs. G. Ciccimara Cardini Di Franco A. Abrogi bs.
Jan. 12	*Amazilia (Pacini)	J. Fodor-Mainvielle s. G. David t. Cecconi G. Chizzola
Feb. 21	*Federico II re di Prussia (Mosca)	J. Fodor-Mainvielle s. A. Comelli-Rubini ms G. David t. A. Nozzari G. Ciccimara E. Orlandini s. Cecconi De Bernardis
Mar. 20	**Sansone (Basili)	F. Eckerlin s. Ferlotti s. A. Nozzari t. M. Benedetti bs.G. Ciccimara E. Orlandini s.
May. 08	Semiramide	J. Fodor-Mainvielle s. C. Lipparini A. Nozzari t. M. Benedetti bs. E.Orlandini s

SUMMER AND AUTUMN 1824 AND WINTER 1825 VIENNA-KARNTNERTORTHEATER

Jun. 24	Il Barbiere di Siviglia	J. Fodor-Mainvielle s. D. Donzelli t.
Jul. 12	*Elisa e Claudio	G. Dardanelli s. F. Eckerlin ms. D. Donzelli t. A. Ambrogi bs.
Jul. 17	Semiramide	J. Fodor-Mainvielle s.
Jul. 31	Il Matrimoio Segreto?	J. Fodor-Mainville s. G. Dardanelli s. A. Comelli-Rubini ms. G. B. Rubini t.
Aug. 18	Adelina? (Generali)	

Aug. 18	*L'Inganno Felice*	J. Fodor-Mainvielle s. G. B. Rubini t.
Aug. 28	*Le nozze di Figaro*	J. Fodor-Mainvielle s. G. Dardanelli
		C. Ungher s. G. Donzelli t. (as Almaviva)
		A. Ambrogi bs.
Sep. 06	*Le Lagrime d'una Vedova*	G. B. Rubini t.
	(Generali)	
Sep. 18	**Doralice* (Mercadante)	F. Eckerlin s. G.B. Rubini t. D.Donzelli t.
Oct. 06	*Mose in Egitto*	G. Dardanelli s. J. Fodor-Mainvielle
	(as Farone)	C. Ungher s. G. David t. A. Ambrogi bs.
		G. Ciccimara t. Rauscher
Nov. 05	**Le nozze di Telemacco*	J. Fodor-Mainvielle s. A. Comelli-Rubini
	(Mercandante)	G. David t. G. Donzelli t. G. B. Rubini t.
		A. Ambrogi bs. F. Eckerlin ms. G. Dardanelli
Nov. 20	**Il Podesta di Burgos*	J. Fodor-Mainville s. C. Ungher s. Di Franco
		G. B. Rubini t. Bassi bs. A. Ambrogi bs.
Nov. 30	*La Cenerentola*	J. Fondor-Mainvielle s. C. Unger s. A. Comelli-
		G. B Rubini ms. Bondra s. Di Franco
Dec. 27	*Le Cantatrici Villane*	H. Sontag s. G. Dardanelli s. G.B.Rubini t.
	(Fioravanti)	C. Ungher s. Bassi bs. Rauscher
Jan. 19	*La gazza ladra*	J. Fodor-Mainvielle s. G. B. Rubini t.
	(as Fabrizio)	P. Botticelli bs. Bassi bs.
Feb. 17	*Agnese* (Paer)	J. Fodor-Mainvielle s. C. Ungher s.
		G. B. Rubini t. Bassi bs. P. Botticelli bs.
Mar. 01	*Il Turco in Italia*	J. Fodor-Mainvielle s. C. Ungher s.
		G. Ciccimarra t. P. Botticelli bs.
Mar. 21	*I Pretendenti Delusi?*	G. B. Rubini t.
	(Mosca)	

1825-26 SEASON NAPLES-TEATRO SAN CARLO - G.Festa Conductor.

Apr. 08	*Semiramide*	J. Fodor-Mainvielle s. Giud. Grisi ms.
		G. Ciccimarra t. M. Benedetti bs.
		E. Manzocchi ms. G.Chizzola t. M. Orlandi
May 12	**Bianca e Faliero*	A. Tosi s. Giud. Grisi ms. G. David t.
		M. Benedetti bs. E. Manzocchi m G. Chizzola t.
Jun. 02	*L'Inganno Felice*	J. Fodor-Mainvielle s.C.Ungher s.G.David t
		G. Fioravanti ?
Jun. 06	*Maometto II*	A. Tosi s. C. Ungher s. G.David t.
		G. Ciccimarra

Jul. 06	*Amazilia* (Pacini)	J. Fodor-Mainvielle s. G.Chizzola t. G. G. David t. E. Manzocchi ms. Pizzoni (later A.Tosi s. G. David t.)
Jul. 17	*Inno con ballo* (Pacini)	J. Fodor-Mainvielle s. A. Tosi s. G. David t.
Aug. 04	**Didone Abbandonata* (Mercadante)	A. Tosi s. E. Manzocchi ms. G. David t. M. Benedetti bs. G. Chizzola t. E. Manzocchi ms?
Aug. 06	*Il matrimonio segreto*	J. Fodor-Mainvielle s.(later A. Tosi s G. Dardanells. (later Biasoli) A. CoRubini (later E. Manzocchi ms.) G. B. Rubini (later G. David t.)A. Ambrogi bs.

1825 NAPLES TEATRO SAN CARLO

Aug 19	***Francesca da Rimini* (Luigi Carlini)	J. Fodor-Mainvielle s. G. David t. G. Ciccimarra G. Chizzola t. E.Manzocchi
Oct. 04	***Gli Italiani e Gl'In dinai* (Carafa)	A. Tosi s. A. Comelli-Rubini ms. G. David t E. Orlandini
Nov. 19	***L'Ultimo Giorno di Pompei*	A. Tosi s. E. Manzocchi ms. G. David t.
Nov. 30	*Il Barbiere di Siviglia*	
Dec. 29	***Ipermestra* (Mercadante)	A. Tosi s. G. David t. Riva M.Benedetti bs. G. Chizzola
Jan. 10	*La Schiava in Bagdad* (Pacini)	C. Unger s. L. Monelli t. A. Ambrogi bs.
Jan. 15	*Tazia* (Balducci)	A. Comelli s. C. Ungher s. G. David t.

1825-26 SEASON NAPLES-TEATRO DEL FOND0
(Concurrent with season at the San Carlo)

Apr. 18	*Il Barbere di Siviglia*	
Spring	*Il Signore del Villaggio*	J. Fodor-Mainvielle s. E. Manzocchi ms L. Monelli t. Casaccia bs. Fioravanti bs.
May?	**Il Podecta di Burgos*	J. Fodor-Mainvielle s. E. Manzocchi ms. L. Monelli t. G. Fioravanti bs. Casaccia bs.
Aug.?	**La Schiava in Bagdad*	C. Unger s. L. Monelli t. A. Ambrogi bs. G. Chizzola Riva
Oct.	*La Finta Amante* (Paisiello)	C. Unger s. L. Monelli t.

SPRING AND SUMMER 1826 NAPLES-TEATRO SAN CARLO - G. Festa conductor.

Date	Opera	Cast
Mar. 26	*Semiramide*	H. Meric-Lalande s. E. Manzocchi ms. G. Ciccimarra t. M. Benedetti bs.
Apr. 19	***Il Solitario ed Elodia* (Pavesi)	H. Meric-Lalande s. E. Manzocchi ms. G. Ciccimarra t. G. Chizzola t. M. Benedetti
May 30	***Bianca e Gernando*	H. Meric-Lalande s. E. Manzocchi ms. G. B. Rubini t. Berrettoni A. Manzocchi ms G. Chizzola t. M. Benedetti bs.
Jul. 02	*Amazilia* (Pacini)	H. Meric-Lalande a. G. B. Rubini t. G. Chizzola t.
Jul. 06	***Elvida* (Donizetti)	H. Meric-Lalande s. G.B. Rubini t. B. Lorenzani s.E. Manzocchi ms. G.Chizzola t
Jul. 19	* *Alahor in Granata* (Donizetti) (as Alahor)	H. Meric-Lalande s.B.Lorenzani. E.Manzocchi ms. B. Winter t. G. Chizzola t.
Aug. 03	*L'Ultimo Giorno di Pompei*	H. Meric-Lalande c. E. Manzocchi ms. G. B. G. B. Rubini t. (later G. David t.) M. Benedetti bs

SPRING AND SUMMER 1826 NAPLES-TEATRO DEL FONDO
(Concurrent with the season at the San Carlo)

Date	Opera	Cast
May 15	*Il matrimonio segreto?*	A. Comelli-Rubini ms. G. Fioravanti bs. G. B.Rubini t. D. Bertozzi t Di Franco
Jun 26	***L'abate dell'Epee* (Mosca, V)	A. Comelli-Rubini ms D. Bertozzi t. Elssler G. B Rubini t. G. Fioravanti bs. De Franchi

AUTUMN 1826 MILAN-TEATRO ALLA SCALA

Date	Opera	Cast
Sep. 11	*Amazilia*	L. Garcia s. L. Lombardi. S. Monelli t. C. Poggiali bs. T. Ruggeri s.
Sep. 25	*Elisa e Claudio*	G. Dardanelli s. Gai ms. F. Piermarini t. A. Ambrosi bs.
Oct 07	*Il matrimonio segreto*	M. Garcia s. Franchini s. Sacchi ms. S. Monelli t. A. Ambrosi bs.
Oct 27	*La Serva Padrona* *Il matrimonio segreto*	G. Dardanelli s.(Double bill) Benefit D. Bertozzi

AUTUMN AND WINTER 1826-27 NAPLES-TEATRO SAN CARLO

Date	Opera	Cast
Nov. 19	***Niobe* (Pacini	G. Pasta s. C. Ungher s. G. B. Rubini t. A? Manzocchi ms. B. Winter t. M. Benedetti G. Chizzola Del Vecchi E. Orlandini s

WINTER, SPRING AND SUMMER 1827 VIENNA-KARNTNERTORTHEATER

Feb. 20	*Amazilia (Pacini)	H. Meric-Lalande s. S. Monelli t.
Mar. 02	Semiramide	H. Meric-Lalande s. Schechner ms.
		G. Ciccimarra t.
Mar. 18	L'Inganno felice	? Schechner ms. L. Monelli t. Santini bs.
Mar. 28	*L'Aio nell Imbarazzo	H. Meric-Lalande s. A. Berettoni bs.
Apr. 16	Agnese	H. Meric-Lalande s. S. Monelli t.
Apr. 25	Mose	H. Meric-Lalande s. G. David t. Ambrogi bs.
May 02	La Gelosia Corretta??	
May 09	Il matrimonio segreto	G. Dardanelli s. Ditti s. G. David t.
		A. Ambrogi bs.
May 22	*Gli Arabi nelle Gallie	H. Meric-Lalande s. G. Dardanelli s.
	(Pacini)	G. David t. A. Berettoni bs.
June 01	Zelmira	H. Meric-Lalande s. de Vecchi ms. G. David t.
		B. Winter t. A. Ambrogi bs.
July 18	L'Ultimo Giorno Pompei	A. Tosi s. G. David t. G. Ciccimarra t.
Aug. 01	Il Barbiere di Siviglia	F. Corry-Paltoni ms. S.Monelli t. L. Pacini bs.
		A. Berettoni bs.
Aug. 16	L'Inganno felice 2/cast.	Greis s. L. Monelli t. Radicchi
		A. Berettoni bs.

AUTUMN AND WINTER 1827-28 NAPLES-TEATRO SAN CARLO - G.Festa conductor

Oct. 04	*Gli Arabi nelle Gallie	A. Tosi s. A. Manzocchi ms. G. David t.
	(Pacini)	G. Chizzola bs. Ricci Capranico
Nov. 06	La Cenerentola	F. Corry-Paltoni ms. A. Manzocchi A. Bonfigli
		G. Paltoni bs.
Nov. 19	**Margherita d'Inghilterra	A. Tosi s. E. Manzocchi s. B. Winter t.
	(Pacini)	M. Benedetti.bs. G.Chizzoli bs. Capranico
Dec. 26	L'Ultimo Giorno di	A. Tosi s. A. Manzocchi ms L. Bonfigli t.
	Pompei	M. Benedetti bs.
Jan. 01	**L'Esule di Roma	A. Tosi s. B. Winter t. E. Ricci s.
		A. Manzocchi ms. G. Campagnoli.b.
		G. Chizzola bs Capranico

SPRING 1828 VIENNA-KARNTNERTORTHEATER

Mar. 19	Il Barbiere di Siviglia	
	La Cenerentola	
	L' Inganno felice	
Apr. 04	La gazza ladra	

SPRING SUMMER AND AUTUMN 1828 MILAN-TEATRO ALLA SCALA

May 17	Il matrimonio segreto	C. Ungher s. T. Ruggeri s. Dotti ms. S. Monelli t. L. Biondini bs.
May 26	La cenerentola	F. Corri-Paltoni ms. S. Monelli L.Biondini
July 12	L'Esule di Roma	H. Meric-Lalande s. D. Spiaggi b. Winter t. T. Ruggeri s. L. Lombardi. Rossignoli
Aug. 02	La Prova d'un Opera seria	F. Corri-Paltoni ms. S. Monelli t. G. Luzio
Sep. 06	La Cenerentola	F. Corri-Paltoni s. S. Monelli t. L. Biondini bs. D. Spiaggi b
Sep. 14	La Prova d'un opera seria	F. Corri-Paltoni s. S. Monelli t. L.Pacini bs.
Sep. 23	Il matrimonio segreto	C. Unger s. L. Biondini bs. Dotti s. S. Monelli t. T. Ruggeri s.
Sep. 27	Il maldicente (Pavesi)	C. Ungher s. B. Winter t. L.Pacini bs. L. Lombardi
Oct. 31	La Pastorella Feudataria (Vaccai)	L. Ferlotti s. B. Winter t. L. Biondini bs. D. Spiaggi b. C. Lange s.
Nov.	15**L'Orfana della Selva (Coccia)	H. Meric-Lalande s. C. Ungher s. B. Winter L. Biondini bs. D. Spiaggi b. L. Pacini bs. T. Ruggeri s.

CARNIVAL 1828-29 NAPLES-TEATRO SAN CARLO - G.Festa conductor

Dec. 12	L'esule di Roma	A. Tosi s. G. B. Rubini t. G. Campagnoli bs.
Jan. 01	L'Ultimo Giorno di Pompei	A. Tosi s. G. B. Rubini t. M. Benedetti bs.
Jan. 12	**Il Paria (Donizetti)	A. Tosi s. G. B. Rubini t. E. Ricci s G. Campagnoli bs. G. Chizzola bs.
Feb. 23	Il matrimonio segreto	A. Tosi s. E. Sedlacek s. G. B. Rubini t. G. Campagnoli bs.
Feb. 27	Il giovedi grasso	E. Sedlacech s. A. Comelli-Rubini ms. M. Carrano G. B. Rubini t. G. Lucio.
Mar. 11	**Saul (Vaccai)	A. Comelli-Rubini ms. M. Carraro G.B.Rubini t. M. Benedetti bs. G. Chizzoli bs
Mar. 20	Mose in Egetto (Faraone)	A. Tosi s. E. Sedlacech s. G. David t. M. M. Benedetti bs. G. Chizzola bs. G. Mazza Metelli t. Eden s.

CARNIVAL 1828-29 NAPLES-TEATRO DEL FONDO

Feb. 22	Il matrimonio segret	E. Sedlacech s. A. Manzocchi ms. G. B. Rubini t. G. Campagnoli bs.

Feb. 26	**Il giovedi Grasso*	A. Comelli-Rubini ms. G. B. Rubini t.
		G. Campagnoll bs
Mar. 30	La dama bianca	A. Tosi s. G.B. Rubini t. Del Vecchi
	(Boieldieu)	G. David t. A. Manzocchi

SPRING 1829 NAPLES-TEATRO SAN CARLO - G. Festa Conductor

Apr. 19	L'esule di Roma	A. Tosi s. B. Winter t. G. Campagnoli bs.
May 13	Gli arabi nelle Gallie	L. Boccabadati B. Winter G.David t
		M. Benedetti bs.
May 30	La vestale (Spontini)	A. Tosi s Eden s B. Winter G.David
		M. Benedetti bs.

SPRING 1829 PARMA-TEATRO REGIO F. Melchiorri conductor.

May 16	**Zaira* (Bellini)	H. Meric-Lalande s. T. Cecconi ms.
		C. Trezzini t. G. Inchindi b.
May 30	Semiramide	H. Meric-Lalande s. T. Cecconi ms.
June 13	Il Barbiere di Siviglia	H. Meric-Lalande s. D. Reina t. G. Cavalli
June 27	**Colombo* (L. Ricci)	H. Meric-Lalande s. T. Cecconi me.
		T. Alexander t.

SUMMER, AUTUMN AND WINTER 1829-30 NAPLES-TEATRO SAN CARLO - F. Festa conductor

Jul. 07	Bianca e Gernando	A. Tosi s B.Winter t. M. Benedetti bs.
July 22	L'esule di Roma	A. Tosi s. B. Winter t. M. Benedetti bs.
Aug 09	La Prova d'un opera seria	A. Tosi s. B.Winter t. G. Luzio B.
Aug. 19	**Teresa Navigero*	A. Tosi s. B. Winter t. Ambrosini G.Chizzoli t.
	(Guglielmo)	
Oct. 11	Margherita d'Inghiterra	A. Tosi s. B. Winter t. M. Benedetti bs.
Jan. 19	L'Orfana della Selva	A. Tosi s. E. Sedlacek s. B. Winter t.
		G. Campagnoli bs. G. Luzio b.
Nov. 19	*Il Contestabile di	A. Tosi s. L. Boccabadati s.
	Chester (Pacini)	Arrigotti t. Eden s. Ambrosini G.Chizzola t.
Dec. 30	L'Ultimo Giorno di Pompei	A. Tosi s. B. Winter t. M. Benedetti bs.
Jan. 01	Il Barbiere di Siviglia	J. Fodor-Mainville s. B. Winter t.
		G. Campagnoli bs. G. Luzio bs.
Jan. 28	**I Portugueai in Goa*	A. Tosi s. B. Winter t. G. Campagnoli bs.
	(Benedict)	G. Chizzola t.
Feb. 07	**I Pazzi per Progetto*	L. Boccabadati-Gazzuoli s. M. Carrano ms.
		G. Luzio bs. Fioravanti bs.

Mar. 06	**Il Diluvio Universale*	L. Boccabadati s. M. Carrano ms. B. Winter t.
		G. Ambrosini bs. G. Arrigo. bs.
		G. Chizzola t. L. Salvi. M. Carraro bs.

SUMMER, AUTUMN AND WINTER 1829-30 NAPLES-TEATRO DEL FONDO
(Concurrent with the season at the San Carlo)

Jul. 25	La Prova d'un Opera seria	L. Boccabadati s.
	*L'Orfana della Selva	A. Tosi s. E. Sedlacek. B. Winter
	(Coccia)	G. Campagnoli bs. G. Luzio bs. Ambrosini bs.
		Fabaini s.
Dec. 28	Il Barbiere di Siviglia	J. Fodor-Mainville s. B. Winter t.
		G. Campagnoli bs. G. Luzio bs.

SPRING AND SUMMER 1830 LONDON-KING'S THEATRE (London debut)

May 13	Il matrimonio segreto	H. Meric-Lalande s. Bellchambers s. M. Mali ms.
		bran ma. (later Specchi ms.) D. Donzelli t.
		Santini bs.
May 22	Semiramide	H. Meric-Lalande s. M. Malibran ms.
		A. Curioni t. Ambrogi bs.
Jun, 03	Don Giovanni	H. Meric-Lalande s. Bellchambers s.
		M. Malbran ms. (later Blasis s.) D. Donzelli t.
		Santini bs.
Jun. 17	Il Turco in Italia	Blasis a. A. Curioni t. Santini bs.
Aug. 03	L'Inganno Felice	H. Meric-Lalande s. D. Donzelli t.
		V?.Santini bs.

AUTUMN AND WINTER 1830-31 PARIS-THEATRE ITALIEN

Nov. 02	Il matrimonio segreto	E. Tadolini s. Corradi s. Rossi ms. G. David t
		G. Zucchelli bs.
Nov. 20	Il Barbiere di Siviglia	M. Malibran ms.
Nov. 27	La gazza ladra	M. Malibran ms. P. Michel ma. G. David t.
		G. Zucchelli bs.
Dec. 07	L'Ultimo Giorno di Pompei	H. Meric-Lalande s. G. David t. Paganini t.
Dec. 02	La Cenerentola	M. Malibran ms. D. Donzelli t. G. Zucchelli bs.
Jan. 22	La Prova d'un Opera seria	M. Malibran ms.
Feb. 12	Don Giovanni	H. Meric-Lalande s. E. Tadolini a.
		M. Malibran ms. Bordogni t. G. Zucchelli bs.

WINTER, SPRING AND SUMMER 1831 LONDON-KING'S THEATRE

Il Barbiere di Siviglia
Il matrimonio segreto

Mar. 17	**L'Ultimo Giorno di Pompei*	Wood s.(later H. Meric-Lalande s.) G. David t.
		(later G. B. Rubini t.) Galli bs.
May 12	*Medea in Corinto*	G. Pasta s. Ayton s. A. Curioni t.
		G. B. Rubini t.
Jun. 02	*Semiramide*	G. Pasta s. A. Comelli-Rubini ms. Curioni t.
		F. Galli bs.
Jun. 09	*Don Giovanni*	H. Meric-Lalande s. Castelli s. G. Pasta s.
		A. Curioni t. Santini bs
Jun. 23	*L'Italiana in Algeri*	Raimbur ms. G. B. Rubini t. Santini bs.
Jul. 02	*Otello?*	G. Pasta s. A. Curioni t. G. B. Rubini t.
		Santini bs.
Jul. 08	**Anna Bolena*	G. Pasta s. Beck s. Gay s. G. B. Rubini t.

SUMMER, AUTUMN AND WINTER 1831 PARIS-THEATRE ITALIEN

Sep. 01	**Anna Bolena*	G. Pasta s. E. Tadolini s. G. B. Rubini t.
Sep. 10	*Il matrimonio segreto*	E. Tadolini s. Rossi s. Amigo s. G.B.Rubini t.
	Otello??	Berettoni bs.
Oct. 02	*Il Barbiere di Siviglia*	Caradori-Allan s.(later Raimbur ms.)
	G. B. Rubini t.	
Oct. 24	*La Prova d'un Opera seria*	G. Pasta s. (later M. Malibran ms.)
	G. B. Rubini t. Graziani bs.	
Nov. 01	*Don Giovanni*(as the Don)	H. Schroeder-Devrient s. E. Tadolini s.
		Caradori-Allan s. G. B. Rubini t. Graziani bs.
Nov. 08	*La gazza ladra*	M. Malibran ms. G. B. Rubini t.
		Santini bs.
Nov. 12	*La Cenerentola*	Caradori-Allan s. Nicolini t. Santini bs.
Jan. 1	*Semiramide*	Melas s.
Mar. 12	**Comingio Romito*	H. Schroeder-Devrient s. Casimir G. B.Rubini t.
Mar. 29	**L'Aio nell'Imbarazzo*	E. Tadolini s. Raimbur ms. G. B. Rubini t.
		Graziani bs.

SPRING 1832 LONDON-KING'S THEATRE

Apr. 28	*Il Barbiere di Siviglia*	L. Cinti-Damoreux s. G.Donzelli t. de Angeli bs.
	(Lablache sang Figaro)	Giubilei bs.
May. 03	*Don Giovanni Ist Act*	(Lablache sang Don Giovanni) De Begnis bs
	Il matrimonio segreto	(Lablache sang Geronimo)
	Ist Act only.	

SUMMER, AUTUMN AND WINTER 1832-33 NAPLES-TEATRO SAN CARLO - G.Festa conductor

Jun. 19	Il Barbiere di Siviglia	T. Raimbaux s.(later M. Malibran) ms.
		G. David t. G. Campagnoli bs. G. Luzio bs.
Jul. 02	La Prova d'un Opera seria	T. Raimbaux s. D. Santolini ms. G. David t.
		G. Luzio bs.
Jul. 06	Anna Bolena	G. Ronzi de Begnis s. A.D'Anvers-Toldi ms.
		D. Santolini ms. N. Ivanoff t.L. Lombardi
Aug. 24	La Cenerentola ?	
Aug. 30	Fausta	G. Ronzi de Begnis s. D. Reina t.
		G. Campagnoli bs.
Nov. 03	La gazza ladra	M. Malibran s. D. Santolini ms. G. David t.
		G. Campagnoli bs. G. Festa cond.
Oct. 04	L'esule di Roma	G. Ronzi de Begnis s. B. Winter t.
Oct. 11	Il matrimonio segreto	M. Malibran ms. A. D'Anvers Toldi ms.
		G. David t. A. Ambrogi bs. Garcia-Ruiz
Nov. 06	**Sancia di Castiglia	G. Ronzi de Begnis s. D. Santolini ms.
		G. Basadonna t.
Nov. 19	Semiramide	G. Ronzi de Begnis s. D. Santolini ms.
		G. Basadonna t.
Dec. 03	Il Felice Imeneo	G. Ronzi de Begnis s. T. Raimbaux ms.
	(Pacini)	N. Ivanoff t. G. David t. G. Basadonna t.
Jan. 12	**Gli Elvezi (Pacini)	G. Ronzi de Begnis s. N. Ivanoff t.
		A. Ambrosini bs. (A.Ambrogi?) L. Lombardi t
Feb. 03	Contestabile di Chester	G. Ronzi de Begnis s. A.D'Anvers Toldi ms.
		G. Basadonna t

SUMMER, AUTUMN AND WINTER 1832-33 NAPLES-TEATRO DEL FONDO
(Concurrent with the season at ths San Carlo)

Aug.	La Cenerentola	M. Malibran ms. Tati t. A. Ambrogi bs,

SPRING, SUMMER, AUTUMN AND WINTER 1833-34 NAPLES--TEATRO SAN CARLO- G.Festa

Apr. 07	*Guglielmo Tell	G. Garcia-Ruiz s. St. Ange ms. T. Raimbaux ms.
		N. Ivanoff t. A. Ambrogi bs. M. Benedetti bs.
		N. Tauro F. Tati t. L. Lombardi t.
Apr. 18	La Cenerentola	M. Malibran s. D. Reina t.
Apr. 21	Semiramide	M. Malibran s. D. Santolini ms.
		G. Basadonna t. M. Benedetti bs.
May 22	Anna Bolena	G. Ronzi de Begnis s. A.D'Anvers-Toldi ms.
		D. Santolini ms. N. Ivanoff t. L. Lombardi t

May 30	**Fernando, Duca Valenza*	G. Ronzi de Begnis s. D. Reina t.E. Speranza S. Andaver L. Lombardi t.
Aug. 15	Il Contestabile	G. Ronzi de Begnis s. A. D'Anvers-Toldi ms. G. Basadonna t
Oct. 04	L'esula di Roma	G. Ronzi de Begnis s. D. Reina t.
Nov. 15	La Prova d'un Opera seria	M. Malibran ms. G. Luzio bs.
Nov. 19	La gazza ladra	M. Malibran ms. D. Santolini ms. L. Lombardi t. G. Luzio bs.
Nov. 30	**Irene* (Pacini)	G. Garcia-Ruiz ms. M. Malibran ms. G. David t. D. Reina t. A. Ambrogi bs. M. Benedetti bs. L. Lombardi t.
Dec. 19	Gli Aragonesi a Napoli	G. Garcia-Ruiz s. St. Ange. M. Malibran G. David t. D. Reina t. A. Ambrogi bs.
Jan. 09	Zampa	A. Toldi s. D. Santolini ms. G. David t. G. G. Luzio bs. Savietti
Jan. 19	**La Figlia dell'Arciere* (Coccia)	M. Malibran ms. D. Reina t. L. Lombardi De Nuovo Manzi de Rosa
Jan. 25	Il matrimonio segreto (1 act only)	A. Toldi s. G. Garcia-Ruiz s. M. Malibran ms G. David t. A. Ambrogi bs.
Jan. 30	Il Barbiere di Siviglia	M. Malibran ms. G. David t. A. Ambrogi bs. G. Luzio bs.

SPRING, SUMMER AND AUTUMN 1833-34 NAPLES-TEATRO DEL FONDO
(Concurrent with the season at the San Carlo)

Oct. 29	**Bianca di Belmonte*	Masi s. Santange. ms. D. Reina t. Ricci
Nov. ?	*Zampa	A. D'Anvers-Toldi s. D. Santolini ms. G. David t, G. Luzio bs.
ND	Il Marito Disperato (Cordella)	T. Raimbaux s. Accenti s. Salvetti s. Fioravanti G. Lucio bs G. Basadonna t.

SPRING AND SUMMER 1834 NAPLES-TEATRO SAN CARLO - G. Festa conductor.

May 30	*I Normanni a Parigi (Mercadante)	C. Ungher s. A. Del Sere s. B. Winter t. D. Raffaelli Dagnini
Jun 19	L'esule di Roma	A. Delsere s. B. Winter t. A. Ambrogi bs.
Jul 06	*Don Giovanni (as the Don)	C. Ungher s. A. Del Serre s. F. Persiani s. L. Salvi t. F. Crespi bs. N. Costantin bs.
ND.	Don Giovanni (as Leporello)	C. Ungher s. A. Del Serre s. F. Persiani s. L. Salvi t. F. Crispi bs. N. Costantin bs.
July 19	Anna Bolena	G. Ronzi de Begnis s. A. Duprez s. G. Duprez t.
Aug. 17	L'elisir d'amore	F. Persiani c. L. Salvi t. A. Ambrogi bs.

SPRING AND SUMMER 1834 NAPLES-TEATRO DEL FONDO
(Concurrent with the season at the San Carlo)

Mar. 30	Le Cantatrice Villani	F. Persiani s. F. Tati t. G. Luzio bs
Apr. 13	L'Elisir d' amore	F. Persiani s. L. Salvi t. A. Ambrogi bs. Zappucci
June 30	La Serva Padrona	C. Ungher s.
Aug. 02	Zampa	F. Persiani s. L. Salvi t. G. Luzio bs.

SUMMER 1834 LIVORNO-TEATRO DEGLI AVVALORATI

Aug.	Il matrimonio segreto	C. Ungher s. A. Duprez t. G. Duprez t. D. Coselli bs.
ND.	Il Barbiere di Siviglia	C. Ungher s. G. Duprez t. C. O. Porto bs. D. Coselli bs.

AUTUMN AND WINTER 1834-35 PARIS-THEATRE ITALIEN - I. Parisini conductor

Oct. 02	La gazza ladra	G. Grisi s. N. Ivanoff t. A. Tamburini b.
Oct. 14	Il Barbiere di Siviglia?	G. Grisi s. G. B. Rubini t. A. Tamburini b
Oct. 30	La Prova d'un Opera seria	G. Grisi s. Fink-Lohr s. N. Ivanoff t. Santini bs.
Nov. 08	Mose in Égitto	Fink-Lohr s. Schuts s. G. B. Rubini t. N. Ivanoff t. A. Tamburinl b.
Dsc. 02	Anna Bolena	G. Grisi s. Schutz s. N. Ivanoff t
Jan. 01	Otello	G. Grisi s. G. B. Rubini t. N. Ivanoff t. A. Tamburini b.
Jan. 24	**I Puritanl	G. Grisi s. G. B. Rublnl t. A. Tamburini b
Mar. 12	**Marino Faliero	G. Grisi s. G. B. Rubini t. A. Tamburini b.
Mar. 21	La Cenerentola	T. Rambeau G. B. Rubini t. A. Tamburini b.

SPRING AND SUMMER 1835 LONDON-KING'S THEATRE - M. Costa conductor

Apr. 09	La gazza ladra	G. Grisi s. N. Brambilla ms. N. Ivanoff t. A. Tamburini b.
Apr. 23	Anna Bolena	G. Grisi s. Seguin s. M. Brambilla ms. N. Ivanoff t.
Apr. 30	Don Giovanni (As Leperello)?	G. Grisi s. Fink-Lohr s. Seguin s. G. B. Rubini t. A. Tamburini b.
May 06	Otello	G. Grisi s. G. B. Rubini t. N. Ivanoff t. A. Tamburini b.

May 14	*Marino Faliero*	G. Grisi s. G. B. Rubini t. A. Tamburini b.
May 21	*I Puritani*	G. Grisi s. G. B. Rubini t. A Tamburini b.
June 02	*La Prova d'un Opera seria*	G. Grisi s. N. Ivanoff t.

SPRING 1835 LONDON-THEATRE ROYAL DRURY LANE
(Concurrent with the season at the King's theatre)

June 04	*La gazza ladra*	G. Grisi s. M. Brambilla ms. N. Ivanoff t. A. Tamburini b.

SPRING AND SUMMER 1835-36 PARIS-THEATRE ITALIEN - I. Parisini conductor

Oct. 01	*I Puritani*	G. Grisi s. G. B. Rublni t. A. Tamburini b.
Oct. 06	*Il Barbiere di Siviglia*	G. Grisi s. G. B. Rubini t. A. Tamburini b.
Oct. 15	*Anna Bolena*	G. Grisi s. E. Albertazzi ms. N. Ivanoff t.
Oct. 20	*La Prova d'un Opera seria*	G. Grisi s. G. B. Rubini t.
Nov. 03	*La Cenerentola*	E. Albertazzi ms. G. B. Rubini t.A.Tamburini
Dec. 08	*Norma*	G. Grisi s. L. Assandri s. G. B. Rubini t.
Jan. 04	*La gazza ladra*	G. Grisi s. E. Albertazzi ms. N. Ivanoff t. A.Tamburini b.
Jan. 19	*Otello*	G. Grisi s. G. B. Rubini t. N. Ivanoff t. A.Tamburinl b.
Feb. 04	*Marino Faliero*	G. Grisi s. G. B. Rubini t. A. Tamburini b.
Mar. 09	*Don Giovanni*	G. Grisi s. L. Assandri s. E. Albertazzi ms. G. B. Rubini t. A. Tamburini
Mar. 22	**I Briganti* (Mercadante)	G. Grisi s. G. B. Rubini t. A. Tamburini b.

SPRING AND SUMMER 1836 LONDON KING'S THEATRE

Apr. 09	*La gazza ladra*	E. Grisi s. G. B. Rubini t. A. Tamburini b.
Apr. 16	*Norma*	G. Grisi s. L. Assandri s. B. Winter t.
Apr. 21	*Mose in Égitto*	Colleoni-Corti s. L. Assandri s. G. B. Rubini t. A. Tamburini b.
Apr. 30	*I Puritani*	G. Grisi s. G. B. Rubini t. A. Tamburini b.
May. 14	*Otello*	G. Grisi s. G. B. Rubini t. B. Winter t A. Tamburini b.
June.03	*Le Siege de Corinthe* (in It.)	G. Grisi s. G. B. Rubini t. B. Winter t. A. Tamburini b.
June 09	*Marino Faliero*	G. Grisi s. G. B. Rubini t. A. Tamburini b.
June.18	*Anna Bolena*	G. Grisi. L. Assandri s. A. Seguin s. G. B. Rubini t.

Appendices 601

June.20	*Don Giovanni*	G. Grisi. G. Puzzi s. (later L. Assandri s.)
		E. Grisi s. A. Seguin ms. G. B.Rubini t
		A. Tamburini b
July 02	**I Briganti*	G. Grisi s. G. B. Rubini t. A. Tamburini b.
July 16	*La Prova d'un Opera seria*	G. Grisi s. G. B. Rubini t.

AUTUMN AND WINTER 1836-37 PARIS-THEATRE DES ITALIENS

Oct. 01	*I Puritani*	G. Grisi s. G. B. Rubini t. A. Tamburini b.
Oct. 15	*La Cenerentola*	E. Albertazzi ms. N. Ivanoff t.
		A. Tamburini b.
Oct. 22	*Norma*	G. Grisi s. L. Assandri s. G. B. Rubini t.
Oct. 29	*Il matrimonio segreto*	Taccani s. L. Assandri s. E. Albertazzi ms.
	(Also Theatre Royal Louvois)	G. B. Rubini t. A. Tamburini b.
Nov. 12	*Anna Bolena*	G. Grisi s. Taccani s. L.Schieroni s.
		N. Ivanoff t.
Nov. 20	*La gazza ladra*	G. Grisi s. Amigo s. N. Ivanoff t.
		A. Tamburini b.
Dec. 03	*Il Barbiere di Siviglia*	Taccani s. G. B. Rubini t. A. Tamburini b.
Dec. 12	*Otello*	G. Grisi s. G. B. Rubini t. N. Ivanoff t.
		A. Tamburini b.
Jan. 14	***Malek Adel* (Costa)	G. Grisi s. E. Albertazzi ms. G. B. Rubini t.
		A. Tamburini b.
Feb. 02	*La Prova d'un Opera seria*	G. Grisi s. N. Ivanoff t.
Mar 07	***Ildegonda* (Marliani)	G. Grisi s. G. B. Rubini t.
Mar. 12	*Mose in Egitto*	G. Grisi s. E. Albertazzi ms. G. B. Rubini
		A. Tamburini b.

SPRING 1837 PARIS-ACADEMIE ROYALE DE MUSIQUE (OPERA)

Mar. 27	*La Prova d'un Opera seria*	G. Grisi s. N. Ivanoff t.

SPRING AND SUMMER 1837 LONDON-KING'S THEATRE - M. Costa conductor

Apr. 08	*I Puritani*	G. Grisi s. G. B. Rubini t. A. Tamburini
Apr. 11	*Norma*	G. Grisi s. L. Assandri s. G. B. Rubini t.
Apr. 15	*La gazza ladra*	G. Grisi s. F. Wyndham ms. N. Ivanoff t.
		A. Tamburini b.
Apr. 18	*La Cenerertola*	E. Albertazzi ms. G. B. Rubini t.
		A. Tamburini b.
Apr. 27	*Don Giovanni*	G. Grisi s. L. Assandri s. E. Albertazzi ms.
		G. B. Rubini t. A. Tamburini b.

May 04	Il matrimonio segreto	G. Grisi s. L. Assandri s. E. Albertazzi ms, G. B. Rubini t. A. Tamburini b.
May 06	Otello	G. Grisi s. G. B. Rubini t. N. Ivanoff t. A. Tamburini b.
May 18	*Malek Adel (Costa)	G. Grisi s. E. Albertazzi ms. G. B. Rubini t. N. Ivanoff t. A. Tamburini b.
Jun. 15	La Prova d'un Opera seria Romeo e Giulietta	G. Grisi s. G. B. Rubini t. (later N.Ivanoff t.) Giannoni s. G. Pasta s. G. B. Rubini t.
Jun. 29	Anna Bolena	G. Grisi s. L. Assandri s. E. Albertazzi G. B. Rubini t. (later N. Ivanoff t.)
Jul. 06	Medea in Corinto	Giannoni s. G. Pasta s. G. B. Rubini t. Curioni t.
Jul. 18	*Ildeonda	G. Grisi s. G. B. Rubini t. A. Tamburini b.
Jul. 20	Mose in Egitto	L. Assandri s. E. Albertazzi ms. G.B.Rubini t. A. Tamburini b.

AUTUMN AND WINTER 1837-38 PARIS-THEATRE DES ITALIENS

Oct. 03	La gazza ladra	G. Grisi s. Amigo s. N. Ivanoff t. A. Tamburini b
Oct. 10	La Cenerentola	E. Albertazzi ms. Zamboni t. A. Tamburini
Oct. 14	Norma	G. Grisi s. L. Assandri s. Zamboni t. G. B. Rubini t.
Oct. 28	I Puritani	G. Grisi s. G. B. Rubini t. A. Tamburini b.
Nov. 14	Anna Bolena	G. Grisi s. L. Assandri s. N. Ivanoff t.
Nov. 21	Il matrimonio segreto	F. Persiani s. L. Assandri s. E. Albertazzi ms G. B. Rubini t. A. Tamburini b.
Dec. 10	La Prova	G. Grisi s. N. Ivanoff t. Ferlini b.
Dec. 21	Otello	G. Grisi s. L. Assandri s. G. B. Rubini t. N. Ivanoff t. A. Tamburini b.
Jan. 13	Don Giovanni	G. Grisi s. F. Persiani s. E. Albertazzi ms. G. B. Rubini t. A. Tamburini b.
Feb. 24	*Parisina d'Este	G. Grisi s. G. B. Rubini t. A. Tamburini b.

SPRING AND SUMMER 1838 LONDON-HER MAJESTY'S THEATRE

Apr. 21	Otello	G. Grisi s. G. E. Rubini t. Tati t. A. Tamburini b.
Apr. 26	I Puritani	G. Grisi s. G. B. Rubini t. A. Tamburin b
May. 03	Norma	G. Grisi s. E. Albertazzi ms. Tati t.

May. 11	Don Giovanni	G. Grisi s. F. Persiani s. E. E. Albertazzi
		G. B. Rubini t. A. Tamburini b. Morelli bs.
May. 29	Anna Bolena	G. Grisi s. E. Albertazzi ms. G. B. Rubini t.
Jun. 7	Mathide di Shabran	F. Persiani s. Eckerlin s. G. B. Rubini t.
		A. Tamburini b.
Jun.14	Il matrimonio segreto	F. Persiani s. Seguin s. E. Albertazzi ms.
		G. B. Rubini t. A. Tamburini b.
Jun. 21	Le nozze di Figaro	G. Grisi s. F. Persiani s. E. Alberazzi ms.
		A. Tamburini b.
Jul. 10	Malek Adel	G. Grisi E. Albertazzi ms. G. B. Rubini t.
		A. Tamburini b.
Jul. 12	La Prova d'un opera seria	G. Grisi G. B. Rubini t.
Jul. 19	**Falstaff (Balfe)	G. Grisi s. E. Albertazzi ms. G. B. Rubini t.
		A. Tamburini b.
Aug. 02	La gazza ladra	G. Grisi s. G. B. Rubini t. A. Tamburini b.

AUTUMN AND WINTER 1838-39 PARIS-THEATRE DES ITALIENS

Oct. 02	Otello	G. Grisi s. G. B. Rubini t. N. Ivanoff t.
		A. Tamburini b.
Oct. 16	La gazza ladra	G. Grisi s. N. Ivanoff t. A. Tamburini b.
Oct. 30	Norma	G. Grisi s. E. Grisi ms. N. Ivanoff t.
Nov. 13	Don Giovanni	G. Grisi s. F. Persiani s. E. Albertazzi ms.
		G. B. Rubini t. A. Tamburini b.
Nov. 24	La Donna del lago	G. Grisi s. E. Albertazzi ms. G. B. Rubini t
		N. Ivanoff
Jan. 17	*L elisir d'amore	F. Persiani s. N. Ivanoff t. A.Tamburini
Jan. 19	I Puritani	G. Grisi s. G. B. Rubini t. A. Tamburini b.
Mar. 04	Le nozze di Figaro	G. Grisi s. F. Persiani s. E. Albertazzi ms.
		N. Ivanoff t. A. Tamburini b.

SPRING AND SUMMER 1839 LONDON-HER MAJESTY'S THEATRE

Apr. 09	I Puritani	G. Grisi s. G. B. Rubini t. A. Tamburini b.
Apr. 13	La gazza ladra	G. Grisi s. G. B. Rubini t. A. Tamburini b.
Apr. 27	Anna Bolena	G. Grisi s. Monanni s. E. Grisi ms.
		G. B. Rubini t.
May 02	Don Giovanni	G. Grisi s. F. Persiani s. Monanni s.
		G. B. Rubini t. A. Tamburini
May 09	Otello	P. Viardot ms. G. B. Rubini t. F.Tati t.
		A. Tamburini b. E.Bellini-Passanti s. G.Galli bs

May 14	*La Prova d'un Opera seria*	G. Grisi s.
May 16	*Le nozze di Figaro*	G. Grisi s. F. Persiani s. E. Grisi ms Tati t.
		A. Tamburini b.
May 28	*Norma*	G. Grisi s. E. Grisi ms. Tati t. Mario t.
Jun. 06	**Lucrezia Borgia*	G. Grisi s. E. Grisi ms. Monanni s.
		Mario t. A. Tamburini b.
Jun. 13	*L'elisir d'amore*	F. Persiani s. Mario t. A. Tamburini b.
Jun. 15	*La Cenerentola*	P. Viardot ms. G. 8. Rubini t. A. Tamburini
Jul. 11	*Guglielmo Tell*	F. Persiani s. E. Grisi ms. G. B. Rubini t.
	(as Guglielmo Tell)	F. Lablache bs.

SUMMER 1839 MANCHESTER-THEATRE ROYAL - M. Costa conductor

Aug. 12	**Anna Bolena*	G. Grisi s. Monanni s. E.Grisi ms. G.B.Rubini t.
Aug. 13	**I Puritani*	G. Grisi s. G. B. Rubini t. A. Tamburini b

AUTUMN AND WINTER 1839-40 PARIS-THEATRE DES ITALIENS

Oct. 01	*Lucia di Lammermoor*	Odeon Theatre, special engagement
Oct. 08	*Otello*	P. Viardot ms. G. B. Rubini t. Sinico t.
		(later R. Mirate t.) A. Tamburini b
Oct. 17	*L'elisir d'amore*	F. Persiani s. Mario t. A. Tamburini b.
Oct. 24	*La Cenerentola*	P. Viardot ms. G. B. Rubini t. A. Tamburini b
		Morelli bs.
Oct. 24	**Ines de Castro*	F Persiani s. E. Albertazzi ms. G. B.Rubini t.
Jan. 04	*Norma*	G. Grisi s. E. Albertazzi ms. R. Mirate t.
Jan. 20	*Don Giovanni*	G. Grisi s. F. Persiani s. E. Abertazzi ms.
		G. B. Rubini t. A. Tamburini b.
Feb. 17	*Le nozze di Figaro*	G. Grisi s. F. Persiani s. E. Albertazzi ms.
		A. Tamburini b.
Mar. 16	*I Puritani*	G. Grisl s. G. B. Rubini t. A. Tamburini b.

SPRING AND SUMMER 1840 LONDON-HER MAJESTY'S THEATRE

Apr. 07	*Norma*	Tosi s. E. Grisi ms. Ricciardi t. Coletti
Apr. 25	*I Puritani*	G. Grisi s. G B. Rubini t.
May 05	*Otello*	G. Grisi s. G. B. Rubini t. Ricciardi t.
		A. Tamburini b.
May 07	*La gazza ladra*	G. Grisi s. Castelli ms. Ricciardi t.
		G. B. Rubini t. A. Tamburini b.
May 14	*La Prova d'un Opera seria*	G. B. Rubini t.
May 21	*Don Giovanni*	G. Grisi s. F. Persiani s. E. Grisi ms. G.
		B. Rubini t. A. Tamburini b. Morelli bs.

May 28	Le nozze di Figaro	G. Grisi s. F. Persiani s. E. Grisi ms. A. Tamburini b.
May 30	*Ines de Castro	F. Persiani s. G. B. Rubini t.
Jun. 09	Il Barbiere di Siviglia	G. Grisi s. G. B. Rubini t. A. Tamburini B.
Jun. 19	L elisir d'amore	F. Persiani s. Mario t. A. Tamburini b.
Jun. 23	Lucrezia Borgia	G. Grisi s. E. Bellini ms. G. B. Rubini t. A. Tamburini b.
Jun. 11	Il matrimonio segreto	G. Grisi s. F. Persiani s. Tosi ms. G. B. Rubini t. A. Tamburini b.
Jul. 21	Anna Bolena	G. Grisi s. De Varny s. E. Grisi ms. G. B. Rubini t.
Jul. 23	La Donna del Lago	G. Grisi s. E. Grisi ms. G.B. Rubini t. Mario t.

AUTUMN AND WINTER 1840-41 PARIS-THEATRE DES ITALIENS

Oct. 6	Norma	G. Grisi s. Nencini s. R. Mirate t. (later Mario t.)
Oct. 15	I Puritani	G. Grisi s. G. B. Rubini t. A. Tamburini b.
Oct. 31	*Lucrezia Borgia	G. Grisi s. Bianchi ms. Mario t. R. Mirate t.
Nov. 12	L'elisir d'amore	F. Persiani s. Mario t. A. Tamburini b.
Jan. 05	La gazza ladra	G. Grisi. R. Mirate t. A. Tamburini b.
Jan. 1	Mose in Égitto	F. Persiani s G. B. Rubini t. A. Tamburini b. C. Magliano R. Mirate t. M. Amigo s.
Jan. 25	Don Giovanni	G. Grisi s. F. Persiani s. E. Albertazzi ms. G. B. Rubini t. A. Tamburini b.
Feb. 13	Il matrimonio segreto	E. Grisi s. F. Persiani s. E. Albertazzi ms. G. B. Rubini t. Campagnoli bs.
Mar. 08	Otello	G. Grisi s. G. B. Rubini t. R. Mirate t. A. Tamburini b.

SPRING AND SUMMER 1841 LONDON-HER MAJESTY'S THEATRE - M. Costa conductor

Apr. 17	Norma	G. Grisi s. Granchi ms. Mario t.
Apr. 22	I Puritani	G. Grisi s. G. B. Rubini t. A. Tamburini b.
Apr. 29	Otello	P. Viardot ms. G. B. Rubini t. Flavio t. A. Tamburini b.
May 04	Anna Bolena	G. Grisi s. Granchi s. E. Grisi ms. G.B. Rubini t.
May 06	Il matrimonio segreto	G. Grisi s. F. Persiani s. P. Viardot ms. G. B. Rubini t. A. Tamburini b.
May 20	Don Giovanni	G. Grisi s. F. Persiani s. S. Loewe s. G. B. Rubini t. A. Tamburini b.

May 25	L'elisir d'amore	F. Persiani s. Mario t. A. Tamburini b.
Jun. 10	Le nozze di Figaro	G. Grisi s. F. Persiani s. E. Grisi m Flavio t. A. Tamburini b.
Jun. 17	Lucrezia Borgia	G. Grisi s. E. Grisi ms. Mario t. A. Tamburini b.
Jul. 06	La Cenerentola	P. Viardot ms. G. B. Rubini t. A. Tamburini
Jul. 17	Il Barbiere di Siviglia	G. Grisi s. Mario t. A. Tamburini b. Giubile bs.
Jul. 22	Il Turco in Italia	F. Persiani s. G. B. Rubini t. A. Tamburini b
Aug. 06	Marino Faliero	S. Loewe s. G. B. Rubini t. Mario t. A. Tamburini b.
Aug. 12	La gazza ladra	G. Grisi s. E. Grisi ms. Flavio t. A. Tamburini b.

SUMMER 1841 LIVERPOOL-THEATERE ROYAL - J. Benedict conductor

| Aug. 21 | I Puritani | G. Grisi s. Mario t. F. Lablache b. |

SUMMER 1841 DUBLIN-THEATRE ROYAL

Aug. 30	I Puritani	G. Grisi s. Mario t. F. Lablache b.
Aug. 31	Norma	G. Grisi s. E. Grisi ms. Mario t.
Sept. 2	La Prova d'un Opera seria	G. Grisi s. E. Grisi ms. F. Lablache b.
Sep. 10	Il Barbiere di Siviglia	G. Grisi s. Mario t. F. Lablache b.

AUTUMN AND WINTER 1841-42 PARIS-THEATRE DES ITALIENS

Oct. 9	L'Elisir d Amore	F. Persiani s. Mario t. A. Tamburini b.
Oct. 12	I Puritani	G. Grisi s. Mario t. A. Tamburini. b.
Oct. 23	La Cenerentola	E. Albertazzi ms. R. Mirate t. A. Tamburini b.
Nov. 4	Norma	G. Grisi s. E. Albertazzi ms :
Nov. 16	Il Turco in Italia	F. Persiani s. R. Mirate t. A. Tamburini b.
Nov. 23	Il Barbiere di Siviglia	G. Grisi s. Mario t. F. Lablache b
Dec. 09	Lucrezia Borgia	G. Grisi s. E. Albertazzi ms. Mario t. A. Tamburini b.
Jan. 27	Don Giovanni	G. Grisi s. F. Persiani s. Donati t. A. Tamburini h.
Feb. 15	Le Cantatrici Villani	F. Persiani s. E. Albertazzi ms. R. Mirate t. F. Lablache b.

SPRING AND SUMMER 1842 LONDON-HER MAJESTY'S THEATRE - M. Costa conductor

| Apr. 16 | L'elisir d'amore | F. Persiani s. Mario t. Stella t. G.Ronconi b. |
| Apr. 30 | Torquato Tasso | E. Ronconi s. C. Guasco t. G. Ronconi b. |

May. 10	*Lucrezia Borgia*	E. Frezzolini s. Gramaglia ms. A. Poggi t.
May. 17	*Le Cantatrici Villani*	F. Persiani s. E. Frezzolini s. Stelle. t
		F. Lablache b.
Jun. 07	*Il Barbiere di Siviglia*	F. Persiani s, C. Guasco t,
		F. Lablache b. G. Ronconi b.
Jun. 06	*Don Giovanni*	E. Frezzolini s. F. Persiani s. Moltini s.
		G. B. Rubini t. G. Ronconi b.
Jun. 23	*I Puritani*	F. Persiani s. G. B. Rubini t. G. Ronconi.b
Jun. 30	*Mose in Égitto*	F. Persiani s. E. Ronconi s. G. B. Rubini t.
		C. Guasco t. G. Ronconi b.
Jul. 09	*Anna Bolena*	E. Frezzolini s E. Ronconi s. E. Grisi ms.
		G. B. Rubini t.
Jul. 14	*Il matrimonio segreto*	F. Persiani s. Moltini s. Gramaglia ms.
		G. B. Rubini t. F. Lablache b.
Aug. 04	*Cosi fan Tutte*	F. Persiani s. Moltini s. Granchi ms.
		G. B. Rubini t. G. Ronconi b.
Aug. 11	*Otello*	F. Persiani s. G. B. Rubini t. Stella t.
		G. Ronconi b.

SUMMER 1842 DUBLIN-THEATRE ROYAL

Sep. 05	*I Puritani*	G. Grisi s. Mario t. F. Lablache b.
Sep. 12	*Norma*	G. Grisi s. E. Grisi ms. Mario t.
Sep. 14	*Anna Bolena*	G. Grisi s. A. Hayland s. E. Grisi ms.
		Mario t.

AUTUMN AND WINTER 1842-43 PARIS-THEATRE DES ITALIENS

Nov. 17	**Linda di Chamonix*	F. Persiani s. M. Brambilla ms. Mario t.
		A. Tamburini b. F. Lablache b.
Dec. 01	*Lucrezia Borgia*	G. Grisi s. M. Brambilla ms Mario t.
		A. Tamburini b.
Dec. 13	*Le cantatrice Villani*	F. Persiani s. P Viardot ms. R. Mirate t.
		F. Lablache b.
Jan. 04	***Don Pasquale*	G. Grisi s. Mario t. A. Tamburini b
Jan. 23	*La gazza ladra*	P. Viardot ms. M. Brambilla ms. L. Corelli
		A. Tamburini b.
Feb. 07	*Don Giovanni*	G. Grisi s. F. Persiani s. Nissen s.
		L. Corelli t. A. Tamburini b.
Feb. 20	*Otello*	G. Grisi s. Mario t. L.Corelli t. A.Tamburini b.

SPRING AND SUMMER 1843 LONDON-HER MAJESTY'S THEATRE - M. Costa conductor

Apr. 18	*Norma*	G. Grisi s. Moltini s. C. Conti t.
Apr. 20	*Semiramide*	G. Grisi s. M. Brambilla ms. C.Conti t.
		L. Fornasari b. E. Bellini
Apr. 27	*Il Barbiere di Siviglia*	G. Grisi s. Mario t. L. Fornasari b.
		F. Lablache b.
May 05	*Don Giovanni*	G. Grisi s. F. Persiani s. Moltini.s
		Mario t. L. Fornasari b. F. Labalche b.
May 11	*La gazza ladra*	G. Grisi s. M. Brambilla ms. Mario t.
		L. Fornasari b.
May 18	*I Puritani*	G. Grisi s. Mario t. L. Fornasari b.
May 23	*Lucrezia Borgia*	G. Grisi s. M. Brambilla ms. Mario t.
Jun. 01	**Linda di Chamonix*	F. Persiani s. M. Brambilla ms. Mario t.
		L. Fornasari b.
Jun. 20	*L'elisir d'amore*	F. Persiani s. Mario t. F. Lablache b.
Jun. 29	**Don Pasquale*	G. Grisi s. Mario t. L.Fornasari. b.
Jul. 27	*La Cenerentola*	G. Grisi s. Mario t. L. Fornasari b. Panzini

WINTER 1844 PARIS-THEATRE DES ITALIENS

Jan. 04	*Don Pasquale*	G. Grisi s. Mario t. G. Ronconi b.
Jan. 08	*Il Barbiere di Siviglia*	F. Persiani s. Mario t. G. Ronconi b.
Feb. 05	*La gazza ladra*	G. Grisi s. M. Brambilla ms. L. Corelli t.
		L. Fornasari b.
Feb. 15	*Otello*	G. Grisi s. Mario t. L. Salvi t. G Ronconi b.
Mar 18	*I Puritani*	G. Grisi s. Mario t. G. Ronconi b.

SPRING AND SUMMER 1844 LONDON-HER MAJESTY'S THEATRE

Apr. 09	*I Puritani*	G. Grisi s. Mario t. L. Fornasari b.
Apr. 11	*Don Pasquale*	G. Grisi s. L. Corelli t. (later Mario t)
		L. Fornasari b.
Apr. 18	*Semiramide*	G. Grisi s. Favanti m. L. Corelli t.
		L. Fornasari b.
Apr. 25	*Norma*	G. Grisi s. Favanti ms. Mario t.
May. 02	*Don Giovanni*	G. Grisi s. F. Persiani s. Favanti ms. L.
		L. Corelli t. L. Fornasari b. F. Lablache b.
May 23	*Il matrimonio segreto*	G. Grisi s. F. Persiani s. Favanti ms Mario t
		F. Lablache b.
May 30	*Il Barbiere di Siviglia*	F. Persiani s. Mario t. L. Fornasari b.
		F. Lablache b.

Jun. 15	*Lucrezia Borgia*	G. Grisi s. Favanti ms. Mario t. (later N. Moriani t.)
Jun. 20	**Don Carlos* (Costa)	G. Grisi s. Mario t. L. Fornasari b.
Jul. 04	*Otello*	G. Grisi s. Mario t. L. Corelli t. L. Fornasari b.
Jul. 11	*Anna Bolena.*	G. Grisi s. Rosetti s. Favanti ms. N. Moriani t.
Jul. 25	*La gazza ladra*	G. Grisi s. Favanti ms. Mario t. L. Fornasari b.

AUTUMN AND WINTER 1844-45 PARIS-THEATRE DES ITALIENS

Oct. 10	*Il Barbiere di Siviglia*	F. Persiani s. Mario t. G. Ronconi b.
Oct 24	*I Puriani*	G. Grisi s. Mario t. Ronconi b.
Nov. 07	*Don Pasquale*	G. Grisi s. Mario t G. Ronconi b.
Nov. 26	*I Canatrice Villane*	F. Persiani s. Manara s. L. Corelli t. G. Ronconi b.
Jan. 23	*Don Giovanni*	G. Grisi s. F. Persiani s. Manara s. L. Corelli t. L. Fornasari b.
Feb. 10	*Otello*	G. Grisi s. Mario t. G. Ronconi b.
Feb. 17	*Norma*	G. Grisi s Manara s. G. Basadonna t.

SPRING AND SUMMER 1845 LONDON-HER MAJESTY'S THEATRE M. Costa conductor

Apr. 08`	*Norma*	G. Grisi s. Rosetti s. Mario t.
Apr. 10	*Don Pasquale*	G. Grisi s. Mario t. L. Fornasari b.
Apr. 17	*Semiramide*	G. Grisi s. M. Brambilla ms. L. Corelli t. L. Fornasari b.
Apr. 26	*Il Barbiere di Siviglia*	G. Grisi s. Mario t.(later L. Corelli t.) L. Fornasari b. F. Lablache b.
Apr. 30	*L'elisir d'amore*	A. Castellan s. L. Corelli t. F. Lablache b
May. 01	*I Puritani*	G. Grisi s. Mario t. Fornasari b.
May. 15	*La gazza ladra*	G. Grisi s. M. Brambilla ms. Mario t. L. Fornasari b.
May. 20	*Don Giovanni*	G. Grisi s. A. Castellan s. R. Basso-Boro s. Mario t. L. Fornasari b. F. Lablache b.
May. 24	*Linda di Chamonix*	A. Castellan s. M. Brambilla ms. N. Moriani t. F. Lablache bs.
Jun. 10	*Lucrezia Borgia*	G. Grisi s. M. Brambilla ms. N. Moriani t.
Jun. 19	*Otello*	G. Grisi s. Mario t. L. Corelli t L. Fornasari b.

| Jul. 10 | Anna Bolena | G. Grisi s. Rosetti s. M. Brambilla.ms. N. N. Moriani t. |
| Jul. 17 | Cosi fan tutte | A. Castellan s. R. Basso-Borio s. Rossi-Caccia s. Mario t. F. Lablache b. |

AUTUMN AND WINTER 1845-46 PARIS-THEATRE DES ITALIENS

Oct. 2	I Puritani	G. Grisi s. Mario t. G. Ronconi b.
Oct. 19	Norma	G. Grisi s. L. Brambilla s. L. Corelli t.
N.D.	Il Barbiere di Siviglia	F. Persiani s. Mario t. G. Ronconi b. J. Tagliafico bs.
Dec. 28	Don Pasquale	G. Grisi s. Mario t. G. Ronconi b.
Feb. 03	Il matrimonio segreto	F. Persiani s. T. Brambilla s. M. Brambilla ms. Mario t. G. Ronconi b.
Feb. 08	Semiramide?	G. Grisi s. M. Brambilla ms.
Mar. 16	Otello	G. Grisi s. Mario t. G. Ronconi b.

AUTUMN 1845 ST. CLOUD
(Concurrent with Paris season)

| Oct. 20 | Il Barbiere di Siviglia | F. Persiani s. Mario t. G. Ronconi b. J. Tagliafico bs. |

SPRING AND SUMMER 1846 LONDON-HER MAJESTY'S THEATRE M.Costa cond

Apr. 14	I Puritani	G. Grisi s. Mario t. L. Fornasari b.
Apr. 16	Don Giovanni	G. Grisi s. A. Castellan s. G. Sanchioli ms. Mario t. L. Fornasari b.
Apr. 23	Il Barbiere di Siviglia	G. Grisi s. Mario t. L. Fornasari b. F. Lablache b.
Apr. 28	Norma	G. Grisi s. Corbari s. L. Corelli t.
Apr. 30	Don Pasquale	G. Grisi s. Mario t. L. Fornasari b.
May 07	La gazza ladra	G. Grisi s. G. Brambilla ms. Mario t. L. Fornasari b.
May 14	La Prova d'un Opera	G. Grisi s. L. Corelli t. F. Lablache b.
May 21	L'elisir d'amore	A. Castellan s. L. Corelli t. F. Lablache b.
May 28	Il matrimonio segreto	G. Grisi s. A. Castellan s. G. Sanchioli ms. Mario t. F. Lablache b.
Jun. 16	Lucrezia Borgia	G. Grisi s. S. Brambilla ms. Mario t.
Jul. 06	Semiramide	G. Grisi s. G. Sanchioli ms. L. Corelli t. L. Fornasari b

Jul. 09	Anna Bolena	G. Grisi s. Corbari s. G. Brambilla ms.
		Mario t.
Jul. 28	*L'ajo nell'imbarazzo	A. Castellan s. Mario t. L. Fornasari b.
		F. Lablache b.

WINTER 1847 PARIS-THEATRE DES ITALIENS

Jan. 05	Don Pasquale	G. Grisi s. Mario t. G. Ronconi b.
Jan. 18	Il Barbiere di Siviglia	F. Persiani s. Mario t. G. Ronconi b.
Feb. 01	Don Giovanni	G. Grisi s. F. Persiani s. Corbari s.
		Mario t. F. Coletti b.
Feb. 15	I Puritani	G. Grisi s. Mario t. G. Ronconi b.
Mar. 01	Il matrimonio segreto	F. Persiani s. G. Brambilla s. M. Brambilla ms.
		Mario t. J. Tagliafico bs.
Mar. 15	Otello	G. Grisi s. Mario t. G. Ronconi h.

SPRING AND SUMMER 1847 LONDON-HER MAJESTY'S THEATRE—M. BALFE CONDUCTOR

Apr. 15	I Puritani	A. Castellan s. I, Gardoni t. F. Coletti b.
Apr. 22	L'elisir d'amore	A. Castellan s. I. Gardoni t.
Mar. 27	La figlia del reggimento	J. Lind s. I. Gardoni t.
Jun. 15	Norma	J. Lind s. G. Fraschini t.
Jul. 20	**I Masnadieri	J. Lind s. I. Gardoni t. F. Coletti b.
		(G. Verdi conducting)
Aug. 14	Le nozze di Figaro	J. Lind s. A. Castellan s. F. Coletti b.
		Staudigl bs.

AUTUMN AND WINTER 1847-48 PARIS-THEATRE DES ITALIENS

Oct. 02	Don Giovanni	G. Grisi s. F. Persiani s. Corbari s. Mario t.
		F. Coletti b.
Oct. 19	I Puritani	G. Grisi s. Mario t. G. Ronconi b.
Oct. 30	Il Barbiere di Siviglia	F. Persiani s. Mario t. G. Ronconi b.
		J. Tagliafico bs.
Dec. 19	La Cenerentola	M. Alboni ms. I. Gardoni t. G. Ronconi b.
Dec. 30	L'elisir d'amore?	
Feb. 07	La gazza ladra	G. Grisi s. M.Alboni ms. Cellini t. F.Coletti b.
Mar. 20	Don Pasquale	G. Grisi s. Mario t. G. Ronconi b.
Mar. 31	Otello?	

SPRING AND SUMMER 1848 LONDON-HER MAJESTY'S THEATRE

Apr. 13	Lucrezia Borgia	S. Cruvelli s. Schwarz ms. I. Gardoni t.
May 20	Linda di Chamonix	E. Tadolini s. Schwarz ms. S. Reeves t.
		I. Gardoni t. F. Coletti b. F. Lablache b.

Jun. 8	*L'elisir d'amore*	J. Lind s. I. Gardoni t. Belletti b.
Jun. 20	*Don Pasquale*	E. Tadolini s. F. Labocetta t. Belletti. b.
Jul. 13	*Le nozze di Figaro*	J. Lind s. S. Cruvelli s. Schwarz ms. G. B. Belletti b. F. Coletti b.
Jul. 29	*I Puritani*	J. Lind s. I. Gardoni t. F. Coletti b

WINTER 1849 PARIS-THEATRE DES ITALIENS

Jan. 06	*La Cenerentola*	M. Alboni ms. Bordas t. G. Ronconi b.
Feb. 08	*Semiramide?*	
Mar. 08	*Don Pasquale*	A. Castellan

SPRING AND SUMMER 1849 LONDON-HER MAJESTY'S THEATRE

Apr. 10	*Norma*	T. Parodi s. Julian van Gelder s. (later M. Alboni ms.) Bordas t.
Apr. 12	*Il flauto magico*	J. Lind s. I. Gardoni t. Bordas t. F. F. Lablache b.
May 01	*La favorita*	T. Parodi s. (later M. Alboni ms.) I. Gardoni t. F. Coletti b.
May 15	*Il Barbiere di Siviglia*	M. Alboni ms. (later H. Sontag s.) I. Gardoni t. G. B. Belletti b.
May. 22	*Semiramide*	T. Parodi s. M. Alboni ms. Bartolini t. F. Coletti.b.
May. 24	*La gazza ladra*	M. Alboni ms. E. Calzolari t. F. Coletti b.
May. 31	*Don Giovanni*	T. Parodi s. Julian van Gelde s. M. Alboni I. Gardoni t. F. Coletti b.
June 14	*Il matrimonio segreto*	T. Parodi s. Julian van gelder s. M. Alboni ms. E. Calzolari t. F. Lablache b.
Jun. 21	*Lucrezia Borgia*	T. Parodi s. M. Alboni ms. N. Moriani t.
Jun. 27	*Don Fasquale*	M. Alboni ms. E. Calzolari t.G.B. Belletti b.
Jul. 7	*Linda di Chamonix?*	H. Sontag s. Casaloni ms. I. Gardoni t. F. Coletti b.
Jul. 25	*Otello*	H. Sontag s. N. Moriani t. E Calzolari t. G. B. Belletti b.
Aug. 7	*Le nozze di Figaro*	H. Sontag s. T. Parodi s. M. Alboni ms. Bartolini b. F. Coletti b. G. B. Belletti b.

WINTER 1850 PARIS-THEATRE DES ITALIENS

Jan. 5	*La Cenerentola*	E. D'Angri ms. G. Lucchesi t. G. Ronconi b.
Jan. 10	*Il Barbiere di Siviglia*	F. Persiani s. (later E. D'Angri ms.) G. Lucchesi t. G. Ronconi b.

Feb. 07	Il matrimonio segreto	F. Persiani s. S. Vera-Lorini s. E. D'Angri ms.
		G. Lucchesi t.
Feb. 14	Don Giovanni	S. Vera-Lorini s. F. Persiani s.
		G. Lucchesi t. G. Ronconi b.
Mar. 14	Don Pasquale	F. Persiani s. P. Brignoli t. G. Ronconi b.

SPRING AND SUMMER 1850 LONDON-HER MAJESTY'S THEATRE

Apr. 04	Don Pasquale	H. Sontag s. E. Calzolari t. G.B. Belletti b.
Apr. 09	Il Barbiere di Siviglia	H. Sontag s. E. Calzolari t. G.B. Belletti b.
		F. Lablache b.
Apr. 11	Don Giovanni	T. Parodi s. Julian van Gelder s. H. Sontag s.
		E. Calzolari t. F. Coletti b. F.Lablache b.
Apr. 27	Linda di Chamonix?	
May. 09	I Puritani	H. Sontag s. (later E. Frezzolini s.)
		C. Baucarde t.(later I.Gardoni t.) F. Coletti b.
May. 21	Lucrezia Borgia	E. Frezzolni s. Bertrand ms. C. Baucarde t.
Jun. 01	L'elisir d'amore	E. Frezzolini s. E. Calzolari t.G.B. Belletti b.
Jun. 08	**La Tempesta (Halevy)	H. Sontag s.T.Parodi s. C.Baucarde t.
		F. Coletti b.
Jul. 04	Il matrimonio segreto	H. Sontag s. E. Frezzolini s. T. Parodi s. E.Calzolari t.
		F. Lablache b.
Jul 18	La prova d'un opera seria	E. Frezzolini s. Calzolari t.
Aug 10	Le nozze de Figaro	
Aug. 13	Norma	Fiorentini s. Julian van Gelder s. I. Gardoni t.

AUTUMN AND WINTER 1850-51 PARIS-THEATRE DES ITALIENS

Nov. 19	Norma	Fiorentini s. (later R. Montenegro s.)
		Giuliani s. E. Calzolari t.
Dec. 06	Il Barbiere di Siviglia	H. Sontag s. E. Calzolari t.
		(later I Gardoni t.) Ferranti b.
Dec. 17	Lucrezia Borgia	Fiorentini s. Bertrandi ms. N. Ivanoff t.
		(later I. Gardoni t.)
Jan. 04	Don Pasquale	H. Sontag s. E. Calzolari t. Colini b.
Jan. 17	L' Elisir d'Amore	C. Duprez s. E. Calzolari t. Ferranti b.
Feb. 25	*La Tempesta	H. Sontag s. Bertrandi ms. I. Gardoni t.
Feb. 26	L'Italiana in Algeri?	
Mar. 01	Il matrimonio segreto	H. Sontag s. Giuliani s. Bertrandi ms.
		E. Calzolari t. Ferranti b.
Mar. 29	**Le Tre Nozze (Alary)	H. Sontag s. Giuliani s. Bertrandi ms.
		I. Gardoni t. Ferranti b,

SPRING AND SUMMER 1851 LONDON-HER MAJESTY'S THEATRE

Apr. 22	*L'Elisir d'amore*	C. Duprez s. E. Calzolari t. F. Coletti b.
May. 8	**Le Tre Nozze*	H. Sontag s. Bertrandi ms. I. Gardoni t.
May. 15	*Don Giovanni*	S. Cruvelli s. (later Julian van Gelder s.) Fiorentini H. Sontag s. (later M Alboni ms) E. Calzolari t. F. Coletti b.
May. 22	*Il Barbiere di Siviglia*	H. Sontag s. E. Calzolari t. Ferrant b. (later Lorenzo b.)
May. 31	*Norma*	S. Cruvelli s. Julian van Gelder s.Pardini t
Jun. 05	*Don Pasquale*	H. Sontag s. E. Calzolari t. (later I. Gordoni t.) Ferranti b.
Jun. 28	*La Prova d'un Opera seria*	Ugalde s.
Jul. 03	***Florinda* (S.Thalberg)	S. Cruvelli s. E. Calzolari t. S. Reeves t. F. Coletti b.
Jul. 12	*La Cenerentola*	M. Alboni ms. E. Calzolari t. Ferranti b.
Jul. 31	*La gazza ladra*	M. Alboni ms. Bertrandi ms. E. Calzolari t. F. Coletti b.
Aug. 26	*Anna Bolena*	M. Barbieri-Nini s. Julian van Gelder s. Bertrandi ms. E. Calzolari t.

WINTER 1852 PARIS-THEATRE DES ITALIENS

Mar. 06	*Il Barbiere di Siviglia*	S. Cruvelli s. E. Calzolari t.G.B.Belletti b.
Mar. 13	*La cenerentola*	E. D'Angri s. E. Calzolari t. G.B.Belletti b.

SPRING AND SUMMER 1852 LONDON-HER MAJESTY'S THEATRE

Apr. 17	*Norma*	S. Cruvelli s. I.Gardoni t.(later A Bettini t
Apr. 22	*Il Barbiere di Siviglia*	S. Cruvelli s. (later A. De la Crange s.) E. Calzolari t. Ferlotti b.(later De Bassini)
May. 01	*La Cenerentola.*	E. D'Angri ms. (later Favanti ms.) E. Calzolari t. G. B. Belletti b.
May. 29	*La Prova d'un Opera*	A. de la Grange s. E. Calzolari t,
Jun. 03	*Don Pasquale*	A. de la Grange s. E. Calzolari t. Ferranti b
Jul. 08	*I Puritani*	A. de la Grange s. I. Gardoni t. A. De Bassini b.
Jul. 15	*Otello*	A. de Grange s. G.Bettini t. E. Calzolari t. A. De Bassini b.

AUTUMN AND WINTER 1852-53 ST.PETERSBURG-IMPERIAL THEATRE

Oct. 20	*Don Pasquale*	G. Medori s. Stechi-Botcardi t. G. Ronconi b.
Nov. 07	*La Cenerentola*	E. de Meric Lablache ms. (later P.Viardot ms.) E. Tamberik t. G. Ronconi b.

Nov. 29	*I Puritani*	F. Marai s. Mario t. s. Ronconi b.
Dec. 11	*Il Barbiere di Siviglia*	P. Viardot ms. Mario t. G. Ronconi b.
		J. Tagliafico bs.
Mar. 01	*La Prova d'un Opera*	P. Viardot ms. G. Ronconi b.

WINTER 1853 ST. PETERSBURG-HERMITAGE PALACE

| Mar. 07 | *La figlia del reggimento* | M. Lablache s. Mario t.G.Ronconi b. |
| | (debut of Marie Lablache) | J Tagliafico bs. *(as Ortensio) |

AUTUMN AND WINTER 1853-54 ST. PETERSBURG-IMPERIAL THEATRE

Oct. 15	*Il Barbiere di Siviglia*	A. de la Grange s. E. Calzolari t. G. Ronconi b.
Nov. 11	*Don Pasquale*	G. Medori s. E. Calzolari t. G. Ronconi b.
Dec. 02	**Il Marito e l'Amante*	G. Medori s. E. De Meric ms. E. Tamberick t.
		A. De Bassini b.
Dec. 08	*Linda di Chamonix?*	A. de la Grange s. E. de Meric-Lablache ms.
		E. Naudin t. G. Ronconi b.
Dec. 17	*L'elisir d'amore*	A. de la Grange s. E. Calzolari t. G. Ronconi b.
Dec. 22	*Don Giovanni*	G. Medori s. E. de Meric Lablache ms.
		F. Marai s E. Tamberlik t. A. De Bassini bs.
Jan. 21	*Anna Bolena*	G. Medori s. F. Marai s. E.de Meric Lablache ms.
		E. Calzolari t.
Feb. 18	*I Puritani*	A. De la Grange s. E. Calzolari t. G. Ronconi b.
Feb. 25	*La Prova d'un Opera seria*	A. De la Grange s. E. Calzolari t. G. Ronconi b

SPRING AND SUMMER 1854 LONDON-CONVENT GARDEN/CONDUCTOR M.COSTA

May. 09	*Il Barbiere di Siviglia*	A. Bosio s. Mario t. G. Ronconi b.
May. 11	*Don Giovanni*	S. Cruvelli s. (later P. Viardot ms.)A. Bosio s.
		F. Marai s. E. Tamberlik t. G. Ronconi b.
May. 18	*I Puritani*	A. Bosio s. Mario t. G. Ronconi b.
		(later O. Bartalini b.)
Jun. 01	*Norma*	G. Grisi s. F. Marai s. E. Tamberlik t.
Jun. 29	*Don Pasquale*	G. Grisi s. Mario t. G. Ronconi b.
Jul. 03	*La Prova d'un Opera*	P. Viardot ms. G. Stricoli t. G. Ronconi b.
Jul. 13	*La Favorita*	G. Grisi s. Mario t. G. Bartilini b. M.
Jul. 13	*Otello*	P. Viardot s. E. Tamberlik t. G. Ronconi b.

AUTUMN AND WINTER 1854-55 ST PETERSBURG IMPERIAL THEATRE

Oct. 04	*Il Barbiere di Siviglia*	A. de la Grange s. E. Calzolari t. G. Ronconi b. J. Tagliafico bs.
Nov. 03	*L'elisir d'amore*	F. Marai s. E. Calzolari t. G. Ronconi b.
Dec. 08	*Don Pasquale*	A. de la Grange s. E. Calzolari t. G. Ronconi
Dec. 10	*I Puritani*	A. de la Grange s. E. Calzolari t. G. Ronconi b.
Dec. 11	*Der Freichutz* (in Italian)	A. de la Grange s. E. de Meric-Lablache ms. E. Tamberlik t. Didot b.

SPRING AND SUMMER 1855 LONDON-COVENT GARDEN CONDUCTOR M. COSTA

May. 05	*L'Elisir d'Amore*	A. Bosio s. I. Gardoni t. F. Graziani b.
May. 17	*I Puritani*	A. Bosio s. Mario t. F. Graziani b.
May. 24	*La Favorita*	G. Grisi s. Mario t. F. Graziani b.
May. 31	*Don Giovanni*	H. Rudersdorff s. F. Marai s. A. Bosio s. Mario t. A. Tamburini b.
Jun. 14	*Il Barbiere di Siviglia*	P. Viardot ms. (later J. Gassier s.) E. Bellini s. Mario t. (later Lorici t.) A. Tamburini b. A. Formes bs.
Jun. 28	*Don Pasquale*	G. Grisi s. Mario t. A. Tamburini b.
Jul. 19	**L'Etoile du Nord* (in Italian)	A. Bosio s. F. Marai s. H. Rudersdorff I. Gardoni t. A. Formes bs.

AUTUMN AND WINTER 1855-56 ST. PETERSBURG-IMPERIAL THEATRE

Oct. 22	*L'elisir d'amore*	F. Marai s. E. Calzolari t. J. Tagliafico bs
Nov. 07	*I Puritani*	A. Bosio s. E. Calzolari t. A. De Bassini bs
Nov. 19	*Don Pasquale*	A. Bosio s. E. Calzolari t. A. De Bassini bs
Dec. 15	*Il Barbiere di Siviglia*	A. Bosio s. E. Calzolari t. A. De Bassini bs J. Tagliafico bs.
Jan. 26	**L'Etoile du Nord* (in Italian)	A. Bosio s. F. Marai s. E. Calzolari t. A. Bettini t. De Bassini bs.

SUMMER 1856 MOSCOW-TEATRE BOLSHOI

Aug. 30?	*L'elisir d'amore*	
Sep.	*I Puritani*	A. Bosio s. E. Calzolari t. A. De Bassini bs
Sep. 08	**Don Pasquale*	F. Marai s. E. Calzolari t. A. De Bassini bs
Sep. 17	*L'Elisir d'amore*	A. Bosio s. E. Calzolari t. A. De Bassini bs

AUTUMN AND WINTER 1856-57 ST. PETERSBURG-IMPERIAL THEATRE

Nov. 08	*Il Barbiere di Siviglia*	A. Bosio s. E. Calzolari t. A. De Bassini bs I. Marini bs.
Dec. 19	*Don Pasquale*	F. Marai s. A. Bettini t. A. De Bassini bs.
Dec. 27	*Don Giovanni*	A. Bosio s. M. Lotti della Santa s. F. Marai s. E. Calzolari t. A. Bassini bs
Jan. 03	*L'Italiana in Algeri*	E. de Meric-Lablache ms. E. Calzolari t. I. Marini bs
N.D?	*L'Elisir d'Amore*	F. Marai s. E. Calzolari t.

CHRONOLOGY B
LABLACHE PERFORMANCES BY COMPOSER

WORLD PREMIERES ** LOCAL *

	COMPOSER	YEAR	TITLE OF OPERA		FIRST ENTRY
1	AIROLDI				
	FEB	1821	ADRIANO IN SIRIA **	1	PALERMO*
2	ALARY				
	MAR 29	1851	TRE NOZZE **	2	LONDON
3	BALDUCCI				
	JAN 15	1826	TAZIA	3	NAPLES
4	BALFE				
	JUL 19	1838	FALSTAFF **	4	LONDON
5	BASILI				
	MAR 20	1824	SANSONE**	5	NAPLES
6	BELLINI				
	MAY 30	1826	BIANCA AND GERANDO **	6	NAPLES
	MAY 16	1829	ZAIRA **	7	PARMA
	JAN 24	1835	I PURITANI **	8	PARIS
	DEC 8	1835	NORMA*	9	PARIS
7	BENEDICT				
	JAN 28	1830	I PORTOGHESI IN GOA **	10	NAPLES
8	BOIELDIEU				
		1837	LA DAME BIANCA	11	NAPLES
9	CARAFA				
	N.D.	1816	IL VASCELLO D'OCCIDENTE	12	PALERMO
	DEC 26	1821	LA CAPRICIOSA** E IL SOLDATO	13	ROME
	JUN 28	1823	ABUFAR	14	VIENNA
	OCT 4	1825	GLI ITALIANI** E GL INDIAI	15	NAPLES
10	CARLINI				
		1817	MARIA STUARDA*	16	PALERMO
11	CIMAROSA				
	JUN 28	1824	IL MATRIMONIO SEGRETO	17	VIENNA
		18	LE TRAME DELUSA	18	NAPLES

12	COCCIA				
	JUN 8	1822	ARRIGHETTO	19	MILAN
	NOV 15	1828	L'ORFANA DELLA SELVA **	20	MILAN
	JAN 19	1834	LA FIGLIA DELL'ARCIERE **21		MILAN?
13	CONTI				
		1826	OLIMPIA*	22	NAPLES
14	CORDELLA				
	SPRING	1833	IL MARITO DISPERATO	23	NAPLES
15	COSTA				
	FEB 7	1829	MALVINA**	24	
	JAN 14	1837	MALIK ADEL**	25	PARIS
	JUN 20	1844	DON CARLOS**	26	LONDON
16	DE LUCA	1815	L'APPUNTAMENTO NOTTURNA PER BURLA	27	MESSINA
17	DONIZETTI				
	JUL 6	1826	ELVIDA** (1)	28	NAPLES
	JUL 19	1826	ALAHOR DI GRANATA*	29	NAPLES
	APR 2	1827	L'AJO NELL IMBARAZZO*	30	VIENNA
	JAN 1	1828	L'ESULA DI ROMA ** (2)	31	NAPLES
	JAN 12	1829	IL PARIA ** (3)	32	NAPLES
	FEB 27	1829	IL GIOVEDA GRASSO ** (4)	33	NAPLES
	FEB 5	1830	IL PAZZI PER PROGRETTO ** (5)	34	NAPLES
	MAR 6	1830	IL DILUVIO UNIVERSALE ** (6)	35	NAPLES
	JUL 8	1831	ANNA BOLENA *	36	LONDON
	NOV 4	1832	SANCIA DI CASTIGLIA **(7)	37	NAPLES
	AUG 30	1832	FAUSTA	38	NAPLES
	APR 13	1834	L'ELISIR D'AMORE *	39	NAPLES
	MAR 12	1835	MARINO FALIERO ** (8)	40	PARIS
	MAR 4	1837	GEMMA DI VERGY	41	NAPLES
	FEB 24	1838	PARISINA D'EST *	42	PARIS
	JUN 6	1839	LUCREZIA BORGIA*	43	LONDON
	OCT 1	1839	LUCIA DI LAMMERMOOR (ODEON)	44	PARIS
	APR 30	1842	TORQUATO TASSO	45	LONDON
	NOV 17	1842	LINDA DI CHAMOUNIX **(9) [1]	46	PARIS
	JAN 4	1843	DON PASQUALE **(10)	47	PARIS

[1] *Linda* revised version

		JUN 5	1849	LA FILLE DU REGIMENT	48	LONDON
		JUL 11	1854	LA FAVORITA	49	LONDON
18	FARINELLI					
		N.D.	1818	GINEVRA DEGLI ALMIERI	50	PALERMO
19	FIORAVANTI					
				LE CANTATRICA VILLANE	51	NAPLES
			1812	LA MOLINARE	52	PALERMO
			1831	COMINGIO ROMITO	53	
			1816	RAUL SIGNOR DI SEQUI	54	PALERMO
			1817	LA MORTE DI ADELAIDE	55	PALERMO
20	FREDERICI					
		N.D.	1820	ZAIRA?	56	PALERMO
21	GENERALI					
			1816	LA CALZOLAIA	57	PALERMO
			1816	IL SERVO PADRONE	58	MESSINA
			1817	I BACCANATI DE ROMA	59	PALERMO
			1823	LE LAGRIME D'UNA VEDOVA		NAPLES
22	GENOVESE					
		OCT?	1833	BIANCA DI BELMONTE	60	NAPLES
23	GNECCO					
		SEP 14	1828	PROVA D'UN OPERA SERIA	61	MILAN
24	GUGLIELMI					
			1818	AMALIA E CARLO?	62	PALERMO
		AUG 19	1829	TERESA NAVIGERO**	63	NAPLES
25	HALEVY					
		JUN 15	1850	LA TEMPESTA**	64	LONDON
26	HEROLD					
		NOV	1833	ZAMPA*	65	NAPLES
27	MANDANICI					
		DEC 9	1833	GLI ARAGONESI IN NAPOLI	66	NAPLES
		JAN 12	1833	CANTATA FOR FERDINANDO II	67	NAPLES
28	MARLIANI					
		MAR 7	18??	ILDEGONDA NEL CARCERE**	68	PARIS
29	MAYR					
		MAR 8	1822	MEDEA IN CORINTO	69	MILAN
		JAN	1821	LA ROSA BIANCA E ROSA	70	PALERMO
		N.D.	1820	IFIGENIA?	71	PALERMO
		N.D.	1818	CORA?	72	PALERMO

30	MELLARA					
		1818	ZILIA?*	73	PALERMO
31	MERCADANTE					
	OCT 30	1821	ELISA E CLAUDIO **	74	MILAN
	DEC 26	1822	AMELETO **	75	MILAN
	SEP 23	1823	COSTANZA ED ALMERISKA **	76	NAPLES
	MAY 22	1820	VIOLENZA E COSTANZA *	77	PALERMO
	SEP 18	1824	DORALICE **	78	VIENNA
	NOV 5	1824	LE NOZZE DI TELMACCO **	79	VIENNA
	NOV 20	1824	IL PONDESTA DI BURGOS **	80	VIENNA
	SPRING	1825	IL SIGNORE DELL VILLAGGIO ?	81	NAPLES
	JUL 31	1825	DIDONE ABBANDONDA	82	NAPLES
	DEC 29	1825	IPERMESTRA **	83	NAPLES
	MAR 30	1834	I NORMANNI A PARIGI*	84	NAPLES
	JUL 2	1836	I BRIGANTI *	85	LONDON
32	MEYERBEER					
	CARNIVAL	1822	L'ESULA DI GRANATA	86	MILAN
		18??	STELLA DEL NORD?	87	
	JUL 19	1855	L'ETOILE DU NORD**	88	LONDON
33	MOSCA					
	N.D.	1818	LA GIOVANTU D'ENRICO 11?	89	PALERMO
	N.D.	1818	ATTILA IN AQUILEA?	90	PALERMO
	N.D.	18	GLI SPOSI IN CIMENTO	91	
	N.D	1819	L'IMPOSTORE O IL MARCOTONTA?	92	PALERMO
	OCT 10	1821	LA SCIOCCA PER ASTUZIA	93	MILAN
	APR 8	1822	LA DAMA LOCANDIERA**	94	MILAN
		1818	FEDERICO II	95	PALERMO
	MAR 21	1824	I PRETENDENTI DELUSI	96	VIENNA
	JUN 26	1826	L'ABATE DELL'EPEE**	97	NAPLES
34	MORLACCHI					
	OCT 2	1821	DONNA AURORA	98	MILAN
35	MOZART					
	NOV 1	1831	DON GIOVANNI	99	PARIS
	JUN 21	1838	LE NOZZE DI FIGARO	100	LONDON
	APR 12	1849	IL FLAUTO MAGICO	101	LONDON
	JUL 6	1855	COSI FAN TUTTE	102	LONDON

36	NICOLINI				
	N.D.	1818	QUINTO FABIO?	103	PALERMO
	N.D.	1819	IL TRIONFO DI GIULIO CESARE?	104	PALERMO
37	PACINI				
	FEB 6	1823	LA VESTALE **	105	MILAN
	JUL 6	1825	AMAZILIA*	106	NAPLES
	JUL 17	1825	INNO CON BALLO	107	NAPLES
	NOV 19	1825	L'ULTIMO GIORNO DI POMPEI**(1)	108	NAPLES
	JAN 1	1826	LA SCHIAVA DI BAGDAD	109	NAPLES
	NOV 1	1826	NIOBE ** (2)	110	NAPLES
	OCT 4	1827	GLI ARABI NELLE GALLIE*	111	NAPLES
	NOV 19	1827	MARGHERITA REGINA D'INGHILTERRA ** (3)	112	NAPLES
	JUN 11	1828	IL CAVALIERI DI VALENZA*	113	MILAN
	NOV 23	1829	IL CONTESTABILE DI CHESTER*	114	NAPLES
	DEC 3	1832	IL FELICE IMENEO	115	NAPLES
	JAN 12	1833	GLI ELVEZI (4)	116	NAPLES
	MAY 30	1833	FERDINANDO DUCA DI VALENZA**	117	NAPLES
	NOV 30	1833	IRENE ** (5)	118	NAPLES
38	PAER				
	N D	1818	AGNESE?	119	TURIN
	N.D.	1818	CAMILLA?	120	PALERMO
	N.D.	1817	LEONORA ?	121	
39	PALMA				
		1812	L'EREDE SENZA EREDITA	122	NAPLES
40	PAISIELLO				
	OCT?	1825	LA FINTA AMANTE	123	NAPLES
			LA VESTALE	124	
			IL SOCRATTO IMMAGINARIO	125	
	OCT 27	1826	LA SERVA PADRONA	126	MILAN
41	PAVESI				
	APR 19	1826	SOLITARIO ED ELODIA**	127	NAPLES
	N.D	1816	SER MARCANTONIO	128	PALERMO
	SEP 27	1828	IL MALDICENTE O LA BOTTEGA DA CAFFE	129	MILAN

Appendices

42	PERSIANI				
	DEC 24	1839	INEZ DE CASTRO	130	PARIS
43	PORTOGALLO				
	N.D.	1817	IL RITORNO DI SERSE?	131	PALERMO
44	PUCCITTA				
	JAN 26	1821	LA FESTA DEL VILLAGGIO**	132	ROME
45	RADICATI				
	N.D.	1818	CASTORE E POLLUCE	133	PALERMO
46	RAIMONDI				
	1837		GLI ARLIFIZJ PER AMORE???	134	NAPLES
47	RICCI				
	JUN 27	1829	Il COLOMBO**	135	PARMA
			MARITOE L'AMANTE	136	
	N.D.	1818	MISANTROPIA E PENTIMENTO?	137	
48	ROSSINI				
	N.D	1817	IL CAMBIO DELLA VALIGIA?	138	PALERMO
	N.D	1818	DEMETRIO E POLIBIO?	139	PALERMO
	AUG	1820	TANCREDI *	140	PALERMO
	N.D.	1817	CIRO IN BABILONIA	141	PALERMO
	AUG 15	1821	LA CENERENTOLA DEBUT	142	MILAN
	OCT 18	1818	IL BARBIERE DI SIVIGLIA	143	NAPLES
	JUL 19	1818	LA PIETRA DEL PARAGONE	144	PALERMO
	JUN 19	1822	L'OCCASIONE IL LADRO	145	MILAN
	OCT 27	1823	OTELLO	146	NAPLES
	JUN 2	1823	ZELMIRA	147	VIENNA
	AUG 30	1820	LA DONNA DEL LARGO *	148	PALERMO
	NOV 30	1823	SEMIRAMIDE *	149	NAPLES
	AUG 18	1824	L'INGANNO FELICE	150	VIENNA
	FEB 20	1820	MOSE IN EGITTO *	151	PALERMO
	JAN 19	1825	LA GAZZA LADRA	152	VIENNA
	MAR 1	1825	IL TURCO IN ITALIA	153	VIENNA
	MAY 12	1825	BIANCA E FALLIERO	154	NAPLES
	JUN 19	1825	MAOMETTO SECONDO	155	NAPLES
	SPRING	1829	MOSE E FARAONE	156	PARMA
	JUN 23	1831	L'ITALIANA IN ALGERI	157	LONDON
	APR 7	1833	GUILIELMO TELL *	158	NAPLES
	JUN 3	1836	SIEGE DE CORINTHE	159	LONDON
	JUN 7	1838	MALHILDE DI SHABRAN	160	LONDON

49	RUSSO				
	N.D.	1819	LA DIFESA DI GIOA?	161	PALERMO
50	SPONTINI				
	MAY 30	1829	LA VESTALE	162	NAPLES
51	THALBERG				
	JUL 3	1851	FLORINDA**	163	LONDON
52	TURINA				
	N D	1822	UNA CASA DA VENDERE	164	TURIN
53	VACCAI				
	MAR 11	1829	SAUL **	165	NAPLES
	OCT 31	1828	LA PASTORELLA FEUDATORIA	166	MILAN
54	VERDI				
	JUL 22	1847	I MASNADIERI **	167	LONDON
55	WEBER				
	WINTER	1856	DER FREISCHUTZ	168	ST PETERSBURG
56	WEIGL				
	OCT	1819	IL RIVALE DI SE STESSO *	169	PALERMO
57	ZINGARELLI				
	JUN 22	1837	ROMEO E GIULIETTA	170	LONDON

LABLACHE'S ORATORIO AND RELIGIOUS REPERTORY:

58	HANDEL		THE MESSIAH	171	ENGLAND
59	HAYDN		THE SEASONS	172	ENGLAND
60	MOZART	1809	REQUIEM (Memorial for Haydn)	173	NAPLES
61	ROSSINI	1842	STABAT MATER	174	ENGLAND
62	MENDELSSOHN		ELIJAH	175	ENGLAND

---

* The data for Palermo can not all be confirmed.
 1824 Autori diversi : La Fondazione di Partenope

☙☙☙

CHRONOLOGY C
LABLACHE FAMILY CONCERTS AND OPERA TOURS

The concerts of Luigi Lablache, Frederic Lablache and Madame Frances Lablache combined. Luigi Lablache's opera performances appear in chronology A. Only British opera performances are added for Frederic. This chronology can in no way be definitive and only attempts to cover the enormous range of their tours. This chronology would not be possible without the help of Tom Kaufman.

MILAN

1823	Accademie Milan	Luigi Lablache De-Sessi Monelli

LONDON

May 15 1830	Lady Jane Walsh Berkley Square	Debut-Lablache first English Concert (private}
May 19 1830	Kings Rooms	Lablache(public)debut in England Lablache Malibran Lalande Stockhauser Wood Donizelli de Begnis Santini
May 20 1830	Morning Concert King's Rooms	Lablache Malibran Stockhauser Mrs. W. Knyvett
May 20 1830	Evening Concert Hanover Rooms	Lablache sang 'Largo al factotum'
May 21 1830	Concert	Lablache Malibran Blasis Knyvett
May 24 1830	Morning Concert	Lablache Lalande Donizelli Curioni Pennega Blasis
May 30 1830	King's Theatre	Lablache
Jun.01 1830	King's Theatre	Lablache
Jun.07 1830	Drury Lane Theatre	Lablache Santini Betts
Jun.18 1830	Morning Concert King's Theatre	Lablache Santini Begnis Malibran
Jun.18 1830	Evening Concert Sir G. Warrender	Lablache Malibran Stockhauser Blasis Begnis
Jun.21 1830	King's Theatre	Lablache Malibran de Beroit
Jun.23 1830	King's Theatre	Lablache Donizelli de Beroit
Jun.24 1830	King's Theatre Last act *Semiramide* *Beethoven's Battle Symphony* Haydn's *Seasons*	Lablache Lalande Malibran Betts Phillips Bochos

Jun.25 1830		Concert	Lablache
Jun.28 1830		King's Theatre	Lablache Malibran Donizelli Blasis Santini Beroit Moscheles
Jul.05 1830		King's Theatre	Lablache Malibran Blasis Begnis Donizelli Beroit

PARIS CONCERTS

Jan.07 1831		Salle Mme Merlin	Lablache Blanchard Mme de Sparre Rossini at the piano David Malibran Raimbaux *Matilda di Shalbran* Donizelli David
Jan.10 1831		Salon de e M. Bonfils	Lablache David Tadolini Zuchelli Malibran
Jan.12 1831		Concert a la Court Palais Royal	Lablache Malibran Meric Lalande David Donizelli Nourrit Levasseur
Jan.19 1831		Concert à la Court Palais Royal 'Air de Patria' *Tancredi*	Lablache Malibran *Sémiramide* Raimbaux Nourrit Zuchelli Donzelli David Lablache Malibran Raimbaux
Jan.26 1831		Schlesinger	Lablache Malibran David (Rossini piano)
Apr.27 1831		Concert a la Court Palais Royal	Lablache Malibran *Semiramide* [duet] (Louis Phillip rule)
Apr.31 1831		Salle Mme Merlin Act II *Semiramide*	Lablache *Prova di Opera Seria*
May.05 1831		King's Theatre	Lablache Inverarity Rubini Masson Knyvet Stockhausen Parry Hummel
Jun.06 1831		Philarmonic concert	Lablache Rubini Seguin Stockhausen Mori
Jun. 1831		Concert St.James	Lablache Pasta Santini Comelli Rubini
Jun.24 1831		King's Theatre	Lablache Pasta Rubini Inverarity Braham Cawse De Begnis Stockhausser Paganini
Jul.18 1831		Kings's Theatre	Lablache Pasta Rubini Santini De Begnis

PARIS

Sep.25 1831		Theatre Italien Grand Concert *La Pietra di Paragone* *Et Moise in Egitto*	Lablache Tadolini Malibran Raimbaux Amigo Santini Rubini Aerizi Bordogni Beriot
Oct.14 1831		Concert a la Court	Lablache
Nov.21 1831		Palais Royal Emperor Don Pedro of Brazil, Princess de Lewchtenberg	Lablache Malibran Mme Lazine *Semiramide* [duet]

Dec.14 1831	Concert a la Court Palais Royal	Lablache Rubini Malibran Rubini *Semiramide* [duet] Lablache Malibran Chollet Schunke Labarre [harp]d'Erard
Dec.25 1831	Grand concert Theatre Italien *Moïse* [Quintet] *La Pietra di Paragone* [Trio] *Tancredi*	Lablache Malibran Rubini Casadoni Raimbaux Schroder-Devrient Santini Hertz de Beriot Bordogini Tadolini Bordogni Lablache Santini Raimbaux
Jan.01 1832	Grand concert Theatre Italien	Lablache Malibran Schroeder-Devrient Rubini Tadolini Raimbaux
Mar.28 1832	Salon de M. Petzold Grand concert	Lablache Raimbaux Rubini Bordogni Tadolini Derosa Michel Berettoni
Apr.04 1832	Salon de M. Pape	Lablache Dorus-Gras Rubini Graziani Raimbaux
Apr.10 1832	Theatre Chantereine	Lablache Rubini Labarre Herz

LONDON

Apr.27 1834	Drury Lane Theatre	Lablache Grisi Tamburini
Feb,02 1835	Paris Palais Tuileries	Lablache Rubini Lablache
Apr.15 1835	Drury LaneTheatre	Lablache Grisi Rubini Ivanoff Tamburini
May 18 1835	Kensington Palace	Lablache Grisi Malibran Ivanoff Rubini Tamburini
May 25 1835	Buckingham Palace	Lablache Malibran Grisi Ivanoff Rubini Tamburini (Princess Victoria's Birthday)
Jul.03 1835	Covent Garden	Lablache Grisi Ivanoff Tamburini
Jul.15 1835	London Concert Rm	Lablache Grisi Stockhauser Rubini Balfe Malibran Tamburini De Beriot Benedict
Jul.15 1835	Stafford House	Lablache Grisi Malibran Rubini Tamburini Ivanoff Costa

PARIS

Oct.02 1835	Paris Les Invalides Requiem for Bellini	Lablache Rubini Ivanoff Tamburini

LONDON

Apr.31 1836	King's Theatre	Lablache Grisi Novello Rubini Tamburini
May 02 1836	King's Theatre	Lablache Grisi Malibran Novello Rubini Tamburini Balfe

May 06 1836	King's Theatre	Lablache Grisi Rubini Tamburini Balfe
May 11 1836	King's Theatre	Lablache Grisi Malibran Novello
May 16 1836	King's Theatre (Frederic's Debut)	Lablache F.Lablache Grisi Rubini Tamburini Degli Antoni
May 20 1836	King's Theatre	Lablache F.Lablache Grisi Rubini Malibran Tamburini
May 27 1836	St. James Palace	Lablache Grisi Malibran Rubini Ivanoff Tamburini
Jun.17 1836	King's Theatre	Lablache Grisi Assandri Bishop Rubini Ivanoff Tamburini
Jun.18 1836	King's Theatre	Lablache F. Lablache Grisi Malibran Assandri Colleoni Corti Rubini Ivanoff Tamburini
Jun.20 1836	King's Theatre	Lablache Grisi Assandri Rubini Ivanoff
Jun.23 1836	King's Theatre	Lablache Grisi Malibran Novello Rubini Ivanoff Tamburini Giubilei
Jun.27 1836	King's Theatre	F.Lablache Grisi Ivanoff Rubini Angeli Tamburini De Angioli
Jun.28 1836	King's Theatre	Lablache Grisi Rubini Curioni Ivanoff
Jun.30 1836	King's Theatre	Lablache F. Lablache Grisi Assandri Rubini Ivanoff Balfe Giubilei
Jul.01 1836	King's Theatre	Lablache Grisi Rubini Tamburini
Jul.04 1836	King's Theatre	Lablache F. Lablache Grisi Caradori Ivanoff Rubini Balfe Tamburini Giubilei
Jul.05 1836	King's Theatre	Lablache Grisi Malibran RubiniAssandri Ivanoff Tamburini
Jul.13 1836	Stafford House	Lablache Grisi Tamburini Rubini
Jul.15 1836	St. James Palace	Lablache Grisi Rubini Tamburini
Jul.29 1836	Stafford House	Lablache Grisi Rubini Tamburini

ON TOUR

Sep.12 1836	Manchester Festival	Lablache Malibran Caradori-Allan Ivanoff De Beriot
Sep. 1836	Norwich Festival	Lablache
Apr.21 1837	King's Theatre	Lablache Grisi Caradori-Allan Ivanoff Tamburini Rubini

May 08 1837	King's Theatre	Lablache Grisi Albertazzi Balfe Assandri Caradori-Allan Tamburini Novello Rubini Thalberg piano
May 13 1837	King's Theatre	Lablache Grisi Wood Abertazzi Ivanoff Tamburini Rubini Costa
Jun.09 1837	King's Theatre	Lablache Grisi Pasta Novello Albertazzi Rubini Tamburini Balfe
May 30 1837	Kings Theatre	Lablache Grisi Novello Schroeder-Deverient
Jun.09 1837	King's Theatre	Lablache Grisi Pasta Novello Rubini Albertazzi Tamburini Balfe
Jul.28 1837	Buckingham Palace	Lablache Grisi Pasta Rubini Tamburini
Aug.17 1837	Buckingham Palace	Lablache Grisi Albertazzi Tamburini

PARIS

Jan.24 1838 [Queen of France King of Belguim]	Palais des Tuileries	Lablache Grisi Persiani Rubini Tamburini

LONDON

May 04 1838	Her Majesty's	Lablache Grisi Rubini Ivanoff Tamburini
May 11 1838	Her Majesty's Theatre	Lablache Grisi Persiani Albertazzi Rubini Ivanoff Tamburini
May 16 1838	Hanover Square Rooms	Lablache Grisi Shaw Bishop Rubini Tamburini
May 18 1838	Buckingham Palace	Lablache Grisi Persiani Rubini Tamburini
May 25 1838	Her Majesty's Theatre	Lablache Grisi Seguin Ivanoff Albertazzi Tamburini
May 28 1838	Her Majesty's Theatre	Lablache Grisi Persiani Balfe Albertazzi Ivanoff Rubini Tamburini
Jun.06 1838	Lansdowne House	Lablache Grisi Persiani Rubini Tamburini
Jun.08 1838	Her Majesty's Theatre	Lablache F. Lablache Grisi Persiani Cinti-Damoreau Rubini Ivanoff Albertazzi
Jun.20 1838	Drury Lane Theatre	Lablache F. Lablache Grisi Cinti-Damoreau Ivanoff Tamburini

Jun.22 1838	Buckingham Palace	Lablache Grisi Albertazzi Rubini Tamburini
Jun.26 1838	Her Majesty's Theatre	Lablache Grisi Persiani Albertazzi Rubini Tamburini
Jul.01 1838	Westminster Abbey	Lablache Grisi Rubini Tamburini

ON TOUR

Sep.04 1838	Manchester Theatre	Lablache F. Lablache Grisi Albertazzi Royal Ivanoff
Sep.07 1838	Manchester Theatre	Lablache F. Lablache Grisi Albertazzi Royal Ivanoff
Sep.11 1838	Gloucester Shire Hall	Lablache Grisi Knyvett Ivanoff
Sep.12 1838	Gloucester Shire Hall	Lablache Grisi Knyvett Shaw Ivanoff
Sep.13 1838	Gloucester Shire Hall	Lablache Grisi Shaw Ivanoff Tamburini

PARIS

Dec 15 1838	Concert Theatre de la Renaissance	Lablache Viardot(debut) Rubini Ivanoff
Mar.17 1839	Salle Hertz Conductor Donizetti	Lablache Grisi Tadoloni Persiani Duprez Rubini Albertazzi Ivanoff Tamburini
Apr.04 1839	Paris La Musicale	Lablache Viardot Ivanoff Herz De Beriot

LONDON

May 08 1839	Her Majesty's	Lablache F. Lablache Grisi Persiani Rubini
May 10 1839	Her Majesty's Theatre	Lablache F. Lablache Grisi Persiani Viardot Rubini Albertazzi Ivanoff Tamburini
May 13 1839	Buckingham Palace	Lablache Grisi Persiani Viardot Tamburini
May 22 1839	Her Majesty's Theatre	Lablache F.Lablache Grisi Albertazzi Stockhausen Birch Ivanoff Tamburini Rubini Roser-Balfe F.Wyndham Costa
Jun.03 1839	Her Majesty's Theatre	Lablache Grisi Persiani Viardot E. Grisi Rubini Tamburini
Jun.05 1839	Her Majesty's Theatre	Lablache F.Lablache Grisi Persiani Viardot Rubini Ivanoff Tamburini
Jun.07 1839	Her Majesty's Theatre	Lablache Grisi Persiani Dorus-Gras Rubini Ivanoff Tamburini

Jun.14 1839	Buckingham Palace	Lablache Grisi Persiani Viardot Tamburini
Jun.21 1839	Fife House	Lablache Grisi Persiani Viardot Rubini Tamburini
Jun.26 1839	Her Majesty's	Lablache Grisi E. Grisi
Jul.05 1839	Her Majesty's	Lablache Persiani Viardot Tamburini
Aug.13 1839	Buckingham Palace	Lablache Grisi Rubini Tamburini Viardot
Aug.19 1839	English Opera House	F. Lablache Grisi Persiani E. Grisi Rubini Ivanoff Tamburini

MANCHESTER

Jan.14 1840	Manchester Theatre Royal	F. Lablache Mad. F. Lablache Holden Chatterton

PARIS

Jan.31 1840	Concert Palais Royal Duc'Orleans	Lablache Grisi Rubini Viardot P.Garcia
Jan.02 1840	Concert Th' Italien	Lablache Rubini Tamburini

LONDON

Feb.07 1840	Hanover Square Rms	F. Lablache Mad. F. Lablache Bizzi E. Grisi Benedict Thalberg (Piano)
Feb.27 1840	FreeMason Rooms	F. Lablache Mad. F. Lablache Williams Anderson Birch
Mar.14 1840	*Sonnambula* Her Majesty's Theatre	F. Lablache Persiani Rubini Rubiccardi
Apr.02 1840	Her Majesty's Theatre	F. Lablache E. Grisi Guibilia Rubini Rubiccardi
Apr.20 1840	Her Majesty's Theatre	F. Lablache Persiani Rubini Rubiccardi
Apr.30 1840	Hanover Square Rooms	Lablache Grisi Mario Birch Rubini Tamburini Masson Birch
Apr.30 1840	Her Majesty's Theatre	Lablache Grisi Rubini Costa Persiani
May 20 1840	Hanover Square Rooms Prince Albert Concert	Lablache Grisi Birch Masson Rubini F.Lablache Parry
May 29 1840	Her Majesty's Theatre	Lablache F. Lablache Grisi Persiani Dorus-Gras Rubini Tamburini
Jun.08 1840	Her Majesty's Theatre	Lablache F. Lablache Grisi Persiani Dorus-Gras Tosi Rubini Tamburini

Jun.12 1840	Buckingham Palace	Lablache Rubini Prince Albert Queen Victoria
Jun.22 1840	Her Majesty's Theatre	Lablache Grisi Persiani Tamburini Rubini Coletti
Jun.25 1840	Freemason's Tavern	F. Lablache Parry E. Grisi Grisi
Jun.26 1840	Her Majesty's Theatre	Lablache Grisi E. Grisi
Jun.29 1840	Maryebone Institution	Lablache F. Lablache Persiani Tamburini
Jul.11 1840	Her Majesty's Theatre	Lablache F. Lablache Hertz Rubini E. Grisi Rubini Morelli
Aug.10 1840	Buckingham Palace	Lablache Grisi Mario Rubini Tamburini
Aug.18 1840	Blackheath Green Man Assembly Rooms	F. Lablache Mario Persiani Rubini Coletti

ON TOUR

Sep.08 1840	Birmingham Festival *La Gazza Ladra* Hereford Festival *La Prova Opera Seria*	F. Lablache Dorus-Gras Cardori-Allan Lablache Brahm Birch Phillips Lablache Cardori-Allan Hawes Birch Williams Lablache Brahm Birch Phillips
Nov.03 1840	Islington Concert	
Nov.05 1840	Southampton Royal Victorian Assembly Rooms	F. Lablache Mad. F. Lablache Birch
Nov. 1840	Oxford	F. Lablache Mad F.Lablache Lockley Marshall[violin] Bladgrove Richardson

LONDON

Dec.07 1840	Islington Concert	F. Lablache Severn Woodyatt Ward Read
Jan.28 1841	Concert	F. Lablache Mad. Hobbs Birch
Feb.04 1841	Woodford Concert	F. Lablache Mad. F. Lablache
Mar.02 1841	Princess rms	F. Lablache Mad. F. Lablache
Mar.03 1841	Exeter Hall	F. Lablache
Mar.12 1841	Manchester	F. Lablache Mad. F. Lablache
Mar.19 1841	Paris Concert	Lablache Rubini Tamburini Albertazzi

LONDON

Apr.23 1841	Royal Society of Female Musicians	Mad. F. Lablache
Apr.28 1841	Hanover Square Rooms	Lablache Grisi Persiani Viardot Rubini
May 12 1841	Hanover Square Rooms	Lablache Grisi Birch Viardot Rubini

Appendices

May 12 1841	Her Majesty's Theatre	Lablache F. Lablache Grisi Persiani Rubini
May 14 1841	Hanover Square Rooms	F. Lablache Steele Dorus-Gras Richardson Chaterton Parry Birch Listz
May 17 1841	Her Majesty's Theatre	Lablache F. Lablache Grisi Mario Persiani Loewe Viardot Dorus-Gras Rubini
May 17 1841	Buckingham Palace	Lablache F. Lablache Grisi Mario Persiani Loewe Viardot Dorus Gras Rubini
May 24 1841	Her Majesty's	Lablache Grisi Persiani Caradori-Allen Viardot Loewe Dorus-Gras Rubini Tamburini
May 31 1841	Her Majesty's	Lablache F. Lablache Grisi Mario Persiani Dorus-Gras Schroeder-Devrient
Jun.02 1841	Her Majesty's Theatre	Lablache F. Lablache Grisi Mario E. Grisi Persiani Loewe Viardot Rubini Loewe Rubini Tamburini
Jun.04 1841	Her Majesty's Theatre	Lablache F. Lablache Grisi Mario Persiani Viardot Rubini
Jun.05 1841	Stafford House	F. Lablache Mad. F. Lablache Rubini Balfe Mad.Balfe Dorus-Gras Kemble Dorus(FL)Vieuxtemps(VLN) Szepanoski Godefroid (HP) Liszt (PF) Benedict Rachel
Jun.16 1841	Her Majesty's Theatre	Lablache F. Lablache Mad. F. Lablache Persiani Rubini Tamburini Grisi E. Grisi Dorus-Gras

ON TOUR

Aug.19 1841	Birmingham	Lablache F. Lablache Grisi Mario
Aug.21 1841	Liverpool *I Puritani*	F. Lablache Grisi E. Grisi Mario Benedict
Aug.23 1841	Manchester *La Sonnambula*	F. Lablache Grisi E. Grisi Mario Benedict
Aug.24 1841	Liverpool	Lablache F. Lablache Grisi Mario
Aug.25 1841	Manchester	Lablache F. Lablache Grisi Mario

Aug.26 1841	Liverpool	Lablache F. Lablache Grisi Mario
Aug.30 1841	Dublin *I Puritani*	Lablache F. Lablache Grisi E. Grisi Mario Benedict
Aug.31 1841	Dublin *Norma*	Lablache F. Lablache Grisi E. Grisi Mario Benedict
Sep.02 1841	Dublin *Sonnambula*	F. Lablache Grisi E. Grisi Mario Benedict
	La Prova D'un Opera Seria	Lablache F. Lablache Grisi E. Grisi Mario Benedict
Sep.04 1841	Dublin *I Puritani*	Lablache F. Lablache Grisi E. Grisi Mario Benedict
Sep.06 1841	Dublin *Norma*	Lablache F. Lablache Grisi E. Grisi Mario Benedict
Sep.07 1841	Dublin *Sonnambula*	F.Lablache Grisi Mario E. Grisi Benedict
Sep.09 1841	*I Puritani & Gazza Ladra*	Lablache F. Lablache Grisi E. Grisi Mario Benedict
Sep.10 1841	*Il Barbiere*	Lablache F. Lablache Grisi E. Grisi Mario Benedict
Sep.15 1841	Glasgow Assembly Rooms	Lablache F. Lablache Grisi Puzzi
Sep.15 1841	Glasgow Royal Threatre	Lablache F. Lablache Grisi E. Grisi Mario Benedict Puzzi
Sep.17 1841	Edinburgh Waterloo Rooms	Lablache F. Lablache Grisi E. Grisi Mario Puzzi Benedict
Sep.18 1841	Edinburgh Waterloo Rooms	Lablache F. Lablache Grisi E. Grisi Mario Puzzi Benedict
Sep.20 1841	Newcastle Assembly Rooms	Lablache F. Lablache Grisi E. Grisi Mario Puzzi Benedict
Sep.20 1841	Newcastle Theatre Royal	Lablache F. Lablache Grisi E. Grisi Mario Puzzi Benedict

PARIS

Jan.26 1842	Palais des Tuileries Soiree	Lablache Grisi Albertazzi Persiani Mario Mirate Dotti Morelli Rosa-Balfe Balfe Campagnoli
Jan.31 1842	Salle Hertz	Lablache Persiani Rosa-Balfe
Feb.15 1842	Paris *Le Cantatrici Villane*	Lablache F. Lablache Persiani Mirate

LONDON

May.06 1842	Grand Morning Concert	Lablache F. Lablache Fezzolini Potini
May 20 1842	*Le Cantatrici Villane*	Lablache F. Lablache Persiani Frezzolini Stella
May 20 1842	Buckingham Palace	Lablache Persiani Moltini Frezzolini Ronconi
May 23 1842	Haymarket	Lablache F. Lablache Persiani E. Grisi
May 23 1842	Her Majesty's	Lablache Mario Moltini
May 28 1842	Royal Society of Female Musicians	F. Lablache Mad. F. Lablache
May 30 1842	Mad Dulken Concert	Lablache F.Lablache Birch
Jun.04 1842	Royal Society of Female Musicians	F.Lablache Mad F.Lablache
Jun.07 1842	Her Majesty's *Il Barbiere*	Lablache F. Lablache Persiani Guasco Ronconi
Jun.11 1842	Royal Society of Femalze Musicians	F.Lablache Mad F.Lablache
Jun.24 1842	Her Majesty's	F. Lablache Persiani Rubini Heinfetta
Jul.00 1842	Her Majesty's *Stabat Mater*	Lablache F. Lablache Guasco Rubini Graziani Mesdames Grammaglia Costa Persiani Ronconi Poggi
Jul.09 1842	Cambridge House	Lablache Mario Rubini Ronconi
Jul.14 1842	Her Majesty's *Il Matrimonio Segreto*	Lablache F. Lablache Persiani Moltini Grammigilia Rubini
Jul.18 1842	St. James Theatre	Lablache F. Lablache Grisi Mario
Jul.19 1842	Her Majesty's Theatre	Lablache F. Lablache Grisi Mario
Aug.05 1842	Her Majesty's Theatre	Lablache F. Lablache Grisi Mario

ON TOUR

Aug.08,09,10	Dublin	
Aug.22 1842	Manchester	Lablache F. Lablache Grisi Mario
Aug.23 1842	Liverpool	Lablache F. Lablache Grisi Mario
Aug.24 1842	Manchester	Lablache F. Lablache Grisi Mario
Aug.29, 30	Edinburgh	
Sep.05 1842	Dublin *I Puritani*	Lablache F. Lablache Grisi E. Grisi Mario Costa

Sep.06 1842	Dublin	Lablache F. Lablache E. Grisi Mario
Sep.07 1842	Dublin	Lablache F. Lablache E. Grisi Mario
Sep.08,09,10	Dublin	Lablache F. Lablache E. Grisi Mario
Sep.12 1842	Dublin *Norma*	Lablache F. Lablache E. Grisi Grisi Mario Costa
Sep.14 1842	Dublin *Anna Bolena*	Lablache F. Lablache Grisi MarioCosta
Sep 15 1842	Dublin *I Puritani*	Lablache F.Lablache Grisi Mario Smeaton
Sep.16 1842	Dublin *Il Barbiere*	Lablache F. Lablache Grisi Mario Costa
Sep.17 1842	Dublin *Anna Bolena*	Lablache F. Lablache Grisi Mario Costa
Sep.19 1842	*La Sonnambula*	F. Lablache Grisi Mario Costa
Sep.22 1842	Brighton	Lablache F. Lablache Grisi Mario

PARIS

Nov.17 1842	*Linda di Chamonix*	Lablache F. Lablache Mario Persiani Brambilla Fornasari
Dec.13 1842	*Le Cantatrici Villane*	Lablache F. Lablache Viardot Persiani Mirate

LONDON

Apr.27 1843	Her Majesty's *Il Barbiere*	Lablache F. Lablache Persiani Fornasari
May 05 1843	Her Majesty's	Lablache F. Lablache Grisi Persiani
May 15 1843	Her Majesty's *La Sonnambula*	F. Lablache Mario Persiani
May 17 1843	Her Majesty's Theatre	F. Lablache Mario Hawes Cardori-Allan Staudigl Prince Albert Phillips
May 26 1843	Her Majesty's Theatre	Lablache Persiani Moltini Fornasari Staudigl
Jun.01 1843	Her Majesty's *Linda di Chamonix*	Lablache F. Lablache Mario Persiani Fornasari
Jun.12 1843	Her Majesty's *Staber Mater* *L'Elisir d'Amore*	Lablache F. Lablache Grisi Mario Brambilla Montini Costa Fornasari
Jun.26 1843	Her Majesty's *Prova opera seria*	Lablache F. Lablache Mario
Jul.13 1843	Her Majesty's *William Tell*	F. Lablache

Jul.22 1843	Her Majesty's *Il Barbiere*	Lablache F. Lablache Grisi Mario Fornasari
Aug.10 1843	Her Majesty's *Italian Selections* *I Puritani*	F. Lablache Mario Brambilla Cialli Lablache F. Lablache (Riccardo) Grisi Mario Fornasari
Aug.17 1843	Her Majesty's *Don Giovanni*	Lablache F. Lablache Grisi Mario

ON TOUR

Aug.23 1843	Liverpool	Lablache F. Lablache Grisi Mario
Sep.19 1843	Birmingham Town Hall	

LONDON

Jan.08 1844	Her Majesty's Theatre	F. Lablache Mad. Lablache
Jan. 1844	Her Majesty's Theatre	Lablache F. Lablache Grisi Mario Persiani Favanti Corelli (Debut)
Feb.21 1844	Hanover Square Rooms	F. Lablache Mad. F. Lablache
Feb.29 1844	Soiree Mad Dulken	F. Lablache Mad. F. Lablache
Mar.04 1844	Hanover Square Rooms	F. Lablache M. Benedict Garcia Brizzi Weiss Ferrari
Mar.19 1844	Her Majesty's *Zampa*	F. Lablache Bellini Corelli Felice Persiani
Mar.28 1844	Her Majesty's *L'Elisir d'Amore*	Lablache F. Lablache Persiani Corelli
Apr.23 1844	Her Majesty's *La Sonnambula*	F. Lablache Persiani Mario
May 23 1844	Her Majesty's *Il Barbiere*	Lablache F. Lablache Persiani Mario Fornasari
Jun.10 1844	Her Majesty's Theatre	Lablache F. Lablache Grisi Mario Persiani Gras Staudigl Thillon Salvi Shaw Corelli Benedict Brizzi Fornasari
Jun 14 1844	Her Majesty's Theatre	Lablache Grisi Castellan Persiani Favanti Mario F. Lablache Mad. F. Lablache Inchindi Corelli Benedict
Jun.21 1844	Her Majesty's Theatre	Lablache F. Lablache N. Lablache Grisi Favanti Castelan Fornasari

Date	Venue	Performers
Feb. 1845	Concert	F. Lablache
Feb.19 1845	Princess Rooms	Lablache F. Lablache Mad. F. Lablache Lucombe Negri
Feb.19 1845	Princess Rooms	Lablache F. Lablache Mad. F. Lablache Lucombe Negri Albertazzi Parry
Feb.26 1845	Woodford Concert	F. Lablache Mad. F. Lablache Hobbs Dulcken
Feb.27 1845	Melodist Club	F. Lablache Sinclair
Mar.18 1845	Concert	F. Lablache Birch Ranforth Seguin
Apr.16 1845	Hanover Square rms	Lablache F. Lablache Staudigl Caradori-Allen
Apr.17 1845	Montague House	Lablache Grisi Mario
Apr.24 1845	Concert	Lablache F. Lablache Moriani Castellan
Apr.26 1845	*Il Barbiere*	Lablache F. Lablache Grisi Mario Fornasari
Apr.30 1845	*L'Elisir d'Amore*	Lablache F. Lablache Castellan Corelli
May 02 1845	Buckingham Palace	Lablache Grisi Mario Castellan Staudigl
Jun.06 1845	Her Majesty's Theatre	Lablache F. Lablache Grisi Mario Dorus-Gras Castellan Corelli
Jun.16 1845	Her Majesty's Theatre	Lablache F. Lablache Grisi Mario Moriani Castellan Dorus-Gras Corelli Fornasari
Jun.21 1845	Hanover Square Rooms	Mad. F. Lablache Dorus-G (Piano)
Jul.04 1845	Hanover Square	F. Lablache Dorus-Gras
Jul.17 1845	*Cosi Fan Tutte*	Lablache F. Lablache Rita Castellan Borio Rossicaccia

ON TOUR WITH JOHN PARRY CONDUCTOR BENEDICT

Date	Venue	Performers
Aug.21 1845	Leamington	Lablache F. Lablache Grisi Mario
Aug.22 1845	Brighton	Lablache F. Lablache Grisi Mario
Aug.23 1845	Brighton	Lablache F. Lablache Grisi Mario
Aug.25 1845	Manchester	Lablache F. Lablache Grisi Mario
Aug.29 1845	Birmingham	Lablache F. Lablache Grisi Mario
Aug.29 1845	Leamington	Lablache F. Lablache Grisi Mario
Sep. 1845	Chester	Lablache F. Lablache Grisi Mario
Sep.01 1845	Newcastle	Lablache F. Lablache Grisi Mario
Sep.02 1845	Scarborough	Lablache F. Lablache Grisi Mario
Sep.03 1845	Sheffield	Lablache F. Lablache Grisi Mario

Sep.04 1845	Leeds	Lablache F. Lablache Grisi Mario
Sep.05 1845	Liverpool	Lablache F. Lablache Grisi Mario
Sep.06 1845	Wolverhampton	Lablache F. Lablache Grisi Mario
Sep.08 1845	Liverpool	Lablache F. Lablache Grisi Mario
Sep.09 1845	Manchester	Lablache F. Lablache Grisi Mario
Sep.10 1845	Liverpool/Harrogate	Lablache F. Lablache Grisi Mario
Sep. 1845	Birmingham	Lablache F. Lablache Grisi Mario
Sep.11 1845	Manchester	Lablache F. Lablache Grisi Mario
Sep.12 1845	Newcastle	Lablache F. Lablache Grisi Mario
Sep. 1845	Bury St Edmunds	Lablache F. Lablache Grisi Mario
Sep.17 1845	Norwich	F. Lablache Grisi Mario
Sep. 1845	Plymouth	F. Lablache Grisi Mario
Sep.22 1845	Blackheath	Lablache F. Lablache Grisi Mario
Sep.25 1845	Bristol VictoriaLablache F. Lablache Grisi Mario	
Sep. 1845	Reading	Lablache F. Lablache Grisi Mario
Sep. 1845	Cheltenham	Lablache F. Lablache Grisi Mario
Sep. 1845	Exter	Lablache F. Lablache Grisi Mario
Sep. 1845	Bath	Lablache F. Lablache Grisi Mario
Sep. 1845	Clifton	Lablache F. Lablache Grisi Mario
Sep.27 1845	Brighton	Lablache F. Lablache Grisi Mario

LONDON

Apr.23 1846	Her Majesty's *Il Barbiere*	Lablache F. Lablache Grisi Mario
Apr.27 1846	Hanover Square Rooms	F. Lablache Mad. F. Lablache Williams Parry Lucombe
May 04 1846	Philharmonic Society	F. Lablache Williams NovelloSteele Lockley
May 14 1846	Her Majesty's *Prova d'Opera Seria*	Lablache F. Lablache Grisi Corelli
May 21 1846	Her Majesty's *L'Elisir d'Amore*	Lablache F. Lablache Grisi Corelli
May 28 1846	Her Majesty's *Il Matrimonio Segreto*	Lablache F. Lablache Grisi Mario
Jun.15 1846	Benedict Concert	Lablache F. Lablache Corelli Castellan
Jun.07 1846	Oxford Concert	F. Lablache Mad. F. Lablache Parry
Jun.24 1846	Concert	F. Lablache Mad. F. Lablache Corelli Fornasari

Jun.27 1846	Melodist Club	F. Lablache
Jul.02 1846	Her Majesty's *Semiramide*	Lablache F. Lablache Grisi Mario Corelli Sanhioli
Jul.24 1846	Des Vaux House	Mario
Jul.28 1846	Her Majesty's *A'jo nell'Imbarazzo*	Lablache F. Lablache Grisi Mario Castellan Fornasari

ON TOUR WITH JOHN PARRY CONDUCTOR BENEDICT

Aug.04 1846	Manchester Tour	F. Lablache Grisi Mario Hawes Staudigl
Aug.08 1846	Manchester Tour	F. Lablache GrisiMario Staudigl Hawes
Aug.25 1846	Birmingham Town Hall	F. Lablache Grisi Mario Staudigl Hawes
Aug.26 1846	Birmingham Town Hall	F. Lablache Grisi Mario Staudigl Hawes
Aug.27 1846	Birmingham Town Hall	F. Lablache Grisi Mario Staudigl Hawes
Aug.31 1846	Manchester Free Trade Hall	F. Lablache Grisi Mario Staudigl Hawes
Sep.02 1846	Manchester Free Trade Hall	F. Lablache Grisi Mario Staudigl Hawes
Sep.03 1846	Manchester Mozart's *Requiem*	F. Lablache Grisi Mario Staudigl Hawes
Sep.12 1846	Shewsbury Coral Society	F. Lablache Grisi Mario
Sep. 1846	Wolferhamton	F. Lablache Grisi Mario Sloper
Sep.14 1846	Liverpool	F. Lablache Grisi Mario Sloper
Sep.19 1846	Derby Atheneum	F. Lablache Grisi Mario Sloper
Sep.19 1846	Derby Royal	F. Lablache Grisi Mario Sloper
Sep.19 1846	Cheltenham	F. Lablache Grisi Mario Sloper
Sep.21 1846	Liverpool Royal	F. Lablache Grisi Mario Sloper
Sep.23 1846	Bristol Bowl	F. Lablache Grisi Mario Sloper
Sep.24 1846	Greenwich Lecture Rooms	F. Lablache Grisi Mario Sloper
Sep.30 1846	Bath, Leeds, Chester, Buxton, Hereford, Macclesfield,	Newcastle,Brighton, Reading

LONDON

Jan.02 1847	Beaumont Institution	F. Lablache Mad. F. Lablache Mad. Bishop
Jan.09 1847	Concert	F. Lablache Mad. F. Lablache

Jan.18 1847	Stoke Newington	F. Lablache Mad. F. Lablache
Feb.08 1847	London Tavern	F. Lablache Mad. F. Lablache Parry
Feb.09 1847	Lyceum Theatre	F. Lablache Mad. F. Lablache Parry Phillips Albertazzi
Feb.10 1847	Beaumont Institution	F. Lablache Mad. F. Lablache Williams
Mar.11 1847	Her Majesty's Theatre	F. Lablache Colletti Bouche Gardoni Solari
Mar.12 1847	Ancient Concert	F. Lablache Gardoni Lockey Bassano
Mar.15 1847	Mile End Road	F. Lablache Mad. F. Lablache
Mar.17 1847	Charity Concert	F. Lablache Mad. F. Lablache Hawes
Mar.18 1847	*Sonnambula*	F. Lablache Castellan Solari Bouche Gardoni Guilbei
Mar.27 1847	Hanover Square Rooms	F. Lablache Mad. F. Lablache Parry Piatti
Mar.30 1847	Haymarket	Lablache Albertazzi Birch Poole Rainforth Novello Phillips Joachin
Apr.03 1847	Concert	
Apr.17 1847	Philharmonic Society	F. Lablache
Apr.19 1847		F. Lablache Rainsforth Hawes Williams
Apr.22 1847	*L'Elsir d'Amore*	Lablache F. Lablache Gardoni Castellan
May 03 1847	Buckingham Palace	Lablache Alboni Castellan Gardoni Gni
May 05 1847	Hanover Square Rms	Lablache Alboni Gardoni Mario Tambui
May 13 1847	*La Sonnambula*	F. Lablache Gardoni Lind Solari
May 27 1847	*La Figlia*	F.Lablache Gardoni Lind Solari
May 28 1847	Buckingham Palace	Lablache Grisi Alboni Mario Tamburini Lind
Jun.08 1847	Hanover Square	Mad. F Lablache Birch Parry Dorus-Gras
Jun.11 1847	Her Majesty's	Lablache F. Lablache Vera Parry
Jun.14 1847	Apsley House	Lablache Grisi Alboni Mario Tamburini
Jun.16 1847	Princess Rooms	F. Lablache Mad. F. Lablache Parry
Jun.17 1847	Her Majesty's	F. Lablache Lind
Jun.30 1847	Buckingham Palace	Lablache

MADAME JENNY LIND TOUR OF THE PROVINCES-HER MAJESTY'S ORCHESTRA

Aug.28 1847	Liverpool *La Sonnambula*	F. Lablache Lind Gardoni Solari

Sep.01 1847	Liverpool	F. Lablache Lind Gardoni Solari
	La Figlia	
Sep.06 1847	Liverpool	F. Lablache Lind Gardoni Solari
	La Sonnambula	
Sep.13 1847	Liverpool	F. Lablache Grisi Mario Parry Benedict
	La Figlia	
Sep. 1847	Norwich	
Sep. 1847	Bath Theatre Royal	F. Lablache Mad. F. Lablache Lind Solari Balfe
Sep. 1847	Bristol	
Oct.02 1847	Exeter	F. Lablache Lind

LONDON

Feb.11 1848	London Concert	Lablache F. Lablache Novello
Apr.17 1848	`Her Majesty's	Lablache F. Lablache Tadolini Vera Coletti Cruvelli Poole Gardoni Thalberg
May 15 1848	Stafford House	Lablache Mario Tamburini Chopin Prince Albert Queen Victoria
May 20 1848	Her Majesty's	Lablache F. Lablache Tadolini
	Linda	Gardoni Coletti
Jun.19 1848	Hanover Rooms	F. Lablache Mad. F. Lablache Pyne Reeves Ludcombe Parry Williams
Jun.24 1848	*Robert Diable*	F. Lablache Mad. F. Lablache Lind Gardoni Poole
Jun.26 1848	Her Majesty's	Lablache F. Lablache Beadolini
Jun.27 1848	Freemasons Hall	F. Lablache Farren Bassano Ransforth
Jun.28 1848	Buckingham Palace	Lablache Grisi Mario Viardot Alboni Gardoni Tamburini
Jul.01 1848	Benedict Concert	Lablache F. Lablache Pardi
Jul.03 1848	Her Majesty's	Lablache F. Lablache Thalberg
Jul.04 1848	Her Majesty's	Lablache F. Lablache Rainsforth Tadolini
Jul.05 1848	Oxford Festival	Lablache Tadolini
Jul.17 1848	Buckingham Palace	Lablache
Jul.19 1848	Willow Bank	Lablache Grisi Mario Alboni Castellan Roger Tamburini
Aug.12 1848	Her Majesty's	F. Lablache Lind Gardoni
	Figlia	

Aug.15 1848	Her Majesty's *I Puritani*	F. Lablache Lind Reeves Alboni

MADAME JENNY LIND TOUR OF PROVINCES-HER MAJESTY's ORCHESTRA

Sep 04 1848	Norwich	Lablache
Sep.05 1848	Birmingham	F. Lablache Lind Roger Balfe Belleti
Sep.07 1848	Liverpool	F. Lablache Lind Roger Balfe Belletti
Sep.09 1848	Manchester	F. Lablache Lind Roger Balfe Belletti
Sep.14 1848	Hull-York	F. Lablache Lind Roger Balfe Belletti
Sep. 1848	York	F. Lablache Lind Roger Balfe Belletti
Sep.23 1848	Edinburgh Concert	F. Lablache Lind Roger Balfe Belletti
Sep.25 1848	Edinburgh Opera *Sonnambula*	F. Lablache Lind Roger Balfe Belletti
Sep.28 1848	Edinburgh *Lucia*	F. Lablache Lind Roger Balfe Belletti
Oct.02 1848	Glasgow *Figlia*	F. Lablache Lind Roger Balfe Belletti
Oct.04 1848	*La Sonnambula*	
Oct.06 1848	Glasgow Concert	F. Lablache Lind Roger Balfe Belletti
Oct.12 1848	Dublin *Puritani*	F. Lablache Lind Roger Balfe Guidi Belletti Bottura Grimaldi
Oct.14 1848	*Figlia*	F. Lablache Lind Roger Balfe Guidi Belletti Bottura Grimaldi
Oct.16 1848	*Lucia*	F. Lablache Lind Roger Balfe Guidi Bottura Belletti Grimaldi
Oct.21 1848	Concert Rotundo	F. Lablache Lind Roger Balfe Guidi Belletti Bottura Grimaldi
Oct.24 1848	*Figlia*	F. Lablache Lind Roger Balfe Guidi Belletti Bottura Grimaldi
Oct.27 1848	Birmingham	
Oct.30 1848	Brighton Concert	F. Lablache Lind Roger Balfe Guidi Belletti Bottura Grimaldi
Nov.01 1848	*La Sonnambula*	F. Lablache Lind Roger Balfe Guidi Belletti Bottura Grimaldi
Nov.03 1848	*Figlia*	
Nov.08 1848	Southampton Victorian Rooms	F. Lablache Lind Roger BalfeGuidi Belletti Bottura Grimaldi
Nov.10 1848	Clifton	
Nov.13 1848`	Exeter	F. Lablache Lind Roger Balfe Guidi Belletti Bottura Grimaldi

Nov. 1848	Bath		
Nov.16 1848	Bath		
Nov.18 1848	Clifton		
Nov.23 1848	Cheltenham	F. Lablache Lind Roger Balfe Guidi Belletti Bottura Grimaldi	
Nov.27 1848	Gloucester		
Nov.29 1848	Leamington		
Dec.01 1848	Oxford Sheldonian	Lind	
Dec.04 1848	Leeds	F. Lablache Lind Roger Bouche Colletti	
Dec.19 1848	Manchester	F. Lablache Lind Roger Bouche Colletti	
Dec.21 1848	Manchester		
Dec.28 1848	Birmingham Gardoni	F. Lablache Lind Roger Bouche Colletti	
Jan.29 1849	Exeter Hall London	Lablache F. Lablache Lind Vera Balfe Bassano Durlacher Belletti Thalberg (Piano)	
Feb. 1849	Edinburgh	Lablache Vera Thalberg (Piano) Tour	
Feb.22 1849	Manchester Hardgreaves Choral Society	Lablache Lablache [Nicolas] Vera Bassano Thalberg (Piano)	

LONDON

Feb.21 1849	Hanover Square	F. Lablache Mad. F. Lablache Lind Osborne Sainton (violin) Dulcken piano
Feb. 1849	Amiens Concert	Lablache Persiani
Apr. 1849	Her Majesty's	F. Lablache Alboni
May 07 1849	Hanover Square Royal Society of Female Musicians	Mad. F. Lablache Treffz Dolby Bassano
May 09 1849	Buckingham Palace	Lablache Lind Angri Parodi Mario
May 28 1849	Her Majesty's	Lablache F. Lablache Alboni Colletlle
May 28 1849	Societa Harmonica	F. Lablache Dolby Pacini Guasco Forbes
Jun.01 1849	Buckingham Palace	Lablache Grisi Alboni Mario Gardoni Colleti Hayes
Jun 22 1849	Her Majesty's Benedict Concert	Lablache F. Lablache Alboni Vera Hayes Williams M. Williams Mario
Jul.18 1849	Hanover Sq Rms	Lablache Mario Gardoni Reeves Grisi
Aug.01 1849	Her Majesty's	Lablache F. Lablache Sontag Calozari Parodi Giuliani Hayes Thalberg (Piano)

ON TOUR

Aug.21 1849	Manchester	Lablache F.Lablache Sontag Calzolari
	I Puritani	Moriani
Aug.23 1849	*Don Pasquale*	Lablache F. Lablache Sontag Calzolari Belletti Moriani Conductor Balfe
Aug 25 1849	*Il Barbiere*	Lablache F. Lablache Sontag Calzolari
Aug.25 1849	*Otello*	Lablache F. Lablache Sontag Moriani
Aug.27 1849	Liverpool Concert	Lablache F. Lablache Belletti Balfe
Aug.28 1849	Liverpool *Elija*	Grisi Hayes Viardot Alboni
Aug.28 1849	Liverpool Concert	Mario Corbari Tagliafinco Treffz
Aug.29 1849	Liverpool	Lablache F. Lablache Grisi
Aug.30 1849	*Messiah*	Lablache F. Lablache AlboniGrisi Viardot Williams Treffz Mario Corbari Formes Tagliafico Botolini Polonini
Aug.31 1849	*Stabat Mater*	Lablache F. Lablache Grisi Alboni Williams Viardot Mario Treffz Cobari Botolini Polonini Tagliafico
Aug 31 1849	Fancy Dress Ball	Lablache F.Lablache Grisi Alboni Hayes Williams Mario Viardot

ON TOUR

Sep.04 1849	Birmingham Music Festival Town Hall	Lablache F. Lablache De Meric De Treffz Hayes Reeves Mario Sontag Williams Thalberg (piano) Reeves Calzolari
Sep.05 1849	Birmingham Festival	Lablache De Meric Lablache Hayes
Sep 05 1849	Birmingham Festival	Lablache F. Lablache Hayes de Meric
Sep.07 1849	Birmingham Festival	Lablache Hayes Castellan Alboni Sontag
Sep 07 1849	Dress Ball	
Sep. 1849	Bury St. Edmunds Assembly Rms	Lablache F. Lablache Sontag Belletti Calzolari Thalberg
Sep.23 1849	Ryde Isle of Wight	Lablache F. Lablache Thalberg(piano)
Sep.24 1849	Royal Victoria Rms	Lablache F. Lablache Sontag Belletti
Sep.25 1849	Ryde Town Hall	Lablache F. Lablache Sontag Belletti Thalberg (piano)
Oct.14 1849	Plymouth	Lablache F. Lablache Belletti Sontag Calzolari Thalberg (piano)
Oct.16 1849	Bath	Lablache F. Lablache Sontag Belletti Thalberg (piano)

Oct. 1849	Cheltenham	Lablache? F. Lablache Sontag Belletti	
	Bristol	Lablache? F.Lablache Sontag Belletti Calzolari? Thalberg (Piano)	
Oct. 1849	Salisbury	Lablache? F.Lablache Sontag Belletti	
Oct. 1849	Exeter	Lablache F. Lablache Belletti Sontag Calozari Thalberg (Piano)	
Oct. 1849	Glasgow	Lablache? F.Lablache Sontag Belletti Calozolari Thalberg (piano)	
Oct.18 1849	Liverpool	Lablache F. Lablache Sontag Belletti Calozolari Thalberg (Piano)	
Nov.01 1849	Norwich	Lablache? F.Lablache Sontag Belletti) Calozolari Thalberg (Piano)	

LONDON

Mar.1850	Beethoven Rooms	F.Lablache Hayes Birch Thalberg (piano)
	3 concerts Beethoven Rooms Dorlacher	
Apr.02 1850	*Lucia Lammermoor*	F. Lablache Hayes Belletti Reeves
Apr.10 1850	Princess Rooms	F. Lablache Mad. F. Lablache Poole
Apr.16 1850	Hanover Square	Mad. F. Lablache Reeves Poole Hayes
Apr.18 1850	*Nozze di Figaro*	F. Lablache Hayes Reeves Sontag
Apr.241850	Her Majesty's	F. Lablache Baucardi Sontag Belletti
May 13 1850	Her Majesty's	Lablache F. Lablache Coletti Sontag Hayes Reeves Calzolari Giuliani
May 15 1850	Hanover Square	F. Lablache Mad. F. Lablache
May 21 1850	Her Majesty's	Lablache F. Lablache Mad. F. Lablache
May 22 1850	Her Majesty's *Lucrezia Borgia*	Lablache F. Lablache Coletti Bettini Fezzolini Bertrand
May 23 1850	*Don Giovanni*	Lablache F. Lablache Coletti Calzolari Sontag Fezzolini Giuliani
May 26 1850	*Lady Cecilia*	Lablache F. Lablache Grisi Mario Sontag
	Belgrave Square	
Jun.05 1850	Hanover Square Rms	Mad. F. Lablache Williams Birch Hayes Benedict
	Royal Society of Female Musicians	Mad F.Lablache Sequin Pyne
Jun.07 1850	Hanover Square Rms	Lablache Mad. F. Lablache Belletti
Jun.21 1850	Her Majesty's	F. Lablache Belletti Hayes Bertrand
Jul.01 1850	Buckingham Palace	Lablache Grisi Mario Castellan

Jul.13 1850	Her Majesty's	Lablache F. Lablache Coletti Birch Belletti Sontag Thalberg
Jul.13 1850	Lyceum Theatre	Mad. F. Lablache Birch Bassano Reeves Leffler Allcroft
Jul.18 1850	Her Majesty's *Figlia del Reggimento* *Prova d'un opera seria*	F. Lablache Sontag Gardoni Ferrari Double Bill Lablache Frezzolini Calzolari
Aug.05 1850	Isle of Wight Osborne House	Lablache Mario
Aug.15 1850	Her Majesty's *Don Giovanni*	Lablache F. Lablache Coletti Calzolari Sontag Fiorentini Giuliani
Jan.27 1851	Exeter Hall	F. Lablache Mad. F. Lablache Poole Sim Reeves and wife
May 02 1851	Her Majesty's *Don Giovanni*	Lablache F. Lablache Lind Balfe Belletti Thalberg (piano)
May 03 1851	Her Majesty's *Lucrezia Borgia*	F. Lablache as Petrucci
May 12 1851	Buckingham Palace Concert	Lablache Castellan Grisi Duprey Mario Gardoni Lorenzo Massol Calozolari
May 16 1851	Crosby Hall	
May 28 1851	Buckingham Palace	Lablache
May 31 1851	Buckingham Palace Second State Concert	Lablache Mario Grisi Pyne Castellan Gardoni Formes Costa
Jun.02 1851	Mad. Puzzi Concert	Lablache F. Lablache Sontage Solari Reeves Coletti Duprey Calzolari
Jun.01 1851	Her Majesty's	Lablache F. Lablache Mad. F.Lablache Sontag C. Duprey Reeves Massol
Jun.07 1851	Queen Anne Rms	Lablache F. Lablache Grisi Tamberlik
Jun.16 1851	Her majesty's Concert	Lablache F. Lablache Sontag Calzolari Duprez Reeves Colletti Cruvelli etc
Jun.30 1851	Her Majesty's Concert	Lablache F.Lablache Sontag Reeves Calzolari Cruvelli Gardoni Duprey etc
Jul.19 1851	Buckingham Palace	Lablache Grisi Mario Castellan Formes Gardoni
Jan.17 1852	Hanover Square Rms	F. Lablache Mad. F. Lablache
Jan. 1852	British School	F. Lablache Williams Collins Choir Islington
Apr.10 1852	Exeter Hall	F. Lablache Mad. F. Lablache E. Garcia
May 01 1852	Exeter Hall	Mad. F. Lablache Pyne Novello Forbes

May 10 1852	Buckingham Palace	Lablache Grisi Mario Cruvelli	
May 15 1852	Queen Anne Rms	F. Lablache Mad. F. Lablache	
May 17 1852	Hanover Square Rms	F. Lablache Mad. F. Lablache	
May 20 1852	Her Majesty's *Matrimonio Segreto*	Lablache F.Lablache (Selection)	
May 22 1852	Her Majesty's	Lablache F. Lablache Belletti Reeves	
Jun.04 1852	Buckingham Palace	Lablache Mario	
Jun.05 1852	Willis Rooms	Mad. F. Lablache	
Jul.03 1852	Queen Anne Rooms	F. Lablache Mad. F. Lablache Taccaca	

ON TOUR

Sep.13 1852	Manchester	F. Lablache Grisi Mario Susini Galvani
Sep.14 1852	Liverpool	F. Lablache Grisi Mario SusiniGalvani

DUBLIN

Sep.17 1852	*Lucrezia Borgia*	F. Lablache Grisi Mario
Sep.20 1852	*I Puritani*	F. Lablache Grisi Mario
Sep.21 1852	*Don Pasquale*	F. Lablache Grisi Mario
Sep.24 1852	*Don Giovanni*	F. Lablache
Sep.25 1852	*L'Elisir d'amore*	F. Lablache Bertrandi Brawn Susini Galvini

ON TOUR

Sep.27 1852	Limerick	F. Lablache Grisi Mario Susini
Sep.28 1852	Cork	F. Lablache Grisi Mario Susini
Sep.29 1852	Cork	F. Lablache Grisi Mario Susini
Sep.30 1852	Clomel	F. Lablache Grisi Mario Susini
Oct.01 1852	Waterford	F. Lablache Grisi Mario Susini
Oct.02 1852	Wexford	F. Lablache Grisi Mario Susini
Oct.04 1852	Dublin *I Puritani*	F. Lablache
Oct. 1852	*Don Giovanni*	F. Lablache Grisi Mario
Oct.06 1852	Dublin *Lucia Sonnambula*	F. Lablache Grisi Mario Bertrand
Oct.07 1852	Belfast	F. Lablache Grisi Mario Susini
Oct.08 1852	Belfast	F. Lablache Grisi Mario Susini
Oct.11 1852	Glasgow	F. Lablache Grisi Mario Susini
Oct.12 1852	Edinburgh	F. Lablache Grisi Mario Susini

Date	Venue	Performers
Oct.17 1852	Aberdeen	F. Lablache Grisi Mario Bertrand Susini
Oct.18 1852	Hull	F. Lablache Grisi MarioBertrand
Dec. 6 1852	Brighton Concert	

LONDON

Date	Venue	Performers
Jan.24 1853	Exeter Hall	F. Lablache Fiorentini Dolby Favanti
Apr.23 1853	Willis Rooms	F. Lablache Mad. F. Lablache Themar
May 07 1853	New Beethoven Rms	F. Lablache Mad. Macfarren Piatti
May 10 1853	Princess Rms.	Mad.F.Lablache Favanti Boddoni
May 28 1853	Royal Princess Rms	Mad. F.Lablache Favanti Williams
May 29 1853	Hanover Square Rms	F. Lablache Mad. F. Lablache Boddoni
Jun.01 1853	Music Hall	F. Lablache Mad. F. Lablache Boddoni
Jun.04 1853	New Beethoven Rms	F. Lablache Mad. F. Lablache Dolby
Jun.06 1853	Hanover Square Rms	F. Lablache Dolby Pyne Sloper Piatti
Jun.24 1853	Hanover Square Rms	F. Lablache Mad. F. Lablache Novello Reeves Viardot Gardoni Williams
Jul.28 1853	Bedford Square	F. Lablache Mad. F. Lablache Ward
Jul. 1853	Reunion Des Arts	F. Lablache Mad. F. Lablache Birch
Aug.20 1853	Exeter Hall	F. Lablache Mad. F. Lablache Reeves D'Angri Viardot Disten Dolby Gardoni
Apr.02 1854	Grove End Road Concert Rooms St John's Wood	F. Lablache Mad.F. Lablache Nappi Regondi
May 08?1854	Hanover Square Rooms	Mad F. Lablache Birch Pyne Rainsford
Jun.22 1854	Hanover Square Rooms	F. Lablache Mad.F. Lablache Ferrari
Jun 24 1854	Her Majesty's	Lablache Grisi Bosio Alboni Sloti
Jul.10 1854	Queen's Rooms Hanover Square	F. Lablache Gardoni Mad. F. Lablache

ON TOUR 1855

Date	Venue	Performers
Aug.28 1855	Birmingham Music	Lablache Grisi Mario Castellan Bosio
Aug.29 1855	Birmingham Music	Lablache Grisi Mario Castellan
Aug.30 1855	Birmingham Music	Lablache Grisi Mario Castellan Bosio
Nov.ND 1856	Brighton Pavilion	F.Lablache Hayes Corelli Brahm Paque Ernest Osborne-conductor

RUSSIA

Date	Venue	Performers
Jan.01 1857	St Petersburg Russia	Lablache Lotti Maray Bosio Tagliafico Calzolari

IRELAND

Jan.14 1857	Dublin	F. Lablache Hayes Corelli Millardi
Jan.24 1857	Cork Athenaeum 2 concerts	F. Lablache Hayes Corelli Millardi Ernest Osborne-conductor
Jan.26 1857	Belfast	F. Lablache Hayes Corelli Millardi Osborne-conductor
Jan.30 1857	Belfast	F. Lablache Hayes Corelli Millardi Osborne-conductor

LONDON

Feb.10 1857	New Beethoven Rooms	F. Lablache Birch Mori Benedict
Feb.14 1857	Mad. Oury's	F. Lablache Mad F. Lablache Ciabatti Hepworth Piatti Balfe-conductor (F. Lablache sang "the Arrow")
Mar.10 1857	New Beethoven Rooms	F. Lablache Birch Piatti
Apr.20 1857	Beaumont Institution Mile End	F. Lablache Mad. F.Lablache Novello Thillon Reeves Hatton-conductor
May 01 1857	Crystal Palace Concert	F. Lablache? Grisi Devries Marai Parepa-Rosa Bosio Mario Ronconi Neri-Baradi Formes Gardoni Poloni Costa-conductor
Jun.29 1857	Hanover Square	F. Lablache Novello Bassano Reeves Piatti Vera Kuhe Benedict-conductor?
Jun.29 1863	Lablache Concert	F. Lablache, Mad. F. Lablache Lind- Goldschmith Thalberg (Piano) Piatti Li Calsi-conductor.
ND 1879	Concert	F. Lablache

☙☙☙

Notes

BOOK ONE—CHAPTER ONE

[1.] Weinstock, 1966, *OPERA*, 689.
[2.] Most dictionaries list Luigi Lablache born in 1794, which is incorrect. See inside mausoleum in the cemetery Maisons Laffitte near Paris 1795-1858.
[3.] Copy of birth certificate in Naples.
[4.] Stanley-Little, T.C. Unpublished memoirs. N.D. Hand Written 1940-50s. Titled: *The Great Lablache.*(no page numbers)
[5.] Ibid.
[6.] Family records.
[7.] Ibid.
[8.] Ibid.
[9.] Ibid.
[10.] Ibid.
[11.] Seward, 1986, 18-19.
[12.] Simon de la Blache, has not been traced. Simon Lablache has. It is beyond the scope of this book to trace the de la Blache family.
[13.] Archives of Marseilles.
[14.] Records traced by Adrian de Friston. 1958, (Royal College of Arms London).
[15.] Caterina Maria Francesca Bietagh. Daughter of Tobia and Giuseppe Reale. Baptized at the Church of S. Maria della Neva, 28th of September, 1770.
[16.] Parrocchia di Santa Maria della Neve. Nella Chiesa di S. Giuseppe a Chiaja. Riveria a Chiaja, Napoli. Copy of the marriage certificate, obtained on September 25th, 1902, by James Stanley-Little. Signed by parroca S. G. Raffaele.
[17.] Record on file from James Stanley-Little.
[18.] Bullard, 1962, 189.
[19.] Trevelyan, 1976, 70-71.
[20.] Correct date of birth, December 6th, 1795. From a copy of Register in the Church of St. Maria degli Angeli, Naples. (Luigi Nicola Giuseppe filio di Nicola Lablache e Francesca Bietagh, abitante strada Chiaia, è stato batteggato dal parrocco.)
[21.] Memoirs. Author.

CHAPTER TWO

22. Headlam, 1906, 4.
23. Stanley-Little, T.C. 6.
24. Ibid., 6.
25. Headlam, 1906,
26. Hamilton and Stewart, 1957, 8.
27. Simpson, 1983. 77.
28. Seward, 1987, 19-20.
29. Stanley-Little, James. *Romance of the Lablaches.* Empire. 1913.
30. Alessandro Pinotti, father-in-law of Luigi Lablache.
31. Stendhal, 1959. *Rome, Naples and Florence.* (Reprint) 402.
32. Stanley-Little, T.C. 16.
33. Hibbert, 1985, 242
34. Stanley-Little, T.C, 15
35. Hamilton and Stewart, 1957, 78.
36. Ibid.
37. Hamiliton and Stewart, 1957, 80-81.
38. Pocock, 1968, 77.

CHAPTER THREE

39. Florimo, 1882, 460.
40. Ibid.
41. They were both thrown in prison.
42. Stanley-Little, T.C., 6.
43. Lofts, 1978, 79.
44. Florimo, 1882, Stanley-Little, T.C., family records.
45. Lofts, 1978, 79, Ferdinand sent Nelson to control Ruffo.
46. Florimo. 1882 p. 460
47. Ibid. 168
48. Simpson, 1983, 77.
49. Stanley-Little, James.
50. Stendhal, 1959, *Rome, Naples and Florence.* 412.
51. *The New Grove Dictionary of Opera.* Cimarosa. 868
52. Research in 2006, found him in Mahe, Seychelles. Andre Joseph Simon Lablache. Born Madrid 1766. Nicola may have been a twin.
53. Florimo, 1882, 465.
54. This portrait is a miniature in Paris at Madame Balsan's House.
55. Florimo, 1882, 469.

CHAPTER FOUR

56. Hamilton and Stewart, 1957,
57. Seward. 1987, 99. King of Naples Joachim Murat Napoleon entered Naples on the 6th of September, 1808.
58. Florimo, 1882.
59. Stendhal-Coe. 1970 Reprint Appendix 1. By time Mozart was six he was already touring Europe with his father.
60. Baker, Theodore:. 1900, 383.
61. *The Musical World*, 1866, November, 24th, 743. *A Visit to the conservatory of Music at Naples.*
62. Florimo, 1882, 469.
63. Ibid.
64. Location not known, other reports say possibly Salerno.
65. Florimo, 1882, 470. King of Naples Joachim Murat Napoleon entered Naples on the 6th of September 1808.
66. Castle Nuova is in the centre of Naples close to the harbor. The Castle St.Elmo is on the hill.
67. Florimo, 470.
68. Ibid. Ref, (1)" These small theatres give several performances a day, and are mostly patronised by the lower classes, who paying very little come to enjoy themselves, laugh a lot because these productions are expressly written for this purpose."
69. Clipping N.D., 3. Family records.
70. See early portraits. Before 1823.

CHAPTER FIVE

71. The San Carlino Naples. There is no proper chronology of this theatre.
72. Florimo, 471.
73. This is mentioned in *Le Voci d' Oro.*
74. Florimo, 1882.(Naples Theatre Chronology). A Pinotti, was a well known singing actor and comedian. Records indicate that he sang at the following theatres in Naples: The Naples S. Ferdinando, the theatres Nuovo and Fondo. His wife also sang with him. It is not known if he ever sang at the Naples San Carlino. He sang in Messina. (See Lablache Chronology) and possibly Palermo. The other members of the Pinotti family sung all over Italy.
75. Elizabeth and Rosina Pinotti were believed to be sisters. Both had careers spanning the first quarter of the century. Birth or death dates unknown. Besides singing at the Neapolitan theatres Nuovo, Fondo, and the San Carlo, they sang in other parts of Italy.(See notes on each singer).

76. B. Cassinelli, A. Maltempi, M. Pozzoni, 1993. Rubini's debut was at the Teatro Fondo in Rossini's *L'Italiana in Algeri*.
77. Marriage Certicate. Copy Lablache Archives, Florida.
78. Florimo, 1882, 471-472.
79. Acton, 1959, 695
80. Stendhal, 1970, 422
81. Isabella Colbran.(1785-1845) Mistress of Barbaja, later Rossini's wife, was the daughter of Gianini Colbran, Court Musician to the King of Spain. Later seperated from Rossini and divorced.
82. Weinstock, 1987, *Rossini,* 423, 499-500
83. Stendhal, 1970, 542.
84. Details of Frédéric's birth on his will. (Died 1887)
85. Florimo, 1882, 483. Details given by Florimo were short of two. Lablache had thirteen children, only eight survived to adulthood: Federico, Nicola, Errico, Domenico, Francesca, Maria, Marianna, Rosina. Details of Rosina's death from *The Musical World,* are the only knowledge that we have of her). Also family records.
86. Rossilli, 1984, 30-33.
87. Ibid, 30.
88. *The Musical World*. n.d. Clipping.
89. Roscioni, 1987.
90. Maguire, 1989.
91. Gossett, 226, *Grove Opera Dictionary*. 1994.
92. *Dwight's Musical Journel*: Clipping.
93. Messina theatre.
94. *Allgemeine Musikalische Zeitung.* Early Issues.
95. Teatro Fondo, Teatro Nuova, Teatro San Carlo and possibly others. Many of the performances are found in: Florimo's *La Scuola di Napoli,* (4 vols., Naples, 1880-4).
96. This information was kindly provided by Danny Hitchcock, of the Sigismund Thalberg Society. Francesca Lablache (1816-1895) became the wife of Sigismund Thalberg.(1812-1871)
97. Both Lablache and Pinotti were in Palermo December 3rd. 1816.
98. Trevelyan, 1973, 5.
99. Tiby, 1987, Note 14, 121: Correcting Florimo (*Scuola musicale di Napoli*, ed. 1871. p. 2075.Lablache." Debutto, si in quell 'opera, ma al San Fernando e non al Carolino." (Ser Marcantonio del Pavesi a Ferdinando) Stefano Pavesi(1779-1850). wrote 70 operas.
100. Ibid, 1987, 40.

101. Ibid, 1987, 118. Note 14.
102. The orginal rare libretti is in the collection of Bruce Brewer, showing the original cast.
103. Uccello, 1986, 89.
104. Stendhal, 1959, *Rome Naples and Florence.* 16-17.
105. Ashbrook, 1982, 602 (note).
106. Stendhal, 1959, *Rome Naples and Florence.* 16-17.
107. Tiby, 1987, 126.
108. Ibid, 1987, Notes: (Smyth, 47). 73.
109. Ibid, 1987, 118. Note Tiby:16 The same opera was given again in 1823 at the San Carlo. See chronology.
110. Weinstock, 1987, *Rossini*, 85
111. *The Musical World*, 1848, 83
112. Stendhal, Coe, 1970. *Life of Rossini.* 320.
113. Ibid, 325.
114. Appolonia, 1992, 92-93.
115. Ibid, 93-98
116. Stendhal, 1970, *Life of Rossini*, 152.
117. *The Musical World*, March 1854, 165-166. (Death notice and biography).
118. Brewer, *The Donizetti Society Journal* 4. 1980. 125, (*Il cigno di Romano*).
119. *The Musical World*, 1847, 691

CHAPTER SIX

120. Stendhal, 1970, *The Life of Rossini*, 134
121. Hughes, 1956, 194.
122. Black, 1982, 7.
123. Stendhal, *Rome, Naples and Florence*, 354.
124. Ibid, 360.
125. Charles Burley Clipping N.D.
126. Catalog 1991 "Rossini a Napoli," 1815-1822. Written by Sergi Ragni.
127. *The Musical World*, 1847, 691, also Hughes, 1956, 195
128. Stendhal, 1970, *The Life of Rossini.*
129. Cambiasi. 1906. 310, 311.
130. Josephson, 1946, 62.
131. Ibid. 62.
132. Ibid, 204.
133. Ibid, 205.
134. Ibid, 64-65.

135. Palmer, 1972, 201. Quoted from Metternich's Memoirs.
136. Palmer, 1972, 201. Quoted from Metternich memoirs. Also Weinstock, 1966, *OPERA*.
137. Weinstock, 1966, *OPERA*, Article on Lablache.
138. Palmer, 1972, 199.
139. Cambiasi, 1906, 310-311.
140. Tiby, 1987. Chronology.
141. Cambiasi, 310-311.
142. Rosenthal, Warrack, 1983, (Second Edition) 65.
143. Della Porta, 1983, 134.
144. Leading Stage designer of his time.

CHAPTER SEVEN

145. Hibbert, *Rome*, 1985.
146. Weinstock, Rossini, 1987, 107-108.
147. Family Tree.
148. Berta? The cast for that performance is not complete.
149. Cambiasi, 1906, 310-311.
150. Chronology Theatre Carignano.
151. Cambiasi., 1906, 310-311.
152. A.M.Z, 1823.
153. Krebiehl, 1921.
154. Warrack, John: *Carl Maria Von Weber*. New York, 1968, 292.
155. Ibid.

CHAPTER EIGHT

156. Chorley, 1984 reprint, vol.1, 18
157. Florimo. 1882, 473.
158. Weinstock, 1971, *Bellini*, 26
159. Black, 1982, 52.
160. Ibid. 50
161. Rossilli, 1984, 62
162. Rosenthal and Warrack,1983, (Second edition) 98, 370, 435, 443.
163. Impressario Joseph Glossip.
164. Luigi's Mother was still alive in 1824.
165. By Tonio, he possibly means the nephew of Lablache, Tonio del Marra who was caretaker of the estates in Naples. Lucio del Marra was believed to be Tonio's son.

166. Letter to D. Domenico. Barbaja, in the Autografo collection in the S. Pietro A Maiella, Naples. No.109459.
167. Warrack, 1968, 293.
168. Pleasants, 1966, 194
169. Marek, 1970, 630.
170. *The Musical World,* 1838, Clippings.
171. Marshall, N.D *Lablache*: bio in *The Universal Dictionary.*
172. *The Musical World*, also Florimo, 1882, 474.
173. Reed, 1985, 56.
174. Deutsch, N.D. 667
175. Brown, M., *New Grove Dictionary*, 1983, 64
176. Florimo, 1882.
177. Reed, 1985, 57.
178. Ibid.
179. Ashbrook, 1983, 294.

CHAPTER NINE

180. Roscioni 1987. 195.
181. Osborne, 1994, 99.
182. Roscioni, 1987, 194-195.
183. *The Concise Oxford Dictionary of Opera*, p.98
184. Lablache was very successful in this opera.
185. *The Musical World, Memoir of Cimarosa.* January 1840. 20-21.
186. The designs for the Milan production were by Alessandro Sanquirico.
187. Black, *The Donizetti Journal*, 1988, 98-99.
188. Florimo, 1881-82, 474.
189. Trevelyan, 1976, 1, There were eruptions of Vesuvius after the AD 79, that distroyed Pompeii. In later years the cycle began in 1631. In 1761, 1765-66, 1775, 1779, June 1794, 1822, 1832, 1838, 1850, 1872, 1906, 1944 and again recently.
190. Cheke, Family notes here.
191. Weinstock, 1971, *Bellini.* 215
192. Florimo, 1881-82, 474
193. Weinstock, 1971, *Bellini*, 31-33.
194. Really his second opera; his first was *Adelson e Salvini*, performed only by students in the conservatory.
195. Weinstock, 1963, *Donizetti*, 48.
196. Ibid. 50.

[197.] Sir Augustus Harris was the son of stage manager Harris of Convent Garden. In 1879 he became lessee of Drury Lane.
[198.] Nicolas and Emilie were married 1854, in Paris.
[199.] Weatherson, Queen Elizabeth Hall, July 1982, program notes.
[200.] Florimo, 1881-82, 474.
[201.] Weinstock, 1963, *Donizetti* 373. *Il Conte Ugolino—"La bocca sollevo dal fiero"* for *basso cantante* with piano occompaniment, dedicated to Luigi Lablache (January-February, 1828). Published by Ricordi, Milan, in *Antologia musicale*, 1843, No.2.

CHAPTER TEN

[202.] Ashbrook 1983, 52.
[203.] Roscioni, 1987, 194.
[204.] Ashbrook, 1983, 53.
[205.] Seward, 1986, 165.
[206.] Hughes, 1956, 128.
[207.] Ibid., 130.
[208.] Roscioni, 1987, 213-215
[209.] Black, 1982, 24. First performance was a the San Carlo on the 6th of February not the Teatro Fondo. Roscioni, in *Il Teatro di San Carlo* lists the 5th of February. 3 times. Ashbrook accepts Black's dates as being correct. Page 58, note 194. Weinstock and Charles Osborne, Florimo, Regli give the first performance as taking place at the Teatro Fondo.
[210.] Ashbrook, 1983, 58, 313.
[211.] Weinstock, 1963, *Donizetti,* 69.
[212.] Ibid., 324. Quoted by Prince Agostino Chigi.
[213.] Hissing and whistling were very common in the l9th century Italy.
[214.] Acton, 1959, 695. King Francesco of Naples.
[215.] Lablache letter in June 1847, from England. Lablache Archives.

BOOK TWO—CHAPTER ELEVEN

[216.] New Grove Opera, 1992, 1172. Rosenthal, 1964, 259.
[217.] *The Morning Post,* Clippings: May 1830
[218.] Ibid.
[219.] *The London Times.* Clipping, May 14th 1830.
[220.] Ibid. 4.
[221.] Chorley, 1862, (reprint 1984) 15.
[222.] Queen Victoria.

CHAPTER TWELVE

[223] Northwest of Paris.
[224] *Musical World*, 1839, 446.
[225] Bushnell, 1979, 121.
[226] Chorley, 1862, (reprint 1984) 6.
[227] Brombert, 1977, 79.
[228] Bushnell, 1979, 44. Countess Merlin was born in Havanna, as Maria de la Merced Santa Cruz y Montalva.
[229] Merlin, 1844, Vol.1, 36-37.
[230] Karasowski, 1939, 228-9.(New edition) Polish 1882.
[231] Ibid, 234-5
[232] Ibid, 372.
[233] Ibid, 372
[234] Niecks, 1888, 165.
[235] Weinstock, 1981, *Chopin,* 206,285.
[236] Brombert, 1977, 62-63

CHAPTER THIRTEEN

[237] Sheppard and Axelrod, *Paganini*, 1979. June 3rd, 1831.Newspaper clippings, review in London's *Morning Post,* 360. *The London Times,* June 2nd, 1831.
[238] Ibid, 352.
[239] *The London Times*, Clipping June 1831.
[240] *The London Times*, review of *L'Ultimo di Pompei*, March clipping. 1831.
[241] Ibid, note
[242] *The London Times*. Clipping. June 13, 1831.
[243] Kuhe, W. 1896.
[244] Walker, A., 1970, 45.
[245] *The Musical World*, 1840, 165.
[246] Osborne, 1994, 197.
[247] Weinstock, 1971, Bellini, 97.
[248] Ibid, 97.
[249] Ashbrook, 1982, 63.
[250] Ibid., 65-66.
[251] *The Musical World*, 1840, 165.
[252] Chorley, 1865, (Reprint 1984) 17-18.
[253] The Times. July 1831, Clipping.
[254] Rosenthal, 1958, 683, *Anna Bolena* was performed in 1852 at Covent Garden, but not with Lablache.

255. Niecks, 1888, (Reprint) 216.
256. Ibid. 217
257. Ibid., 226.
258. Ibid., 228-229.
259. Vienna, March 27, 28, 1827, at the Vienna Karntnertortheater.
260. *The London Times.* Clipping: *Il Barbiere di Seviglia.* Compressed into one Act, 1st Act of *L'Esule di Roma.*
261. Trevelyan, 1973, note from *Princes under the Volcano*
262. Bushnell, 1979, 136.

CHAPTER FOURTEEN

263. *The London Times*, Clipping. May 1832.
264. *The London Times*, Clipping. March 30th, 1832.
265. Cheke, 1993, 105.
266. Josephine Bonnard de Méric, born 1801.
267. *The London Times*, February through July.
268. Cheke, 1993, Glossip was born on January 27th 1793. 43.
269. Ibid. Féron, or Fearon, or Ferron, Elizabeth (born 1797-1853), 45.
270. Luigi Frederick Lablache, actor and grandson and name sake of the great Luigi Lablache, was employed by Harris at Drury Lane in the 1880s.
271. Cheke, 1993, 69.
272. Lablache Archives, Playbill.
273. Abigaile Betts. Born in London:(1800-1866). She was a great Aunt of the author's Mother. Betts sang with all the great singers of the time including Malibran and Lablache, she was one of the princpal vocalists of the Drury Lane theatre from 1827-1838, also singing at Covent Garden the Theatre Royal Dublin and many theatres in the provinces.
274. Arthur, Edward and John Betts. Both listed in the dictionary of violin makers. 145,
275. Lablache Archives, Original playbill.
276. Levy, O'Rourke, 1880.
277. Lablache Archives, Playbills.
278. Beaumont, 1938, 73.
279. Ibid. 288.
280. *The London Times*: Clipping, May 1832.
281. Bushnell, 1979, 136-137.
282. Ibid., 137.

Notes   661

[283.] Roscioni 1987, 228-230. Lablache chronology.
[284.] Bushnell, 1979, 139.
[285.] Ibid, 143.
[286.] Weinstock, 1963, *Donizetti*, 75-76. Quote from Italian republican leader. Giuseppe Mazzini.(82,11,313)
[287.] Brewer, Rubini Society, Paris.
[288.] Bushnell, 1979, 141.
[289.] Roscioni, 1987, 228. Anna Bolena claimed 18 *rappresentazioni*.
[290.] Bushnell, 1979 143.
[291.] Florimo, 1881.
[292.] Bushnell, 1979, 143-144.
[293.] Ibid.
[294.] Weinstock, 1963, *Donizetti*, 84.
[295.] Ibid., 331.
[296.] Ibid.
[297.] Florimo, This anedote also appears under the title: *Over provided*. Crowest 1902, p.273. The Palace of Capodimonte is now a museum.

CHAPTER FIFTEEN

[298.] Roscioni, 1987. 1833-34,
[299.] Parry, J. 1935.
[300.] Morning Post, Clipping, Summer, 1833.
[301.] He toured England with Liszt.
[302.] Rosenthal and West, 1992, 533.
[303.] Bushnell, 1979, 164.
[304.] Ibid.
[305.] Rossilli, 1984, 62. Malibran according to Dr. Rossilli's charts earned a monthly fee of F. 20. 730 (francs) in 1834, the highest fee, compared to Lablache who was earning only F.2.175, in 1825.
[306.] Ibid, 64-65. Pasta was earning in London F.57,500, plus her benefit in 1827. The fees paid in London were double or treble anything in Italy.
[307.] Fanny Persiani was the daughter of a tenor Nicola Tacchinardi. She married Giuseppe Persiani.
[308.] Richardson. 1959, 52.
[309.] Museum Carnavalet Paris, Dantan collection.
[310.] Possible extract from *Journal des Debats*, 3/10/1831, 389-391.
[311.] Pleasants, February 20, 1971. *Opera News*. 24-25.

CHAPTER SIXTEEN

312. Weinstock, 1971, *Bellini*, 159.
313. Ibid., 163.
314. Ibid., 183.
315. Translated from the French.
316. Weinstock, 1963, *Donizetti,* 104.
317. Ibid., 105
318. Maguire, Simon, 1987, *Norma and Bel Canto*, Covent Garden Program.
319. Weinstock, 1971, *Bellini,* 170.
320. Brombert, 1977, 334-5.
321. Weinstock, 1963, *Donizetti*, 107
322. Brombert, 1977, 73.
323. *The London Times.* Clipping.
324. Chorley, Reprint 1984, 92-93.
325. Warner, 1979. Lablache: The Doge in *Marino Faliero,* 70. Elmiro in *Otello.* 71. Georgio in *I Puritani*, 72. Portrait of Lablache by Princess Victoria, 74. Grisi: as Norma, 67. as Elena in *Marino Faliero,* 68-69. Grisi in *I Puritani* with Lablache, 72.
326. Ibid, 93.
327. Chorley, Reprint 1984, 93.

BOOK THREE—CHAPTER SEVENTEEN

328. Ibid, 93-94.
329. Ibid., 66
330. Rowell, 1978. 14
331. Rushmore, 1949, Opera News, January 31, 8.epa
332. Esher, 1908,(editor)
333. Massingham, N.D. 39-40. Quoted from Raumer, England in 1835.
334. Weinstock 1971, *Bellini*, 203-204.
335. Ibid. 104. Dr. Dalmas, a member of the Faculté de Médicine and awarded the Legion d'honneur.
336. Ibid., 205-206
337. Ibid., 209.
338. Ibid.
339. Ibid.
340. Ibid., 210.
341. Ibid., 206.

[342]. Program London's Royal Opera House. Maquire, 1987, *Norma,* (350th performance)
[343]. Ibid.
[344]. Warner,1979, 67.
[345]. Rowell, 1978, 32.
[346]. Heath, circa 1849, (reprinted 1977) 35-36.

CHAPTER EIGHTEEN

[347]. Woodham-Smith, 1972, 118.
[348]. Rushmore, 1949, *Opera News,* January 31st. 10.
[349]. Ibid., 10.
[350]. Woodham-Smith, 1972. 118.
[351]. Weaver, 1980, Quoted on page 53, from: *The Girlhood of Queen Victoria* Viscount Esher, Murray, (1912)
[352]. Rowell, 1978, 14.
[353]. Warner, 1979, 75.
[354]. Ibid.
[355]. Rowell, 1978, 14.
[356]. Rushmore, *Opera News*, January 31st. 10.
[357]. See lithograph and photo.
[358]. Bushnell, 1979, 201.
[359]. Fitzlyon, 1987, 204.
[360]. Ibid., 205.
[361]. Husk, 1881, 50.
[362]. Written for Lablache by Rossini.
[363]. Reported in *The London Times,* Summer, 1836.
[364]. Fitzlyon, 1987, 226.
[365]. Ibid, 233.
[366]. Ibid, 227.
[367]. Osborne, 1994, 253.
[368]. Ibid., 253.
[369]. Ibid., 1994, 251.
[370]. Frédéric Lablache sang three Donizetti operas: *L'Elisir d'amore, Betly* and *Il Campanello*: 1837 at the English Opera House, (Lyceum) and the theatre Royal Dublin. See *London Times.*
[371]. Weinstock, 1963, *Donizetti, 124.*
[372]. Warner, 1979, 64.
[373]. Ibid.

[374.] *The London Times.* Clipping
[375.] *The Musical World*, January 24th 1837,95.
[376.] Playbill, Covent Garden, New York City Library. (*Quasimodo*)
[377.] Original Play Bills. New York Public Library. Billy Rose collection.
[378.] *The Musical World*, February 1837, 138.
[379.] Ibid., April, 1837. 80.
[380.] Married London, July, 1839.

CHAPTER NINETEEN

[381.] Hibbert, 1985, 21.
[382.] Ibid., 21.
[383.] Ibid., 23.
[384.] Macaulay, 1848-61.
[385.] Hibbert, 1985, 26.
[386.] Rosenthal and Warrack, 1978., 296. Rebuilt in 1834.
[387.] Weaver, 1987, 69.
[388.] Weinstock, 1963, *Donizetti,* 126.
[389.] Levy and O'Rourke, 1880, 95.
[390.] Ibid., 98.
[391.] Ibid., 102.
[392.] *The Musical World*, May, 1838, 52
[393.] Ibid, 52.
[394.] Wechsberg, 1973, 71.

CHAPTER TWENTY

[395.] Ibid.
[396.] Ibid.
[397.] Hibbert, 1985, 33.
[398.] Mackenzie-Grieve, 1955, 316.
[399.] Ibid, 33.
[400.] Ibid, 32.
[401.] *The Musical World*, April 9. 232, 1840. Sir, George Smart was one of the trustees.
[402.] Rosina was buried in Mason Laffette, Paris.
[403.] *The Musical World*, May 1838,268.
[404.] Wechsberg, 1973, 68.
[405.] Rowell, 1978, 128.

406. *The Musical World*, July 19, 1838. 212-215
407. Rogers, 1977 (Reprint) 51.
408. Weinstock, *Luigi Lablache, OPERA*, 1966.
409. Wechsberg, 1973, 73.
410. Warner, 1979, 68.
411. Ibid, 69.
412. Ibid 71.
413. *The London Times*, April 23, 1838.
414. The original letter is in the Museo Teatro La Scala Milan.
415. Mordden, 1985, 110.
416. Ashbrook, 1983, 329.
417. *Dwight Musical Journal,* Boston. August 12, 1871. A sketch of Mario by himself. Under title Mario's farewell. (London, July 19, 1871.)
418. Chorley. 1862, 174.
419. Ibid, 275.
420. *Dwight's Musical Journal*. Boston. August 12, 1871. 77.
421. Chorley, 1862, 278.
422. Rogers, 1977 (Reprint) 101-102.
423. Maynard, 1890.
424. Rogers, 1977, 64.

CHAPTER TWENTY-ONE

425. Rowell, 1978, A Calendar of Victoria's Theatregoing, 129.
426. Maguire, 1989, Preface.
427. Ibid.
428. Toured 1895, with *Carmen, Frou-Frou, Denise, Romeo and Juliet.*
429. Rowell, 1978, A Calender of Queen Victoria's Theatregoing, 128.
430. Ibid., 129
431. Forbes, 1985, 41.
432. Rowell. 1978, 25.
433. Ibid, 24.
434. Ibid., 25, 129
435. Ibid, 128.
436. *Leisure Hour*, 1876, Clipping.
437. Fitzlyon, 1964, *(The Price of Genius.)*
438. Rowell, 1978, 33
439. Original Playbill. *William Tell*, Lablache Archives.
440. Clipping

441. Weinstock, 1987, *Rossini*, 205.
442. *The Musical World,* August 1839, 219.
443. Forbes, 1985, 42.
444. Newman, 1933-46, Vol.I, 212-213.
445. Family records, Lablache Archives.
446. Engel, 1886.
447. Florimo, 1880-84. 490.
448. Dodds, 1952, 150-152

CHAPTER TWENTY-TWO

449. Hibbert, 1985, *Queen Victoria. 54-55-57.*
450. Ibid, 63.
451. Bushnell, 1979, 182.
452. *Dwight Musical Journal.* Boston, June 19th 1852. Translated from a German newspaper.(Clipping)
453. Engel, 1886, 164
454. Walker, 1970, 56.
455. Engel, 1886, 164.
456. Spark, 1888, 160.
457. Photocopy of marriage certificate, 1843, Lablache Archives.
458. Josephson, 1946, 452.
459. Of François Bouchot paintings two are in the Martino Museum in Naples. Grisi's portrait is in the tower of the Royal College of Music London. The portrait of Francesca Bouchot whereabouts is unknown. French portrait artist also painted Emilio Belgiojoso (1840) Malibran and Balzac.
460. Holoman, 1989, Clipping.
461. *The Musical World*, 1841, 358.
462. Original Manuscript in Lablache Archives.

CHAPTER TWENTY-THREE

463. Levy, 1880, 75.
464. Ibid., 93.
465. Ibid., 94.
466. Ibid., 99.
467. Ibid., 111-115.
468. Ibid., 115
469. Ibid., 116.

470. Ibid.
471. Florimo, 1882, 478.
472. Ibid, 479.
473. They returned to Dublin September,1842,but not 1843. Frédéric Lablache returned in 1844 with Grisi and Mario. Luigi seems to have never returned. Frédéric came back in 1848 again with Jenny Lind.
474. *The Musical World*, Clippings.
475. Shultz, 1962, 45.
476. Alter. 1979, 277-278.
477. Josephson, 1946, 452, note 2, R. Vigneron.
478. Richardson, 92, 285.
479. Josephson, 1946, 452.
480. Ibid, 452.
481. Stendhal's *La Chartreuse de Parme.* 1944.
482. Alter, 1979, 255-256.
483. Ibid., 280

CHAPTER TWENTY-FOUR

484. Ibid., 218-220.
485. Ibid. 224.
486. Ibid. 227
487. Ibid. 229
488. *Illustrated London News*. Vol 8, 124-125 July 2, 1842.
489. Ibid, 140
490. Latham, 1901, 50.
491. Rowell, 1978, 37.
492. Ibid.
493. *The Musical World.* Clipping.

CHAPTER TWENTY-FIVE

494. Budden, Julian, 1984, 4. *Don Pasquale* EMI recording liner notes.
495. Tiby, 1957, Tiby corrects Florimo. *Ser Marcantonio*, was sung by Lablache and is recorded and conserved in the municipal library of Palermo. A way to be sure of a date in 19th century Italy is to look in original libretti.
496. Ashbrook, 1983, 303.
497. In Vienna the world premiere was on May 19th, 1842.
498. Weinstock, 1963, *Donizetti* 191.

499. Ashbrook, 1982, 174-175.
500. Ibid, 194.
501. Weinstock, 1963, *Donizetti* 189.
502. Ibid.
503. Madame Goüin Balsan.
504. Ardoin, 1984. Gaetano di Parigi: San Francisco Opera Programme article, September 7-December 9th.
505. Ashbrook, 1982, 175,(note from the collected letters of Zavadini 463, 4th January 1843, p.646).
506. Ibid, 175, (Note Zavadini letter 465, 5th January 1843. p.648).
507. *The Illustrated London News,* June 24, 1848.
508. Ibid, 175. Gautier, (*L'art dramatique en france depuis vingt-cinq ans*) p.322.
509. Lablache Archives owns the two originals. Both Lithographs on music covers.
510. Weinstock, 1963, *Donizetti* 195.
511. Ibid.
512. Michotte, 1906, p.64.
513. Florimo, 1882, *Le Camelie di Don Pasquale,* 147.
514. Museo Rubini, Letter translated into English.
515. In the late Madame Balsan, Paris Collection.
516. Maria Rosa Francesca Nicolet Lablache. Born 1816 in Palermo.
517. *The Musical World*, November 1843, P. 256.
518. Ibid.
519. Rowell, 1978, 130.
520. Chorley, 1862, 225.
521. *The London Times,* June 30th, 1844. Clipping.
522. Florimo, 1882, 491-492.
523. The country home of Aguado outside Paris.
524. Michotte, 1906, p.64.
525. Florimo, 1882, 491-492.

CHAPTER TWENTY-SIX

526. Hibbert, *Queen Victoria* (To Leopold March 25, 1845) 96.
527. Ibid, (To Lord Melbourne April 25,1845) 96
528. Ibid, 97.
529. *Hampshire Advertizer*. Clipping.
530. Brannon, 1990.
531. Latham, 1901.

Notes

532. Florimo, 1882, 486. Also:, Crowest, *"One better"*, 1902, 305.
533. Wallace Collection London: Snuff boxes on the second floor, records are vague to which or if all belonged to Lablache. Family history.
534. Weinstock, *Donizetti*, 1963, 270
535. *The Musical World,* May, 1845, 200.
536. Ibid, June 26th, 302.
537. Ibid, 303.
538. Ibid, September, 17, 1845. 499.
539. Ibid, 460.
540. Ibid.
541. Ibid. 427.
542. Rogers, 1914, Reprint 1977. Lablache, 46.
543. Lumley, 1864, Reprint da Campo Press, 1976. 90-94
544. Ibid. 89-90.
545. *The Musical World*. Clipping.
546. Kaufman, *The Donizetti Society* Journals. *Persiani* Article.
547. Levy, 1880. 121.
548. Kaufman, Chronology of Mario. Unpublished. Mario sang *Otello* first in 1843 on February 20th at the Theatre-Italian. Also Forbes, 1985. 61. Mario's Otello was in good taste. Gautier sprang to his defence.
549. Forbes, 1985, 70.
550. Chorley, 1862, 258
551. Forbes, 1985, 71.
552. Ibid, 71. *Morning Post*, clipping.
553. Ibid.
554. Lumley, 1864 (reprint da Campo 1976.) 122.
555. Chorley, 1862

CHAPTER TWENTY-SEVEN

556. Richard Dyer; San Francisco Opera program. *Nabucco*
557. Chorley, 1862, 282.
558. *Illustrated London News* Clipping.
559. Holland, H.S. & Rockstro, Lind W.S., 1893.
560. Pleasants, 1966, 198.
561. Chorley, 1862, 270.
562. Forbes, 1985, 78.
563. *The Musical World. 1846*
564. Chorley, 1862, 275.

CHAPTER TWENTY-EIGHT

565. Shultz, 1962, 115.
566. Pleasants, 1966. 188.
567. Kuhe, 1896, Clipping.
568. Sitwell, 1955, 147.
569. Shultz, 1962. 117.
570. Benét, 1939, 252.
571. Rowell, 1978, 131-132.
572. *The Musical World*, Clipping.
573. Walker, F,. 1982 reprint, 161. Summer of 1847.
574. Ibid. 158-159.
575. *Illustrated London News*. Clipping.
576. Walker, F., 1982 reprint, 162
577. Original two page letter in Lablache Archives
578. Luigi Lablache's sons.
579. The Lablache House in Naples
580. *The Musical World*. Clipping.

CHAPTER TWENTY-NINE

581. Weinstock, 1981, *Chopin*, 147.
582. Ibid, 145.
583. Woodham-Smith, 1972, 298.
584. Rowell, 1978, 132.
585. Ibid. 37.
586. Russell, 1964, 190
587. Ibid., 197
588. Ibid.
589. *The Musical World*; September 29th. 1849, 614. Reprinted from the: *Bury and Suffolk Herald*
590. Weinstock, 1966, *OPERA,* 356.
591. Rosenthal, 1958, 82.
592. Cheke, 1993, 208-209.
593. Ibid, 213.
594. Russell,F. 1964, 200-202.

CHAPTER THIRTY

[595] *The Musical World*, April 13, 1850.
[596] Ibid, April 1850, 213.
[597] Ibid 1850, 236
[598] Lumley, 1864, 286-287.
[599] Rowell, 1978, 133.
[600] Ibid, 133.
[601] Ibid, 36-37.
[602] Hibbert, 1985, Hibbert only mentions three gun attacks. 69-70, 81n, 227,272.
[603] Rosenthal, 1976, *Covent Garden*, 100.
[604] Chorley, 1862, 116-119. Vol. 2.
[605] *Illustrated London News*, July 15, 1850, 426.
[606] Chorley, 1862, 117. Vol 2.
[607] Royal Archives, Queen Victoria's Journal.
[608] Tyler-Whittle, 1980. 30.
[609] The Duchess of York, Stoney, 1991, 133. RA QVJ 26 August 1854. Note 4. It was most likely Lablache was there in August of 1854.
[610] Royal Archives, Queen Victoria's Journal
[611] Dominique de Friston family records
[612] *The Musical World,* May, 1851, 310.
[613] Lumley, 1864.
[614] Ibid. 301
[615] Ibid, 300.
[616] *The Musical World,* May 15, 1851.
[617] Ibid, Clipping.
[618] Chorley, 1862. 134-136.
[619] *The Musical World,* August, 1851, 603.
[620] Ibid.
[621] Cheke, 1993, 230.
[622] *The Musical World,* September, 1852, 573

BOOK FOUR-CHAPTER THIRTY-ONE

[623] Letter located in La Scala Museum. Beginning of letter not included.
[624] Letters in the collection of Madame Balsan, Paris.
[625] Levy, O'Rourke, 1880.
[626] Ibid, 156-157.
[627] Translated by the late Prof. Dennis Stevens.

628. Russian Newspapers *Severraya Pehala*—translated by April Fitzlyon.
629. The original letter is in the Rubini house.
630. *The Musical World*, March, 1853, 16.
631. Collection of Madame Balsan, Paris.
632. Timoleone Alexander. 2nd husband of Josephine de Méric.
633. Collection of Madame Balsan, Paris.
634. Translation by Miss Valentina Mironova.
635. *The Musical World* 1854 clipping.
636. Both Letters located at H. Baron in London. Italian originals missing.
637. Original letter in La Scala Museum.
638. Florimo, 1882.

CHAPTER THIRTY-TWO

639. *The Musical World* 1854. 531
640. Farwell, 1972, 69.
641. *The Musical World*. April 1854.
642. Dominique was in the Crimea. Nicholas LaBlache did not enter the army.
643. See photo in uniform
644. *The Musical World*, July 1, 1854, 531.
645. Ibid.
646. Ibid.
647. In the North of Italy
648. Obituary in *The Musical World*, July 22, 1854 and also Dwight's Musical Journal Clipping.
649. Ibid.
650. Farwell, 1972, 68.
651. See Marriage certificate, Lablache Archives.
652. Ivanov, 1895 (In Russian) Vols. I & II. (Translated to English).
653. *The Musical World*, 1854, Serov.
654. Ivanov, 1895.
655. Cheke, 1993, 247.
656. Letter belongs to the late Madame Balsan. Paris.
657. Dr. Dulcamara in *L'Elisir d'amore*.
658. Ivanov, 1895
659. Ibid.
660. Ibid.
661. Ibid.
662. John Watt's Collection London.

[663.] Lablache Archives
[664.] Toye, 1987, 204.
[665.] Ibid., 204, 207
[666.] Unpublished diaries, belonging to a descendant of Sir Julius Benedict.

CHAPTER THIRTY-THREE

[667.] Ivanov, 1895.
[668.] Ibid.
[669.] Ibid.
[670.] Ibid.
[671.] Kaufman, Donizetti Journals, *Italian Performances in Vienna*.
[672.] Cheke, 1993, 259-60.
[673.] Rogers, 1977. 52.
[674.] Cheke, 1993, 259.
[675.] Ibid., 260. Letter belongs to the late Madam Balsan, Paris.
[676.] Madame Balsan collection, Paris.
[677.] Kuhe, 1896, 84.
[678.] Philadelphia Obituary of Lablache.
[679.] *The Musical World*, 1857.

BOOK FIVE-CHAPTER THIRTY-FOUR

[680.] Letter, unpublished. Madame Balsan.
[681.] Florimo, 1882, 483.
[682.] *The Athenaeum*, February 6, 1858, 186.
[683.] Ibid. Mar 6, 1858, 313.
[684.] Florimo, 1882, 484.

CHAPTER THIRTY-FIVE

[685.] New York Public Library. (Pazdirek, F. 1900-1910, 18.)
[686.] *The Musical World*, 1843, October, 351. On another page there is another advert: "Lablache's *Tutor for the Bass voice*. The price was 24 shillings, with a portrait of the author. Published by Chappell, 50 New Bond St., London. A new edition of Lablache's *Celebrated Method of Singing*, with exercises expressly arranged to suit Low Voices.
[687.] Pazdirek, F. 1900-1910. 18.
[688.] Crowest, 1878, 287.

689. Ibid., 258.
690. Florimo, 1882, 480.
691. Brian Meringo was a researcher working with the Balsan Collection in Paris.
692. All these records have been photocopied and are in the Lablache Archives.
693. They may have come from Paris.
694. The house is listed in "Le guide du patrimoine ile de France," by Hachette.

CHAPTER THIRTY-SIX

695. *Naples Guide Book*, 1900.
696. Zaré Thalberg sang five years at Covent Garden. She left later for Spain to join her family.
697. Rosenthal, 1983, 497. Cited here, but incorect.
698. Vitale, 1972, *Nuova Rivista Musicale Italiana*.
699. We have no facts this is the same house he was born in, only it is the same street. Florimo states: "Lablache was born on the Riviera Chiaia, at the corner of the Arco Merelli."
700. The Posillipo house was part of the auction of the estate of Lablache.
701. Thalberg obtained the house in the family auction of Lablache's estate.
702. Thalberg submitted his product for the jury of the Universal Exhibition 1867.
703. Kuhe, 1896.
704. August 16, 1862.
705. *The Musical World*, 1872, Clipping. And Spark, Musical Memories, 172.
706. Ibid., 1873.
707. Barbiera, 1930, 326.
708. Ibid., 236
709. Pocock, 1968, Nelson died October 21, 1805. 118, 120.
710. Naples newspapers. 1895. The will was contested.
711. Record lists of the auction do not detail music by name, just by value. Over 1000 pages of items.

CHAPTER THIRTY-SEVEN

712. Documentation found by Brian Meringo, Paris.
713. The Lablache house was 39 Rue Albine.
714. *The Musical World,* 1860's. Clipping.
715. Ibid, December, 1877, 795.
716. Brian Meringo was a researcher working with the Balsan Collection in Paris.

717. RA VIC/MAIN/QVJ/1879:18 May.
718. RA VIC/MAIN/QVJ/1881:24 June.
719. Harding, 1965, 161.
720. Married July 23, 1885 at Osborne House on the Isle of Wight.
721. The Battu family are buried next to Dominique Lablache in Pere LaChaise cemetary in Paris.
722. *The Musical World*, July 1857, 459.
723. *Strand Musical magazine* Vol.I January-June, 1895.
724. *The Musical World,* 288.
725. *The Athenaeum*, 1879, 419.
726. Some of these pieces are published in F. Pazdirek List, 1900-1910. See author's listing of Frédéric's works in appendix.
727. Macfarren, 1905, 201
728. Pazdirek, F. 1900-1910. Listings of some of F. Lablache's compositions. *Requiem Mass*, Vocal Score 8vol paper cover 3-n, paper boards Novello.
729. Fanny Rose was the author of two children's books, *Starlight Stories* and *A Wayside Posy*, (Illustrated by Kate Greenway). Published by Griffin and Farren, London, 1884 and 1885.

CHAPTER THIRTY-EIGHT

730. Johann von Rokitansky was born 6th of March 1835 died 1909 Vienna. Johann's debut in Prague in *La Juive*. 1862, 1863, Vienna two years. Concert debut in England 1856. Sang in England for four seasons from 1865. Then again in 1876-77. Retired in 1892. Became a professor of music in the Vienna Conservatory. Died at Schloss Castle Laubegg, Styria, in November 1909.
731. www.pubmedcentral.nih.gov/articlerender.fcgi?artid=1073956, perhaps authored by L.F. Haas.
732. Victor von Rokitansky (born 9 July 1836) published *Uber Sanger und Singen* in 1894. He died Vienna 17 July 1896.
733. *Musical World*, March 1866, 170.
734. Ibid., April 15, 1876, 284.
735. Weinstock, 1987, *Rossini*, 482 (note from p. 369)
736. Ibid. 367-369.
737. Forbes, 1985, 194.
738. Ibid. 199.
739. *The Musical World,* Dec 4 1869, 829-930.
740. Stanley-Little. *Empire Review.*

[741] Granger, 1981, 12.
[742] *Era,* Theatrical Newspaper. London, January 27, 1983, 10.
[743] Lived 1877-1946.
[744] Lived 1883-1871.
[745] Granger, 1981, 12.
[746] *The London Times,* 1896-1908. Also London's *Era* and *Variety.* Same years.
[747] As a surname. Many members of the family carry the Lablache name *incorporated* into their names.
[748] Granger, 1981, 13.
[749] Ibid, 407.
[750] Ibid.
[751] Granger died of complication's of cancer and emphysema.
[752] James Granger, Lindsey and Tracy, Samantha.

ଔଔଔ

Bibliography

ACTON, HAROLD: *The Last Bourbons of Naples*. London, 1959.
ABBATE, CAROLYN and PARKER, ROGER: *Analyzing Opera, Verdi and Wagner*. California, 1989.
ALLSOBROOK, DAVID IAN: *Liszt, My Travelling Circus Life*. Illinois, 1991.
ALTER, ROBERT: *A Lion for Love, A Critical Biography of Stendhal*. New York, 1979.
APPOLONIA, GIORGIO: *Le Voci di Rossini*. Italy, 1993.
ARDITI, LUIGI: *My Reminiscences*. London, 1896.
ARNOTT, JAMES F. and ROBINSON, JOHN W.: *English Theatrical Literature 1559-1900, A Bibliography (incorporating R.Lowe's Bibliography)*. London, 1888.
ASHBROOK, WILLIAM: *Donizetti and his Operas*. London, 1983.
BACCHELLI, RICCARDO: *Rossini*. Italy, 1941.
BAEDEKER, KARL: *Southern Italy and Sicily*. London, 1912.
BAKER, THEODORE: *Baker's Biographical Dictionary of Musicians*. London,1900
BARBIERA, RAFAELLO: *La Principessa Belgiojoso*. Milan, 1930.
BEALE, THOMAS WILLERT: *The Light of Other Days*. London, 1890.
BEAUMONT, CYRIL W.: *Complete Book of Ballets*. New York, 1938.
BENSON, E.F.: *Queen Victoria*. London, 1935.
BLACK, JOHN: *The Italian Romantic Libretto, a study of Salvadore Cammarano*. Edinburgh, 1984.
Donizetti Operas in Naples. 1822-1848. London, 1982.
"The Eruption of Vesuvius in Pacini's L'Ultimo Giorno de Pompei", Donizetti Society Journal. Vol.6. London, 1988.
BLANCHARD, ROGER and DE CANDE, ROLAND: *Dieux, Divas de L'Opéra*. Paris, 1957.
BONAVENTURE, ARNALDO: *Teatro Musicale Italiano*. Livorno, 1913.
BRANNON, PHILLIP: *Southampton, Beauties of the Port and Town of Southampton,* (Introduction by Derek Whatley and John Edgar Mann). Southampton, 1990.

BREMONT, ANNA: *The World of Music: The Great Singers.* New York, 1902.
BREWER, BRUCE: *"Il cigno di Romano",* Donizetti Society Journal Vol.4. London, 1980.
BROMBERT, BETH ARCHER: *Christina, Portrait of a Princess.* New York, 1977.
BROOK, DONALD: *The Romance of the English Theatre.* London, 1946.
BROWN, JAMES D. and STRATTON, S.: *British Musical Biography: A Dictionary.* London, 1897.
BROWN, MAURICE: *Schubert (New Grove Biography Series).* New York, 1983.
BUDDEN, JULIAN: *Don Pasquale.* Recording liner notes. 1984.
BULL, SARA C.: *Ole Bull, A Memoir.* New York, 1883.
BULLARD, F.M.: *Volcanoes.* Texas, 1962.
BUNN, ALFRED: *The Stage, vols 1,2,3.* London, 1840.
BUSHNELL, HOWARD: *Maria Malibran.* University Park, PA, 1979.
CAMBIASI, POMPEO: *La Scala,* 1778-1906. Italy, 1906.
CARAPEZZA, PAOLO EMILIO: *"Palermo". New Groves Musical Dictionary.* London, 1995.
CASTIL-BLAZE, (FRANCOIS HENRI JOSEPH BLAZE): *L'Opéra-Italien.* Paris, 1856.
Theatres Lyriques de Paris: L'Academic Imperiale de Musique. Paris, 1855.
CELLETTI, RODOLFO: *The History of Bel Canto.* Oxford, 1993.
CHEER, CLARISSA LABLACHE: *"Donizetti and Lablache, 200 Years Celebration",* Donizetti Society Journal, vol.7. London, 2002.
CHEKE, DUDLEY: *Josephine and Emilie.* London, 1993.
CHORLEY, HENRY F.: *Thirty Years' Musical Recollections.* London, 1862.
CLARENCE, REGINALD: *The Stage Cyclopaedia, A bibliography of plays.* London, 1909.
CLAYTON, ELLEN C.: *Queens of Song.* New York 1856.
CLEMENT, F. and LAROUSSE, P.: *Dictionnaire Lyrique ou Histoire des Operas.* Paris, 1905.
COOPER, THOMSON: *Biographical Dictionary.*vol.II (Geo.Bell)1892
COWDEN, ROBERT H.: *Concert and Opera Singers.* Westport, CT, 1985.
COX, H.BERTRAM AND C.L.E: *Leaves from the Journals of Sir George Smart.* London, 1907.
COX, REV. T.C: *Musical Recollections of the last Half Century.* London, 1872.
CRANKSHAW, EDWARD: *The Shadow of the Winter Palace, Russia's Drift to Revolution 1825-1917.* New York, 1976.
CROWEST, FREDERICK J.: *A Book of Musical Anecdotes.* London, 1878.
CURTISS, JOHN SHELDON: *Russia's Crimean War.* North Carolina, 1899. Reprint, 1979.

DALE, ANTONY: *The Theatre Royal Brighton.* London, 1980.
DAVID, EWEN: *The Dictionary of Composers.* New York, 1981.
DAVISON, J.W.: *From Mendelssohn to Wagner.* London, 1912.
DE FILIPPIS, F. and ARNESE, R.: *Cronache del Teatro di S.Carlo. 1737-1960* Vol.1. Naples, 1961.
DELLA PORTA, DARIO: *Dentro Donizetti.* Bergamo, 1983.
DERWENT, LORD G.H.: *The Light of Rossini,* London, 1934.
  Rossini and Some Forgotten Nightingales. London, 1934.
DEUTSCH, OTTO ERICH: *Schubert.* London, 1947.
DORE, GUSTAVE: *Les Russes ou histoire dramatique pittoresque.* Paris, 1967.
DODDS, JOHN, W.: *The Age of Paradox. A Biography of England, 1841-1851.* New York, *1952.*
EAMES, WILBERFORCE: *A Bibliographical Account of English Theatrical Literature.* Washington, D.C., 1888.
EDWARDS, H. SUTHERLAND: *The Prima Donna.* London, 1888.
ELKIN, ROBERT: *The Old Concert Halls of London.* London, 1955.
ENGEL, LOUIS: *From Mozart to Mario,* London, 1886.
ESCUDIER, LEON: *Literature Musicale.* Paris, 1863.
  Mes Souvenirs. Paris, 1868.
ESCUDIER, MARIE: *Etudes Bibliographiques sur les Chanteurs contemporains.* Paris, 1840.
  Vies et Aventures des Cantatrices Celebres. Paris, 1856.
ESHER, VISCOUNT (editor): *The Girlhood of Queen Victoria, A Selection from Her Majesty's Diaries between the Years 1832 and 1840.* In Two Volumes. London, 1912.
ESHER, VISCOUNT and BENSON, ARTHUR C. (editors): *The Letters of Queen Victoria, A selection from her Majesty's correspondence between the years of 1837 and 1861.* In Three Volumes. London, 1908.
FANAN, Georgio: *Drammaturgia Rossiniana.* Rome, 1997.
FANTEL, HANS: *The Waltz Kings.* New York, 1972.
FARWELL, BYRON: *Victoria's Little Wars.* London, 1972.
FENNER, THEODORE: Opera in London. Carbondale, IL, 1994.
FITZLYON, APRIL: *The Price of Genius.* London, 1964.
  Maria Malibran. London, 1987.
FLORIMO, FRANCESCO: *La Scuola Musicale di Napoli, vols* 3-4. Naples, 1882.
FORBES, ELIZABETH: *Mario and Grisi.* London, 1985.
FOUQUE, O.: *Histoire du Theatre Ventadour.* Paris, 1881.
FRASER, FLORA: *Emma.* New York, 1986.
GANZ, A.W.: *Berlioz in London.* London, 1950.

GATES, W.F.: *Anecdotes of Great Musicians.* New York, 1905.
GATTEY, CHARLES NEILSON: *Queens of Song.* London, 1979.
GATTI, CARLO: *Il Teatro alla Scala, nella storia e nell'arte (1778-1963).* Milan, 1964.
GAUNT, WILLIAM: *The Aesthetic Adventure.* London, 1945.
The Victorian Olympus. London, 1952.
GAUTIER, THEOPHILE: *L'Historie de l'Art Dramatique en France depuis 25 Ans.* Paris, 1858-59.
GIRARDI, MICHELE and ROSSI, FRANCO: *Il Teatro La Fenice, 1792-1936. Chronologia degli spettacoli.* Venice, 1989.
GOSSETT, PHILIP: *Anna Bolena and the Artistic Maturity of Gaetano Donizetti.* London, 1985.
GRAHAM, GERALD S.: *A Concise History of the British Empire.* New York, 1970.
GRANGER, STEWART: *Sparks Fly Upward.* New York, 1981.
GROVES, GEORGE: *A Dictionary of Music and Musicians.* New York, 1908 *(edited by Fuller Maitland).*
HALL, G.K.: *Dictionary and Catalog of Music of the Boston Public Library.* Boston, 1972.
HAMILTON, GERALD and STEWART, DESMOND: *Emma in Blue.* London, 1957.
HARDING, JAMES: *Saint-Saëns.* London, 1965.
HEADLAM, CECIL: *The Story of Naples.* London, 1906.
HEATH, CHARLES: *Beauties of Opera and Ballet.* London, circa 1844. (reprinted New York, 1977).
HERIOT, ANGUS: *The Castrati in Opera.* London, 1975.
HIBBERT, CHRISTOPHER: *Queen Victoria and her Letters and Journals.* New York, 1985.
Rome, the Biography of a City. New York, 1985.
Nelson. London, 1994.
HOBHOUSE, HERMIONE: *Albert, Prince Albert His Life and Work.* London, 1983.
HOEFER, J.C.F.: *Nouvelle Biographie Generale.* Paris, 1858.
HOLLAND, H.S. and ROCKSTRO, W.S.: *Jenny Lind the Artist.* London, 1893.
HOLOMAN, D. KERN: *Berlioz.* Cambridge, Massachusetts, 1989.
HOWARD, DAVID and STEPHEN: *Lord Nelson, the Immortal Memory.* London, 1989.
HUDSON, LYNTON: *The English Stage, 1850-1950.* London, 1973.
HUGHES, SPIKE: *Great Opera Houses.* London, 1956.

HUSK, WILLIAM HENRY: *Templeton and Malibran.* London, 1881.
IOVINO, ROBERTO: *Domenico Cimarosa.* Milan, 1992.
IVANOV, M.: *The First Decade of the Italian Theatre of St.Petersburg in the 19th century 1843-53.* St Petersburg, 1895.
The Second Decade of the Imperial Theatre in St Petersburg 1853-63. St. Petersburg, 1895.
JOHNSON, JANET LYNN: *The Theatre Italian and Theatrical Life in Resoration Paris, 1818-1827 Vol 1.* Dissertation University of Chicago, 1988.
JOSEPHSON, MATTHEW: *Stendhal.* New York, 1946.
KARAWOWSKI, MORITZ: *Frédéric Chopin, His Life and his Letters.* (Translated by Emilie Hill, William Reeves). London, 1939.
KAUFMAN, THOMAS, G.: *Verdi and His Major Contempories.* New York, 1990.
"*Italian preformances in Vienna*", *Donizetti Society Journal* vol 4. London, 1980.
"*Giulia Grisi, A re-evaluation*", *Donizetti Society Journal* vol 4. London, 1980.
KENNEY, CHARLES L: *A Memoir of Michael William Balfe.* London, 1875.
KIMBELL, DAVID: *Italian Opera.* Cambridge, 1991.
KREHEIBL, H.E.: *The Life of Ludwig Von Beethoven* by A.H. Thayer. 3 vols. New York, 1921. Edited and revised translation by Kreheibl.
KUHE, WILHELM: *My Musical Recollections.* London, 1896.
KUTSCH, K.J. and RIEMENS, LEO: *GroBes Sangerlexikon.* Munich, 1993.
LABLACHE, L.: "*Lablache on English Music*", *The Musical World.* London, 1837.
LANCELLOTTI, ARTURO: *Le voci d'oro.* Italy, 1953.
LARIONOFF, P. and PESTELLINI F.: Maria *Malibran e i suoi tempi.* Italy, 1937.
LATHAM, MORTON: *Alfredo Piatti.* London, 1901.
LEONE, GUIDO: *L'Opéra a Palermo dal 1653 al 1987.* Italy, 1988. *L'empire du dernier tsar 1896-1912.* Italy, ND.
LEVY, RICHARD N. and O'ROURKE, J.: *Annals of the Theatre Royal Dublin.* Dublin, 1880.
LINCOLN, W. BRUCE: *Nicholas I, Emperor and Autocrat of all the Russias.* Indiana and London, 1978.
LOEWENBERG, ALFRED: *Annals of Opera.* Cambridge, 1943.
LOFTS, NORA: *Emma Hamilton.* London, 1978.
LUMLEY, BENJAMIN: *Reminiscences of the Opera.* London, 1864.
MACAULAY, LORD: *History of England.* London, 1849-61.
MACFARREN, WALTER CECIL: *Memories.* London, 1905.

MACKENZIE-GRIEVE, AVRIL: *Clara Novello.* London, 1955.
MAGUIRE, SIMON: *Vincenzo Bellini and the Aesthetics of Early Nineteenth-Century Italian Opera.* New York, 1989.
MAMMUCARI, RENATO: *Napoli e I suoi colori.* Italy, 1989.
MANCINI, FRANCO: *Il Teatro San Carlo,* 2 vols. Naples, 1987.
MARCO, GUY: *A Research and Information Guide.* New York, 1984.
MAREK, GEORGE, R: *Beethoven, Biography of a Genius.* New York, 1970. *Schubert.* New York, 1985.
MASSINGHAM, HUGH and PAULINE: *The London Anthology.* London, 1950.
MAUROIS, ANDRE: *Lelia, ou la Vie de George Sand.* Paris, 1952.
MAYNARD, WALTER: *The Light of Other Days.* London, 1890.
MELISI, FRANCESCO: *Catalogo dei libretti per musica dell'ottocento 1800-1860.* Lucca, Italy, 1990.
MERLIN, MARIA DE LAS MERCEDES: *Memories of Madame Malibran.* London, 1844.
MICHOTTE, EDMOND: *Richard Wagner's Visit to Rossini.* Paris, 1860. *An Evening at Rossini's in beau-Sejour.* Paris, 1858. Translated from the French and annotated, with an introduction and appendix, by Herbert Weinstock. Chicago, 1968.
MORDDEN, ETHAN: *Opera Anecdotes.* New York, 1988.
MORRIS, LLOYD: *Curtain Time.* New York, 1953.
MOUNT EDGCUMBE, LORD RICHARD: *Musical Reminiscences.* London, 1834.
NEWMAN, ERNEST: *The Life of Richard Wagner.* London, 1933-47, Vol I-IV.
NIECKS, FREDERICK: *Frédéric Chopin, As a Man and Musician.* 2 vols. New York, 1888.
NIGGL, PAUL: *Musiker Medaillen.* Darmstadt, 1965.
ODELL, GEORGE C.: *Annals of the New York Stage, vol 3.* New York, 1928.
ORGA, ATEZ: *Chopin, His Life and Times.* Neptune City, NJ, 1980.
ORREY, LESLIE: *Bellini.* New York, 1969.
OSBORNE, CHARLES: *Bel Canto Operas.* Portland, *1994.*
OSBORNE, RICHARD: *Rossini.* London, 1986.
PARRY, JOHN: *Victorian Swansdown-Extracts from* the *Early Travel Diaries of John Orlando Parry.* London, 1935.
PAZDIREK, FRANZ: *Vienna Universal Handbook.* Vienna, 1904-1910.
PEARSE, MRS GODFREY and HIRD, FRANK: *The Romance of a Great Singer.* London, 1910.

PLEASANTS, HENRY: *The Great Singers.* New York, 1966.
POCOCK, TOM: *Nelson.* New York, 1968.
PORTER WARE, W., and LOCKARD, THADDEUS C., JR.: *P.T. Barnum Presents Jenny Lind.* Louisiana, 1980.
POUGIN, ARTHUR: *Marie Malibran.* Paris, 1911.
PRATT, WALDO SELDEN: *The History of Music.* New York, 1907.
RASI, LUIGI: *I comici italiani.* Florence, 1897-1905.
REED, JOHN: *The Schubert Song Companion.* New York, 1985.
RICHARDSON, JOANNA: *Stendhal.* New York, 1974.
Theophile Gautier, His Life and Times. New York, 1959.
ROGERS, FRANCIS: *Some Famous Singers of the 19th Century.* New York, 1914.
ROSCIONI, CARLO: *Il teatro San Carlo.* 2 vols. Italy, 1987.
ROSENTHAL, HAROLD: *Two Centuries of Opera at Covent Garden.* London, 1958.
ROSENTHAL, HAROLD and JOHN WARRACK: *The Concise Oxford Dictionary of Opera.* (second ed.). London, 1983.
The Mapleson Memoirs. London, 1966. (editor)
ROSENTHAL, HAROLD AND EWAN WEST: *The Oxford Dictionary of Opera.* Oxford, 1992.
ROSSELLI, JOHN: *The Opera Industry in Italy from Cimarosa to Verdi: The role of the Impresario.* London, 1984.
ROSTAND, CHARLES: *Liszt.* Translated by John Victor. London, 1972.
ROWELL, GEORGE: *Queen Victoria Goes to the Theatre.* London, 1978.
ROYER, ALPHONSE: *Histoire de L'Opéra.* Paris, 1875.
RUSSELL, FRANK: *Queen of Song.* New York, 1964.
RUSSELL, JACK: *Nelson and the Hamiltons.* New York, 1969.
SCHONBERG, HAROLD C.: *The Great Pianists.* New York, 1963.
The Glorious Ones. New York, 1985.
SEWARD, DESMOND: *Napoleon's Family.* New York, 1986.
SHEPPARD, LESLIE and AXELROD, DR. HERBERT R.: *Paganini.* New Jersey, 1979.
SHULTZ, GLADYS DENNY: *The Swedishish Nightingale.* New York, 1962.
SIMPSON, COLIN: *Emma.* London, 1983.
SITWELL, SACHEVERELL: *Liszt.* London, 1955.
SMITH, KAREN: *Constantin Guys: Crimean War Drawings 1854-1856.* Cleveland, OH, 1978.

SMITH, WILLIAM, *The Italian Opera and Contemporary Ballet in London.* London, 1955.
SOUBIES, A.: *Le Theatre-ltalien de 1801 a 1913.* Paris, 1913.
SPARK, WILLIAM: *Musical Memories.* London, 1888.
STANLEY-LITTLE, JAMES: *"Romance of the Lablaches". Empire Review.* London, 1913
STEINER-ISENMANN, R.: *Gaetano Donizetti.* Stuttgart, 1982.
STENDHAL,(PSEUD. OF MARIE-HENRI BEYLE) *Rome, Naples and Florence.* Translated by Richard N. Coe. London, 1959.
*The Life of Rossini. T*ranslated by Richard N. Coe, London, 1970.
Melanges Intimes et Marginalia, 2 vol. Paris, 1936.
The Charterhouse of Parma. New York, 1944.
The Scarlet and Black. London, 1953.
STONEY, BENITA and HER ROYAL HIGHNESS, THE DUCHESS OF YORK: *Victoria and Albert, A Family Life at Osborne House.* New York, 1991.
STRATMAN, CARL J.: *British Dramatic Periodicals 1720-1960.* New York, 1962.
STRATTON, STEPHEN: *Mendelssohn.* New York, 1910.
SUBIRÁ, JOSÉ: *Historia y Anecdotario del Teatro Real.* Madrid, 1949.
THORNBURY, GEORGE WALTER: *Old and New London.* London, 1872.
TIBY, OTTAVIO: *Il Real Teatro Carolino e L'Ottocento.* Italy, 1957.
TINTORI, GIAMPIERO: *La Scala, Cronologia completa.* Milan,1964.
L'Opéra Napoletana. Milan, 1958.
TOYE, FRANCIS: *Rossini, The man and his music.* New York, 1987.
*Rossini and a study in Tragi-comed*y. London, 1934.
Verdi. New York, 1946.
TREVELYAN, RALEIGH: *The Shadow of Vesuvius.* London, 1976.
Princes under the Volcano. London, 1973.
TYLER-WHITTLE, M.S.: *Victoria and Albert at Home.* Manchester, 1980.
UCCELLO, GIUSEPPE: *Lo spettacolo nei secoli a Messina 1724-1908.* Palermo, 1986.
VINCENZI, MARCELLA: *La Musica a Napoli.* Naples, N.D.
VITALE, VINCENZO: *"Sigismundo Thalberg a Posillipo". Nouova Rivista Musicale Italiana.* (October/December 1972). Translated by Daphne Stevens-Pascucci.
WALKER, ALAN(editor): *Franz Liszt.* New York, 1970.
WALKER, FRANK: *The Man Verdi.* Chicago, 1982.
WARNER, MARINA: *Queen Victoria's Sketch Book.* London, 1979.

WATTS, JOHN (editor): *Donizetti Journals, vols 1-3.* London, 1974-1977.
WEATHERSON, ALEXANDER (editor): *Donizetti Journals, Vols 4-6,* London, 1980-1988.
WEAVER, WILLIAM: *The Golden Century of Italian Opera.* London, 1980.
Verdi: London, 1977.
WECHSBERG, JOSEPH: *The Waltz Emperors.* New York, 1973.
WEINSTOCK, HERBERT: *Bellini.* New York, 1971.
Donizetti. New York, 1963.
Rossini. New York, 1987.
Chopin. New York, 1981.
"*Lablache, L.*": *OPERA,* London, 1966.
WHITEHOUSE, H.R.: *A Revolutionary Princess, Christina Belgiojoso-Trivulzio, her Life and Times.* London, 1906.
WIDÉN, GUST: *Lablache, en bild fran sangens guldalder. (Nagra anteckningar vid hundraarsminnet af Luigi Lablache).* Sweden, 1897.
WILSON, A.E: *The Lyceum Theatre.* London, 1952.
WILSON, ANGUS: *The World of Charles Dickens.* London, 1972.
WOODHAM-SMITH, CECIL: *Queen Victoria.* New York, 1972.
ZAVADINI, GUIDO: *Donizetti.* Bergamo, 1948.

PERIODICALS, JOURNALS AND NEWSPAPERS CONSULTED

UNITED KINGDOM
Queen Victoria's Journals—Royal Archives
The Athenaeum
The Belfast News-Letter
The Bury and Suffolk Herald
Daily Echo Southampton
The Dublin Evening Mail
The Era
The Figaro
The Graphic
Hampshire Advertizer
Hampshire Chronicle
The Harmonicon
The Illustrated London News
The Leicester Post
The Liverpool Daily Post

The London Dramatic Magazine
The London Enr'acte
The London Examiner
The London Journal
The London Times
The Manchester Guardian
The Mirror London, 1834
The Morning Post
The Music Hall and Theatre Review
The Musical World London
Opera London
The Pall Mall Magazine
The Scotsman
The Stage
The Strand Magazine
The Theatre
The Theatrical Journal
The Variety

ITALY
Gazzetta dei teatri Milano
Gazzetta Musicale di Milano
Gazzetta Musicale di Napoli
Nuova Rivista Musicale Italiana

U.S.A.
The American Musical Journal
The Boston Daily Evening Transcript
The Chicago Tribune
Dwight's Journal Boston
The Los Angeles Times
The Daily Picayune, New Orlean
New Orleans Bee
The New York Times
The Opera Quarterly, Durham, NC
Opera News New York
The Philadelphia Bulletin
San Francisco Alta
The Washington Post

FRANCE
Galignani's Messenger
L'Avante-Scene
Le Journal des Débats
Le Journal de Paris
Le Menestrel
L'Union

GERMANY
Allgemeine Musikalische Zeitung

RUSSIA
Le Journal de Saint-Petersbourg
Severnaya Pchela (The Northern Bee) St.Petersburg

LIBRARIES AND MUSEUMS

UNITED KINGDOM
Greenwich Naval Museum Library
London British Library
London Collindale Library
London Marylebone Library
London National Portrait Gallery
London Royal Academy Portrait Division
London Royal College of Music
London University Library
London Westminster Library
Bath Library
Bournemouth Library Dorset
Cheltenham Library
Mitchell Library Glasgow
Salisbury Library Wiltshire
Southampton Library Hampshire
Winchester Library Hampshire

FRANCE
Bibliothèque de l'Opéra
Bibliothèque Historique de la Ville de Paris

National Library Paris
Paris Museé Carnavalet

ITALY
Accademia Nationale di Santa Cecilia Rome
Conservatorio di Musica San Pietro a Majella Naples
Museo Donizetti Bergamo
Museo Teatrale alla Scala Milan
The Archivio di Stato Naples
*The Rossini Found*ation Pesaro

SWEDEN
Kungliga Biblioteket Stockholm

U.S.A.
Beverly Hills Library Los Angeles
Harvard Library Boston
Library of Congress, Washington, DC
Long Beach Central Library California
Long Beach Public Library California
Metropolitan Opera Collection, New York
New York Public Library
Palos Verdes Library California
Pierpoint Morgan Library New York
Princeton University Library New Jersey
Torrance Library California
U.C.L.A. Library Los Angeles
U.C.L.A. Music Library Los Angeles
U.S.C. Library Los Angeles
U.S.C. at Long Beach Library California

☙☙☙

Index

A

"A te o cara" 208, 259, 283, 286
Aboukir Bay (Battle of the Nile) 11
Abufa (Carafa) 48
Adelaide (Beethoven) 221
Adelaide (Queen of England, aunt of Queen Victoria) 115
Adelaide di Borgogna (Rossini) xv
Adelson e Salvini (Bellini) 66, 657
Aeneid (Virgil) 58
Agnese (Paer) 46, 583, 589, 592, 622
Aguado, Alexandre-Marie (Marquis de las Marismas) 302
Aïda (Verdi) 260, 512
Alahor in Granata (Donizetti) 68-9
Albani, Emma 211, 514
Albert (Prince of Saxe-Coburg) 222, 268, 313, 337-8, 347, 358, 370-1, 441, 447
Alboni, Marietta 339, 343, 349-52, 354, 372, 428, 443, 487, 490
Alceste (Gluck) 509
Alexander, George 234
Alexander, Timoleone 73, 672
Alexander I (Czar of Russia) 41-2, 73, 292, 431, 455, 462, 685
Alexander II (Czar of Russia) 455, 457, 460, 462
Amazilia (Pacini) 56, 63, 71-2, 588, 590-2, 622
Ambrogetti, Giuseppe 111
Ambrogi, Antonio 26, 46, 48, 147, 151
Ameleto (Mercadante) 46, 621

Ancelot, Jacques-Arsene 162
Anderson, Hans Christian 330
Anna Bolena (Donizetti) 52, 130-4, 137, 141-2, 159, 164, 173, 175, 207, 218, 222, 229, 248, 295-6, 326-7, 572-3
Arditi, Luigi 512, 517, 677
Arne, Thomas Augustine 138
Arrighetto (Coccia) 46, 586, 619
Artemisia (Cimarosa) 15
Ashbrook, William xix, 62, 131, 249, 298
Assandri, Laura 215
Athenaeum 126, 171, 250, 255, 260-1, 263, 270, 326, 347, 480-1, 490, 517, 650, 673, 675, 685
Attila (Verdi) 260, 621
Auber, Daniel 140, 255, 264, 278, 453, 511
Avellino (Princess) xiv, 16-17

B

Baldassare 438, 443
Balfe, Michael 139, 220, 230, 242-3, 255, 281, 344, 350-1, 361, 453, 462, 466
Barbaja, Domenico 26, 34-5, 42-3, 47, 51-3, 55-6, 66-8, 70-1, 138, 142, 151-4, 156, 365, 654, 657
Barili-Patti, Caterina 211
Basili, Francesco 50, 588, 618
Bassini, Achille de 455-8, 614-15
Battle of Culloden Muir 1
Battu, Leon 510

Battu, Marie 510-11, 516, 522, 547, 582
Battu, Pantaleon 510
Baumeister, Mathilde 521
Beatrice (Princess of United Kingdom) 133, 252, 289, 495, 514-15
Beethoven, Ludwig van 681
Begnis, Giuseppe de 97, 137, 141, 280, 597-8, 626
Belasco, David 529
Belgiojoso, Christina 121, 166-7, 508, 685
Bella Molinara see La Molinara (Paisiello)
Belletti, Giovanni 312
Bellini, Vincenzo 26-7, 51, 66-8, 73, 130, 132-3, 162-7, 169, 210-15, 219-22, 237-8, 254-5, 265-6, 656-7, 662, 682
Belloc-Giorgi, Teresa 42-3, 97
Belluomini, Joseph 226
Benedetti, Michele 33, 38, 142
Benedict, Julius 74, 230, 252, 260, 281-2, 315, 332, 453, 503, 520, 673
Beriot, Charles Auguste de 120, 141, 149, 157
Berlioz, Hector 58, 144, 170, 255, 266, 277, 394, 499, 679-80
Bernhardt, Sarah 234
Betly (Donizetti) 228, 237, 281, 663
Bettini, Jeremiah 456-7
Betts, Abigail 73, 138, 242, 261, 660
Betts, Arthur 138
Betts, John 138, 660
Beyle, Marie-Henri *see* Stendhal
Bianca e Falliero (Rossini) 63, 259
Bianca e Gernando (Bellini) 66-8
Bietagh, Giuserra Reale 1
Bietagh-Lablache, Catherine Maria Francesca *see* Lablache, Francesca (mother of Luigi Lablache)
Birmingham festival 276, 331-2, 357, 449, 632
Blache, Falcoz Alexander de la 3
Blache, Simon de la (Count) 2, 651
Bohemian Girl, The (Balfe) 139, 351

Boileau, Nicolas 40
Boito, Arrigo 514
Bolshoi Theatre 305, 426, 458
Bonaparte, Joseph-Napoléon (King of Naples and Sicily) 17
Bonaparte, Louis-Napoléon *see* Napoléon III (Emperor of the French)
Bonaparte, Napoléon 8, 17-18, 24, 39-40, 72, 145, 158, 273, 279, 296
"Bonnie Prince Charlie" 1
Borghese, Gian Battista 73
Bosio, Angiolina 211, 306, 441-2, 447-9, 455-6, 458-9
Bouchot, François 104-5, 194, 275, 289, 306, 504, 572-3, 666
Braham, John 209, 234, 258, 261
Brayda (Marquis) 17
Breadon-Lablache, Jane Clementine (wife of Luigi Frédéric) 112, 508, 512, 524-7, 532
Buckingham palace 210, 220-1, 234, 240, 265, 267-8, 311, 313, 339-40, 370-1, 514, 521
Bunn, Alfred 220, 678
Burley, Charles 38, 655
Byron, Lord George 40, 577, 679

C

Callas, Maria 254
Calzolari, Enrico 354, 374, 450
Cammarano, Salvatore 228, 237
Campanini, Italo 512, 523, 527
Cantata (Handel) 509, 569
Capoul, Victor 512
Caradori-Allan, Maria 133, 208, 596
Carafa, Michael Enrico 29, 45, 48, 66, 212, 583, 586-7, 590, 618
Carlini, Luigi 30
Carmen (Bizet) 255, 527-9, 532, 665
"Casta Diva" 295, 343, 355
Castellan, Jean-Anais 357
Castignace, Giuseppe 20

Index

Caters, Ernest de 429, 456, 458, 513-14, 516
Championnet, Jean Étienne (Vachier) 13
Charles III (Duke of Bourbon) 36
Cherubini, Luigi 56, 133, 212, 264, 278, 357
Chiara di Rosenberg (Ricci) 230
Chizzola, Gaetano 68, 72
Chopin, Frederic 124
"Chorus of Dervishes" (Beethoven) 509
Ciccimarra, Guiseppe 26, 588-92
Cicero, Marcus Tullius 58
Cimarosa, Domenico 12-15, 23, 27-8, 40, 52, 63-4, 94, 117, 287, 332, 652, 657, 681, 683
Cinti-Damoreau, Laure 134, 137-9, 260
Ciro in Babilonia (Rossini) 30
Coccia, Carlo 46
Colbran, Isabella 33, 38, 48, 68, 266, 317, 654
Colombo (Ricci) 73, 594, 623
Coltran, Theodore 342, 480
Comelli-Rubini, Adelaide 46, 54, 127, 184
Compte Ory (Rossini) 139
"Con pazienza" (Fioravanti) 259, 288, 332
Constanza ed Almeriska (Mercadante) 50
Corrado D'Altamura (Ricci) 321
Cosi fan tutte (Mozart) 138, 293-5, 332, 458, 511, 607, 610, 621, 638
Costa, Michael iv, 221, 229, 231-2, 257, 295, 321, 323, 328, 357, 364, 370-1, 435-6, 449, 453, 601-2
Covent Garden 68, 230-1, 257, 337-8, 347, 363-6, 440-1, 443, 447, 449, 451-2, 455, 502-3, 510-11, 515-16, 659-60
Crane, Walter 524
Crescentini, Girolamo 214
Crimean War 432-3, 435, 440, 444, 457, 678, 683
Cruvelli, Sophie 372, 375

D

D'Angri, Elena 306, 358, 375, 502-3
Dabadie, Henry Bernard 260
Dabadie, Louise-Zulm 260
Danse iroquoise 518, 571
Dardanelli, Girolama 26, 30, 34, 53
David, Giovanni 26, 30, 47-8, 67, 102, 122, 148, 151, 154, 260, 583-5, 587-98, 626, 679-81
De Candia, Giovanni Matteo *see* Mario
De Caters, Marie, Baroness *see* Lablache, Marie de Caters (daughter of Luigi Lablache)
Deborde-Lablache, Catherine 4
Der Freischutz (Weber) 47-8, 255, 445, 521, 624
Devil's Disciple, The (Shaw) 532
Didone Abbandonata (Mercadante) 63, 590
Die Rauber (Schiller) 220
Dimitresco, Jean (Ion) 513
Don Carlos (Costa) 321
Don Giovanni (Mozart) 115, 121, 133-4, 137, 140, 157, 235, 247, 270, 286, 291, 293-5, 322, 332, 373-4, 441
Don Pasquale (Donizetti) xv, 29, 137, 251, 264, 296, 298-303, 307-8, 310, 322, 327, 348, 354, 361-2, 442, 573
Donizetti, Gaetano 68-72, 74-5, 130-3, 143-4, 162-5, 169, 228, 235-7, 254-6, 263-4, 291-2, 298-302, 344-6, 661-4, 667-9, 677-8
Donna Aurora (Morlacchi) 43
Donzelli, Domenico 26, 30, 43, 46, 53, 101, 112-13, 120-2, 315, 423-4, 497, 579, 584-9, 595
Doyle, Arthur Conan 524
Drury Lane Theatre Royal 139, 231, 242, 247, 256-7, 261, 366, 525-6, 532, 658, 660

Duprez, Caroline 372-3
Duprez, Gilbert-Louis 137, 228, 254, 277, 373, 510

E

Ecuba (Manfroce) 25
Elijah (Mendelssohn) 331, 335, 349, 354, 356, 449
Elisa (Mayr) 120
Elisa e Claudio (Mercadante) 42, 46, 53-4, 66, 120, 139, 237-8, 281, 295, 621
Elisabetta, regina d'Inghilterra (Rossini) 24, 34, 39
Elizabeth II (Queen of England) xviii, 513
Elvida (Donizetti) 68, 263, 591, 619
Emmerson, Jane *see* Lablache, Jane Clementine (wife of Luigi Frédéric)
Empire Theatre 528
English Opera House 138, 149, 232, 234, 631, 663
Ernani (Verdi) 326, 339
Eugénie (Empress of the French) 514
Euryanthe (Weber) 48, 54

F

Fabre, Guiseppina 30
Farinelli, Giuseppe 64
Faust (Gounod) 511-12, 521, 527
Fechter, Charles 234
Federico II Re di Prussia (Mosca) 50
Félix, Elisabeth Rachel 124, 365, 431, 491
Ferdinand I (King of the Two Sicilies) 7, 10-11, 14, 17, 26, 29, 34, 36, 38, 41-2, 63, 66, 145
Ferdinand IV of Naples *see* Ferdinand I (King of the Two Sicilies)
Ferdinando Duca di Valenza (Pacini) 147
Féron, Elizabeth 68, 138, 230
Fidelio (Beethoven) 220, 222, 521

Fioravanti, Valentino 28, 157, 259, 479
Fioravanti, Vincenzo 37, 484-5
Florimo, Francesco 2, 51
Florinda (Thalberg) 375, 614, 624
Fodor-Mainville, Josephine 26, 48-9, 52-3, 74, 579
Foli, Allan James 521
Francesco I (King of Austria) 292
Franz Joseph I (Emperor of Austria) 520
French Revolution xiii, 2, 7-8, 10, 27, 39, 296
Frezzolini, Giuseppe 144, 349
Frohman, Charles 528, 532
Frohman, Daniel 529
Frohman, David 529
Frou Frou (Meilhac and Halévy) 527, 530, 665

G

Galli, Filippo 130
Garcia, Manuel 26, 34, 46, 67, 114, 121, 136, 141, 244, 289, 315, 324, 334-5, 579
Garcia, Pauline *see* Viardot, Pauline
Gardoni, Italo 335, 339-40, 342, 349, 448-9, 521, 611-14, 616, 644
Gassier, Edouard 521
Gautier, Theophile 158, 680
Generali, Pietro 28
Gerster, Etelka 512
Giannina e Bernardone (Cimarosa) 28
Gilardoni, Domenico 66, 69, 74-5
Giselle (Gautier) 158
Giulietta e Romeo (Vaccai) 137
Giulietta e Romeo (Zingarelli) 214, 232
Gli elvezi, ovvero Corrado di Tochemburgo (Pacini) 147, 597, 622
Gli l'Italianie Indinai (Carafa) 66
Gli sposi in cimento (Mosca) 23
Glinka, Mikhail 130
Glossip, Joseph 138
Gluck, Christoph Willibald 509

Gnecco 229, 276, 620
Goethe, Johann Wolfgang von 7
Goldschmidt, Jenny Lind *see* Lind, Jenny
Gounod, Charles 119, 255, 550
Grand Opera House 134
Grange, Anna de la 375
Granger, Stewart 524, 531-3, 566-7, 582, 676, 680
Grecis, Nicola de 43
Grisi, Carlotta 158, 363, 368-9
Grisi, Ernesta 158, 239, 251, 282, 286, 288
Grisi, Giulia 157-8, 207-8, 214-16, 229, 234, 242-5, 255-6, 259-61, 81-9, 296-7, 305-8, 312-19, 322-3, 326-33, 522, 572-4
Grisi, Giulietta 208
Guglielmo Tell. see Guillaume Tell (Rossini)
Guido e Ginevra (Tommasi) 456
Guillaume Tell (Rossini) xv, 139, 147, 154, 207, 221, 225, 227, 257, 260-1, 266, 295, 338, 347, 450, 522
Gustave III (Auber) 373

H

Haggard, Rider 524
Halévy, Fromental 278, 367-8
Hamilton, Lady Emma 11, 34, 681
Handel, Georg Frederic 209, 227, 509, 578-9, 624
Harrison, William 234
Hauk, Mini 512
Haydn, Joseph 19, 57, 209, 226, 343, 488, 624
Hayes, Catherine 356, 361, 363, 365
Heine, Heinrich 124, 163, 166
Her Majesty's Theatre 129, 138, 220, 231, 242, 250, 257-8, 261, 264, 268, 293, 325-6, 364-6, 370-1, 373-4, 453-4
Herman, Henry 526

Herold, Ferdinand 321
Hoango (Lavigna) 28
Hohler, Tom 521
Hugo, Victor 124, 158, 255-6, 456

I

I Brigante (Mercadante) 219
I Capuleti e i Montecchi (Bellini) 73
I due Foscari (Verdi) 339
I Lombardi (Verdi) 326, 332, 339, 367
I Masnadieri (Verdi) 220, 338-40
I Pazzi per progretto (Donizetti) 74
I Portuguesi in Goa (Benedict) 74
I Puritani (Bellini) 162, 164-9, 171, 207-8, 211, 222, 232, 254-5, 268-9, 286-7, 295, 348-9, 426-7, 457-8, 573-5, 662
Il Barbiere di Siviglia (Rossini) 30, 34, 38-9, 42-5, 47-8, 50, 53, 61, 66, 73-4, 76, 111, 159-60, 249, 287, 322-3
Il Campanello di notte (Donizetti) 228, 235, 237, 281, 444, 663
Il Contestabile di Chester (Pacini) 147
Il Degona (Marliani) 229
Il Diluvio universale (Donizetti) 74-5
Il fanatico per la musica (Fioravanti) 259, 272, 288, 332, 343
Il Giovedi grasso (Donizetti) 71-2
Il Matrimonio Segreto (Cimarosa) 48, 64, 117-18, 134, 226, 270, 287, 294, 315, 332, 574
Il Paria (Donizetti) 75
Il Ritorno di Pulcinella dagli Studi di Padova (Fioravanti) 37
Il Rivale de se stesso (Weigl) 32
Il Seraglio (Mozart) 520
Il Servo padrone (Generali) 28
Il sogno di Partenope (Mayr) 38
Il Solitario ed Elodia (Pavesi) 66
Il teatro San Carlo 682-3
Il traditor deluso 59-60

Il Trovatore (Verdi)   237, 260, 446, 449-50, 455-6, 458-9, 503, 510, 512
Il Turco in Italia (Rossini)   34, 115, 225, 589, 606
Il Vascello d'occidente (Carafa)   29
Il Ventaglio (Raimondi)   37
Imperial Theatre   304-5, 356, 426-7, 432, 681
Industrial Revolution   128, 366
Inez de Castro (Persiani)   270-1, 340
Irene (Pacini)   156, 598, 622
Irving, Henry   234, 524-5, 528, 530
Israel in Egypt (Handel)   227, 357, 449
Ivanoff, Nicholas   147, 171, 208, 212, 221-4, 227, 229, 231
Ivanoff, Nicolas   147, 171, 208, 223-4, 227, 229, 254, 317, 597, 599-603, 613, 627-30

J

Jacobite   1, 8
Jones, Henry Arthur   526

K

Kärnthnertor Theater   26, 47-8, 56, 59
King's theatre   76, 111-15, 125-6, 128, 130, 132-3, 135, 137, 140, 170, 177, 207-8, 219, 222-3, 229-30, 232
Kipling, Rudyard   524

L

L'Africaine (Meyerbeer)   511
L'Ajo nell'imbarazzo (Donizetti)   62, 134, 264, 344
L'appuntamento notturna per burla (Luca)   28
L'Assedio di Calais (Donizetti)   211, 228
L'Assedio di Corinto (Donizetti)   75, 139, 142, 207

L'Elisir d'amore (Donizetti)   62, 137, 144, 217-18, 234-5, 237, 247-52, 255, 264-5, 281, 293, 300, 348-9, 447-8, 458, 574
L'erede senza eredita (Palma)   23
L'Esule di Granata (Meyerbeer)   46
L'Esule di Roma (Donizetti)   69, 137, 139, 660
L'Étoile du Nord (Meyerbeer)   449, 455-6
L'Impostore o il marcotondo (Mosca)   32
L'Inganno Felice (Rossini)   34, 63, 71
L'Italiana in Algieri (Rossini)   34, 237
L'Occasione fa il ladro, ossia il cambio della valigia (Rossini)   46
L'ultimo giorno di Pompei (Pacini)   56, 65-6, 71-2, 127
La Calzolaia (Generali)   29, 583, 620
La Capriciosa e il Soldato (Carafa)   45
La Cecchina see Lablache, Francesca (daughter of Luigi)
La Cenerentola (Rossini)   42-3, 46, 48, 134, 159, 280, 315, 426
La clemenza di Tito (Mozart)   295
La contadina bizzarra (Castignace)   20
La Contessa Villana (Rossi)   37
La Dame Locandiera (Mosca)   46
La Danza (Rossini)   222, 336
La Donna del largo (Rossinil)   43
La Favorita (Donizetti)   264, 339
La Festa del Villaggio (Puccitta)   45
La Figlia del reggimento see *La Fille du régiment* (Donizetti)
La Fille du régiment (Donizetti)   255, 337, 339, 344, 443
La Fondazione di Partenope (autori diversi)   50
La Gazza ladra (Rossini)   32, 117, 142-3, 150, 156-8, 170, 222, 231, 247, 276, 281
La Juive (Halévy)   364, 366, 675
La Molinara (Paisiello)   23, 485

Index

La muette de Portici (Auber) 511
La Noyade (Auber) 140
La Pietra del Paragone (Rossini) 30, 34, 39, 46
La prova di un'opera seria (Gnecco) 121, 159, 229, 276, 332, 375, 426
La Scala di Seta (Rossini) 34
La Sciocca per Astuzia (Mosca) 43
La Scuola Musicale di Napoli (Florimo) 1, 51, 679
La Sonnambula (Bellini) 37, 130, 132, 147, 167-8, 220, 222, 227, 252, 281-2, 322, 342-3, 350-2, 513, 641, 643
La straniera (Bellini) 142, 292
La Sylphide (Taglioni) 139-40
La tempesta (Halévy) 365, 367-70
La Traviata (Verdi) 260, 456, 458, 512
La Vestale (Spontini) 25, 587, 622, 624
La zingara (Donizetti) 52
Lablache, Adelaide (sister of Luigi) 16-17
Lablache, Anna (granddaughter of Luigi) 510, 512-13
Lablache, Dominique (son of Luigi) 429, 440, 446, 479, 502, 511, 515-16, 672
Lablache, Emilie *see* Méric-Lablache, Emilie de (daughter-in-law of Luigi)
Lablache, Francesca (daughter of Luigi) 2, 28, 275, 289, 306, 460, 480, 486
Lablache, Francesca (mother of Luigi) 1-2, 4-5, 12, 14-15, 651
Lablache, Francesca Rosa Marie Nicolette *see* Lablache-Thalberg (Bouchot), Francesca (daughter of Luigi)
Lablache, Frédéric (son of Luigi) 211, 228-9, 238-9, 281-2, 296-7, 312-13, 315, 322, 330-1, 338-9, 347-9, 351-2, 356-7, 360-1, 363, 516-19
Lablache, Fredrico Licterius Paul Nicola *see* Lablache, Frédéric (son of Luigi)
Lablache, Henri 135, 376, 425, 429, 480, 513
Lablache, Jane Clementine *see* Breadon-Lablache, Jane Clementine (wife of Luigi Frédéric)
Lablache, Louise Emilie 512, 522, 551
Lablache, Luigi Frédéric (grandson of Luigi) 255, 523, 660
Lablache, Nicola (father of Luigi) 1-5, 9, 12-16, 68, 135, 341, 444, 651
Lablache, Nicola (son of Luigi) 45, 68, 135, 341, 429-30, 444
Lablache, Nicola Pierre Andre *see* Lablache, Nicola (son of Luigi)
Lablache, Rosina (daughter of Luigi) 457
Lablache, Simon (grandfather of Luigi) 3-4, 651
Lablache, Simone Raimondo Tobia Andrea Giuseppe (brother of Luigi) 4
Lablache, Teresa (wife of Luigi) 23-4, 28-9, 45, 452, 457
Lablache-Brayda, Clelia (daughter of Luigi) 16-17, 582
Lablache chronology 653, 661
Lablache-de Caters, Marie Isabelle de (daughter of Luigi) 120, 140, 266, 356, 376, 429-31, 443, 514-15, 679
Lablache-Rokitansky, Thérèse Frances (granddaughter of Luigi) 363, 519-20
Lablache-Singer, Marianna (daughter of Luigi Lablache) 513, 515, 654

Lablache-Stewart, Elizabeth Frederica Charlotte (great-granddaughter of Luigi) 531
Lablache-Thalberg (Bouchot), Francesca (daughter of Luigi) xvii, 2, 28, 45, 275, 289, 306, 460, 479-80, 486, 502, 513, 654
Laporte, Pierre 111, 125-6, 223, 261, 269, 291-2
"Largo al factotum" (Rossini) 44, 126, 160-1, 280
Lavigna, Vincenzo 28
Le cantatrici villane 293, 574
Le nozze di Figaro (Mozart) 230, 235, 237, 270, 295, 348, 353-4, 363
Le Prophète (Meyerbeer) 347, 363, 365, 444, 458
Le Siège de Corinthe (Rossini) 63
Le trame deluse (Cimarosa) 23
Leopold II (Emperor of Austria) 64
Les Huguenots 221, 234, 283, 347, 364-6, 511, 520-1
Les Huguenots (Meyerbeer) 221, 234, 283, 364, 511, 520-1
Li Calsi, Joseph 517
Lind, Jenny 159, 221, 245, 264, 289, 323, 328-30, 334-7, 339-43, 345, 347-52, 358, 360, 365-6, 405-6, 573
Linda di Chamounix (Donizetti) 263-4, 292, 299, 344, 348, 353, 356, 446, 619
Liszt, Franz 124, 128, 166, 169, 258, 264, 266, 271, 273-4, 336, 346, 355, 661, 677, 683
Lohengrin (Wagner) 521
Louis XVI (King of France) 8
Love in a Village (Arne) 138
Luca, Giovanni de 28, 332, 583, 619
Lucia di Lammermoor (Donizetti) 52, 130, 137, 169, 236-7, 247, 252, 255, 297-8, 344, 361, 373

Lumley, Benjamin 268, 291-2, 321-4, 328-30, 334-5, 340, 350, 352, 360, 364, 366-7, 372-3, 423, 466, 669, 671
Luzio, Gennaro 74

M

Madelena (Abbess of Sessa) 479
Madelena (sister of Luigi) 479
Magic Flute, The (Mozart) 221, 352
Maid of Artois, The (Balfe) 139, 220, 242
Malek Adel (Costa) 229, 232, 322, 601-3
Malibran, Eugene 227
Malibran, Maria 45, 112, 117, 120, 122, 136, 138-42, 149, 155, 157-8, 219-20, 224, 226-7, 244-5, 270, 678-9
Malibran-de Bèriot, Maria 111-14, 120-4, 133-4, 138-43, 147, 149-51, 155-8, 219-20, 224-7, 241-2, 244-5, 258-9, 270, 497, 678-9, 681-3
Manfroce, Nicola 25
Maometto II (Rossini) 63, 219
Mapelson, James Henry 512
Marai, Fanny 444, 449, 456-8, 615-17
Maria-Carolina (Queen of Naples and Sicily) 5, 14-15, 65
Maria Padilla (Donizetti) 291
Maria Stuarda (Carlini) 30
Maria Stuarda (Niedermeyer) 458
Maria Theresa (Empress of Austria) 7
Marie Antoinette (Queen of France and Navarre) 8, 14
Marie Louise (Empress of France) 72-4
Marini, Ignazio 33, 51
Marino Faliero (Donizetti) 164-5, 167, 169, 171, 194-5, 218, 222, 264, 300, 572-3, 599-600, 606, 619, 662

Index

Mario (Prince of Tenors) 250-3, 255-6, 281-3, 286-8, 295-6, 303-4, 309-10, 315-16, 322-3, 326-8, 330-3, 346-7, 356-7, 364-6, 604-11, 615-16
Marliani, Marco 229, 601, 620
Marx, Karl 358
Masmaniello (Auber) 140
Mass in C major (Beethoven) 509
Matilde di Shabran (Rossini) 44
Maximilian of Prussia 292
Mayo, Frank 529
Mayr, Giovanni Simone *see* Mayr, Johann Simon
Mayr, Johann Simon 38, 43, 46, 68, 120, 127
McKenzie, Nazarena *see* Thalberg, Zaré
Medea in Corinto (Mayr) 46, 127, 133, 317
Medrano, Giovanni 36
Mefistofile (Boito) 514
Mendelssohn, Felix 335
Mercadante, Saverio 26, 42-3, 46, 50, 53-4, 63, 66, 87, 95, 119, 139, 219, 225, 237, 264, 281
Méric, Joséphine de 66, 68, 137-9, 211, 356, 426, 430
Méric-Lablache, Emilie de (daughter-in-law of Luigi) 66, 68, 73, 138, 306, 356-7, 426, 444, 446-7, 450, 456-9, 510-13, 520-3, 527, 658, 678
Méric-Lalande, Henriette 67-9, 73, 98, 114, 122
Merlin, Marie de la Mercedes 121-2, 142, 309, 659
Merry Wives of Windsor, The (Nicolai) 520
Messiah, The (Handel) 209, 331-2, 357, 580
Metastasio, Pietro 59-60
Metropolitan Opera House 211, 512, 688

Metternich, Clemens von 292, 656
Meyerbeer, Giacomo 119, 134, 255, 347, 360, 363-6, 444, 449, 456
Milton, John 226
Mongini, Pietro 521
Moonlight Sonata (Beethoven) 509
Morelli, Filippo 111, 261-2
Morlacchi, Francesco 43, 586, 621
Mosca, Luigi xiv, 23, 32, 46, 50, 583-6, 588-9, 591, 621
Mosè e Farone (Rossini) 32-3, 139, 222, 293, 295, 505
Mosè in Egitto (Rossini) 32-3, 505
Mozart, Wolfgang Amadeus 18, 28, 48, 50, 56, 115, 138, 157, 160, 230, 287-8, 294-5, 351-2, 357, 373-4, 487-8
Much Ado about Nothing (Shakespeare) 524
Murat, Joachim 20, 24, 653
Murska, Ilma di 211, 521
Muzio, Emmanuele 338

N

Nabucco (Verdi) 73, 260, 325, 669
Naldi, Marie 111, 579
Napoléon III (Emperor of the French) 257, 425, 514
Neipperg, Adam Count von 72
Nelson, Lord Horatio 5, 11
Nethersole, Olga 527, 531, 534, 558
Nicholas I (Czar of Russia) 356, 376, 431, 455, 457, 681
Nicolai, Otto 520
Nicolini, Antonio 36
Nilsson, Christine 512, 514, 521, 523, 527
Norma (Bellini) xviii-xix, 9, 73, 120, 133, 147, 214-17, 264-5, 284-6, 295-6, 314, 351-2, 441-2, 513, 573-4, 662-3

Northern Star, The. see L'Étoile du Nord (Meyerbeer)
Nourrit, Adolphe 260
Novello, Clara 208, 224, 231, 242, 682
Nowosielski, Michael 111
Nozzari, Andrea 244

O

O la capanna svizzera (Donizetti) 228
Oberon (Weber) 520
Oft in the Stilly Night (aria) 238
Olivo e Pasquale (Donizetti) 137
Osborne House 268, 311-12, 340, 370, 414, 647, 675, 684
Otello (Rossini) 20-1, 35, 38, 53, 120, 133-4, 141-2, 154, 158, 244-7, 259, 262, 280, 314, 450, 572-3
Our American Cousin (Taylor) 530
Overture op. 124 (Beethoven) 56

P

Pacini, Giovanni 26, 43-4, 63, 65, 71-2, 96, 127, 142, 147, 155-7, 271
Paer, Fernando 46
Paganini, Niccolo 18, 44, 124-30, 138, 221, 228, 258, 271-2, 274, 481, 659, 683
Paisiello, Giovanni 23, 27, 52, 64, 95, 111, 487-8
Palma, Silvestro 23
Pandolfini, Francesco 521, 523
Paradise Lost (Milton) 226
Paris opera 63, 139, 251, 265, 522
Parkinson, Norman 513
Parry, John Orlando 147-9, 151-5, 273, 293, 315, 331, 333, 355, 570, 661, 682
Parthenopian Republic 12

Pasta, Guiditta 52, 67, 113, 123-4, 127, 130-3, 141, 158-9, 215, 244, 264, 280, 296, 329, 573-4, 661
Patti, Adelina 211
Pavesi, Vincenzo Stefano 29, 66, 298, 654
Pelissier, Olympe 266, 292, 317
Pepoli, Carlo 162, 166
Père Lachaise Cemetary 212, 360, 516, 522, 675
Pergolesi, Giovanni Battista 579-80
Persiani, Fanny Tacchinardi 322
Persiani, Giuseppe 270
Philip V (King of Spain) 7
Piatti, Alfredo 221, 294, 517, 681
Pignatelli, Donna Francesca Ferrara (Princess of Pignatelli) xvii
Pignatelli, Fernando Ferrara (Prince of Strongoli) xvii
Pignatelli, Mario (Prince of Strongoli) 15
Pignatelli, Vincenzo Ferrara (Prince of Strongoli) 503
Pimental, Eleanora 15
Pinotti, Elisabetta 23-5, 28, 34, 39, 582
Pinotti, Rosa 23, 28
Pinotti, Rosina 23, 42, 159, 441, 457, 653-4
Pinotti-Lablache, Teresa *see* Lablache, Teresa (wife of Luigi)
Poliuto (Donizetti) 444
Polyeucte (Gounod) 514
Ponte, Lorenzo da 365
Posillipo xvii, 24, 76, 152, 275, 291, 429, 502, 504, 542-3, 674, 684
Potocka, Delphine 123-4
Prince of Tenors *see* Mario
Puccitta, Vicenzo 45, 586, 623
Puente, Giuseppe del 523
Pulci-Dora, Nobili Francesca 503
Puritani Quartet 170, 221, 229, 245, 253, 268-9, 282, 291, 451, 462

R

Raimondi, Pietro 37
Raul signore di Sequi (Fioravanti) 28
Reeves, Sims 258, 349, 357, 361, 363, 375
Requiem (Cherubini) 56, 277-8, 359, 449, 487-8, 640, 675
Requiem Mass in D minor (Mozart) 19, 28, 56-7, 277-8, 357, 359-60, 449, 485-90, 518
Riccardo 211, 637, 677
Ricci, Federico 321
Ricci, Luigi 37, 230, 237
Righetti-Giorgi, Gertrude 42
Rigoletto (Verdi) 260, 444, 446, 450, 456, 458-9, 511-12
Robert, Edouard 120
Robert il Diavolo (Meyerbeer) *see Robert le Diable* (Meyerbeer)
Robert le Diable (Meyerbeer) 134, 221, 251-2, 265, 336-7, 343, 364-5, 511, 521
Robert the Devil see Robert le Diable (Meyerbeer)
Roberto Devereux (Donizetti) 237, 247, 259, 344
Roger, Gustave 220, 347, 349-50, 453, 510, 677
Rohan (Prince) 257, 453, 510
Rokitansky, Johann von 519-20, 675
Rokitansky, Karl von 519
Rokitansky, Therese von *see* Lablache, Therese. (grandaughter of Luigi Lablache)
Rokitansky, Victor von 519-21, 675
Romani, Felice 63, 73, 212, 237, 254
Romeo und Juliet (Gounod) 521
Ronconi, Giorgio 292-3, 351, 364, 426-8, 444, 448, 455
Ronzi, Giuseppina 97, 141, 280
Rosenthal, Harold 364
Rossi (Countess) *see* Sontag, Henrietta
Rossi, Gaetano 49, 349, 352, 680
Rossi, Lauro 37
Rossi, Luigi 12
Rossini, Gioacchino 24-7, 29-30, 32-5, 38-40, 42-9, 54-6, 61-4, 69-71, 119-20, 122-4, 132-4, 156-9, 210-13, 259-61, 291-3, 654-6
Royal Academy of music 230, 516
Rubini, Giovanni Battista 67-8, 123-4, 127-8, 130-4, 167-8, 221-2, 251-4, 258-62, 269-73, 281-4, 293-7, 587-91, 593-4, 596, 599-607, 626-8
Ruffini, Giovanni 29
Ruins of Athens, The (Beethoven) 509

S

Saint-Saens, Camille 514
Saintine, Joseph-Xavier Boniface 162
Salieri, Antonio 53
Sancia di Castiglia (Donizetti) 143
Sanquirico, Alessandro 43
Sansone (Basili) 50
Santley, Charles 234, 521
Saul (Vaccai) 72
Scalchi, Sofia 512, 523
Scarlatti, Alessandro 52
Schiller, Friedrich von 220, 260, 339
Schroder-Devrient, Wilhelmine 123, 134
Schubert, Franz 18, 47-8, 56, 59-61, 92, 678-9, 682
Scott, Sir Walter 131, 236, 256, 577
Seguin, Arthur 367
Sembrich, Marcella 211
Ser Marcantonio (Pavesi) 29, 39, 298, 583, 622, 654, 667
Seraglio (Mozart) 520
Serov, Alexander 444-5, 450, 672
Severini, Carlo 120
Shakespeare, William 40, 46, 244, 256, 279, 367, 369, 445, 525

Shakespeare Memorial Theatre 524
Shaw, George Bernard 524, 532-3
Siddons, Mrs. Mary F. Scott 525
Silver King, The (Jones and Herman) 526
Singer, Henry 514-15, 582
Sinico, Clarice 512, 521, 604
Sirletti, Luigi 30
Sloper, Lindsay 517
Smith, William James Parkinson 513
Sontag, Henriette 54-6, 100, 245, 274, 306, 352-4, 357, 360, 363-4, 368-9, 372, 374, 428, 443, 492
Sothern, Edward Askew 529-30
Spark, William 453
Sparks Fly Upward (Granger) 524
Spontini, Gaspare 25, 594, 624
Stabat Mater (Rossini) 291, 293, 295, 297, 322, 354, 443, 514, 522, 579, 624
Stael, Germaine de 73
Stagno, Roberto 512, 521
Stanley-Little, James xviii, 523-4, 531, 582, 651-2
Stanley-Little, T. C. xviii, 523, 534, 651-2
Stendhal 9, 15, 31, 33-4, 36-7, 39-40, 102, 289-90, 652-5, 667, 677, 681, 683-4
Stewart, James Lablache *see* Granger, Stewart
Stonehenge 355, 574
Strakosch, Max 513
Strauss, Johann 169, 221, 240, 244, 279
Strepponi, Giuseppina 73, 211
String trio in E flat (Beethoven) 509
Sullivan, Barry 524
"Suoni la Tromba" 165-6, 284, 301, 442
Sutherland, Joan 211, 254
Symphony no. 9 (Beethoven) 56
Syracuse (Prince) 29, 257, 453, 528, 530

T

Tagliafico, Joseph 349
Taglioni, Amalia Galster 140
Taglioni, Filippo 139-40, 236, 262-3
Taglioni, Marie 120, 139-40, 207, 236, 261-2, 266, 356, 363, 366, 376, 411, 429-31, 443, 456, 458, 480
Taglioni, Salvatore 484
Tamberlik, Enrico 441, 445, 450-1, 455, 458
Tamburini, Antonio 142, 160, 164-5, 207-8, 220-1, 231-2, 234-5, 243, 252-4, 259-60, 269-70, 272-3, 281-2, 299-300, 304-5, 317
Tancredi (Rossini) 34, 39, 67, 120, 272, 280, 357, 585, 623, 626
Teatro alla Scala, Milan 68, 680
Teatro Apollo, Rome 32
Teatro Argentina 25, 44-6
Teatro Carignano, Turin 46
Teatro Carolino, Palermo 30-1, 39, 68, 71, 120, 211, 654
Teatro della Canobbiana 26
Teatro Fenice, Naples 73, 149
Teatro Fiorentini 23
Teatro Fondo, Naples 13, 23-5, 34, 36-7, 50, 56, 71-2, 74, 76, 141, 144, 148, 157, 248, 653-4, 658
Teatro Munizione, Messina 28, 583
Teatro Partenope 36-8, 50, 624
Teatro San Carlino, Naples 23
Teatro San Carlo, Naples 23-5, 33-9, 43, 50-1, 65-72, 74, 76, 137-8, 141-3, 147, 149-51, 154-7, 236-7, 590-1, 598-9, 653-5
Teatro San Ferdinando, Palermo 28, 298
Terriss, William 234
Terry, Ellen 234, 524, 528, 534
Terry, Kate 234
Tete Rondes et Cavaliers (Ancelot and Saintine) 162
Thalberg, Francesca 398, 400, 481, 509, 540

Thalberg, Sigismund xvii, 273-5, 277, 281, 293, 309-10, 336, 346, 352, 354, 375, 453, 460, 495, 500, 502-6
Thalberg, Zaré 502-3, 674
Theatre Monnaie 511
Theatre Nuovo 228
Theatre Royal 224-5, 237, 239, 280-1, 288, 295-6, 322, 342, 350, 663, 681
Théâtre-Italien 29, 67, 117, 120, 127, 133-4, 139, 157-8, 162, 214-15, 229, 247-8, 259-60, 298-9, 510-11, 522
Tietjens, Teresa 372, 520-2
Tit for Tat (Mozart) 138
Tolbecque, Auguste 129
Tommasi, Chevalier 456
Torquato Tasso (Donizetti) 130, 238, 281, 293
Tosi, Adelaide 67, 69, 72, 74, 137
Trebelli-Bettini, Zelia 512, 514, 520-1, 523
Turina, Joaquín 46, 587, 624

U

Un avventura di Scaramuccia (Ricci) 230, 235, 237-9
Un giorno di regno (Verdi) 325
"Un segreto d'importanza" 221, 287, 295, 315
Una Casa da Venere (Turina) 46
Unger, Caroline 26, 46, 48, 53, 56, 157

V

Vaccai, Nicola 72, 137, 593, 624
Verdi, Guiseppe 27, 38, 73-4, 119, 211, 220, 244, 255, 292, 325, 338-40, 444, 450, 455-6, 459, 683-5
Vespri (Verdi) 260

Viardot, Pauline 260, 263, 265, 305, 364
Victoria (Queen of England) 207-10, 217-19, 232-4, 239-40, 242, 244-6, 254-7, 267-8, 311-12, 337, 370-1, 441-3, 513-15, 662-3, 679-80, 683-5
Vienna Opera House 520
Virgil 12, 58
Vitale, Vincenzo 504, 684
Voltaire 49, 73

W

Wagner, Richard 119, 255, 265, 521, 682
Weber, Carl Marie von 48, 54, 255, 445, 624, 684
Wilde, Lady Jane Francesca 524
Wilde, Oscar 524-5
William IV (King of the United Kingdom) 115, 233
William Tell see Guillaume Tell (Rossini)
Wilton-Lablache, Frances (wife of Frédéric) 230-2, 235, 238-9, 257, 264, 268, 306, 313, 339, 452, 517, 570, 582
Windsor castle xviii, 267, 311, 377, 514-15, 574
Winter, Berardo 69, 74, 137, 482, 486
Wyndham, Fanny *see* Wilton-Lablache, Frances (wife of Frédéric)

Z

Zaira (Bellini) 73, 585, 594, 618, 620
Zamboni, Luigi 46, 160
Zampa (Herold) 321-2, 461-2, 521, 598-9, 620
Zelmira (Rossini) 43, 48, 158, 328, 456, 587, 592, 623